# The BRAZILIANS

## Also by Joseph A. Page

Perón: A Biography (1983)

The Law of Premises Liability
(1976; Second Edition 1988)

Bitter Wages:
The Nader Report on Disease and Injury on the Job
(Coauthor with Mary Win O'Brien)(1973)

The Revolution That Never Was:
Northeast Brazil, 1955–1964 (1972)

# The BRAZILIANS

## Joseph A. Page

**DA CAPO PRESS**
A Member of the Perseus Books Group

Many of the designations used by manufacturers and sellers to distinguish
their products are claimed as trademarks. Where those designations appear
in this book and Da Capo Books was aware of a trademark claim, the designations have been printed in initial capital letters.

*Library of Congress Cataloging-in-Publication Data*

Page, Joseph A.
 The Brazilians / Joseph A. Page.
  p.  cm.
 Includes bibliographical references (p.   ) and index.
 ISBN 0-201-40913-5
 ISBN-10: 0-201-44191-8   ISBN-13: 978-0-201-44191-8 (pbk.)
  1. National characteristics, Brazilian.  2. Ethnology—Brazil.
 3. Brazil—Economic conditions—1985–  4. Brazil—Social
 conditions—1985–  5. Brazil—Religious life and customs.
 I. Title.
 F2510.P34  1995                                    94-45812
 305.8'00981—dc20                                      CIP

Da Capo Press is a member of Perseus Books Group

Cover design by Jean Seal
Cover illustration by Catherine Neal
Text design by Jean Hammond
Set in 10.5-point Meridien by Clarinda

Visit us on the World Wide Web at www.dacapopress.com

*Para a Martha, minha musa maga*

# Contents

## *Part Four*
# Spiritual Brazil

## *Part Five*
# In Search of What Makes Brazilians Brazilian

# Preface

As a wine tastes of its own grape, a book bears the stamp of its author, a truism that is particularly relevant to the pages that follow. There is no way I can view the subject matter I have chosen other than through the lens of personal experience. The Brazilians parading through these pages will be my Brazilians, as seen and interpreted through my eyes. Thus, I have an obligation to offer readers some explanation of my involvement with Brazil and its people.*

For me the land its citizens call Brasil, but we in the English-speaking world insist upon referring to as Brazil, can never cease evoking a kaleidoscope of memories and a spectrum of emotions based on experiences spanning three decades. From the moment I arrived at the Guararapes Airport in Recife in June of 1963, the living organism that is Brazil laid siege to my sensibilities. The assault went far beyond what might be expected from the stifling heat (which I suffer badly), the unfamiliar language, and the oversized dimensions of nearly everything. I found myself stimulated as never before, constantly bombarded by the sights, sounds, smells, moods, and rhythms of this "new world in the tropics."

---

* Brazilians may call me a "Brazilianist," a reference to academics, mostly from the United States, who specialize in Brazilian studies and who began to come to Brazil on research projects in the 1960s, and have produced a large body of scholarly literature about the country.

I do not consider myself a Brazilianist. This book is not intended to be a work of scholarship, and although I am a professor of law, my academic interests are unrelated to Brazilian studies. I would prefer to place myself within the tradition of a long line of foreigners who have visited or lived in Brazil, have been seduced by the land and its people, and who have attempted to set down their impressions and reflections for the benefit of other non-Brazilians.

Over the years various traveling companions have enriched what for me has been a never-ending process of discovery. Ralph Nader, who shared the 1963 odyssey with me, contributed both style and substance. His restless curiosity prodded me to venture beyond passive fascination and facile explanation. We threw ourselves with youthful abandon into a quest to make some sense of Northeast Brazil at a moment when the whole region seemed in ferment. The search took us to settings far removed from the precincts of the Harvard Law School, which we had escaped five years earlier. We marveled at the hilltop mansion in Apipucos, on the outskirts of Recife, where sociologist Gilberto Freyre had re-created with loving care the ambience of Brazil's colonial past; at a British Club where no one spoke English, and at a Lebanese Club where no one spoke Arabic; and at a political rally we viewed from a platform on the back of a flatbed truck, where we towered over a row of local politicians in front of us, gazed out at an audience of expressionless peasants, and dodged the swarms of oversized tropical insects that were drawn to the lights.

Next it was the turn of a Harvard College undergraduate named Jeff Bingaman, a fellow student in a Portuguese language class I audited during the academic year (1963–64) I spent at Harvard in pursuit of a Master of Laws degree. Jeff, now a U.S. Senator from New Mexico, helped me view things with a fresh sense of wonderment. Exploring the city of Salvador, capital of both the state of Bahia and of Afro-Brazil, we saw the incomparable Master Pastinha, seventy-four years old, blind in one eye, barely five feet tall, displaying his skills at *capoeira*, a style of foot-fighting that originated in Angola and has been converted into a form of dance; the mysterious rites of *candomblé*, an African religion; and the launching of *balões*, or cloth-covered candles resembling miniature hot-air balloons, which then floated wistfully over the bay of Salvador at sunset during the feast days of Saints Peter and Paul.

On our last morning in the city, we could not resist visiting the medical school for a look at its ghoulish treasure, the heads of the legendary outlaw Lampeão, his mistress Maria Bonita, and other members of his gang. When the authorities finally ambushed and gunned down the bespectacled Lampeão and his associates in 1938, they decided to decapitate the corpses and display the severed heads throughout the interior of the Northeast, in order to convince skeptical backlanders that Lampeão, a hero to many, had truly departed this life. Afterward, the heads found their way to the medical school of the University of Bahia, where they were preserved in jars of formaldehyde and became a tourist attraction.

It was a holiday, and the school was closed. With earnest hyperbole, we told the watchman we had come thousands of kilometers just to see Lampeão's head, and were leaving Salvador in a few hours. With the graciousness for which Brazilians are justly beloved, he yielded to our persistent entreaties and let us pass, wide-eyed, through the basement room where the grisly trophies were kept on display.*

In recent years my wife, Martha Gil-Montero, has invested our trips to Brazil with a dimension lacking in my prior visits. Her lifelong passion for Brazilian music helped me to learn to appreciate the genius of Vinicius de Moraes, Tom Jobim, Maria Bethânia, Maria Creusa, Milton Nascimento, Caetano Veloso, and many others. As she researched her book *Brazilian Bombshell: The Biography of Carmen Miranda*, I had the opportunity to become acquainted with some of the luminaries of the Brazilian entertainment world— Emilinha Borba, Braguinha, Dorival Caymmi, Grande Otelo, and Sinval Silva, to name a few. Caught up in the swirl of Rio Carnivals, we danced the samba in the streets with local revelers, convulsed at the costumes and antics of the transvestite "Carmen Miranda Band," and watched samba-school parades that elevated the term "dazzling" to unimagined heights.

On my second trip to Brazil I was involved in an incident that might easily have aborted my then embryonic love affair with the country. In June 1964, a scant two months after a military coup had toppled the government of President João Goulart and shortly following my arrival in Recife, I found myself detained and interrogated by the police, who were convinced that I had been involved in "agitation" during my 1963 sojourn in the city. When I denied this and demanded that the U.S. Consulate be notified of my ar-

---

* Several years later, Lampeão's surviving relatives persuaded the government that the exhibit was unchristian, and the heads received a proper burial.

rest, they confined me to a squalid cell in a dungeon, where I could hear the cries of prisoners being beaten. It took the intervention of U.S. Vice-Consul Peter de Vos (who would later serve as U.S. Ambassador to Mozambique, Liberia, Tanzania, and Costa Rica) to secure my release, twenty-four hours after my arrest.

Thoroughly traumatized, I resolved to leave the country immediately and permanently, but after a night's sleep, my terror subsided. It soon became evident that I was in no further peril. The incident had not gone far enough to force the authorities to expel me from Brazil in order to justify what they had done, and I was willing to refrain from making a public protest and to accept their explanation that a mistake had been made.

As visit piled upon visit (there have been sixteen in all) over the course of thirty years, these and other adventures and encounters have formed a coral reef of memories. Brazil the "infinite country" seems to hold a limitless store of surprises, delightful as well as shocking, my appetite for which has yet to be slaked.

The images remain vivid to this day. Among them:

- a night at the Moulin Rouge, the liveliest spot in Recife's downtown red-light district, where clean-cut American sailors create a turbulent sea of white as they dance wildly with prostitutes of every racial hue, oblivious to a human trunk with muscular arms outstretched in supplication, its deformed, useless legs tucked out of view, its head tilted back and gazing upward at the revelers, the face so exquisite it could have come from an Italian renaissance painting;

- a drive through the rain forest of Rondônia during the burning season, when the air is so thick with smoke it blocks out the rays of the midday tropical sun and casts a ghoulish pall over charred tree trunks looming mournfully on both sides of the road;

- the thrill of sitting in Rio de Janeiro's monumental Maracanã stadium, where Jeff and I watch Mané Garrincha, one of Brazil's soccer immortals, as he comes within inches of scoring on a corner kick, and where Martha and I share the delirium of ninety thousand spectators at a "Fla-Flu" (a game between traditional Rio rivals Flamengo and Fluminense), and cheer the legendary Zico as he returns from a knee injury to make three goals for the ruby red and black;

- the exhilaration of walking along Rio's Copacabana Beach on New Year's Eve, where more than a million devotees of the African goddess Iemanjá place candles and offerings of cosmetics on tiny rafts, launch them out to sea, wade in the surf, and raise joyous shouts of *"Muito Axê"* ("May you have everything that makes you happy");

- a visit to idyllic Alcântara in the northern state of Maranhão, in colonial times a thriving town inhabited by Portuguese nobility and wealthy locals, but abandoned by them soon after abolition and taken over by freed slaves, whose descendants have converted the town into one of Brazil's most pleasant tourist centers, where palatial homes and churches in various stages of decay serve as ghostly reminders of a bygone era;

- a trip to Curionópolis, the rowdy boomtown just outside the gold mine at Serra Pelada, where a group of gentle nuns mourn the death of one of their sisters, killed by a stray bullet when a hired gunman tried to assassinate a rural labor leader who was standing next to her at a bus stop;

- attending an afternoon of worship at the Vale do Amanhecer (Valley of the Dawn) just outside Brasília, where the cape-clad followers of the late Tia (Aunt) Neiva, a truck driver who claimed she could be present on several planets simultaneously, gather around a small pond to receive forces emanating from the sun, moon, and elsewhere in the universe;

- sitting on a curbstone on the Rua 7 de Setembro across from the lighthouse at the entrance to the bay of Salvador, chatting with Sônia as she prepares Afro-Brazilian delicacies on a makeshift stove for passersby, munching on an *acarajé,** enjoying the

---

\* White beans ground into a paste, mixed with onion, garlic, and salt paste, and fried in *dendé* (palm oil) until the outside is crisp and reddish.

cool breeze whipping in from the ocean, and thinking how obscene it would be for fast-food outlets to replace these mag-
nificently turbaned, full-skirted *baianas* (Bahian women);

- watching a young woman as she sits out of motorists' view behind a sign at a traffic intersection during the rush hour in Brasília, smacking with the flat edge of a stick the open palms of a
  little boy and girl, who then dash into the street with tears
  streaming down their cheeks and a pained expression on their
  faces, beg from motorists pausing for a red light, dart back behind the sign, deliver to the woman the money they have received, and hold out their hands for another smack;

- a descent by train in 1971 from São Paulo down a steep escarpment and through billowing clouds filled with deadly pollutants on the approach to Cubatão, an industrialized hellhole
  of a region that would soon gain notoriety as Brazil's "Valley
  of Death";

- edging forward in the evening traffic along the Praia do Flamengo in Rio, past a man pulling a cart on which two puppies
  sit calmly next to a large white mouse;

- sampling my first *feijoada* (the Brazilian national dish made
  from black beans and pork) at the home of Paulo Freire in
  Recife in June of 1964, on the day before the army would arrest and jail the gentle, innovative educator whose literacy
  method would earn him worldwide renown;

- discovering other Brazilian delights such as *guaraná*, a soft
  drink made from the little round fruit found on shrubbery in
  the Amazon basin; *cupuaçu*, a sweet substance that might rival
  chocolate if a way could be found to produce it cost effectively;
  and, of course, the nectarlike *caipirinha*, a cocktail made of
  lime, sugar, and *cachaça* (a white rum made from sugar cane).

On at least two occasions, fate played a major part in helping
me write this book. Upon my return from a trip to Brazil in February and March of 1986, I left all my notes (two full, fat note-
books in all) and clippings in a paper shopping bag on the floor of
my office. That evening a cleaning person picked up the bag and
tossed it into the trash. I figured out what had transpired only min-

utes after a disposal truck had compacted all the garbage and litter from the Georgetown University Law Center and had left for the university campus.

A frantic drive across town brought me to the truck just as it was about to depart for the District of Columbia dump in Lorton, Virginia. The driver, Yardley Jackson, and his assistant, James M. Bradley, informed me that my only recourse would be to follow them to the dump and then look for my things as they unloaded what amounted to several days' trash from the entire Law Center. The prospects did not seem bright, but the men encouraged me to give it a try.

I followed them to Lorton and joined them in the cab of the truck as they entered the forbidding landscape of the enormous dump. We were directed to a spot that a bulldozer was approaching as it moved refuse into fifteen-foot piles, so there was not much time to search. Miraculously, the shopping bag, torn but intact and still holding its contents, slid out of the truck with the first wave of trash, and I was able to recover it.

I would have thought that the odds were prohibitive that a similar mishap could occur, but I was mistaken. That October, while riding a bus in Rio de Janeiro, I absentmindedly left behind a thick copybook with notes from my recent trip to Amazônia, São Luís, Recife, and Salvador. When I discovered the loss, I dashed to the nearby U.S. Consulate, where one of the secretaries calmed me down and helped me to remember the color and posted destination of the bus. As luck would have it, its last stop, in the neighborhood of Urca at the foot of the Sugar Loaf, was across the street from the home of the American cultural attaché, Wally Keiderling. A hurried call was made to Carminha, his housekeeper, who dashed out, caught the bus just as it was arriving, and retrieved the notebook.

There are numerous individuals without whose help this book could never have been written and to whom I would like to extend my profound gratitude.

For providing special assistance:

In Washington: Eimar Avillez, Robert Goodland, Javier Illanes, Peter Jakab, John Laskey, Jeff Leonard, Vera Machado, Paul Maloof, Richard Morse, José Neistein, Antônio Pimenta Neves, Luiz

Antônio de Oliveira, Miriam Parel, Edgardo Reis, Matthew Shirts, Carlos Eduardo Lins da Silva, Brady Tyson, Chuck Weiss, Enrique Wetzler, *Américas* magazine, the Biography Group of Washington, and João Francisco Bezerra, my Portuguese teacher at the Brazilian-American Cultural Institute.

In São Paulo: Cláudio Abramo, Ignácio de Loyola Brandão, the Canalle family, Célia Castelló, Fábio Konder Comparato, Norman Gall, Eros Grau, Samirah Dayeh Heide, Leila Iannone, Flávio Jorge, Marilena Lazzarini, Pedro Paulo de Sena Madureira, José Mindlin, Joyce Mitchell, Renato Ortiz, Haquira Osakabe, Leigh Payne, Father Bill Rheinhard, Renato Tucunduva, the Tucunduva family, and the Center for Nippo-Brazilian Studies.

In Rio de Janeiro: José Almino, Márcio Moreira Alves, Rosenthal Alves, Ana Maria Bahiana, Antônio Rangel Bandeira, Marina Bandeira, Rui Bello, Maria Luisa Braga and her friends Alzira and Moisés, Bruce Bushey, Sérgio Cabral, Antônio Callado, Cristiane Cammerman, Roberto Carvalho, Ralph della Cava, Márcia Clark, Roberto da Matta, Rubem Fernandes, Ana Figueiras, Peter Frye, Heloisa Buarque de Hollanda, Francisco Ivern, S. J., Wally Keiderling, Father Ed Leising, Cindy Lessa, Alfredo Machado, Sérgio Machado, Creúza Maciel, João Carlos Magaldi, Yvonne Maggie, Paulo Moraes, Susana de Moraes, Thompson Motta, Frances O'Gorman, Edina Palatinique, Maria Augusta Rodriguez, Donna Roginski, Lenni Silverstein, Márcio Souza, and the Reverend Ed Tims.

In Recife: Martin Adler, Marco Aurélio de Alcântara, Miguel Arraes, Carlos Bakota, Antônio Magalhães, Liêdo Maranhão, Waldemar Oliveira Neto, Cláudio, Solange, and Teresa Souto, and Ana Vasconcelos.

In Brasília: Francisco Ferreira, Felipe Illanes, Cesare La Rocca, Rubens Ricupero, and Plínio Sampaio.

In Salvador: Nancy and Solange Bernabó, Carybé, Juanita Elbein, David Kurakane, V. de Costa Lima, and Father Dave O'Brien.

In Porto Velho: Gabriel Lima Ferreira, Wim Gruenwaldt, Jim LaFleur, and Brent Milliken.

In Porto Alegre: Ondina Fachel Leal, John Matel, and Paulo Azevedo Moura.

In Curitiba: Carlos Guillen and Sandra Turra.

In Campinas: Eustáquio Gomes.

In São Luís: Sérgio and Mundicarmo Ferretti.

In Manaus: Ronald Colavecchio, S. J.

For reading chapters of the book and offering useful suggestions: Lonnie Athens, Marcello Hallake, Carlos Hasenbalg, Tom Krattenmaker, Jim Malley, S. J., Mari Matsuda, Chris Parel, Ginger Patterson, Lynn Stout, and Edie Weiss.

Heartfelt thanks go to my agent, Carl Brandt, and to my splendid editor, Don Fehr. A special nod of appreciation is due Pat Jalbert, who supervised the production of the book, and to Maggie Carr, for a terrific job of copyediting.

For taking me to see the film *Black Orpheus*, I owe a debt of gratitude to Tom and Elizabeth Lambert.

Finally, I must acknowledge what planted the seed from which my interest in Brazil blossomed. A Christmas gift from my cousin Amy Corbisiero when I was eleven years old—Richard Halliburton's *Book of Marvels*—fired my imagination with pulsing descriptions of the mighty Iguaçu Falls and the "Queen of Cities," Rio de Janeiro, and made me resolve to experience these exotic locales for myself one day. I have never once regretted that decision.

# Introducing Brazil

*T*here once was a time when the word "Brazil" conjured up fond memories of Carmen Miranda and her "tutti-frutti hat"; some song lyrics about "an awful lot of coffee"; the cool, lilting rhythms of "The Girl from Ipanema"; Fred and Ginger, "flying down to Rio"; and the bipedal wizardry of soccer's "King" Pelé.

By the early 1990s, however, mention of Brazil was evoking images of street children being preyed upon and slaughtered by private death squads composed of off-duty policemen, and chain saws and fires destroying the world's largest remaining rain forest.

Over the past decade, the tropical Eden to which many of us at one time or another secretly longed to escape has been frightening off tourists who have seen or heard news reports of violence in Brazilian cities and have decided to travel elsewhere.*

Indeed, Brazilians themselves seemed to have lost much of the optimism, once the bedrock of their national character. As one of the country's most prominent authors observed in a letter to me in 1987: "By all means, start the book already. Pretty soon you won't have a country to write about, mark my words! . . . Get to work, man, or you'll be writing archeology before you know it." Tom Jobim, the internationally famous Brazilian composer of popular music, was quoted as saying that the best way out for his compatriots is the airport of Rio or São Paulo. A million of them have followed his advice and abandoned their homeland in search of bet-

---

* During the tourist season (November to March) of 1985–86, at least twenty tourist each day experienced criminal assaults, according to the police unit charged with protecting visitors. Between 1988 and 1993, an estimated five hundred thousand tourists stayed away from Brazil, and caused the country to lose about $400 million in tourist revenue.

1

ter lives abroad. An estimated 332,000 have migrated to the United States.

Once Brazilians confidently asserted that their economy was like the bumblebee: according to all the laws of science it should not be able to leave the ground, yet it somehow managed to fly. When the monthly inflation rate passed 45 percent in March of 1994 and threatend to pass 5,500 percent for the year, few took comfort either in this analogy or in the popular joke that Brazil cannot fall into the abyss because Brazil is bigger than the abyss.

Yet by the end of 1994, Brazilian self-assurance was on the rise again as the inflation rate dipped sharply, the national stock market boomed, and a new presidential administration gave rise to the perennial hope that Brazil at last stood poised to assert its vast potential, and that the tarnish its image had recently acquired might evaporate like the morning dew.

The romantic vision embraced by many outsiders has always been somewhat misleading, for Brazil and things Brazilian have never been exactly what they seemed. This has held true ever since 1500, when the first Portuguese explorers to cross the South Atlantic named the land mass they discovered the Island of the True Cross. Some years later mariners stumbling upon the entrance to what is now Guanabara Bay suffered a similar misperception. They thought they had arrived at the mouth of a great river, which they called Rio de Janeiro (the River of January).

Delusive appearances have recurred with metronomic regularity throughout the social history of Brazil. Black slaves seeking to preserve their heritage disguised *capoeira* (Angolan foot fighting) as a dance, and transformed the rich cuisine they once prepared as offerings to their ancestral gods into dishes ostensibly cooked for their masters, but which, in fact, they intended to share on the sly with their own African divinities. Brazilian efforts in the nineteenth century to create the impression that they were complying with British demands to terminate the slave trade in Brazil, when they had no intention to do so, made popular a descriptive phrase that has survived to the present day—*para inglês ver,* meaning "for the English [or, indeed, anyone] to see."

The phenomenon of misperception persists to the present day. One of the most beautiful women in Brazil was, until a 1989 sex-change operation, a man. Americans seeing *capoeira* for the first time commonly assume it is break dancing. The well-publicized sensuality that Brazil seems to exude—and that reaches its apotheosis in the frenzy of the annual Carnival in Rio—in fact hides the repressive and repressed attitudes about sex that permeate much of Brazilian society.

Thus images of Brazil cannot always be taken at face value. The former dominant perception of the country as a friendly playground or an exotic refuge in the tropics took no account of the social and economic inequities that consigned much of the population to lives of poverty, disease, and ignorance. It also missed the serious side of Brazil, the slumbering leviathan with the potential to become a great power, ever on the verge of awakening to claim its rightful place among nations.

Since outsiders have traditionally misinterpreted what they see in Brazil, it is conceivable that Brazil's current negative image abroad is yet another erroneous impression drawn by foreigners. This is certainly what Brazilians would like to believe. However, it also could be that at long last the real Brazil has begun to emerge from the romantic mists that have long clouded the judgment of nonnative observers. Or the truth may lie somewhere in between.

It is easy to underappreciate the dimensions of things in Brazil. The Baixada Fluminense (Fluminense Lowlands), a group of poverty-stricken municipalities in the steamy flats just outside Rio de Janeiro, is home to more than three million people, its population exceeding that of Nicaragua. Guatemala, the largest country in Central America, has but 50 percent of the population of the megalopolis of São Paulo.

Number five on the list of the world's geographically largest nations, Brazil resembles a continent more than a country. Its length added to its breadth approximates the distance that separates New York from London. Lisbon is closer to Moscow than Belém, a city in northern Brazil, is to Porto Alegre in the south. At one time the municipality of Altamira in the Amazon basin matched France in size. If one discounts Alaska, Brazil is about 185,000 square miles larger than the United States. It occupies just under one half of the area of South America and borders all but two of the other eleven nations of the continent.

The cliché that it is a land of startling contrasts holds true. Brazil's far-flung borders include one third of the earth's remaining tropical forests, drought-stricken backlands occupying 10 percent of its territory, a mineral-rich central plateau and rolling plains in the temperate south, and a river basin that discharges into the Atlantic Ocean a volume of water equal to that flowing through all the rivers of Europe.

There are more Brazilians than all but five of the world's nationalities. They are a young people; the 1980 census found that nearly one half of them are under twenty years of age. More babies are born in Brazil each year than in the United States and the former Soviet Union combined. Brazil is the largest Roman Catholic country on earth, and only Italy has produced more bishops. It has the largest black population outside Africa, and more Japanese live in Brazil than anywhere else except Japan.

Before the current recession wreaked havoc, Brazil had the eighth largest market economy in the world. There were only five nations that exported more armaments, five that produced more aircraft, and eight that manufactured more motor vehicles. Brazil was the second largest iron-ore producer, the sixth largest gold producer, the seventh largest steel producer, and the eighth largest producer of aluminum. It ranked first in production of sugar, second in production of soybeans and cattle, and third in production of corn.

Among the planet's privately owned television networks, Brazil's Rede Globo yields only to CBS, NBC, and ABC. The network's well-crafted *telenovelas* (soap operas) enjoy high ratings in Latin America, Western and Eastern Europe, and even the People's Republic of China. They hold their own in competition with programs exported from the United States.

In the 1960s and 1970s, Brazil in some ways resembled the United States at the end of the nineteenth century as it pushed with explosive energy into its vast hinterlands ("the last last frontier," as a French journal once put it). This was the image that inspired

John Huston's final words in the 1979 film *Winter Kills*. In the role of an unscrupulous billionaire, just before he falls to his death he shouts to his son: "Take our money out of the Western banks and put it in South America. . . . Brazil. . . Brazil. . . they're the next ones up."

Indeed, there was once a sanguine vision of Brazil that held that the nation possessed sufficient human and natural resources to enable it to overtake the United States as an economic power; that while the twentieth century has been the "American century," the twenty-first would belong to Brazil. Looking with great anticipation beyond tomorrow has long been a shared article of faith for Brazilians who embraced the slogan "Brazil, Country of the Future." However, with typical self-deprecation, many were wont to add such caveats as "but the future never comes," or "ours is a land of unlimited impossibilities."

There might have been resignation as well as frustration lurking behind these wry reservations, for Brazil faces obstacles far more formidable than those the United States had to surmount in its climb to adulthood. For example, when North Americans opted to industrialize, technology was relatively simple and inexpensive, and hence easy to acquire or replicate. Brazil's commitment to large-scale industrialization did not occur until well into the twentieth century, at a historical moment when technology had become exceedingly complex, costly, and difficult to import.

Moreover, although social and economic disparities existed in the United States in the late nineteenth and early twentieth centuries, they were minor compared with the yawning chasm that now separates Brazil's "haves" and "have-nots." Poverty has become so pervasive and has reached such dire proportions that the social fabric is tearing to shreds. The relatively recent shift of Brazil from a primarily rural to a primarily urban society has added to the strain, as metropolitan centers struggle in vain to accommodate an influx of migrants from the countryside, and to stem the rising tide of crime and other social disorders.

The Brazilian political system, its evolution stunted by two decades of military dictatorship (1964–85) and a long tradition of corruption, has given the impression of being incapable of responding to the current crisis. The economy, moreover, has been wracked by chronic inflation and groans under the enormous, conflicting needs of investment for long-term growth and expenditures for programs to alleviate current social problems.

The latter have become a matter of critical concern, as Brazil is now a leading producer of human misery. Every six seconds a Brazilian baby dies from a diarrhea-related disease. Every thirty minutes one Brazilian contracts leprosy and another tuberculosis. Tropical diseases are rampant: the country has an estimated one million cases a year of malaria and ten million cases of schistosomiasis, which attacks the intestines and liver. The number of Brazilians carrying the HIV virus that causes AIDS is reckoned to range between five hundred thousand and one million.

In 1983, 47 percent of Brazil's eighteen-year-olds could not pass the physical examination for compulsory military service. A 1988 survey by the Brazilian Health Ministry disclosed that only 33 percent of Brazilians at age eighteen had all their teeth.

Chronic nutritional deficiencies have taken a grim toll. The average height of a Brazilian male is the equivalent of the average height of a fifteen-year-old boy in the United States, while the average height of a Brazilian woman matches that of a twelve-year-old American girl.

About two thirds of all Brazilians have been classified as poor. Of the families that make up this "miserable majority," 71 percent lack running water, 79 percent have no refrigerator, and 85 percent live without sewage disposal.

One half of Latin America's illiterates are Brazilian. Total illiteracy claims 20 percent of the population, and functional illiteracy reaches double that figure. Out of the total number of Brazilians ten years old or older, fewer than 18 percent have completed four years of primary education. Of the sixty-five million Brazilian children below the age of nineteen, more than half are not attending school. To put this in a slightly different perspective, of the more than seventy-five million Brazilians qualified to vote, 40 percent are either illiterate or semiliterate, and 68 percent do not have a primary education—figures that do not bode well for the viability of democracy in Brazil.

Brazil's per capita income puts it in 105th place among all nations—behind Barbados, French Guiana, Surinam, Gabon, and Paraguay. A World Bank study several years ago found that Brazil had the world's highest concentration of wealth, with the richest 10 percent of the citizenry enjoying 50.6 percent of the nation's income. A more recent survey concludes that the poorest 50 percent of Brazil's population and the richest 1 percent have approximately the same share of the national income. Five percent of the population owns 80 percent of the land.

Economic hardship has inspired new enterprises, such as the illegal sale of young children to foreign couples. One source has estimated the 1988 outflow at fifty per week. As a British magazine advertising a television documentary on the subject phrased it, "It's not only coffee Brazil is exporting these days."

A few years ago it was fashionable for Brazilians to refer to their country as "Belindia," an amalgam of the productive capacity of Belgium and the poverty of India. By the early 1990s, use of the term Belindia had faded and was replaced by talk of the "Africanization" of Brazil.

Brazil has a unique Janus-like quality that enables it to gaze into both the past and the future. Brazilians have simultaneously experienced such disparate phenomena as an outbreak of bubonic plague and a growing AIDS epidemic. The unbridled violence of their frontier towns mirrors that of the American "Wild West"; while a disastrous radiation accident in central Brazil in 1987 evoked memories of Chernobyl.

This enables one to observe in Brazil not only American history repeating itself but also what might lie ahead for American society. For example, the homelessness that has become a feature of life in American cities has been endemic in Brazil over the past decade or two. The poverty affecting ever-increasing numbers of American children has long afflicted large numbers of Brazilian children. The actual violent crimes, and the perceptions of violence, that are beginning to inhibit foreign tourists from visiting the United States is replicating the negative effect violent crime has been having on tourism in Brazil. The "savage capitalism" that greatly exacerbated social and economic disparities in Brazil during the 1970s in certain ways foreshadowed the decade of the 1980s in the United States.

Indeed, it may not too be far-fetched for Brazilians to suggest to their neighbors to the north, "We are you yesterday, and we are you tomorrow."

Of course, to compare Brazil to the United States, Belgium, India, or the less developed countries of Africa overlooks the qualities that set Brazil apart from these and most other nations. The special characteristics of "Brazilianness" have contributed significantly to the current plight of South America's ailing giant. They are what make Brazilians Brazilian, and what will ultimately make or break Brazil.

The distinctive features of Brazilianness emerge from human factors, the singular interplay between Brazilians and their physical environment, and the magic that permeates both land and people. These are the aspects of Brazil that have long seduced and inspired foreign observers. Here are a few examples:

- Stefan Zweig, the Austrian novelist who found refuge in Brazil as the perpetrators of World War II menaced Europe, was so taken by Brazilian society that he penned the classic *Brazil: Land of the Future* (in which he called Brazil "one of the most lovable countries of our world");

- Orson Welles found Brazilian folk culture so fascinating (and life in Rio de Janeiro so congenial to his sybaritic tastes) that he recorded an epic coastal voyage by a fisherman from the Northeast and explored the origins of the samba in his unfinished documentary *It's All True;*

- the stark drama in the lives of juvenile delinquents in São Paulo inspired Argentine-born director Héctor Babenco to film the gripping *Pixote;*

- Marcel Camus, the French filmmaker, discovered in the hillside slums of Rio the setting for his celluloid gem *Black Orpheus;*

- Mario Vargas Llosa, the Peruvian author-turned-politician-turned-author, applied his prodigious talents to capturing and brilliantly bringing to life the messianic fervor and violence of a nineteenth-century Brazilian backlands revolt in his novel *The War of the End of the World;*

- Elizabeth Bishop, the American poet, found Brazil was so full of surprise and stimulation that she composed some of her best verse while living there for nearly two decades.

It is difficult not to fall under the spell cast by Brazilians. Jack Harding, in his 1941 travel book *I Like Brazil*, noted, "Anyone who does not get along with [them] had better examine himself; the fault is his." Cordiality is a defining characteristic of their behavior. They radiate an irresistible pleasantness, abundant hospitality, and unfailing politeness, especially to foreigners.

The gentleness factor is ubiquitous. Even the Brazilian political leader who brought the country to the verge of fascism, President Getúlio Vargas, radiated this quality. A plump-faced, benevolent "father-of the-poor" figure, he could not have been more different in style than his contemporaries (some would say soul mates) Adolf Hitler and Benito Mussolini.

The tender and delicate touches that mark the Brazilian way of conducting interpersonal relations in no way contradict the sense of the grandiose often projected by Brazilians.* In a land with natural wonders such as the world's largest river drainage system, the world's largest fluvial island, and the world's largest swamp, it should be no surprise that Brazilians have been able to boast of man-made phenomena like the world's largest hand-excavated hole, the world's largest soccer stadium, the world's largest hydroelectric dam, and what is probably the world's largest illegal gambling operation.

The Brazilian affinity for grandeur may derive in part from history. Brazil is the only Latin American country to have gone from colony to empire; upon achieving independence, the new nation could proudly boast of having emperors. And remarkable rulers they turned out to be! The two emperors who ruled Brazil during the nineteenth century were larger-than-life figures, a father and son with little in common, yet both were distinctly Brazilian in their personalities—the one energetic and insatiable in his lust for life, the other bookish, gracious, and endearing.

These two sides of the Brazilian national character—cordiality and grandiosity—coexist harmoniously. Indeed, to borrow an insight from Brazil's contribution to North American jurisprudence,

---

* Elizabeth Bishop once alluded to this characteristic when she noted that "there is no word in Portuguese for 'understatement.' "

law professor Roberto Mangabeira Unger, the most original feature of Brazilian culture is the conviction that one can be at once sweet and great.

The amiable Brazilians cope amazingly well. In the face of discomforts and hardships that might drive others to protest or even open revolt, they exhibit forbearance and an extraordinary degree of adaptability. Perhaps these qualities developed as a reaction to the futility of openly challenging Brazil's traditional class structure, rigid laws, and unresponsive bureaucracy. Perhaps these traits reflect a sense of fatalism that the Moors brought to Portugal during the Middle Ages, and the Portuguese later brought with them to the New World.

Brazilians characteristically seek subtle ways to circumvent difficult situations. Instead of resorting to confrontation, they prefer to use what they call the *jeito* or *jeitinho*, a difficult to translate term referring to what a French scholar once described as "an ingenious maneuver that renders the impossible possible; the unjust just; and the illegal legal." It is a rapid, improvised, creative response to a law, rule, or custom that on its face prevents someone from doing something. The *jeitinho* personalizes a situation ostensibly governed by an impersonal norm.

On the other hand, the maxim that in Brazil appearances often deceive fully applies to both the greatness and the sweetness of the Brazilian people. Lurking behind their sense of grandiosity is an inferiority complex exemplified by the pronouncement of poet Oswaldo de Andrade: "My country suffers from a cosmic incompetence." Brazilians are wont to ignore their own virtues and fixate on their shortcomings. As the writer Nelson Rodrigues has observed, "We are Narcissuses in reverse, who spit on our own image."

Feelings of inferiority once caused many Brazilians to deprecate their own indigenous culture and look first to Europe and then to the United States for models to imitate. Such attitudes helped hold back the process of industrialization, since Brazilians could not bring themselves to believe that goods produced at home could match those they imported from abroad.

In addition, beneath the Brazilian vocation for greatness lurks a traditional habit of indulging in excessive rhetoric and display, and, as a Brazilian intellectual once pointed out, a childlike tendency to project the sort of utopian dreams that might consume a young boy reading about Napoleon or Alexander the Great but not comprehending the effort that would be required to emulate their accomplishments.

Indeed, Brazilians rely much more on improvisation and spontaneity than on sustained effort proceeding from careful planning and preparation. This is yet another aspect of the immaturity that on the one hand adds youthful exuberance to the charm they exert but on the other hand keeps them from achieving greater economic and social progress.

The celebrated sweetness of Brazilians often obscures the dark side of their nature—a capacity for extreme violence that runs like a murky undercurrent throughout the history of the land, from the colonial period up to the present day. Examples abound: the extermination of Indians; the suppression of slave revolts; the execution of rebels seeking Brazil's independence from Portugal; the slaughter of peasants challenging the system of landholding in the countryside; the contemporary urban crime wave, most of which, in truth, amounts to an undisguised form of class warfare waged by the poor against the rich; the so-called "death lottery," a macabre form of protest by inmates of a seriously overcrowded prison, whereby they drew lots and killed the "winner" in order to call public attention to their plight; and the systematic assassination of street children. Indeed, the voiceless and ceaseless neglect that has consigned thousands of young people to living on city streets and in brothels amounts to a more subtle but no less significant expression of societal brutality.

Brazilian cordiality has also created misimpressions in the area of race relations. On one level blacks and whites can display in their dealings with one another a genuine human warmth that blurs color lines and has produced a high degree of social integration, a major achievement—if not *the* major achievement—of Brazilian society. Yet this does not mean that Brazilians live in a "racial democracy," as many have convinced themselves. The ease with which individuals of different racial backgrounds intermingle has served to obscure recognition of the existence of a subtle and not-so-subtle racism that makes it difficult for blacks to enjoy the same political, social, and economic opportunities as whites.

The legacy of slavery perhaps goes beyond the lingering racism infecting contemporary Brazilian society. It may contribute, at least in some part, to the low value Brazilians place on human life (including their own). They often manifest a reckless indifference to (or, better yet, an unabashed preference for) physical risk. The behavior of Brazilians once they grab hold of the steering wheel of an automobile is one example. Another may be found in the practice of young (mostly poor) people who "train surf," or stand atop moving trains—a pursuit depicted graphically in the otherwise forgettable film *Exposure*. Although other psychological factors surely share responsibility for this trait, by accepting the dehumanizing of one sector of the country's population through their long toleration of involuntary servitude, Brazilians may have subconsciously depreciated the worth they placed on each human life.

There are other societal ills that can be traced at least in part to slavery. For example, the slave owner could do as he pleased with his slaves without having to answer to anyone for the consequences of his actions. The master-slave relationship replicated the medieval relationship between the Portuguese king and his subjects, and it came to define the link between the powerful and the powerless in Brazil. Large landowners in rural Brazil claimed this privilege, as did the republican governments and dictatorial regimes that ruled the country. Indeed, a sense of being above the law became a prerogative of the nation's haves. The notion of impunity—the avoidance of personal responsibility—became deeply ingrained in Brazilianness and has proved to be a barrier to development.

The vastness of Brazil has made inevitable the crystallization of strong regional differences among Brazilians. According to the accepted stereotypes, *paulistas* (people from the state of São Paulo) are hardworking and entrepreneurial; *cariocas* (residents of Rio de Janeiro) carefree and funloving; *mineiros* (inhabitants of the state of Minas Gerais) cautious and frugal; *nordestinos* (northeasterners) introverted; and *gaúchos* (people from the extreme south) fiercely independent. Yet these distinctions have served to enrich rather than to fractionalize the country.

The explanation for Brazil's capacity to gain strenth through diversity may lie in the fact that Brazilian society has long exerted a vigorously centripetal force—no doubt a legacy from Portugal, which throughout its history has demonstrated a remarkable tolerance for cultural, religious, and racial diversity. The ease with which non-Portuguese immigrants have been assimilated perhaps best illustrates this characteristic. Over the past century and a half Brazil has welcomed Italians, Germans, Spaniards, Syrians, Lebanese, Japanese, and others. Once in the melting pot, immigrants (or, to be more accurate, their children) have become totally Brazilian. Even American southerners resettling in Brazil immediately after the fall of the Confederacy experienced this transformation.

There are other elements that agglutinate Brazilians. The Portuguese language provides one common bond. There are variations in regional accents but no regional dialects, despite the vast size of the country. The mother tongue spoken in Portugal "resembles nothing so much as windsurfing from consonant to consonant," as one observer has noted. Softened and made mellifluous by the slaves imported from Africa, the Portuguese one hears in Brazil is a delight to the ear.

The rituals and traditions of the Roman Catholic Church, to which an estimated 90 percent of the population at least nominally adheres, also serve to hold Brazil together. Another unifying force is soccer. The country eats, drinks, and dreams *futebol,* as it is called. Not only is the sport practiced in every corner of Brazil, but some of the important professional teams, such as Flamengo of Rio de Janeiro, have large national followings. The television networks in recent years have become a critical homogenizing element, especially with their *telenovelas,* which enthrall viewers from every social class, from gold-mining towns in the Amazon frontier to the glass and concrete apartment complexes of São Paulo.

Although deep diversities of opinion and amoebalike parties that constantly fractionalize and reorganize characterize politics in Brazil, one factor shared by Brazilians from virtually all points on the political spectrum is a passion for development—a deeply felt conviction that Brazil's future depends upon the acceleration of material growth and progress. This tenet sets Brazil apart from the Hispanic countries of the hemisphere and is perhaps a legacy of the Portuguese, who during their golden age as a world power indulged a taste for the pragmatic rather than the speculative. It also explains, at least in part, the affinity that many Brazilians feel toward the United States.

Despite the constancy of traditional values, especially within the family and in the countryside, Brazilians embrace modernism with unrestrained enthusiasm. Examples of this passion include the magnificent airport of Belo Horizonte, the spectacular shopping malls that stand as temples of consumerism in large cities throughout the country, and, most dramatically, the futuristic design and architecture of Brasília.

The construction of a new capital on a barren plateau in the interior of the state of Goiás was like Brazil's attempt to sketch on a clean slate, and gave free rein to Brazilians' power of imagination and to their vision of a dynamic tomorrow. There is an interesting paradox here. The idea (and the name) of Brasília dates back to 1822, yet at the same time Brasília is very much a city without a past, and as such it symbolizes an absence of historical memory, yet another facet of Brazilianness.

Developmentalism and a taste for newness are youthful traits befitting a young country. Brazilians, however, go one step further. As singer Caetano Veloso once observed in an interview in *The New Yorker*, "Staying young is an idea that is present all over the world, but in Brazil it is an obsession." This is especially true in Rio de Janeiro, with its tropical sun and glorious beaches, where life is a perennial beauty contest and the desire to preserve juvenescence impels most society matrons over forty years of age to submit themselves at least once to the scalpel of the cosmetic surgeon.

Environment has played a major role in shaping salient features of Brazilianness. As an American writer once observed, Brazilians are "drowned in beauty." The warm climate and lush landscape of the tropics have helped create an overripe sensuality that permeates every level of society. The resplendence of the land has contributed to the popular, if tongue-in-cheek, saying "God is a Brazilian."*

---

* As a counterpoint, a joke often told by Brazilians has one of the angels complaining to the Lord about the disproportionate physical splendor and resources He allocated to Brazil, and the concomitant absence of natural scourges such as hurricanes and floods. "Ah, but wait 'til you see the people I'm going to put there," was the Lord's reply.

The abundance of natural resources has convinced Brazilians that the land will continue to yield limitless wealth capable of sustaining Brazil's march to inevitable greatness. This mind-set merges calamitously with what the Brazilian subconscious has retained of the mentality of Portuguese rulers, explorers, and colonists who saw in Brazil only riches to extract, and had no intention of investing anything in return. The result is a careless attitude toward nature that has pushed Brazil toward the brink of ecological disaster.

Thus a constant flow of industrial and domestic waste is destroying Guanabara Bay, the once glorious gateway to Rio de Janeiro. Cubatão, an industrial enclave nestled at the foot of the plateau that holds the nearby metropolis of São Paulo, once could claim the dubious distinction of being the most polluted city in the world. The destruction of the Amazon rain forest by the slash-and-burn land-clearing techniques practiced by settlers forced by economic exigency to migrate from other regions of Brazil, and by mining techniques that pay little heed to ecological consequences, may yet convert the jungle into a desert.

It is paradoxical that despite this thoughtless exploitation and neglect of the environment, Brazilians relate warmly to their native land. Their popular songs often reflect a genuine and touching affection for Brazil, an emotional attachment that comes directly from the heart and is quite distinct from the type of chauvinistic national pride upon which mindless patriotism often feeds. A measure of the gravity of the current economic crisis is that it is causing Brazilians to emigrate to Europe, Japan, and the United States in increasing numbers.

Brazilians have a penchant for joyfulness. The spirit of carnival, not merely as exercised in the world-famous bacchanalia of Rio de Janeiro but in the popular street celebrations of cities like Salvador and Olinda, sets a universal standard for exuberance. Brazilian fans at the quadrennial World Cup soccer championships always bring with them a contagious enthusiasm that proves irresistible to spectators from other countries. According to Joãozinho Trinta, the creative genius who revolutionized Rio's annual carnival extravaganza, "If you consider the planet as a living entity, Brazil is its heart; thus, Brazil's function is to bring happiness to this earth."*

Brazilians often reach other emotional extremes as well. They can be unabashedly mawkish. The heights this sentimentality can attain are illustrated by an anecdote, reported in the *Washington Post*, about a foreign journalist who was suffering his second holdup in Rio when one of the assailants suddenly embraced him. The robber might have participated in the prior crime or perhaps merely recognized his victim from somewhere. He gave the journalist his money back. The combination of sentiment and a deep yearning for someone or something sorely missed produces *saudade*, a uniquely Brazilian expression for "nostalgia."

Emotional outbursts in Brazil can have devastating results. The loss of a critical soccer match—such as the defeat inflicted by the Uruguayans on the Brazilian national team before 173,850 fans in Rio's Maracanã Stadium in the championship game of the 1950 World Cup—can provoke mass depression and even suicides. The lingering agony and untimely demise of President-elect Tancredo Neves in 1985 touched off an unfettered outpouring of collective anxiety and grief.

There is perhaps no better example of the sudden and extreme mood swings Brazilians are capable of than the recent responses to an Associated Press (AP) poll of the most dramatic sports stories of 1994. AP subscribers in more than thirty nations around the globe put in second place the tragic, accidental death of Brazilian race driver Ayrton Senna, whose fatal crash in April 1994 left his compatriots mired in a deep depression, while the top story was Brazil's July 1994 World Cup soccer victory, which brought the nation to the heights of euphoria.

The death throes of Tancredo (Brazilians often refer to politicians and celebrities by their first names) also summoned forth a remarkable display of another aspect of the Brazilian national character, a profound spirituality colored by both mysticism and excess. As the seventy-five-year-old politician underwent a series of ab-

---

*This quality does not appeal to everyone. Catherine Deneuve once remarked, "Brazil doesn't attract me. It's too consistently carefree."

dominal operations, the prayers of Roman Catholics, Protestants, and members of Afro-Brazilian and Oriental cults asked for (and expected) divine intervention in the form of a miraculous recovery. As the *New York Times* reported, "A man dragged a large wooden cross along the hospital sidewalk. Another followed, flagellating himself with a whip. People have walked by on wounded knees, fumbling rosaries, praying, chanting out loud." Those who believed in mental telepathy set up "national chains of energy" to transmit "positive currents" to the fatally stricken leader.*

The three peoples whose blood commingles in the veins of most Brazilians have contributed much to the peculiar brand of religiosity that has taken root in Brazil. The Portuguese colonists brought with them a Roman Catholicism that was much "softer" and more tolerant than the brand practiced by their Iberian neighbors, the Spaniards. The vastness of Brazil and a shortage of priests led to a lack of supervision and discipline in religious practice, which in turn permitted, especially in the interior, the emergence of a folk Catholicism blending superstition and archaic beliefs, such as messianism.

The slaves imported from West Africa to work on sugar plantations managed to preserve their ancestral religious orthodoxies and rituals even though they were forced to convert to Roman Catholicism. They merged their deities, called *orixás*, with Catholic saints and created a unique syncretism, marrying superficial elements of Catholicism with the fundamental tenets of their cults. The latter have not only survived to the present day but have attracted followers of every race and social class.

The Indian heritage includes belief in spirits and in the extraordinary powers of shamans, or medicine men, who can communicate with the dead, foresee the future, and cure illnesses. This tradition demonstrated its continuing vitality in 1986 when national attention focused on the plight of a famous naturalist, Augusto Ruschi, who was suffering from serious liver problems and

---

* If these events smacked of the surreal, how much more surrealistic were widely circulated reports that the actual cause of the president-elect's death was an infection he contracted from one of the many onlookers who were unaccountably allowed to be present in the operating room during his surgery?

nosebleeds as a result of contact with a rare poisonous frog. Conventional medical treatment having failed to help, the president of Brazil personally intervened, summoning the chief of an Amazon tribe and its medicine man first to a meeting with him in Brasília, and then sending the duo to Rio de Janeiro, where they applied herbs and special smoke to the ailing Ruschi. The press, which had been covering the affair in meticulous detail, happily reported that the Indians had restored their patient to health. (He died four months later from renal insufficiency.)

The tendency of Brazilians to believe in magic, or at the very least to exercise a remarkable tolerance for such beliefs, bridges past and future. Nowhere is this phenomenon more evident than in "Mystic Brasília," to borrow the title of a brochure once published by the Department of Tourism of the Federal District. Brazil's capital has drawn to it a surprising number of individuals and groups espousing ufology, parapsychology, alternative medicine, and other ornaments of the Age of Aquarius. Books have been written using numerology and pointing to the prevalence of pyramid shapes in the city to argue that Brasília is in fact an Egyptian city, foreordained to become the capital of the world in the third millennium. The use of official publications to promote such chiliastic notions suggests that people in high places take them seriously.*

This widespread preoccupation with the preternatural has led some Brazilians to describe Brazil as surrealistic (or to go further and invoke an often-quoted comment, falsely attributed to French President Charles de Gaulle, that "Brazil is not a serious country"). There is undoubtedly a strong trace of the Brazilian inferiority complex underlying these characterizations. But the magic that Brazilians embrace has not prevented the nation from showing signs of emerging as an industrial power; it is merely another face of Brazil. Indeed, Brazil's destiny may be to demonstrate that it can be at once surreal and great.

---

* The "Mystic Brasília" brochure bears the stamp of the Department of Tourism of the Federal District and an introduction by then Governor José Aparecido, who later served as Ambassador to Portugal and was named foreign minister by President Itamar Franco. Illness prevented him from assuming the latter post.

To do so, however, Brazil must overcome its contemporary crisis, which in fact represents the most recent and deepest nosedive in a giddy roller-coaster ride that Brazilians have experienced over the past three decades. The hopefulness that burgeoned in late 1994 suggests that Brazil may once again have made the transition from plunge to climb.

An understanding of where the Brazilians presently find themselves requires a brief retracing of the hectic journey that has taken them from euphoria to instability, from repression to economic miracle, from high hope to disillusion, and back again to the initial stages of what could be a meteoric recovery.

In the late 1950s, the dynamic leadership of President Juscelino Kubitschek launched Brazil on a path toward rapid economic development. "Fifty years in five" was the ambitious order of the day issued by Juscelino as he adopted policies that encouraged industrial expansion. He also gave substance to a long-standing national dream by constructing in the middle of nowhere a modernistic new capital, Brasília, which would help open up the country's interior.

Juscelino's optimism and enthusiasm were highly contagious. Brazil's triumph in the 1958 World Cup soccer championship in Sweden (followed by the capturing of a second title in Chile in 1962) and the worldwide popularity of the bossa nova (a felicitous marriage of Brazilian samba and American jazz) convinced many Brazilians that their "tomorrow" had at last dawned.

The performances of Juscelino's successors, however, dampened the nation's mood. Jânio Quadros, winning the presidency as an "antipolitician" reformist, turned out to be quirky and erratic. His mysterious, unexpected resignation after less than a year in office shook the country and brought to the nation's highest office Vice President João Goulart, a populist deeply distrusted by the armed forces and the economic elite. Goulart inherited an economy wracked by inflation—the legacy of Juscelino's spending spree—and proceeded to reduce it to even greater shambles. His efforts to redistribute wealth and shift the balance of political power to the Left were often clumsy and provoked predictable resistance from those who prospered from the status quo. His policies and demagogic style frightened the middle and upper classes so thoroughly and created such widespread unrest that the military overthrew him in 1964.

Brazil thereupon entered a long night of authoritarian rule. Military interventions in the past had always been temporary—exercises of the armed forces' self-appointed (yet widely accepted) role as guarantors of public order. But this time the military refused to step aside, and one general-president followed another. Although some trappings of democracy remained, the military held the country in an iron grip and vowed to purge the body politic of "communism and corruption." The leaders did not hesitate to utilize measures such as censorship, arbitrary arrest, and torture. Hundreds of individuals, ranging from Communist party members to ex-President Kubitschek, had their political rights summarily suspended. The repression reached its nadir during the late 1960s and early 1970s.

The only institution strong enough to resist the regime was the Roman Catholic Church. Following the courageous examples set by Recife's Archbishop Hélder Câmara and São Paulo's Cardinal Paulo Arns, a significant number of bishops, priests, and nuns came forward to defend the human rights of those targeted by the regime.

During this same period, responding to policies that promoted industrialization through private investment and stifled workers' wage demands, the economy grew at an astonishing annual rate of nearly 11 percent. By 1973 the country was exporting $10 billion worth of goods, up from less than $3 billion in 1968. The world soon began to take notice of what came to be known as the "Brazilian miracle."* For the upper and middle classes, the giddy optimism of the Kubitschek era returned in full force.

Not to be outdone by Juscelino, the generals launched their own exuberant projects and gave free rein to what Brazilians call their "pharaonic complex." The trans-Amazon highway, a massive hydroelectric complex at Itaipú on the border with Paraguay and

---

* No less an authority than U.S. economist Milton Friedman was among those who saluted the "miracle" and its apparent taming of inflation by a device known as indexing, which adjusted prices and wages upward to keep pace with the current rate of inflation.

Argentina, the Rio Niterói Bridge across Guanabara Bay, and a nuclear power plant were its most notable expressions.

Brazil, however, was the Third World's leading petroleum importer, and the quadrupling of oil prices in the wake of the 1973 Middle East conflict caused the bubble to burst. The growth rate tailed off sharply, balance-of-payments deficits ballooned, inflation began to soar, and by the late 1970s the country was mired in a deep recession. Brazil's foreign debt raced past the $100 billion mark, the largest in the underdeveloped world, and rising interest rates abroad made full service payments unthinkable. The mood of those whom the "miracle" had profited now matched that of the lower classes, whose economic position had in fact worsened substantially during the rapid growth spurt (a result that demonstrated beyond cavil that rising tides do not always lift all boats).

Unable to stem the downturn, the armed forces decided that the time had come for the gradual restoration of civilian rule. The regime lifted censorship, permitted left-wing exiles to return, eased restrictions on political activity, and planned to have a special electoral college choose the next president. The move toward redemocratization unleashed tremendous popular enthusiasm, as millions of Brazilians took to the streets in 1984 to demand direct presidential elections. The regime clung to its plan but lost control of the process, and the opposition candidate won an overwhelming victory.

On January 1, 1985, the first baby of the new year was celebrated by the media as a symbol of the era that was about to dawn, and he was named Tancredinho, in honor of the man who was soon to become the nation's president-elect. But in mid-March the baby, who lived in a Rio de Janeiro slum, died of pneumonia and dehydration. It was a bad omen.

Tancredo Neves's fatal illness, which prevented him from taking office, was a cruel twist of fate, because he gave every indication of being the right person in the right place at the right time. A seasoned politician skilled in the art of accommodation, he might well have been able to guide his country through the difficult days ahead. With his passing the euphoria with which the country had been hailing the departure of its military rulers was deflated, but only temporarily.

Vice President José Sarney, a provincial politician who had supported the military regime and whom Tancredo had tapped in order to balance the ticket, assumed the presidency. After a somewhat
hesitant start, Sarney gained tremendous popularity with an economic program aimed at stemming the growing menace of inflation by decreeing a price and wage freeze. But when the
government had to lift the cap on prices in late 1986, because of
serious shortages of food and other consumer goods, and inflation
soared, Sarney did not have the faintest idea what to do next. Most
of the country's politicians, moreover, displayed an incapacity for
anything except political gamesmanship. Reports of corruption and
waste at all levels of government appeared with increasing frequency in the press and added to a growing mood of discontent.
Popular revulsion peaked when President Sarney flew 150 guests
to Paris, where they lavishly celebrated, at the Brazilian taxpayers'
expense, the bicentennial of the French Revolution.

Social inequities, meanwhile, reached potentially explosive
levels. The sporadic looting of food supplies and the riots triggered
by failures in the rail system indicated that the patience of the nation's have-nots had limits. Personal security became a matter of
major concern for all Brazilians, as the crime rate joined inflation
in an upward climb. Heavily armed gangs of drug traffickers in Rio
de Janeiro took control of large slum areas, where they even began to furnish municipal services.

Against this backdrop, the Brazilian Congress devoted almost
two years to the drafting of a new Constitution to replace the authoritarian document the military had promulgated as the supreme
law of the land in 1967. A surreal aura enveloped the process, as
the federal lawmakers who formed the constituent assembly
charged with drafting the document seemed to assume that constitutional fiat in and of itself could somehow transform the country, and that constitutional guarantees that all citizens would have
equal access to basic rights would somehow concretize these aspirations.

The lengthy, minutely detailed charter approved on September 2, 1988, touched upon almost every aspect of life in Brazil. It
curtailed the powers of the chief executive, reduced the presidential term from six years to five, reduced the voting age to sixteen,

and capped annual interest rates at 12 percent, a provision that could not possibly be taken seriously in an economy where the monthly inflation rate was at least twice that figure.

On the other hand, the new Constitution ignored some urgent problems, such as the imbalance in the relative congressional representation enjoyed by different regions of the country. Thus, one third of Brazil's population continued to control two thirds of the members of the Chamber of Deputies—an arrangement that the military regime had purposefully imposed and that fixed power in the hands of politicians from the less developed rural states. Thus, a deputy from São Paulo would need more than two hundred thousand votes to be elected; while one from the state of Roraima in Amazônia would need only about five thousand.

At a time when Brazil seemed to cry out for a period of institutional stability, the new Constitution injected jarring uncertainties into the political panorama. It provided for a plebiscite in 1993 to determine not only whether the country should move to parliamentary government (similar to the systems used in Western Europe), but also whether the country should transform itself into a constitutional monarchy or remain a republic.* It also would permit the 1993 Congress to enact constitutional amendments by a simple majority vote.†

One of the notable innovations of the new "Magna Carta" affected the ground rules for presidential elections. If no candidate obtained an absolute majority of the vote, a second election would pit the two front-runners against one another.

When the elections came up in 1989, Brazilians had not cast their ballots for a president for almost thirty years. Back in 1960 they chose a quintessential outsider who promised to sweep away corruption and reinvigorate democratic rule. Although the election of Jânio Quadros had provoked disastrous consequences, the electorate of 1989 proved susceptible to a similar pitch, and history began to repeat itself in a number of ways.

---

* Both republicanism and presidentialism prevailed.

† Instead of rewriting the Constitution to make it more realistic and workable, Congress proved incapable of dealing with the opportunity presented in 1993 and made few changes in the document.

In a bewildering field of more than twenty candidates, one man stood out, helped in no small part by strong support from Brazil's largest television network. Fernando Collor de Mello, the thirty-nine-year-old ex-governor of the small northeastern state of Alagoas, and ex-mayor of Maceió, its capital—and a strong supporter of the Sarney government until the economy soured—broke out of the pack early in the race.

The public knew him because of his highly publicized hunt for "maharajahs," the name given to state officials who collected fat paychecks without ever showing up for work, and for his other efforts to eliminate waste and corruption in his home state. He was able to capitalize on a youthful, telegenic appearance and the national mood of revulsion toward the spendthrift government and the tradition of politics as a vehicle for the enrichment of politicians and their families.

The rest of the field was comprised of familiar warhorses, and a few fresh faces, such as that of Luís Inácio da Silva (known popularly as Lula). A former São Paulo metalworker, Lula had cut his political teeth in labor struggles during the 1970s and had served a term as federal deputy. He carried the banner of the Workers' party, a coalition of union and grassroots activists, Catholic militants and left-wing intellectuals.

As the campaign progressed, it was clear that the economy had become a "basket case." Indeed, the monthly inflation rate hit 34 percent in September of that year. Collor proposed no specific steps to deal with the crisis. He put himself forward as a populist conservative, pledging to open Brazil's economy to the free market, to sell off unprofitable state enterprises, and to cut down the size of the federal government; at the same time he promised to spend more on social welfare.

After a heated campaign that produced some moments of memorable mudslinging (Collor's people paid an ex-lover of Lula's to come forward and claim that she had rejected his requests that she abort the child she was carrying—a daughter Lula had always acknowledged), Collor emerged victorious by about five percentage points, and Brazil stood poised to enter yet another new era.

Many Brazilians saw Collor as their own John F. Kennedy. He had good looks and projected a youthful vitality (and devil-may-care recklessness) that seemed to reflect the defining characteristics of his native land. People were willing to overlook his inexperience and the fact that he had no political base in the Congress. The opportunism that had fueled his political career was discounted, as were his close ties to a small northeastern state reputed to be one of the most politically violent and primitive in the country.*

The new president pledged to trim three hundred thousand jobs from the federal payroll and privatize many of the state-owned enterprises that had long been a drain on the federal budget. He also launched yet another ambitious economic plan that would, in his words, "kill the tiger [of inflation] with one shot."

The plan was the brainchild of Zélia Cardoso de Mello (no relation), Collor's young Minister of the Economy. Among other belt-tightening measures she imposed upon Brazilians was a freeze on withdrawals from all bank accounts for one year. The hardships it imposed on middle- and upper-income Brazilians were substantial. (For example, many people who had entered contracts to purchase homes or apartments could not access their savings to pay for them.) Several suicides and heart attacks were linked to the new program, but most Brazilians, as good-natured as ever, were willing to accept as necessary evils the financial burdens they had to bear. Inflation eased, but only temporarily. Soon the "tiger" returned with a vengeance.

Collor provided diversion with his presidential style. He flew military jets, rode jet-powered water skis, and donned T-shirts with political or inspirational messages for his morning jogs. The presidential sideshow took on aspects of a soap opera when his marriage appeared to sour and he conducted a press conference at which he revealed he had removed his wedding band.

The "Brasília Follies," as they could have been called, escalated when Zélia, seeking respite from the intractable problems created by the persistence of inflation and recession, embarked on a love affair with Justice Minister Bernardo Cabral. The couple let the world know they were an item by dancing cheek to cheek to the

---

* Indeed, his father, a senator from Alagoas, had once killed a bystander during a gunfight with a political opponent on the floor of the Senate.

music of the bolero "Bésame Mucho" at Zélia's 1990 birthday party. The liaison between the fifty-eight-year-old married man and the attractive (and much younger) single woman set tongues wagging on several continents and gave some Brazilians an opportunity to exercise their sense of humor.*

President Collor could not permit the affair to continue. Since at this point in time the economy took precedence over the justice system, he asked for Cabral's resignation and kept Zélia at her post. When her economic plan continued to show no positive results, she too lost her job.†

The adventures and misadventures of Zélia Cardoso de Mello turned out to be a minor farce in light of what was to follow. In May 1992 Fernando Collor's younger brother, Pedro, went public with charges of corruption against one of the president's closest associates, and Brazil soon began to wallow in a sea of mud dubbed "Collorgate."

According to Pedro Collor, Paulo César Farias—or P.C., as he was known to all—had used his intimate access to the new president to set up an elaborate system of kickbacks that required individuals and corporations doing business with the federal government to divert to him as a surcharge a substantial percentage of the sums of money they expected to derive from their dealings with Brasília. The stocky, mustachioed entrepreneur P.C. had been closely associated with Fernando Collor during the latter's earlier political career in Alagoas and had served as treasurer of the Collor presidential campaign. At this time, although he held no office, he was said to be busily trading on what he represented as his access to the president.

Pedro Collor claimed initially that he was pointing the finger at P.C. because the latter had begun to threaten certain Collor fam-

---

* When Zélia landed with an official party at the military airport in Brasília a short time later, the air force band, on hand to greet the group, launched into "Bésame Mucho."

† Her first public appearance after resigning was on a TV comedy show that had often lampooned her. She gave a tearful defense of her performance in office and later married the star of the program. Cabral, who had unilaterally terminated his relationship with the Minister of the Economy, paid for his "sins" by becoming the chief target of a torrid best-seller based on interviews granted by Zélia.

ily business interests that Pedro was responsible for administering. But the family immediately tried to silence him. The president was particularly eager to keep his brother quiet; he went so far as to arrange for his mother to discharge Pedro from his job and raise doubts about his sanity. This served only to aggravate matters, as Pedro then went public with fresh accusations that Fernando had once attempted to seduce his wife and had introduced him to cocaine.

By now it was apparent that the presidential affair compared favorably with any plot ever concocted for Brazil's famous *telenovelas*. The media, having given Fernando Collor a "free ride" during the presidential campaign, now pursued the story with a zeal and thoroughness unique in the history of Brazilian journalism. No patch of muck remained unraked, and daily disclosures kept the country alternating among states of amusement, shock, disbelief, and disgust.

Fernando Collor's involvement in the scandal soon became painfully apparent. P.C. had channeled a portion of the kickback funds back to the president to pay for such items as the lavish personal expenses of the First Lady, a Parisian apartment for the president and himself, and the opulent remodeling of the president's private residence in Brasília. The president maintained his innocence, but few believed him. The evidence established at best his tacit approval of (and at worst his connivance in) the shameless looting. The man who had become famous as a fighter against corruption now looked like the fox who had the keys to the henhouse.

Congress brought impeachment charges, the first time this had ever happened to a Brazilian president, and Collor did his best to win congressional support in the time-honored way—by attempting to buy votes with promises of presidential largesse. But public opinion had been aroused, and protesters took to the streets to demand his ouster. Accepting the inevitability of removal from office, Fernando Collor resigned, leaving intact Juscelino Kubitschek's distinction of being the last Brazilian president to serve out his term.

There was public jubilation, but it was short-lived. Collor had selected as his running mate an obscure politician who was thought to bring certain electoral strength to the ticket. When Vice President Itamar Franco succeeded to the highest office in the land, it was soon apparent that he was as ill-equipped as Sarney had been to deal with the problems facing Brazil.*

At heart a populist, Itamar sincerely wanted to help Brazil's have-nots, but he was uncomfortable with the idea that tough measures were needed to modernize the economy and streamline the government. Moreover, he did not seem to realize the extent to which inflation victimized the poor. (Brazilians with money could always play the financial markets and actually come out ahead during inflationary cycles.) The country drifted aimlessly under his weak leadership.

At the same time the national taste for exposing corruption had not abated with the ouster of Fernando Collor, and investigations by the press and congressional committees brought to light all kinds of fresh scandals implicating Brazilian politicians. The new mood extended to the business community, and the government began to pursue tax evaders aggressively for the first time.

Itamar Franco managed to maintain the image of an honest man, but his erratic personal behavior nullified whatever advantages he might otherwise have reaped from his probity. At the 1994 Rio Carnival, he permitted one of the participants in the parade to join him in his box, where he let her stand next to him and raise her arms to salute the crowd. Widely published photographs revealed that all she was wearing at the time was a T-shirt that failed to cover her private parts.

The *Economist* magazine once referred to Brazil as a "stumbling elephant in the van of the charge towards affluence by the most development-ripe dozen countries among the poor two thirds of the world." But it had by now become painfully evident that Brazil had gone from the point position to the rearguard of development in Latin America. The economies of Chile, Argentina, and Mexico were thriving, while the Brazilian gross domestic product had fallen by 1 percent in 1992. Spain had passed Brazil on the list of the world's largest market economies, and other nations were

---

* Alma Guillermoprieto, in an article in *The New Yorker*, wrote of "the odorless, flavorless Itamar Franco, who seems incapable of more than pained expressions of dismay as the great ship of state sinks slowly into a mudbank."

poised to follow. In 1989 Brazil had the eighth most competitive economy among developing nations; by 1993 it had dropped to fourteenth. Brazil's inflation, meanwhile, soared into first place. (In March 1994, inflation increased at a rate of more than 45 percent.) Instead of being a Third World country poised to leap into the "First World," Brazil gave every indication of being in a free fall toward the "Fourth World."

In addition, there were abundant signs that the reservoir of goodwill Brazilians traditionally enjoyed abroad was beginning to evaporate. Foreign criticism of human-rights violations and environmental devastation in Brazil had intensified to the point where Brazilians began to protest what they saw as "Brazil-bashing." This negative trend might have reached its nadir on a bumper sticker spotted in England and declaring: Fight for the Rain Forests—Burn a Brazilian.

A tongue-in-cheek article in the *New York Times Magazine* (purportedly a "Historian's Guide to American History" published in the year 2008) noted that the Taiwanese had purchased Brazil at the start of the twenty-first century—a sad commentary on the present state of the international reputation of what was once the "Country of the Future."

Meanwhile, Itamar kept changing Ministers of the Economy, with no effect on the inflation rate. In June 1993, he named Fernando Henrique Cardoso to the post. It was a move that smacked of desperation in one sense, since the new minister had no financial or administrative experience. But he did bring to the job a keen, dispassionate mind and an understanding that putting Brazil's economic house in order should be the government's number-one priority.

An internationally-renowned sociologist who had made a successful transition from intellectual to politician in 1978 and had gained respect as a federal senator from a São Paulo-based party that was slightly to the left of center, Fernando Henrique perceived a national-leadership vacuum as well as a mood of apprehension and paralysis on the part of Brazil's upper and middle classes in the face of the apparent inevitably of a victory by Lula in the presidential elections scheduled for October 1994. It was obvious that the electorate would not accept any of the shopworn candidates offered by the existing political parties, nor, after the Collor debacle, were they likely to warm to a media-created nominee. There was an opening for someone who could offer more than promises. Fernando Henrique seized the moment.

He developed an economic plan that called for the creation of a new currency, a reduction in government spending, the privatization of state-owned companies, the continuation of negotiations begun in 1990 to restructure Brazil's foreign debt, and the opening of the Brazilian market to foreign imports—the latter an initiative meant to force Brazilian industry to compete. Inflation continued unabated in early 1994. Fernando Henrique revised the plan by pegging the monetary system to a unit of value that was itself pegged to the dollar, and resigned his position to run for the presidency.

Both his plan and his political gamble paid off handsomely. Inflation fell off sharply, and Brazil reached an agreement that restructured its obligations to foreign banks and brought to an end the debt crisis that had been looming, like the sword of Damocles, since 1982. Fernando Henrique crept up on and then overtook Lula in the polls, as Brazilians adjusted to a stable economy and once again began to feel optimistic about their future. A victory in the World Cup soccer tournament held in the United States in the summer of 1994 reinforced the new national mood.

Lula at first failed to grasp the damage the economic recovery was doing to his candidacy, and then tried to argue that the government and big business were holding down the inflation rate in artificial ways to secure the election of Fernando Henrique.* The latter, on his part, ran a controlled campaign and avoided gaffes like the one he committed during an unsuccessful campaign for mayor of São Paulo, when he admitted on television that he did not believe in God. He won enough votes to win in the first round.

The prospect of an economically sound Brazilian economy attracted an influx of foreign capital. The government began to lower tariff barriers, especially those that hindered commerce with Ar-

---

* Lula was unable to capitalize on the fact that Fernando Henrique's successor as Minister of the Economy admitted to this in early September in an interview he did not realize was going out on live television.

gentina, Paraguay, and Uruguay, and Brazil's trade surpluses mounted. Talk of Brazil as the "Country of the Future" once again resounded throughout the Western Hemisphere.

However, the fact that after the elections the government had to call upon the army to occupy Rio de Janeiro slum areas that had fallen under the control of gangs of drug dealers cast a chill over the mood of optimism, at least for those who paid heed to both parts of "Belindia." And magazine photos of garbage pickers eating large, roasted rats on spits served as a grim reminder of the social ills that a true national recovery would have to address.

This book examines Brazilianness, with particular emphasis on the context of the current crisis and the events leading up to it. It both explains to non-Brazilians the unique character of the Brazilian people and explores how national character may have contributed to the dilemma in which the country now finds itself.

Brazilians themselves have long struggled with the problem of self-definition. The enormous size of the country, its regional diversity, and the richness of its culture complicate the task at hand. Indeed, a description and analysis of every aspect of Brazilianness could fill several volumes. Therefore, comprehensiveness will have to yield to selectivity, with respect both to themes and approaches to them.

Part One examines the ethnic and racial components of Brazilian society; Part Two tells stories about rich and poor Brazilians; Part Three looks at the phenomenon of violence in Brazil; Part Four considers Brazilian spirituality; and Part Five presents some miscellaneous aspects of Brazilianness.

# Who Are The Brazilians?

# Chapter 1

# The Portuguese

*A* search for Brazilianness must begin with the remarkable people who gave the Brazilians their language, religion, and some essential components of their national character. Indeed, the glue that held Brazil together after it achieved independence—in contrast to the centrifugal forces that fragmented Spain's colonial empire—had a markedly "made-in-Portugal" stamp.

Yet the relationship between Brazilians and their mother country is ambivalent at best. Jokes poking fun at the Portuguese enjoy a high degree of popularity in Brazil. Brazilian television soap operas and miniseries dealing with historical themes often depict the Portuguese in a disparaging light. Brazilian municipalities named after Portuguese cities and towns are exceedingly rare (in contrast to designations such as New London, Manchester, Cambridge, Oxford, Windsor, and Greenwich found in North America). Brazilians seem to take little pride in the fact that the ancestors of most of them came from a tiny country with a truly glorious past.

Because of its geographical location on the crossroads between Europe and Africa, the land that eventually produced the nation of Portugal attracted a steady influx of invaders. The first outsiders came from the north about ten centuries before the birth of Christ. The primitive Iberians left a lasting mark, since the peninsula to which they emigrated on the southwestern edge of the European land mass still bears their name. Celts, Phoenicians, Greeks, Carthaginians, and Romans followed in turn, the latter establishing themselves in what is now southern and central Portugal, the

35

province of Lusitania, which would provide an enduring synonym (Lusitanians) for "Portuguese." At the end of the fifth century new invaders began to appear, first the Vandals and then the Visigoths. By this time the inhabitants of the peninsula had embraced Christianity, and they succeeded in converting their pagan conquerors. In 711 the Moors crossed the Straits of Gibraltar from North Africa and brought with them their Moslem faith. Eventually they installed themselves throughout much of the peninsula.

Adding to the racial mix were small colonies of Sephardic Jews who appeared in Lisbon and other port cities during the Moslem conquest. They managed to gain economic and political influence as merchants, tax collectors, court physicians, astrologers, and middlemen between Christians and Moslems. During the Inquisition many of them accepted conversion and became "New Christians," although many viewed with skepticism their claims to be bona fide Christians.

The Portuguese nation emerged from the struggles by rulers of the earldom of Portugal, a portion of the peninsula the Moors had not conquered, to expel the "infidels" and resist the hegemonic designs of Castile, whose king was claiming the Portugese Crown and ruling over the most powerful of the peninsula's Christian kingdoms. It was not until 1250 that the Portuguese reconquered their territory from the Moors. Then in 1385 they defeated the Castilians and at last secured their independence.

With youthful zest, fueled at first by religious fervor and later by a lust for riches, the new nation began to reach out beyond its borders. The Portuguese pursued the Moors into North Africa and captured the city of Ceuta in 1415. At the same time they proceeded to take advantage of their geographical position on the outer rim of Europe. Seafaring came naturally to the Portuguese, and their beloved Prince Henry (popularly known as "Henry the Navigator") invested heavily in the honing of their maritime capabilities. The Lusitanians soon became masters of the art of ocean navigation. They also developed the caravel, a ship that could sail against the wind.

Venturing out into the Atlantic Ocean and making their way gradually down the shoreline of Africa, they discovered and established colonies on Madeira and the Azores, the former off the coast of Africa, the latter due west of their homeland. Their success inevitably attracted the attention of other maritime nations of Europe, and soon little Portugal faced stern competition. The Spanish leapt into the exploration business and seized the Canary Islands, off the northwest coast of Africa. In 1492 a Genovese named Christopher Columbus sailing westward under the auspices of the Spanish Crown found what he thought was a direct sea route across the Atlantic to India. This put Spain into potential conflict with Portugal. The Pope encouraged both sides to work out a settlement. The result was the Treaty of Tordesillas, signed under papal auspices in 1494: Portugal was to control all lands, newly discovered or to be discovered, lying east of a line running north and south 1,110 miles west of the Cape Verde Islands; Spain assumed authority over everything to the west of the line.

The location of the line turned out to carry enormous significance: it put a large slice of Brazil within the Portuguese hemisphere. Indeed, this apparent stroke of good fortune has aroused suspicion (as yet unproven) in some quarters that Portuguese navigators veering widely off the bulge of Africa had already sighted the Brazilian coast and had relayed information to the royal court, which had kept the news a secret as it negotiated the treaty.

Several years later Vasco da Gama made his historic voyage around the Cape of Good Hope to India, and Portugal's golden age was at hand. Outflanking the Moslem countries situated on the overland routes between Europe and the East, the intrepid Portuguese eventually reached China and Japan and were able to ship goods from the Orient more cheaply over the sea lanes they had mastered. They also opened up trade with Africa and set out to produce sugar and wine in their colonies on Madeira and the Azores. Caravels laden with spices, silk, perfume, porcelain, gold, ivory, and other valuable commodities (including slaves) were soon streaming into Lisbon.

The discovery of Brazil seemed at first to be but a footnote to this success story. In 1500 Pedro Cabral set sail from Lisbon with thirteen ships. His mission was to replicate the journey of Vasco da Gama. But adverse winds blew the vessels off their course as they tried to hug the shoreline of Africa, and on April 22 Cabral's sailors spotted what they believed to be an island, which they named Vera Cruz (True Cross).

In fact, Cabral had stumbled upon what is now the southern coast of the state of Bahia. Sailing northward in search of shelter for his ships, he found a small harbor, to which his men gave the name Porto Seguro (Safe Port). The local inhabitants, apparently peaceable and totally without guile, observed the newcomers with great curiosity. The Portuguese planted a cross, replenished their water supply, and left behind two exiles, who were instructed to learn the native language and customs. One ship returned home with a report of the discovery. The rest of the fleet resumed the voyage to India.

The royal court greeted the news of Cabral's find with indifference. More important things were happening in the Orient. The fact that Vera Cruz apparently contained neither gold nor precious stones put it near the bottom of Portugal's priorities. Subsequent explorations confirmed that Vera Cruz was no island, and revealed the abundance of brazilwood, the raw material for a valuable red dye. Lusitanian merchants began to exploit this resource, which in time gave the new land its permanent name.

The profits that could be earned from the brazilwood trade soon attracted entrepreneurs from countries that refused to recognize the Treaty of Tordesillas. The French made increasingly frequent appearances along the Brazilian coast. The few trading posts established by the Portuguese proved insufficent to prevent these incursions, so in the 1630s Lisbon decided to colonize Brazil as a means of protecting it against foreigners.

The first permanent Portuguese residents of Brazil were the outcasts left behind by Cabral, other exiles put ashore by later expeditions, and sailors who survived shipwrecks in the waters off the coast. These men went totally "native," cohabiting with Indian women who often treated them as gods and freely bore their offspring. They were the first Europeans to experience the seduction of tropical Brazil, and the knowledge they acquired would prove valuable to Portugal's colonization efforts.

The first official colonists put down roots in São Vicente, near what is today the port of Santos in the state of São Paulo. Other settlements were founded to the north along what turned out to be a three-thousand-mile coastline. Because incursions from other European powers threatened the vast new territory, the Portuguese Crown realized that colonization would be the only way it could retain access to the wealth of Brazil, but instead of directly underwriting the effort of occupying the colony, the Crown decided to let others do the job. So Brazil was divided into fifteen so-called captaincies, parallel strips of land bordered to the east by the sea and to the west by the line of the Treaty of Tordesillas. Each captaincy stretched at least ninety miles along the coast. The king bestowed them to distinguished noblemen or commoners who had rendered outstanding service to the Crown.

There were elements of both feudalism and capitalism in the system of captaincies. The captaincy was hereditary and subjected the grantee to the absolute authority of the Crown, which reserved for itself a monopoly over the brazilwood trade and the right to collect certain taxes. But the grantee had the right to profit from agricultural enterprises set up in the captaincy—an arrangement that gave him incentives to invest. He could also distribute lands, and he undertook responsibility for populating, administering, Christianizing, and defending his domain.

Except for São Vicente in the south and Pernambuco in the Northeast, where the soil was especially suited for the growing of sugarcane and the grantees were wealthy, dynamic individuals, the captaincies floundered. Most of the original grantees had no experience in governance and lacked the resources to defend their domains and carry out other administrative tasks that should have been the responsibility of the Crown. The natives often turned out to be uncooperative, unlike those who had watched Cabral's men come ashore (some tribes even practiced cannibalism on their enemies), and they stubbornly resisted "pacification." Moreover, protecting the coast against the French turned out to be much more difficult than anticipated.

But despite its shortcomings, the captaincy system left a lasting imprint on Brazil. Six of Brazil's current states bear the names of the captaincies from which they evolved. Moreover, because of a shortage of colonists, grantees often subdivided their captaincies into huge estates, which they then parceled out to family and friends—a practice that produced a pattern of landholding that has profoundly influenced (some say severely retarded) the social and economic development of rural Brazil.

The failure of the captaincies forced the Crown to rethink its colonial policy. The decision was reached to maintain the captaincies as administrative units but to centralize control over them. In 1549 a governor-general appointed by the king and given broad authority arrived in the scenic Bahia de Todos os Santos (Bay of All Saints), conveniently located between São Vicente to the south and Pernambuco to the north, and set about to found the town of Bahia (or Salvador, as it would later come to be called), the new capital of the colony. He brought with him a party of one thousand, which included soldiers, bureaucrats, artisans, and six Jesuit priests who were to take charge of the Christianization of Brazil.

The new structure of colonial governance proved provident, for it enabled the Portuguese to repel a serious attempt by the French to plant a permanent colony in the vicinity of Guanabara Bay. French settlers had cut São Vicente off from the rest of Brazil and were exploiting the extensive brazilwood groves found near the bay. After a two-year siege, the Portuguese governor-general managed to oust the French in 1567 and establish the settlement of Rio de Janeiro.

The colony as a whole thrived under the guidance of the governors-general, who acted as the king's representatives. They encouraged agriculture and created special incentives for the production of sugar for export. A shortage of workers in the cane fields created difficulties, especially when colonists began to use Indians as slave laborers. The Portuguese Crown had promised the Pope to civilize and protect the Indians, and the Jesuits sought to carry out this commitment, which often brought them into conflict with the planters' need for cheap labor. The controversy over enslavement of the Indians, the latter's inability to adapt to regimented work in the fields (they were nomads and rejected the sedentary life), and the steady growth of the sugar industry combined to force the colonists to look to Africa for slave laborers. Soon the massive importation of black slaves began in earnest.

An important implication of the new centralized system of administration was the Portuguese Crown's direct involvement in the growth of the colony. No longer would the king rely on others to finance the development of Brazil. The royal court not only invested in its overseas territory but also encouraged immigration. In the second half of the sixteenth century the number of Lusitanians in Brazil increased from thirty-five hundred to thirty-five thousand.

The Portuguese who settled in the New World were a varied lot. Members of the nobility could be found among the grantees of captaincies and owners of large landholdings within the captaincies. Prosperous commoners also benefited from sizeable land grants. Some of the peasants who emigrated became small landowners, and others inhabited urban settlements. Exiles banished from their homeland because they had violated the strict laws of Portugal constituted another slice of Brazilian society. They were nonconformists, often from influential families; some found success in their new lives; others became the dregs of their communities. Finally, a number of "New Christians" migrated to the coastal cities and soon played a key role in the production and export of Brazil's sugar.

The Portuguese crossing the Atlantic in the sixteenth century brought with them various traits that would contribute to the evolution of Brazilianness. The adventurers responsible for Portugal's maritime empire were self-reliant individualists who neither accepted nor imposed upon others the constraints of discipline or organization but nonetheless recognized their place within the hierarchical society of medieval Portugal. They responded both to the spiritual imperatives of their Christian faith and to the crass materialism that fueled the commercial enterprises upon which they were embarking.

One of the key strengths of the Portuguese colonists was adaptability, a characteristic honed over the centuries during which foreign invaders occupied portions of the Iberian peninsula. In addition, there was a physical aspect to this capacity for accommodation. The climate of Portugal tends to be more African than European; thus the Lusitanians had little difficulty adjusting to the tropical climate of Brazil.

The Portuguese who migrated to Brazil often tended to hold manual labor in disdain, a natural corollary of their refined sense of dignity bred by the success of Portugal's imperial adventures. Also the Portuguese had been relying on black slaves to perform most domestic work for about a century, so they had accumulated a sense of entitlement to a life free from drudgery.

The long contact between the Portuguese and the Moors had produced some remarkable psychological consequences. The Portuguese male had grown to idolize the Moorish woman as the embodiment of feminine beauty. Perhaps it was the reaction of a conquered people to its conquerors. The Moorish princess—dark-skinned, long-haired, mysterious, and supremely erotic—became a staple of Portuguese legend and an object of hidden fantasies. To Portuguese adventurers and colonists, the naked Indian women they encountered in Brazil were a dream come true. These females were close enough to the idealized Moorish princess both in appearance and behavior (both, for example, enjoyed bathing in rivers and combing their tresses), and at the same time submitted willingly to the sexual advances of the Portuguese. This led to the beginning of a process of miscegenation, which would assume greater dimensions as a result of sexual relations between white colonists and African slaves.

The Moors also may have contributed to certain distinctively Oriental aspects of Portuguese society. A fondness for display, the de facto polygamy practiced by heads of households, the excessively patriarchal focus of home life, and the domestic seclusion of women were Moorish legacies that the Portuguese brought with them to Brazil. The latter traits would contribute to the evolution of perhaps the most important of Brazil's contemporary institutions, the family, which defines personal, social, and economic relations for most upper- and middle-class Brazilians.

The Portuguese peasants who migrated to the New World served as conduits for a wealth of legends that went far beyond tales of Moorish princesses. They provided an abundant heritage of folklore that would enrich popular culture in Brazil. One of the more fascinating myths emerged from a historical event that had serious, real-life repercussions for the Brazilian colony.

King Sebastian of Portugal, a religious fanatic who saw himself as Christ's warrior, led his army against the Moslems in Morocco and suffered a disastrous defeat in 1578. Sebastian himself perished on the field of battle. Yet many of his compatriots believed that one day he would return to them in triumph as a messiah. The legend of King Sebastian survived among Portuguese peasants and their descendants, some of whom settled in the interior of Brazil. In the nineteenth century what had come to be known as Sebastianism was responsible for several violent uprisings in the rural Northeast.

The demise of King Sebastian had a more immediate impact. He left no immediate heirs, and the throne of Portugal soon fell into the hands of one of his distant relatives, King Philip II of Spain. Although Philip was not given to meddling in the affairs of the Brazilian colony, Spain's enemies now became Portugal's. The Dutch seized Bahia in 1624. They were driven out the following year, but in 1630 they captured Pernambuco. Soon they controlled most of the Northeast.

Occupation by the Dutch brought with it a certain degree of progress. The new rulers made efforts to expand the sugar industry and encourage the local production of foodstuffs. The city of Pernambuco (later to be called Recife) was introduced to urban planning. For the first time scientific studies of the tropics were launched. But the Portuguese colony resisted the Protestant intruders, both from within the occupied territory and from without. In the early 1640s Portugal successfully rebelled against Spanish rule, established a new royal dynasty, and temporarily patched up its differences with the Netherlands. The Brazilians, however, continued their struggle against Dutch domination, a struggle in which not only white settlers but also blacks and Indians participated. In 1654 they finally succeeded in ousting the Dutch.

The victory had psychological implications. The colonists for the first time felt the strong impulses of national unity, not as Portuguese subjects but as Brazilians. They had defeated the Dutch by themselves. Self-esteem began to replace their sense of inferiority to the Portuguese.

The expulsion of the Dutch marked not only what many consider the birth of Brazilian nationhood but also the emergence of a military mystique that would have lasting effects throughout the country's history. The struggle seeded not only the Brazilian nation but also its army. When the latter took shape as a distinct institution, its leaders would look back on the victory over the Dutch occupiers as the crucible that forged a solid bond between Brazil and its military.

The Crown had facilitated this symbiosis by refraining from committing units of the Portuguese army to defend the colony. Portugal sent a few professional officers to Brazil, and they conscripted troops from the ranks of social outcasts, but what was called Brazil's "paid" army hardly sufficed to protect the colony from external threats. Therefore, Lisbon authorized the creation of local militias, whose members were drawn from all levels of colonial society. Over time the militias inevitably became involved in local politics, and eventually produced a new breed of military men.

The victory against the Dutch was primarily the work of the militias, whose ranks mirrored the multiracial composition of colonial society. Success provided grist for their conviction that Brazil belonged to them at least as much as to the Portuguese Crown.

The penetration of the interior of the subcontinent also contributed heavily to the fortification of the Brazilian psyche. Unlike the United States, where vast plains extended as far west as the Rocky Mountains and a network of navigable rivers facilitated the opening of the West, the topography of Brazil presented formidable obstacles to the first adventurers and settlers who sought to move beyond the coastal zones of the colony. The central highlands rising precipitously not far from the coast blocked access to the heartland of the colony. Moreover, most of the rivers run inland instead of to the ocean and are often impossible to navigate.

The opening of the Brazilian interior was a complex process that had begun with the first Portuguese explorers who ventured inland in search of fabled Indian treasures or the lost colony of warrior women from whom the Amazon River took its name. Efforts to keep the French from establishing a foothold in northern Brazil encouraged the Portuguese to make forays into the Amazon region. The search for land suitable for raising cattle led renegades and mixed-blood cowboys away from the coastal sugar-growing zone of the Northeast and into the interior. The unification of the thrones of Spain and Portugal relaxed the enforcement of restrictions on trade between Brazil and the rest of South America, and overland routes soon linked the colonies.

But the most dramatic and significant probes into the vast, forbidding hinterlands of Brazil were the work of an extraordinary breed of adventurers known as *bandeirantes* from the frontier town of São Paulo in the original captaincy of São Vicente. São Paulo was not far from the coast, but its location atop a plateau descending steeply to the sea gave it a healthy measure of isolation that stimulated self-sufficiency and growth. Its early inhabitants raised livestock and engaged in subsistence farming. Many of them had Indian blood in their veins.

It was a desire to acquire Indian slaves that motivated the first expeditions from São Paulo into the interior. Those who participated were called *bandeirantes,* a medieval Portuguese expression for members of a small mobile assault force. Adopting Indian dress, weapons, and tactics, these fearsome raiders embarked on expeditions that often lasted for several years. The *bandeirantes* decimated settlements the Jesuits had established for the Guarani Indians in what is now Paraguay (a bloody page of history recorded vividly in the film *The Mission*), roamed throughout the center of Brazil, helped fight against the Dutch in the Northeast, and even reached the Amazon River.

There were many who looked upon the *bandeirantes* as semi-civilized savages. But these intrepid individuals had two remarkable accomplishments to their credit: Their journeys opened the way for the settlers who followed, and were instrumental in pushing Brazil's borders far beyond the line of the Treaty of Tordesillas. In addition, they ushered in a new era in the development of Brazil because the *bandeirantes* discovered gold in the highlands several hundred miles to the north of Rio de Janeiro.

Rumors about deposits of precious metals and stones had long fired the imaginations of explorers who braved the vast interior of Brazil. In the last decade of the seventeenth century, these dreams materialized, and news of a substantial gold strike triggered a wild rush into an area that would become known as Minas Gerais (General Mines). People from all over Brazil (including large numbers of slaves), Portuguese immigrants, and even Europeans seeking their fortunes joined the original *bandeirantes* in panning for alluvial gold in the riverbeds and then scouring riverbanks and nearby slopes. Little heed was paid to securing adequate supplies of foodstuffs for the unruly hordes of prospectors, and on two separate occasions famines ravaged the mining camps. Moreover, rivalry between the *bandeirantes* and the newcomers provoked a virtual civil war in the first decade of the eighteenth century.

Explorations to the northwest produced further discoveries of gold in the regions known as Mato Grosso and Goiás. Moreover, in the northern part of Minas Gerais gold seekers stumbled upon deposits of diamonds. The Portuguese Crown levied a 20 percent tax (the so-called royal fifth) when miners traded in their gold dust or nuggets, which by law were required to be brought to smelting houses and converted into bars that were then sold to the royal mint in Lisbon. Brazilians devised many ways to avoid this obligation, and shipments of contraband gold flourished.

The gold boom in Brazil came at a propitious moment, inasmuch as the sugar industry was in crisis. Competition from the Caribbean had cut deeply into Brazilian sugar exports, which made up about three fifths of the colony's total foreign commerce. In the eighteenth century Brazilian mines yielded two million pounds of gold, or about 80 percent of the world's supply.

Yet in the long run the boom did Portugal more harm than good. The revenues earned from gold production were not prudently invested. An orgy of wasteful spending led to inflation. The Portuguese used gold and diamonds to import manufactured goods from England. As historian E. Bradford Burns notes, "It has been observed with some sagacity and a little exaggeration that Brazilian gold mined by African slaves financed English industrialization." In addition, the gold rush drained manpower from Portugal's farms and cities.

Brazil fared little better. Its riches ended up in overseas coffers, and the lure of gold and diamonds created labor shortages in the agricultural sector. Portugal tightened its political and administrative control over the colony in an effort to maximize the Crown's revenues from the mines. The most significant long-term gain from the boom was that Brazil at last was looking away from the coastal region and into its enormous heartland. The new captaincies of São Paulo, Minas Gerais, Mato Grosso, and Goiás were created, and a number of new towns sprang to life in the interior.

Production of gold peaked in 1750. The Brazilians failed to develop any but the most rudimentary mining technology, and the closed-door policy imposed by Portugal on its colony prevented the importation of foreign equipment. This was but one of the negative effects of the increasingly autocratic rule exercised by the Crown.

Although the system of governors-general—later to be called viceroys—was a great improvement over the captaincies, it proved inadequate to the enormous task of governing Brazil. The size of the colony made centralized administration from Bahia exceedingly difficult, and the Portuguese lacked the genius for organization that the situation required. Moreover, the top officials appointed by the royal court were often incompetent or corrupt, qualities that permeated all ranks of the bureaucracy. The failure to establish effective control over the day-to-day management of government left the various captaincies to their own devices and fostered, in turn, provincialism and regionalism.

In 1763 the capital of Brazil was transferred from Bahia to Rio de Janeiro. The move did little to improve the supervisory authority of the viceroy. It reflected Portugal's concern with its running dispute with Spain over the border separating southern Brazil from the Spanish colonies along the Río de la Plata.

As the eighteenth century drew to a close, Brazil had just about reached its present size. The Amazon basin had at last been secured against the claims of the French, Dutch, British, and Spanish. Boundary agreements with Spain confirmed the incorporation of what is now the southern state of Rio Grande do Sul into Brazil in return for Portuguese withdrawal from the north bank of the Río de la Plata. Rough estimates have put the population of the colony at this time in excess of three million.

In addition to its production of sugar, gold, and diamonds, Brazil was now growing substantial quantities of cotton and tobacco. The raising of livestock was also assuming importance in the economy of the colony.

Portugal's colonial policy sought to milk Brazil rather than to develop it. The Crown insisted on monopolizing trade with its colony and prohibited the creation of industries that would compete with those in Portugal. Thus Brazil had to export its sugar, cotton, tobacco, and gold and to import manufactured goods from its homeland.

The mother country also struggled to curtail ideas that might subvert the status quo. Printing books and newspapers in Brazil was forbidden. No universities were founded in the colony. The entry of foreigners was strictly regulated.

In the latter part of the eighteenth century, the Crown began to transfer army units across the Atlantic, principally to protect the southern border of the colony but in part because of a growing suspicion that the men who led the local militias shared the national consciousness that was spreading throughout Brazil.

This turned out to be a prudent move, as dissatisfaction with Portuguese rule and the examples set by the American and French Revolutions inevitably sparked Brazilian efforts to shake off the shackles of colonialism. The most famous of these was a secret plot aimed at securing Brazil's independence devised by a group of poets, planters, merchants, militia officers, and priests in Minas Gerais. The authorities quickly crushed the incipient rebellion in 1789 and made an example of its leader, a dentist named Joaquim José da Silva Xavier (popularly and aptly known as "Tiradentes," or "Toothpuller"), who was also a second lieutenant in the militia. They quartered him and hung the pieces of his body on signposts.

Because of the conspiratorial nature of these early independence movements, they did not attract broad support within the colony. Furthermore, they were short-circuited in 1808 by the most dramatic single event to unfold in Brazil since the arrival of Cabral. The troops of Napoleon Bonaparte poured into Portugal and forced the entire royal court to flee abruptly across the Atlantic to Brazil. The Portuguese presence now assumed an entirely different cast. The implications for Brazil and Brazilianness would be far-reaching.

The story of the hegira of the royal family had elements of comic opera and was recounted most entertainingly by Bertita Harding in her delightful monograph *Amazon Throne*. The refugees included Queen Maria, who was insane; her son João, who had taken over as regent; João's Spanish wife, Carlota Joaquina; and their six children. Their escape was so precipitous that trunks containing the royal wardrobe were left behind on a Lisbon dock. When they arrived in the Bay of All Saints, the regent and his family were infested with lice and in a state of total unkemptness. The residents of Bahia, taken completely by surprise, scurried to find soap and clean clothing for their distinguished guests.

Shifting the capital of Portugal across the Atlantic was not a new idea. Brazil provided a more strategic location for administering a worldwide empire than did the western edge of Europe. Yet it took Napoleon's army marching on Lisbon to precipitate the move. The British also lent the beleaguered nation a hand by providing a naval escort for the thirty-six Portuguese vessels carrying the royal family and its entourage of fifteen thousand. The struggle against Napoleon would be better served if the queen and the regent remained out of French hands. Moreover, in return for the support of the British, João agreed to grant them commercial privileges in Brazil.

Less than a week after his arrival in Bahia, Dom João* signed a decree opening up Brazilian ports to foreign trade. He also lifted the bans on industry and foreign residents in Brazil. Clearly a new era in Brazilian history was at hand.

Nowhere was the change more evident than in Rio de Janeiro, where the royal family installed itself several months later. A number of Frenchmen and Englishmen had accompanied the royals across the Atlantic, and they too established residences in the city. Their cosmopolitan presence, and that of the European diplomats who were soon assigned to Rio, had an immediate impact on the city.

Dom João immediately set about to transform this tropical backwater into a European metropolis worthy of a royal court. He established a national library, an academy of fine arts, a royal school of medicine, a print shop, a national bank, a mint, and botanical

---

* Dom is a Portuguese expression of respect, used in reference to royalty and high Church officials.

gardens. He saw to the construction of a huge aqueduct, which carried a copious supply of fresh water to the city. He also set out to upgrade Brazilian society (and at the same time enrich the royal treasury) by freely dispensing titles to those of his colonial subjects who could afford them.

The presence of the royal family in Brazil gave a great psychological boost to Brazilians. It marked the first (and only) time that any European monarchs had trodden upon the soil of their American possessions. The excitement and pride spread throughout Brazil and in turn made it easier for the Crown to establish an even more centralized government in the colony. Although the bureaucracy that Dom João created in Rio de Janeiro was controlled at the top levels by Portuguese officials who had accompanied the royal family from Lisbon, Brazilians held lower positions and could at least become familiar with the organs of government that ruled them.

In addition, the royal court brought with it a passion for things French that soon spread to Brazil's upper and intellectual classes. This infatuation would develop firm roots and have a significant impact on the development of Brazilian culture.

Relocation invigorated Dom João. He assumed the throne in 1816 when the mad Queen Maria finally died. More important for the locals, he chose to be crowned João VI of Portugal and Brazil, thereby transforming the latter into a kingdom, coequal in status to its mother country. A cautious, indecisive ruler while in Lisbon, he governed wisely and at times forcefully from his new palace in Rio de Janeiro. Manifesting the effects of a royal gluttony fueled by an uncontrollable appetite for fried chicken, the corpulence of the good-natured Dom João did not diminish the vigor he now applied to the task of administering his Brazilian domain.

The one cross he had to bear in the New World was the comportment of his wife, Carlota Joaquina. The Spanish Princess had been ten years old when she was given in marriage to the eighteen-year-old heir to the throne of Portugal. The union turned out to be a mismatch, to say the least. She was precocious, mischievous, and full of life; he was stodgy, obese, and repressed. She had grown to love the luxury and sophistication of royal life in Lisbon, so the primitive conditions she encountered in America totally disgusted her. She never forgave Brazil for the indignity of having to have her lice-infested head shaved before she stepped ashore in Bahia.

Carlota Joaquina sought consolation in affairs of the heart. As she reached her mid-thirties, her features took on a somewhat masculine form and, in the words of Bertita Harding, "all over her body a state of hirsute anarchy seemed to have set in." She had always been a passionate woman, given to extramarital adventures, but now she was consumed by a sexual appetite that rivaled her husband's craving for fried chicken.

For several years her favorite lover was a handsome young man whom Dom João had appointed to head the new Bank of Brazil. The man's wife finally intervened, putting an end to the liaison. Carlota Joaquina, in a queenly rage, arranged for the assassination of her rival. Dom João ordered an investigation of the crime, and when he discovered that its author was his wife, he ordered that she be locked up in a convent. But when his oldest son Pedro married the Austrian Archduchess Leopoldina of the Hapsburg dynasty later that year, the monarch found it advisable to release his wife from confinement. She returned to the court and resumed her licentious ways.

By this time an army of Portuguese and British troops under the command of the Duke of Wellington had driven the French from Portugal, and a council of regency had assumed control of the country. The winds of liberalism were beginning to blow across the Iberian peninsula, and pressures for the installation of representative, constitutional government were mounting.

Although Dom João was not eager to leave his new home, he was equally reluctant to face growing opposition in Brazil. Brazilians were tired of his handing out government and military appointments, as well as commercial concessions, to Portuguese immigrants. They had also grown weary of the Queen's scandalous behavior. Advocates of constitutional rule in Brazil were becoming more and more vocal.

In 1821 the king installed Prince Pedro as his regent, in charge of the internal affairs of Brazil, and returned to Lisbon with the rest of the royal family. Dom Pedro was twenty-three years old at the time. He had spent his formative years in the New World, and in many ways he was more Brazilian than Portuguese.

In Portugal King João had to confront a revolutionary movement that convoked a legislative assembly known as the Côrtes in
an effort to limit the power of the monarchy. Although the Brazilians were permitted to send representatives to the Côrtes, the Portuguese members treated them with disdain. The Portuguese
sought to restore Brazil to its prior status as a subservient colony
and ordered that Prince Pedro return to Portugal. Having tasted the
importance their status as a kingdom had given them, Brazilians
were of no mind to turn back the clock. They were delighted when
Dom Pedro announced his intention to stay in Brazil.

A spirit of independence now permeated the Brazilian elite.
Most of Spain's American colonies had by that time shed their colonial chains. Brazil could hardly ignore what was happening elsewhere on the continent. On September 7, 1822, as Dom Pedro was
traveling from São Paulo to Rio de Janeiro, he received a transatlantic directive from the Côrtes announcing that it had greatly diminished his authority. In a grand gesture, he drew his sword and
declared: "Independence or death!" In October a convention proclaimed him emperor of Brazil, and on December 1 he was crowned
constitutional monarch of the new nation.

It took about a year to secure the complete withdrawal of Portuguese troops, a triumph achieved with remarkably little bloodshed (thus producing the notion that Brazilians were a nonviolent
people). Moreover, Brazil maintained national unity despite its
enormous size and despite the precedent set by Spain's South
American empire, which split into nine distinct countries upon
gaining independence. This unity has to be numbered among the
Portuguese legacies to Brazil. The Portuguese distaste for organization (rigid or otherwise) resulted in a lack of centralized control
that in turn permitted considerable local autonomy. Thus the coming of independence did not fan the flames of separatism in the
far-flung regions of the country. In addition, the presence of the
royal family turned out to be a strongly unifying influence.

Brazil's first emperor was a character worthy of the exuberant
land whose throne he inherited. Though not Brazilian by birth, he
loved Brazil with a fierce passion that matched his appetite for phi-
landering. The marriage arranged for him in 1817 with the cul-
tured, amiable Archduchess Leopoldina did not interfere in the

least with his favorite diversion. It is not known how many love children the tall, dark-eyed, handsome Pedro sired, but he seemed to personify and encapsulate the tradition of the prolific Portuguese explorers and settlers who went before him. His long, open, and tempestuous affair with the beautiful Domitila de Castro Canto e Mello (more commonly known as the Marquise de Santos) scandalized the entire country.

In 1824 Pedro I supported the adoption of a Constitution that vested broad powers in the hands of the emperor. This set the stage for a series of ongoing battles with the new legislative assembly, composed of landowners and representatives of commercial urban interests. Dom Pedro's stubbornness and his continuing reliance on Portuguese advisors did not endear him to the political opponents he was creating.

Even more damaging to his popularity was the way he handled foreign relations. He paid off part of Portugal's debts in return for the latter's recognition of Brazil's independence, committed Brazil to disadvantageous trade agreements with Great Britain, and plunged the country into ill-conceived military adventures that resulted in the loss of some southern territory (and the creation of Uruguay as a buffer state between Brazil and the new nation of Argentina). Moreover, his involvement in the intrigues over the successor to the Portuguese Crown when his father died in 1826 (there were the inevitable rumors that Carlota Joaquina had poisoned her husband) underscored the fact that he had never really abandoned his "Portugueseness," which became a matter of acute concern to the newly independent Brazilians.

Things came to a head in April of 1831 when street demonstrations in Rio de Janeiro protested a change that the emperor had made in his cabinet. Out of weariness and frustration Dom Pedro decided to abdicate his throne. He set sail for Lisbon and left behind his five-year-old son to assume the duties as Brazil's sovereign.

The Constitution provided for a period of regency until "little Pedro," as he was called, reached the age of eighteen. But the decade of the 1830s was a turbulent one, with a number of regional rebellions threatening the national unity. There seemed but one way out of the morass. In 1840 a number of political leaders decided to offer the crown to the young prince. He agreed, and on July 22 the fourteen-year-old boy took an oath to uphold the Constitution (which he was at that very moment in the process of violating—a delightfully Brazilian irony). A year later he was formally crowned Pedro II, emperor of Brazil.

The new monarch, though a born-and-bred Brazilian, may still be numbered among Portugal's gifts to its former colony because of his royal lineage. He underwent a rigorous education that instilled in him a lifelong passion for learning. Intellectually curious, bookish, thoughtful, genteel, and romantic, he was as different from his father as chalk from cheese. Fluent in English, French, German, and Spanish, he also prided himself on his sure-handed grasp of Latin, Greek, Hebrew, and even Sanskrit.

Blue-eyed and softly handsome, he grew to a great height (six feet four inches), with a full beard that at first matched his light hair and then made him look increasingly distinguished as it whitened. His preoccupation with the life of the mind caused him to neglect his health, but he still managed to survive to a ripe old age.

Upon assuming the throne, Pedro II had to confront the question of marriage. Emissaries from the court in Rio scoured Europe for a suitable match. The anguish his mother had suffered from the womanizing of Pedro I, combined with the political instability now endemic to South America, made the royal families of Europe reluctant to send a daughter to Brazil. A long search produced only Thereza Christina, the homely scion of King Francis I of Naples. In the words of Bertita Harding, "she was short, stocky, sallow of skin, coarse-featured, and she walked with a limp." Thereza lunged at the opportunity. Dom Pedro agreed after seeing a portrait that did the princess much more than justice. After a proxy marriage in Naples, the bride journeyed to Brazil. When Dom Pedro boarded the vessel that had brought her to him as it sat anchored in Guanabara Bay, the eighteen-year-old emperor was so dismayed at the sight of the real Thereza that he contemplated sending her back. His sense of duty ultimately prevailed, and he went through with the formal wedding ceremony.

The empress remained at her husband's side throughout his long reign. She grew comfortable in the role and soon won Brazilian hearts with her kindness and maternal manner.

Pedro II proved to be a valuable representative of his young country. Afflicted with incurable wanderlust, the emperor traveled widely abroad. The unpretentious and inquisitive nature of the royal tourist endeared him to onlookers wherever he went.* On trips to Europe and the United States, where he helped celebrate the centennial of American independence, he developed friendships with such luminaries as Alexander Graham Bell, Henry Wadsworth Longfellow, Victor Hugo, and Louis Pasteur. During his numerous junkets Dom Pedro helped to both create and propagate the stereotype of the cordial, amiable Brazilian.

The long and relatively peaceful reign of Pedro II was a period of transition in Brazil. Coffee replaced sugar and gold as the major source of the country's wealth. The government encouraged massive immigration from Europe. The process of industrialization began. Steam transport and the telegraph brought the nation closer together. The major blemishes of the era were a bloody war with Paraguay in 1865–70 and the long delay in abolishing the shameful institution of slavery.

The monarchy eventually became an anachronism, and however much Brazilians loved Dom Pedro as a person and as a symbol, they could no longer tolerate him as their sovereign. In late 1889 the tired, aging emperor and his wife found themselves forced to repair in exile to Portugal. Less than a month later, Thereza died of a heart attack. On December 5, 1891, Pedro, II succumbed to pneumonia in a hotel room in Paris.

The Portuguese contribution to Brazil did not end with the monarchy. Between 1884 and 1970, immigrants from Portugal numbered more than 1.5 million, or 30 percent of the total influx. They, like the other settlers from abroad, participated in the movements that transformed the face of Brazil during the twentieth century. Particularly successful were the Portuguese families who built fortunes in the food marketing business in Brazil.

No discussion of Portugal's legacy would be complete without mention of a remarkable little girl who came to Rio de Janeiro from

* One of his favorite diversions was wandering, unannounced, into synagogues and reading aloud from the Talmud.

Portugal at the age of two and grew up to become not only Brazil's most popular radio singer of the 1930s but also one of Hollywood's brightest and most enduring stars—Carmen Miranda.

Although the Lusitanian component of Brazilianness is strong, certain sharp discrepancies still separate the two cultures. The Portuguese have a predilection for melancholy, as evidenced dramatically by the *fado*, a type of folk song drenched in sadness. Brazilians (and their music) exude gaiety. The celebration of Carnival in Portugal has long since passed into relative unimportance, at least in comparison to the madness that grips much of Brazil during its pre-Lenten festivities. Portuguese cuisine no longer exerts a strong influence on Brazilian cooking.

To understand why these cultural differences exist, it is necessary to examine in detail the other major contributor to the sum total of features that make Brazilians Brazilian. The African presence in Brazil is as much a defining element of the national character as the Portuguese, if not more so. The interrelationship between the African and European components of Brazilian society is at once a source of great richness and challenge.

# Chapter 2

# The Africans

*I*t was a gripping human-interest story tailor-made for television: the inadvertent switching of newborn babies by hospital employees, whose carelessness came to light by pure chance three years later. Both families involved in the incident had grown attached to their babies, and the little boys themselves were by now happily and securely settled in their homes. During the legal proceeding to determine custody, a judge heard testimony from the two sets of parents, who agonized over their predicament, and from neighbors who supported the status quo. The judge ruled that each youngster be turned over to his natural parents, who would have the right to visit the child they had given up only after a six-month period of adjustment. TV news programs milked every dollop of pathos from the exchange, as those touched by the incident expressed their unrestrained dismay.

In the course of the reportage, no one saw fit to remark on the evident fact that one of the boys was black and had been accepted at birth without question by white parents; while the other was white and had been raised unhesitatingly by dark-skinned parents.

It is unlikely that this could have happened anywhere else but in Brazil, where miscegenation has been a common and accepted practice dating back to the arrival of the first Portuguese explorers. As Jorge Amado put it in his novel *Os Pastores da Noite (Shepherds of the Night)* (and what he wrote about his native state applies equally to most of the other regions of Brazil): "It's impossible to separate and catalogue all the blood strains of a child born in Bahia. Suddenly a blonde appears among mulattoes or a little Negro baby among whites. That's the way we are, praise be to God!"

A panoramic view of the Brazilian people would reveal skin colorations of every conceivable hue, from the blackest black to the milkiest white, and from the copper-toned tint of the Indian to the pale yellow of the Oriental. Moreover, no intermediate shade lacks ample representation. Out of the long tradition of miscegenation between individuals of Portuguese and African descent has evolved the Brazilian mulatto, one of the most distinctively attractive variations of the nation's racial mix. In the Amazon region the union of Portuguese settlers (and later migrants from the Northeast) with Indians has produced the *caboclo*. Inhabitants of the Northeast often display the combined heritage of their Indian, African, and Portuguese ancestors, along with occasional traces of the blonde Dutch who occupied the region during the seventeenth century. The veins of those who populate the interior of southern Brazil may bear the blood of Indians, blacks, migrants from São Paulo, immigrants from the Azores, and people who crossed the borders separating Brazil from the Spanish colonies that later became Uruguay and Argentina.

It is difficult to know with certainty how many contemporary Brazilians bear within them the physical effects of four centuries of miscegenation, since the official census records only the responses volunteered by each individual (in categories predetermined by the government), and self-perception may not always correspond with biological reality. In 1980, out of a total population of 119 million, 46 million classified themselves as brown, signifying some African ancestry. This compares with 65 million who reported that they were white (many of whom undoubtedly had some African or Indian ancestry), and 7 million who declared that they were black (many of whom undoubtedly can count whites or Indians among their forebears).

Miscegenation has significantly complicated the relationship between whites and blacks, the predominant ingredients of the Brazilian populace. Some look upon miscegenation as the key to racial harmony and the cornerstone of a single *mestiço* (racially mixed) society. For them racial mixture is at the core of Brazilianness. Others view miscegenation as camouflage for serious social and economic inequities that are the fruits of a peculiar yet virulent strain of racism infecting Brazilian society.

Those who, like Jorge Amado, celebrate the fact that theirs is a *mestiço* country can point to African contributions accepted by all Brazilians as important components of their Brazilianness. *Feijoada*, the national dish of Brazil (black beans, rice, assorted meats, a green-leaf vegetable called *couve*, and manioc flour), comes directly from the slave quarters of colonial sugar plantations. The samba, the national dance, uses rhythms and movements of African origin. Afro-Brazilians have profoundly influenced the evolution of Carnival. The Portuguese language spoken by all Brazilians owes its melodic inflection as well as many of its expressions to the African presence in Brazil. The spirituality of the Brazilian people bears the distinct signature of the *orixás* (African gods and goddesses).

The strong African elements that permeate Brazilian culture, the presence of African blood in the veins of a large percentage of the population, and the affability with which Brazilians normally interact have given non-Brazilians the impression that Brazil is a land where people of different races, in the words of Austrian novelist Stefan Zweig, "live in fullest harmony with one another." The African-American magazine *Ebony* put it a bit more circumspectly in the subheading of a 1965 article entitled "Does Amalgamation Work in Brazil?": "The formula is not perfect but so far it works the best."

Moreover, many Brazilians have long clung to the belief that, to quote author Érico Veríssimo's 1945 dictum, they "have no color problem." The descriptive expression they have proudly attached to this sanguine view of race relations in Brazil is "racial democracy."

Yet in its edition of May 11, 1988, commemorating the centennial of the abolition of slavery in Brazil, the weekly magazine *Veja* noted that data from the 1980 census taken by the Brazilian Institute of Geography and Statistics showed that a black doctor earned 22 percent less than a white doctor; black schoolteachers earned 18 percent less than their white colleagues; a black bricklayer earned 11 percent less than his white counterpart. Shifting from microscope to telescope, the magazine reported that "out of every ten Brazilians, four are black, but out of every ten poor Brazilians, six are black."

The truth of the matter is that racism deeply permeates Brazil's social fabric. Dramatic incidents illustrating this reality abound:

- Benedita da Silva, having achieved in 1986 the distinction of becoming the first black woman to be elected to the federal Chamber of Deputies (the equivalent to the United States House of Representatives), received anonymous letters declaring that "the Negress' place is in the kitchen";

- Antônio Carlos Cortes, a black attorney from Porto Alegre, had to use sundry legal maneuvers to surmount the various obstacles thrown in the way of his client Deise Nunes de Sousa as she won her way through various beauty contests to become the first Afro-Brazilian to be crowned "Miss Brazil";

- Zezé Motta, a black actress, incurred angry reactions from some viewers when a *telenovela* in which she starred depicted her in a serious interracial romance with a white actor;

- in Vitória, the capital of Espírito Santo, Ana Flávia de Azaredo was racially insulted by an apartment manager and punched in the face by the manager's son, neither of whom realized that the young black woman they were attacking for delaying the elevator in which they were riding was the daughter of the governor of the state.

The physical and psychological violence police customarily employ when dealing with dark-skinned suspects is hardly a secret in contemporary Brazil. Merely being black is enough to place a person under suspicion. Black men who jog face the constant threat of being stopped by the police, and if they do not have their identity cards with them, they risk being taken into custody.

These and other manifestations of racism support the position of those who argue that Brazil has had no "color problem" only because blacks have accepted their consignment to the bottom of the ladder in Brazilian society (or, to put it more bluntly, they know their place); that racial prejudice in Brazil lies in the insistence that there is no racial prejudice in Brazil; and that "racial democracy" has always been a myth (some would call it an ideology) concocted to mask or even reinforce social, economic, and political inequities.

These, then, are the two sides of a complex racial dilemma. Brazil is undeniably *mestiço*, in the sense that African (and Indian) elements form an integral part of the national culture. Nevertheless, the country does in fact have a race problem, with subtleties and complexities that are uniquely Brazilian. To grasp both the realities of race relations in Brazil and the illusions surrounding them, it is necessary to begin at the beginning.

The first slave ship arrived in Brazil in 1538. The rapid growth of the sugar industry in the Northeast had created a demand for labor that the Portuguese colonists and the nomadic natives were unwilling or unable to satisfy. The importation of slaves from Africa, therefore, became indispensable if the colony was going to take root and prosper. In the course of three centuries about 3.5 million blacks (six times the number brought to the United States) survived the ordeal of the Atlantic crossing.

Slavery in Brazil featured all the cruelty inherent in an institution based on the forcible subjugation of one race by another. Working conditions in the fields, and later in the mines, were often appalling. Black men were treated like beasts of burden. Black women were often forced to slake the carnal appetites of their masters. Corporal punishment was freely dispensed and at times sunk to the level of blatant torture.

In the words of Arthur Ramos, a psychiatrist who became one of the earliest Brazilian specialists in Afro-Brazilian studies,

> Physical deformities such as body mutilations, scars and sores were common enough, the result of ill treatment, excessive labor and defective hygiene. The welts from beatings, scars on the back and shoulders, buttocks and neck, deformities of the legs, arms and head as well as injuries due to the type of work performed, constituted features which distinguished the slave population.

The psychological damage inflicted upon slaves was no less devastating. Both in Africa after they were captured and upon their arrival in the New World, blacks were segregated and sold on the basis of their physical qualities, thus causing the destruction of family and tribal units. In addition, members of traditionally hostile tribes found themselves thrown together indiscriminately, which occasionally provoked violent clashes among groups of slaves on the plantations. The horrors of involuntary servitude became insupportable for some who chose to take their own lives as an affirmation of their humanity.

Many have argued that slavery in the Portuguese colony had a distinctively Brazilian cast, in that it featured not only cruelty but also compassion. Waldo Frank, to cite but one example, has claimed that there was a great difference between the black slaves of Brazil and those of the United States "[b]ecause the latter have known lust and greed of their masters; the former lust and greed no less, but tenderness also."

Claims of tenderness must be handled with great caution and a large dose of skepticism. They represent, above all, a characterization from white commentators and derives mainly from a somewhat skewed perception of the feelings of slave owners toward blacks.

To the extent that kindness existed as an element of race relations in colonial Brazil, it primarily benefited the domestic slave. Landholding patterns, especially in the Northeast, concentrated ownership in the hands of relatively few people. Each proprietor was a patriarch who ruled over his domain with absolute authority. Slaves who worked in the "big house" became, in a sense, members of the family, around which all plantation life revolved. They raised their master's children, who, in the words of sociologist Gilberto Freyre, learned from them "a human kindness greater, perhaps, than that of which whites were capable, and a depth of tenderness of which Europeans do not know the like." They gossiped with the owner's wife and served as companions to his daughters, who were kept in virtual seclusion until they married. Black girls also introduced white boys to the mysteries and delights of physical love, a practice so prevalent that it left its mark on the national subconscious, in the form of the exaltation of the *mulata* as the paragon of female sexuality in Brazil.

A certain degree of tenderness on the part of some Portuguese colonists toward slaves who served in their households (as opposed to those who toiled in their fields) was an inevitable part of the susceptibility of the settlers to the cultural influences exerted by their African "possessions." Lusitanians had always adapted to the ways of strangers, so it was natural that they should prove receptive to African folklore, customs, and traditions. In the close confines of plantation society, white babies had black nannies and servants who sang African lullabies and told them stories learned from their African ancestors. When these babies took sick, the slave women would give them medicines derived from their knowledge of African plants, and would hang charmed amulets around their necks. When the mistress of the mansion or one of her daughters had problems of the heart, she would go to her maid, who searched out sacred herbs or love potions that would help her. In an intimidating environment similar to Africa in many ways, it was natural that whites would come to rely upon their slaves.

Whatever tenderness toward slaves that existed during the slavery era could be located in the minds of the slave owners, nominal Catholics who were able to turn a blind eye to the inherent evil of involuntary servitude and convince themselves that they were kindly disposed toward the slaves who served them in their households. This disposition served a historical purpose, since it facilitated the absorption of African culture into the mainstream of Brazilian culture.

Feelings of warmth traveled a one-way street, however. It is difficult to believe that such feelings could have been genuinely reciprocated by people trapped in a subjugated status. Indeed, any attempts by masters to stimulate tenderness in the hearts of their human chattel advantaged only the slave owners, since evoking compassion from the subjugated Africans could serve as a means of social control of the slave population, who were a numerical majority. Most masters probably preferred to cultivate their image as kindly father figures and to deflect hatred by having their foremen administer corporal punishment. Since the latter were most often mulattoes or freed blacks, this pecking order fostered conflicts between members of exploited groups and diverted hostility that might otherwise have been directed at slaveholders. (Indeed, as part of this divide-and-rule strategy, colonial authorities would often send Indians to recapture runaway slaves, and use blacks to fight against hostile Indian tribes.)

A final contributor to the emotional landscape of race relations in colonial Brazil was the peculiarly Portuguese attitude toward miscegenation. The Portuguese male who came to the New World indulged to the fullest his taste for dark-skinned women. The earliest adventurers and colonists took advantage of the eagerness of Indian women to submit to their advances. With the arrival of slaves from Africa, black women joined their Indian sisters as sexual objects.

Yet the relationship between women of color and male settlers at times went beyond the mere servicing of the latter's carnal needs. The continuing shortage of white women in the colony (exacerbated by the tendency of plantation owners to put their daughters in convents rather than permit them to marry below their station in life) resulted in the cohabitation of interracial couples and occasional interracial marriages. In addition, masters who had taken slaves or former slaves as mistresses often recognized and emancipated the offspring of these liaisons and even permitted them to inherit property on the same basis as legitimate children.

One of the best known examples, which has now passed into legend, involved a tall, seductive ex-slave named Xica da Silva. She became the lover of an official sent by the Crown to preside over Portugal's monopoly of the production and sale of precious metals in Minas Gerais—a task that enabled him to amass an enormous fortune. The couple produced thirteen children, all of them legitimized by their father.*

While many contemporary observers maintain that slavery in Brazil was as harsh and repugnant as its counterpart in the United States, one key difference between involuntary servitude in the two countries was that Brazilian slaves had better opportunities to gain freedom. This, perhaps more than any other factor, opened the way for the creation of a multiracial society that came to assume a life of its own.

The condition of free blacks and mulattoes within this society was far from ideal. A. J. R. Russell-Wood has documented numer-

---

* The Portugese official fell so madly in love with Xica that he catered to her every whim, to the point of building for her an artificial lake and a miniature sailing vessel—she had never seen the ocean—as well as a castle surrounded by trees he imported from Europe.

ous examples of racial prejudice drawn from the colonial period: laws discriminating against free blacks and mulattoes with respect to dress codes and the bearing of firearms; discriminatory treatment of blacks by law-enforcement officials; barriers to blacks' entry into public service, the military, and religious orders; and the prevalent use of deprecatory expressions to describe persons with African blood.

Mulattoes faced additional obstacles. As Russell-Wood has noted,

> Both whites and blacks spoke disparagingly of the products of inter-racial alliances, seeing mulattos as the embodiments of the least desirable characteristics of either race. It was to mulattos that both whites and blacks turned to find the quintessence of moral turpitude, laziness, and arrogance. To be . . . a mulatto was to find oneself in a social and racial "no-man's land."

Some mulattoes, proud of the white blood in their veins, refused to perform manual labor because it was associated with blacks. In places where this was the only employment available to them, they could end up leading dissolute lives marked by drunkenness and poverty. Others climbed the social ladder by taking advantage of their own intelligence and drive, the lightness of their skin, and any commercial and educational opportunities they encountered. After a generation or two, the most successful often crossed the color line, rewrote their family histories, and became "white," a process described with great wit and perception by João Ubaldo Ribeiro in his masterful novel *Viva o Povo Brasileiro* (published in English under the title *An Unforgettable Memory*).

Individual mulattoes were able to achieve remarkable success during the colonial period and afterward. One of the most notable was Antônio Francisco Lisboa (1738–1814), nicknamed Aleijadinho (Little Cripple). The illegitimate offspring of a Portuguese architect and his slave, Aleijadinho suffered from leprosy, which mutilated his hands, but he nonetheless managed to sculpt intricate, highly original statues in wood and sandstone. His work adorns the façades and interiors of numerous churches in Minas Gerais.

Another remarkable mulatto was Joaquim Machado de Assis (1839–1908), whom many consider the greatest writer Brazil has ever produced. The offspring of a brown-skinned house painter and a Portuguese mother, he combined humor, irony, and a strong sense of pessimism, the latter perhaps deriving from his being afflicted with epilepsy. His novels, written in the latter half of the nineteenth century, are widely read and admired even today (although in the years immediately following his death, it was considered bad form to mention his racial derivation).

A third outstanding mulatto, André Rebouças (1838–98), was a distinguished engineer who managed to be at the same time a leader of the abolitionist movement and an ardent monarchist. Among Brazil's earliest advocates of agrarian reform, he opposed the Republic because he predicted (correctly) that it would be dominated by Brazil's landowning elite. He went into exile with Pedro II and later committed suicide on the Portuguese island of Madeira. One of Rio de Janeiro's most heavily used highway tunnels and an avenue in São Paulo bear his name.

The institution of slavery in Brazil inflicted long-term damage on masters as well as slaves. Together with the obvious cruelty inherent in the system of forced labor was the sadomasochistic nature of the relationship between white men and the black women they took as sexual objects, and between white boys and the young blacks who were given to them as playthings as well as playmates. Among the lasting effects these practices have had on the Brazilian psyche are the debasement of human life (evidenced by the individual Brazilian's preference for conduct that may put himself and others at great risk) and the development of a taste for anal intercourse, which has assumed deadly implications with the onset of the AIDS epidemic.

The institution of slavery pervaded all levels of society in colonial Brazil. All but the poorest whites owned at least one slave. This degree of dependence on forced labor might have made life in Brazil more comfortable, but it also fostered indolence and lethargy—traits hardly conducive to the future development of the colony.

The slaves brought in chains to Brazil came from different regions of Africa, and the degree of their cultural development varied widely. Some had known only their own tribes and believed in the existence of spirits and demons. Others had lived in sophisticated kingdoms ruled by dynastic regimes. A few were followers of Islam and could read the Koran. Slaves contributed more than just muscle in the fields and mills. As E. Bradford Burns has noted in *A History of Brazil,*

> They brought with them or learned in the New World many skills essential for the growth of Brazil. They were the carpenters, painters, masons, jewelers, sculptors, locksmiths, tailors, cobblers, and bakers. They made technical contributions in metallurgy, mining, cattle-raising and agriculture.

Some of them took advantage of the relative ease with which Brazilian slaves could earn their freedom, and not only cast off the shackles of slavery but also returned to West Africa, where they used their skills to build houses in the exuberant baroque style popular in Brazil during this epoch.

Just because blacks had qualities that made them prized as slaves—their hardworking disposition and capacity to survive in a tropical environment—did not mean that they quietly accepted their status as chattel. In all parts of the colony runaway slaves assembled in small groups known as *quilombos;* in urban areas they took refuge in safe houses. In the countryside the *quilombos* were often modest-sized settlements, some of which replicated the African villages from which the blacks had been torn.

During the seventeenth century, some twenty thousand blacks created the most famous of all the *quilombos,* the so-called Republic of Palmares, which flourished in the interior of Northeast Brazil for several decades. It was a virtual state within a state, reviving African traditions and demonstrating the capacity of ex-slaves to create for themselves a social order and a highly civilized community. Because of its symbolic significance and the frequent raids made by its black warriors seeking to liberate slaves on nearby plantations and bring them back to the *quilombo,* the authorities viewed Palmares as a serious threat to the security of the colony and made repeated attempts to destroy it. A military expedition led by the infamous *bandeirante* Domingos Jorge Velho finally overwhelmed Palmares in 1695, slaughtered its inhabitants, and left it in ashes.

Another way blacks could fight for their freedom was by volunteering for service in armed struggles for the defense of Brazil, and they often distinguished themselves in the process. In the seventeenth century black regiments led by the intrepid ex-slave Henrique Dias opposed and helped expel the Dutch forces that had been occupying much of the Northeast for decades. In 1711 black troops participated in the defense of Rio de Janeiro, which was under siege by the French. Countless black soldiers shed their blood in the War of the Triple Alliance (1865–70), in which Paraguay rashly took on Brazil, Argentina, and Uruguay at the same time and both suffered and inflicted extensive casualties.

In addition to fighting for Brazil, slaves demonstrated an increasing willingness to fight for their own lives during the nineteenth century, when the number of slave revolts multiplied. Political instability in the 1830s as a result of the uncertain regency of Pedro II no doubt encouraged these uprisings, as did the growing distaste for slavery among large sectors of Brazilians. In addition, by that time most slaves had been born in Brazil, spoke Portuguese, were familiar with the country's laws and customs, and saw no reason why they should have to live as chattel rather than as human beings.

In typical Brazilian fashion the process that brought slavery to an end was glacial and nonviolent. Pressure from Great Britain (itself motivated by economic self-interest) led to the passage of laws in Brazil limiting the importation of slaves, but half-hearted enforcement and nationalistic resentment at the high-handed manner in which the British were interfering in Brazil's domestic affairs rendered these enactments ineffective. Indeed, during the period from 1830 to 1850, the illegal slave trade was responsible for the smuggling of some half a million Africans into Brazil.

It was not until 1850 that the Brazilian government passed a statute that forthrightly put an end to the transatlantic shipment of slaves. In 1866, during the War of the Triple Alliance, the government decreed that slaves who joined the army would be freed; in 1871 the Law of the Free Womb emancipated the children of slaves (and at the same time caused the dissolution of many black families when children had to be separated from their enslaved parents); in 1885 slaves who had reached the age of sixty-five received their freedom; and, finally, in 1888 Brazil became the last country in the western world to put a complete end to the institution of slavery.

The tendency of Brazilians to forget about the past was evident in their attitudes toward abolition. Three years to the day after the proclamation of the so-called "Golden Law" decreeing abolition, the government ordered the burning of its slavery archives, a collection of materials that would have shed inestimable light on the social history of Brazil. (One explanation for the destruction of these records was to avoid claims for indemnity being brought against the government by slave owners who had suffered economic losses as a result of abolition.) Collective amnesia also caused Brazilians to disregard the effects of slavery on those who had been enslaved, and thus no measures were taken to help blacks adjust to their new status.

At the same time Brazilian intellectuals were accepting without question European theories that explained the "superiority" of Western civilization in terms of race—a convenient justification for the wave of European imperialism being wreaked throughout much of Africa and Asia. This was an era when upper-class Brazilians aped French culture and peered down their noses at anything Brazilian. Thus many were willing to lay major blame for what they perceived as their own national inferiority on the presence of a large black and mulatto population.

In the opinion of many, however, the "problem" contained the seeds of its own solution. The continuing process of miscegenation, they were convinced, would improve the level of social development in Brazil, not by producing a unique *mestiço* society, but rather by gradually whitening the population. Thus it would simply be only a matter of time before the common practice of interracial marriage would produce a people "white" enough to approximate the European ideal. (In 1923 a federal deputy would predict that "the Negro in Brazil will disappear within seventy years.") To facilitate this process, the government did everything it could to encourage immigration from Europe.

Consistent with this policy of racial bleaching was the official discouragement of efforts to preserve African culture. The police even resorted to the violent suppression of African religions: invading properties belonging to spiritist cults, arresting practitioners, and destroying or impounding items used during worship. The repression reached a peak intensity during the 1920s, providing grist for Jorge Amado's treatment of race relations in his novel *Tenda dos Milagres (Tent of Miracles)*.

Although the regime of Getúlio Vargas engaged in sporadic efforts to stifle cults during the 1930s, a new spirit of nationalism was abroad in the land, and it encouraged manifestations of Brazilian popular culture, to which the descendants of African slaves had made and were making important contributions. But their influence did not receive its proper due until the seminal work of Gilberto Freyre forced Brazilians to come to terms with their racially mixed heritage.

It would be difficult to overstate the importance of the publication of Freyre's 1933 masterpiece *Casa-Grande & Senzala (The Masters and the Slaves)*. A sociological study of the formation of Brazilian society in the sugar-growing regions of the country during the colonial period, the book explained how Portuguese colonizers, Indians, and African slaves interacted to create a distinct ethnic mix. Displaying what French critic Roland Barthes would call "an obsessive feel for substance," Freyre brought analytical tools from sociology and a variety of other disciplines to bear on virtually every aspect of the phenomena he was exploring. His magisterial vision ranged across history, economics, religion, and ethics as well as diet, sexuality, and folklore.

In assessing the black presence in Brazil, Freyre gave his fellow Brazilians persuasive reasons to replace their shame with pride. He described the positive impact blacks had had on Brazil's social fabric and national identity, and at the same time he called into question the negative traits that had commonly been attributed to them (and convincingly linked those traits to the institution of slavery).

*Casa-Grande & Senzala* struck a telling blow at the source of the inferiority complex that had long afflicted the upper and educated classes. It introduced Brazilians to their own cultural past and instilled in them a sense of their own worth as a people. They would never be the same again.

The man who accomplished this signal feat came from a family that could trace its roots back to seventeenth-century Brazil. Born in 1900 in Recife, Gilberto Freyre was educated by private tutors and then at a secondary school run by Baptist missionaries. He later traveled to Texas, where he attended Baylor University. After earning a master's degree from Columbia, he continued his studies in Europe. Upon his return to Brazil, he taught sociology and involved himself in political activity, which in 1930 made it necessary for him to take refuge in Portugal and the United States. There he became a visiting professor at Stanford. When the political climate in Brazil permitted him to reenter his home country, he brought back with him the idea for *Casa-Grande & Senzala*, which soon gained him worldwide recognition.

Of the more than forty other books he wrote, the best known are *Sobrados e Mucambos (Mansions and Shanties)* and *Ordem e Progresso (Order and Progress)*, which followed up on themes he had touched upon in *Casa-Grande*.

Although he traveled widely, Gilberto Freyre was most comfortable in his eighteenth-century manor house perched on a hillock in Apipucos, on the outskirts of his native Recife, where he resided until his death in 1987. At home, in the midst of abundant vegetation, he painstakingly re-created the atmosphere he had described and analyzed in many of his books. "It was like living a chapter of *Casa Grande*," American author John Dos Passos once wrote after a visit. During the holidays of Saints John, Peter, and Paul in late June, guests invited to the Apipucos mansion could sip a special cherry liqueur that Freyre himself had concocted (only he knew the formula), sample assorted delicacies made from corn, and watch local children in peasant costumes perform traditional dances.

The ambience at Apipucos was consistent with Freyre's idyllic vision of plantation life in colonial Brazil and provided the intellectual foundation for a notion that had been evolving since abolition: that post-slavery Brazil was developing a unique "racial democracy" integrating whites, blacks, and people of mixed blood into an egalitarian social system.

Yet what Freyre had in mind was something far from egalitarian. Although he celebrated the African contributions to Brazilianness, he was very clear in assigning them a subordinate role. For
Freyre, Brazil represented the evolution of *Portuguese* civilization,
which flourished in equatorial settings on three continents because
of its capacity to absorb African and Asian elements. He called this
civilization "Luso-tropical." Its principal characteristics remained
European and Christian, but its singularity lay in the fact that it
was not exclusively either European or Christian. Thus Freyre did
not make Africans or Indians equal partners in what he dubbed
the "new world in the tropics."

"Racial democracy" became a catchphrase for democratic governments and authoritarian regimes alike. It served as a convenient
way to dismiss racial issues and to avoid confronting the country's
failure to come to grips with the stark fact that centuries of slavery
had deprived Afro-Brazilians of the ability to compete on an equal
footing for jobs and social status. The phrase implied that since Brazil was truly a land of equal opportunity, nonwhites had the responsibility to take advantage of what the country offered them
and improve their own lives, and if they failed to do so, it was their
own fault. Those who called into question this glossy view of race
relations ran the risk of being branded anti-Brazilian.

Perhaps the earliest publicized protest against racial prejudice
came to light in 1904, when a Rio de Janeiro newspaper reported
complaints that a well-known local theater was discriminating
against blacks through their hiring practices. It was not until the
1920s that Rio de Janeiro's clubs permitted blacks to play on their
soccer teams. The Brazilian navy and foreign service long excluded
blacks from jobs that would put them in contact with foreigners.
For years classified advertisements in newspapers included the descriptive "good appearance" to convey the message that only persons with light skin need apply.

It is, of course, true that after abolition, laws overtly discriminating against Afro-Brazilians ceased to exist, and Brazil did not
experience the sort of legally sanctioned segregation that marred
black-white relations in the United States. Indeed, Brazilians like
Veríssimo who saw no "color problem" in their country were perhaps comparing Brazil to the "Colossus of the North." Yet this judg-

ment, even if it once had validity, has been rendered obsolete by the significant gains recorded by many African Americans over the past several decades, while the status of Afro-Brazilians has remained virtually unchanged.

In addition, the Brazilian way of doing things enables Brazilians to avoid the sort of overt, hostile racism found in the United States. An employer, a landlord, or a private-school official who does not want to hire, rent to, or admit blacks will politely insist that there are no vacancies, practices vividly documented in 1967 by the magazine *Realidade*, which sent a black and a white reporter to apply for the same jobs, apartments, and private-school slots for their children in various parts of Brazil and recorded the responses they received.

This does not mean, of course, that openly expressed prejudice does not exist. To cite but one example, private social clubs, which provide recreational facilities for upper- and middle-class Brazilians, have routinely refused admittance to blacks. Such clubs allow members to develop the sort of personal ties that inevitably carry over into other aspects of life, where one friend might be in a position to do a favor for another. Being excluded from such networking inflicts obvious disadvantages, since the personalization of relationships that occurs on every level of Brazilian life is a key element of Brazilianness.

There are many who maintain that whatever prejudice Afro-Brazilians face stems from color rather than race. Marshall João Batista de Mattos, the grandson of a slave and the first black to achieve the army's highest rank, made this point in another *Realidade* article during the 1960s when he averred, "If an individual is of Negro origin but this doesn't show in the color of his skin, he won't suffer any restriction." An ex-nun who works with residents of a Rio *favela* (shantytown) describes how a black woman from the neighborhood married a light-skinned man and gave birth to eight children, each with a different coloration. Two of the boys, whose intelligence and comportment did not differ to any significant degree, attended the same class in primary school. The teacher put the lighter-complexioned boy in the front row and doted upon him but made his dark-skinned brother sit in the back row and treated him with indifference.

However, the distinction between race prejudice and color prejudice may be more apparent than real. According to Carlos A. Hasenbalg, an Argentine-born sociologist and the author of several studies of racial inequality in Brazil, social and economic indicators show that whites are much better off than mulattoes; while mulattoes are only slightly better off than blacks. Nelson do Valle Silva's recent study of income differentials among blacks, mulattoes, and whites attributed a substantial portion of the differences to discriminatory labor-market practices, and a measurement of this discrimination led to the startling conclusion that mulattoes actually suffered more from discrimination than did blacks.

Given the discrepancy between the so-called racial democracy and the persistence of racial injustice in Brazil, it was inevitable that some blacks would eventually resort to collective action as a reaction against racism and as a means of promoting the interests of Afro-Brazilians. Their stance amounted to an outright rejection of the notion, espoused by Gilberto Freyre and others, that Brazilian society had successfully absorbed the descendants of slaves.

The first initiative they pursued was the founding of the Brazilian Black Front in São Paulo in 1931. Seeking to protest the existence of racial discrimination and to secure for black people their full political and social rights, the Front published a newspaper, sponsored demonstrations, and even tried to become a political party. However, it failed to mobilize widespread support among working-class blacks, and it alienated many because of the neo-Fascist tone it began to adopt. In addition, the historical moment proved inopportune. In 1937 the regime of Getúlio Vargas banned all political organizations, and the Brazilian Black Front died in its infancy.

When World War II ended and the Vargas dictatorship collapsed, the black movement remained dormant, despite the efforts of a few intrepid individuals. During the subsequent era of democratic rule, which lasted until 1964, Afro-Brazilians did not engage in any collective political activity, and no attempts were made to revive the Brazilian Black Front.

Blacks played no role in the drafting and ratification of the 1946 Constitution, which for the first time guaranteed equal rights to all citizens regardless of color; nor in the enactment of the nation's first antidiscrimination law in 1951. Indeed, an ultimate irony is that what inspired the new legislation was the refusal of a São Paulo hotel to admit Katherine Dunham, a black dancer from the United States.

An obsession with national security permeated the military regime that seized power in 1964, so it became exceedingly risky to raise one's voice in protest against any kind of perceived social inequity in Brazil. Criticizing racial prejudice in Brazil—or even raising doubts about the existence of racial democracy—was viewed as subversive by those in power.

Nevertheless, during the 1970s a number of factors combined to give impetus to the resuscitation of a black movement in Brazil. The civil-rights struggle in the United States in the 1960s had captured the imagination of black Brazilians. The presence of ambassadors from the emerging nations of Africa inspired in Afro-Brazilians a growing consciousness of their African heritage. Slogans such as "Black is beautiful" became popular, and in 1976 a Black Rio movement that took inspiration from American soul music, dance, hair and dress styles, and handshakes spread from lower-class black youths to university students. The military government loosened its control over the political process, and the new climate encouraged blacks to speak openly about racial issues.

In 1978 the death of a black worker at the hands of the police and the expulsion of four black boys from a volleyball team sponsored by a private club outraged blacks in São Paulo and furnished the spark that led to the formation of the Unified Black Movement Against Racial Discrimination, an organization that quickly attracted adherents from other parts of the country. Black leaders participated in the campaign for popular presidential elections during 1983 and 1984 and addressed many of the rallies that brought millions of Brazilians into the streets. The governor of São Paulo created the Council for the Development and Participation of the Black Community, the first state organ in Brazil to be given responsibility for dealing with racial problems.

The vision of Brazil as a racial democracy came under sustained and withering fire during 1988, the centennial of the abolition of slavery in Brazil. In observing the anniversary of the Golden Law of May 13, 1888, which granted freedom to the 750,000 blacks still bound by the chains of involuntary servitude, the mass media gave extensive coverage to reports documenting the existence of disparities along racial lines in every aspect of Brazilian life; to the discontents expressed by increasingly outspoken blacks; and to documenting persistent manifestations of racism in many forms and on many levels. This was by no means the first time these matters had been brought to the public's attention. But never before had there been such intense and systematic focus on Brazil's race problem.

Most blacks who are conscious of their past would have preferred not to celebrate May 13, in 1988 or in any other year, since they hold that the day on which Princess Isabel signed the law abolishing slavery (her father, the Emperor Dom Pedro II, was ill and out of the country at the time) did not really mark the liberation of Afro-Brazilians. Indeed, the various cultural and political organizations that compose the black movement in Brazil have designated November 20 as their holiday. This was the day on which Zumbi, the leader of the Palmares *quilombo,* was believed to have hurled himself from a cliff to avoid capture by government forces determined to put an end to a black outpost of freedom that had survived and prospered for decades.

Whatever latent reservations blacks may have harbored about celebrating the centennial found ample justification as early as 1984, when the Ministry of Justice announced the formation of a special commission that would publish five books to commemorate the abolition. The chairman of the group was to be Prince Pedro Gastão de Orleans, a direct descendant of Princess Isabel. In a display of astonishing insensitivity, the ministry did not name a single black to the new commission. When this omission drew protests, the secretary of the commission announced that he would try to find an Afro-Brazilian with a doctorate in history (and with slavery as his or her area of specialization) to include in the group, although no other member of the commission had been required to possess similar qualifications. Afro-Brazilians nonetheless resolved to take advantage of 1988 as an occasion to bring the race problem—which their fellow Brazilians (white, black, and mulatto alike) had long refused to recognize—into the national spotlight.

During this same period, black priests convinced the National Conference of Catholic Bishops to dedicate their 1988 Fraternity Campaign to the theme of the plight of Afro-Brazilians. Their hope was to make racial justice a subject for discussion and reflection in churches throughout the country. They succeeded, for the most part, but not without some controversy. Dom Eugênio Sales, the conservative cardinal of the city of Rio de Janeiro, withdrew his diocese from the campaign and substituted his own theme: "Every race but only one people."

Moreover, a booklet prepared by a committee of black priests and seminarians stirred up a firestorm of criticism when it identified as a "false hero" Luís Alves de Lima e Silva, better known as the Duke of Caxias, whom the Brazilian army considers its hero. The booklet charged that he purposefully sent thousands of black soldiers to their death during the War of Paraguay. Several prominent historians immediately disputed this allegation.

A parade scheduled for May 11 as part of the centennial celebrations in downtown Rio de Janeiro gave the Brazilian army cause for concern because the place where the Duke of Caxias is buried was along the announced parade route. In a scene reminiscent of the military dictatorship, a large contingent of troops took to the streets and prevented the five thousand marchers from going anywhere near the tomb.

Despite the impetus provided by these events and the publicity generated by the commemoration of the centennial of the abolition of slavery, the black movement in Brazil has remained fragmented and weak, plagued by internal divisions that have impeded the development of a consensus about both strategy and tactics. Particularly problematic has been the split between those who see political action as the primary vehicle for achieving racial justice, and those whose priority is the development of an Afro-Brazilian consciousness through efforts to preserve the cultural heritage of black Brazilians.

The latter movement dates back at least to the 1940s, when groups such as the Black Experimental Theater of Rio de Janeiro came into being. It sought to broaden awareness of the contributions of persons of African descent to the political and social history of Brazil, as well as to encourage the evolution of Afro-

Brazilian culture in such diverse fields as music, dance, religion, art, and literature.

The political wing of the black movement has encountered tremendous frustration because of its failure to score more than token successes in the electoral arena, despite the fact that people of color constitute the majority in the Brazilian populace. Nowhere is this more apparent than in the heartland of Afro-Brazil—the city of Salvador, where blacks and mulattoes compose 80 percent of the population, but the mayor and more than 90 percent of the city council are white; and the state of Bahia, where the governor is white and the congressional delegation, as reported in the *New York Times*, "looks as though it just stepped off a plane from Portugal."

The forms racism has assumed in Brazil have made it difficult for the black movement to find obvious targets for large-scale mobilization. (Indeed, protests against apartheid in South Africa were easier to organize.) The movement has yet to reach and galvanize the great masses of Afro-Brazilians who live in dire poverty, a shortcoming dramatized by the dismal failure of blacks to turn out to support fellow blacks running on racial issues during the 1980s elections.

One of those who tasted frustration in this period was Abdias do Nascimento, a pioneer in the struggle against racial discrimination in Brazil. His story provides useful insights into the dynamics of Brazil's black movement.

He was born in 1914 in Franca, a city located in the far north of the state of São Paulo, near the border of Minas Gerais. His father worked in a shoe factory; his mother was a candy maker and a wet nurse for the children of the local landowners.

"One of my earliest memories is of black women who lived on an abandoned coffee plantation not far from town. They would come to Franca looking for work. They dressed all in white, very clean, as though they were wearing uniforms. I thought they were beautiful. Once we spent a whole day at their plantation. I ate a special kind of food, made from corn. This was my introduction to African culture."

Abdias's father was very Catholic.

He wanted me to become a priest. When I said I wanted to get an education and enter a profession, he told me about a young black who had the same ambition and worked very hard to become a physician. But no one wanted to be treated by a black doctor, and he had no patients. He became so dispirited that he hanged himself.

Undaunted, Abdias went to public high school and studied accounting. In 1930 he volunteered for the army as a way of escaping Franca. Several years later, he and a friend were prevented from entering a bar in São Paulo because of their race. A brawl ensued, as a result of which Abdias was discharged from the army for disorderly conduct.

Although he had been studying economics during his spare time, he soon developed a passion for the theater. During a trip to Lima, Peru, he attended a performance of Eugene O'Neill's *The Emperor Jones*. A white actor in blackface played the title role. Nonetheless, the experience touched Abdias deeply. "In Brazil blacks on the stage were used only in decorative parts. I began to realize what theater could do."

He spent some time in Buenos Aires, where he studied the dramatic arts, and then returned to São Paulo. There he discovered to his dismay not only that criminal charges had been filed against him as a result of the brawl, but also that he had received a two-year prison sentence in absentia.

The result was that he was confined in a maximum-security penitentiary, where he helped to found the prison theater. This was his first opportunity to train and direct actors. At the same time he worked on appealing his conviction, on the ground that he was a soldier at the time of the incident, and hence civilian courts had no jurisdiction over him. After having served out almost the entire sentence, he won his appeal and was released.

He went to Rio, where he worked as an actor, and in 1944 he cofounded the Black Experimental Theater. Reflecting on his experiences, Abdias observed, "We were pioneers, opening new roads. No one believed a black could be anything except someone white people laughed at. But we created a whole new atmosphere, and soon whites began to write for our Theater."

One of Abdias's achievements as an actor was his performance in Vinicius de Moraes's play *Orfeu da Conceição*, which was later adapted as the film *Black Orpheus*. Abdias was not entirely happy with either the play or the motion picture. "There are plenty of myths in African culture," he observed. "Why did they have to use something out of Greek mythology? And what's more, when Orpheus decides to descend into Hell to look for Eurydice, where does he go? To a temple of Afro-Brazilian religion!"

Abdias became a leading figure in Brazil's black movement, in both its cultural and political areas. Because he spoke out frequently on race-related issues, the military regime forced him into exile in 1968. He spent the next fourteen years at universities in the United States.

Upon his return he entered politics and in 1982 was elected to the federal Chamber of Deputies, where he became the only member who identified himself as a black and who pressed for legislation specifically targeting racial problems. But the radical, highly emotional rhetoric he employed blunted his effectiveness within the Congress. Moreover, he lacked a real power base of his own within the community. His victory at the polls had been owing to the success enjoyed by the party that had put him up as a candidate, and when that party fared poorly in the 1986 elections, Abdias was one of the casualties.

On the other hand, Benedita da Silva, a tall, handsome, hefty woman with a marvelously resonant voice, has demonstrated that Afro-Brazilians may yet be able to use the electoral process for their collective gain. But she is no ordinary politician. As she likes to point out, being black, a woman, and a slumdweller gives her membership in three disadvantaged groups.

"I began my political militancy very early, because politics is something you do from the day you're born," she pointed out in an interview in her office in Brasília. "Early on you discover there is a difference between being a black woman from the slums and a rich white man. Early on you learn that to be black is to be ugly, to be a woman is to be good for nothing but raising children, to be poor is to be marginal. I have tried to say 'Enough!' to all this."

One of thirteen siblings, Benedita was born in 1940 in a *favela* overlooking Rio's Rodrigues de Freitas Lagoon. Her grandmother had been a slave. Her mother worked as a freelance laundress and also served as a priestess in an Afro-Brazilian cult. Her father washed cars. Benedita found her first job at the age of ten and married at sixteen. Of the five children to whom she gave birth, only two survived. She has outlived two husbands, married for the third time, and now lives in Chapéu da Mangueira, a slum that overlooks Copacabana Beach.

Her political career began when she went to work in various community movements and came into contact with Dom Hélder Câmara, at the time an auxiliary bishop in Rio and an outspoken advocate for the poor. From these experiences she discovered that public authorities pay attention to slumdwellers only after they organize. In the late 1970s she was one of the founding members of the Workers' party, which put great stress on developing close contacts with grassroots organizations. In 1982 she was elected to the city council of Rio de Janeiro, and four years later, in a low-budget campaign that depended almost exclusively on word-of-mouth publicity, she won a seat in the federal Chamber of Deputies and became the first black woman ever to achieve that honor.

Benedita is one of a handful of deputies who consider themselves a part of Brazil's black movement, and she has forcefully raised racial issues in the Congress. However, the strong ties she maintains with her other constituencies, which cut across racial lines, provide a base of support that makes her a force to be reckoned with and a budding figure on the national political scene.

When she began her national political career she was well aware of the pitfalls before her. "My presence in the Congress is a historic moment for women and for blacks in Brazil. The danger— and you can already see it materializing—is that I will be converted into a folkloric figure. That happened to Mário Juruna.* I'm not going to let it happen to me."

In 1992 Benedita da Silva made a strong run for mayor of Rio de Janeiro. In the first round she topped the field, but because she failed to win more than 50 percent of the votes, she had to face the second-place finisher in a runoff, which she lost. In 1994 she

---

* Juruna was an Indian who was elected to Congress from Rio de Janeiro in 1984 and who lost his seat in 1986. His story will be told in more detail in Chapter Three.

attracted more than two million votes in a successful campaign for the Senate.

While candidates primarily identified with the black movement have fared badly at the polls, blacks seeking office on the basis of their ability to represent all their constituents have scored some impressive wins. In 1990 voters elected three Afro-Brazilians to governorships, one of them in the state of Rio Grande do Sul, where whites have an overwhelming majority.

One of the difficulties besetting the political wing of the Brazilian black movement is uncertainty about what specific policies to pursue. It has not surprisingly turned out to be easier to denounce injustice than to develop remedies to deal with it. The 1988 Constitution makes racism a serious crime and enables the Congress to enact laws spelling out the details, but the benefits of this change may be more symbolic than real. The legal system in Brazil is cumbersome and has never been a particularly useful weapon against social injustice. Moreover criminalizing discrimination means that all the protections generally afforded criminal defendants will be available to those accused of racial offenses.

Since Afro-Brazilians have increased their contacts with the civil-rights movement in the United States, it should come as no surprise that they are debating the feasibility of proposing American panaceas such as affirmative action. Even if one puts aside for a moment the political difficulties of enacting such measures in Brazil, the fact remains that such measures may be ill suited in the Brazilian context. For example, given the racial mix in Brazil, who would qualify for benefits under affirmative action?

Indeed, the problem of defining who is black—given the heritage of nearly five centuries of miscegenation—turns out to be a serious impediment not only to the fashioning of specific race-based programs, but also to the growth of the black movement in Brazil. Color lines in Brazil are exceedingly difficult to draw, because Brazilians have customarily rejected the American practice of categorizing as black anyone with the slightest trace of African ancestry. Indeed, they have perhaps gone to the opposite extreme by creating a host of words and expressions for the various skin shadings that distinguish Brazilians. As a reaction to this, Afro-Brazilian militants are now embracing the American custom in an effort to attract even the lightest mulattoes into their camp.

The Brazilian attitude toward color, on the other hand, has opened up the possibility for a certain degree of social mobility that many consider an effective safety valve against the pressures of social unrest. Marriage to someone of a lighter color is seen as an opportunity to better the lot of one's children. Moreover, persons whose pigmentation falls on the border between recognized categories often decide for themselves to which group they belong and most often opt for the lighter classification. The tendency of successful fairer-complexioned mulattoes to do this has inspired the popular saying "Money whitens."

Thus, the mestizo character of Brazilian society has not dislodged the underlying assumption that whiteness is the ideal to which all should aspire, a conviction that predated the bleaching policy of the early twentieth century. By assimilating certain aspects of African (and Indian) culture, Brazilian society has created not a racial democracy in the political, social, and economic sense of the term, but rather an exceedingly subtle form of white supremacy.

There are signs that forces within the black movement may be trying to push Brazil in the direction of a dual-culture society. Efforts to re-Africanize Afro-Brazilian religions by purging them of elements they acquired in the western hemisphere are but one illustration of this trend.

There is something unmistakably tragic in manifestations of the beginnings of racial polarization in Brazil. It represents an inevitable reaction to the country's stubborn refusals to recognize the concept of racial democracy for what it is and to address the chronic ills attributable to slavery.

White Brazilians need to acquire a greater sensitivity to racial issues and to stop viewing them solely from a white perspective. To profess extravagant admiration for Pelé, the black soccer superstar internationally celebrated as the greatest player in the history of the game, does not necessarily demonstrate racial tolerance. There is only one Pelé (and his indifference to the problem of racism has earned him bitter, if subdued criticism from a number of Afro-Brazilians). As American scholar Carl N. Degler has observed,

If the Brazilian emphasis upon individual exception permits some blacks to rise above their fellows, despite their color, it has also two other effects. It does not alter the white's impression of Negroes in general and it does not help to advance the status of blacks in general.

To use what whites view as expressions of endearment (such as *meu nego,* or "my black") toward their dark-skinned fellow Brazilians may not always delight the object of affection. To view the *mulata* as a national symbol of sexuality is in fact profoundly demeaning, since it may convey the subtextual message that the worth of women of color derives only from their status as sex objects.

On the other hand, Brazilian blacks who express a preference for the kind of open racial discrimination they associate with the United States because it would be easier to confront and combat are too hastily discounting the distinct advantage Brazil has over its neighbor to the north in the matter of race relations. As a young African-American musician put it,

> After spending six months in Brazil, I became quite comfortable living in a single Afro-Brazilian culture to which everyone belongs. When I returned home, it was like a dash of cold water in my face. I was very quickly reminded that the U.S. is a dual-culture society. A line exists, and you are either on one side or the other.

The opportunity still exists for Brazilians to create a genuinely *mestiço* society in which biracialism does not serve as a figleaf, and in which neither white nor black elements predominate, but rather both contribute on an equal footing to the emergence of a truly "new world in the tropics." But all signs point to the need to develop a fresh commitment to racial equality, before time runs out.

# Chapter 3

# The Indians

$\mathcal{N}$o one knows with any degree of certainty how many Indians were living within the present borders of Brazil when Cabral and his men anchored in Porto Seguro in 1500. The upside estimate is 6 million. A more realistic projection, hazarded by a British scholar who has published two highly regarded volumes on the history of indigenous Brazilians, might be 2.4 million. After nearly five centuries of contact with "civilization," Brazil's entire Indian population today can fit neatly, though perhaps not comfortably, in the seats, benches, and standing-room sections of Rio de Janeiro's Maracanã soccer stadium.

The native contribution to Brazilianness may be somewhat less pronounced than that of the Portuguese and the Africans, but it is not insignificant. The high cheekbones and coppery skin possessed by many Brazilians proclaim the Indian blood that flows in their veins. Indian customs and characteristics have penetrated deeply into Brazilian behavior. Indian myths form a part of the Brazilian subconscious.

At the same time, the tribal way of life that makes Indians Indian has suffered a fate no different from that of aborigines elsewhere in the hemisphere. What has amounted to a genocidal process of attrition dates back to the arrival of the first white men, and the abuse and killing of native Brazilians has gained fresh impetus in recent decades as Brazil has opened up its frontiers in an effort to tap the vast resources of the Amazon basin.

From time to time Indians still use bows and arrows to defend themselves against those who intrude on their lands, but they have also learned to fight back with modern weapons. Some tribes now videotape encounters with government officials, in order to preserve a record of the promises being made to them. With an eye toward television coverage on the evening news programs, groups of aborigines converged on Brasília, painted their bodies and donned feathers at a protest demonstration as the 1988 constituent assembly (containing not one single native Brazilian) debated constitutional provisions that would affect the rights of Indians. The 1989 tour of Chief Raoni, who accompanied British rock star Sting on visits to Pope John Paul II, Prince Charles, and French President François Mitterrand, helped enlist international sympathy for the plight of his people.

In setting national priorities, Brazil's elite have always put their own comfort and enrichment ahead of the native Brazilians' struggles to preserve their way of life. In every confrontation between "progress" and the interests of the Indians, the latter have had to yield. Indeed, efforts from abroad on behalf of the tribes have at times been labeled foreign plots to impede Brazil's access to important natural resources and to keep Brazil underdeveloped.

But the exploitation of Brazilian rain forests over the past several decades has not only had a devastating effect on the Indians who depend on them for sustenance; it has also proved to be economically wasteful and ecologically disastrous. There is no little irony in the fact that as Brazilians have begun to realize this, they are also discovering that their Indian compatriots have much to teach them about how to preserve and live in harmony with the jungle environment. It has taken nearly five centuries, over the course of which Indians have endured all kinds of atrocities, for this insight to dawn.

Anthropologists have classified native Brazilians into two main types: tropical-forest Indians, who inhabited the rain forests of the Amazon and the coastal plains and lived off agriculture and fishing; and so-called marginal-culture Indians, nomadic inhabitants of the plains and plateaus who hunted, gathered, and fished. These indigenous peoples spoke four main languages and a number of other unrelated tongues. The first Portuguese explorers and colonists came into contact with tropical-forest Indians, mainly belonging to Tupi tribal groups.

The European intruders initially viewed the native Brazilians as "noble savages," unspoiled children of nature, innocent and hospitable, exotic and handsome, carefree and sensual. The sight of naked painted bodies in the midst of lush vegetation had a hypnotic effect on men who had just survived the rigors of a transatlantic crossing. The willingness with which Indian women gave themselves to the white strangers no doubt contributed heavily to the enthusiastic response of the Europeans to the native people.

But very soon the honeymoon had ended. The newcomers pursued their imperial designs, and the Brazilian Indians turned out to be, in fact, rather warlike. Tribal groups fought among themselves and with other tribes. Prisoners were enslaved, ritually clubbed to death, and eaten. Such behavior supplied the Europeans with a pretext for resolving to "civilize" the indigenous peoples they encountered. Of course, the policies inflicted upon the Indians by the white intruders coincidentally served to promote the interests of the latter in extracting as much wealth as possible from the New World.

The sugar plantations the Portuguese began to create along the Brazilian coast required a great deal of manpower, and the colonists themselves felt that manual labor was beneath their dignity. Although the Indians did not mind performing specific tasks in exchange for goods such as metal tools, they saw no point in doing steady work to accumulate things for which they had no need. Since the Indians could not be lured into long-term employment, the Portuguese decided to subject them to involuntary servitude. At first the colonists bartered for prisoners whom one tribe had seized during battles with another tribe and were about to eat. Then the settlers encouraged intertribal warfare in order to increase the supply of captives. When this tactic didn't yield sufficient laborers to meet the demand, the colonists began to enslave Indians directly.

Native Brazilians, however, did not adjust easily to work on sugar plantations. Although tropical-forest Indians lived in villages, they customarily moved whenever the local supply of game ran low or the topsoil in the area eroded. The nomadic nature of their lives induced a sense of freedom that made it difficult for them to accept the constraints of forced labor. Moreover, within their society taking care of crops and performing menial tasks were women's work. The males were warriors, hunters, fishermen, and craftsmen. They considered forced labor in the cane fields extremely degrading.

The Portuguese Crown opposed the enslavement of Indians and entrusted the Jesuits with responsibility for protecting them. Priests sent to the New World established missions where they assembled, converted, educated, and sheltered aborigines. These settlements were fascinating experiments in social engineering, wherein the Jesuits attempted to Europeanize the Indians. They suppressed indigenous values that ran counter to the teachings of the Church yet absorbed some elements of the collective structure of Indian society. The Jesuits and the plantation owners were in constant conflict over the issue of the Indians' fate, but the Jesuits were badly outnumbered by those who sought to enslave the Indians. Later, beginning in 1628, raids by *bandeirantes* decimated the Jesuit missions.

Portuguese colonization had a catastrophic impact on native Brazilians. Tribal warfare intensified, not only because of the colonists' need to provoke skirmishes to increase the numbers of captured prisoners who could be bartered into slavery, but also because of the conflicts between the Portuguese and their European rivals. Each European contender cultivated tribal groups as allies in a bloody contest for domination of Brazil. As more colonists and large numbers of African slaves arrived, the Indians were forced to migrate inland. This often put them in conflict with other tribes.

The Portuguese generally did not hold the Indians in high esteem. In addition to consigning them to involuntary servitude, they used native women to slake their carnal needs. The mixed-blood offspring created by these unions then occupied the lower rungs of the colonial society.

Despite the cruelty and exploitation inflicted by Portuguese settlers upon the Indians, the latter nonetheless succeeded in leaving their mark on the evolving society in the New World, and on the evolution of Brazilianness, in a number of distinctive ways.

One of the distinctive characteristics of the aborigines was their scrupulous personal hygiene, which contrasted sharply with the slovenliness of sixteenth-century Europeans. Indians took river baths several times a day. Native women, moreover, liked to apply coconut oil to their hair and to sleep in hammocks. The colonists eventually absorbed these habits, which survive among contemporary Brazilians.

The newcomers borrowed from the Indians in a number of other respects. Explorers used the Indians' small canoes for river transport. A type of flour the aborigines made from the ubiquitous and easy-to-grow manioc root served as a staple for the colonists, who came to prefer it to wheat. Indian corn and cashew nuts were among the other native foods settlers adopted. The Indian method of wrapping fish in banana leaves and roasting it over open coals underwent a process of Africanization that produced one of the adornments of Brazilian cuisine, the *moqueca,* or "fish stew." The Indians introduced the Portuguese to tobacco smoking, and tobacco eventually became one of the colony's principal export crops. Indian names for places, plants, and animals quickly made their way into the Portuguese language.

The aborigines' love of freedom and abhorrence of regimentation burn in the soul of modern Brazilians. Their wanderlust is also visible today in the internal migrations that continue to shape and reshape Brazilian society. As one writer has observed, "Almost every Brazilian man has at least one itching foot." The northeasterners who trek to São Paulo and the southerners who make their way to the western Amazon region follow in the tradition of tribes that roamed the length and breadth of the land. Between 1940 and 1990, some 57 million Brazilians migrated from one state or territory to another.

Even the eating of human flesh, as practiced by some Brazilian aborigines, contributed in a rather unique way to the development of Brazilianness. An intellectual movement that arose in the mid-1920s issued a so-called Cannibalist Manifesto, advocating the digestion and Brazilianization of concepts originating abroad. Anthropophagy, they argued, was a peculiarly Brazilian capability that would produce ideas and styles that were truly original. Thereafter, many Brazilians would count this metaphoric cannibalism as one of their national traits.

Some Indian characteristics merged with and fortified Portuguese and African attributes. For example, natives used a slash-and-burn approach to agriculture that paralleled the extractive mentality of the Portuguese settlers, who sought only to take from the land and gave no thought to long-term consequences. The individuality of the native Brazilian matched that of the colonists from Portugal. Brazilian music and Carnival have evolved from the aborigines' love of music and splendid costume joined with African and European elements. The Indian's belief in spirits and in supernatural relationships between humans and animals meshed neatly with similar convictions held by Africans—which accounts for the traces of animism and totemism one finds deeply imbedded in the Brazilian psyche. Indeed, the popularity of the *jogo do bicho* (an illegal lottery in which players bet on animals that represent numbers) may have roots in Brazil's Indian culture.

The most important figure in tribal society was the *pagé*, or "medicine man," who interpreted the supernatural for a people who entertained no doubts about the omnipresence of spirits affecting every aspect of their lives. The *pagé* also foretold the future and cured the sick. He performed the latter function by the prescribing of jungle herbs and, more often, by faith healing.

Portuguese settlers and their descendants, struggling for survival in a strange, often menacing environment, proved understandably receptive to native beliefs and practices. They learned to use Indian medicines and placed great store in faith healing, which even today remains a source of hope and comfort for Brazilians of every social class.

Perhaps the greatest single contribution of the Indians was their indispensable service in the opening of the interior of Brazil. Without the help of native guides, bearers, hunters, and canoers, explorers could never have penetrated the vast reaches of the Amazon basin, nor could settlers have pushed into the hinterlands of central and southern Brazil. Indians were intimately involved, either as participants, victims, or both, in the slaving expeditions of the *bandeirantes*, the conquest of the Amazon for the Portuguese Crown, the founding of large cattle ranches in the interior of the Northeast, and the great gold and diamond rushes of the eighteenth century. These were milestones in the formation of modern Brazil. Because of this advance into the interior the Portuguese concluded a 1750 treaty with Spain that fixed the boundaries of Brazil far beyond the limits set by the Treaty of Tordesillas.

There was, of course, a sad irony to all this, since the Indians were abetting their own gradual destruction as a people. Yet the extermination of the native population did not serve any of the immediate interests of the colonists and the crown. As John Hemming has pointed out in *Red Gold*, the first of his two volumes on the history of the Brazilian aborigines,

> Nobody wanted the Indians to die out. Land on the Amazon was valueless without people to penetrate its forests or man its canoes. The settlers demanded Indians as hired or slave labour. Missionaries wanted them as Christian converts, to swell and glorify their missions. The royal authorities wanted them as subjects, to be used if necessary on public works or fighting to defend Portuguese possessions against other colonial powers or hostile tribes.

Yet bloody clashes and the spread of diseases such as influenza and smallpox, which were transmitted by Europeans and Africans, and to which the Indians had virtually no natural resistance, took a frightful toll.

In the middle of the eighteenth century native Brazilians suffered yet another serious setback. The Jesuits had come under mounting criticism, in both Brazil and Portugal, for their zealous defense of the Indians and their resistance to the implementation of the 1750 treaty, which called for some dislocation of their remaining missions. In addition, Portugal's declining economy suffered further strain by the need to rebuild Lisbon, which an earthquake had leveled in 1755. Sebastião José de Carvalho e Mello, better known in the annals of European history as the Marquis of Pombal, had become de facto dictator of Portugal by this time and had developed an obsessive hatred of the Jesuits, who he believed were plotting against him. He decided to expel them from Brazil, not only to end their supposed insubordination, but also as a ploy to augment the royal treasury, because he intended to confiscate Jesuit property and goods in the colony and sell them.

Thus Brazilian Indians lost their principal source of protection and support. In addition, Pombal secured the promulgation of laws that supposedly "liberated" the Indians of northern Brazil by forbidding their enslavement and bestowing upon them the same rights and privileges enjoyed by other colonists. The purpose of these decrees was to integrate the natives into the Luso-Brazilian community by encouraging them to speak Portuguese, to dress in the European style, and to intermarry with non-Indians. So-called Indian directors replaced the missionaries as representatives of the Crown in the various native communities. But instead of looking out for the interests of the Indians, the directors exploited the Indians shamelessly, to such a degree that in 1798 the director system was abolished.

For about one hundred years the Indians of northern Brazil, which constituted most of the surviving tribal units in the country, were generally left to their own devices. Some had managed to avoid contact with "civilization"; others, supposedly converted to Christianity and western values by the missionaries, eventually slipped back into their native cultures.

It was during this period that Brazilian literature was going through its "Indianist" phase. Authors glorified the aborigine and emphasized the character defects of the Portuguese explorers and settlers—in a sense a return to the theme of the "noble savage," but for the purpose of nourishing national pride and identity. As John Hemming has noted in *Amazon Frontier*, the second of his two-volume history of the native Brazilians, "Indians were becoming curiosities rather than a serious threat. . . . Now that there was nothing to fear from [them], urban intellectuals could afford to ro-manticise about them." The Indianist writers distorted the past and ignored the brutal realities of contemporary Indian life. José de Alencar produced the classic novel *O Guarani*, which composer Car-los Gomes later adapted into Brazil's most famous opera of the same name, portraying the native Brazilian as a repository of virtue. None of this, of course, was very comforting or even relevant to the real-life Indians, who in the mid-nineteenth century were about to undergo yet another calamity—a rubber boom that would convulse the Amazon basin for five decades.

Wild rubber trees grow with great profusion in northern Bra-zil. The Indians used the liquid extracted from them to waterproof their canoes. The colonists made boots from rubber. Yet the prod-uct remained something of a novelty item until 1840, when the American Charles Goodyear invented a process of vulcanization that prevented rubber from becoming sticky in heat and brittle in cold. In a short time rubber became a major or crucial ingredient in the manufacture of rainwear, steam engines, electric insulation, and tires. With the spread of the Industrial Revolution and the growing popularity of the bicycle and the automobile, the world-wide demand for rubber skyrocketed. Although latex (the liquid from which rubber is fashioned) could be drawn from trees found in other parts of the world, the milky substance obtained from the wild Brazilian trees produced by far the best quality rubber.

Along with the demand for rubber came a new class of entrepreneurs who flourished in Belém, near the mouth of the Amazon, and Manaus, a river port nearly one thousand miles from the ocean. Their most pressing need was for rubber tappers, workers who could roam the rain forest and extract latex from the wild trees. Once again the Indians became targets for a vicious form of de facto enslavement. Once again they proved to be an inadequate source of manpower. This time the alternative was to be found in the drought-lashed, overpopulated backlands of the Northeast, from which thousands of laborers were enlisted. They soon found themselves trapped in debt peonage, forced to work in a "green hell" fraught with physical dangers. The Indians resisted the encroachments of the *seringueiros,* as the rubber tappers were called, and bloody conflicts ensued. As usual, the indigenous peoples came out on the losing end. The *seringueiros* hunted down and killed many of them. The entrepreneurs (by now known as rubber barons) were much more efficient. They organized the massacre of some forty thousand Indians—an outrage that provoked international condemnation in 1912.

The end of the rubber boom brought a halt to the atrocities, at least for the moment. In 1876 a British agent named Henry A. Wickham, posing as an orchid hunter, managed to smuggle seeds of rubber trees out of Brazil. They were transported to east Asia and planted. Thirty years later groves of cultivated rubber trees in Asia began to produce latex, and the Brazilian monopoly came to an end.* The rubber barons, who had converted Manaus from a

---

* There was a smidgen of poetic justice here. In 1727, a Brazilian smuggled some coffee-plant seeds out of French Guiana, in violation of French law, and brought them into Brazil. They made possible the creation of the colony's first coffee plantation.

collection of jungle huts into a bustling city with a celebrated opera house—and who were so wealthy they could afford to send their laundry to Paris—saw their empire collapse in ruin.

As the rubber boom was drawing to a close, the Brazilian government changed its attitude toward the Indians. An army officer named Cândido Mariano da Silva Rondon was primarily responsible for the new policy. A heroic figure who exemplified the sweetness and greatness that is Brazil at its finest, Rondon was uniquely suited to his life's work among the Indians.

He was born in the interior of Mato Grosso, a land of prairies where herds of cattle roamed. His father was descended from the *bandeirantes*, his mother from several Indian tribes. At the age of sixteen he entered a military school in the royal palace in Rio de Janeiro, an institution permeated by the progressive ideas of Dom Pedro II. There Rondon came under the influence of the positivist philosophy of Auguste Comte, which emphasized the essential worth of humanity. He decided he would apply these enlightened views to Brazil's indigenous peoples, who he became convinced were a reflection of human civilization that ought to be preserved rather than exterminated.

His military service took him on a series of excursions to central Brazil and the Amazon basin. He put up over eleven hundred miles of telegraph wire and was instrumental in the discovery of fifteen new rivers. In the course of his adventures he imposed upon those under his command a simple maxim with respect to the Indians his expeditions encountered: "Die if you must, but never kill." Although hostile natives fatally wounded several of his men, he refused to use force in retaliation, and as a result he succeeded in gaining the trust of tribes with which he came into contact. World renown came to him when he accompanied former United States President Theodore Roosevelt on a trek through the Amazon jungle.

Rondon and other like-minded officers persuaded the government to set up an agency to be charged with the protection of Indian communities. In 1910 the federal Service for the Protection of the Indians (SPI) came into being, and Rondon was made its first director. The function of the SPI was not to administer the affairs of the tribes, but rather to safeguard the tribes against outside encroachments and to permit them to preserve their traditional culture. Under the leadership and inspiration of Rondon, SPI agents created posts in the frontier regions and succeeded in convincing the Indians of their good intentions.

But idealism was not enough. The SPI could, in fact, do very little when cattle ranchers, nut gatherers, and settlers pushed their way into tribal lands. This was especially true in southern Brazil, where immigrants creating agricultural colonies put irresistible pressure on the few surviving Indian communities. In the Amazon region the new policy had pacified the Indians, but the peace that Rondon had achieved turned out to be illusory. Between 1900 and 1967, ninety-eight indigenous tribes ceased to exist.

Rondon himself lived a long and distinguished life. The Brazilian government made him a marshal in the army and named the territory (now the state) of Rondônia after him. To the Indians and those who have joined the struggle to preserve the Indian way of life he is a legend. He died in 1958.

The passing of Rondon coincided with a change in the orientation of the SPI. Army officers and bureaucrats who did not share his humanitarian ideals began to infest the agency and turned it into what many would call the Service for the Prostitution of the Indians. In 1967 the military government ordered an investigation of the SPI and a year later released the results. Brazilians and non-Brazilians alike were genuinely shocked by the news, which constituted one more sorry chapter in a long history of atrocities perpetrated against Brazil's Indians.

The report found that Indian agents, land speculators, and property owners conniving with them were systematically slaughtering Indians. The new twist to this old story was that the killers were using modern technology, in the form of bacteriological warfare (issuing Indians clothing infected with smallpox, measles, influenza, and tuberculosis germs) and aerial bombardments. The enslavement of aborigines, the use of Indian girls as sexual objects, and the theft of land from the tribes were other instances of wrongdoing cited by the report. A number of SPI officials were criminally indicted. The service itself was disbanded and replaced by a new agency called the National Indian Foundation (FUNAI).

The action taken by the military government headed off efforts by foreign critics to persuade the United Nations to investigate the plight of aborigines in Brazil. But in 1969 the military regime came under new leadership and launched a program whose effects on what remained of Brazil's indigenous population would be more far-reaching and negative than what had occurred owing to the malfeasance of the SPI. The country's rulers set out to develop the untapped resources of its jungles and rain forests, and as a first step the government announced plans to build a transcontinental highway across the Amazon basin.

Over the next several years Brazilian army engineers constructed an ambitious network of roads that opened up the entire region to exploitation, in the form of cattle raising, mining, and other extractive enterprises. Funds from outside sources such as the World Bank and the Inter-American Development Bank made possible the creation of a highway system that opened up hitherto inaccessible areas. This also exposed many Indians to the dangers of contact with civilized society. Once again disease ravaged various tribes, and Indians whose lives had been disrupted could be seen begging along the new roads.

The crisscrossing of the Amazon basin with highways threatened the efforts of the Villas Bôas brothers to save indigenous cultures from extermination. Inspired by Rondon, Orlando and Cláudio Villas Bôas had led a group of Indianists in urging the government to set aside areas of land where tribes could follow their traditional ways of life yet also receive medical protection against disease. The Xingu National Park, established in 1952 in northern Mato Grosso, became the first of a number of such reservations.

The goal of the Villas Bôas brothers was to enable the Indians to avoid extinction and to preserve their culture. They believed that abrupt and uncontrolled contact with the rest of Brazilian society would be disastrous for the native peoples, but that it would be impossible to isolate them completely from the rest of the country. Only through gradual integration would they have at least a fighting chance to survive.

But Brazil's military rulers took a different view. They resolved not to let anything stand in the way of the development of the Amazon region and the exploitation of its apparently limitless resources. The Indian policy they imposed in the early 1970s sought the rapid assimilation of native Brazilians into the social and economic mainstream. As critics pointed out, this meant that those Indians who managed to survive the integrative process would enter the lowest levels of Brazilian society and would provide cheap labor for landowners and entrepreneurs.

The boundaries of the Indian reservations proved to be no obstacle to the rapid development of Brazil's last frontier. Roads skirted or intruded upon them. Settlers were inevitably attracted by the opening of new land. When they moved in, the Indians occasionally fought back with primitive weapons. Once again, they were no match for determined men using modern arms. The deforestation caused by migrants swarming into the western Amazon region, the ecological devastation wrought by thousands of gold seekers drawn to the area in the 1980s and 1990s, the flooding of tribal lands as a result of massive hydroelectric projects, and the very recent discovery of oil in the jungles of Brazil's far north have all added to the cataclysmic forces now threatening to impose a "final solution" on native Brazilians.

International protests against Brazil's treatment of its indigenous peoples and against the deforestation of the tropical rain forest (the latter to be examined in more detail in Chapter Twelve) helped persuade the Brazilian government in the early 1990s to demarcate reservations for several of the tribes. But the pressures exerted by freelance goldminers and others eager to extract natural resources on or near Indian land has continued to increase, and it remains very difficult for the federal government to enforce laws protecting native Brazilians.

Brazilian Indians have had little to say about their legal status. Until recently they were excluded from participation in the political process because Brazilians could qualify as voters only by passing a literacy test; this requirement was not abolished until 1986. The most notable public figure to emerge from their ranks in recent years was a creation of the mass media, more folkloric than real, one more bad joke perpetrated by "civilization" on native Brazilians.

Mário Juruna came on the national scene in 1976. A chief of the Xavante tribe in Mato Grosso, Juruna traveled to Brasília to petition the government for supplies. He encountered the standard bureaucratic evasions, but instead of giving up in despair, he began using a tape recorder to preserve his conversations with officials. Then the press discovered him. He was wonderful copy—thirty-nine-years old, wearing bones through his ears, and speaking his mind in a blunt way, capturing what many Brazilians felt about the military regime. He attained celebrity status as a folk hero, but more as a symbol of citizen distrust of government than as a champion of the rights of Indians. In 1982 the Democratic Labor party took advantage of his popularity by running him as a candidate for federal deputy from the state of Rio de Janeiro, and he won.

Juruna was as outspoken and as colorful as ever in the Congress, but he accomplished very little of substance for his people. Nothing in his background had prepared him for the task of building legislative alliances, and his colleagues showed little concern for the problems of native Brazilians. By now the public seemed more interested in stories about Juruna's adjustment to life away from his tribe, and the three wives he had simultaneously accumulated. He became a target for television comedians.

In the 1986 elections the Democratic Labor party did poorly, and the voters of Rio rejected their Indian deputy. Juruna returned to Brasília. Overweight, suffering from diabetes, and displaying white hairs that his people normally acquire only when they reach old age, he went to work for FUNAI, and his tape recorder was put on display in the Indian Museum of Campo Grande. In June 1992, when the United Nations held its Earth Summit in Rio de Janeiro, he appeared with a large cougar skin to protest what he called the commitment of environmentalists to protect animals at the expense of human beings.

However much some environmentalist abroad want to idealize Brazilian aborigines as noble savages, the sad fact remains: modern civilization has proved irresistible to many Indians. Exposure to technology such as automobiles, airplanes, television, and radio has convinced some Indians to prefer modernity over their traditional ways. The Kayapos, for example, have decided to exploit the gold and lumber on their tribal lands for profit, rather than to preserve the natural state of things. In the process they have demonstrated that they can cause nearly as much damage to the environment as any other Brazilians.

There are numerous parallels between the treatment afforded Brazil's Indians and the lot of indigenous peoples elsewhere in the hemisphere at the hands of the first European colonizers and those who governed the nation-states that subsequently evolved. There are also parallels between the experiences of immigrant groups who came to the United States, Canada, and Hispanic America in the ninteenth and twentieth centuries and the fate of the intrepid Europeans and Asians who crossed oceans during that same period and landed in Brazil.

# Chapter 4

# The Immigrants

*T*hey converged on the port of Santos with tickets in hand, bags packed, savings depleted, and expectations aflame, eager to board ships that would take them to farms they had recently purchased in Japanese-occupied Southeast Asia. It was a supreme act of faith, and a by-product of the efforts of the *kachigumi*, or "victory group," composed of members of Brazil's Japanese community who refused to accept the defeat of Japan in World War II.

Convinced that media accounts of an Allied victory in 1945 were outright lies, members of the victory group opted to embrace reports circulating clandestinely in their communities, such as the "news" that sixty-five thousand captured American soldiers, under the supervision of Japanese troops, were repairing the wartime damage Japanese planes had inflicted on the Panama Canal. Nippo-Brazilians fell easy prey to announcements that Japan needed their expertise in tropical agriculture for the "conquered territories," and that credibility enabled unscrupulous hustlers to sell them tickets on nonexistent voyages and titles to nonexistent properties.

Having endured the humiliations inflicted on them during the surge of Brazilian nationalism in the 1930s, and once again after Brazil had declared war against Japan and entered the war against the Axis in 1942, they waited patiently on the docks of Santos for phantom vessels that would never arrive.

The postwar era was a watershed for the Japanese colonies in Brazil. It marked a painful, at times bloody, transition between the early decades of struggle in a cruel, bewildering environment, and the attainment of the most notable success of any of Brazil's numerous immigrant groups. The saga of the Japanese in Brazil also provides dramatic evidence of how Brazilian society has been able to absorb, and in turn gain enrichment from, cultural and racial diversity. The Japanese were not the first immigrants to arrive from abroad, but in some ways they have been the most interesting.

Credit for the first non-Portuguese immigrant colony must go to King João VI, who established the royal court in exile in Rio de Janeiro in 1808. His son, Crown Prince Dom Pedro, married the Austrian Archduchess Leopoldina, a number of whose retainers spoke German and put down roots in Brazil. But Dom João went further and encouraged permanent colonies. Immigrants from Switzerland and the Rhineland established small settlements in the state of Bahia in 1818, and two years later they founded the town of Nova Friburgo in the mountains not far from the capital.

During the 1820s German immigrants began to make their way to southern Brazil. They were responding to solicitations from Dom Pedro, now emperor of Brazil, who wanted to populate the territory flanking the former Spanish colonies of La Plata. By 1830 about seven thousand Germans had entered Brazil, the great majority opting to live in the south, where the climate approximated that of Europe.

Dom Pedro's son and successor to the throne gave further encouragement to immigration. It was during the reign of Dom Pedro II that the most famous and prosperous of all German colonies, which became the cities of Blumenau and Joinville, were established in the southern state of Santa Catarina. In addition, after the American Civil War, the emperor offered inducements that attracted as many as twenty thousand white southerners from the United States. Some settled in the Amazon region; but the majority made their way to the state of São Paulo, where they founded the town of Americana.

The biggest obstacle to immigration to Brazil during the nineteenth century was the existence of slavery. Those who considered starting life anew in Brazil realized that they would be competing with slave labor. In addition, Protestants hesitated to put down roots in a country whose established religion was Roman Catholicism.* Moreover, the mistaken notions that all of Brazil lay in the tropics and that the weather there was uniformly debilitating may also have discouraged prospective colonists.

With the abolition of slavery in 1888, the need for labor on coffee plantations caused Brazil to open wide its doors and beckon to Europe. The preference for immigrant workers over ex-slaves reflected racial theories that Brazilian intellectuals had imported from across the Atlantic at the end of the nineteenth century. The country's elite believed that it was in their country's best interest to "whiten" its population. European immigration would provide the bleach.

The influx of immigrants continued up to the outbreak of World War II. Italians, more Portuguese, Spaniards, and Germans came in large numbers. There was also a steady flow from the Middle East, Eastern Europe, and Russia.

An 1890 federal law reveals that Brazil's immigration policy was openly racist: Africans and Asians were prohibited from entering Brazil without special congressional approval. But the Constitution of 1891 gave the states autonomy on matters of immigration and colonization, and pressure from coffee growers forced the state of São Paulo to permit immigration from Japan on an experimental basis.

The first Japanese contract workers made the long trip to Brazil in 1908. There were 781 of them, crowded aboard the *Kasato Maru,* which arrived on June 18. They were on their way to coffee plantations in the countryside of the state of São Paulo, which was suffering from a shortage of labor. The Italians who had migrated to Brazil at the turn of the century had proved unreliable workers; they brought with them European notions of anarchism and socialism, constantly moved from plantation to plantation, and thus created an unstable situation for the growers. Moreover, complaints about the treatment of Italian colonists had moved the Italian government to prohibit further migration to Brazil in 1902.

---

* It was not until 1863 that Protestant clergymen were legally licensed to perform civil marriage ceremonies.

The newly arriving Japanese were more docile. Mainly lower-class agricultural workers, they had been encouraged to emigrate because of population pressure at home. Confronting an unfamiliar language and a culture totally different from their own, they endured harsh exploitation at the hands of their employers.

As time passed, an increasing number of Japanese immigrants managed to leave the coffee plantations and become tenant farmers, or saved enough money to purchase small farms of their own. Others formed agricultural cooperatives. They put their skills to good use at a time when the city of São Paulo was growing rapidly, and by 1935 Japanese farmers and laborers were responsible for 35 percent of vegetable and fruit production in Greater São Paulo.

The decade of the 1930s saw a marked increase in immigration from Japan. Most of the new colonists settled in the state of São Paulo. In the interior a number of towns, such as Alvarez Machado, Arujá, and Mirandópolis, came to be populated exclusively or almost exclusively by Japanese.

The great majority of Japanese immigrants, like their counterparts from Italy, hoped to earn and save enough cash to return to their native land. But this dream materialized for very few. Those who could afford to do so realized they would have difficulties re-adapting to Japanese society, which they knew would relegate them to the lowly status from which they had fled. Many of those willing to go back were not able to save enough money to purchase passages back to Japan.

During these decades of struggle, the first generation of Japanese immigrants resisted assimilation. They continued to speak Japanese, to read Japanese-language newspapers, and to cling to ancestral customs, such as the use of matchmakers to arrange marriages. The also founded Japanese schools for their children.

But with the advent of the nationalistic regime of Getúlio Vargas, who had seized dictatorial power in 1930, the government placed restrictions on all of Brazil's immigrant groups. The teaching of foreign languages in school to students below the age of ten was forbidden (the age limit was raised to fourteen in 1939), and in 1940 the government banned the publication of newspapers in foreign languages.

When Brazil declared war on Japan and the Axis powers in 1942, Japanese residents found themselves under further constraints. Although they were not deported to detention centers, as were Japanese citizens in the United States, the authorities kept them under constant surveillance. They were even prohibited from speaking Japanese in public. "My parents told me not to say a word of Japanese outside our home or the police would arrest me," recalled a woman who lived through those difficult days and is now an official in a São Paulo bank. "It was a traumatic experience. Whenever I walked by a sign written in Japanese, I would avert my eyes."

As the Emperor Hirohito announced to his subjects that Japan was surrendering, members of the Japanese community in Brazil were celebrating the "report" that the Japanese navy had sunk the entire Allied fleet in the Sea of Japan. Fanatics from the *kachigumi* (victory group), to which a great majority of the community belonged, targeted those who sought to come to terms with Japan's downfall and who had organized what their adversaries dubbed the *makegumi*, or "defeat group." In 1946 terrorist attacks claimed the lives of fourteen "defeatists." Later that year the Constituent Assembly writing a new Constitution for Brazil reacted by considering a provision that would have prohibited any more Japanese immigrants from entering Brazil. (It was ultimately rejected.) But members of the *kachigumi* remained in their own world. As late as 1952, a poll revealed that 25 percent of the Nippo-Brazilian community still clung to the belief that Japan had won the war.

Reality inevitably prevailed among the *nisei*, or second-generation Japanese. With Japan prostrate and their lives already rooted in the environment into which they had been born, the *nisei* realized that their future belonged to Brazil. Although they had learned to speak Japanese at home, they attended Brazilian schools and were exposed to Brazilian culture. Moreover, their parents stressed the value of a university education and encouraged them to enter professions, such as law, medicine, architecture, and engineering, that traditionally enjoyed great prestige in Brazil. It was during this period that many Japanese moved from the countryside to the city of São Paulo and its suburbs.

Like their parents, however, the *nisei* did not have an easy time of it. Their families, for the most part, were of modest means. Moreover, many of them were ashamed of Japan's defeat and the excesses perpetrated by the *kachigumi*. They felt that their Japanese identity was a negative factor and tried to downplay it.

Brazilian society's ability to absorb people of different cultures aided the *nisei* in their effort to adjust to Brazil. An ability to adapt, which may date back to the time when the Moors occupied Portugal, characterizes Brazilians of every social class. Thus, it was nothing out of the ordinary for them to accept the Japanese, as they had accepted immigrants from Germany, Italy, Spain, the Middle East, and many other lands.

Assimilation was not a painless process. To the Brazilian peasant, the Japanese settlers simply did not look Brazilian. In the prewar era, the literature of the *cordel* (pamphlets containing folktales and political commentary aimed at lower-class, rural readers) occasionally portrayed Japanese in a derogatory light and as performing strange feats, such as turning tomatoes into cabbages—no doubt expressions of concern, bewilderment, and perhaps even envy at the agricultural skills of the Japanese. Brazilian farmers, accustomed to depending on the government for help, at times criticized the achievements of their self-reliant Japanese counterparts.

In spite of these obstacles, the successes achieved by the Japanese in Brazil have been extraordinary. In 1988 16 percent of the students at the University of São Paulo had Japanese surnames. Three *nisei* have served as cabinet ministers in the federal government; others have held positions as mayors and legislators on both state and municipal levels, and as high officials within the business community.

Moreover, Nippo-Brazilians have continued their outstanding work in the agricultural sector. Cotia, a farm cooperative whose twenty thousand associates may be found in fourteen states, is the twenty-sixth largest enterprise in Brazil and the most prosperous operation of its kind in all of Latin America. Spreading its knowhow freely, the cooperative cultivates two hundred fifty kinds of fruits, vegetables, and grains and most recently introduced the kiwi to Brazilian menus.

Brazil's Japanese community now supplies roughly 70 percent of all fruits and vegetables consumed in the city of São Paulo and its environs. Indeed, the total acreage its members own and cultivate in Brazil is greater than the total farm acreage in all of Japan.

From the ranks of the Japanese immigrants and their descendants have come a number of distinguished individuals. The stories of their lives illustrate the varieties of the experience of Brazilianization. Among them are artist Tomie Ohtake, journalist Hideo Onaga, jurist Kazuo Watanabe, and filmmaker Tizuka Yamasaki.

Unlike the overwhelming majority of her compatriots in Brazil, Tomie Ohtake was an accidental immigrant. Her older brother had come to Brazil as a tourist in the early 1930s and had liked the country so much that he decided to stay. In 1936 Tomie, then twenty-three years old, took the forty-five-day voyage from Japan to Santos to visit him. The outbreak of hostilities in Asia made it impossible for ordinary travelers to book return passage to Japan. Tomie stayed, married an associate of her brother, went to live in a lower-middle-class section of São Paulo, took Brazilian citizenship, and raised two sons.

During her secondary-school education in Kyoto, Tomie had studied Oriental art history and had taken routine drawing classes. Her love for art persuaded her to consider a career as an artist, but her father insisted that she fulfill her traditional duties as a Japanese woman by becoming a wife and mother. It was not until years after coming to Brazil, when her children had reached an age when they required less attention from her, that she decided to take up painting seriously. She began to take lessons in 1952, at the age of thirty-nine, sending her boys outside to play soccer while she worked.

Her progress was remarkable. Without any formal study and basically self-taught, Tomie Ohtake became one of Brazil's most respected and widely praised artists, presenting her first exposition in 1957 and eventually gaining recognition on four continents as a world-class abstractionist. She is a preeminent figure among a group of outstanding artists of Japanese origin who have made far-reaching contributions to contemporary Brazilian culture.

The striking, delicate, yet forceful quality of her work reflects a fusion of two worlds. "The Japanese tradition is very strong in my blood," she has observed. "It is apt to surface at any moment and in any manner. In Brazil, which is very young, traditions are not so heavy, and one feels freer here." As a critic once said of the artist's first lithographs, "Tomie now adds to her original values a dynamic and hot rhythm which she has extracted from her new country." Marília Martins, a Rio journalist, has noted that "in the tropics, [Tomie's] quintessential Japanese quality became pure vibration."

Tomie Ohtake lives and works in the Campo Belo neighborhood of São Paulo in a spacious retreat designed by one of her sons, a successful architect, and tucked discreetly behind a garage among middle-class two-story dwellings. Shy and self-conscious about her lack of total fluency in Portuguese, she expresses herself with a force of imagination and creativity that merges Japanese sensitivity with the exuberance of her adopted land.

Hideo Onaga is a prototypically Brazilianized *nisei*. His father, however, was no ordinary immigrant. A naval engineer born on the island of Okinawa, he obtained permission to leave his Japanese merchant ship during a stopover in Peru in 1908. After three years of work, travel, and adventure in the Andes, he crossed the northwestern frontier of Brazil and eventually made his way to Rio de Janeiro.

There, without disclosing his educational background, he took a job as a butler for a wealthy *carioca* family. One of his employer's sons was having difficulty in school, so he asked his new butler to help the boy with mathematics. Impressed by what he thought was his servant's native intelligence, the boy's father asked what Japanese eat. The butler replied that the staple food in Japan was rice. Demonstrating the power of stereotypical thinking, the father ordered that his son be fed rice every day.

The senior Onaga eventually settled in São Paulo, where he married an immigrant from Tokyo, published a Japanese-language newspaper until the 1940 ban of foreign language newspapers, and then opened a boardinghouse for out-of-town Japanese students attending school in the city. He became a prominent and highly respected figure in the immigrant community.

Hideo remembers his father requiring the family to speak only Japanese at home. "I speak it better" was one reason his father gave for his insistence. The other was a reluctance to spoil the correct Portuguese the children were learning at school. Hideo was one of the first *nisei* to attend the University of São Paulo, where he studied during World War II. He then became the first *nisei* to enter the field of journalism outside the Japanese-language media.

His career spanned four decades. Beginning at the bottom in 1941 as a copy editor for a large São Paulo newspaper, he soon became a reporter, and in the next fifteen years he achieved recognition as one of the best journalists in the city. After serving for five years as head of the editorial offices of several São Paulo dailies, he took over the editorship of *Visão* magazine in 1959. Over the next decade and a half he guided the fortunes of various important magazines and newspapers. Thereafter he worked as an advisor to Shigeaki Ueki, the *nisei* business leader, during Ueki's terms as federal Minister of Mines and Energy and president of Petrobrás, the state oil company, and as Ueki's associate in private ventures.

Hideo Onaga has long advocated that the immigrant community fully integrate itself into Brazilian society. He is strongly opposed to the notion of "hyphenated Brazilians." "In 1945 I was asked to run for federal deputy in order to represent the Japanese colony in Congress," he stated in 1987. "I refused. I told them I would be a Brazilian deputy or no deputy at all."

Sharing Hideo's conviction that total integration into Brazilian society provides the best hope for the future of the descendants of Japanese immigrants in Brazil is Kazuo Watanabe, another pioneering *nisei*, who has the distinction of being the first judge of Japanese origin to serve on the equivalent of the Supreme Court in the state of São Paulo.

Open and articulate, Dr. Kazuo is a typical *nisei* in that his parents were settlers on a coffee plantation. They eventually moved to the city of Bastos, a place founded by immigrants and at one time populated entirely by Japanese. Born in Bastos, Kazuo Watanabe spoke only Japanese until he was six years old and learned Portuguese at school. While attending the University of São Paulo, he belonged to *nisei* clubs, which he saw as aiding the process of integration. "We had dances and played soccer," he has reminisced. "The clubs were a bridge between the Japanese and Brazilian cultures."

Dr. Kazuo points out that Japan is still a very closed society and that some Brazilian *nisei* who have studied there on scholarships have been discriminated against and treated as "second-class Japanese." "When I return to Japan, I insist on speaking Portuguese with an interpreter. I am respected as a foreigner. This wouldn't happen if I attempted to converse in Japanese, which I now speak badly."

The sense of propriety felt by first- and second-generation Nippo-Brazilians at one time produced feelings of shame when anyone with a Japanese surname attracted attention for engaging in antisocial or criminal behavior. Dr. Kazuo sees it as an indicator of progress that this is no longer true. "It used to be a cause of great scandal in the community if a Japanese was arrested as a smuggler; now, no one gives it a second thought."

The emergence of Tizuka Yamasaki as a public figure is testing the new self-assurance of Nippo-Brazilians. Strong-willed, candid, nonconformist, and enormously energetic, Tizuka is one of Brazil's hottest young filmmakers and television directors. Her low-budget masterpiece, *Gaijin*, captured in vivid and striking terms the experience of the first Japanese immigrants. Having once rejected her Japanese heritage, Tizuka turned the making of *Gaijin* into a quest for identity.

Her father, an adventurer and the black sheep of his family, emigrated to Brazil from Japan during the 1930s. He died while Tizuka was still a child. Her *nisei* mother grew up in a completely Japanese environment, isolated from the rest of Brazilian society.

At an early age Tizuka decided to break with the hierarchical traditions of the community into which she had been born. She refused to learn Japanese and left her home in São Paulo to live and study on her own at universities in Brasília and Niterói. At the latter she took a course from Nelson Pereira dos Santos, perhaps Brazil's most influential film director, and as a result she decided to pursue a career in film. Nelson became her mentor, and she worked as his assistant. *Gaijin*, based on the life of her maternal grandmother, was her first feature film.

Despite the process of assimilation she shared with other *nisei,*
Tizuka had always felt like a stranger, but this feeling conflicted
with her sense of being a Brazilian. *Gaijin,* which turned out to be
both cathartic and a search for her roots, enabled Tizuka to resolve
this inner contradiction.

The title of the film derives from the Japanese word for "foreigner"; it is the term Japanese immigrants used when they referred
to Brazilians. "For me," she declared in a 1986 interview, "the film
showed that all Brazilians, except the Indians, are *gaijins.*" Thus she
was able to declare, to the consternation of some members of the
community from which she had emerged, "I am not a Japanese; I
am a Brazilian."

Tizuka is a keen observer of the assimilation process. "Brazilians are great jokers," she has observed. "They love to make self-
deprecatory jokes about everything that happens to them. The
Japanese is incapable of engaging in this kind of humor. The *nisei*
in São Paulo have big problems with this." On the other hand, in
making *Gaijin,* Tizuka discovered that she had to use Japanese,
rather than *nisei,* actors to play the leading roles, because the latter
had become too Brazilianized. Their gestures were so expansive and
their demeanor so expressive that it was extremely difficult for
them to portray characters as introverted as the early immigrants.
At the same time, using Japanese actors allowed Tizuka to incorporate into her film the culture shock that Japanese actors would
experience working in Brazil with Brazilians.

Their origins have made many Brazilians of Japanese descent diligent, honest, and efficient. This has not prevented them from
adopting certain Brazilian characteristics. As the head of the Japanese Chamber of Commerce in São Paulo told a *New York Times*
reporter, "We work harder than most Brazilians, but we gain some
Brazilian habits. We have a chat, maybe we slip up a little, postpone something to the next day."

*Sansei* (third-generation Nippo-Brazilians) are on the whole
fully integrated into Brazilian society. They feel no pressure or obligation to enter the traditionally "respectable" professions. Many,
like Tizuka, are following careers in the arts. *Sansei* enter into racially mixed marriages as freely as do other Brazilians. (Records

kept by the Center for Nippo-Brazilian Studies show that nearly half of the *sansei* have wed Brazilians who are not of Japanese descent.) They participate in Carnival parades and Afro-Brazilian religions.

At the same time, the respect that *sansei* enjoy because of the accomplishments of Brazilians of Japanese origin and because of the economic success that Japan has attained has instilled in some of them a new sense of pride. There is a renewed interest in the Japanese language and culture among the *sansei*. "My children now complain because they have Brazilian rather than Japanese first names," Kazuo Watanabe has commented wryly.

Yet although Japanese investments in Brazil have increased (in 1988 they were estimated to be about $4 billion dollars) and Japanese companies such as Honda and Sony have a strong presence in São Paulo, there is little contact between Japanese executives based there and Brazilians of Japanese origin. "Japanese representatives of the multinational corporations look down on the *nisei* and *sansei*," Tizuka Yamasaki has observed. "However, they need them as intermediaries for doing business in Brazil."

The current economic crisis in Brazil has created another opportunity for some Nippo-Brazilians to renew their ties with Japan. In search of remunerative employment, many have returned to the land of their parents or grandparents in response to a 1990 Japanese law facilitating the return of *nisei* and *sansei* for a period of up to three years.* The outflow to Japan is estimated at 160,000, which is more than 10 percent of the entire Nippo-Brazilian population.

The experience of the *dekassegui* (the Japanese term for "people who go abroad to work") is demonstrating vividly the fruits of the assimilation process in Brazil. Transplanted Nippo-Brazilians in Japan have established soccer teams and radio programs that broadcast Brazilian music, as well as shops where Brazilian goods are sold. Their Brazilianness—noisy, joyful, open, spontaneous, and occasionally, to borrow a phrase used by the Brazilian magazine *Veja*,

---

* Emigration is not limited to the Japanese community in Brazil. The prosperity of the European Economic Community has been attracting Brazilians of Portuguese, Italian, and Spanish descent.

"ethically indelicate"—has created problems for them with the Japanese locals, who often discriminate against them.

Migrant workers in Japan, even those doing drudge work, can save a thousand dollars a month or more. Brazilians of Japanese descent have been sending most of their savings back to Brazil. (In 1991 alone they remitted about $1.5 billion.) But by late 1993 the recession in Japan had caused many of them to lose their jobs and return to Brazil earlier than they had planned.

Despite their acculturation, the descendants of Japanese immigrants remain sensitized to the subtle kinds of racism that target them in Brazil. For example, television advertisements and *telenovelas* (soap operas) still occasionally present caricatures of Nippo-Brazilians who laugh while speaking Portuguese with a heavy, often exaggerated, Japanese accent.

More serious is the resentment that some young non-Japanese Brazilians feel toward *sansei* and *nisei* who compete successfully for admission to universities and technical schools. On May 8, 1988, the *New York Times* quoted complaints on the part of non-Japanese Brazilians that the Nippo-Brazilians were only "average students" but presented "unfair competition" because they "work so hard." The popular joke "To get into the university, you have to take preparatory courses and kill a Japanese" reflects not only the Brazilian sense of humor but also presents a subtextual concern.

The Japanese presence has added a great deal to Brazil. In addition to their oft-cited achievements in agriculture, Japanese immigrants have affected the Brazilian diet by popularizing the consumption of rice and vegetables. Ethnic Japanese own and run banks and factories in São Paulo and elsewhere. Bars promoting the peculiarly Japanese institution of karaoke (open-microphone sessions during which anyone can sing) have become very fashionable. Brazilians have also embraced Japanese martial arts. There is even a stadium in São Paulo where Brazilians of Japanese origin play baseball every weekend.

Katsunori Wakisaka of the Center for Nippo-Brazilian Studies thinks that such examples may oversimplify the real benefits that Japanese have brought to Brazil. "Today we have a population of more than a million persons of Japanese descent who are integrated into Brazilian society and the Brazilian system of values, who work and suffer every day like other Brazilian citizens and who have contributed, like all the other immigrant groups, to the modernization of Brazil."

A celebration of the achievements of Brazilians of Japanese origin should by no means be interpreted as undervaluing the significance of the contributions from immigrants from other countries. Colonists and descendants of colonists from Italy and Germany, for example, have left and continue to leave their imprint on the economic and social development of the country.

The first Italians to arrive in Brazil were sugar growers who had originally migrated to the Madeira Islands and who settled, during the middle decades of the sixteenth century, in what would later become the state of São Paulo. Later, small numbers of Italians arrived, attracted by the new cosmopolitanism of Rio de Janeiro, which had blossomed because of the presence of the Portuguese royal family. Among their ranks were artists, intellectuals, entrepreneurs, and individuals who had been exiled from their homeland as a result of participation in struggles for the liberation and unification of the Italian peninsula. Among them was Giuseppe Garibaldi, a young, romantic adventurer who would later fight on the side of the province of Rio Grande do Sul in its effort to win independence from Brazil. The future national hero of Italy was deeply influenced by his experiences in the south of Brazil. He honed his skills as a warrior, developed a rugged constitution, and took a Brazilian wife.

Immigration from Italy did not reach massive proportions until late in the nineteenth century. Of the estimated five million immigrants who entered Brazil between 1820 and 1930, almost 35 percent came from the Italian peninsula. Although the first groups of Italian settlers were contracted to work on coffee plantations, Italian workers with technical skills subsequently made their way to São Paulo, where they played a key role in the industrialization that transformed the city into South America's mightiest metropolis. The Portuguese spoken in São Paulo carries inflections that give testament to one cultural contribution of the Italians. The colorful ethnic neighborhood of Bexiga is another of their gifts to the city.

Italian immigrants played key roles both as laborers and as entrepreneurs in their new country. They participated in early struggles to unionize and could also be found in the ranks of businessmen who took full advantage of the opportunities that abounded in the New World. The most famous of the latter, Francisco Matarazzo, became a kind of *paulista* Rockefeller. (His story will be told in Chapter Five.)

Italo-Brazilians did much to enrich Brazil's cultural life. The most notable of them, Cândido Portinari, stood at the forefront of a group of artists, composers, and writers who in the 1930s managed to free themselves from European influences and put a uniquely Brazilian stamp on their creative work.

Both of Cândido's parents were of peasant stock. At the end of the nineteenth century they joined the wave of Italians migrating to Brazil, and ended up on a coffee plantation on the outskirts of a small town in the interior of the state of São Paulo. Cândido, the second of twelve children, was born in 1903.

He remained in school only until he was big and strong enough to work on the plantation. In his spare time he played soccer with his friends in the town plaza, a pastime that left him with a broken leg and a lifelong limp. He also liked to draw pictures, a pursuit that fired so much enthusiasm in him that when an artist came to town to redecorate the interior of the local church, Cândido convinced the man to let him paint stars.

At the age of fifteen his parents sent him to study at the National School of Fine Arts in Rio de Janeiro. They had no money to give him, so he had to take a job in a third-class boardinghouse to make ends meet. It was not an easy life, but he eventually won some prizes and a fellowship to continue his studies in Europe, where he remained for three years.

When he returned to Brazil, he brought back with him a wife (she was Uruguayan) and a surprisingly small number of completed paintings. But the re-encounter with his homeland, and especially with his birthplace, seemed to stir his creative juices, and he soon began to paint at a prodigious pace. In the words of *New York Times* reporter Warren Hoge, Portinari "fill[ed] his canvases with scenes and themes covering the country's earliest history, its slave trade, small-town life, gold prospectors, farming, construction, religious processions, circuses, jungle wildlife, urban slums, racial mixture and backlands bandits." His personalized vision captured Brazil in all its greatness and sweetness, with all its conflicts and tractability.

In the course of his career, Portinari produced a body of brilliant work that includes not only his perspectives on Brazilian reality, but also portraits and sacred art. His murals and paintings adorn the United Nations headquarters in New York, the Hispanic Institute of the Library of Congress in Washington, D.C., the Governor's Palace in São Paulo, and the Ministry of Education building in Rio de Janeiro.

Portinari labored prodigiously but could never escape his roots. As his biographer Antônio Callado put it, he "seemed like a gardener. Or a planter of coffee, like his father and mother. He toiled on his paintings from dawn to dusk. Afterward, he let his work flourish on its own." The artist often neither signed nor dated his canvases. As a result, it has been very difficult to determine how many he completed (the best guess is more than four thousand) and where they are now.

Painting eventually killed him. Doctors told him that the oils he was using contained lead and that the paint was poisoning him, but he kept on working and died from the insidious disease at the age of fifty-nine.

Cândido Portinari is the epitome of success realized by Italians and Italo-Brazilians in Brazil. But human immigrants from Italy had no monopoly on achievement, as the story of the remarkable pigeons of Porto Velho demonstrates. Brought from Turin to Brazil in 1907 by an Italian who came to the western Amazon region to work on the Madeira-Marmoré railroad, these feathered adventurers took up residence in the terminal in the capital of what is now the state of Rondônia and have managed to adapt to and thrive in a tropical environment. Their descendants remain in the high-roofed station (now a museum) and have become as much a tourist attraction as the ancient locomotive that still makes a seven-kilometer run every Sunday.

For some Americans the most famous contemporary Brazilian of German origin may be Oscar Schmidt, the irrepressible long-range shooter on the Brazilian national basketball team that defeated the United States in the Pan-American Games of 1987. For Brazilians, that distinction may belong to Dom Paulo Arns, the progressive Cardinal of São Paulo. For tourists, the honor may fall to Hans

Stern, a German Jew who escaped from the Nazis in 1939, landed penniless in Brazil, and built from scratch what is now one of the world's largest international jewelry businesses, which bears his name.

The lasting contributions made by German immigrants and their descendants have been more collective than individual. In Brazil's three southernmost states, they established communities that even today often retain the appearance of tidy, well-scrubbed German towns. Many brought with them the Protestant faith and helped it to take root in Brazil. In addition they were instrumental in the founding of Brazil's first breweries; in the launching of VARIG and VASP, the country's first airlines; and they provided the driving force behind the rapid growth of the shoe and textile industries in southern Brazil.

In absolute terms, German immigrants were not nearly so numerous as Italian and Spanish immigrants. Between 1890 and 1919 more than a million Italians entered Brazil, as compared to only 56,834 Germans. Many of the latter remained in settlements that were isolated from Brazilian society, and hence for a long time Germans were able to resist assimilation. (The same phenomenon occurred in self-contained colonies of Japanese, Poles, and Italians.)

Descendants of the U.S. southerners who fled from the ashes of the Confederacy and took refuge in Brazil have also emerged from the melting pot as 100 percent Brazilian and have generally prospered. Their presence attracted missionaries who made substantial contributions to the growth of Protestantism in Brazil, and who founded MacKenzie University in São Paulo. The best known American-Brazilian in the country today is Rita Lee, a rock-'n'-roll singer.

Other ethnic groups have added to the mix. The experience of Spanish immigrants from Galicia has been recorded in the brilliant novel *The Republic of Dreams*, by one of their descendants, Nélida Piñon. Many of São Paulo's most dynamic entrepreneurs are of Middle Eastern origin, as is Tasso Jereissati, the businessman who did an outstanding job as governor of the northeastern state of

Ceará.* Brazil's Jewish community has produced, among others, José Mindlin, founder of an industrial conglomerate and owner of the country's most valuable collection of antiquarian books; Jaime Lerner, the dynamic mayor who revitalized the southern city of Curitiba; and Moacir Scliar, the witty novelist from Porto Alegre.

The process of Brazilianization has spawned presidents of Italian and German origin—Emílio Médici and Ernesto Geisel—both of whom were generals who served as chief executives during the recent military regime. They cannot, however, claim to be the first descendants of foreign-born Brazilians to govern the republic. That honor belongs to Juscelino Kubitschek, the grandson of a Czechoslovakian immigrant.

Even though the Brazilian melting pot has produced remarkable results, the Brazilian attitude toward ethnic diversity provides useful insights into the nature of Brazilianness. Nowhere has this attitude been better encapsulated than in a pair of television commercials for the soft drink Tang. Gently good-humored and irreverent in a manner that would never play in the United States, the ads show a family of Japanese sitting around a kitchen table, speaking an animated Italian (with Portuguese subtitles) and behaving very Italian; and a family of blacks in the same sitcom environment, speaking a subtitled German, dressed in German folk costumes and behaving very German. Only in Brazil . . .

---

* Brazil's most famous Middle Easterner may be Nacib, one of the main characters in Jorge Amado's classic novel *Gabriela, Cravo e Canela (Gabriela, Clove and Cinnamon)*.

## Part Two

# The Pyramid of Power in Brazil

# Chapter 5

---

# The Haves

*O*ver the past decade and a half, Brazil's upper class has not done badly for itself, at least in comparison with the rest of the country. During the 1980s the wealthiest 10 percent of the population increased its share of the national income from 46.6 to 53.2 percent; while the shares of the bottom 50 percent fell from 13.4 to 10.4 percent. People with money were able to profit from the steep rate of inflation by speculating in government bonds, gold, dollars, and real estate.

But the wealthy have also experienced a decline in quality of life, most dramatically because of the increased incidence of crime, which has taken on aspects of a class warfare waged by the poor against the rich. A wave of kidnappings in recent years has instilled fear even among those wealthy enough to afford bodyguards and other security measures for themselves and their families.

Another problem for Brazil's haves is that their privileged status has been tainted by ethical concerns surfacing as a result of the circumstances surrounding the fall of President Fernando Collor in 1992. Collor's demise was not just a political milestone in Brazilian history; it also laid bare, in the most vivid way imaginable, the corruption that defined the symbiotic relationship between the government and the nation's elite.

An administration that began by promising to modernize the economy, privatize deficit-ridden state enterprises, and wean businessmen from their addictive dependence on the state collapsed in the wake of relentless revelations of kickbacks, or under-the-table payments made by companies or individuals directly or indirectly to the president or his close associates in payment for the privilige of doing business with the public sector. Even the most jaded observers were dismayed.

Indeed, when Mário Amato, the president of São Paulo's Federation of Industries, made the indiscreet admission, "We are all corrupt," and the highly respected Antônio Emírio de Moraes, whose family's holdings were worth billions of dollars, confessed sheepishly that his company had paid bribes to secure favors from the Collor administration, Brazilians could not help but begin to face up to the harsh reality that such corruption has existed in the country since the arrival of the first Portuguese settlers.

Corruption has traditionally been a defining feature of the country's politico-economic system, which functions for the benefit of a relatively small elite at the top of the societal pyramid, while a mass of poor people remain trapped at the base. Entrepreneurs often overcharge the government for the goods and services they provide, and government officials often receive kickbacks from individuals and corporations doing business with the state. The rot that caused Collor's presidency to crumble was novel only in its size and scope, in the glare of publicity it attracted, and in the widespread outrage it provoked.

Moreover, the worsening economic crisis in Brazil has provided critics with additional grist for their condemnation of the upper class. The wealthy, they argue, have always held power in Brazil and have always used it to further their own immediate interests, without regard for the welfare of their less fortunate compatriots and without regard for the long-term needs of the country. Thus, the sins of selfishness and shortsightedness on the part of the haves bear heavy responsibility for the country's current economic predicament.

On the other hand, there are those who point out with equal cogency that dynamic elements within the Brazilian elite have been instrumental in bringing about the remarkable growth that has made Brazil one of the most advanced industrial powers of the Third World. The most dramatic evidence of this spurt toward development is in the center south of the country—the Belgium of Belindia. There one can find remarkable success stories involving bold, hard-driving entrepreneurs, many of them immigrants or the children of immigrants, who have built businesses that have generated tremendous wealth for both themselves and the country.

Thus Brazil presents a peculiar paradox. It owes much of its economic growth to talented businessmen, yet fundamental flaws in the way economic power is distributed and exercised have helped to trap the country in the morass in which it now finds itself. The degree to which the Brazilianness shared by all Brazilians has contributed to the country's economic flaws as well as to its achievements is worth exploring.

In 1549, when the system of captaincies (described in Chapter One) proved inadequate to the challenge of administering its giant possession in the New World, the Portuguese Crown installed in Bahia a governor-general to rule the colony as the personal representative of the king. His main task was to defend Brazil against incursions by foreigners. He was also responsible for collecting taxes and administering the king's justice. Later, in the eighteenth century, the title governor-general was changed to viceroy.

The system by which Portugal governed its colony produced an interesting contradiction. On the one hand, the Crown claimed absolute dominion over Brazil and its inhabitants and installed an administrative structure designed to carry out its dictates in an authoritarian way. Yet at the same time it willingly tolerated the growth of a class of large landholders who exercised virtually unchecked dominion over those who lived on and near their estates.

Behind the relationship between Lisbon and the colony, in the words of Brazilian historian Caio Prado, Jr., was the conception of the Portuguese state

> as a vast organic body with the King as its head, leader, father, representative of God on earth, supreme dispenser of all graces and favors, rightful regulator of all activities, or, more precisely, of all personal and individual "expressions" of his subjects and vassals.

Thus, what evolved in Brazil during the colonial period was a centralized administration subject to strict supervision and control by Portuguese authorities acting in the name of the Crown. In theory that administration could exercise absolute power over most aspects of life in the colony. But no effort was made to adapt the stewardship to the peculiar conditions found in Brazil, with its vast expanses and scattered settlements, as well as the enormous distance between Brazil and Portugal.

Of course, the ocean that separated the mother country from its subjects in the New World often delayed the transmission of detailed instructions drafted in Lisbon, so colonial authorities had opportunities for exercising some discretion of their own. Moreover, the functionaries of the centralized administration, located in Bahia, faced obstacles in communicating with and exercising control over the local officials and colonists in the vast outlying areas of the king's colony.

The fact that the welter of decrees and regulations imposed on the colony could not be enforced in more than a highly selective way, and hence could for the most part be safely ignored, created a cavalier attitude toward legality that still exists in Brazil. In addition, enforcement by local authorities became a matter of discretion, to be exercised on the basis of considerations other than the pursuit of evenhanded justice.* In many ways, the status of the large landholder mirrored in miniature the status of the monarch. Thus the notion the King could do no wrong, which set the Crown above the law and provided it with a cloak of impunity, was transformed into an attitude assumed first by plantation owners and later by the country's political and economic elite. Individuals with power, like the king, did not have to bear personal responsibility for what they did. Sadly, this condition has survived to the present in Brazil and continues to impede social and economic development.

The Portuguese Crown looked on Brazil almost exclusively as a source of revenue, mostly to be gained from export duties levied on products leaving Brazilian ports, import duties on products entering Portugal, and taxes on the transfer of precious stones and metals. Little heed was paid to other aspects of colonial governance. Thus the royal court looked benignly on the plantation owners who

---

* The pithiest description of this phenomenon came from a twentieth-century governor of a northeastern state, when he pronounced the famous dictum "To my enemies, the law; to my friends, facilities."

ruled their huge properties with an iron hand and established dominion over vast areas of the interior. The King realized that he had to depend on these powerful figures for the defense of the colony, and that they were an important source of the wealth Lisbon was sucking from the New World. He may also have been pragmatic enough to realize the impossibility of subjecting them to close and effective control.

The centralized colonial government made its presence felt in the capital (first Salvador, and later Rio de Janeiro) and in port cities where commerce was regulated. But on the sugar and tobacco estates in Pernambuco, Bahia, and Rio de Janeiro, and on the cotton farms in Maranhão, absolute authority rested with the landowner, who stood at the center of a patriarchal social structure that functioned without substantial interference from the colony's administrators.

This limitation on the de facto powers of the governor-general (and later the viceroy) did not prevent the growth of what Caio Prado, Jr., has called "the monstrous, awkward, and inept bureaucratic machine that was the colonial administration." There were innumerable decrees to comply with, especially in the areas of taxation and economic regulation, and they generated a need for an ever-increasing number of government functionaries to interpret and enforce them. The notary public, whose job it was to stamp official documents, became a figure of great importance. The administration of the colony became a paradigm not only of inefficiency but also of graft and corruption, as local officials siphoned off public funds and otherwise took financial advantage of their positions.*

During the nineteenth century, from the installation of the Portuguese royal family in Rio de Janeiro to the ouster of Dom Pedro II in 1889, Brazil underwent dramatic changes in the way it was ruled. King João VI set up a government-in-exile, complete with all the various bureaus and departments that had been function-

---

* The pervasive presence of red tape survives to the present day. Brazilians generally deal with it indirectly, by resorting to *jeitinho*. Indeed, an entire profession—private facilitators known as *despachantes*—has emerged to guide people through bureaucratic mazes.

ing in Lisbon, and in 1816 he pronounced Brazil a kingdom. After the monarch returned to Portugal and his young son Pedro replaced him, the Brazilians declared their independence, and the country became a "constitutional empire."

In an effort to secure the loyalty of the upper class, Dom Pedro I chose members of the local elites with links to the plantation economy to replace the Portuguese officials who had filled the most important positions in the government. He was also generous in bestowing titles, which helped transform the economic elite—both old families and parvenus—into an aristocracy.

As they evolved into an upper class with airs commensurate with their sense of self-esteem, the elite adopted a negative attitude toward Brazilianness and glorified anything European, reserving a special affection for France and its culture. This *moçambismo*, as their outlook came to be called, encouraged travel and study abroad, and the use of French as a second language.

While Dom Pedro I catered to the upper class, he did not create a parallel military elite drawn from the same stratum of colonial society. Both he and his father appointed Portuguese members of their retinues to high army posts and kept native-born officers in inferior positions. This, in turn, caused resentment among Brazilians who had opted for military careers, and disdain toward native-born military men on the part of the new Brazilian upper class.

In response to Brazilian desires for a greater degree of self-government, Dom Pedro I established an elected legislative assembly, with suffrage limited by qualifications based on property ownership and income. The emperor retained considerable authority, however, because he was able to count on a general acceptance of the monarchy as the guarantor of national unity and public order.

Soon a pair of political parties came into being. The Conservatives represented the landowners and advocated protectionist measures for both agriculture and the industries that were beginning to emerge. The Liberals, who also had links to the landed elite, sought to emulate the English model of development and supported free trade. Neither party developed a coherent set of principles or imposed partisan unity on its members.

*     *     *

The face of the Brazilian elite underwent remarkable changes during the nineteenth century. The importance of the sugar industry declined because of foreign competition, and coffee growers replaced the northeastern sugar-plantation owners as the country's dominant economic force (although cotton growers briefly came to the fore during the American Civil War, when the prices they could charge for their exports soared). Coffee production spread to the states of Minas Gerais, Rio de Janeiro, and São Paulo. Because of "King Coffee," the latter would soon become the nation's economic center of gravity.

The new coffee elite tended to be more forward-looking than the sugar growers had been. They were not so dependent on slavery as the sugar barons, and they supported liberal free-trade policies. Many of the coffee growers became fabulously wealthy, and the emperor recognized their achievements by bestowing titles of nobility on them.

This was also an era during which Brazil's cities blossomed. The presence of the royal court in Rio de Janeiro encouraged the growth of the municipality, to the extent that by midcentury it was the largest in South America. São Paulo and Recife likewise expanded and developed. Wealthy landowners often established residences in the cities (the coffee barons built lavish mansions along the Avenida Paulista in São Paulo), and spent more and more time in the urban environnment. They sent their sons to law school in the cities, which then proved more attractive as places to live than the plantations where these young men had spent their childhoods.

The cities spawned a new middle class made up of merchants, bureaucrats, lawyers, bankers, military officers, and artisans, and also provided a haven for intellectuals. All these groups tended to worship at the altar of progress, as defined by the positivist philosophy of the Frenchman Auguste Comte, and looked to European and North American models for their inspiration.

Also during this period the process of industrialization began in earnest. João VI, upon his arrival in the New World, had lifted the prohibition that the Portuguese Crown had placed on manufacturing within Brazil. But it was not until the second half of the nineteenth century that the number of factories began to grow.

They turned out textiles as well as food, chemical, metal, and wood products.

Although they pushed hard for growth and change, Brazil's earliest "developmentalists" left intact the political power of the large landholders. No attempt was made to alter the inequitable distribution of land in the countryside. The emphasis on the export sector brought profits to only relatively few Brazilians, who used their wealth to import luxury items from abroad, thus making the Brazilian economy totally reliant on foreign markets. No effort was undertaken to develop a domestic market for products manufactured in Brazil.

This preference for foreign goods was yet another manifestation of *moçambismo;* it also evidenced a sense of inferiority. Brazilian manufacturers were deemed incapable of matching the quality of products imported from abroad. Indeed, it was not uncommon for local producers to sell their goods under counterfeited foreign labels.

What developed during this period bears certain resemblances to the fruits of military rule in the 1970s. As historian E. Bradford Burns points out, "Growth indicates simply and exclusively numerical accumulation"; whereas "[d]evelopment signifies the maximum use of a nation's potential for the greatest benefit of the largest number of the inhabitants." Applying these criteria, he concludes that the growth achieved by Brazil in the nineteenth century "contributed to retarding development, impoverishing the masses, and increasing dependency."

The traits and attitudes that pushed Brazil to choose growth over true development are not difficult to identify. They include lack of foresight, a characteristic that dates back to the colonists who came to the New World to acquire for themselves as much wealth as possible in as short a period of time as possible; self-centered greed, which marked those who made it to the top of the economic and social pyramids and came to believe that the state existed to enhance their accumulation of private wealth rather than to promote the public good; and an elitist contempt for those below them—in large part a legacy of slavery.

Moreover, corruption continued to permeate the relationship between the government and the private sector. This was particularly evident in the case of an entrepreneurial activity that flourished from 1830 to 1850, despite its illegality. During that span of time Brazilian slavers brought half a million Africans into the country. Given the scale of their enterprise, it can hardly be called clandestine. Government functionaries were routinely bribed, and the leading traffickers maintained close ties with people in high places. One of them even managed to obtain a title for himself.

Another important sector of Brazilian society underwent a transformation during the latter part of the nineteenth century. Military officers took it upon themselves to serve as ultimate arbiters of political disputes and guarantors of the Constitution. They became (and continue to be) haves in their own right, imposing their will at times by the spoken or unspoken threat of physical force, and at times by the actual use of it. The birth of a military mystique that equated the armed forces with Brazil's nationhood has been described in Chapter One. It took two hundred years for this mystique to mature into a full-fledged justification for the military's institutional entry into politics.

A reciprocal lack of respect developed between Brazil's civilian and military elites in the process. Powerful civilians were not above using the armed forces for their own political ends. Thus military leaders were persuaded to join in the movement that ousted Dom Pedro I, but they also served in high political posts during the reign of Dom Pedro II. Yet civilian leaders still looked down on them, perhaps in part because most of the members of the armed forces tended to come from the ranks of the middle class. Moreover, there had been no epic battles in the struggle against Portugal, so the military had no towering heroes who could command greater respect for their institution.* Indeed, civilian leaders supported the creation of a national guard to replace the militias and contemplated dissolving the army. The military, in turn, came to look down on civilian politicians, whom they viewed as not placing the interests of the nation above personal ambitions.

---

* The outstanding military figure of this period, Luís Alves de Lima e Silva (the Duke of Caxias), participated in the movement to expel Dom Pedro I but gained his lofty reputation by steadfastly supporting Dom Pedro II and keeping the army and navy loyal to the emperor.

The 1865-70 war against Paraguay was a watershed event for the military, for its aftermath provoked such discontent among the officer corps that they turned against the imperial government. Feeling that politicians did not appreciate their wartime sacrifices and upset at what they perceived as inadequacies in the military budget, the younger officers turned eagerly to the philosophy of positivism and became convinced that Brazil needed a republican form of government that could bring about modernizing reforms and maintain social stability.

Making common cause with landowners who were upset at the government's refusal to compensate them for the value of the slaves freed in 1888, Brazil's men in uniform emerged from the barracks to oust Dom Pedro II and install a republic, under a new flag that bore the positivist slogan Order and Progress. The immediate provocation for this action was their belief that the government was about to dissolve the armed forces, but they also acted to preserve their institution, whose well-being they equated with the well-being of the nation. From then on, they would see themselves as watchdogs responsible for the stability of Brazil and the permanence of its armed forces—a unitary function in their eyes.

What came to be known as the "Old Republic" lasted until 1930. With the Constitution of 1891, the extreme centralization was replaced by an extreme form of local autonomy, to the extent that states could levy export and other taxes, contract foreign loans, and organize their own militias. This new power arrangement benefited the large states—mainly São Paulo and Minas Gerais—which would provide most of the presidents during this period. Suffrage was extended to all literate males over the age of twenty-one.

The Old Republic, for all its talk of transforming Brazil, left virtually intact the social and economic system that had evolved under the monarchy. The export of agricultural products remained the backbone of the economy. Coffee remained king, although the rubber barons of Amazônia had their moment in the sun during a short-lived rubber boom (to be described in greater detail in Chapter Twelve). The sugar planters of the Northeast maintained their grip on the region's economy, and cacao producers in the state of Bahia enjoyed periods of prosperity. Profitability depended in large part on the availability of cheap labor. The rich who profited from the export of these goods remained oblivious to the needs of the rest of the population.

The expansion of the right to vote served to enhance the power of the patriarchal landowners of the interior. Because of their (or their ancestors') service in the national guard, they adopted the conceit of calling themselves colonels and controlled the votes of their extended families as well as those of all the people who lived on their lands. The political oligarchy that ran the state governments, especially in the Northeast, had to gain the support of the colonels by dispensing favors to them, in the form of jobs or investment opportunities. The state governments, in turn, formed alliances among themselves that determined the outcomes of presidential elections.

Politics at every level came to be dominated by a web of patron-client relationships, very similar to those underlying the basic power structure of rural Brazil, where landowners related to those under them on the social scale in a very personal way, and social inferiors sought the protection of members of the dominant class. It was but a small step for Brazilians to look on their relationship with the government in much the same way. (Indeed, the role of the republican government was but another version of the paternalistic, favor-dispensing role of the Portuguese monarch.) Brazilians used personal contacts to secure advantages from the state, which in their view existed to serve them. The long-term effects of the dependency that was being fostered was of no concern, since they were receiving immediate gratification.

The coffee barons set an example by securing from the government laws and regulations that helped prop up the price of their crop. Limitations were placed on the planting of new coffee trees in order to prevent overproduction, and when coffee prices fell, the government would purchase beans from the growers at an inflated price and then hold onto them until prices recovered.

During the Old Republic, the plantation elite continued to cast a decisive influence over all important political and economic decisions, but one could also detect that some important changes were taking place. Immigration, as described in Chapter Four, reached flood-tide proportions and set the stage for the eventual shaping of a new elite. The military remained politically active. Several presidents came from army backgrounds, and in the 1920s young officers, impatient with the domination exercised by the coffee barons rebelled openly against the government (a phenomenon to be explored in detail in Chapter Seventeen). Moreover, industry experienced a steady growth, spurred by the scarcities of imported goods created by World War I, when it was impossible to import manufactured goods from Europe.

Nonetheless, the oligarchs who controlled Brazil's economy continued to be shortsighted. They made no effort to alleviate the country's reliance on the export of primary goods, and they saw to it that wages remained depressed. This served to maximize profits, but it also impeded the growth of a domestic market that could absorb products manufactured in Brazil.

Another example of the myopia of the elite was its failure to reform the educational system, which favored the rich by providing free education at the various faculties of higher education while it neglected the system of primary schooling for the poor. In addition, university education remained antiquated, in the sense that it stressed the theoretical and the encyclopedic. The sort of technical training that would be useful to Brazil's nascent industries was virtually nonexistent.

Early in the twentieth century, the Liberal and Conservative parties disappeared, to be replaced by parties similarly lacking in substantive content and often regionally based. São Paulo and Minas Gerais maintained their domination over national politics, although by backing military candidates Rio Grande do Sul emerged as a force to be reckoned with. (The strong army presence along the borders in southern Brazil facilitated alliances between the *gaúcho* oligarchy and the armed forces.)

Widespread dissatisfaction with the distribution of political power in Brazil led to the demise of the Old Republic. The President, a *paulista* named Washington Luiz, wanted another *paulista*, Júlio Prestes, to succeed him. But the political bosses of Minas Gerais, who believed that control of the presidency should alternate between their state and São Paulo, objected strenuously. Leaders from other states took advantage of the controversy by reiterating their objections to the monopoly long asserted by the *paulistas* and the *mineiros*.

President Luiz managed to secure the nomination of Prestes as a candidate in the 1929 elections, and he defeated Getúlio Vargas, a canny politician from Rio Grande do Sul. But there were loud claims of electoral fraud. Shortly thereafter, the assassination of the opposition's former vice presidential candidate by the son of one of his political enemies then galvanized the opposition into armed rebellion.

Faced with the threat of civil war, the military exercised its arbitration function by siding with the insurgents. In what became known as the Revolution of 1930, they overthrew the government of Washington Luiz before the president-elect could take the oath of office, and, they then installed Vargas as head of a provisional administration.

Although the regime of Getúlio Vargas lasted for fifteen years and would eventually bring an end to the power monopoly exercised by the coffee oligarchs, the latter did not at first oppose the revolution. A worldwide economic crisis had depressed coffee prices, and the government's response, in their view, had been weak and ineffectual. But by 1932 they had become disenchanted enough with Vargas to support an unsuccessful revolt against him in São Paulo.

The man his compatriots liked to call simply Getúlio realized both the importance of coffee to the Brazilian economy and the need to terminate the country's dependence on a single crop. He forgave the planters for their participation in the 1932 uprising and adopted measures to help them, but at the same time he sought to achieve diversification by encouraging cotton production and the raising of livestock.

More important from the long-range perspective, Vargas accelerated the pace of industrialization. He adopted a protectionist policy that put limits on the importation of foreign goods, made credit and tax exemptions freely available to domestic manufacturers, and imposed wage controls. He also invested government funds in infrastructure projects (railroads and shipping, for example) and in basic industries. Among his major contributions were plans for a government-owned steel mill in Volta Redonda, between Rio de Janeiro and São Paulo (it finally opened in 1946), and the establishment of the Vale do Rio Doce Company, a state enterprise charged with exploiting iron-ore deposits in Minas Gerais.

Vargas left intact laws and regulations that protected Brazilian manufacturers from foreign imports. Brazilian tariffs were among the highest in the hemisphere. These incentives not only encouraged domestic production; but also, since they protected local entrepreneurs from competition with foreign-made goods, they contributed to inefficient business practices and the production of substandard goods. As a consequence, Brazilian consumers had to pay more for inferior products.

In addition to expanding the government's role in the promotion of industrial development, Vargas increased the degree of control exercised by the government over private industry. His corporatist philosophy led him to force producers to join state federations, and he created a number of regulatory agencies that set production quotas and prices. Businessmen became accustomed to receiving all manner of special favors from the government, including subsidies, low-interest loans, and guarantees of fixed returns on investments. These practices cultivated in many entrepreneurs a distaste for financial risk—a characteristic that held back the evolution of capitalism in Brazil.

These policies, in turn, necessitated an enlargement of the federal bureaucracy, which Vargas accomplished by using the powers of patronage at his disposal. The dispensing of these posts not only reduced middle-class unemployment and fortified the political support he enjoyed, but also expanded the possibilities for red tape in all areas of government regulation. Vargas thus played into Brazil's long bureaucratic tradition.

It was during the Vargas dictatorship that the face of the Brazilian elite began to change again, at least in the south. The heyday of the coffee barons had passed, and a new aristocracy was beginning to take shape. Its sources of wealth were industry and commerce. In many instances, the new aristocrats rose from the ranks of the immigrants who had streamed into Brazil at the turn of the century. Perhaps the most famous was Francisco Matarazzo.

Matarazzo was born into a middle-class family of modest means in the region of Calabria on the southern coast of Italy. As a young man, after having secured a high-school education, he entered the business of making and selling lard. In 1881, at the age of twenty-five, he decided to make the long journey to Brazil, not to work on a coffee plantation, as many of his compatriots had done, but rather in search of business opportunities. The lighter bringing him ashore at Santos sank, and he lost the stock of lard he was bringing with him, so he had to begin from scratch.

He went first to Sorocaba, a commercial town in the interior of the state of São Paulo where other Italian immigrants had established themselves as merchants. With help from them, as well as from family and friends in Italy, he opened a store and began to buy and sell hogs. Soon he began to produce lard. At the time, Brazil was purchasing all its cooking fat from abroad. Matarazzo innovated by packing his product in tins rather than barrels. Within a short time his lard operation had scored a remarkable triumph over its foreign competitors.

Tranferring his base of operations to the city of São Paulo, he joined two of his brothers in launching a wheat-import business. In 1900 he built a flour mill, with the help of British capital. Four years later he constructed a textile plant, and then cotton-seed mills, so that he could make his own sacks. His business strategy was one of vertical integration—the control of all elements of his operation. Thus he bought his own ships, which brought in from abroad the raw materials he needed, and he even built docks for them in Santos.

Matarazzo had a disarming way about him, and he could beguile even those predisposed to dislike him. Warren Dean, in his excellent study of industrialization in São Paulo, describes Matarazzo as

> a tough and energetic man as well as a charming one. Photographs of him reveal a proud, unsmiling face, its expression intelligent and self-conscious, as though he knew that his appearance impressed others as much as his wealth. He shaved his head as he grew bald, wore a small moustache, and always kept his strong, athletic figure, so that he appeared to be a soldier rather than a businessman.

World War I stimulated the growth of Brazilian industry, and before long Matarazzo had put together a conglomerate called United Industries. By 1925 he and his relatives owned slightly less than 50 percent of the 150,000 shares constituting ownership of an empire that would extend to ships, railway cars, trucks, chemicals, distilling, metallurgy, salt and sugar refining, meat packing, and insurance. It was said that he was a man with a factory for every day of the year, 365 in all. People began to call him the Prince of São Paulo. As a result of contributions he made to Italian charities, the King of Italy made him a count.

Like other Brazilian entrepreneurs, Matarazzo employed many family members in the corporate conglomerate he founded. Following the practice of other successful immigrants in Brazil, he brought enterprising young men from his native Calabria to work for him. He set an example that was not easy to follow, since he often toiled a seven-day week.

What he first saw during a visit to Italy in 1923 made him an open admirer of Benito Mussolini. A newspaper article reported that Matarazzo gave the Fascist salute at a dinner in Guarujá, a resort not far from São Paulo. According to Warren Dean, "It is probable that he became a member of the [Fascist] Party."

In 1928 Matarazzo helped found the Center (later to be called the Federation) of Industries of the State of São Paulo and was elected its first president—an indication of the prestige he enjoyed among his peers. When he died in 1937, his son Francisco Matarazzo, Jr., inherited both the business and his father's title.

The Matarazzos were in many ways typical of the immigrant-entrepreneurs who helped industrialize Brazil.* Like others who came from Europe or the Near East and built empires from the ground up in the New World, they were intelligent, hardworking, aggressive, and ambitious; eager to gain social status and wealth for their families; and not held back by the cultural and political factors that kept the established elite tied to the traditional plantation economy.

---

* They did have their quirks. According to Richard Morse, "The bleak and impeccably dressed Francisco, Jr., controls his empire from a pigskin-paneled office that is fitted with a buzzer system to summon top executives, who, on leaving, must bow their way backward from his presence." Like his father, Francisco, Jr., refrained from open involvement in Brazilian politics.

The authoritarian regime of Getúlio Vargas imposed a hiatus on electoral, partisan politics in Brazil. But as World War II came to an end and a return to democratic rule seemed unavoidable, the president created not one but two political parties to act as vehicles for his further ambitions. The Social Democratic party (or PSD, to use the Brazilian acronym), brought together the state machines, mostly in the rural states, that had always supported Vargas. The Brazilian Labor party (PTB) was urban based and looked to the working class for its constituency. (The PTB will be described in some detail in Chapter Eight.) Vargas's opponents formed the Democratic National Union (UDN), a party that appealed to conservatives nostalgic for the Old Republic.

There were other, smaller parties that came into being, but the PSD, PTB, and UDN would dominate the national political scene for nearly two decades. The parties did not stand for any particular ideologies or policies but instead came to rely on the strength of the personalities that were able to dominate them. For this reason both politicians and voters did not hesitate to switch parties as they would change shirts.

With the demise of the Vargas dictatorship in 1945, a series of elected governments sought to accelerate the pace of development in Brazil. A principal motor of this process was a spirit of nationalism that had animated many of the policies of the Vargas regime and now continued to push Brazil toward economic self-sufficiency.

Brazilian nationalists believed passionately in state planning, industrial growth, government control over the country's natural resources, and restrictions on investments from abroad. They decried foreign ownership of basic industries and public utilities. Some of them frankly preferred a socialist model; others thought their goals could be accomplished within the framework of a capitalist economy.

The Brazilian elite held no brief for socialism. The large landowners knew that it would lead to agrarian reform and the loss or reduction of their holdings. The industrialists knew that socialism would bring even more government controls. Moreover, the captains of Brazilian industry were already beginning to come under attack by nationalists who charged that they were too closely associated with and dependent on foreign (mainly North American) interests.

On the other hand, there was much in developmental nationalism that appealed to industrialists. Nationalists defended the laws and regulations that shielded industrialists from competition with foreign imports; they also favored the continued use of government incentives and outright grants to private business as a means of stimulating the economy. Government-subsidized credit and below-cost transportation were among the favors businessmen had long enjoyed, and the nationalists did not seek to eliminate these privileges. Moreover, infrastructure investments in transportation and energy promoted the interests of domestic producers. Finally, the industrial elite lacked sufficient capital to invest in basic industries such as oil and steel, so they did not seriously oppose the creation of state enterprises in these areas.

Indeed, some industrialists embraced the cause of developmental nationalism and were regarded as "left-wing entrepreneurs," an oxymoron perhaps anywhere else but in Brazil. The most prominent of this group was José Emírio de Moraes, who built an empire out of a modest business into which he married in 1925.

José Emírio was born in 1900 in Nazaré da Mata, a town in the sugar-growing region of the state of Pernambuco. His father, the owner of two sugar plantations, died when José was but eighteen months old, and his mother took over the management of the properties. When he got older, she decided to send him to study engineering at the Colorado School of Mines in Golden, Colorado.

The boy adapted easily to the United States. He absorbed not only American know-how but also self-sufficiency, as he worked part-time to defray his living expenses. Upon returning home he decided not to enter the sugar business, but instead to put his engineering skills to work first for the state of Minas Gerais, and then for a private company.

In 1924, while on a vacation in Switzerland, José Emírio met and began to court the daughter of a Portuguese immigrant, Antônio Pereira Ignácio. A self-made man, Pereira Ignácio had created various industrial enterprises, much in the way Matarazzo had done, and in 1917 he had bought at auction a failed textile mill called Votorantim, near Sorocaba in the interior of the state of São Paulo. He took an immediate liking to José Emírio and made him the administrator of Votorantim. A year later the young engineer married Pereira Ignácio's daughter.

José Emírio had a flair for business. During the years of the depression he diversified Votorantim's operations by reinvesting its profits. In 1936 the company moved into cement manufacturing, which turned out to be highly lucrative because the numerous construction projects the Vargas regime was undertaking required large purchases of the product. Later José Emírio obtained from Vargas customs exemptions that enabled him to import from the United States machinery for a chemical plant he and fellow investors were building in São Paulo.

José Emírio's nationalism intensified during his struggle to construct the country's first aluminum plant. Up to that time the Brazilians had been mining bauxite and exporting it abroad, where it was made into aluminum and then imported back into Brazil. The price the Brazilians obtained for their raw material was, of course, much lower than the price they paid for the finished metal—a common phenomenon in the Third World. When José Emírio decided that Brazilians should produce the finished metal themselves, he found that the U.S. and Canadian firms that controlled the manufacture of the aluminum shipped to Brazil were reluctant to sell him the machinery he needed, and that the Canadian company that supplied electrical energy in São Paulo was hesitant to provide him with the power his new factory would require. He succeeded in finding an Italian company willing to sell him machinery, and he constructed his own power plant to furnish the energy he needed.

Along with Francisco Matarazzo, José Emírio was one of the first directors of the Center of Industries for the State of São Paulo. But unlike the Count, José Emírio became a highly visible figure on the political landscape. In 1932 he supported the São Paulo uprising against the Vargas regime. Later he won election to the Brazilian Senate from his native state of Pernambuco, where his financial backing also helped put a populist candidate in the governor's palace in 1962. He even served briefly as President João Goulart's Minister of Agriculture.

The fortunes of Votorantim, as well as those of Brazil's industrial elite in general, rode the crest of the boom created by the developmentalist policies pushed during the presidency of Juscelino Kubitschek in the late 1950s. The founding of an automobile industry in São Paulo, the construction of Brasília, and the building of the Belém-Brasília highway were among the projects that stimulated industrial growth. But they also unleashed an inflationary spiral that produced economic instability, which in turn contributed substantially to the overthrow of President João Goulart in 1964.

The military dictatorship that replaced Goulart set out to control inflation. One of its major weapons was putting a cap on workers' wages that served to decrease their real income. The regime also sought to attract foreign investment, which provoked criticism from Brazilian nationalists. At the same time, an effort was made to increase exports, not only by spurring the development of Brazil's natural resources, but also by encouraging the export of domestically manufactured goods.

Finally, the generals indicated that they would wean Brazilian businessmen from their addiction to government handouts. This initiative could be summed up in the dictum of Minister of Planing Roberto Campos to the effect that capitalism had not failed in Brazil; it had never been attempted.

But as Thomas E. Skidmore has observed in his excellent book *The Politics of Military Rule in Brazil, 1964–85*, Brazil's new rulers did not attempt to alter the industrial structure they had inherited. Instead they chose to invigorate the existing consumer-durables industry by increasing domestic sales of goods such as automobiles and refrigerators through devices such as the easing of credit restrictions. But since the purchasing power of workers continued to diminish, only people at the high end of the earnings scale could afford these items. Increased consumer demand for expensive durables led to the expansion of productive capacity, which in turn fostered the need to increase demand even further—all of which served to perpetuate the country's highly uneven distribution of income.

Helping the haves to become more affluent and pauperizing the have-nots by reducing workers' salaries was the inevitable outcome of most of the economic initiatives pursued during the two decades of military rule. Critics called this "Hood-Robin economics"—robbing from the poor and giving to the rich.

Despite the military regime's promises to give authentic capitalism a try, in significant respects the country's military rulers moved Brazil in the opposite direction. The number of state enterprises grew, existing state enterprises expanded, bureaucracy flourished more than ever, and the government's overall involvement in the economy increased. One explanation for this phenomenon might lurk in the middle-class (and generally Catholic) backgrounds that instilled in Brazil's military officers a deep distrust of capitalism and the profit motive that matched, in its intensity, their distaste for Communism.

During this period young people with training in economics or business administration assumed key positions within the government, the state-controlled industries, and the private sector. At the height of the boom, they were commanding salaries that were among the highest in the world for equivalent work. In part this was owing to the shortage of professionals with their practical skills, owing to the fact that most students at Brazilian universities traditionally pursued degrees in law, medicine, architecture, and engineering.

Those who went to work for the government helped to shape and execute the grand schemes that produced what came to be known as the "Brazilian miracle." Although they derived their authority from the military regime that employed them, they brought their own ideas and styles to the jobs to which they were assigned.

Prototypical of this new breed was Antônio Delfim Netto, a short, stocky, owlish economist who taught at the University of São Paulo and came into the government at the urging of Minister of Planning Roberto Campos. Holding various key positions during the dictatorship and displaying an aptitude for bureaucratic maneuvering that enabled him to amass considerable power (and a coterie of faithful acolytes), Delfim Netto became known as the Father of the Brazilian Miracle. Politically accountable to no one but the generals who appointed them, he and his associates could safely ignore the human costs of the economic policies they were pursuing. Thomas Skidmore has dubbed him "the technocrat par excellence."

With the gift of hindsight it is possible to second-guess a number of the moves made by Brazil's "miracle workers." The policies aimed at developing the Amazon basin, for example, exacted serious human and ecological costs, a matter to be examined in greater depth in Chapter Twelve. The mechanization of agriculture forced peasants off the land and into the cities, where they have created vast new social and economic problems, a subject to be explored at length in Chapter Seven. The development of an arms industry that exported goods worth billions of dollars depended on the continuation of tensions in trouble spots around the globe, but international conflicts had an element of uncertainty that made them an unreliable long-term source of income.

This was the era of the "pharaonic binge," during which the regime launched some thirty-three grandiose projects, each with an expected price tag of $1 billion dollars or more, in fields such as industry, communications, agriculture, mining, transportation, energy, steel, and petrochemicals. The economists supporting the government made wildly optimistic projections about the various "megaprojects," which in turn made it easy to justify the massive borrowing that helped to balloon Brazil's crushing debt. Optimism also led to the unrealistic belief that the country could expand its agricultural production to the point where it could feed the Brazilian people, generate massive export earnings, *and* furnish plant-derived substitutes for petroleum products.

The decision to rely on the production of automobiles to develop the Brazilian economy probably dates back at least to the Kubitschek administration. The generals pushed ahead with this industrial policy, and soon Brazil became the world's ninth-largest producer of motor vehicles. Yet the negative effects of emphasizing the production of motor vehicles have been significant.

In addition to regressive income distribution, a point that has already been noted, automobile production contributed to a deterioration in the quality of life in some of the older cities, which suffered badly from the effects of heavy traffic and air pollution. It also committed Brazil to a highly inefficient form of public and mass transportation, given the country's dependence on oil imports. Indeed, Brazil's vulnerability to sharp increases in oil prices on the world market would eventually doom the "miracle."

Moreover, with the onset of an economic crisis triggered by the rising cost of petroleum purchased abroad, the government increased the money supply to help create badly needed domestic capital and support its domestic programs. This set off an inflationary spiral far dizzier than the one that had preceded (and provided one of the justifications for) the overthrow of João Goulart.

Other spectacularly dubious initiatives were launched. One of the most notable was the decision to develop nuclear power. The progress-at-any-cost mentality that was motivating Brazil's generals and their civilian supporters led to the negotiation of contracts, first with Westinghouse and then with the government of West Germany, for the construction of eight nuclear plants. Billions of dollars were spent to obtain what turned out to be outdated equipment and technology. Only one facility has been completed, in Angra dos Reis. Brazilians call it a "nuclear pachyderm" because of the constant breakdowns that have rendered it virtually useless.

During the "miracle" era, the growth of state enterprises and the launching of government-financed "pharaonic" projects completely overshadowed what was happening within the private sector. Norman Gall has pointed out in an article in *Forbes* magazine that the regime relegated private industry "to a kind of coattails capitalism, in many instances cravenly dependent on government purchases, incentives, price-fixing, bureaucratic approvals and special export and development programs." Brazilian businessmen, in point of fact, had always suckled at the teats of the government. The bond merely reached new levels of intensity and intimacy during the military dictatorship.

If there was one entrepreneur who benefited most handsomely from business dealings with the government, it was probably Sebastião Ferraz de Camargo Penteado, a *paulista* who built a road-subcontracting business from scratch during the 1930s and eventually became a billionaire as a result of participating in some of the "pharaonic" projects launched by the military regime. The Itaipú hydroelectric dam, the trans-Amazon highway, and the eight-mile bridge linking Rio de Janeiro with Niterói on the other side of Guanabara Bay were among the undertakings in which he had a large piece of the action.

One group that benefited directly, and in a positive way, from the government's ownership and control of basic industries in Brazil was the capital-goods sector, which manufactured heavy equipment used in the production of primary goods such as petroleum, energy, and metals. Instead of purchasing this equipment from abroad, as had been done in the past, the regime began to rely on Brazil private entrepreneurs, and many of them earned handsome profits from the opportunities presented to them.

During the military dictatorship, products manufactured by both the public and private sectors replaced commodities as the country's foremost exports. But exports did not increase quickly enough to generate earnings sufficient to offset Brazil's balance-of-payments deficit (created mostly by the need to pay for oil imports), or to pay interest charges on the foreign debt.

The 1980s came to be called the "lost decade" because during this time the twin scourges of inflation and recession plunged the country into hopeless debt. For a number of years the generals had been talking about a return to civilian rule, and in the late 1970s they had begun to relax some of the restrictions they had placed on civil liberties. As the economic situation worsened, the military became increasingly eager to extricate itself from the mess it had created. Moreover, as censorship gave way to freedom of the press, reports of corruption within the regime and the state enterprises added to the pressures generated by the rising expectation, on the part of a majority of Brazilians, that the authoritarian system imposed by the generals would soon be consigned to the dustbin of history.

A number of entrepreneurs also joined in the chorus of voices advocating an end to military rule. The business elite had done well for themselves during the "miracle" and had generally supported the economic and political policies of the regime. Now that the country had plunged into a recession, and neither the generals nor their civilian allies seemed to have any idea how to deal with it, many executives suddenly discovered that they preferred civilian government after all.

An intriguing aspect of the transition to democracy in 1984 was the key role played by a prominent São Paulo businessman whose taste for politics made him unique among Brazilian entrepreneurs. Although members of the economic elite, such as José Emírio de Moraes, had held elective office in the past, none embraced the political life with so much gusto, and generated so much controversy, as Paulo Salim Maluf.

His father, Salim Farah Maluf, arrived in Brazil from Lebanon in 1910 with the equivalent of $6 in his pocket. Following in the footsteps of Francisco Matarazzo and other immigrants who created fortunes in the New World, Salim founded both a clan and several profitable enterprises. When he died in 1943, his eldest son, Roberto, left school to take charge of the family business. Eight years later, Roberto and his younger brother Paulo, then only twenty years old, launched Eucatex, a company that fashioned, from the wood of the eucalyptus, fiber-based hardboards used in construction. The new firm prospered and diversified, producing minerals, steel, chemicals, and insulation materials.

The Maluf brothers were a study in contrasts. Roberto was dour, introverted, and totally devoted to Eucatex (to the extent that he collected figurines and other artifacts in the shape of turtles, the original symbol of the firm). Paulo was outgoing, possessed of a photographic memory, a graduate in civil engineering from the University of São Paulo, and an excellent horseman as well as a gifted classical pianist. He also nourished ambitions that went far beyond participating in the management of Eucatex and the business ventures of the rich Lebanese-Brazilian family into which he married.

His opening came as a result of his friendship with a fellow equestrian, General Artur Costa e Silva, who served as the second president of the military regime. Costa e Silva first appointed Maluf to the presidency of a federal bank and then, in 1969, made him mayor of São Paulo. The millionaire-businessman's link to the dictatorship, and the fact that his term of office coincided with a period of harsh repression against dissent, earned him the undying enmity of those who suffered at the hands of the regime. In addition, he attracted criticism on his own by demonstrating a flair for unrestrained self-promotion that many found unseemly.*

After serving as secretary of transportation for the state of São Paulo, Maluf set his sights on the governorship. This was at a time when governors were chosen by an electoral college rigged in favor of proregime candidates. Thus Maluf had only to secure the nomination of the party that supported the dictatorship. To do so, he had to weather a scandal based on accusations that a firm owned by his wife's family had gone into bankruptcy immediately after having secured substantial loans from a government bank.

The generals running Brazil opposed Maluf's candidacy, and the economic elite of São Paulo had serious reservations about him. Nevertheless, Maluf managed to snare the nomination, and he became governor of São Paulo in 1978. With Brazil's richest state under his control and a personal fortune at his disposal, he set about establishing himself as the country's foremost civilian politician. Since the regime had committed itself to a process of gradual democratization, the prospect of a presidential election involving civilian candidates in the not too distant future explains much of Maluf's conduct in office.

He founded a state oil company (which discovered very little oil), devoted much of his budget to public works, donated ambulances and water-well drilling crews to impoverished municipalities in the Northeast, traveled extensively both in Brazil and abroad, and invited prominent Brazilians to make all-expense-paid trips to São Paulo to receive medals from him. At the same time he cultivated the image of an efficient chief executive who knew how to administer the government of a state with a gross domestic product larger than that of any country in Latin America except Brazil itself.

The fact that he had pressed forward with his candidacy in defiance of the wishes of the generals running Brazil gave him a certain amount of cachet, as did the right-wing populism he espoused.

---

* For example, he presented automobiles to the players on Brazil's 1970 world-champion soccer team. This provoked a lawsuit on the part of a citizen claiming that Maluf had illegally used governent funds for the purchase of the cars, and in 1981 a court finally ordered Maluf to indemnify the municipal fisc.

In 1982 he resigned the governorship and was elected federal deputy with more votes than any other candidate in the country. He was now poised to make a run for the presidency. The regime announced that indirect elections for the highest office in the land would be held in 1984. An electoral college, the composition of which would ensure the choice of an aspirant acceptable to the military, would do the voting. Thus, nomination by the proregime party would seem to be tantamount to election.

Maluf set about winning that nomination. He campaigned tirelessly throughout the length and breadth of Brazil. Stories of favor-peddling, by now his stock-in-trade, now gave way to charges that he was actually trying to buy the support of electors. A joke making the rounds at the time put it like this: when he comes near you, keep your hands on your pockets, not to prevent him from removing something, but to stop him from putting something in.

His political enemies, who were legion, made persistent but fruitless efforts to uncover solid proof linking him to corruption. They charged, for example, that Eucatex secured advantageous (and perhaps even dubious) loans from a government financial institution, but even if this were true, this did not set him apart from countless other businessmen who took advantage of the peculiar way capitalism functioned in Brazil. Nonetheless, Maluf had trouble shedding the image of a wheeler-dealer who would stop at nothing to become Brazil's first civilian chief executive in nearly two decades. (Some suspected that ethnic prejudice may have contributed to the animosity toward him.)

The specter of a Maluf presidency fired massive street demonstrations calling, in vain, for direct presidential elections. When the ex-governor of São Paulo won the nomination of the pro-government party, political conservatives and members of the economic elite who would be expected to support an "official" candidate declared their support for the opposition's nominee, Tancredo Neves, whom the electoral college then picked to be the next president.

Losing an election that had apparently been rigged in his favor did not dull Paulo Maluf's appetite for politics in the least. With the restoration of full democracy, he became a perennial also-ran, campaigning for governor of the state of São Paulo in 1986 and 1990, mayor of São Paulo in 1988, and president of the republic in

1989. In race after race he projected in person as well as on television an unflagging fervor that more than occasionally strayed across the line into shamelessness or bathos.

Maluf's "happy-warrior" image differed sharply from that of one of his rivals in the São Paulo business community, Antônio Emírio de Moraes. When Antônio Emírio tried his hand at politics, he discovered to his dismay that entrepreneurial skills did not always tranfer to the electoral arena.

Like his father, the redoubtable José Emírio (who passed away in 1973), Antônio Emírio also graduated from the Colorado School of Mines. He then entered the family business and became the superintendent-director of Votorantim, whose mechanical and metallurgical divisions he managed.

A tireless administrator who took no vacations, drove his own car, paid for lunches out of his own pocket, and delegated little to subordinates, Antônio Emírio played a major role in building Votorantim into the largest private-sector industrial conglomerate in Brazil. Readers' polls conducted by a business magazine named him the country's "businessman of the year" eight years in a row, and he has made *Forbes* magazine's list of the world's billionaires. Unlike Maluf, he shied away from publicity. Unlike his father, he was not an "industrialist of the left," although his political views were somewhat more progressive than those of most Brazilian entrepreneurs.

Antônio Emírio did not hesitate to speak out on public issues, and in 1984 he openly opposed Maluf during the latter's run for the presidency. Antônio Emírio's name was often mentioned on lists of potential candidates for high office. In 1986 he took the plunge and ran for governor of São Paulo. It was, as he put it in a 1987 interview, a "terrible experience. I won't ever run again." Whereas the thick-skinned Maluf, as was his wont, relished the rough-and-tumble of the campaign; Antônio Emírio found it an ordeal, especially when he and his family became the objects of personal attacks. Smiling came across as a painful exercise for him, and his evident lack of enthusiasm was an unfortunate message to send to voters, no matter how highly many of them might have regarded him. He did not do well in the final tally.

*        *        *

Both Paulo Maluf and Antônio Emírio de Moraes have been atypical Brazilian entrepreneurs in their willingness to engage openly in the electoral process, but their participation in family-owned enterprises puts them on common ground with a substantial number of the economic elite. Family groups control 280 of the country's 300 largest domestic firms. This phenomenon, a relic from Brazil's patriarchal past, poses a serious obstacle to the development of a modern capitalist economy.

The early phases of Brazilian industrialization were characterized by the emergence of powerful individuals, such as Francisco Matarazzo, who by their energy, intelligence, and force of personality built up enterprises that became highly, if not totally, dependent on them. In this respect business entities replicated the authoritarian structure of the large plantations and ranches of the countryside, where a single owner exercised absolute control over his property and the uses to which it was put. Large landholders dealt on a personal basis with other members of the elite, as well as with local, state, and federal officials. They used these latter ties to secure subsidies and other forms of favorable treatment for their businesses.

But the patriarchal model has proved ill-suited not only to the orderly transfer of control after the death of the founding father, but also to the requirements of large-scale private enterprises in the modern world. The fate of the once-mighty Matarazzo empire provides a vivid example of the shortcomings of the antiquated system of corporate governance in Brazil.

Francisco Matarazzo, Jr., ran the family enterprise in an extremely authoritarian way, as his father had done before him. By the early 1970s, at the height of the Brazilian "miracle," its assets totaled more than $1 billion. But the Count passed away at age seventy-seven in 1977, and a bitter family squabble ensued. The deceased patriarch had left control of the business to his youngest daughter, Maria Pia, and her three brothers challenged their father's will in court.

Although the male Matarazzos were unsuccessful in their suit for control, the family feud introduced an element of instability into the enormous conglomerate. Maria Pia made a number of administrative changes, but she ruled the company in the autocratic tradition of her father and grandfather, and in doing so she failed to make the sort of structural reforms that were long overdue. In a few short years, the net worth of the Matarazzo group had plunged to $500 million, and the company was so heavily in debt that it filed for bankruptcy on behalf of a number of the firms it controlled.

Of course, the recession that hit the Brazilian economy in the 1980s had much to do with the demise of the Matarazzo empire. Moreover, the military regime had encouraged private businesses to borrow dollars heavily during the 1970s, and the devaluation of Brazil's currency in 1983 made it all but impossible for many firms to meet their debt obligations. Nevertheless, the fact that the Matarazzo group never modernized made it vulnerable to sharp downturns in the business cycle, and neither its size nor its long history could keep it from the brink of disaster.

The Matarazzos took desperate measures to keep the business from collapsing. In 1988 they entered into a joint venture whereby they supplied the land, on which the flagship operation of their mighty industrial empire had once been located, for yet another chic shopping center in São Paulo.

In 1989 the family engaged in an unseemly dispute with São Paulo officials when they tried to sell their mansion on Avenida Paulista, a thoroughfare that had once been lined with the ornate residences of coffee barons and industrialists and was now hemmed in by a phalanx of glass and steel high-rise office buildings. Property values along the avenue are said to be the highest in all Brazil. With members of the clan selling off personal possessions to keep the business afloat, the prospect of receiving $120 million for the premises was alluring, but Luiza Erundina, the socialist mayor of the city, declared the mansion a historical monument.

Undoubtedly Erundina was seizing an opportunity to address what she viewed as historical wrongs perpetrated on the working class during the "golden era" of São Paulo's industrial growth as well as during the more recent "miracle." She claimed she would expropriate the palatial structure, which had once been modified by an architect who had done work for Benito Mussolini, and turn it into a "museum of worker culture." The Matarazzos vowed to resist. When dynamite was discovered on the premises, the police set up a twenty-four-hour watch to protect the mansion from being destroyed by its owners.

Brazil's style of corporate governance has been a constant problem for the country's private sector for a very long time. The founders of powerful family companies were tireless, intuitively intelligent men who devoted their lives to the creation of industrial empires. But many of them not only refused to relinquish power during their lifetimes but also failed to prepare their heirs for the succession that would one day have to occur. Indeed, consulting groups now do a thriving business offering courses in business administration for offspring who have inherited businesses and have no idea what to do with them.

Companies' tendencies to maintain family control as well as autocratic management have frustrated the top-notch executives who were not members of a business clan. Those with talent tended to move on, taking with them managerial skills that family firms could ill afford to lose, especially as it became increasingly necessary for Brazilian companies to compete in a global economy.

Just as families relied on their patriarch to administer the businesses they owned, so private firms relied on the state to fill the role of patriarch for Brazilian entrepreneurial ventures. This relationship helped businessmen with ambition and talent to build empires that were instrumental in the industrialization of the country, but at the same time it created a system highly susceptible to corruption.

It was never a secret that doing business with the government at the national, state, or municipal levels could necessitate the payment of outright bribes or percentage kickbacks to high officials, just as it was a matter of common knowledge that high officials enriched themselves by accepting these payments and sometimes also by dipping freely into the public till. Indeed, perhaps the most notorious practitioner was São Paulo politician Adhemar de Barros, who campaigned openly (and successfully) under the slogan "He steals, but he gets things done."

The scandals that brought down Fernando Collor gave Brazilians a long, hard look at how the system operates. They produced a moral crisis of sorts, as opinion polls revealed loss of confidence in the country's institutions, as well as a loss of self-esteem among ordinary citizens who recognized that important elements of Brazilianness were at the root of the problem.

One of the casualties of the scandals was Votorantim, the largest industrial complex in Brazil, which was forced to split up because of the matter. The investigation of Paulo César Farias, the Collor intimate whose corrupt practices eventually implicated the president and forced his resignation, brought to light payments made to the notorious P.C. by the giant conglomerate. Although Antônio Emírio de Moraes was called on to admit to and explain these payments, the person responsible for them was his older brother, José Emírio de Moraes Filho. In the wake of this public embarrassment, the Votorantim group split apart, and the heirs of the patriarch José Emírio went their separate ways.

As the 1994 presidential elections approached, it became clear that Brazil's business community had no obvious candidate to place in the field against Lula, the Workers' party nominee who was once again raising the banner of the Left. Paulo Maluf, who in 1992 had won a surprise victory in the São Paulo mayoral contest, was willing to put himself forward again, but he attracted his usual modicum of national support. With Lula leading in the early polls, Brazilian entrepreneurs had no choice but to back Fernando Henrique Cardoso, a lifelong social democrat whose academic publications utilized Marxist analysis and seemed to place him firmly on the left side of the political spectrum.

Fernando Henrique, however, was now running on a platform Brazil's haves felt comfortable with, since he was promising to hold down inflation, loosen government controls on business, reduce government spending, and privatize sectors of the economy previously under state ownership. When he won a resounding victory, those at the top of the pyramid of power in Brazil breathed a sigh of relief.

But Fernando Henrique, as a convert to the cause of the free market economy, was in fact proposing to challenge Brazil's entrepreneurs by introducing the country to bona fide capitalism. He was advocating the reduction of tariff bariers that had traditionally protected local industries—a free-trade policy that would subject Brazilian businesses to competition from powerful multinational corporations. His program also left no room for the type of government largesse to which Brazil's haves had grown accustomed.

It remains to be seen, first, whether Fernando Henrique will actually implement all the measures he has advocated and, if so, how Brazilian entrepreneurs will respond. "Business as usual" in Brazil has long meant no risk and easy access, for personal gain, to the levers of political and economic power. To force a change in this mindset would truly be revolutionary.

# Chapter 6

# Controlling Brazilian Minds

## *A Case Study of the Globo Network*

*A*n article in the *Los Angeles Times* once called him a "South American Citizen Kane," but the differences that separate Roberto Marinho from the title character in the Orson Welles classic, as well as those that distinguish him from the real-life tycoon who inspired Welles's masterwork, are much more interesting than the resemblances. Indeed, comparing Marinho with Charles Foster Kane and William Randolph Hearst can illustrate the pitfalls of viewing and interpreting Brazilians through an American lens.

Each in his own way, the three men have become symbols of the all-powerful media baron. Hearst and Kane, his on-screen counterpart, used inherited wealth to build communications empires that spanned the United States. They put together chains of newspapers, magazines, and radio stations, and reigned as peerless practitioners of the art of yellow journalism from the late nineteenth century until well into the twentieth.

Roberto Marinho, who inherited a Rio newspaper from his father, turned out to be a much later bloomer. Although for many years he wielded some influence on the national scene, he remained very much a secondary figure, outshone by other media luminaries. But when opportunity beckoned in the 1970s, he converted the national television network he had created a decade earlier into a virtual monopoly, and thereby reached an apogee of power far beyond that attained not only by his Brazilian rivals but also by William Randolph Hearst.

Hearst and Kane were egocentric individualists who embraced progressive views early in their careers. They were quintessential outsiders, gadflies to the establishment, and indifferent to the hostility generated by the unpopular stands they occasionally took. Hearst was an active politician who served two terms as a United States congressman and was a candidate for mayor of New York City, governor of New York State, and president of the United States. When he was not seeking public office for himself, he worked ceaselessly to influence officeholders.

Roberto Marinho is an egocentric conservative who has long served as a pillar of Brazil's power structure. Though not in the least reluctant to use the vast means at his disposal to advance his political and economic agendas (long a hallmark of Brazilian journalism), he has always cultivated the image of a very private person, the epitome of the serious businessman, and has remained as far removed from the public eye as his position permits.

Hearst, tall and handsome, impulsive yet painfully shy, had a long, notorious liaison with film star Marion Davies and even founded a movie studio to further her career. In *Citizen Kane*, Charles Foster Kane, the character played by Welles, builds an opera house to promote his paramour's career. Both men did not hesitate to fill the pages of their newspapers with unrestrained adulation of their respective protégées.

The short, bald, dour-faced Marinho engaged in a winter romance with a Rio socialite who had won the Miss France beauty contest in 1938 and became his third wife. The affair might provide excellent grist for one of the *telenovelas* (serialized dramas) his network has become famous for, but, of course, he would never countenance such a production.

The original title of *Citizen Kane*, as well as the name Hearst gave to some of his newspapers, was "American," a reflection of both the self-image and the pith of fictional character and flesh-and-blood magnate alike. Roberto Marinho shares with them a staunchly pro-American outlook, although at the same time and in many respects he has remained archetypally Brazilian.

*O Globo*, the Rio de Janeiro daily with the largest circulation in Brazil, is undoubtedly Roberto Marinho's personal favorite among the various components of the empire he has created (which also includes finance, insurance, publishing and recording companies, cattle ranches, and shopping centers), because Marinho considers himself first and foremost a print journalist by profession. But what makes him the most powerful man in Brazil is the crown jewel in the $1 billion Marinho family conglomerate: the television network that reaches almost every town in the country, occasionally posts viewer ratings of 100 percent, has attracted advertising revenues in excess of $600 million, and has exported programs to 128 countries.

The origins of the Marinho family fortune date back to the last decade of the nineteenth century and the first decades of the twentieth. Newspapers and periodicals during this period were sprouting like dandelions after a summer rain; indeed, in 1912, some 1,377 of them were published in the country, and 1,275 of these had come into being since the proclamation of the republic in 1889. The ferment that had roiled the country during the struggles for abolition and the institution of a republican form of government continued unabated during the formative years of the new regime.

The public debate between monarchists and republicans provided a powerful stimulus for the founding of new publications, and a revolt (to be described in detail in Chapters Nine and Thirteen) by religious northeasterners who refused to accept the authority of the newly formed republic inspired sensational, distorted reportage aimed at inflaming public opinion against the rebels. This was the birth of yellow journalism in Brazil. (Coincidentally, at about the same time that much of the Brazilian press was hysterically urging the Brazilian government to make war on the rebellious backlanders, the Hearst newspapers were using the same style of reportage to exhort the American government to make war on Spain.)

The press throughout this period served primarily as a vehicle for opinion. Most journals were outlets for intellectuals who had particular political axes to grind. Indeed, a symbiotic relationship developed between the press and the government, as a number of public officials came from the ranks of those who had previously edited or written for newspapers.

But journalism soon began to evolve, becoming less an outlet for ad hoc pamphleteering and more of a profession. In addition, the larger metropolitan dailies underwent the same process of growth and modernization that much of the rest of industry was experiencing, and their preoccupation with the pursuit of profits began to mirror that of other commercial enterprises. One result was the slanting of articles and editorials in response to direct or indirect payments or favors from business groups or government officials seeking to influence public opinion. Individual reporters were poorly paid and hence were particularly susceptible to blandishments. Newspaper owners were no less likely to succumb to bribes.

One of the new breed of professional journalists was Irineu Marinho, a hard-driving Rio de Janeiro reporter who founded his own daily, *A Noite (The Night)*, in 1911. He innovated by using lengthy feature articles and illustrations, and his newspaper built up a substantial circulation. Marinho subsequently lost control of *A Noite*, but he then launched another new daily, *O Globo (The Globe)* in 1925.

A scant twenty-one days after *O Globo* first appeared on the streets of Rio, Irineu Marinho died. The newspaper passed into the hands of Roberto, his eldest son, a twenty-year-old university student at the time. The journalistic career of Roberto Marinho had begun one year earlier when his father published on the front page of *A Noite* a letter of political commentary Roberto had written from Portugal to a friend. Roberto continued his studies after his father's death and also performed various subordinate jobs on the newspaper. In 1931 he took over active, full-time management of *O Globo*.

Ownership of a large Rio daily gave him some degree of political influence, but it was minor compared to the power and prestige that was being accumulated by one of his rivals. Indeed, Roberto Marinho soon found himself in the long shadow of another man who was well on his way to becoming Brazil's foremost newspaper and magazine publisher (and who was often referred to as the "Hearst of Brazil"), Francisco Assis Chateaubriand Bandeira de Mello.

Chateaubriand, Marinho's senior by twelve years, could not have been more unlike his young competitor in a number of ways. On the one hand, Chateaubriand was a typical *nordestino*, deeply imbued with regional traits such as a violent disposition, unbridled machismo, and an unswervingly authoritarian bent. On the other hand, in many respects he was an original—flamboyantly eccentric, precocious, mercurial, shockingly crude, and keenly intellectual. This unique makeup set him apart sharply from Marinho, the shadowy, reclusive, deliberate, late-blooming *carioca.*

Born in the state of Paraíba, Chateaubriand* as a boy had to overcome rickets and a painful stammer. He worked as a journalist to help support his family while he studied law at the University of Recife, and grew to love the profession, especially as it provided him with the opportunity to engage in polemics, a pursuit for which he displayed considerable talent.

In 1917 the diminutive Paraiban followed the example of other bright, ambitious *nordestinos,* and moved to Rio de Janeiro, where he continued his career as a journalist (for a while serving as editor-in-chief of the daily newspaper *Jornal do Brasil*) and at the same time practiced law.

During this period he represented the interests of foreigners who were seeking to acquire an iron-mining concession in Brazil. Serving these clients was consistent with his firm belief that Brazil could not achieve its potential without opening its doors widely to investment from abroad. He also used his contacts within the local business community to raise the money that enabled him to purchase *O Jornal,* a conservative morning newspaper.

While Roberto Marinho was struggling to make a success of *O Globo,* Assis Chateaubriand went about the business of creating a media empire. He soon acquired a São Paulo newspaper; a second Rio daily that appeared in the evening and featured sensationalist news that made it popular among Rio's lower classes; and the magazine *O Cruzeiro* (inspired by *Life*). *O Cruzeiro* not only pioneered the art of photojournalism in Brazil, but also became the country's

---

* The name Chateaubriand was legally adopted by his grandfather, who had founded a school and named it after the French author and statesman Vicomte François René de Chateaubriand. The locals began to refer to the grandfather as "José de Chateaubriand," often mispronouncing the French appellation, and he grew fond of the sound of it. Later in life Assis Chateaubriand would embrace the conceit that his forebears were Normandy pirates.

first nationally circulated magazine. For three decades it would serve to define Brazil's image of itself.

Other newspapers around the country gradually came under the control of Chateaubriand, who named his group the Diários Associados (Associated Dailies). He wielded absolute control over what went into his publications, and for many years he wrote editorials and columns that appeared simultaneously in all of them. This enabled him to carry on personal feuds and satisfy personal whims. Invective was his stock in trade. He used his media empire to heap abuse upon figures such as the Francisco Matarazzos (senior and junior) and José Emírio de Moraes.

The line imposed by Chateaubriand upon his publications promoted private enterprise and foreign investment. They vigorously opposed totalitarianism of both the Right and the Left. Chateaubriand was an early backer of Getúlio Vargas,* turned against him when Vargas's authoritarian tendencies surfaced, and then made peace with the dictator.

Chateaubriand, unlike Marinho but like William Randolph Hearst,† dabbled in politics. In 1952, after a whirlwind campaign, he was elected Senator from Paraíba, and in 1956 he switched states and won a Senate seat from Maranhão. (In Brazil, as in England, a candidate for the national congress need not reside in the state he seeks to represent.) He resigned the latter post in 1957, when President Juscelino Kubitschek appointed him ambassador to Great Britain.

In many ways Assis Chateaubriand reflected a manic Brazilianness. He was very individualistic, very extroverted, totally un-

---

* Chateaubriand was so eager to take an active part in the Revolution of 1930 that he attempted to reach the insurgents in Rio Grande do Sul by an overland route. When he reached a small town held by the rebels, he was mistaken for a government spy and arrested. His captors did not believe he was Assis Chateaubriand and were about to execute him when one of them remembered that there was a correspondent for the Diários Associados in the town, and that the owner of the chain signed every press card. A comparison of the prisoner's signature with that on the correspondent's press card saved Chateaubriand's life.

† Chateaubriand resembled Hearst in one other interesting respect. Both recognized at a very early stage the tremendous potential of aviation. Indeed, Chateaubriand became the first Brazilian to fly in an airplane in Brazilian airspace when he accompanied a French aviator on a flight over Recife on June 10, 1913.

predictable, loud, outrageous, erratic, and always issuing orders with no concern for details. "Working for him was like performing on the flying trapeze," was the way one ex-employee put it.

The people close to him had to be on constant alert to keep him from doing irrational things. Once at an airport in southern Brazil he ran into an *O Cruzeiro* reporter who was carrying with him photographs and material for an important article for the next issue. Chateaubriand insisted that the reporter forget about his assignment and accompany him on a trip to Belém, (in those days a long journey, even by air), because he didn't want to go by himself. The reporter excused himself to go to the men's room and then slipped out of the airport to escape his employer. Chateaubriand never held such acts of constructive insubordination against his underlings.

While Assis Chateaubriand towered over his competitors, Roberto Marinho was content to remain with the rest of the pack. *O Globo* continued to follow an ultraconservative line spiced by a vitriolic brand of anticommunism. *O Globo*'s owner acquired no other newspapers, and it was not until 1944 that he launched his first radio station in Rio de Janeiro. He did demonstrate a characteristic that would prove essential later when he built his TV empire— a willingness to associate himself with highly competent people. For example, Herbert Moses, who helped Irineu Marinho found *O Globo* in 1925, remained intimately involved with the paper for nearly forty years. Known as the "electric mosquito" because of his slight build and enormous energy, Moses was a prestigious journalist and tireless fighter against government censorship of the press.

Like most other publishers, including Chateaubriand, Roberto Marinho used his newspaper to promote business interests with which he had ties. In the case of *O Globo*, this meant helping out Rio's Portuguese importers and merchants, who controlled a substantial amount of the retail trade in the region. Thus the paper supported orthodox economic policies that called for balancing the budget, restricting the money supply, and eliminating restrictions on foreign capital.

Having adjusted to playing second fiddle to Assis Chateaubriand, in the two decades after World War II Roberto Marinho found himself outshone by another press superstar, Carlos Lacerda.

The meteoric Lacerda did not build a publishing empire to compete with the Diários Associados and *O Globo*. Instead, as if he were living in the earlier age when the two professions overlapped, he became the country's foremost journalist-politician. A charismatic *carioca* with a flare for invective, Lacerda was a cutting-edge conservative who in the 1950s and 1960s played one of the leads in the political dramas that gripped the country, and who managed to relegate to supporting roles not only Marinho but also Chateaubriand.

Lacerda had been an outspoken opponent of the Vargas dictatorship during the late 1930s. With youthful exuberance and courage, he worked closely with the Communist party (which he came close to joining) in the struggle against fascism in Brazil, and ended up behind bars on a number of occasions. Later, after suspending his political activity, he became a star reporter for Chateaubriand's *O Jornal*, of which he was named city editor in 1943.

When his superiors refused to print an interview he had conducted with a respected politician who was harshly critical of the regime (Chateaubriand was reconciled with Vargas at the time), Lacerda left the Diários Associados and began contributing a regular column to a rival daily. He also returned to politics, as Getúlio Vargas loosened his grip on the nation and permitted free elections in 1945. By now Lacerda was as anticommunist as he was anti-Vargas, and he made fiery radio broadcasts that tore into his foes. In 1946 he was elected to the city council of Rio de Janeiro. Three years later he launched his own newspaper, *Tribuna da Imprensa (Tribune of the Press)*.

Commingling the professions of journalist and politician, Carlos Lacerda went on to accomplish the extraordinary feat of bringing down (or being instrumental in the bringing down of) three Brazilian presidents: Getúlio Vargas, Jânio Quadros, and João Goulart. Yet he failed to realize his burning ambition to place himself in the presidential palace.

When Getúlio Vargas made his comeback and was elected to the presidency in 1950, Lacerda targeted him with a steady stream of acerbic attacks in newspaper columns, as well as radio talks, even to the point of encouraging the military to intervene. (Marinho and Chateaubriand did the same.) The drumfire continued unabated throughout Vargas's term. Lacerda became so much a symbol of the anti-Vargas forces that friends of the president, unbeknownst to Vargas, organized an assassination attempt on the editor. Lacerda was wounded but not fatally. In the resulting uproar, Vargas came under such pressure that he committed suicide.

Having served two terms in the federal Chamber of Deputies, Carlos Lacerda decided to run for governor of the state of Guanabara (the city of Rio de Janeiro) in 1960. At the same time he supported the presidential candidacy of the eccentric Jânio Quadros. Both men were elected. But the alliance between them did not survive Jânio's first year in office. The president's erratic behavior, his pro-Castro leanings, and his alleged ambition to become a "Brazilian de Gaulle" turned the governor against him, and in August 1961 Lacerda violently attacked Quadros in a radio address. Shortly thereafter Quadros suddenly and unexpectedly resigned.

Lacerda's third victim was João Goulart, Jânio's vice president, who took over leadership of the country in spite of opposition from Lacerda and other powerful right-wing elements. A populist politician who had served as Vargas's Minister of Labor, Goulart survived the threat of civil war and a constitutional amendment that for a while limited his authority as president. But he proved incapable of dealing with increasing social unrest and an economy beset by inflation, and he eventually fell victim to a military coup that Lacerda and his allies encouraged and abetted.

As governor of Guanabara, Lacerda ordered his state security apparatus to participate in the repression that followed the 1964 coup. He clearly expected that the military would soon step aside and restore the political process. His eyes were on the prize, and he made no secret of his intention of running in the scheduled 1965 presidential elections.

But the generals had other ideas. They first postponed the elections and then decreed that the Congress would select the next chief executive—which meant that the military would dictate the choice, since Congress was now under its control. Lacerda joined the opposition. His term of office had expired, and he no longer owned the *Tribuna da Imprensa*, but he still enjoyed the paper's support and also was able to use television to publicize his views. In 1967 the regime barred him from TV, and one year later it suspended his political rights. He died of a heart attack in 1977.

Meanwhile, Roberto Marinho, like the rest of the conservative newspaper owners, opposed Goulart and welcomed his overthrow. *O Globo* then became an enthusiastic supporter of the military government. At the same time, Marinho took an entrepreneurial initiative that would make him one of the wealthiest men in the world. He decided to create a television network.

His would not be the country's first TV network. Assis Chateaubriand, who introduced television to Brazil in 1949, had put together a chain of TV stations in Rio de Janeiro, São Paulo, Belo Horizonte, Brasília, Recife, and elsewhere. But the Chateaubriand people were slow to take the new medium beyond its infancy. Television programming continued to target only those wealthy enough to purchase sets, and little effort was made to cultivate a mass audience. Moreover, existing technology did not yet permit simultaneous telecasts. Even with the advent of videotaping in 1962, it was still necessary to ship recorded programs from city to city, and the enormous size of Brazil made this a cumbersome process.

As Roberto Marinho set about building his Globo network, fate intervened on his behalf. Assis Chateaubriand suffered a cerebral thrombosis that confined him to a wheelchair. The "Old Captain," as his friends liked to call him, had begun to withdraw from the active management of his media empire some years before the disabling stroke. Rather than keep the business within the family, he attempted to pass control of it to a group of associates. But his sons squabbled because they wanted to safeguard what they felt was their patrimony, scandal tainted disputes over transfers of shares in the business, and the decentralized nature of the enterprise led to chaos.

The vulnerability of the Chateaubriand empire left an opening on which Roberto Marinho was able to capitalize. But it would be wrong to credit the subsequent success of Rede Globo (the Globo network) entirely to luck. Although the collapse of the competition helped, it was Marinho's business acumen that contributed most to his meteoric rise.

In his excellent doctoral dissertation on the Brazilian television industry, Joseph Straubhaar points to six factors that impeded the development of national networks in Brazil in the early 1960s: a total focus on local markets; a lack of discipline among member stations; a failure to use networkwide advertising; an ignorance of what a mass audience of viewers wanted to watch; the limited availability of financial resources; and poor financial management. When he took the plunge into TV, Roberto Marinho addressed the first four factors himself, and he obtained outside help to deal with the other two.

A study of the industry in its current form convinced Marinho that he should establish a presence in the country's major markets, link together a chain of stations with centralized rather than local management, and take full advantage of the potential for selling advertising on a national level. He made several brilliant hires and delegated to his managers the authority to develop programming with the widest possible audience appeal.

As he moved forward in accordance with a carefully conceived plan, Roberto Marinho clearly distinguished himself from Assis Chateaubriand, who had always relied on improvisation in reaching business decisions. Marinho, making careful calculations about how to maximize his profits, was acting like a modern North American, European, or Japanese entrepreneur.

His particular genius was in sensing the vast earnings to be made in the sale of TV airtime to advertisers, especially during periods of economic expansion. He was also shrewd enough to think in long-range terms, which led to his decision to plow profits back into Rede Globo, a strategy his competitors failed to employ. His perspicacity has been underappreciated by many of his compatriots, however, because of the loud and bitter controversy that erupted over his effort to obtain financial and technical assistance from abroad.

What would come to be known as the "Time-Life affair" had its genesis in a decision by Roberto Marinho to seek the help of foreign investors in creating his TV network. Long an admirer of the United States, he wanted to take advantage of American capital and know-how, the latter of particular importance to him as he prepared to go beyond what then existed in Brazil. He therefore negotiated an eleven-year deal with Time-Life Broadcasting Inc., which had not been able to put together into a network the TV stations it owned in the United States but was eager to gain a foothold overseas. Time-Life would provide the newly organized network with funding and technical help, in return for a 30 percent share of Globo's annual profits.

But there was a legal problem to be confronted: the Constitution prohibited foreigners from owning, in whole or in part, mass-media enterprises. A cautious sort, Marinho not only obtained opinions from his own attorneys but also consulted President João Goulart personally about the contract. After the 1964 coup, he then contacted the new president, Army Marshall Humberto Castelo Branco, and explained the terms of the arrangement. Neither Goulart nor Castelo Branco voiced any objections. Marinho and Time-Life went ahead quietly with their deal, and in 1965 Globo acquired a Rio de Janeiro television station, the first step in the forging of the Globo network.

Ironically, it was then Governor Carlos Lacerda who blew the cover off the Globo network's link with Time-Life. During Lacerda's stormy political career, *O Globo* had occasionally chided him for his temperamental excesses, but Lacerda had long admired Marinho, even to the point of nominating him in 1956 for Columbia University's Maria Moors Cabot Award (given to Latin American journalists). But his respect for Marinho did not prevent Lacerda from confirming what many had suspected for some time.

As part of a continuing postcoup crackdown on suspected subversion, Lacerda's police arrested a Cuban who they said was a Castro agent. He turned out to be a Time-Life employee assigned to work with Globo television in Rio. Under questioning, he revealed the details of the arrangement, which Lacerda then denounced to the Ministry of Justice in Brasília.

Before long, the matter became public knowledge, and Roberto Marinho found himself at the center of a swirling controversy. Prominent politicians and much of the nation's press attacked him for violating the Constitution and facilitating foreign control over Brazil's mass media. Both the Ministry of Justice and the Congress conducted investigations into his dealings with Time-Life.

The brouhaha was an intertwining of economic and political elements. Some of the loudest accusers were Marinho's competitors. His aggressive talent raids on existing Rio TV stations had stirred considerable resentment, especially from the Chateaubriand chain. Moreover, the launching of a Spanish-language edition of *Life* magazine in Latin America had seriously damaged the earnings of the Spanish edition of Chateaubriand's *O Cruzeiro*, because powerful U.S. companies doing business in the region switched their advertising from the Brazilian publication to its American rival. Thus the Chateaubriand people also had a score to settle with Time-Life. A federal deputy who was also a director of the Diários Associados led the assault on the Globo deal.

The "Old Captain" himself, still able to contribute occasional pieces for his newspapers, lashed out in print at Marinho, whom he called "incurably feeble-minded" and "Roberto the African," the latter a reference to Marinho's dark complexion. Chateaubriand conveniently overlooked his lifelong championing of the cause of foreign investment in Brazil. He also kept secret the fact that just prior to the publicity given to the Time-Life contract with Marinho, he had sent a representative to the United States to sound out the American Broadcasting Company about the possibility of a similar deal. (This was one of the more startling disclosures made by Fernando Morais in his excellent biography *Chatô: O Rei do Brasil (Chatô: The King of Brazil)*, published in 1994.)

At the same time, left-leaning politicians who had not been purged gave vent to their repressed anger at the 1964 coup, which most of them believed could not have succeeded without help from the United States. The regime permitted a certain amount of free expression during the first phase of the dictatorship, and what remained of the Left took full advantage of it. Since they could not criticize the military directly, they targeted the Globo network and its American associates.

In addition, many of the critics were sincerely concerned about foreign penetration of their country's mass media. There had already been controversy about the economic and cultural effects of the sale of publications such as the Portuguese-language edition of *Reader's Digest* in Brazil. The power to shape ideas and attitudes— indeed, Brazilianness itself— seemed at stake. The strong sense of nationalism at the core of their political beliefs matched the equally passionate nationalism of conservatives such as Carlos Lacerda. As a result Marinho took hits from all points on the ideological spectrum. (One of the harshest broadsides came from the typewriter of Carlos Lacerda. Entitled "The Al Capone of the Press," the article appeared in Chateaubriand's *O Cruzeiro.*)

Much of the debate was legalistic. Did the arrangement between TV Globo and Time-Life give the latter part-ownership of the former (a set-up that would have violated Brazil's Constitution), or was the arrangement more in the nature of a loan? Reacting to his opponents' charges, Marinho altered the terms of the deal in 1965, so that Time-Life purchased the building out of which Globo television operated, in exchange for a share of TV Globo's profits, instead of a fixed amount of rent.

This arrangement did not satisfy Marinho's critics, who kept on the offensive. The military regime saw nothing wrong with what Marinho was doing, but at the same time the leaders wanted to put an end to the controversy. In the end the generals opted for procrastination, which provided Marinho with enough time to extract as much as he could out of the deal.

By 1969 both Time-Life and Marinho concluded that it was in their best interests to part company. Up to that point, Time-Life had received no profits from the Globo network's operation, since Marinho had been reinvesting earnings. Marinho paid back the loan, which best estimates put at around $6 million. To do so, he had to borrow from a Brazilian bank, which required him to put up virtually everything he owned as security. His son once told an American magazine that as part of the deal he had to cosign a declaration to the effect that his father was of sound mind. (He later denied having said this.) The elder Marinho in fact knew very well what he was doing. He was subsequently able to pay off the note, as a result of the success of his network.

Today it is commonplace for Brazilians to credit the meteoric rise of the Globo network to the Time-Life contract. In part this may reflect the sense of inferiority that often shapes their self-estimations. In their view, no Brazilian could possibly achieve what Marinho and his associates did; therefore, the Globo people must have been dependent on outsiders.

This belief flies in the face of facts. As Joseph Straubhaar has convincingly demonstrated in his dissertation, the Brazilian contribution to the triumph of the Globo network was substantial and indispensable. The money from Time-Life certainly helped, and the advice the Americans offered with respect to financial management put Globo on a much sounder footing than any of its competitors. But it was the creative work of Brazilian executives that shaped network programming; and it was Roberto Marinho who had the good sense to give his people free rein and to reinvest corporate earnings. The net result was a highly professional, polished, modern operation.

The Globo network did not really take off until after the termination of its relationship with Time-Life. By that time Marinho had already acquired stations in São Paulo and Belo Horizonte, and thus he covered the most important market areas in the country. TV Globo was already scoring impressively in the ratings, and the two Brazilian executives—Walter Clark and José Bonifácio de Oliveira Sobrinho—who were most responsible for the network's programming strategy were already in the fold. By 1968 TV was consuming 44.5 percent of mass-media advertising expenditures, up from 24.7 percent in 1962. But these factors merely set the stage for what was to follow.

On December 13, 1968, in response to growing political and social unrest, the military government issued the notorious "Institutional Act No. 5" (or "AI-5", as it was called), which ripped away most of the democratic veneer the generals had left in place after the coup, and initiated a period of harshly authoritarian rule. Under AI-5 and subsequent institutional acts and decrees, the regime purged Congress of dissident deputies, destroyed what was left of the independence of the judiciary, and imposed stringent censorship on the media.

One of the policies to which the dictatorship gave particular emphasis was national integration, mainly as a means of securing the country against what it saw as the threat of subversion from within and from without. The most visible aspect of this grand design was a road-building program intended to link the far north and northwest, in the Amazon basin, with the rest of the nation. A less obvious but equally important measure was the inauguration of a system of microwave links between cities and regions that would permit the simultaneous transmission of TV signals to all parts of the country. The Globo network turned out to be the only private group fully capable of utilizing this technological advance.

Roberto Marinho remained a fervent supporter of the military regime, even in its most repressive phase. He earned the gratitude of the generals, and they in turn rewarded him handsomely. Not only was the Globo network allowed to transmit via microwaves, but Marinho's company also was favored when the government handed out licenses for new TV stations. This special treatment enabled the Globo network to expand, as it acquired outlets in Brasília, Recife, and elsewhere. By 1980 the network had thirty-six affiliates.

During this same period, television was becoming the country's primary means of mass communication, which should have come as no surprise in light of the high rate of functional illiteracy in Brazil. After a decade of regular telecasting, the *Jornal Nacional (National Journal)*, the evening news program Globo television inaugurated in 1969, had attained the status of a national institution, earning the distinction of being the country's most widely shared single source of information. The tilt taken by the program was inevitably and unfailingly favorable to the regime. The fact that the government was a repressive dictatorship and censored the media (even to the point of cutting or prohibiting some of the Globo network's own programs) did not unduly perturb Roberto Marinho.

The regime, meanwhile, was making low-interest loans available for the purchase of TV sets, and the number of homes reached by television skyrocketed, especially when the economic policies adopted by the military produced the so-called "Brazilian miracle" of 1969–73 (described in more detail in the Introduction). The generals also encouraged the development of color TV, in order to enable Brazilians to view in living color the quadrennial World Cup soccer tournament from West Germany in 1974.* Globo television was the only Brazilian network with sufficient resources to be able to switch immediately to color transmission.

The programming strategies conceived by Clark and Bonifácio de Oliveira (or Boni, as he came to be known) were achieving remarkable results. With increasing reliance on Brazilian talent and shows produced by Globo (rather than tapes imported from the United States and programs put together by independent producers), the Globo network attracted an enormous audience and used North American marketing techniques to sell time to advertisers eager to reach viewers.

The *telenovela*, or serialized drama, contributed heavily to the extraordinary success of the Globo network. (The phenomenon of the *telenovela* merits an in-depth look, which will be provided in Chapter Eighteen.) Although this type of programming did not originate in Brazil, it underwent, mainly at the hands of the Globo people, a process of Brazilianization that made it wildly popular among Brazilians and one of the staples of the network.

Roberto Marinho's TV operation was highly disciplined and centralized, with its Rio headquarters exercising close control over all the affiliates. At the same time, Marinho gave Clark and Boni substantial leeway in carrying out their ideas, in contrast to what often occurred in family-owned enterprises, where family members often interfered in day-to-day business matters.

Success bred success. The highly professional atmosphere and excellent facilities of the Globo network made it easy to lure many of Brazil's finest entertainers, actors, writers, and directors. The enormous audience shares posted by the network attracted even more advertisers. The competition floundered, as the disintegration of the Chateaubriand chain continued apace and no other groups emerged to give Globo more than a token run for its money. Centralization was one of the military's most cherished tenets, so the leadership saw nothing amiss about the development of a media monopoly.

---

* The hope was that the nationwide euphoria produced by the Brazilian victory in 1970 would be repeated, to the indirect benefit of the dictatorship. Unfortunately, the team failed to cooperate, because it was eliminated in the semifinals.

By the time the generals decided to relinquish power and permit the restoration of democratic government, Roberto Marinho's empire was securely in place. In 1980, more than fourteen million Brazilian households had TV sets, and about two thirds of the entire population was believed to have access to television. Globo was attracting from 60 to 90 percent of the nation's viewers. Television was now consuming more than half of all mass-media advertising expenditures, of which the Globo network attracted the lion's share.

The decade of the 1980s was a time of transition and turbulence for the country, as civilians took the reins of power from the military and full democracy returned to Brazil; while at the same time social unrest intensified and the economy stagnated. For Roberto Marinho it was the period during which his power and prosperity crested. He found it as easy to develop beneficial relationships with the new government as he had done with the military regime. He also used his vast influence to help swing the balance in Brazil's first free presidential election in thirty years, and he greatly expanded his network's global reach by selling its *telenovelas* to more than fifty countries and purchasing a TV station that transmitted into the Italian market.

Marinho had set himself apart from the rest of the pack of Brazilian businessmen by relying to a considerable degree on private-sector initiatives to expand the Globo network, rather than by placing himself in a position of near total dependence on the largesse of the government. But this did not mean that he ignored the substantial benefits to be gained from ingratiating himself with high government officials (to the point of not permitting the use of the term "military regime" on the Globo network until the evening of the indirect election of a civilian president on January 15, 1985). When the generals returned to their barracks, Marinho skillfully cultivated their successors.

One of his first moves in this direction was to support the presidential candidacy of Tancredo Neves. Although Neves emerged from the ranks of the opposition, he was a cautious, mainstream politician. Moreover, the "official" candidate, Paulo Maluf, was not very popular, even within the military, and therefore the "tancredization" of Globo, as people liked to call it, reflected pragmatic good sense (and self-interest) on the part of its owner.

When Tancredo triumphed in the indirect election, Marinho was instrumental in assuring that the crucial (to him) post of Minister of Communications would go to a close friend, Antônio Carlos Magalhães, the ex-governor of Bahia and an old-fashioned political boss. José Sarney, upon assuming the presidency after the sudden, untimely demise of Tancredo, kept his predecessor's cabinet choices. As a result, Roberto Marinho made some profitable business deals with help from the government, Sarney enjoyed strong support from the Globo network, and a Bahia TV station owned by the family of Magalhães became a part of Globo television.

Brazilian law has limited Marinho's ability to influence direct elections (in which candidates are chosen by the public at large rather than the Congress). When a campaign officially begins, all candidates receive a certain amount of free time on every television channel, and no political advertising is permitted on TV. Therefore, the Globo network has had to confine itself to the slanting of campaign news. Similar restrictions do not apply to newspapers and magazines.

In his home state of Rio de Janeiro, Roberto Marinho has been notoriously unsuccessful in imposing his will on the electorate. Veteran populist Leonel Brizola has twice won the governorship despite the intransigent opposition of *O Globo*, Marinho's daily paper, and the Globo network, which generally treats Brizola as a nonperson. Brizola, on his part, has found political capital in attacking Marinho, and has inspired crowds of his supporters to chant slogans against the network.

Marinho has had more luck on the national level. In the 1989 presidential campaign, the Globo network was an early and enthusiastic supporter of Fernando Collor de Mello, who began the contest as a little known but highly photogenic politician from the northeastern state of Alagoas. As Collor's luck would have it, Marinho had once made some real-estate deals with his father, and, better yet, Collor's family happened to own an Alagoan TV station affiliated with the Globo network.

Globo's favorable coverage helped Collor pull away from the pack in the first round of voting. During the runoff between Collor and Luís Inácio (Lula) da Silva, the Globo network did little to hide its bias in favor of Collor. On the crucial night before the final vote, Globo edited footage of a Collor-Lula debate to eliminate the strongest points made by Lula, as well as a gaffe committed by Collor. This was done per the explicit instructions of Roberto Marinho, who circumvented TV Globo's news director. (The news director resigned shortly afterward, but his assistant, who had done the actual editing, was later rewarded, first by the new Collor administration, which gave him exclusive interviews and information, and later by Marinho, who put him in charge of Globo's news division.)

The influence of Roberto Marinho and his Globo network may be measured in cultural as well as political terms. Globo programming reaches almost every town in Brazil. It has shaped the way Portuguese is spoken throughout the country, the way people dress, and the way people behave. In so doing, it has diminished regional differences. Some would say it is homogenizing Brazil.

A scene from the film *Bye, Bye, Brazil* captures this phenomenon superbly. As a tent-show caravan pulls into a small town in Amazônia, its loudspeaker proclaims the arrival of the troupe, a ploy that normally fills the streets, but this time there is no reaction. The streets remain empty. The owner of the show notices TV antennas on the rooftops ("fishbones," he calls them), and ruefully realizes he is no match for this kind of competition.

By 1987 Roberto Marinho began to appear on the list of the world's billionaires published by *Forbes* magazine. His TV network embraced 54 affiliated stations, employed more than seven-thousand people, and exported programs to 128 countries on five continents. He also owned an 80 percent interest in the European Italian-language network Telemontecarlo. His radio network included 16 AM/FM and 4 short-wave broadcasting stations. Globo was also producing records and videotapes. Its publishing house was churning out 45 different magazines and nearly 200 books a year. *O Globo* continued to be one of the country's most influential newspapers. The family fortune also included finance companies, cattle ranches, and shopping centers.

The creation of the Roberto Marinho Foundation in 1977 provided vivid evidence of Marinho's ability to borrow North American models. His rival Assis Chateaubriand had been an avid collector of paintings and had been instrumental in developing and stocking the São Paulo Museum of Art. While Chateaubriand's philanthropic initiatives had mirrored those of certain North American multimillionaires earlier in this century, Marinho took a more modern, pragmatic approach and opted to channel his major charitable activity through a foundation that would bear his name.

The Roberto Marinho Foundation has as its goal the promotion of education, culture, and sports at the community level. It uses telecommunications as well as other media to foster social development and to improve the quality of life for Brazilians. Rede Globo gives more than ample publicity to the work of the foundation.

Roberto Marinho has never been afflicted by an excess of modesty. Indeed, in some respects *O Globo* is his own "vanity press." The newspaper always refers to him as "Journalist Roberto Marinho," or "our comrade," as if he were just one of the boys. When Marinho writes a major piece or receives an honor, members of Brazil's political and economic establishment dutifully send him letters of congratulations, which *O Globo* then reprints in full.*

Marinho sired four male offspring by his first wife. All bear the name Roberto. Roberto Irineu, João Roberto, and José Roberto work for the Globo empire. Paulo Roberto died in an auto accident in 1969. In 1989 Marinho divorced his second wife and wed a wealthy widow prominent in Rio de Janeiro's high society.

Like many other entrepreneurial success stories in Brazil, the Globo empire is to a considerable degree the work of one extraordinary individual. However, this achievement has been so overwhelming that it has resulted in the creation of a near monopoly in an area where it would be in the public interest for there to be vigorous competition producing a diversity of perspec-

---

* In 1993 Marinho's prose gained him entry into the Brazilian Academy of Letters, a group of forty intellectuals who call themselves The Immortals and meet once a week for tea and discussion in an ornate building in downtown Rio. They have their own mausoleum and fill vacancies in their ranks with elections that have the trappings of the selection process for an elite club. They take themselves very seriously, and on ceremonial occasions they don uniforms with plumes, sashes, and fancy buttons.

tives. In other words, Rede Globo has been too good for the good of Brazil.

The authority wielded by Roberto Marinho puts at risk the functioning of democracy in Brazil. He has been very straightforward in admitting that he calls the shots for his TV network and his newspaper. "Yes, I use this power," he once told a *New York Times* interviewer, "but I always do so patriotically, trying to correct things, looking for the best paths for the country and its states." The problem is that not everyone in Brazil has the same conception of patriotism and the national interest that Roberto Marinho does, but unlike everyone else, Roberto Marinho can make his views known to the nation whenever he pleases on the Globo network.

One solution to the problems created by Globo's hegemony is to bring in competition. To a certain degree this is beginning to happen. Sílvio Santos, the one-time Rio street vendor who put together the SBT, or Sistema Brasileiro de Televisão (Brazilian TV System), has seen his network grow steadily until it is now second only to the Globo network. The host of a Sunday variety show that features hour after hour of games, giveaways, interviews, and specialty acts, Santos has built up an enormous following among Brazil's lower classes. The son of a Turkish-born mother and a Greek father (his real name is Senor Abravanel), Santos reaches an estimated audience of thirty million with a program awash in bad taste and triviality. Indeed, Globo and the other networks have virtually abandoned Sundays to him.

A shrewd businessman, Santos has set SBT's sights beyond Sundays and now competes vigorously with Globo by televising high-quality foreign films, shows, and *telenovelas*. SBT has also upgraded its news division. But whether it can prevail against Globo's headstart and economic muscle remains to be seen.

Another threat to Globo is the mortality of Roberto Marinho. As has happened with the Chateaubriand empire and with many other large enterprises that are monuments to the genius of an individual, the disappearance of the founding father very often results in the eventual collapse of the business. This is because the founder, while alive, monopolizes power and prestige, symbolizes the enterprise, and holds it together. Roberto Marinho, like Chateaubriand before him, totally dominates his conglomerate. His three sons hold high positions within the organization, but they remain in their father's shadow. Thus, despite its modern trappings, Globo possesses a Brazilian characteristic that may over the long run be a cause of its unraveling.

# Chapter 7

# The Have-Nots

*I*f there is one sight that succinctly captures the stark contrast between the Brazil of the haves and the Brazil of the have-nots, it is the view from the roof of the Hotel Nacional in São Conrado, a seaside nook hemmed in on three sides by dramatic hills that isolate it from the rest of Rio de Janeiro.

Along the beachfront, near the ultramodern glass cylinder that is the hotel, deluxe apartment buildings fringed by tennis courts, swimming pools, and a golf course provide a backdrop for daredevils on hang gliders as they swoop earthward from nearby peaks and drift gently to earth on the glistening sand.

Yet if one gazes inland, toward the north and slightly to the east, a different reality intrudes. The shacks of Rocinha, which perhaps as many as three hundred thousand Brazilians call home, spill down the side of the rocky barrier that separates São Conrado from the chic neighborhood of Gávea, and come to a halt at the edge of the highway that emerges from the nearby tunnel that provides swift and direct access to the rest of Rio de Janeiro.

Rocinha and São Conrado are two distinct worlds. The inhabitants of both may speak the same language and occasionally mingle on the beach or on the streets near the Hotel Nacional. They may even root for the same soccer team and watch the same programs on television. But the apartment dwellers of São Conrado enjoy privileges of wealth and social status that permit them to live comfortably behind secure walls and fences, and to enjoy access to decent sanitation, health care, and education. They would never dream of venturing across the highway into the sprawling slum that stares them in the face. They would never risk the steep climb to Rocinha's crest, from which they might contemplate the wall of luxury high-rises that block what would otherwise be a magnificent view of the sea.

If they did, they would encounter a community of survivors, some clinging stubbornly to traditional values and striving to lead honest, decent lives, others accepting their status as social outcasts and engaging in various forms of extralegal or illegal activity, all of them trapped in a society that makes upward mobility a Sisyphean struggle, and in an environment hardly suitable for human habitation.

Rocinha dates back to the 1920s and the founding of a modest settlement near some small farms in forest clearings at the foot of the hill, next to a road that wound its way upward, over the crest, and then down to Gávea. Only in the 1950s, when migrants from the drought-stricken Northeast sought living space reasonably close to the city and began to pour into the area, did Rocinha become a *favela*, or "shantytown," one of countless such settlements in and around Rio de Janeiro.

The migrants invaded unused land, first at the base of the hill and then on its slopes. The homes they initially erected were transient structures of wood, cardboard, and metal, materials easy to dismantle and move in the event the authorities decided to terminate the illegal occupation. Everything was improvised in helter-skelter fashion, with no thought given to consequences. Rocinha just grew . . . and grew . . . and grew.

Today Rocinha represents the classic Rio hillside *favela*, unusual only because of its enormity. The lowest part of the neighborhood is the most developed, having been settled first and having benefited from improvements such as the installation of a system of running water. Once the municipality made these investments in the community, residents could be certain that city hall would not summarily remove them, so they made renovations of their own, and concrete structures with solid foundations began to replace jerry-built shacks. Indeed, a few owners have added upper floors, on some buildings as many as seven, which they rent out to tenants.

At the bottom of Rocinha there are stores, bars, pharmacies, a bank, several churches, and community centers, alive in a loud buzz of ceaseless activity. Commercial enterprises serving the needs of the residents are for the most part informal, in the sense that the power of the government does not reach them. For example, next to a technical school stands a butcher shop, where the proprietor keeps pigs in pens on the roof and slaughters them on the premises, without concern that health inspectors might one day darken his doorway.

Vehicular traffic can transit the narrow streets at the bottom of the *favela*, but only foot traffic can ascend the hill, up a labyrinth of narrow passageways that flank sewage flows. The presence of chickens, pigs, dogs, and cats intensifies the stench. The houses are so close together that certain corridors remain in dark shade for most of the day. It is easy to understand why the police seldom venture beyond the lower reaches of Rocinha, and why firemen could never bring in equipment to fight a blaze.

The higher the elevation, the more dilapidated the dwellings are, a testament to the difficulties of the climb and the lack of access to public utilities. The air drafts at the top of the hill make it a perfect spot for kite flying, a major diversion for Rocinha's children (and a method criminal elements customarily use to signal the commencement of police activity in the *favela*).

Life in slums like Rocinha is an exercise in social Darwinism. Health hazards are as varied as the tropical vegetation, and include assorted diseases caused by excessive humidity, deficiencies in nutrition, vermin bites, and a lack of elementary sanitation. The high density of the population and the fact that large family groups often live together in a single room facilitate the spread of many of these illnesses. Because most residents need to work long hours at menial jobs that don't pay a living wage, they seldom have the time to seek proper medical attention or money enough to purchase medicine.

Moreover, when slumdwellers seek medical treatment, they confront a public-health system mired in a perpetual state of chaos. Clinics and hospitals that attend the urban poor are overcrowded, understaffed, badly equipped, and poorly maintained. They often provide indifferent care and more than occasionally subject patients to additional risks, such as infection from contaminated blood. The situation in the countryside is even worse.

Another peril faced by *favela*-dwellers is the flooding that occurs during the heavy rains that often lash Rio de Janeiro. The narrow walkways become conduits for streaming water, sometimes several feet deep, which gathers garbage and other debris in a wild downward plunge. Frantic mothers snatch up their children, who could easily be swept away by the raging streams, and take shelter in their homes. But the shacks on Rio's hills have no foundations, so the danger that they might wash away, or that neighboring structures might topple down on them, remains constant. Every hillside *favela*, including Rocinha, has experienced this sort of disaster on various occasions.

The physical risks associated with crime are also an integral part of contemporary life in the slums. This is a relatively recent development, as gangs involved in drug trafficking have put down roots in Rio's *favelas* during the past decade (a phenomenon explored more fully in Chapter Nine). When two or more such groups vie for control of an area, bullets fly and the death toll rises. Upon eliminating its competition, a gang will often guarantee the security of *favela* inhabitants, except during raids by the police, who often generate considerable random violence of their own.

A unique feature of Rio's slums is that many of them nestle near the downtown or the beaches. This location provides residents with service jobs easy access to a source of employment. But many other *favelados* (*favela*-dwellers) must live in settlements far from the center of the city and its industrial parks, so they must rely on public transportation to reach their places of employment, commuting on overcrowded trains or buses for one or two hours each way. The rail system has become so dilapidated that it is undependable and occasionally unsafe. The poor people forced to use it risk accidents and long delays, which can cost them work time.

As if physical hazards did not sufficiently test their mettle, *favela*-dwellers must also endure being held in contempt by many of their more fortunate compatriots. The class bias that pervades Brazilian society oppresses the poor in infinite ways, subtle as well as crass. Whenever they venture out of their slum and have to deal with their social superiors—such as doctors in health clinics, teachers in public schools, bureaucrats in government offices, or upper- or middle-class families for whom they work as servants—they risk experiencing some form of degradation that reinforces their sense of inferiority.

Rocinha provides one of the most visible symbols of the poor circumstances in which a majority of Brazil's city dwellers now find themselves. The problems faced by inhabitants of urban slums everywhere have many similarities, although the topographies of the slum areas (and the words used to denominate them) may differ from region to region. Thus, in Rio de Janeiro and its environs poor people live in clusters of shanties known as *favelas*. These bidonvilles may peer down on scenic neighborhoods such as São Conrado, Ipanema, or Copacabana, or on elegant mansions tucked away in a fashionable corner of Botofogo; they may cover the grimy hills of the north side of the city; or they may extend to the horizon on the steamy flatlands of the Fluminense Lowlands, a desolate area once rendered uninhabitable by malaria and yellow fever.

In São Paulo the poor live in enormous ghettoes that form the city's periphery—neighborhoods like Vila Brasilândia, on the hilly northern edge, where a pollution-laden haze obscures the view of distant office buildings and apartments (although their lights are visible at night)—or in shabby, overcrowded tenements called *cortiços* (beehives) near the center of town.

The shanties (or *mucambos*) of Recife form neighborhoods like Nova Descoberta, on a clay hill where residents can escape the misery that surrounds them by looking out on the placid waters of the Atlantic. Those even less fortunate inhabit smaller clusters of *mucambos* perched on stilts over riverbanks. There they can participate in what nutritionist Josué de Castro once dubbed the "crab cycle," by feeding on crabs that have fed on human excrement. "And with this meat, made out of mud," de Castro wrote, "they build the flesh of their bodies and the flesh of their children's bodies. . . . What their bodies throw off is returned to the mud, to be made into crabmeat again."

In Salvador squatters have invaded valleys in a hilly area on the edge of town. Here, in a settlement pattern quite the opposite of what has occurred in Rio de Janeiro, the poor set up their shacks in gullies, with no view of the nearby bay and no access to its cooling breezes. The force of gravity makes garbage removal from these inhabited pits virtually impossible, much to the delight of the local rodent population.

Other big cities, such as Fortaleza, Manaus, Belém, Belo Horizonte, Curitiba, and Porto Alegre have their own extended patches of poverty. Even in the Federal District, where Brasília stands as a monument to Brazil's faith in the future, desolate slums form a satellite ring far enough removed from the carefully planned metropolis that they cannot be seen by the naked eye, but close enough to cast an invisible pall on the sleek capital.

As bad as conditions may be in these urban hellholes, one must keep in mind that many of the people inhabiting them migrated to the cities to escape even worse conditions in the countryside. In the vast reaches of the interior of Brazil, wherever people live off the land, peasants survive as they always have, despite often abysmal poverty.

Simplistic explanations often mislead, but a persuasive case can be made that the root cause of rural destitution in contemporary Brazil is woefully inequitable land distribution, a phenomenon that dates back to the colonial era. When the Portuguese Crown opted for the system of captaincies, a few privileged settlers gained control of enormous expanses of territory. Like the venereal diseases introduced among the native population by the European invaders, this pattern of land tenure spread rapidly throughout the colony. It led to the creation of large sugar plantations in the coastal areas and even larger cattle ranches in the interior.

The ensuing concentration of property ownership fueled a demand for cheap labor, a need satisfied by the importation of African slaves on a grand scale. The net result was the emergence of a society based on an ethos of exploitation and rigid distinctions, first between masters and slaves, and then between rich and poor.

The abolition of slavery brought about only nominal changes. In Brazil's immense countryside the relationship between landowners and a multitudinous peasantry composed of ex-slaves and the descendants of slaves remained feudal in almost every respect. Peasants were totally dependent on and submissive to the rural upper class. Their mind-set remained passive and fatalistic, qualities fortified by traditional Roman Catholic doctrine, which taught acceptance of one's lot in life on earth as a means of gaining eternal salvation.

Rural wage earners received meager salaries and were often trapped in debt peonage because they were forced to purchase necessities on credit at plantation stores that charged exorbitant prices. Living conditions were often primitive, although in much of the country the abundance of tropical vegetation provided some sustenance and helped the poor to survive. Opportunities for even rudimentary education bordered on the nonexistent.

Some peasants were able to rent small plots of land. They paid the owner in cash or crops (or by working several days a week without pay for the landowner). Theirs was an insecure existence, inasmuch as the landlord could expel them whenever he pleased. In some of the more backward areas, the landlord could also force his sexual attentions on laborers' wives and daughters whenever he pleased, and with impunity.

Peasants who journeyed into the vast interior of Brazil and settled on unoccupied land experienced a host of legal and bureaucratic difficulties when they attempted to establish ownership. Neither the Portuguese Crown nor the Brazilian imperial regime took effective steps to encourage the development of a class of small farmers in the vast interior of the country, and the republican governments that followed continued to neglect this possibility. Wealthy individuals with political connections could easily manipulate the judicial system and assert claims backed up by the police or by their own private gunmen. Lower-class settlers had scant hope of prevailing in these unequal contests.

In the middle of the twentieth century, Brazil remained what it had always been, a primarily rural society in which the great majority of those who lived in the countryside were ill-housed, ill-fed, illiterate, disease-ridden, and underproductive. Farming was labor intensive, which made it profitable for landowners because they were able to continue paying starvation wages. This kept workers at a great disadvantage, for their paltry share of the owner's earnings from agricultural production had to feed many mouths.

Family units could survive only by spawning enough children to work in the fields and otherwise contribute to the income of the household. The economic need for large families, along with an ignorance of birth-control methods (and the opposition of the Roman Catholic Church to all forms of contraception), led to a high birth rate. Although a high rate of infant mortality tempered population growth to a certain degree, rural areas often suffered from the presence of too many poor people.

As long as Brazil's peasants had no voice and no political representatives, there was no possibility of reform in the economic and social structure of the countryside. The political arena was hardly a level playing field. Under the Constitution of the first republic, illiterates were not permitted to vote. Rural workers and sharecroppers who could meet the legal qualifications for suffrage traditionally obeyed the dictates of their employers or landlords when they went to the polls.

It was not until the termination of the dictatorship of Getúlio Vargas in 1945 that the breezes of change began to reach the peasantry. The Communist party, newly (but only temporarily) legalized, made some tentative efforts to organize farm laborers. Nothing changed, however, until the late 1950s and early 1960s, with the formation of peasant leagues and rural unions in the Northeast and elsewhere.

The organizers were a diverse lot—card-carrying Communists and miscellaneous Marxists, intellectuals and students, Catholic priests and laity—often in vigorous competition with one another but united both in their judgment that the deplorable conditions in the countryside were symbolic of Brazil's backwardness, and in their call for a radical change in the landowning system. Inspired by the Cuban Revolution, they raised the banner of agrarian reform, although they differed on specifics. The Constitution presented serious obstacles to any redistribution of privately owned land, so it was abundantly clear that without a political transformation there could be no social or economic restructuring in rural Brazil.

The military refused to countenance any such serious threat to the established order, so on March 31, 1964, the army seized power and put an emphatic end to all agitation in the countryside.

Union leaders as well as peasants were arrested and occasionally tortured. The nascent rural labor movement was reduced to shambles.

The new president, Army Marshall Humberto Castelo Branco, was a *nordestino* by birth. He understood the realities of life in the interior and had no particular brief for the landowning elite. One of the first initiatives of his regime was the promulgation of a new land law that aimed to bring about a more evenhanded distribution of land by facilitating the expropriation of unused and underused properties.

But political interference by large landowners, bureaucratic inertia, and the government's failure to allocate sufficient funds for the implementation of an extensive land reform conspired to stall the initative. In addition, those who stood to benefit from such a program could not support it in any organized way because the military continued to repress those who spoke up on behalf of Brazil's have-nots. As a result, the inequitable pattern of land tenure in the countryside remained intact.

Indeed, while paying lip service to the need for agrarian reform, the military regime adopted policies that actually upped the numbers of landless peasants. By emphasizing increased productivity in the agricultural sector, and by subsidizing the manufacture of alcohol fuel from sugarcane in response to the worldwide oil crisis, the government encouraged the use of labor-saving modern technology, which in turn cast more peasants off the land.

Many of those who remained in the countryside became itinerant laborers (*bóias-frias*, or "cold lunches"), living in temporary shacks on the outskirts of villages and waiting for wage contractors to hire them to work a harvest. Whole families formed part of a new rural proletariat, wandering about from place to place, often earning less than the minimum wage (itself an illusory standard, since it generally takes three minimum wages to provide a livable income).

Some *bóias-frias* joined unions that helped them in struggles to enforce wage contracts, which employers often refused to honor, and labor conflicts ensued. But the fact that these workers were constantly crossing state lines made it difficult to organize them into unions based in a single state, and Brazilian law did not permit the formation of interstate syndicates.

In more remote areas of central Brazil and Amazônia rural workers continued to risk falling into the trap of debt peonage. Their salaries, often well below the legal minimum wage, did not cover what they were said to owe their employer for transportation, lodging, and the purchase of food and other necessities, and armed guards prevented them from escaping. A report issued by Americas Watch, a human-rights group, documented a number of cases of forced labor occurring as recently as 1989 and 1990.

Gains in agricultural production served to boost shipments of farm products abroad, so that by the beginning of the 1980s Brazil had become the fourth largest food exporter in the world. But at the same time the country was failing to feed its own people and had reached sixth place on malnutrition indices, behind only India, Bangladesh, Pakistan, the Philippines, and Indonesia.

There was another development that made the sorry plight of many peasants even more desperate. From 1979 to 1983 a severe drought, yet another in a regular, deadly cycle that has been a part of life in the region ever since the first settlers penetrated the area, ravaged the heavily populated interior of the Northeast. It not only forced hordes of peasants to migrate elsewhere but also inflicted untold hardship on those who remained. The catastrophe forced Brazilians once again to direct their attention to a neglected region that has long been a metaphor for their country's backwardness.

To tell the story of Brazil's have-nots without including a description of Northeast Brazil would be like the clichéd staging of *Hamlet* without the Prince of Denmark. If it were an independent country, the Northeast would be the third largest and second most populous nation in South America. In 1955 the number of inhabitants in the region was nearly twenty million. By 1970 it passed the thirty million mark, and in 1990 it exceeded forty-two million. A majority of *nordestinos* live in abject poverty. Indeed, the area contains the largest concentration of wretchedness, both rural and urban, to be found anywhere in the Western Hemisphere.

Occupying the easternmost bulge of the continent, Northeast Brazil extends westward to the tropical forests of the Amazon basin and southward well into the remote central highlands. It embraces a number of coastal cities, including Recife and Fortaleza; a humid strip of sugarcane fields not far from the coast; a hilly and subtropical zone (known as the *agreste*) further inland; and, last but hardly least, the *sertão*, immense, arid backlands covered with prickly, stunted trees and brush the Indians called *caatinga*, or the "white forest."

Originally explored by adventurers looking for precious metals, the *sertão* soon attracted a tough breed of permanent settlers, including runaway and freed slaves. They were hardy souls, willing to confront hostile Indians and endure an inhospitable clime. They had to live with a pattern of landholding that was no different there than elsewhere, with a few wealthy families owning large cattle ranches and riverbank cotton plantations. In addition, these backlanders (called *sertanejos*) had to endure the unique curse of the northeastern interior, cyclical droughts that devastate the region on an average of about once every decade, and sudden, heavy rainstorms that cause widespread flooding and soil erosion.

Some of the extended dry spells took horrendous tolls. One of the first struck in 1692 and killed most of the cattle in the Northeast. One third of the population of the state of Pernambuco died in the drought of 1790–93. In the great drought of 1877–79, it is estimated that half of the people in the state of Ceará perished.

Despite the massive out-migrations provoked by these periodic natural disasters, the population of the *sertão* has remained surprisingly dense. *Sertanejos* tend to be hardworking, honest, primitively religious, suspicious of outsiders, and given to anachronistic speech patterns. They identify so strongly with their environment that many of them stolidly endure whatever tribulations nature imposes on them. If they are forced to emigrate, they never forget where they came from, and they will often return home upon hearing news of rainfall in the *sertão*.

The interior of the Northeast has produced a remarkably singular culture, marked by religious fanaticism, banditry, blood feuds, folk traditions, music, and a hierarchical social structure dominated by local landowners (the *coroneis*, or "colonels") who are a law unto themselves. Brazilians from other parts of the country tend to look on the unique aspects of life in this region with considerable awe, and often through eyes glazed by romanticism and feelings of guilt.

The saga of Antônio Conselheiro, for example, remains firmly fixed in the national consciousness. This backlands prophet, with his long hair, flowing beard, tattered blue robe, and hypnotic stare, provoked tens of thousands of humble *sertanejos* to rise up in a bloody and ultimately unsuccessful rebellion against the national government at the end of the nineteenth century. (He is discussed further in Chapters Nine and Thirteen.)

The long tradition of banditry in the *sertão* is best exemplified by the adventures of Lampeão, the bespectacled leader of a gang of outlaws who defied local, state, and even federal authorities as they roamed the interior during the 1930s. They clad themselves in distinctive leather outfits and acquired a reputation roughly equivalent to that of Robin Hood and his band.

These cultural phenomena have inspired creative works that have enjoyed national success and have further perpetuated the mystique of the Northeast. Graciliano Ramos's novel, *Vidas Sêcas (Barren Lives)*, captures brilliantly the anguish of *sertanejos* in the grip of a drought. Ariano Suassuna, in his *Auto de Compadecida (The Compassionate Virgin's Play)*, brings to life the earthy wisdom and ingenuity of the backlander. The life and times of Lampeão have provided the grist for a number of popular films. Both bandits and prophets provided the inspiration for Glauber Rocha's *cinema novo* (new cinema) classics *Deus e o Diabo na Terra do Sol (Black God, White Devil)* and *Antônio das Mortes*.

Droughts in the Northeast traditionally provoke out-migrations of what are popularly referred to as *flagelados*, or the scourged ones, to other parts of Brazil. During the 1877–79 catastrophe, *flagelados* journeyed by boat to the Amazon basin, where they became rubber tappers. A serious dry spell in 1958 encouraged a flow of refugees to the central plains, where they helped build the new capital, Brasília.

The 1877–79 drought produced for the first time a response on the part of the government that would become a tradition: the solemn promise of help. Dom Pedro II declared he would sell all the crown jewels if that was what it would take to put an end to the suffering. (He never did.) Subsequent droughts produced similar pronouncements, but there have been no substantial inroads made on either the human suffering or its causes.

The federal government's usual response was to set up a program of public works in the *sertão* to combat the effects of drought. Reservoirs would be constructed to facilitate irrigation, but landowners would use their political muscle to have these projects located not on the basis of rational, equitable planning but rather in a way that promoted their own immediate enrichment. Little benefit ever reached the peasants who worked on the newly irrigated soil, and their marginal existence remained unchanged.

Poverty in the Northeast extends beyond the backlands and into the overpopulated coastal areas where sugarcane is grown. Called the *zona da mata* or "wooded zone" (after a forest that vanished long ago), this subregion is home to an industry that has been in a state of crisis since the mid-seventeenth century, when the Dutch, having been expelled from their foothold in northeastern Brazil, exacted revenge by creating their own sugar industry in the New World colonies that they managed to retain.

Economic and political power in the Northeast has always been concentrated with those who controlled sugar production. At first the plantation owners held sway. Later, as new technologies permitted the construction of large sugar refineries, the mill owners attained a position of dominance.

To produce sugarcane and operate the mills, both groups relied on slave labor, and, after abolition, a surfeit of available cheap labor. The wages mill owners paid remained minimal and failed to keep up with rising food prices. Until well into the twentieth century, there were no legal protections, such as minimum-wage laws, to which rural workers could resort. Theirs was a wretched lot, made bearable only by the comfort provided by *cachaça*, a strong alcoholic drink made from sugarcane.

The mill owners, on the other hand, lived lives of conspicuous consumption and did not reinvest their profits. As a result, sugar production in the Northeast remained remarkably inefficient and could not compete on even terms with other sugar growing and refining operations either in Caribbean countries like Cuba or in the state of São Paulo.

The northeastern producers resorted to using their political influence to persuade the state and federal governments to subsidize
them. At times they would employ a crude form of blackmail, arguing that if they did not receive help, they would have to shut
down and thousands of peasants would starve to death. Of course,
when financial assistance was forthcoming, almost none of it trickled down to the peasants, who remained in a state of semistarvation.

Hard times in the *sertão* and in the sugar zone inevitably forced
peasants to out-migrate, and the major pole of attraction for them
was Recife, the capital of the state of Pernambuco, one of the oldest, most attractive, and largest cities in the country.

The modern history of the most important urban center in the
region dates back to the seizure of the Northeast by the Dutch in
the seventeenth century. Instead of occupying Olinda, the capital
of the captaincy of Pernambuco, the invaders installed themselves
in Recife, a fishing village that took its name from a protective reef
just offshore. They then set about modernizing the hamlet in a systematic way—the first effort at city planning in the hemisphere.
The Dutch built the continent's first astronomical observatory and
its first zoo in Recife, erected several palaces, and encouraged the
work of scientists as well as painters. But before they could finish
carrying out their plans to transform the village, they were expelled
from the Northeast.

Recife still managed to grow into a proud regional capital (the
"Brazilian Venice," as some have called it, because of its location at
the confluence of three rivers that flow into the Atlantic), boasting
busy docks, Brazil's oldest newspaper, a fine university, and a vigorous intellectual life. Its proximity to Europe, North America, and
Africa made it an important port of call for shipping, and later a
point of departure for international flights.

But Recife could never escape its debt to the have-nots of the
region. The blood and toil of the peasants made possible the wealth
that allowed plantation and mill owners to lead elegant lives in
Recife, but eventually the have-nots themselves migrated to the
city, especially during droughts or economic downturns. The 1950s
were especially tough years for *sertanejos* and workers in the sugar
zone. Recife, which had always had its share of poverty, found itself overwhelmed by the influx.

It was not just the slums, the unemployment, the hunger, and the sickness that gave Recife its new nickname as the "Calcutta of the Western Hemisphere" (or, as one poet aptly described it, "a vast well of the suffocated"); the city came to develop a distinctive kind of wretchedness not found anywhere else in Brazil.

Perhaps the most dramatic aspect of Recife in the 1950s and 1960s was its infestation of beggars who pawed and tugged prospective donors in the busy downtown district. Their bodies were often grotesquely misshapen, as if by some mad practitioner of the plastic arts, far more ghoulish than anything that has come from the imagination of Hollywood horror-film directors. The forms their bodies assumed could suggest all kinds of images: the Question Mark, with his curved spine; the Number Four, with one leg permanently twisted over the other; the Frog, a woman whose trunk was folded against her thighs, keeping her close to the ground as she hopped from place to place; the Snake, a man with no nose and twisted limbs slithering sideways along the sidewalk; and, worst of all, the Lump, a human blob with flippers, perched on a wheelchair on the Maurício Nassau Bridge, grunting at passers-by.

Another distinctive feature of Recife was the widespread prostitution that catered not only to domestic needs but also to the appetites of the many sailors, both Brazilian and foreign, who looked forward to shore leave in Recife. Reliable numbers are difficult to come by, but in 1961 a French monk who researched the subject extensively estimated that there were some thirty thousand practitioners of the world's oldest profession in Recife. He calculated that 20 percent of them worked at it full-time; while the rest held regular jobs in bars and restaurants (or even were employed as maids in private homes). There were stories that organized rings were luring young girls from the countryside to the city with false promises of respectable jobs, and then forcing them into prostitution.

Creating the sort of contrast one often finds in Brazil, Recife's main *zona*, or red-light district, was located in the business district, not far from the docks, where banks and other commercial enterprises plied their trades by day, and where noisy bars and brothels installed above or next to them served swarms of patrons by night.

The government eventually closed the downtown *zona* when it expanded to the point where it could not easily be controlled.

The drought of the late 1950s combined with depressed economic conditions in the sugar-growing regions to create, for the first time, serious signs of unrest among rural workers and tenant farmers, and the formation of peasant leagues, which evolved from modest mutual-assistance societies to politicized groups advocating radical agrarian reform. Although they were never a real threat to the power structure of the region, they contributed to the social ferment that caused the Brazilian military to stage their 1964 coup.

The have-nots of the Northeast continued to suffer under the new regime. Although attempts were made to use tax incentives to encourage the creation of new industries in the region, the factories that were constructed tended to be capital- rather than labor-intensive, and did not make much of a dent in the unemployment problem. Moreover, the land-reform policies adopted by the generals neither redistributed property to any significant degree nor increased agricultural productivity in the region.

The dry cycles seemed to come more frequently, and in 1979 the Northeast suffered one of its worst droughts ever, an unmitigated disaster that lasted four years and adversely affected the lives of 10 million people. No one knows for certain how many died. (Estimates range from 250,000 to well over a million.) The capacities of Recife, Fortaleza, and other coastal cities strained to the breaking point with the arrival of hordes of desperate *flagelados.* Food riots in interior towns were not uncommon, and one heard stories of starving backlanders eating rats to survive.

In 1990 another extended dry spell began to spread throughout the Northeast, and by 1993 it was afflicting more than 50 percent of the region. Although not so serious as the previous drought, it generated the same kinds of horror stories. Starving farmers occupied government offices in Recife, and the federal government solemnly issued statements about doing something about the problem.

Of the human toll exacted by poverty in the Northeast, the long-term effects of malnutrition in the region are perhaps the most gripping. Deficiencies in daily food consumption in the region have been documented over an extended period of time. A 1957 study by the United Nations Food and Agriculture Organization revealed that the average daily food intake in the Northeast was only 1,990 calories, considerably below the recommended minimum requirement of 2,500. A 1967 investigation in the southern part of Pernambuco's sugar zone uncovered the fact that peasants there were consuming only 1,299 calories per day. A 1983 report by a Brazilian government agency calculated at 1,713 the average daily consumption of calories in the Northeast. A 1983 study by the Institute of Nutrition of the Federal University of Pernambuco found that about 70 percent of families living in the *sertão* consumed less than half the vitamin A the human body requires.

A United States government task force in 1963 demonstrated one result of the chronic underconsumption of nutrients in the region: The body weights of Northeastern boys and girls were 10 percent lower than the standard heights and weights for American children of the same age group. Men and women above forty-five years of age in the Northeast showed a steady decline in body weight. The tendency in the United States is the opposite.

Dr. Nelson Chaves, a Brazilian professor, has written, "The population of the Northeast is of low stature, anemic, and, in the sugar zone, is on the way to dwarfism." A UNICEF study tends to confirm this. It estimates that in the Northeast as many as 3.5 million children may be affected by stunted growth.

Another affliction related to hunger is mental debility, which can result from the undernourishment of children in their first year. A study of infants in the sugar zone disclosed that only 4.4 percent received milk from their mothers after they passed the age of six months. The most common reason was simply that the mother had no milk for breast-feeding. Once deprived of this source of nourishment, these infants were fed a diet seriously lacking in vitamins and proteins. These deficiencies, in turn, produce fatigue, nervousness, a limited attention span, inadequate muscular development, and possible mental retardation.

The infant mortality rate in the Northeast has always been high, especially for the first year of life. In her study of this phenomenon, Professor Nancy Scheper-Hughes has documented its impact on mothers in a town in the sugar zone of Pernambuco, where the average woman endures 9.5 pregnancies, 3.5 child deaths, and 1.5 stillbirths.

Children born weak, sick, and unlikely to survive are left alone, a Darwinistic practice mothers justify on the ground that these babies "want to die." When nature takes its course, deaths are accepted with stoicism and without the shedding of tears. One anthropologist has called this "passive infanticide."

"In a society where triplicates of every form are required for the most banal events," Scheper-Hughes writes, "the registration of infant and child death is informal, incomplete, and rapid." Neighborhood children carry the body to the cemetery, where it is buried in an anonymous grave and quickly forgotten.

On one level, mothers are merely replicating the indifference of their government, which has traditionally left the poor to their own devices, and of the Catholic Church, which has traditionally preached the virtue of patient acceptance of God's will, and which continues to oppose all forms of contraception. Yet there is something sublimely tragic about circumstances that force women to sublimate or suppress maternal love and condition them to shut themselves off from grief.*

The recurring images of wretchedness emanating from the Northeast coexist with indicia of the progress the region has made in the last decade and a half. The economy of the region has been consistently outperforming that of the country as a whole by about 10 percent. There has been a remarkable expansion of industry in the Northeast. Irrigation has permitted once barren land to yield crops for export. A new generation of entrepreneurs has elbowed aside the traditional northeastern sugar-mill and plantation owners, who have retreated to the sidelines and taken with them their white linen suits and autocratic ways. Tourism is flourishing.

Moreover, the face of Recife itself changed dramatically. Gleaming high-rise apartments now stretch for miles along a sandy Atlantic beach, where twenty years ago there were but three tall

---

* This phenomenon does not affect rural women exclusively. In her book *Hillside Women*, Frances O'Gorman tells the story of a Rio slumdweller whose baby died while being taken to a hospital. "To come home by bus," the mother said, "I had to pretend that the baby was alive, because it's against the law to transport a dead person. I couldn't even cry."

buildings. Hotels, restaurants, and shopping centers signal the explosive growth of Boa Viagem, once a sleepy seaside neighborhood on the outskirts of the city.

Yet the signs of progress throughout the Northeast and the new Recife mean only that a considerable degree of economic progress has bettered the condition of the region's haves, who were able to take advantage of the 1969–73 "Brazilian miracle," the tax incentives that facilitated the creation of new industry in the region, and the opportunities Brazilian financial markets provided for investing money. What trickled down to the have-nots was hardly enough to make a meaningful change in the lives of a substantial number of them.

Thus, Recife's once vibrant downtown has been totally abandoned by the upper and middle classes and has become a gigantic bazaar, taken over by *ambulantes* (street vendors), thirty thousand according to one estimate. It is a world of its own, where only the fittest survive. Every conceivable kind of merchandise is peddled, cheaply, without regard to quality, and often on the sidewalk in front of stores that sell the same goods. The *ambulantes* pay no taxes or licensing fees, but they are susceptible to shakedowns by criminal gangs as well as poorly paid policemen and government functionaries. They constantly face the risk of violence at the hands of competitors and thieves.

The labyrinth of narrow streets also provides a setting for *camelôs*, or pitchmen, who use colorful language and seductive sales techniques to peddle wares such as folk medicine (including cures for impotency, an item with special appeal to elderly men). One can encounter other remarkable sights—for example, a whole row of abandoned automobiles that have been converted into workshops for the repair of used products such as electrical goods and watches. And, of course, the usual complement of beggars and homeless people clutter the area.

The plight of the downtown ("our Bedford-Stuyvesant," as one former resident put it) is a visible symbol of the grinding poverty that still afflicts what Ralph Nader once called the "shadow city of Recife." Other aspects include an unemployment rate that may be the highest of any city in the country; the chronic hunger that forces people to pick through the city's garbage dumps in search of food, and to consume popcorn as a stomach-filling staple; the spread of infectious diseases because of the closing of clinics where those with illnesses such as tuberculosis could be interned during their contamination period; the steady deterioration of basic municipal services (that were never adequate to begin with); and a spiraling crime rate attributable in large part to the exigencies of survival.

Those trapped in the web of penury occasionally resort to desperate measures. A local dentist told of a man who obtained some anesthesia from him, to castrate his dog, he said. "The guy kept coming back for more, so I got suspicious and investigated. It turned out he was injecting it into the hands of some of his friends and then hitting their hands with a hammer, so that they could qualify for social-security disability benefits."

Conditions in the *sertão* and the sugar zone produce a steady influx of migrants to the city of Recife. Most of these newcomers make their homes in *mucambos* on the sides of hills or on the banks of a river. In 1989 it was estimated that there were 520 of these settlements within city limits.*

What has happened to Recife and its have-nots may be worse than developments in other major cities, but it is no different in kind. Street vendors, for example, have become pervasive in Rio de Janeiro and São Paulo, where men who had made their way upward into the lower middle class found themselves once again without jobs and back in society's cellar. Urban rot transformed the downtown of Salvador into a depressed area where tourists wander at their peril (although the recent $12 million renovation of the historic center of the city should revitalize the area).

Moreover, city slums formed as a result of the influx of peasants during the past decade and a half share a lack of a sense of community and identity, because immigrants from different parts of the country have problems communicating with one another. This is why immigrants often try to settle with others from their home state.

---

* The names bestowed by slumdwellers on newly formed neighborhoods reflect a surprising degree of awareness of current political and cultural events. They include Iran-Iraq, Skylab II, and the Planet of the Apes.

The picture of Brazil's have-nots is undoubtedly a bleak one, but it is not totally devoid of glimmers of hope. Efforts at self-help are visible in slums throughout the country, suggesting that the poor are abandoning the idea that they must depend on someone in authority to take care of them. They are beginning to struggle collectively to take charge of their own lives, and they are making small but visible improvements in their communities.

In part this progress is owing to the work of grass-roots organizers—middle-class idealists, some connected to the Catholic Church, others committed to helping the poor but cut off from the possibility of engaging in political activity during the military dictatorship. They have turned their energies inward and worked at the grassroots level to help the poor help themselves.

But major credit must go to the participating slumdwellers themselves, since they have assumed positions of leadership in these efforts and have provided the necessary manpower and enthusiasm. The most active participants tend to be women, who are the fiber that holds together both slum families and community initiatives.

The mutual-assistance groups that have mushroomed in urban slums include health clinics, such as one operating in Vila Brasilândia, on the outskirts of São Paulo, where women are trained to teach preventive medicine to other women from the neighborhood; day-care centers, such as an operation in the Rio *favela* of Santa Marta, where youngsters (some of whom are unaccustomed to the light of the sun because their working mothers used to leave them home alone in darkened shacks) are able to play on a rooftop with a glorious view of the Sugar Loaf, Guanabara Bay, and the Rodrigo de Freitas Lagoon; and alternative educational centers, such as the imaginative "Homework Bank" in Rocinha, where schoolchildren have the opportunity to do their daily assignments under supervision and in a reasonably comfortable setting.

In addition to participating in these kinds of specific projects, urban slumdwellers have organized neighborhood associations to deal with matters that require contact with municipal or state authorities. The installation of municipal services, the construction of ramps or funicular carts that permit the removal of garbage from the upper levels of hillside *favelas,* and the improvement of community relations with the police are among the issues that these groups have addressed.

The magnitude of the social and economic morass represented by Brazil's urban slums makes these modest efforts at incremental improvement seem like an exercise in self-delusion. "When I first came here," a foreign priest who worked in Rocinha has observed, "I thought the only solution was to tear everything down and begin again. Now I'm convinced of the opposite: the only solution is to find new forms of urbanization for these poor neighborhoods." In other words, the challenge is to take existing slums as they are, and to channel even more energy, imagination, and public expenditures into the awesome task of bringing them up to a level of decent habitability. The story of Brasília Teimosa suggests that this may not be an impossible task.

During the 1930s, the Brazilian government filled in some land on the northern edge of Boa Viagem, at the mouth of the Jequiá River and facing the Recife waterfront. The original plan was to build an airport, but there was not enough space either for landing strips of the length required by international regulations or for future expansion. Then the land was turned over to the navy, which hoped to build oil-storage facilities, but this project was never realized, and the navy let fishermen establish a colony on what was first called Areal Novo.

In 1958 when a drought in the *sertão* forced tens of thousands of peasants to migrate to Recife, a group of refugees broke through the fence the navy had constructed around the property and erected shacks on the empty land. The police, with help from some of the fishermen, kept expelling the invaders, but the latter refused to acquiesce and kept returning. The occupation became a political issue, as the settlement took the name Brasília Teimosa (Stubborn Brasília), in honor of the new capital under construction in central Brazil and the tenacity of the intruders. Finally the government allowed the migrants to stay and divided the settlement into lots.

Brasília Teimosa became a fetid slum, beyond the purview of travelers along the highway that crossed the Pina Bridge and connected Boa Viagem with the downtown of Recife. Its unpaved streets turned to mud during the rains, and twice a year at the time of the highest tides the shacks nearest the beach would be swept away. By the mid-1960s there were about twenty thousand people living in the settlement.

Despite the hunger, disease, high infant mortality, widespread unemployment, and fear that they might one day be expelled, the residents of Brasília Teimosa maintained their characteristic perseverance. With the help of some Catholic priests they organized and succeeded in convincing the government to install water mains and build a public school. The military regime's crackdown on dissent in 1968 put a damper on the community's efforts to pressure city hall, but only temporarily.

In the mid-1970s rumors that the neighborhood was to be dismantled began to circulate. This time they had some substance. Within a short time the mayor announced a plan to relocate Brasília Teimosa's inhabitants (now numbering thirty thousand), and to build apartment buildings on the site.

The community reacted with demonstrations, which were now possible under the country's more relaxed political climate. City hall was forced to pay heed and announced it would consider any alternative development plans the dissenters could present. The residents' association obtained help from some sympathetic city planners (even Oscar Niemeyer, the architect who designed the original Brasília, contributed to the cause), and "Project Little Teimosa" was born.

The association proposed that residents obtain titles to their homes from the government, that no one could own more than one lot, and that the city rebuild Brasília Teimosa's water-supply system and pave its streets. In 1979 the mayor, well aware that Brazil was back on the road to democracy and wanting to do something for the common people of the city, adopted the plan, and two years later implementation began.

The process was not a smooth one, but during the early 1980s Brasília Teimosa underwent an astonishing transformation. It ceased being a slum and became a tidy, totally urbanized neighborhood, with modest yet sturdy houses instead of temporary shacks. Unemployment remained a problem, but there were enough residents with jobs as drivers, vendors, and domestic servants to create an atmosphere of stability.

Of course the situation of Brasília Teimosa is far from typical. It had an effective residents' association that was in the right place at the right time. The municipal government wanted a pilot community-development project, and Brasília Teimosa provided an ideal site. Nonetheless, the fact that the project succeeded is enough to nourish the possibility that urban Brazil may not have to be on a one-way trip to hopelessness.

# Chapter 8

# Lula and the Workers' Party

## *Who Speaks for the Voiceless?*

*I*n 1989 a bearded ex-metalworker named Lula won thirty-two million votes—47 percent of the total valid ballots cast—in Brazil's first direct presidential election in three decades. Although he lost, the thought that the candidate of the Workers' party had come close to capturing the nation's highest office sent paroxyms into the nerve endings of the elite, which had never before had to confront the possibility of being obliged to relinquish real power to an authentic representative of the country's have-nots.

How Lula became viably presidential is the most recent chapter in the saga of the Brazilian working class, composed of men and women who have provided the muscle behind the country's industrial expansion, faced repression when they first tried to make their voices heard in matters that affected their lives, and, finally, have organized themselves into a force potentially capable of uniting the nation's impoverished majority.

The formation of Brazil's urban working class dates back to the late nineteenth century, when many of the slaves who had won their freedom as a result of service in the war against Paraguay opted to settle in Rio de Janeiro rather than return to the countryside. They occupied some of the hills in the north zone of the city, where they built the first *favelas*.

The flow of Afro-Brazilians into Rio and other urban areas increased at the turn of the century, first because of the abolition of slavery in 1888, and then as a result of the government's decision to encourage immigration from Europe and Japan in response to the demand for labor created by the coffee boom. Instead of using the pool of rural workers made available by emancipation, Brazil's leaders looked abroad to fill the need. (In part this reflected an effort, described in Chapter Two, on the part of the country's rulers to "whiten" its population.) Thus, many ex-slaves had no choice but to migrate to the cities.

A few Afro-Brazilians possessed skills that enabled them to find employment as artisans, but the great majority took menial jobs as laborers or domestic workers. When Brazil began the process of industrialization, members of the native-born lower class in Rio de Janeiro and São Paulo found themselves competing with immigrants who had either entered the country to work on coffee plantations and then made their way to metropolitan areas, or come directly to the cities in search of employment.

By 1920 there were some 275,000 factory workers in Brazil, mostly in small workshops, mostly involved in the production of textiles. About one half of the workforce was located in either Rio de Janeiro or the state of São Paulo. Wages generally remained at or below the subsistence level. Living conditions were appalling, and municipal services lagged far behind the needs of the growing urban population.

The government continued to facilitate immigration, in order to maintain an abundant supply of cheap manpower. The foreign-born elements of Brazil's nascent working class now shared with their black and mulatto comrades the brunt of policies that sought to advance only the interests of the upper class. In addition, if employees resorted to protest in an attempt to improve their wages or working conditions, they risked repression at the hands of the police, who customarily treated the poor with unchecked brutality.

The earliest efforts to organize workers produced mutual-aid societies designed to provide financial benefits for members in the event of accident, illness, or death. Later, European immigrants brought with them and transplanted anarcho-syndicalism, a revolutionary worker ideology that advocated direct action, in the form of strikes and boycotts, by unionized employees.

The worker syndicates enjoyed a modest degree of success in mobilizing workers and shutting down individual factories. Between 1917 and 1920 they even managed to stage a number of general strikes in major cities. Alarmed, the government reacted by deporting foreign-born militants, and by enacting some modest pieces of social legislation.

During the 1920s internal disputes held back the progress of the labor movement. The success of the Russian Revolution inspired the creation of the Brazilian Communist party, which then became part of the Comintern (the name given to the international Communist movement under the control of Moscow). Some anarcho-syndicalists refused to join and opposed the Communists. Later in the decade, unionists who preferred the ideas of Leon Trotsky also abandoned the party.

These theoretical disputes had limited resonance among rank-and-file workers. Arguing over ideas might have appealed to intellectuals, and perhaps even to some first-generation European immigrants who came to Brazil in search of jobs. But the majority of Brazil's urban have-nots were native-born, uneducated, and basically rural in outlook.

Among the values they or their parents had brought with them from the countryside was a tendency to view all relationships, including those with individuals exercising authority, in personal rather than ideological terms—an outlook reflected by customs such as tenants and workers choosing their landlords or employers to serve as godparents for their children. Such practices were a reflection of the dependency that characterized interactions between the powerful and the powerless.

Getúlio Vargas succeeded brilliantly in capitalizing on this mind-set. Upon assuming the presidency after the revolution of 1930, he set about creating a relationship of dependency not only between government and private enterprise, as described in Chapter Six, but also between government and labor. This relationship turned out to be a mirror image of the traditional tie between haves and have-nots in rural Brazil. Peasants who moved to the cities encountered a social structure quite different from the one to which they were accustomed. They had to live in amorphous slums and, as Brazil industrialized, to toil in impersonal workplaces. Thus, it was easy for Vargas to substitute the government as the authority figure that would take care of the needs of employees, just as the landlord or employer had done in the countryside.

Before Vargas, government policy had treated labor problems as matters for the police. Getúlio had the cunning and foresight to perceive that the economic development he sought to achieve would increase the importance of labor, and that co-optation, rather than repression, was the most effective way to control the working class.

One of his first acts was to create a new Ministry of Labor. His first Minister of Labor (Lindolfo Collor, the grandfather of Fernando Collor) was instrumental in drafting a 1931 decree putting the labor movement under the thumb of the government. The Ministry of Labor had the exclusive authority to grant legal recognition to unions, which would then be organized into state federations and national confederations. It also had broad supervisory powers over union finances and governance and could replace union officers at will with appointees of its own.

The new framework was borrowed from the contemporary regime of Benito Mussolini in Italy (and would one day appeal to Argentina's Juan Perón). Many existing unions resisted, denouncing the decree as a step in the direction of fascism, and the government had to resort to heavy-handed tactics in an effort to impose its will on recalcitrant workers.

At first the Communist party joined in the struggle and kept the unions it controlled from seeking recognition by the ministry. Later, as part of the "popular front" policy adopted by the Soviet Union, the party took a more conciliatory line and permitted some of its unions to attain legal status.

In 1935 the Communists organized a movement called the National Liberation Alliance, which drew support not only from the Left and politically conscious members of the working class, but also from middle-class voters disillusioned with Vargas. The alliance advocated such progressive measures as land reform, social insurance, Brazilian control over public utilities, a minimum wage, and trade-union independence. It also militantly opposed a growing number of Brazilians who dubbed themselves "Integralists," wore green shirts, and espoused fascism with a samba beat.

Dismayed by the success of the alliance in mobilizing opposition to his regime, and by the increasingly revolutionary rhetoric of its honorary president, Luiz Carlos Prestes (whose trajectory as an authentic Brazilian hero will be described in Chapter Seventeen), Vargas outlawed the new movement. In a bizarre miscalculation of the breadth and depth of their support, the Communists then precipitated an armed revolt against the Vargas regime in late November of 1935. It was the first time that a Communist party, with the support of Moscow, ever attempted the violent overthrow of a government in the Western Hemisphere. The army easily suppressed the uprising, and Vargas had a pretext for cracking down harshly on the Communists as well as anyone suspected of supporting them.

Congress granted the president emergency powers, which he used to place a tight lid on political activity. In response to both pressure from the Integralists, who wanted him to become their "Führer," and the threat of subversion from the Left (which the regime itself cultivated by releasing a number of militants who had been imprisoned after the 1935 revolt), Vargas decided to put a formal end to democracy in Brazil. In 1938 he masterminded a bloodless coup that canceled elections scheduled for that year, and installed what was termed the *Estado Novo*, or "New State." The president thus became the de facto dictator of Brazil.

Labor unrest, and the possibility that the extreme Left might continue to exploit it, persuaded Vargas to crack down on the Communist party—in a frenzy of repression described vividly by Jorge Amado (during his Stalinist phase) in the three-volume novel *Os Subterrâneos da Liberdade (The Freedom Underground)*—and at the same time to take some modest steps to meet the pressing needs of impoverished workers. His regime reorganized and enlarged the elementary social-security system that had been set up earlier in the decade to provide health care and retirement benefits; it also decreed a minimum wage for the urban workforce. At the same time, the Ministry of Labor tightened its grip on the unions by bureaucratizing them to an even greater degree and making them more dependent than ever on the government. The president's propaganda apparatus began to hail Vargas as the "father of the poor" and the "benefactor of the working class."

The celebrated benefactions turned out to be rather modest. The minimum wage remained at such a low level that a worker could barely survive on it himself, let alone support a family. Employers who were supposed to contribute to the social-security system found ways to circumvent their obligations. With the coming of World War II and Brazil's participation on the side of the Allies, dissatisfied workers had to postpone their demands in deference to wartime exigencies—a situation that Communists readily accepted because of the party's commitment to the needs of the beleaguered Soviet Union.

The victory of the Allies spelled doom for the *Estado Novo* and the Vargas dictatorship. Having sent troops to fight in Europe for the preservation of freedom and democracy, the regime lacked the moral authority to continue its undemocratic grip over the Brazilian people. But the president was not prepared to retire gracefully from the political scene. He arranged for the creation of the Partido Trabalhista Brasileiro (PTB), or Brazilian Labor party, which he would use as a personal vehicle after the military deposed him in 1945. Insofar as it stood for anything substantive, the PTB supported the paternalistic labor policies of the Estado Novo and opposed Communist penetration of the union movement.

The Communist party, meanwhile, achieved legal status in the immediate postwar period. It enjoyed remarkable success in the 1945 elections: its candidate for president took 10 percent of the popular vote; fourteen Communists were elected to the national Chamber of Deputies; and one—the legendary Luiz Carlos Prestes—captured a seat in the Senate.

But the Communist party found itself in the uncomfortable position of participating in the democratic process at the very moment when Brazilian workers were militantly pressing wage demands that had been suspended during the war. As the number of strikes increased, the Communists had no choice but to support them. The government intervened and as part of the crackdown once again outlawed the Communist party.

The elected government that replaced the *Estado Novo* declared a "New Brazil" and convoked a constituent assembly that rewrote the nation's Constitution. But the new supreme law of the land left intact the legal mechanisms that enabled the government to control the labor movement. It also preserved the literacy requirement that excluded from the electorate the great majority of the country's poor people, who composed more than half the population of Brazil.

_1946_. Vargas's successor, General Eurico Dutra, was a conservative who viewed reform with suspicion if not hostility. He slowed down the process of industrialization and opened Brazil to a flood of manufactured goods imported from abroad. As a result, the country's gold and foreign-exchange reserves dwindled and prices rose. Labor unrest, inevitable under the circumstances, was severely repressed, and the government ousted a number of militant union officials.

This paved the way for Vargas to make an astonishing comeback in the 1950 presidential election. Adapting his _Estado Novo_ philosophy to the new political climate, he raised the banner of social welfare, worker participation in the democratic process, and economic nationalism, the latter encapsulated in protectionist policies that encouraged local industry and in an expansion of government control over the country's natural resources. Running as the candidate of the PTB and playing the political game like a virtuoso, Vargas won a stunning victory and returned to the Catete Palace (then Brazil's White House).

Having campaigned on a populist, prolabor platform that attracted a large following among lower-class voters, Vargas now had to make an effort to translate promise into performance. The economic nationalism he espoused struck a sympathetic chord with urban workers, who supported his policy of increasing the number and importance of state-owned enterprises. But there was still the matter of meeting the bread-and-butter concerns of the poor.

A political magician adept at compromise and balancing the demands of various constituencies, Getúlio found himself unable to make headway against the country's economic ills. The real wages of workers had actually dropped during the Dutra years, and now spiraling inflation served to exacerbate social tensions. The president had to loosen the government's hold on the unions, but this permitted Communists and left-wing radicals to assume positions of leadership within the labor movement, and intensified agitation for wage increases.

By mid-1953 the economic situation had deteriorated even further. In response, Vargas shuffled his cabinet in a way that evidenced his decision to set aside the caution that had always tempered his approach to governance. The most dramatic of the new appointments placed João Goulart, at the time the head of the PTB, in charge of the Ministry of Labor.

Darkly handsome and only thirty-five years of age, the man who would soon become known to Brazilians simply by his nickname Jango was viewed with suspicion not only by businessmen but also by the military and many middle-class voters. He was said to be too willing to deal with Communists and radical union leaders in return for their political backing. Moreover, he was a friend of Argentina's Juan Perón, whose authoritarian regime rested on a "vertebral column" of trade-union support, and there were those who accused Goulart of wanting to install the same kind of government in Brazil.

The fact that he was a prosperous rancher did not lessen the worries of his detractors, since contradiction was not unusual within the context of Brazilian politics. His special status as a back-home neighbor and personal favorite of the president made him even more dangerous in their eyes, since it enabled him to claim the mantle of "Getúlio's protégé."

Even before he took over the Ministry of Labor, Goulart was a lightning rod for vitriolic attacks by anti-Vargas forces, and his performance in office served only to produce more froth on the lips of his enemies. He took steps to increase the minimum wage and helped settle a national maritime strike in which the Communists played an active part. He also feuded openly and bitterly with high-level union bureaucrats who owed their positions to previous labor ministers, and reduced government restrictions on the unions (thus making it easier for Communists to participate in their governance). In less than a year criticism of him reached such a crescendo that the military forced Vargas to appoint a new Minister of Labor.

Jango remained a dominant force within the PTB, and when Getúlio suddenly took his own life in 1954, Jango stepped into his mentor's shoes. With strong support from the labor movement and the Left (including the Communists), Goulart negotiated a deal that gave him the vice presidential nomination on a slate headed by Juscelino Kubitschek, the candidate of the Social Democratic party

(PSD). Their victory at the polls provoked calls for a military coup by those who had convinced themselves that the Kubitschek-Goulart ticket was a Communist front. But powerful elements within the army opted for supporting the election results, and the pair took office in 1956.

The PTB at this point continued to lack a coherent philosophy and a comprehensive program (which made it indistinguishable from every other political entity, except the Communist party, in Brazil). It remained personalist and flexible, content to support the developmentalism of Kubitschek. The new president adopted a generous wage policy for urban workers, and in return the vice president used his trade-union contacts to keep the labor movement in line.

During the euphoric years of the Kubitschek administration, the urban workforce expanded to accommodate the process of industrialization Juscelino had intensified. But wages remained low, and the inflation caused by the government's practice of printing new money to pay for its grandiose projects put a cruel squeeze on the poor. The gap between haves and have-nots widened. In 1957 one fourth of Rio's residents inhabited *favelas*.

Those on the Left who claimed to represent the interests of workers and peasants generally embraced some form of economic nationalism that called for state ownership or control of basic industries and vital natural resources, restrictions on the profits that could be taken out of the country by foreign-owned businesses, and resistance to foreign creditors who were urging Brazil to adopt a stabilization program that would reduce social spending by the government and thereby place even more financial burdens on the poor. They also tended to be anti-American, at least in the sense that they harshly criticized what they saw as Brazil's subservient relationship to the United States. These spokesmen for the poor tended to come from the middle or upper classes. Many were intellectuals. Very few could claim to be authentic urban or rural workers.

The mainstream politicians who espoused some or all of these views are best described as populist. They appealed to the urban masses, who were becoming more numerous each year and who responded positively to anyone who pronounced that they should receive a larger share of Brazil's wealth. The haves looked with increasing anxiety on what they viewed as dangerous demagoguery promoting a not-so-hidden agenda—the "Bolshevization" of Brazil.

Yet populism was not the exclusive property of the Left. Politicians with a conservative outlook or with no agenda other than self-enrichment could play the same game and play it well. Exhibit A was Adhemar de Barros, the scion of a well-to-do São Paulo family, who parlayed a colorful personality, political acumen and the uninhibited use of patronage to attract the support of the lower and middle classes and win the governorship of Brazil's wealthiest state. Politicians like Adhemar proved that in free elections they could compete very well against the Left.

João Goulart continued to present himself as a nationalist-populist in the mold of Getúlio Vargas (hardly a leftist), but he now seemed to be leaning much more to the port side of the political spectrum. What his political beliefs really amounted to remains unclear even to this day. As vice president and titular head of the PTB, he accepted the support of the Left and from time to time advocated its line. At the same time he maneuvered cautiously within the political system and demonstrated that he was not averse to making deals with his opponents.

In the 1960 presidential elections Kubitschek was constitutionally barred from seeking reelection, but the prohibition did not apply to the vice president. Goulart ran again for his old office and won, even though the candidate at the head of his ticket went down to defeat. (Brazilian law allowed voters to split their ballot in choosing a president and vice president.)

The new president was Jânio Quadros, a quirky, charismatic "anti-politician" who several years earlier had defeated Adhemar de Barros in a race for the governorship of São Paulo. Campaigning as a reform-minded outsider, he had capitalized on widespread dissatisfaction with the status quo. In the presidential campaign, his symbol was a broom, and his slogan was simply "Jânio's coming."

Once again, voters seemed drawn by the dynamic force of personality—Jânio's long, black hair and hypnotic eyes helped create a mystique that obscured his failure to offer any concrete programs to address Brazil's economic and social ills. On August 25, 1961, after less than a year in office, he suddenly and unexpectedly re-signed, blaming "occult forces" that were frustrating him (forces that wags identified as several brands of Scotch whiskey to which the president was known to be partial).* João Goulart then as-sumed the presidency.

The controversial Jango, who was visiting the People's Repub-lic of China when Jânio stepped down, not only evoked memories of Getúlio Vargas but also bestirred great enthusiasm on the Left— all of which made him anathema to both conservatives and ele-ments within the military and gave concern to the middle class. Many on the right urged the army to intervene, and a full-blown crisis erupted.

In the end the Brazilian capacity for compromise prevailed. Moderates within the military and the Congress agreed on a solu-tion that pro- and anti-Jango elements grudgingly accepted: Gou-lart would become president, but under a parliamentary system of government in which the powers of the chief executive would be reduced. In 1963 there would be a popular referendum to decide whether to maintain the new structure or return to the old one.

What ensued were nearly three years of tumult, as Goulart sought to govern with limited powers and at the same time to con-vince voters to restore full presidential authority. He faced unyield-ing opposition from the same conservative forces that had frustrated Vargas in 1954. Now, with the Cuban Revolution a real-ity, his enemies could invoke the "Communist menace" and link the president to what they claimed were "subversive" groups (most prominently including the Communist party) that supported him.

The Left on its part was hardly of one mind about the tactics it should follow. On one extreme were those who advocated violent upheaval. A more moderate radical sector sought to mobilize work-ers and peasants by organizing them into state federations and na-tional confederations, to bring about a far-reaching land reform, to

---

* The most plausible explanation for Jânio's resignation was that he hoped Con-gress would be pressured not to accept it and to give him additional presidential powers, à la French President Charles de Gaulle. If so, this strategy proved to be a gross miscalculation.

nationalize certain foreign-owned enterprises, and to change the
Constitution to allow illiterates to vote. At the other end of the
spectrum were the moderates, who favored more gradual change
by working within the system and forming electoral alliances with
middle-class voters.

Goulart, at heart a cautious politician, fell within the third,
moderate, group, but he was unable to restrain those who were
arguing for immediate and radical measures to transform Brazil. His
own brother-in-law, Leonel Brizola, who had been elected governor of Rio Grande do Sul, was perhaps the most insistent of the
firebrands who were pressuring him. The tumult over the direction of the country led to a prolonged period of social unrest, which
aroused considerable anxiety not only among the haves, but also
within the middle class and, most significantly, in the high echelons
of the military.

What made matters worse was the economic crisis Goulart had
inherited from his predecessors. The inflation sparked by the cost
of Kubitschek's ambitious projects continued to worsen, and the
political turbulence in the country discouraged both domestic and
foreign investment. Moreover, Brazil found it difficult to attract
new, badly needed loans from abroad, as creditor nations, led by
the United States, pressed for economic stabilization as a prerequisite for furnishing further aid.

Although in January of 1963 Goulart convinced a majority of
Brazilian voters to restore the presidential system, he was not able
to prevent a rapid polarization of the political process and a mobilization of the forces that both opposed and supported him. The
indecision he displayed in the face of political and economic crisis
gave him an appearance of weakness, which became more pronounced as he began to yield more readily to pressures from the
Left.

On March 13, 1964, overconfident leftists persuaded Goulart
to sponsor a mass rally in Rio de Janeiro, at which he gave a highly
charged speech announcing a series of decrees that would nationalize all private oil refineries and expropriate vast amounts of un-
derutilized land. Televised coverage of the event conveyed to
viewers the image of a sweating president, barely able to keep his
emotions in check.

The last straw came at the end of the month, when he permitted his Minister of the Navy to grant amnesty to a group of sailors who had gone on strike to support the formation of a union of naval enlisted men. Coming on the heels of other efforts by the Left to organize noncommissioned officers and enlisted men, this was viewed by most high-level military officers as an intolerable affront to discipline and a serious challenge to their authority.

For some time politicians and businessmen who opposed Goulart had been secretly conspiring to oust him from office, and they had been seeking to enlist the support of the armed forces. Now powerful elements within the military were ready to move against the president, and on March 31, 1964, they struck quickly and decisively. Goulart fled the country, and a new era dawned in Brazil.

The Left crumbled in disarray. The masses in whose name it spoke were neither prepared to resist the forces lined up against them nor disposed to offer even token protest. The improvisation at the heart of Brazilianness had shaped attempts to organize peasants and workers. In the wake of the coup and the subsequent persecution of leftists (real and imagined), the lack of substance behind the revolutionary rhetoric became painfully evident.

Leftists consoled themselves by blaming the United States for the coup. Although Washington applauded the military intervention and even had naval forces on alert not far from the coast of Brazil, the fact is that the overthrow of Goulart required no outside aid. Those who place responsibility on the Yankees are merely reflecting Brazil's inferiority complex, the conviction that Brazilians can accomplish nothing of real significance on their own.

The new regime purged the labor movement of "subversives" but left intact the structure originally imposed by Vargas, so the government could intervene at will in union activities. At the same time, the regime assigned to the unions responsibility for managing medical and dental programs, in order to keep their leaders occupied with administrative matters. In addition, Brazil's military rulers coerced Congress into enacting a law making virtually all strikes and other forms of work stoppages illegal.

The crackdown on the unions was a logical corollary of the economic program adopted by the regime, which put into effect measures designed to stem inflation, to attract foreign capital, and to

encourage domestic investment in productive enterprises; among
the measures included a lid on salaries and the repeal of a law that
gave tenure to employees who had worked for more than ten years
in the same employ. The strategy succeeded, but only up to a point.
In 1968 there were two major strikes, one in Contagem, a suburb
of Belo Horizonte, the other in Osasco, just outside the city of São
Paulo. Both represented protests against the regime's wage policy.
The army and the police used violence to suppress the strikes (although the Contagem workers subsequently received a 10 percent
increase from the Ministry of Labor).

These work stoppages combined with student demonstrations
against the government and other manifestations of social and political unrest to give military hard-liners the pretext they needed
to persuade the regime to tighten its authoritarian grip on the country. Staging a "coup within the coup," they secured the promulgation of a series of decrees, called "Institutional Acts," that imposed
censorship on the mass media, purged the universities of suspected
subversives, destroyed what limited independence the judiciary still
enjoyed, and placed further restrictions on political activity.

These measures set the stage for the "Brazilian miracle" of the
early 1970s, a period of sustained, spectacular economic growth.
Industrial development boomed, causing the workforce to expand.
The new factories that produced automobiles and automotive parts
in and around São Paulo rode the crest of the wave, and the skilled
employees who manned production lines became a privileged segment of the working class, earning enough to purchase cars, refrigerators, and television sets.

The great majority of Brazil's workers, however, saw their purchasing power decrease during these "fat" years, although this
turned out to be a period of significant wealth redistribution in Brazil. Employers put tremendous pressure on workers to increase productivity, which in turn caused the incidence of industrial accidents
to skyrocket. The unions lacked the legal authority to do anything
to improve the plight of their members, the censored press could
neither speak out nor inform, and the political process had been
reduced to a rubber stamp. Moreover, sporadic outbreaks of terrorist activity and guerrilla warfare on the part of radicalized students, intellectuals, and military personnel (described in more

detail in Chapter Nine) failed to bestir the workers and peasants, on whose nominal behalf the actions were undertaken. These uprisings were easily crushed by the armed forces.

Yet at the same time Brazil's have-nots were beginning to stir in the festering slums that had mushroomed in and around the nation's cities. The foci for this grassroots activity were Comunidades Eclesiásticas de Base (CEBs), or "Ecclesiastical Base Communities" (a phenomenon explored at greater length in Chapter Thirteen).

The CEBs were originally designed to provide opportunities for religious reflection by lay Catholic groups in urban slums and rural areas affected by the shortage of priests in Brazil. But they soon became the vehicles that enabled poor people to organize themselves and take collective action to improve living conditions in their own communities. Workers who could do nothing about their situations in the workplace now had a mechanism that allowed them to do something about their situations at home.

What was novel about the CEBs and other community associations that began to take shape in the slums was that they were organized from the ground up, with an active rank and file that participated in decision making and chose its own leaders from within the group. This was a novelty in Brazil—true democracy in action, albeit on a small and local scale. The workers who participated learned important lessons.

In addition, the trade-union movement was undergoing an important transformation during this period. By purging militant leaders, the regime had opened space for a new generation of young workers to take over the direction of the unions. By outlawing strikes, the regime had forced individual unions to address bread-and-butter issues. This in turn forced labor leaders to develop and maintain close contact with the rank-and-file members they were representing. Thus trade unionism in Brazil began to manifest many of the features of the participatory democracy that was developing in grassroots community organizations.

By the late 1970s the regime had loosened its grip and had embarked on a process of liberalization that would one day bring an end to military rule. The young men who had risen to positions of leadership in the labor movement now felt secure enough not only to call strikes and to speak out on behalf of union independence from the government, but also to demand a voice in what was becoming a national dialogue over the reconstitution of democracy in Brazil. It was the first time in Brazilian history that workers became players in matters of national policy. It was also the first time that a bona fide worker would rise to political prominence as the spokesman for his peers.

His name was Luís Inácio da Silva, but everyone called him by his childhood nickname, Lula. For most of Brazil's have-nots, to look at him was to gaze into a mirror. His experiences were their experiences, his suffering was their suffering, and his life was their life. The remarkable success he enjoyed made him a symbol of a type of upward mobility that the country had never seen before.

The story of Lula begins in Garanhuns, a moderate-sized city in the southern highlands of the state of Pernambuco. He was born there in 1946, the sixth of twenty-three children who could trace their parentage to Aristides Inácio da Silva, a poor but fecund farmer. Shortly after Lula's birth, Aristides abandoned his wife, Eurídice, and ran off with a local woman. Like countless other northeasterners, the couple went south, settling in Santos, the busy port near São Paulo, where Aristides worked loading sacks of coffee onto cargo vessels.

In 1949 Aristides brought his new woman and the two children he had sired with her back to Garanhuns. He remained for twenty days, time enough to impregnate the accommodating Eurídice once again, after which he departed, taking with him two of Lula's elder brothers.

Three years later, Eurídice received a letter, ostensibly from Aristides, asking her to bring the family to Santos. The epistle had in fact been written and mailed by one of her two boys, who missed his mother and the rest of the family. She packed Lula, his siblings, and their worldly goods into an open wooden flatbed truck, one of the *paus-de-arara*, or "parrot's perches," that customarily carried impoverished northeasterners on their migrations to other parts of the country, and they inhaled clouds of dust during the grueling two-thousand-mile trip.

Recovering from his surprise at their arrival, Aristides at first installed Eurídice and her children in modest quarters and divided his time between the two families. By 1955 Eurídice had had enough of this arrangement, so she took her brood to São Paulo.*

Lula and seven of his brothers and sisters, along with their mother and three cousins, moved into a one-room apartment in the back of a bar, and they had to share a bathroom with the tavern's patrons. Lula soon went to work on the mean streets of the city, peddling peanuts and pastries. Later he got a job in a dry-cleaning shop. He also managed to complete his primary education, the only one in the family to do so. At fourteen he found work in a factory that produced screws, and at the same time he gained admittance to a state technical school, where he studied to be a mechanic. Working the night shift, he had difficulty finding a place to sleep during the day, which contributed to the momentary drowsiness that overcame him one day while he was working at a machine press and that cost him the little finger on his left hand.

Lula lost his job as a result of the recession brought on by the economic policies of the military regime, and he had to look for another. He found one as a metalworker in a large factory in São Bernardo do Campo, just outside São Paulo. His brother José (known as Frei Chico, or "Friar Chico," because of his monklike haircut) was a committed member of the Communist party, which was operating clandestinely at the time, and tried to interest him in becoming involved in the union, but at this point in his life Lula preferred to play soccer.

In 1969 Lula married a neighbor who worked in a textile factory. Two years later she died during childbirth, and the son she was delivering did not survive. Lula's curriculum vitae was now a fairly accurate reflection of life near the bottom rung of Brazilian society. It gave him a foundation upon which he would build his career as a trade-union official.

Lula's entry into the labor movement was gradual. He had never been a politically aware person. Indeed, his family had supported the various candidacies of Adhemar de Barros. But at the

---

* Aristides remained with his other woman until 1968, when she finally left him. He died from the effects of chronic alcoholism in 1978.

same time he was not blind to what was happening around him, and he understood that he and his fellow employees were being exploited by the company, which had modified the workplace to raise the productivity of individual workers without increasing their salaries. Therefore, his brother's efforts to enlist him finally bore fruit, and he not only joined the local metalworkers' union but also ran for office in it.

Lula found he had a talent for union work, and he managed to avoid the temptation to become one more union bureaucrat. He brought no political preconceptions with him to the job and even displayed a certain amount of naiveté in speaking his mind. But he also established close contact with the rank and file, whose language he spoke, and he instituted a number of changes within the union. In 1975 he won the presidency of the Metalworkers' Union of São Bernardo do Campo and Diadema, which drew its membership from a pool of about one hundred thousand workers. Three years later he was reelected to office, just in time to play a key role in events that were to transform the country.

During the "miracle" of rapid economic expansion in Brazil in the early seventies, the regime had tied increases in the minimum wage to the inflation rate. When the worldwide petroleum crisis brought the "miracle" to an unexpected end, prices began to shoot upward. The government's response was a barefaced falsification of the rate of inflation. Since annual salary adjustments were calculated to reflect increases in the cost of living, by a statistical sleight of hand the military regime could defraud the Brazilian labor force of wage increases on a grand scale, and thereby save industry the cost of paying laborers a living wage. Calculations released by the World Bank eventually exposed the fraud and gave unions the grist for a wage-restoration campaign, which they launched in 1978. Lula and his metalworkers were at its forefront.

In a country where political activity had been severely restricted for nearly a decade and a half, Lula was a breath of fresh air. The media gave ample coverage to the novel spectacle of the swarthy young union leader with the close-cropped beard, stooped shoulders, and slight paunch as he harangued huge assemblies of workers and spoke out, at times brashly, at times with earthy humor, on a range of issues.

Although strikes were still illegal, the working class became increasingly emboldened, first in staging slowdowns and sit-down strikes, and then in carrying out full-scale stoppages. In 1979 an estimated three million workers engaged in strike activity in every region of Brazil, as unions took advantage of the regime's decision to loosen its grip on the reins of power.

The country had by now embarked on the long, cautious, and arduous process of redemocratization. A general amnesty permitted political exiles to return, and the artificial two-party system the regime had decreed in order to create the appearance of representative government was scrapped in favor of a multiparty system. The professional politicians began to engage in their customary maneuvers in the expectation that the country would soon return to politics as usual. The names of the parties might be different, but the game would remain the same, with the emphasis on self-serving accommodation and scant attention paid to ideology or principle.

But Lula and many of his comrades had other ideas. Much to the dismay of both the generals and those politicians who thought they could count on the electoral support of the labor movement, the young workers joined with intellectuals, grass-roots Catholic activists, and miscellaneous left-wingers to form the Partido dos Trabalhadores (PT), or the Workers' party.

The PT, like Lula himself, was a novelty item in Brazilian politics. It represented the interests of a particular segment of society and stood for principles and programs that promoted those interests. It was unabashedly socialist but rejected foreign models of socialism. Although the party began as a vehicle for urban workers and drew its main strength from the industrial suburbs around São Paulo, it made efforts to broaden its base to include not only rural workers but also poor people from all parts of the country.

The PT might not have been the first political party in Brazil to appeal to the working class, but it broke new ground by presenting itself as an organ founded by workers rather than politicians purporting to speak for workers. This enabled it to compete successfully with the Brazilian Communist party, which was now beginning to try to reclaim its role as the authentic voice of the working class in Brazil, and the Communist party of Brazil, a Maoist splinter group.

The regime reacted with horror, exacerbated by discomfort, at the increase in strike activity all over the country. The government did its best to remove the "troublemakers" from positions of leadership within the union movement; the regime even went so far as to arrest Lula and other union militants for inciting an illegal strike in the automobile industry. A military court sentenced them to three and a half years in prison, a move that under the law would also disqualify them from running for elective office. Public protests against the verdict reached a crescendo, and a higher military tribunal set aside the sentence. Lula emerged from confinement to a hero's welcome.

It was at this point that he made the transition from union leader to politician. As the brightest star in the new Workers' party, he was a natural choice to bear its standard before the electorate. In 1982 he ran as the PT candidate for governor of São Paulo. Given the massive numbers of workers and poor people among the state's voters, he and the rest of the leadership of the fledgling party were optimistic about his chances, especially when PT rallies attracted large crowds. "Worker, vote for a worker" was the dominant PT message; the campaign proclaimed Lula "a Brazilian just like you."

The election results came as a shock to the PT. Lula finished fourth and captured less than 10 percent of the vote. Apparently the great majority of São Paulo's have-nots believed that one needed a university degree to qualify for the governorship. Perhaps reflecting a sense of their own inferiority, they might have agreed that Lula was "just like" them, but in their hearts they knew that *they* were not qualified to govern the state.

The 1982 elections were not a complete disaster for the novice political party, since it did elect six candidates to the national Chamber of Deputies and nine to the legislature of the state of São Paulo. Though discouraged, the PT resolved to remain active in the legislative arena. It decided to broaden its appeal to voters, and although maintaining a working-class orientation, it abandoned its "Worker, vote for a worker" slogan and took a less sectarian approach to politics. People who were not urban workers began to run as PT candidates. Moreover, in subsequent campaigns the party softened its tactics and also began to make more effective use of television.

In the 1985 elections, the PT presented candidates for mayor in all but one state capital and did surprisingly well, capturing the city hall of Fortaleza in the important northeastern state of Ceará. In 1986 the Workers' party tripled the seats it held in the Chamber of Deputies and elected state legislators in thirteen states. Lula himself garnered over 650,000 votes in a successful race for the national Congress, gaining more votes than any other candidate. Benedita da Silva, a black community activist from a Rio *favela*, joined the PT bloc of deputies in Brasília and became one of its most effective members. In 1988 Luiza Erundina, a social worker originally from the Northeast, surprised everyone by defeating Paulo Maluf in the 1988 São Paulo mayoral race. Other PT candidates won elections for mayor in Porto Alegre, Vitória (the capital of the state of Espírito Santo), and the important São Paulo cities of Campinas and Santos.

The PT by now enjoyed a reputation as Brazil's only principled political party. Yet a track record in fidelity to principles had disadvantages as well as advantages. On the plus side was the unique aura the PT was developing. Its elected officials were known to be committed to the party's platform and ideology rather than to the pursuit of self-enrichment, and honest administration became a PT trademark. But the PT was so tied to its principles that it eschewed alliances with other parties. (Indeed, it had even refused to support Tancredo Neves in the 1985 indirect election, preferring instead to abstain.) While refusal to compromise may have guaranteed party purity, it also made the PT less effective in advancing the programs and policies it espoused.

Moreover, the Workers' party encountered difficulties in making the transition from opposition to incumbency. During the last years of the military regime, the PT positioned itself in the vanguard of the struggle against the dictatorship. But once democratic rule was restored and the party opted to engage in electoral politics, it not only had to play by the rules; it also had to confront the consequences of success.

In the legislative arena at both the federal and state levels, PT lawmakers could still engage in a certain amount of oppositionist rhetoric, but they also had to take specific positions for which they might be held accountable by voters. The party faced its most difficult challenges in the municipalities administered by PT mayors. They had to govern, and the limited resources generally available to Brazilian mayors made it difficult for PT chief executives to satisfy the competing demands of their constituents as well as other members of the citizenry. Anticapitalist rhetoric would no longer suffice. Specific programs had to be fashioned and carried out, and tangible results would have to be achieved.

On the whole, after some initial stumbling, the party did as well as might reasonably have been expected on the local level, and in the presidential election campaign of 1989 it put forward Lula as its nominee. His chances for success were boosted by the failure of the other parties of the Left and center to produce strong candidates.* In addition, health problems forced the early withdrawal of Jânio Quadros, the right-wing-populist ex-President, who appealed to much the same constituency as Lula.

As the contest came down to the wire, the PT found itself battling with Leonel Brizola, the charismatic brother-in-law of João Goulart, who had established in the state of Rio de Janeiro a political party that advocated a populist line but served primarily as a vehicle for Brizola's gubernatorial and presidential ambitions. There was no love lost between Lula and Brizola. The PT candidate once declared that his rival "would step on his own mother's neck to get elected president." Brizola ran second to Collor in the early stages of the campaign, but he failed to pick up any momentum, and Lula made a late charge.

When the first-round ballots were tallied, Fernando Collor was an easy winner, with 28 percent of the votes, and Lula narrowly edged Brizola for the runner-up spot by fewer than 450,000 votes out of about 72 million cast. Since Collor did not win an absolute majority, he would have to face Lula, *mano a mano*, in a second-round showdown.

---

*The one exception, interestingly enough, was Roberto Freire, the Communist candidate, who came across as the most articulate and intelligent of the lot, but whose party affiliation repelled most voters.

In the face of united opposition from Brazil's elite and with a fraction of the funding available to his rival, Lula mounted a spirited, creditable effort. He refused to respond in kind when Collor engaged in smear tactics (the highly publicized production of Lula's ex-lover, who claimed he had urged her to abort their daughter) despite the availability of counter-ammunition. (Collor himself had sired an illegitimate child, but this fact was not disclosed during the campaign.) Lula could take great satisfaction at having received the votes of 31 million of his fellow citizens.

It is ironic that Lula and the avowedly socialist PT came reasonably close to capturing the presidency of Brazil at a time when socialist movements were in shambles elsewhere on the planet. The collapse of the Communist regimes in Eastern Europe and the Soviet Union threatened to create the impression that Brazil's Workers' party and its supporters were swimming against the tide of history. On the one hand, Brazilian leftists steadfastly refused to abandon their major idols—Fidel Castro and the *sandinistas*—despite overwhelming evidence of deteriorating conditions in Cuba and Nicaragua. On the other hand, they insisted they could govern without reproducing those conditions in Brazil.

During the election Lula gave repeated assurances that he would impose no foreign models on his country. He supported the privatization of certain state-held entities but maintained that the government should continue to own basic enterprises such as the power and oil industries and should continue to play a decisive role in the economy, for example by formulating and executing an industrial policy. Despite the presence of an ultra-Left faction within the party—the "Shiite" or "Apocalypse Now" group, as some dubbed it—the PT remained generally responsive to its rank and file, which gave backbone to Lula's verbal commitment to democracy.

After the election, Lula withdrew for a short while from active public life, but he continued to serve as head of the PT. With the fall of Collor, Lula's national prestige rose, and he became a leading candidate for the presidency in the election scheduled for 1994.

He could now count on the support of a party that could boast of an impressive growth curve over the prior eleven years. In 1982 the PT had elected six federal deputies; over a decade later it had thirty-four. In January 1993 fifty-four PT mayors were in office, an increase of nineteen since the last municipal elections. Moreover, the party had progressed from its original incarnation as the political wing of certain trade unions to a much broader based movement.

Yet any optimism by PT enthusiasts should have been tempered by the realization that Lula won only about 17 percent of the vote in the first round of the presidential elections. Most of the support he received in the runoff was more in the nature of opposition to Collor and less an expression of a positive preference for him. In addition, in his head-to-head race against Collor he did poorly in the state of São Paulo, supposedly a PT stronghold. One explanation posited this result as an expression of dissatisfaction with the performance of the incumbent PT mayor of the city of São Paulo. The fact that the PT has yet to win a state governorship suggests a possible weakness in the scope of the party's electoral appeal.

Another problem facing the PT became evident in the defeat of its candidate Benedita da Silva (profiled in Chapter Two) for mayor of Rio de Janeiro in 1992. Although she had been running strongly in the second round, she lost momentum as a result of a beach riot perpetrated by teenagers from the slums. Her explanation for the riot—stressing the social and economic roots of the despair felt by these young people—might have been sociologically accurate, but it was unacceptable to the frightened middle-class voters suffering the immediate effects of the crime wave in Rio. Benedita's defeat suggested that the Brazilian electorate, at least in the big cities, was so concerned about the problem of physical security that candidates seen as unwilling or unable to take strong measures against crime would lose support. Lula, who shared Benedita's views about the causes of crime in Brazil, ran the risk of alienating even lower-class voters who perceived him as "soft" on the crime issue.

As events came to pass, however, it was on economic issues that Lula proved vulnerable in the 1994 presidential campaign. He and the PT underestimated how much the sharp drop in the inflation rate delighted voters of every social class, and they were unable to fashion an effective response, other than to claim that the government was manipulating economic indicators for political ends. Moreover, Lula and the PT were running on a platform that was totally at odds with the economic approach then being taken in Argentina and Chile, whose governments had drastically reduced state controls over the economy and had adopted free-market policies that seemed to be producing very positive results.

The resounding triumph of Fernando Henrique Cardoso in the October 1994 elections opened the way for a new era in the economic life of Brazil. The fate of the nation's have-nots now seems to depend on whether the new administration will push for the type of reforms that will further impoverish the lower and middle classes, as occurred in the 1970s, or whether the new president's social-democratic instincts will prevent him from forgetting the existence of social and economic injustice in Brazil.

Lula and the PT have reason to take pride in the constructive role they have played in the restoral of democracy in Brazil. Theirs has been the voice of Brazil's voiceless, and with a new phase in the country's history apparently about to begin, they will be needed more than ever to provide a counterbalance to those who think that the solution to the nation's woes is to make the rich richer. What they face is the challenge of fashioning what may be termed a postmodern political strategy that can remain faithful to the goals of social and economic justice without ruining the productive capacity essential to Brazil's survival.

## Part Three

# The Curse of
# Violence in Brazil

# Chapter 9

# The Culture
# of Brutality

*I*n a society marked by a dramatic gap separating the wealthy
and the powerful from those at the base of the social pyramid,
the cordiality that Brazilians exude has made a deep impression on
foreign observers. From the Reverends D. P. Kidder and J. C.
Fletcher, American clergymen who visited the country in the early
1850s, came the following observation of the conduct of Brazilians
traveling on horse-drawn trolleys: "Each person, as he rises to depart, lifts his hat, and the compliment is returned by every individual in the omnibus, although all may be entire strangers. No
one ever enters a large public conveyance in Rio without saluting
those within and receiving in return a polite acknowledgement of
his presence. Very frequently a pinch of snuff is offered to you by
your unknown neighbor." Stefan Zweig, the Austrian novelist,
wrote in 1941: "As soon as one enters this country, it is one's first
pleasant and ever-recurring surprise to find in how friendly and
peaceful a way people live with each other [sic] within this immense space." He went on to wax eloquent about "the native tolerance" of the Brazilians, their "desire for peace" and
"humanitarian behaviour."

The impression that Brazilians were a congenial, gentle, endearing people gained remarkable currency. The warm, lovable,
nonthreatening Brazilian became a deeply entrenched stereotype,
fortified by the public personae of attractive figures such as Dom
Pedro II, Carmen Miranda, and Pelé, and by fictional characters
such as the sweet Brazilian millionaire who falls in love with Au-
drey Hepburn in the film *Breakfast at Tiffany's.*

But over the past three decades, this image has joined the myth of racial democracy in history's dustbin, and a new, diametrically opposite stereotype is beginning to evolve—that of the violent Brazilian, the product of a society that has desensitized itself to brutality.

The shift in Brazil's image began in the 1960s and 1970s, when the military dictatorship resorted to terror, torture, and other forms of repression to impose its will on dissidents. Although the extent of the violence did not match what occurred later in Argentina during the "dirty war" of 1976–78, it was still shocking enough to elicit protests from abroad, especially in response to egregious cases such as the murder of a priest in Recife in 1969, and the army's torturing to death a São Paulo journalist six years later.

In addition to the government's resorting to force as a matter of policy, there were other types of reported violence that began to affect foreigners' perceptions of Brazil during this period: the activities of the "death squads" that were exterminating suspected criminals in the slums of Rio de Janeiro and São Paulo; the killing of rural labor leaders and peasants during conflicts over land in Amazônia; the killing of Indians by settlers and others bent on taking profits from tribal lands; the killing of wives by husbands who claimed they were "defending their honor"; the increase of criminal assaults in Brazilian cities; and the dispensing of "vigilante justice" by citizens fed up with crime.

Over the past several years the media in Brazil as well as abroad have become obsessed with the subject of Brazilian violence, and there has been a plethora of reporting on the subject. Causes célèbres include

- the 1993 execution-style murder of 8 Rio street children as they slept on a downtown sidewalk, followed shortly thereafter by the killing of 21 *favela*-dwellers. Both massacres were attributed to policemen;

- the fatal asphyxiation of 18 prisoners in a São Paulo jail in 1989. After foiling an attempted escape, police stuffed 51 of the participating inmates into a tiny windowless cell and locked the door for three hours. This tragedy was surpassed three years later when São Paulo police invaded a different prison to stop a gang fight and slaughtered 111 prisoners;

- the cold-blooded murder of Chico Mendes, the leader of the rubber tappers of western Amazônia, at the hands of gunmen hired by a local landowner; and

- the videotaped frenzy of members of an angry mob in a rural town in Mato Grosso, as they poured gasoline on and set fire to a trio of kidnappers who had thrown down their arms and surrendered to the authorities.

It is, of course, evident that the economy has played a major role in generating violence in Brazil. The Brazilian "miracle" of the early seventies produced a massive enrichment of the rich at the expense of the poor, and the "lost decade" of the 1980s not only placed even greater burdens on the backs of the poor but also expanded their ranks. The repression unleashed by the military regime was a necessary concomitant to the adoption of economic policies that worsened inequities that already existed within Brazilian society and might otherwise have generated political and trade-union opposition. The armed forces therefore elevated torture and other forms of brutality to the status of unofficial policy.

Eventually the suffering inflicted by the regime stretched beyond the breaking point the endurance and patience of those on society's bottom rung. Moreover, the chaotic growth of Brazil's urban centers had spawned fetid slums that lacked the social controls found in the Brazilian countryside and now became fertile ground for the growth of lawlessness. A factor that contributed to crime was the frustration and despair engendered in many of the poor when they became aware that they would not be able to obtain the consumer goods that they saw advertised on television. Some of the so-called "marginal people" began to react violently, which in turn produced even more violent counterresponses.

Brazil's violence is not rooted in the recent economic crisis, however; the current epidemic is only part of the larger history of violence that began with the founding of the colony. Certain elements of Brazilianness contribute significantly to the phenomenon. Indeed, the notion of the "peaceful" Brazilian is yet another example of a foreign misperception of Brazil.

It is possible to find Brazilianness in all the complex, interrelated strands of contemporary violence. Chapter Seven described the indirect violence suffered by the nation's have-nots, who live a daily existence defined by the constant risk of physical and emotional harm from disease, hunger, thirst, accident, and ignorance. Chapter Ten focuses on a specific group of victims, the nation's children; while Chapters Eleven and Twelve explore another aspect of violence, the destruction of Brazil's natural environment.

This chapter examines violence in its most direct forms. It focuses on a complex system in which the government at the national, state, and local levels uses force against the governed, the haves use force against the have-nots, the have-nots use force against people from every social class (including their own), and victims from every social class use force to protect themselves. These forms of violence have fed off one another, making brutality both routine and ordinary. Adding to the mix and the dynamic are more intimate types of brutality, such as the battering and killing of wives by their husbands, and self-inflicted violence, the consequence of extremely reckless behavior on the part of many Brazilians.

As has been suggested, violence in Brazil has always been an integral part of the historical and social fabric of the country. Indeed, from prehistoric days to the era of Portuguese colonization, and from the dawn of independence to the present, violence has been omnipresent in one form or another, at times lurking beneath the surface, and at other times bursting brutally into view. Despite this reality, the myth of the "nonviolent Brazilian" gained wide currency.

A closer look at the myth reveals that it has served the interests of those holding the levers of power in the country. A people made to believe in its own pacificity is hardly likely to rise up in revolt against its rulers. The ruling elite in Brazil, during the period of empire and the first several decades of republican government, propagated the images of cordiality and nonviolence in order to fortify the status quo.

The myth has also drawn some sustenance from a selective reading of the country's history. Very little blood was shed when Brazil won its independence from Portugal, and when a republican form of government replaced the empire, especially if one compares these transformations with the brutality that similar struggles generated in Hispanic America. Displaying a taste for and skill at compromise and conciliation, Brazil settled its outstanding border disputes at the end of the nineteenth century and the beginning of the twentieth century by negotiating with neighboring countries, rather than by warring with them. The same approach to conflict resolution surfaced at other key moments in history, such as the abolition of slavery.

Yet in fact one can find countless examples of extreme violence threading its way throughout the history of Brazil. As has been described in Chapter Three, the use of force against indigenous peoples has been a constant, whether in the form of outright warfare, or entrepreneurial initiative (by the *bandeirantes* of the seventeenth century and gold miners of the twentieth, to cite but two examples). As is pointed out in Chapter Two, the institution of slavery brought with it not only an inherent brutality but also the use of unrestrained barbarity by slaveholders suppressing revolts by freedom-seeking blacks. Colonial society, with its highly authoritarian, patriarchal structure and rural, often isolated setting, required the use of force to maintain itself in the face of both internal and external challenges.

In the sugar zone and the interior of the Northeast, active as well as passive violence has long been a way of life. Large landholders maintained private armies of gunmen who protected their interests during conflicts with other owners. Bitter and long-lasting family feuds were not uncommon, and some have continued to the present day. Northeasterners traditionally use force to defend their personal or familial honor. Indeed, in 1993 the governor of the state of Paraíba put three bullets in the face of an ex-governor who had accused him of corruption.

The haves of the Northeast used paramilitary might to subjugate the ample pool of peasants and rural workers needed to work the farms and keep up the large estates. These hapless souls found themselves forced to endure starvation wages, disease, and periodic droughts.

There were have-nots who rebelled against their lot, most commonly by forming or joining outlaw bands and waging open war against the people who oppressed them. These bandit backlanders employed a counterviolence that was no less implacable than what they themselves had been made to suffer. Jorge Amado, who normally romanticizes the struggles of the poor, describes the cruelty they perpetrate with shocking frankness in his novel *Seara Vermelha (Red Harvest)*, especially in one memorable scene involving a gang of outlaws who capture a small town and force its inhabitants to attend a dance at which various forms of humiliation, violence, and sexual degradation are visited upon them.

One of the bloodiest episodes in Brazilian history (discussed in more detail in Chapter Thirteen) occurred in the interior of the Northeast during the last decades of the nineteenth century, when a charismatic prophet named Antônio Conselheiro attracted tens of thousands of *sertanejos* to a form of primitive Christianity that eventually challenged the authority of the newly installed republic. The sect took over the town of Canudos in the backlands of Bahia and created their own settlement. Aided by bandits who rallied to their cause, the followers of Antônio Conselheiro repulsed several attacks by the police and the army but finally succumbed to the superior firepower of federal troops, who slaughtered all but four members of the settlement. The rise and fall of Canudos has been immortalized in one of the preeminent works of Brazilian literature, *Os Sertões (Rebellion in the Backlands)*, by Euclides da Cunha.*

Several preliminary hypotheses emerge from this long history of violence. First of all, large quantities of blood have been shed in Brazil during class or social conflicts. Attempts to disrupt the hierarchical order of things seem inevitably to provoke extremely violent responses. Those defending the status quo have proved as ruthless and violent as those trying to disrupt it.

This history of bloodletting in turn belies the myth of the "cordial Brazilian." As Dante Moreira Leite has pointed out in his excellent *O Carácter Nacional Brasileiro (The Brazilian National*

---

* Da Cunha was himself a victim of violence in 1909. His honor having been sullied by an affair his wife was conducting with an army officer, he confronted his rival with a drawn pistol and was mortally wounded in an exchange of gunfire. Seven years later da Cunha's son attempted to avenge his father's death and suffered the same fate. Courts acquitted the officer for both killings on grounds of self-defense.

*Character)*, Brazilians behave cordially toward one another when an interaction poses no threat to the social standing of the participants. A person from the upper class will display warmth toward a social inferior as long as the latter respects the differences between the two. A person from the lower class will display a deferential congeniality toward social superiors as an indication of his or her acceptance of the class division between them.

Thus cordiality serves to mask condescension on the one side and subordination on the other. It also helps to preserve the status quo, so we begin to see why the paradigm of the "cordial Brazilian" has also been a useful ideological construct for those who benefit from the way power is distributed in Brazil.

A second hypothesis explains violence in Brazil as a result of the low value placed on human life by Brazilians. One explanation for this devaluation of life is that it is one of the obvious legacies of the institution of slavery. Moreover, the persistence of rigid divisions between landowner and peasant, employer and worker, and rich and poor have undoubtedly contributed heavily to the notion that inferior beings count very little in the scale of things.

The have-nots have been conditioned to accept this devaluation of their worth by the fatalism the Portuguese brought with them from the Old World; the Roman Catholic teaching that the endurance of suffering in this life is a virtue that can lead to eternal salvation; a sense of impotence before the awesome forces of nature in Brazil; and a conviction, born of long experience, that attempts to make meaningful changes from below in the structure of Brazilian society are Sisyphean at best. It follows, then, that whenever the dispossessed break free from these psychological constraints and in utter desperation enter into open conflict with the forces that oppress them, they feel they have nothing to lose and strike out with unrestrained savagery.

Another factor contributing to the Brazilian disregard for human life is the cloak of impunity that has always protected the powerful in Brazil. Those who do not have to answer for their deeds are more likely to have few compunctions about either inflicting harm directly on others or engaging in conduct that places others at risk. The notion that corrective justice extends to every Brazilian citizen, no matter what his or her social station, has been very slow to make the transition from theory to practice.

Impunity has bred attitudes of irresponsibility and gross neglect that have contributed to another form of violence—the mass disaster (or near disaster). They include the capsizing of an overloaded tour boat in Guanabara Bay on December 31, 1988, in which 54 passengers drowned; the collapse, due to faulty construction and disrepair, of a retaining wall of the upper deck in Maracanã stadium just as a championship soccer game was about to begin, causing spectators to plummet into the reserved seating section; a São Paulo skyscraper fire that took 188 lives and injured 400; and the importing of powdered milk contaminated by radioactivity that had escaped from Chernobyl.

These hypotheses do not apply to the violence that has long been endemic to another region of Brazil, the south, where geographical and historical factors produced a type of brutality that was unique to Brazil. It is worth taking a brief look at this phenomenon, since it provides a useful illustration of Brazil's complexity.

The history of Rio Grande do Sul, a cattle-raising, wheat-growing state in the extreme south of the country and on the borders with Uruguay and Argentina, is soaked in blood. The earliest inhabitants found themselves in constant conflict with warlike Indians, as well as with Spaniards who contested Portuguese control over the sparsely settled region.

These ongoing struggles made violence a part of everyday life—a reality brilliantly captured by Érico Veríssimo in the first segment of his epic novel *O Tempo e o Vento (Time and the Wind)*. They also produced a tough, belligerent, freedom-loving breed of settler in whose veins mingled the blood of soldiers and adventurers, Portuguese colonists and runaway slaves, Spaniards and Indians. The region's horsemen, known as *gaúchos*, were rugged, fearless fighters who worked the countless herds of wild cattle that roamed the immense southern grasslands.

The tradition of violence in Rio Grande do Sul did not fade away once the borders between the Portuguese and Spanish colonies had been permanently fixed in the late eighteenth century. During the regency that ruled Brazil after the abdication of Dom

Pedro I, a number of regional revolts erupted in various parts of the country. At the end of the nineteenth century, a savage civil war between two political factions tore the state apart. All kinds of atrocities were committed by both sides, the most gruesome involving captors using knives to slaughter prisoners by slitting their throats from ear to ear, the manner *gaúchos* used to kill sheep.

The violence marking the history of southern Brazil was qualitatively different from violence occurring elsewhere in the country. It did not arise from class conflicts. The clashes with the Spanish (and even the struggles against the Indians) were in the nature of battles between equals. Nor did the violence have anything to do with the institution of slavery, inasmuch as relatively few slaves were imported into the region, whose economic well-being did not require an abundance of cheap labor.

It is difficult to link the bloodshed that occurred over the centuries in southern Brazil with the current epidemic of violence. The urban crime to be found in Porto Alegre, the capital of Rio Grande do Sul, is no different from the criminal anarchy afflicting other large cities, and the land disputes in the interior of the state follow the same pattern as conflicts in Amazônia and elsewhere in rural Brazil.

In one egregious episode in 1989, crop-dusting planes dropped liquid pesticide on an encampment of landless peasants, including children (4 of whom were fatally poisoned by the spray). The victims of the attack—1,200 families in all—reacted by invading the nearby Santa Elmira Farm. This particular group had been wandering about the interior of Rio Grande do Sul for several years and had previously occupied other private properties. On those occasions state officials had persuaded them to leave with promises of future grants of land. This time, however, unmarked airplanes assaulted the invaders with concussion bombs and tear gas, and then a large contingent of state police, augmented by several hundred armed men belonging to an association of rural landowners, swept through the encampment. They took prisoners, beating or otherwise abusing some of the peasants. Several of the occupiers were made to sit on anthills.

Perhaps the brutality intrinsic to southern Brazil comes out of a unique phase in the country's development, much like the violence that grew up in the American West. Civilization has brought an end to the more primitive forms of violence and is replacing it with new forms.

One of the common features of rural conflicts throughout the country is the involvement of the state, either acting on its own or in conjunction with private interests, on the side of those seeking to protect the existing pattern of landownership in Brazil. The history of Brazilian violence, as has been suggested, reveals numerous instances of official brutality directed against those thought to be threatening the status quo. The state-sponsored brutality that has been evident over the past several decades has contributed in a major way to the climate of violence in Brazil today.

However, the suppression of dissent during the military dictatorship engendered a much more prolonged, focused, and systematic use of violence than any previously employed by a Brazilian government. During its most repressive moments, the Vargas regime had treated political opponents harshly, but the armed forces in the late 1960s and early 1970s far exceeded the levels of savagery to which the *Estado Novo* had descended.

The military coup of 1964 encountered no resistance worthy of note (in large part because of the overconfidence of those who were pushing for radical change). What the military and conservative elements had perceived as a serious, imminent threat by leftists plotting to install a socialist regime in Brazil collapsed in shambles once army troops left their barracks and moved to oust the administrations of President João Goulart and certain "subversive" governors. The violence accompanying the coup was relatively mild. There were mass arrests, but no summary executions, nor was torture widely employed by the armed forces and the police. The physical abuse that did occur in isolated instances was consistent with the treatment Brazilian law-enforcement officials customarily dole out to suspects.

However, by 1969 the human-rights situation in Brazil had deteriorated badly. Elements of the Left had decided to take up arms against the dictatorship, and the armed forces met the threat of force with overwhelming counterforce. Sporadic terrorist actions occurring in the years immediately following the coup had given way to organized guerrilla warfare, on a modest scale but nonetheless sufficient to alarm the military. This was the era of the Tupamaro insurgents in Uruguay, Che Guevara's botched campaign in Bolivia, and the beginnings of left-wing violence in Argentina. Brazil, with its vast empty spaces and overpopulated cities, offered what seemed at first glance to be a ripe opportunity for revolutionary action.

The initial stages of what never amounted to more than an embryonic insurrection involved a series of bank robberies and raids on military facilities, generally for the purpose of stealing weapons, and the assassination of a U.S. army captain in São Paulo.* Those participating in the movement were mostly middle-class students and intellectuals. Ideological differences have always factionalized the Left, and this movement was no different, but its members also clashed because of their own individualism, an ineradicable element of Brazilianness. At the same time they faced the difficulties inherent in coordinating activities during relentless military repression.

The appearance of an armed resistance gave a faction within the military an excuse to push hard for the elimination of the trappings of democratic government that had been permitted to remain in place since the coup. Worker and student protests that had begun to spread gave the hard-liners additional arguments for mounting a crackdown. Finally, the regime was about to embark on economic programs that would produce a massive redistribution of income from the poor and middle classes to the rich, and social peace would have to be preserved at all cost for this policy to succeed.

So the regime unleashed its iron fist. On the antisubversion front, this meant widespread arrests and the methodical use of torture both to extract information and to create a climate of terror. Victims suffered an array of torments, documented in detail in a report based on the regime's own records and subsequently published by the Archdiocese of São Paulo: electric shocks; the "par-

---

* In an imaginative caper, guerrillas stole a safe from the house of the mistress of São Paulo's notoriously corrupt Governor Adhemar de Barros, and inside they found $2.5 million in cash.

rot's perch"* (in which a bound subject was suspended by the limbs from an iron bar); the use of insects, snakes, and chemicals in torture; the beating of children in their parent's presence; and the sexual abuse of female prisoners.

The guerrillas then resorted to kidnapping diplomats in an effort to pressure the regime into trading hostages for prisoners. Although the guerrillas achieved a modicum of success, the military intensified its repression with more arrests and more torture. The leaders of the armed resistance movement soon found themselves targeted by intense manhunts. Most were captured and summarily executed. By 1975 what had passed for an insurgency in Brazil no longer existed; nonetheless the regime continued to condone torture by the security forces as a mechanism for social control.

An argument can been made that what the military regime did was to "democratize" violence. The authorities had always used brutality to suppress the lower classes. When middle- and upper-class students and intellectuals engaged in what was considered dangerous subversion, the military and the police merely subjected them to the same forms of physical abuse they had inflicted as a matter of routine on poor people suspected of criminal activity, or caught in flagrante delicto.

In one sense, the violence perpetrated by the military regime had historical roots. But it also set a tone and provided an impetus for the age of physical insecurity in which Brazilians now live. The brutal treatment meted out to political prisoners from the upper and middle classes merely "democratized" the low value placed on the lives of poor people in Brazil. The cynical view that those with power need not account for their actions, no matter how vile, had always existed in Brazil. It gained further force when Brazilian society failed both to reach a consensus about the excesses of the military regime and to bring to justice those responsible for human-rights abuses.

In 1979, as part of an amnesty that permitted political exiles to return to the country, the military regime made certain that there would be no accounting for the unspeakable barbarities that

---

* In 1993 a monument honoring torture victims and depicting a prisoner suspended from a "parrot's perch" was unveiled in downtown Recife.

had been committed in the name of national security. Unlike what happened later in Argentina, there would be no investigations, no trials. Indeed, the military saw to it that individuals who served prominently in the military dictatorship during its most brutal years would have no difficulty continuing their careers in public service and even in winning elective office under the newly restored civilian rule.

Another form of violence that plagued Brazil during the dictatorship specifically targeted "marginal" elements among the poor. What came to be known as "death squads" may have originated with special police units created in 1958 by the Rio de Janeiro police chief to deal in summary, extralegal fashion with suspected murderers and bandits in the city's slums. But the term itself came into being in the wake of an incident that occurred during the first year of the dictatorship, when a criminal nicknamed Horseface murdered a Rio police detective. The victim's colleagues swore revenge and commenced a manhunt that ended in the town of Cabo Frio, where a large contingent of law-enforcement officers cornered Horseface and riddled him with more than a hundred bullets. The police later announced that the suspect had committed suicide to avoid arrest.

The elimination of Horseface was only the beginning. Soon the bodies of "marginal" people thought to be involved in criminal activities began turning up in abandoned fields, along unlit roadways, or in slum neighborhoods. Often the victims were handcuffed, had nylon cords tied around their necks, and showed marks of torture. Those responsible signed their handiwork with a skull and crossbones and the initials "E.M.," standing for *"Esquadrão da Morte,"* or "Death Squad."

There was no doubt that the authors of these killings were off-duty or retired policemen, acting with impunity because of the tacit complicity of the authorities, who either refused to investigate or saw to it that investigations were never brought to a successful conclusion. Before long the phenomenon had spread to São Paulo and other large cities.

The emergence of death squads reflected in part a growing sense of frustration with the inefficacy of the judicial system, because of antiquated procedures, underfunding, and inadequate manpower. The fact that police departments in Brazil were (and are) improperly trained, understaffed, ill-equipped, and poorly paid undoubtedly also contributed to the frustration.

The authoritarian climate imposed by the military regime was certainly conducive to encouraging the dispensation of summary justice by civilian police. Indeed, the work of the death squads seemed to intensify during the late 1960s and early 1970s, when the dictatorship moved into its harshest phase. In an extraordinary bit of linkage, the army enlisted the leader of the São Paulo death squad to interrogate political prisoners and help hunt down urban guerrillas.

It soon became apparent, however, that the "public-spirited ideals" that some attributed to the death squads did not always explain the motives behind the actions of their members. Some of these supposed dispensers of justice were found to belong to narcotics gangs or prostitution rings, or to be engaged in extorting protection money from gangsters. Others used the death squads to settle private grudges, or even to give vent to their psychopathic tendencies.

These disclosures, in addition to the bad publicity the death squads were attracting abroad (as well as the discovery that on a number of occasions innocent persons had been executed), led the military regime to denounce para-police activities, and state governments to launch investigations of them. Yet very few of the vigilantes were ever brought to justice, and the infrastructure of their organizations remained intact.

It was during the heyday of the death squads in the early 1970s that the urban crime rate in Brazil began to soar, first in Rio and then elsewhere. The police found themselves overwhelmed by the magnitude of the problem. The court system, creaky to begin with, could not keep pace with the increase in criminal prosecutions. The prisons were soon bursting at the seams.

By 1979 Rio had become the ninth most violent city in the world, according to a report published in the *New York Times*. A Gallup poll revealed that between 1979 and 1984, 34 percent of all Brazilians had experienced a criminal assault, a figure that placed Brazil second only to Colombia. These distinctions were achieved in spite of the death squads. In the first three months of 1980, nearly three hundred corpses were attributed to freelance executioners in Rio. But the vigilantes were having little effect on crime in the city and its suburbs. Indeed, they may have been contributing to the general climate of anarchy, thereby encouraging violent crime.

Personal security soon became *the* paramount concern of urban Brazilians, as the poor among them stole to survive, the hopeless killed as a means of expressing radical social criticism, drug traffickers fought with rival gangs for control of slum neighborhoods, kidnapping served as a lucrative enterprise for professionals and amateurs alike, and random gunfire put everyone at risk.

The primary victims of crime in Brazil were, and are, Brazilians from the lower and middle classes. Riding buses, a necessity for many, means confronting the constant danger of being held up, and also the occasional risk of being hurt in the cross fire when armed riders or drivers defend themselves against assailants. On city streets urchins strip the clothing and footwear from unattended middle- and upper-class children and rob the elderly with impunity.

Violent crime can strike at any time and in any place. Crowded city streets offer no refuge, as muggers prey on pedestrians and occupants of motor vehicles while onlookers go silently about their business. Those not wealthy enough to convert their dwellings into fortresses can never be certain that one day intruders might not force their way in and commit violence against them.

Aggressive reporting by the media has brought this vividly home to Brazilians. The magazine *Veja,* for example, published a dramatic photo of two young criminals who had gained access to a middle-class residence in Rio and were holding hostage a fifteen-year-old boy and an eleven-year-old girl in her nightdress, while the criminals tried to negotiate with police. The look of desperation on the faces of the assailants and the terror in the eyes of their helpless victims, as well as a subheading that read "Portrait of the Banality of Evil," spoke volumes about Brazilian reality.

The omnipresent risk of random violence has made urban life ever more frightening. One incident that hit *cariocas* with particular force was the 1992 death of a well-known stage and TV actor-director, who was sleeping in his bed in the fashionable Copacabana district when a stray bullet from a nearby hillside *favela* killed him.

Upper-class Brazilians have espoused the theory that responsibility for the crime explosion in Brazil rests with left-wing radicals who resorted to kidnapping and bank robberies and then served time in prisons, where they taught common criminals the skills they had developed. But this explanation is somewhat facile and does not bear all the weight that it has been given.

There is evidence that political prisoners were held together with common convicts in the prison at Ilha Grande, an island off the coast of the state of Rio de Janeiro, in the late 1960s and early 1970s, and that the latter learned from the former not only how to organize and defend their rights within the penitentiary but also some of the subtleties involved in planning and executing bank robberies and kidnappings. Moreover, this was the period when inmates founded the "Red Command," a network that enabled organized crime to take virtual control of major prisons in the state of Rio de Janeiro and eventually to draw into its ranks some of the major drug traffickers in the region.

But the left-wing prisoners surely have not inspired hardened criminals to rob banks. At best they may have improved the techniques criminals used. Indeed, some young gang members have learned elements of their trade by enlisting in the army, but this hardly makes the military responsible for Brazil's crime wave. Blaming left-wing students and intellectuals conveniently diverts attention from the responsibility the Brazilian elite bears for failing to address the social and economic ills that have produced the crisis.

The increase in violent crime marks a watershed in the country's social development. Previously, most impoverished Brazilians had accepted their lot with resignation and surprising good humor. Foreigners who observed this phenomenon could not help marveling at the capacity of the poor to bear suffering and degradation without protest. But in the early 1970s things began to change, as an increasing number of "marginals" reached a point of such desperation that they abandoned their traditional passivity and resorted to violent crime. This proved that the capacity of the supposedly easygoing Brazilian to cope with whatever hardships were heaped on him had its limits.

There is another way of looking at the crime phenomenon. If the military regime can be said to have "democratized" the torturing of suspected criminals, Brazil's have-nots may be credited with democratizing the violence they encountered in their everyday lives. With the spread of urban crime, all Brazilians have come to share in the physical insecurity that heretofore had been reserved exclusively for the poor.

In response, the dictatorship tolerated the existence of death squads, which at best were meant to fight fire with fire. Just as when the government sanctioned the brutal repression of dissent, the moral message emanating from the state on the topic of death squads was that ends justify means. But unlike the army, which had annihilated the threat of subversion, the death squads were unable to make any real headway against the urban crime wave that swept forward as a direct result of the "savage capitalism" the regime had unleashed.

The crime problem has produced further adverse reactions. Its actual and potential victims have become so frustrated by the government's inability to protect law-abiding citizens that many of them have expressed approval of the work of the death squads. Even lower-class Brazilians, who bear much of the brunt of criminal violence, have seemed willing to applaud the brutal elimination of those among them suspected of engaging in lawlessness. Moreover, small businessmen in slum neighborhoods have not hesitated to pay for the services of vigilante law enforcers.

Resorting to extralegal measures at times has become a life-or-death necessity for ordinary people. One middle-class *carioca* related the story of a friend who found that his automobile had been stolen. A stranger approached him and told him he knew where the car was and would let him know for a price. The man denounced the stranger to the police, who arrested the man, beat him, and secured a confession. Sometime later the stranger telephoned his accuser and promised to take reprisals on the man's children at some unspecified time in the future. The recipient of the threat sought protection from the police, and a policeman replied that there was only one sure way to ensure that his children would be protected, but it would cost money. Payment was made, with the understanding that off-duty policemen would "take care of" the situation. No one ever heard from the stranger again.

Another offshoot of the crime problem has been an increasing tendency for groups of citizens to take the law into their own hands and mete out rough justice to actual or alleged lawbreakers. Lynchings have occurred in slums as well as posh neighborhoods such as Copacabana in Rio de Janeiro, and in cities as well as villages in the countryside. At times enraged crowds have set upon suspects in the immediate aftermath of a crime; at other times avengers have hunted down suspects and committed acts of deliberate retribution. Groups of taxi drivers, for example, have occasionally tracked, pursued, and killed persons they believed were guilty of murdering colleagues.

Impatience with the ineffectiveness of the police and the judicial and penal systems has provided much of the impetus for law enforcement by ordinary citizens. Radio talk-show hosts have intensified the climate of violence by voicing loud support for the death squads and public lynchings, and by calling for the institution of the death penalty in Brazil.

The chronic economic crisis has not only fueled Brazil's crime rate; it has also provoked another kind of private violence on the part of those at the bottom of the social ladder. From time to time slumdwellers have rioted and sacked food stores. This phenomenon has occurred during extended droughts in the interior of the Northeast, when starvation drove *flagelados* to raid food supplies. Now it is beginning to happen in urban centers like Rio and São Paulo. Looting by the poor has also become a common occurrence whenever heavy rains flood the Avenida Brasil, the main artery into and out of Rio, and trucks laden with cargo are immobilized by the rising waters.

Over the past few years, there has been only one real break in the climate of physical insecurity that blankets Rio de Janeiro, and that occurred in June 1992 during the U.N.'s Earth Summit. The army occupied downtown Rio and those parts of town where meetings were being held or delegates were being lodged. Some fifteen thousand heavily armed troops, along with personnel carriers and troops, took up strategic positions in an unusual show of force. For about two weeks *cariocas* could walk the streets of certain sections of the city in total safety. They enjoyed this tranquility while it lasted, but as soon as the soldiers were withdrawn, violent crime resumed. The lesson to be drawn from this has ominous implications for the future of democracy in Brazil.

The private violence inflicted by ordinary criminals, citizen-vigilantes, and looters, as described up to now, is random and disorderly, in contrast to the systematic violence committed by the state. However, there is another form of nongovernmental violence that has assumed a more structured form and has become increasingly widespread in contemporary Brazil. Organized crime, especially in the area of narcotics trafficking, has reached alarming proportions and has put down deep roots in urban slums.

The history of organized crime in Brazil begins with the birth of a remarkable institution at the end of the nineteenth century, when Baron João Batista Viana de Drummond founded Rio de Janeiro's first zoo. To attract patrons, he instituted a lottery system. Each entrant received a ticket that had on it a drawing of an animal, which represented a number, and daily drawings produced winners. The lottery, which was called the *jogo do bicho,* or "animal game," eventually separated itself from the zoo and took on a life of its own.

By the middle of the twentieth century, the *jogo do bicho* had become a permanent fixture of Brazilian life. Everybody knew the names of the twenty-five animals, beginning with the ostrich and ending with the cow, and representing four consecutive numbers. Lower-class Brazilians were particularly fond of the lottery because it cost very little to place a simple bet, which paid off at 18 to 1. Although the government made sporadic attempts to close down or take over the animal game, it remained in private hands. Moreover, it maintained such a spotless reputation for fulfilling its financial obligations to participants that many Brazilians maintained that it was the only honest institution in the country.

Yet the *jogo do bicho* was an illegal operation, under the control of organized crime. The men who ran it were called "bankers." They divided Rio and its environs into baronies and formed a loose confederation. There were occasional turf wars, but since it was in everybody's interest to settle disputes as quickly and amicably as possible, these disturbances did not last very long.

By the late 1980s, the animal game had become a vast national enterprise employing over seven hundred thousand people and grossing more than $150 million a month. The state of Rio de Janeiro was the domain of three hundred bankers who had forty-five thousand people on their payrolls and controlled some three thousand locations where bets were taken. The sight of men and women with animal-game betting slips operating openly at their posts on city sidewalks has always been an indelible part of the Rio street scene. The game has remained illegal, but payoffs to policemen and their superiors have kept things running smoothly. Candidates for public office have routinely sought support from the bankers, who are known to contribute heavily to political campaigns.

With the wealth they were amassing, some of the bankers invested in their customers' communities. In addition to donating money to charities, they underwrote neighborhood samba schools (to be discussed further in Chapter Nineteen), and they even purchased professional soccer teams. Rio's leading bankers have enjoyed considerable prestige among the people whose gambling needs they serve. A handful of them have attained the status of folk heroes.

Yet under this veneer of respectability one could still find traces of blood. In 1981 the Rio police reported that over the past fourteen years fifty murders, seven attempted murders, and two kidnappings involved suspects with links to the *jogo do bicho*. In 1985 another police investigation found about one hundred forty unsolved cases of homicide or disappearances that implicated bankers or their underlings.

The animal game continues to compete successfully with government-sponsored lotteries, in large part because the low cost of betting makes it affordable for all but the poorest of the poor, in part because of its deep roots in the Brazilian psyche (a legacy of Brazil's Indian and African heritages, with their beliefs in supernatural ties between animals and humans).

But in recent years the bankers have had to confront a pair of challenges that pose serious threats to their status. The first comes from the new face of organized crime, with the emergence of "narco-traffickers" in Brazil's urban slums. The second is the more recent animosity toward them, which has gained momentum because of the contemporary wave of public revulsion against all aspects of corruption in public and private life.

The extent to which bankers themselves have been involved in drug trafficking is a matter of some uncertainty. The vast sums at their disposal must have made investing in what would be an even more profitable venture rather tempting, despite the higher risks involved. What is clear is that the bankers have not expanded into drug dealing in any massive or systematic way, at least not at the local level. This has left the door open for others to do so, with the result that thriving narcotics operations, specializing in cocaine and marijuana, have placed a substantial number of the slum neighborhoods of Rio, São Paulo, and other major cities under the dominion of gangs armed with automatic weapons.

Many of the new drug lords are young and black or mulatto. They are products of the slums and have learned their trade on the streets, in detention centers for juveniles, or behind prison bars, where they have come into contact with the "Red Command." They do not hesitate to use violence or even to engage the police in an occasional gun battle. They are clearly a breed and a generation apart from the animal-game bankers.

The drug traffickers have had a heavy impact on the lives of the slumdwellers. When gang warfare erupts, everyone in the area is put at risk, but once a single gang establishes its control over a *favela*, an atmosphere of security and tranquility descends. The drug dealers look down on the petty thieves and muggers who live in their neighborhoods and will often see to it that they ply their trades in the outside world only.

More recently, the dealers have begun to invest in social services. Unlike the *jogo do bicho* bankers, who have given money for schools, day-care centers, and other large-scale, visible projects, the drug dealers tend to dispense largesse irregularly, in the form of medicines, food, and clothing. However, the traffickers expect something in return, for example, hiding places whenever large contingents of police make forays into the slum.

The presence of confident young men carrying weapons, wearing distinctive articles of clothing (baseball caps were popular with them at one point in time), answering to colorful nicknames, and flashing large amounts of cash sets a powerful tone within the slums. The traffickers contrast sharply with hardworking, honest men and women who toil long hours to make miserable wages and must also put up with all kinds of humiliation for their efforts. The message is not lost on the children of the poor.

Indeed, the pressures on children to join the gangs are constant. Some are enlisted directly from the alleys of the neighborhood. Others are recruited while serving time in detention centers for juvenile delinquents. The traffickers use young boys to deliver cocaine to customers and to signal whenever the police enter the neighborhood. Involvement is like stepping into quicksand; once a youngster begins to work in the drug trade, he cannot quit, because he knows too much.

Just as bandits from the backlands and later bankers from the animal game have achieved a certain cachet as folk heroes, the drug traffickers have likewise begun to gain admission into the pantheon of the dispossessed. The Robin Hood aura surrounding some of them has bestirred affection in the hearts of people accustomed to being exploited and humiliated by their social betters. When the drug lord of the Rocinha *favela* in Rio was captured by the police, slumdwellers staged a protest that temporarily closed down the heavily traveled highway tunnel at the foot of their hill.

One drug dealer to gain hero status was the slender, bespectacled José Carlos dos Reis Encina, known to all as Escadinha (Little Ladder), whose gang controlled the Morro de Juramento (Oath Hill) on Rio's north side. Famous for his frequent flights from jail (once he dressed as a priest, another time as a guard), he outdid himself on December 31, 1985, when he staged a spectacular escape by helicopter from an island prison off the coast of the state of Rio de Janeiro.* He later assumed the leadership of the Red Command.

---

* Two weeks later, when Senator Edward M. Kennedy descended in a helicopter to visit a school in one of Rio's slums, some mischievous children began to shout, "It's Escadinha."

One of the more unusual traffickers was Floripes de Souza Oliveira, nicknamed "Brasilândia Nenê," who ran an extensive drug-dealing operation in Vila Brasilândia on the northern periphery of Sâo Paulo. In a land where machismo is pervasive, Nenê proved that women, too, can succeed in the field of violent crime. During the 1970s she first gained notoriety as the "Marijuana Queen," and she went on to rule her own gang with an iron hand for two decades.

A slender brunette partial to blue jeans, she was feared for her fearlessness, which was backed up with the gun she always kept within easy reach. Nenê served prison terms for murder and drug dealing but kept returning home, where she ran a string of bakeries as a cover for various criminal activities, which included money laundering and disposing of stolen goods.

Nenê's career as a crime boss came to an end on the evening of March 1, 1987. As she emerged from a taxi and was about to enter her heavily fortified home, two men dressed in black and waiting in a car parked nearby, their faces covered by bandages, pumped a hail of bullets into her. They were thought to be rival drug dealers, although there were those who suspected police involvement in the killing.

The new generation of drug traffickers has succeeded in shouldering aside the animal-game kingpins. But at least the bankers enjoyed a veneer of respectability they had been able to purchase—an asset that served them well until a single courageous judge in Rio de Janeiro decided that they should no longer be above the law.

A handful of dedicated prosecutors had been trying to make a case against the bankers for eight years. By bribing policemen to destroy evidence and by taking advantage of the opportunities for delay inherent in the Brazilian legal system, the bankers had been able to delay the proceedings for what they hoped would be an indefinite period of time. However, the prosecution adopted the clever tactic of simplifying the case against them, and they had the bad luck to appear before Judge Denise Frossard. On May 21, 1993, this no-nonsense jurist sentenced fourteen of the heads of what the press was now calling the "zoo mafia" to six-year prison terms. The only comfort the defendants could take from the verdict was that the charge of drug trafficking against them had to be dropped for lack of proof.

Judge Frossard's action drew praise from Brazilians weary of seeing the crime and corruption everywhere about them go unpunished.* But when the press reported that the incarcerated bankers were living comfortably behind bars, with access to amenities such as cellular telephones and permission to hold parties and even go on temporary leave to visit relatives on the outside, doubts about how much things had really changed began to surface.

The animal-game racketeers were no longer "untouchables," however, and the government would soon launch another strike against them. A bookkeeper who had worked for Castor de Andrade, the undisputed chief of the "zoo mafia," tipped Judge Frossard off to the whereabouts of his employer's headquarters, and a police raid turned up five vaults containing log books and computer diskettes that not only confirmed widely held suspicions but also surprised even jaded observers.

The seized documents recorded payments to government officials such as President Fernando Collor, the governor of the state of Rio de Janeiro, Rio's mayor, and numerous members of the law-enforcement community, as well as prominent private citizens.† There was also what prosecutors called evidence of a link between Andrade and narcotics traffickers in Cali, Colombia, which renewed suspicions that the bankers had been laundering drug money and were perhaps even facilitating the transit of Colombian cocaine to Europe and the United States.

---

* The magazine *Veja*, in a profile of Judge Frossard, recounts an anecdote intended to put her in a positive light, but which is indicative of the persistence of traditional attitudes about violence. A man broke into her apartment with a gun and attempted to rob her. She managed to escape and at the same time locked him inside. The police arrested him, and she personally conducted the interrogation. When the suspect refused to confess, she took delight in kicking him in the testicles.

† There was no proof that any of the recipients knew they were receiving money from Andrade, other than an admission (and an apology) from Herbert de Souza, an antihunger activist who had accepted money to help support a group fighting AIDS.

The increase in criminal activity by highly organized groups as well as freelance lawbreakers has put a tremendous strain on Brazil's prison system, which was outdated and inadequate even before the current crisis. Today Brazil has three hundred penal institutions built to hold 62,000 inmates but currently housing 130,000.

Mirroring the treatment Brazilian society has always accorded lower-class citizens who disrupt the social order, penitentiaries have traditionally dealt with inmates harshly. The sharp rise in the number of convicts sent to these institutions over the last two decades has led to an increase in the violence the penal system has inflicted on inmates, and this violence has in turn generated sporadic brutal responses by the prison population.

Indeed, in 1972, just prior to the start of the current crime wave, a report by Ministry of Justice investigators detailed the woeful inadequacies of Brazil's prisons, which they found to be filthy, overcrowded, undermanned, and in effect training camps for crime. A year later the military regime announced it would allocate $16.6 million for penal reform. This amount was but a tiny fraction of what the government was spending on its "pharaonic" projects, and this promise turned out to be yet another expression of noble intentions that would never come to fruition.

In 1980 the Minister of Justice himself recognized the bleakness of the situation when he admitted that Brazil's penitentiaries were "dumps for prisoners, where the individual is subject to the basest human degradation." But it was not until 1985, when the press disclosed the existence of a "death lottery" in a prison in Minas Gerais, that the dimensions of the prison crisis became evident.

To protest the overcrowded conditions under which they were being held, inmates announced that they were staging a lottery. The leaders of this macabre movement had put together a list of fellow prisoners they deemed worthy of sacrifice. Each week they would draw the name of a "winner," who would then be strangled with what the inmates referred to as a *teresa* (a rope made of rags tied together). The killing would go on until their demands were met. Fifteen convicts lost their lives in the lottery. The authorities tranferred some prisoners to other facilities, but they could not solve the basic problem of overcrowding without massive expenditures of funds, which simply were not available.

The culture of violence spawned by Brazil's penal system involves prison guards, inmates, and police. Guards often treat prisoners with extreme cruelty. Beatings are not uncommon, nor is solitary confinement for extended periods of time. Understaffing, low pay, and a general lack of education all contribute to the atmosphere of barbarity. The inmates commit all kinds of violence against one another, ranging from simple assaults to homosexual rape to murder. They are also brutal to hostages taken during revolts or attempts to escape.* Whenever circumstances require the state police to intervene inside a prison, the force they apply is often unrestrained, and they may also exact steep retribution once order has been restored.

Two final types of contemporary violence worth noting are private in nature. One occurs within the precincts of that most sacred of Brazilian institutions—the family—and is authored by husbands who intentionally injure or kill their wives. The other is indirectly self-inflicted; it results when Brazilians willingly engage in conduct that subjects them to the risk of serious harm.

There has always been a riptide of violence in Brazilian family life, and it stems from the absolute authority vested in the figure of the patriarch, as well as from a strong tradition of machismo. These foundation stones of male domination have vested in husbands the right to beat (and, in some instances, maim or burn) their wives—a common practice in rural areas (especially in the Northeast) and in urban slums populated by migrants from the countryside. The privilege extends across social boundaries, although wife-

---

*The most highly publicized hostage taking occurred in March of 1994, when inmates at a penitentiary in the state of Ceará seized the Cardinal of Fortaleza, Dom Aloísio Lorsheider, while he was visiting the institution as part of his efforts on behalf of human rights for prisoners. He was released, unharmed, after twenty hours of captivity.

beating in the upper and middle classes has been less frequently publicized.*

When a man kills his wife or his lover, he often escapes punishment by invoking the "defense of honor," which makes male passion, inflamed by grave affronts to one's manhood, a valid excuse for murder. Under the Brazilian legal system, murder is the only crime that requires trial by jury, and juries have wide latitude to decide cases on the basis of their intuitive notions of justice. In wife-killing cases, defense attorneys can argue that their client killed to protect his dignity, which was sullied by the alleged misconduct of his wife, and juries will often acquit the accused on this ground. Moreover, if a man is found guilty and he is a first-time offender (usually the case when wife-killing is involved), the judge may take the defendant's "violent emotion" into account in sentencing him, which often results in mild punishment.

The "defense of honor" is traceable to the Portuguese input into Brazilianness. The saying "jealous as a Portuguese" dates back several centuries and perhaps stems from the Moorish tradition of making wives and daughters subservient to their husbands and fathers. Portuguese colonial law absolved a man who caught his wife in the act of adultery and killed her.

Although the first penal code of the Brazilian empire abolished this legal privilege, it not only remained a customary defense that could be used in murder trials, but over the years it was also stretched to protect men in situations other than in flagrante delicto adultery. Thus a husband might be exonerated for killing his wife when he merely suspected her of unfaithfulness. Brazilian jurisprudence equated defense of honor with self-defense. A husband could protect his male dignity with as much force as he might lawfully use to protect his own life from an imminent threat.

In the late 1970s and early 1980s several highly publicized murder trials in Rio de Janeiro and Belo Horizonte produced acquittals based on the defense of honor. These outcomes not only

---

* Even beauty queens are not exempt. A recent authorized biography has revealed that Martha Rocha, a Miss Brazil and the runner-up in the Miss Universe pageant in 1954, was badly battered by one of her husbands, a well-known millionaire.

outraged women throughout Brazil but also gave considerable impetus to the country's budding feminist movement. Adding fuel to the indignation were reports such as a newspaper crime survey that found that in 1980, 772 women were murdered by their husbands or lovers in São Paulo alone, and few perpetrators of these crimes of passion were ever punished.

In 1991 the Superior Tribunal of Justice, Brazil's highest court in criminal and civil matters, reversed the acquittal of a husband accused of murdering his wife on the ground that the judgment was contrary to the facts presented, and held that discovering a wife's adultery did not give a husband the same legal protections afforded a person whose own life was threatened. The decision was widely hailed, but on retrial the trial judge permitted the defense of honor to be invoked again, and once again the jury acquitted the defendant. This time, under the law, there could be no appeal.

Feminists have had more success in changing the way law-enforcement authorities deal with crimes against women. In 1985 the governor of the state of São Paulo set up the first Division for the Protection of Women within the state police. Officers assigned to the division (often women) investigate complaints of violence against women and may bring criminal charges. Other states have set up similar units. As one activist for women's rights has noted, these new police entities "not only combat crime but also its definition, changing the border of accepted/nonaccepted social behavior."

It is clear that changes in the law and in law enforcement programs aimed at reducing violence against women can bring about incremental progress only, but they will not succeed in any meaningful way until deeply ingrained societal attitudes evolve. There is a direct correlation between the way the judicial system responds to social problems and values cherished by most Brazilians.

Self-inflicted violence resulting from personal recklessness is certainly not peculiar to Brazil. Every nationality has its risk preferrers, as economists like to call them: individuals with a keen taste for peril and a low concern for their own safety. Brazil, however, seems to have more of them than most.

Examples abound. President Fernando Collor enhanced his popularity with the masses when he demonstrated his disdain for danger and engaged in highly publicized stunts such as piloting a jet fighter at more than the speed of sound and riding a motorcycle without a helmet at twice the legal speed limit. Daredevils lie on custom-made skateboards and descend at breakneck speed a two-and-a-half-mile stretch of highway that winds its way down the escarpment that lies between the city of São Paulo and the sea, a roadway so steep that only uphill vehicular traffic is allowed.

Several of the nation's most cherished sports idols are professional race drivers. Emerson Fittipaldi, who won the 1993 Indianapolis 500, and Ayrton Senna, three-time world champion of Formula 1 auto racing,* are not only revered but imitated by ordinary Brazilian motorists.

The recklessness phenomenon crosses class lines. Young men from the *favelas* practice "train surfing," the sport of balancing oneself atop a speeding train. More recently they have invented "bus surfing," which involves standing on the roof of an express bus as it makes the nonstop run between Copacabana Beach and downtown Rio de Janeiro.

Several elements of Brazilianness contribute to this devil-may-care attitude toward risk: a low regard for human life (a by-product of slavery and a corollary of the institutionalization of extreme poverty in Brazil); the compulsion to assert one's machismo and individualism; and an adolescent mind-set that fosters a feeling of invulnerability to harm.

The disregard of risks to themselves has combined with a lack of concern about jeopardizing others to make Brazilians extremely dangerous when they take the wheel of a motor vehicle. As Albert Camus observed in a journal he kept during a 1949 visit, "Brazilian drivers are either joyous madmen or icy sadists." Auto collisions claim the lives of more than fifty thousand victims a year in Brazil. In the city of São Paulo alone, there are more than four hundred fifty accidents a day.

A disdain for traffic laws, which are seldom enforced, contributes to the carnage. Persons responsible for accidents are rarely held accountable, either criminally or civilly, for the results of their reck-

---

* Senna was killed in a crash during a race in Italy on April 30, 1994.

lessness. Safety regulations aimed at promoting highway safety are also routinely ignored. Bus and truck drivers often work long hours without a break, in violation of rules designed to make certain that motorists remain alert, and exhaustion has resulted in a number of highway catastrophes.

The aspect of violence that has most horrified observers both inside and outside Brazil is the systematic brutalization of young people on society's margin. Nowhere does the gap separating rhetoric and reality emerge more starkly than in the contrast between the guarantees afforded children by the 1988 Constitution and the cold-blooded assassination of boys and girls who live on city streets. If there is anything that most vividly symbolizes the perversity of the contemporary wave of violence in Brazil, it is the way it has victimized children. The story is not a pleasant one, but it must be told.

# Chapter 10

# Suffer the Little Children

*I*n 1944 Getúlio Vargas presided over the festive inauguration of a broad thoroughfare named after him and linking Rio de Janeiro's downtown with the north zone of the city. A chorus of thirty thousand children, conducted by world-class composer Heitor Villa-Lobos, raised angelic voices to celebrate the occasion, and had a clear view of the façade of the eighteenth-century Church of Our Lady of Candelária, from whose stately portals the mighty Avenida Presidente Vargas seemed to flow.

Forty-nine years later, another group of children would participate in a noteworthy event in front of the picture-postcard landmark. Instead of singing in a choir, they would play the role of murder victims, and their numbers would be added to the mounting body count of Brazilian children killed on the streets, a phenomenon that has badly marred the image of Brazil.

Shortly after midnight on July 23, 1993, they were sleeping on cardboard mats near the entrance to the floodlit church when two unmarked cars approached. Six men emerged from the vehicles and began to question them. An argument ensued and the men drew their weapons, took aim at the heads of the boys, and fired. The execution-style slaying claimed five lives. Within a short time three other boys were slaughtered in front of the Museum of Modern Art, about a mile away, in all likelihood by the same assassins. The killing was done with cold-blooded efficiency, and the Rio de Janeiro police came under immediate suspicion.

Although the incident provoked outraged headlines in newspapers around the globe and widespread revulsion within Brazil

259

itself, it also drew the approval of a number of Rio residents, who used police hot lines and radio call-in shows to heap praise on the work of the executioners. Indeed, a newspaper poll published shortly after the event disclosed that 16 percent of the city's population supported the killings.

The Candelária massacre was actually a rather prosaic event. In 1992, 424 children in the state of Rio de Janeiro were murdered, and during the first six months of 1993, 320 met the same fate. At the time of the incident in downtown Rio, it was estimated that every day 4 Brazilian children were homicide victims. In 1991 the Institute of Legal Medicine in the state of Pernambuco autopsied the remains of 79 youngsters, age ten to seventeen, who had been shot to death on the streets of Recife. About 80 percent of the bodies had been mutilated.

The universe of "street kids" in Brazil breaks down into two categories: those who actually live on the streets and sleep on sidewalks, under viaducts or in other sheltered locations, and those who sleep at home but roam the streets during the day. Some work, some play, some beg, some sniff glue, and some engage in criminal activity that ranges from petty theft to armed assault to an occasional murder.

Life on the streets for these children carries with it a constant risk of physical harm. One source of danger for them is police violence. A worker for the Pastoral Commission for Minors, an organ of the Archdiocese of São Paulo, told of seeing a policeman push a youngster's face into a wall; the impact left the boy with a broken nose. He related the story of how railroad security guards who had caught an urchin illegally selling merchandise on a train hauled him outside and forced his feet onto the tracks; the boy lost his toes when they were crushed by a passing train. "The police are supposed to deter crime, but in fact they cover it up," he charged. "Adult criminals use the kids in a variety of jobs, and then the police use the kids as scapegoats. They make a show of roughing them up, to prove to the public that they are doing their job."

A São Paulo attorney specializing in juvenile justice pointed out that official violence is seldom punished. "The police are completely out of control," she claimed. "For example, individuals not connected with them may do the actual torturing of suspects inside a police station. It's impossible to trace these people." She described efforts to discover what had really happened to a fourteen-year-old whom the police had detained and whose body turned up a week later; the child's body had been perforated four times and buried under another name. "This sort of thing happens all the time," she said ruefully.

The official violence uniformed police perpetrate on street children pales in comparison to the handiwork of *justiceiros*(vigilantes), off-duty or retired policemen who engage in what some have called an "extermination industry" designed to reduce the numbers of youngsters suspected of engaging in criminal activity. These free-lancers often torture their prey before killing them. Due process of law is the least of their concerns. Some observers have estimated that as many as half of the victims may have been totally innocent of even any suspicion of wrongdoing. Human-rights advocates have alleged that some businessmen hurt financially by the high rate of crime have been underwriting the *justiceiros*—a charge echoed in 1991 by the federal Minister of Health.

Street children must face other physical threats as well. Ordinary citizens upset by the crime wave sweeping Brazil have been known to vent their frustrations on youngsters. The archdiocese worker in São Paulo told of an incident in which an attorney caught and stomped on a fifteen-year-old who had tried to steal a watch from him. The boy vomited bile and died fifteen minutes later. The attorney successfully defended himself against criminal charges. The violence aimed at street kids is in part a response to the violence perpetrated by the children, who are victimizers as well as victims. The cycle is a vicious one: society brutalizes homeless boys and girls, who become brutal themselves. According to a São Paulo social worker, the police have used cigarette-lighter fluid to set fire to children they have picked up in the Praça da Sé in the downtown area. In response, some of the children have taken it upon themselves to spray lighter fluid on passersby at the Praça and then have attempted to ignite it. "It's their form of counter-terrorism," he observed.

The mass media gives ample coverage to violent crime committed by children, with television often conveying images that pack a terrifying impact. For example, in July 1992 newscasts showed a videotape of three boys who looked to be no more than twelve years old surrounding an elderly man in downtown Rio. They first asked him for a match and then demanded money. A look of horror came on his face as they drew knives on him. At that point one of the assailants noticed that someone was filming them, and the trio fled. The old man had the equivalent of about 30 cents in his pocket at the time.

What rachets up public outrage against street urchins even higher is the cloak of impunity that protects children who kill, assault, and rob. The legal system does not brand them criminals but instead uses the more euphemistic term *infratores* (lawbreakers) and does not subject them to punishment. Under a statute enacted in 1990, a lawbreaker under twelve years of age is generally released into the custody of his family or a surrogate family. A lawbreaker over twelve will be sent to a state institution specially designed for adolescents. These facilities are so antiquated and overcrowded that there is constant pressure to release the wrongdoers as soon as possible, and children escape from them regularly.*

At this point it might be useful to place the violence perpetrated by and against street kids in a larger context, that of the sorry plight of all poor children in Brazil. The "savage capitalism" that fueled the Brazilian economy in the late 1960s and early 1970s took an especially harsh toll on the children of the families left behind in the country's rush to development, and the economic crisis of the 1980s made a bad situation much worse. In 1985, out of approximately 3.9 million children born in Brazil, about 320,000 died before reaching their fourth year; 246,000 did not survive their first year, and of these half perished during the first thirty days of life. A study released at the end of 1987 put it more starkly: every four minutes two children less than one year old die in Brazil. According to one estimate, proper preventive care could reduce by two thirds the deaths of children below the age of five in Brazil.

---

* It is ironic that young criminals enjoy the same impunity that has always cloaked the rich and powerful in Brazil. But there are no *justiceiros* or lynch mobs that take it upon themselves to inflict retribution on elite wrongdoers.

A 1992 study by the Brazilian Institute of Geography and Statistics found that 15 percent of Brazilian children under the age of five showed signs of malnutrition. It also concluded that 32 million children under the age of seventeen lived in poverty. This figure exceeds the entire population of Argentina or Canada.

The great majority of poor children must work to support themselves and help their families. Indeed, a recent study has revealed that 8 million children work; they comprise 11.6 percent of the Brazilian workforce. An estimated 2.8 million young people between the ages of ten and fourteen are employed—in violation of the 1988 Constitution, which solemnly proclaims that the minimum work age in Brazil is fourteen. Many of these young workers receive as little as one third of what an adult would earn at the same job, and they are subject to a range of occupational hazards. With their small hands and dexterity, youngsters are considered especially suitable for work in the shoe and glass industries, the latter subjecting children to high oven temperatures and constant noise of up to 195 decibels.

The dangers of the workplace parallel the hazards many poor Brazilian children face at home, where beatings and sexual abuse are not uncommon. Of about one thousand complaints of sexual assaults reported betweem 1988 and 1993 to a São Paulo state agency charged with protecting minors, more than 75 percent of the assaults were alleged to have been committed by relatives. Moreover, it is quite likely that most rapes within family units go unreported.

There is a correlation between domestic violence perpetrated on minors and child prostitution in Brazil. A figure often cited posits that about half a million Brazilian girls are engaged in "the life," as it is called. This figure is probably as exaggerated as the estimate of two million made in 1987 by UNICEF (the United Nations Children's Fund), since reliable surveys have never been conducted. Yet the prevalence of the phenomenon cannot be denied, whatever the exact numbers may be. Poverty and antediluvian attitudes that make ostracism the penalty for loss of virginity before marriage also force young girls to sell their bodies.

In São Paulo and Rio de Janeiro, the seemingly inexhaustible supply of children has kept up with the demand for "pretty babies."

Girls learn quickly never to admit to being more than fifteen years old, lest they lose potential patrons. Many of them admire Madonna and imitate her as best they can. Boys learn to dress as girls or to adopt a macho swagger in order to attract homosexual clients.

Given Brazil's current economic crisis, it is not surprising that many youngsters end up living on the streets. Yet the problem of homeless children in Brazil is not new. Among the reasons cited for child homelessness among the black and mulatto population has been the disruptive impact of slavery on black families and the dislocations brought about by abolition, when freed slaves were turned loose on their own in the countryside and later migrated to urban areas, inevitably left a number of young people to fend for themselves at an early age. One of the first to call national attention to the plight of the abandoned child was Jorge Amado, when he wrote *Capitães da Areia (Captains of the Sand)*, a 1937 novel chronicling (and somewhat romanticizing) the adventures of a gang of youths surviving on the streets in the city of Salvador. Living in tiny shacks, physically abused by a drunken, frustrated father or by the uncaring man with whom their mother is living, forced to seek work and bring money home, many children understandably prefer to run away and fend for themselves on the streets.

What compounds the contemporary dilemma of Brazil's "lost children" is that they are part of an ever-expanding pool of people without hope, a dehumanized subspecies that poses a critical threat to social stability. To capture the essence of the tragedy, one has to forget about the numbers and enter places such as the Vila Maria shelter in São Paulo and look at the faces of the street kids taking refuge there.

The collective as well as the personalized misery encountered in Brazil's urban rookeries and rural backwaters may not shock the sensibilities of those accustomed to viewing Brazilian poverty, but even for veteran observers there is something very unsettling about the sight of youngsters who have been systematically brutalized by the society into which they have been born.

In addition to the obvious fact that virtually all the children are black or brown (another visible legacy of slavery), what produces a dramatic impression on the casual observer is the children's eyes—darting, attentive, curious, and expressive. As Cláudia, a worker at the Vila Maria shelter, explained it, "Observation is their stock in trade. They are keen students of human behavior. They need to know whom to steal from, who might grab them, who might be police. It's a matter of survival for them." When I visited the shelter, they watched me very carefully and wanted to know my identity. Told that I was an American writer, one of the boys approached and guilelessly asked to hear some English spoken. Another gave me a gift of some rosary beads.

The truth painfully emerges: they are really children—affectionate and affection-starved, fragile, playful, innocent, capable of laughter and tears, smiling the irresistible Brazilian smile. Yet the same youngsters can be as dangerous as wild animals—hard-eyed, tough, ruthless, explosive, vicious. Maria Teresa Moura, a social worker in Rio de Janeiro, described another aspect of street children's dichotomous existence. "They mature by necessity and become adults very quickly. But many of them still sleep in the fetal position, often with their thumbs in their mouths. You can find them playing with toy cars like four-year-olds, but with cigarettes dangling from their lips."

The distinctive personalities of the Vila Maria children became obvious even to the casual observer. There was the beautiful Claudinha, thirteen years old and a heavy smoker, beginning to develop as a woman, wearing a lanyard around her forehead, curly-haired, scars disfiguring her face and chest. There was eight-year-old Paulo, elfin, barefoot, blonde, and dark-skinned, his hands heavily bandaged. He had stolen a watch and then refused to sell it to an *intrujão* (an adult who handles pilfered property for the urchins). The latter responded by dousing the boy with gasoline and setting fire to him. As I watched Paulo, he aimed a playful kick at the groin of one of the counselors, and a playful swipe with a shard of broken glass.

The counselors try to interact with the children on the children's own terms. For example, they respect the children's freedom—the most cherished possession of street kids, something that they have fought to win and that is fundamental to their existence. The counselors also respect the strong sense of solidarity and sharing that develop among abandoned children (traits shared by adolescent street-gang members in the United States). They find themselves spending a great deal of time decoding the street vocabulary the youngsters use.

A survey of a group of street kids produced some revealing answers. When asked what they were most afraid of, they named either someone in their family or something quite ordinary, such as cockroaches or cats. When asked what they would most like to do that they hadn't done before, the most common answer was that they would like to play; next on the list was to travel, to places like Japan.

The lives of Brazil's street kids reflect a process of natural selection. Their experience suggests a cruel, if unintended experiment that confirms the tenets of social Darwinism. Leila Iannone, a São Paulo social worker and author, put it succinctly: "The weak die early from disease and violence; the strong survive to adulthood."

Those who do not shrink from the struggle develop a great deal of character, according to a worker for the São Paulo archdiocese. "They are conquering life and have a strong sense of dignity. They hate being pitied and will strongly object when anyone calls them 'abandoned children.' " Indeed, one of their cherished goals is to join the Brazilian mainstream. As a worker for the UNICEF in Brasília noted, "When they get a little money, they prefer to eat at Bob's [a popular fast-food chain] because they see the TV ads for Bob's and want to be like everyone else."

At the same time, they realize full well what society has done and is doing to them. As Maria Teresa Moura observed, "They are aware of the process of their marginalization and clearly perceive how people are judging them." They know that they have no choice but to do what they are doing. In the words of one of the youngsters who attended a "Municipal Encounter of Street Kids" in 1987, "Nobody is born stealing."

That these children regularly resort to drugs should be no surprise. The substance of choice is glue, easy to obtain, inexpensive, and potent. Sniffing it can have serious and irreversibly damaging effects on the brain. Participants at the 1987 "Encounter" gave various explanations for their abuse of this substance: "On the street you have to sniff glue; if you don't, you can't put up with this life";

"Kids sniff glue and forget life, they see [animated] cartoons on the walls, they forget their hunger."

Other factors influencing children to sniff glue include peer pressure, encouragement from the adults who purchase stolen goods from them and use them in other criminal activities, and no doubt a strong desire to make a statement of social protest. Glue sniffing produces a euphoria that fortifies the user's resolve to engage in criminal activity that might turn violent.

Other substances that street kids abuse include ether, stain removers, fire-extinguishing sprays, varnish, and gasoline. Some youngsters even smoke horse manure or inject into their feet a mixture of coffee and water. When they reach puberty, they often switch to using marijuana as a status symbol. Those who move on into organized crime end up using cocaine.

At the Vila Maria shelter, counselors encouraged the children to draw and talk about the realms they inhabit while under the influence of drugs. Voyages to stars, comets, and satellites—obvious reflections of the children's earthly discontents—were the most popular fantasies.

The impact of society's institutions on these young people is seldom positive and often negative. The public school system, for example, cannot deal with them. "The educational system in Brazil is hardly suitable for street kids," commented Maria Cecília Ziliotto, the São Paulo representative of the National Foundation for the Well-Being of Minors. "It's not very good to begin with, and poor children need a great deal of attention, because they get no help at home. Instead, the schools give them even less than they give middle-class youngsters, and in the end they expel the street kids." As a Vila Maria counselor put it, "The street kids are not accepted in the public schools. They come from an entirely different reality and have nothing in common with their classmates."

One set of public entities that does directly touch the lives of underprivileged children is the complex web of federal and state institutions created both to protect the welfare of needy minors and to deal with lawbreakers under the age of eighteen, who by law cannot be held criminally responsible for their misdeeds. Over time, as the poverty of children and the violence perpetrated by and against them have grown, the government has proven incapable of recognizing and remedying the complex web of social ills that are to blame for the sad existences of street children in Brazil.

During the colonial period and up to 1889, when Brazil abolished its monarchy and became a republic, it was thought to be the job of the churches to take care of abandoned and orphaned children. As Brazil's cities grew more populated and crime increased, the elected governments that ruled the country in the first three decades of the twentieth century took the position that urban violence was a matter for the police to deal with and repress. Thus, institutions were created to control and punish delinquent children.

It was not until the authoritarian regime of Getúlio Vargas that social problems were recognized as such. As a result of the new policies developed to confront these problems the Service of Assistance to the Minor (SAM) was created. As a department within the federal Ministry of Justice, it was designed to foster the vocational rehabilitation of youngsters who ended up in detention centers. But a lack of adequate funding and staffing, a spate of corruption, and the physical mistreatment of children by officials and guards earned for facilities operated by the SAM a deserved reputation as "branch offices of hell" and "crime schools."

The military regime that seized power in 1964 adopted what it proclaimed to be a new priority for poor and delinquent children. It abolished the SAM and in its place established the National Foundation for the Well-Being of the Minor (FUNABEM). State governments created similar agencies, called FEBEMs (State Foundations for the Well-Being of the Minor). The responsibilities delegated to FUNABEM included the dispensing of federal funds to state entities, such as São Paulo's FEBEM, and the actual day-to-day administration of detention centers in the city of Rio de Janeiro (a seemingly anachronistic function dating back to the days when Rio was the capital of Brazil).

Despite its efforts to substitute programs assisting children for those that had been trying to punish and control them, despite the organizational changes it made, the military regime did not bring about any significant improvements. The FUNABEM-run facilities often tried to instill a military-like discipline in their charges, who just as often resisted. As economic indicators plunged and the crime rate soared, there was an increase in the use of minors by adults in the commission of serious crimes, which occasionally included murder. The young people whom the police caught were committed to FUNABEM or FEBEM facilities, which often had to release them after a short time because of overcrowding.

The mass media in Brazil seized the opportunity to sensationalize the exploits of juvenile criminals, virtually all of whom were identified as alumni of FUNABEM or the various FEBEMs. One of the most notorious was sixteen-year-old Reinaldo Moreno, popularly known as Naldinho, a frequent fugitive from the São Paulo FEBEM, who was accused of robbery and murder. The newspapers made him into a sort of "superbandit," and he became a symbol for those who advocated a hard line on juvenile crime. The São Paulo police made his recapture a matter of pride. The boy's body, riddled with bullets, eventually turned up in Rio de Janeiro. The circumstances of his death were never clarified, but rumors implicated law-enforcement officials from São Paulo.

The great majority of young people passing through these institutions had never committed any violent crimes. Often the police picked them up for vagrancy or begging. (Christmas and Carnival are regular occasions when the police sweep minors from city streets.) According to Maria Ignês Bierrenbach, a former director of the São Paulo FEBEM, judges often brand as lawbreakers children picked up for vagrancy and brought before them several times, and then they commit them to FEBEM. The stigma that the children then carry makes their integration into the community very difficult.

In 1981 the FEBEM in São Paulo gained worldwide notoriety as the setting for *Pixote*, Héctor Babenco's prize-winning, gut-wrenching cinematic depiction of the fate of a group of young boys who are committed to a reformatory, escape, and lead a life of crime in São Paulo and Rio de Janeiro. The harshness of life in the closed society of the institution mirrors the brutality of the outside world, where the title character, a ten-year-old, snatches purses, deals dope, robs a prostitute's customers, and eventually commits murder.

With the transition to democracy in 1984, efforts were undertaken to ameliorate conditions in the São Paulo FEBEM. One goal of the newly elected state government was to eliminate abusive practices on the part of FEBEM employees who were known to be routinely inflicting physical violence on minors. More ambitious plans sought to change FEBEM's paternalistic, assistance-oriented approach and to create a system that would respect the rights of the children as human beings and citizens. The bureaucracy resisted. Guards who wanted to maintain within FEBEM the authoritarian structure of the society beyond the institution's walls complained that the young inmates were given too much freedom. Moreover, the guards pointed out that the social services FEBEM was now providing for its charges exceeded what society made available to the children of FEBEM guards and functionaries, who were poorly paid for difficult, thankless jobs. Their discontent infected the entire enterprise.

For nearly two years unrest plagued the large FEBEM facility in Belém, one of São Paulo's grey industrial, working-class districts near the Tietê River. Drugs and weapons found their way inside, and young prisoners fashioned "guns" from dark wood and even soap bars. Mutinies and escapes were frequent, the latter occasionally abetted by friends from outside who boldly invaded the confines of the "Quadrilateral," as the complex is called. An ex-internee shot and killed a FEBEM inspector at the institution's gate. A youthful inmate hanged himself.

The inevitable explosion occurred in February of 1986, when a series of riots rocked the facility. Shock troops from the state police eventually entered and used brute force to subdue the young rebels, some of whom were carrying knives, clubs, and stones. But the children managed to reduce to charred shambles the pavillions that housed them.

Until recently, no effort was made to segregate detainees according to the gravity of the crimes they were charged with. A worker at a FUNABEM facility in Rio de Janeiro, where juvenile offenders of all types are housed at random, underscored the senselessness of such an arrangement. "We mix hard-core criminals with kids who are in here for stealing oranges." He pointed out a shy fourteen-year old who had been sent to the institution for getting into a fight in school, and he then described another boy in the same group of inmates. "He was part of a gang which held up a taxi driver, shot him in the head (but didn't kill him), dragged him from the cab, slit open his stomach, put rocks in, and then threw him in a river."

Indeed, the violent crimes attributed to youthful offenders strain the imagination. In the isolation ward of the São Paulo FE-BEM, which houses boys who are ill, subject to discipline, or kept apart for their own protection (rapists, for example, run the risk of dire physical retribution from their peers), two black teenagers share a cell. The seventeen-year-old sits on a bench, doubled over from the injuries he sustained during a barroom brawl, which had aggravated a bullet wound in the spine he had previously suffered at the hands of the police. He is surprisingly articulate and occasionally flashes a fetching grin. He says it pains him to stand erect. The sixteen-year-old, handsome and well-built, is recovering from a bullet wound in the thigh he sustained during a holdup in which he claims not to have been participating. They admit to having killed seven people between them, and each with quiet pride demonstrates the various bullet and knife scars his body bears. Each has been in and out of the "Quadrilateral" on at least eight occasions—an indication of the "revolving-door" nature of juvenile justice in Brazil.

What strikes me most as I listen to them is that they betray no feeling at all for the crimes they say they have committed, and they project a completely antisocial attitude. One of the monitors points out that although the law prevents these boys from being punished, the police in São Paulo know who they are and what they have done; they will be "eternal suspects" and will constantly be subject to police harassment. Thus even if the two turned their lives around and no longer committed crimes, the police would continue to watch and question them.

The seventeen-year-old speaks bitterly, in a soft voice. "There are worse people than us on the outside, but the police don't arrest them because they have money, social position, family, lawyers. Only the poor come to FEBEM."

This is the sorry truth that the minors in these institutions learn merely by looking around. When scions of wealthy or even middle-class families run afoul of the law, they are normally released into the custody of their parents, who promise to procure for them psy-

chological or psychiatric treatment. As a FEBEM monitor remarked, "Statistically speaking, juvenile delinquency on the part
of the rich doesn't exist in Brazil."

In some small ways detainees actually benefit from their stays.
The average weight they gain during the first month at the São
Paulo FEBEM is from six to thirteen pounds. Many for the first time
learn rudimentary hygiene, such as how to use a toothbrush, and
the basics of preventive medicine.

They also receive medical and dental care. At the well-
equipped, well-scrubbed FUNABEM hospital in Quintino, on the
outskirts of the city of Rio de Janeiro, Dr. Carlos José Carvalho
pointed out that malnutrition and infectious diseases are the most
common ailments afflicting institutionalized minors. Of much
greater concern to him was that as of December 1987 eleven young
patients at the hospital had been diagnosed as suffering from AIDS,
apparently contracted through sexual contact and the use of contaminated hypodermic needles.

The state government of São Paulo has been taking additional
steps to improve its programs for poor and delinquent children. The
Youth Administration now supervises all these programs, and it has
initiated a number of reforms. For example, a new entity called
"SOS Children" takes in lost or abandoned youngsters, handles
complaints of violence against children, and does the initial screening of minors accused of breaking the law. Only those suspected of
committing serious offenses are sent to a nearby FEBEM facility. The
administration also operates open houses and shelters for street
kids.

As hopelessly grim as the plight of poor, abandoned, and delinquent
children may be, concerned private citizens are struggling with the
problem on many levels. The courage, persistence, and indomita-
bility of many of these children offer slender rays of hope that a
small percentage of them may be salvaged from society's scrap
heap.

There is currently a vast array of social programs for street kids,
and they take varying approaches to the problem. Some, like the
Movement of Street Boys and Girls, are primarily political and seek
to influence government officials and legislators. Others are solo

efforts, such as that of an air force noncommissioned officer who uses facilities at the airbase at Galeão in Rio de Janeiro to provide activities for impoverished youngsters. Still others are more elaborate, such as the former municipal slaughterhouse that has been converted into a center for the education and training of 350 street kids in Curitiba. Some corporations are beginning to involve themselves in efforts to help bring these youngsters back into the societal fold.

The work of a dynamic, dedicated, courageous lawyer named Ana Vasconcelos typifies the efforts of individual Brazilians. Her project in Recife targets a generally neglected aspect of the tragedy of Brazil's underprivileged children—the plight of street girls.

"People never look at these girls as workers, the way they might perceive boys on the street," Ana has observed. "The girls are seen and treated as sexual objects. The pressure to engage in prostitution overwhelms them. It is very easy for them to earn money by selling their bodies.

"So far three girls here have died from AIDS. We try to give them some sex education and we provide them with condoms, but the adults who patronize them don't want them to use contraceptives. It's a cultural thing. Sperm is considered an instrument of male domination, and the use of a condom is viewed as a form of rejection. There have been instances of girls getting killed for insisting on wearing them.

"The street boys also exploit the girls. They use them to do errands, have sex with them, and physically abuse them. The fantasy of these girls is to find a boy who will love them.

"The girls live a life of permanent violence. They use razor blades to defend themselves. Sometimes they cut themselves as a form of self-flagellation. For them there is a very thin line between love and hate.

"The Church, the rural tradition from which most of them come—indeed, Brazilian society as a whole—fills these girls with a sense of guilt. Our job is to try to instill some dignity and self-worth into them."

Ana's project, called the "House of Passage," is just off the Conde da Boa Vista Avenue in downtown Recife. The building is old and somewhat dilapidated, but Ana and her coworkers have made great efforts to turn it into a refuge where the girls can come and go as they please. The "House of Passage" offers them meals, a locker where they can store their meager possessions, and classes providing rudimentary education and certain job skills. Friday is cleanup day, and a number of the girls assist with the chores. They are mostly black or mulatto. Several are pregnant. Two are sleeping in a stairwell under a piece of canvas, still feeling the effects of the glue they sniffed on the previous night.

Ana drives off with one of the pregnant girls, a fifteen-year-old *mulata* with beautiful grey eyes. Sessa lives with her mother and her two children on the sidewalk in front of the downtown Church of São Francisco. Sessa's mother rents out her grandchildren to a beggar for 50 percent of the children's daily take. Ana is trying to help Sessa negotiate with her mother so that Sessa will be permitted to care for her third child herself.

The challenge of working with Recife's street girls is severely testing Ana. "Every day the problem gets worse," she says. "All we can do is try to help them survive the reality of their daily lives."*

If there is one person who symbolizes the marginalized minor in Brazil, perhaps it is Fernando Ramos da Silva. Born into an impoverished family in Diadema, a working-class suburb of São Paulo, Fernando was twelve years old when he had the good fortune to land the title role in *Pixote*. The film was a great success, and his performance gained high praise. In the words of *New York Times* reviewer Vincent Canby, Fernando "has one of the most eloquent faces ever seen on the screen. It's not actually bruised, but it looks battered. The eyes don't match, as if one eye were attending to immediate events and the other were considering escape routes. It's a face full of life and expression."

At the conclusion of the film, the diminutive Pixote is cruelly rejected by the prostitute with whom he has been working. He

---

*The daughter of a sugar-mill owner in the interior of Pernambuco, Ana has always had a fiercely independent spirit. As a child she ran away several times with itinerant gypsies ("My father would always come to the next town to fetch me"), and the local prostitutes fascinated her ("They were strong women and they were free").

picks up his gun and leaves. The final scene shows him walking by himself along some railroad tracks.

For Fernando Ramos da Silva, life and art were interchangeable. Few acting roles came his way after *Pixote,* and he had to return, jobless, to Diadema. Eventually he made the news again. The police arrested him for burglary and later for carrying a weapon. In 1987 they shot him to death during what they said was a robbery he was committing. He was nineteen.

# Chapter 11

# Abusing Nature's Bounty

*T*he press customarily referred to Cubatão as the "Valley of Death," the "most polluted place on Earth," or "Brazil's Minamata."* For some the city was a symbol of the violence Brazilians had been willing to inflict on themselves in the name of progress. For others it represented the fruits of "savage capitalism" at its worst. Since Brazilians like to poke fun at everything, there was even a popular song describing the varied forms of pollution one could sample during a "Honeymoon in Cubatão," and a Rio punk nightclub called "Cubatão Dusk."

The working-class residents of this industrial complex thirty-five miles from the city of São Paulo have had the sorry distinction of living in a "chemical laboratory" where they serve as test animals for what has turned out to be an experiment to determine both the long- and short-term effects of air and water pollutants on humans. According to measurements taken in 1980 by a government agency, every day the factories of Cubatão were discharging ten thousand tons of toxic gases and particulate matter into the atmosphere. In one slum neighborhood the level of air contamination was twice what the World Health Organization considered capable of producing excess mortality. In 1977 a device installed there by the state government to measure pollutants in the air broke down after eighteen months because it was strained beyond

---

* Between 1932 and 1968 a company dumped tons of mercury into the ocean off the southern coast of Japan near the village of Minamata, a bountiful fishing area. The poison took a thousand lives and inflicted serious illness on thousands more.

its capacity. Moreover, the levels of acid rain in Cubatão exceeded those to be found anywhere on the planet.

The 1980 investigation found that on a daily basis industrial plants were dumping twenty-six hundred tons of poisonous wastes into adjacent rivers, which were all certifiably lifeless. Detergent foam, clouds of steam, and green sludge were the signature elements of Cubatão's waterways, which ceaselessly disgorged deformed, dead fish and assorted foul stenches.

The effects of this ecological violence on the nearly one hundred thousand citizens of Cubatão were predictably disastrous. The incidences of birth defects were said to exceed those to be found elsewhere in the country, and unconfirmed reports of gruesomely deformed infants—babies born without brains, and kittens born without limbs—added to Cubatão's disrepute. The city had Brazil's highest infant mortality rate. As many as half of the city's inhabitants were believed to be suffering from some form of lung disease.

The story of the ruin of Cubatão involves elephantine miscalculation, which may be attributed to a number of uniquely Brazilian tendencies. Indifference to risk, especially as it might affect people on the lower end of the social scale, obviously was a factor. This same attitude has made Brazil a leading importer of dangerous pesticides. The primary victims of these agrochemicals are the farmworkers who are constantly exposed to them; the primary beneficiaries are the multinational companies that dump in Brazil products banned in "First World" countries, or that sell chemcials in Brazil under circumstances in which proper warnings are not given to those who will use them.

Other elements contributing to the misjudgment include an unblinking embrace of modernism, without regard for its possible adverse consequences (a mind-set also conducive to the indiscriminate use of supposedly "state-of-the-art" pesticides manufactured abroad). According to José Lutzenberger, a pioneer in Brazil's environmental movement, his compatriots equate nature with backwardness.

What happened in Cubatão mirrored developments in other parts of the country, where there were abundant signs that Brazilians were well on their way toward destroying their "tropical Eden." One example is the fate of the 140-square-mile Guanabara

Bay, which provides a spectacular setting for Rio de Janeiro. There was a time when much of Rio's social life centered on the bay, whose waters welcomed swimmers, boaters, and fishermen. Today it is a cesspool, a receptacle for the raw sewage discharged from heavily populated slums, and for waste originating in shipyards and nearby factories. The rivers that flow into the bay add more pollutants to the mix of toxic substances. A scenic backdrop that at one time inspired lyrical prose from travelers arriving in Rio by ship* now repels visitors and residents alike.

Cubatão was once a collection of mangrove swamps intersected by rivers and inlets from the nearby sea. During the early years of the captaincy of São Vicente, the need to secure a trail connecting the port of Santos with the highland trading post of São Paulo led to the founding of a small settlement on the bank of the Cubatão River. Canoes brought passengers and freight from the port of Santos to Cubatão, where horses or mules provided transport up the steep escarpment to São Paulo. By the end of the eighteenth century, the shipment of sugarcane from São Paulo down to the sea had reached such a high volume that the government responded by constructing a new road between São Paulo and Santos.

In 1833 Cubatão attained the legal status of a municipality. But prosperity proved elusive. The Santos Lowlands, as the entire region was called, was a breeding ground for a range of debilitating diseases, and although tropical vegetation was abundant, the soil was ill-suited for agriculture. When the completion of the São Paulo–Santos railroad line in 1867 (a remarkable engineering feat) cut the need for intermediate transport facilities, such as inns and posts where fresh horses could be obtained, Cubatão entered a period of decline.

But at the turn of the century, the swamps between the coast and the mountains were finally drained. The urgent need for a sanitation campaign had been dramatized by a yellow-fever plague that once left more than forty British ships adrift, their crews dead or

---

* When Cole Porter, his wife, and actor Monty Wooley approached Rio by ship at dawn and gazed at the view of the city, Porter remarked, "It's delightful." His wife added, "It's delicious." Not to be outdone, Wooley chimed in with, "It's de-lovely." The latter phrase provided Porter with a title for one of his best songs.

dying, in the river upon which the port of Santos is located. By the end of World War I, the Santos Lowlands became a center of banana cultivation and soon was producing more bananas than any other agricultural area of Brazil.

Indeed, there was an idyllic quality about the place. Zélia Gattai, the wife of Jorge Amado, in her charming memoir *Anarquistas, Graças a Deus (Anarchists, Thank God)*, described her first impression of the area: there was "kilometer after kilometer of banana trees implanted on humid terrain. . . . I admired the size of the bunches of bananas, immense, almost lying against the ground, held up by dwarf-like trees." For French anthropologist Claude Lévi-Strauss, who passed by Cubatão in 1935, the region was "an inundated plain, variegated with lagoons and marshes and crisscrossed by innumerable rivers, straits, and canals, the pattern of which is perpetually blurred by a pearly vapor, [a place that] seems like the earth itself, emerging on the first day of creation."

Up to the early 1950s Cubatão had experienced a very modest degree of industrialization, with the construction of a paper plant and a tannery in the second decade of the century. But then the supply of power available to Cubatão increased sharply because of improvements in the flow of water down from a reservoir on the plateau above the town. This development set the stage for a great leap forward—into catastrophe.

From a purely rational point of view, any proposal to install an industrial complex in Cubatão should have been adjudged sheer madness and dismissed out of hand. If there was any spot on this earth where factories should not have been located, it was on these steamy, rain-drenched lowlands tucked against the foot of an escarpment that blocked prevailing winds blowing in from the nearby ocean.

But with the advent of the Kubitschek era of giddy growth, all that mattered were Cubatão's proximity to the megalopolis of São Paulo and to Santos, the largest port in South America, and its access to a bountiful supply of energy. In 1955 Petrobrás, the state oil company, set up a refinery in Cubatão. In rapid succession, a steel mill and plants manufacturing fertilizer, cement, and an array of petrochemicals sprouted chimneys and opened their gates. All in all, some twenty-five Brazilian and multinational companies came to Cubatão, turning the municipality into one of the continent's largest manufacturing complexes, accounting for 16 percent of the total output of Brazilian industry.

The only drawback of all this productivity was that human beings had to operate these factories and live near them. Laborers, many of them from the Northeast, made their way to Cubatão to provide the manpower for the new plants. They erected *favelas* and installed their families next to these workplaces. Neither the companies nor the government did anything to prevent this settlement of the area.

The worst of these slums, called Vila Parisi, was at one time home to fifteen thousand people. Hemmed in on three sides by smoke-spewing stacks, the shanties of Vila Parisi suffered a constant bombardment of toxic pollutants. Moreover, these ramshackle structures roosted on land eighteen inches below sea level. High tides regularly caused flooding, which swept the contents of open sewers through the muddy streets of the settlement.

In sum, the decision to locate an industrial complex in Cubatão evidenced a total lack of regard for even the most basic environmental considerations. But in the 1950s and 1960s, Third World countries were wont to ignore suspected or confirmed hazards in order to set themselves firmly on the path to development. Brazil, with customary exuberance, put itself in the vanguard of the ecologically indifferent.

During the 1970s, ecology appeared on the agendas of many nations of the "First World." The Brazilian response, as typified by remarks made by the Minister of Planning in 1972, was that "Brazil can become the importer of pollution." He was suggesting that foreign companies restricted by environmental legislation in their homelands might consider relocating to Brazil. They would be able to ship to Brazil plants with machinery made obsolete by technology that antipollution laws in their countries had forced to be developed. It was an attractive proposition. "Why not?" the *New York Times* quoted the minister as asking. "We have a lot left to pollute." The Brazilians reiterated their commitment to development, regardless of its consequences, at the 1972 United Nations Conference on the Human Environment in Stockholm.

The potentially serious human health risks posed by air and water contamination did not weigh heavily on the minds of Brazil's policymakers, who dismissed environmental concerns, insisting that the poverty caused by underdevelopment was a greater social hazard than any effects of pollution. They ignored a 1970 study by the municipal government of Cubatão documenting the range of illnesses reported by residents and attributed to atmospheric contaminants. (The first reported case of illness dated back to 1957.) The march toward industrialization proceeded apace. The fact that the victims were primarily ill-paid workers and their families undoubtedly influenced this attitude of malign neglect. The value of life at the low end of the social spectrum in Brazil has never been high. In part this is one of the legacies of slavery. This attitude also proceeds from a long tradition of authoritarianism that has inculcated in the lower classes an attitude of submission to whatever lot their superiors assign to them.

The residents of Cubatão were forced to pay a high price for the progress Brazil achieved from the output of the factories installed in the Valley of Death. Brazil gave very little in return for the sacrifices these people made. Nor did residents have an opportunity to speak out about what was happening to them. In 1968 the military regime designated Cubatão a "national security zone," which meant that the federal government would appoint its mayor, and that the inhabitants of the city could not even exercise the limited rights of self-government other citizens enjoyed during the years of the dictatorship.

The silent violence of environmental pollutants was not the only danger the townspeople faced. In 1984 a pipeline carrying diesel oil from Santos to the Petrobrás refinery in Cubatão ruptured and exploded. The resulting fire spread rapidly to the nearby *favela* of Vila Socó, a conglomeration of wooden shacks perched on stilts rising out of a swamp. The police claimed that as many as one hundred people may have perished in the inferno. Unofficial sources put the fatality toll at between six hundred and nine hundred.

Human beings were not the only casualties in the Valley of Death. Like a giant eraser, air pollution wiped out vegetation on the slopes of the plateau rising above Cubatão. Since there were no roots to anchor the earth, heavy rains would inevitably bring erosion, and with it the grim prospect that landslides might bury *favelas*.

\*       \*       \*

The story of Cubatão is not atypical of Brazil. The carelessness Brazilians have always displayed toward themselves also extends to their attitude toward the environment. As irresponsible as the choice of Cubatão as the site for an industrial complex appears in retrospect, it was no less dubious than the decision to construct Brazil's first nuclear power plant in Angra dos Reis. The reactor sits on a narrow strip of coastal land seventy-five miles south of Rio de Janeiro, near an earthquake fault line and at a point where the Serra do Mar mountain range rises almost directly above the shore. Seasonal rains produce mud slides that often block or tear away the seaboard highway, a condition that would prevent the rapid evacuation of the nearby city in the event of a nuclear accident.

Brazilians live in the midst of such abundance that many have come to believe that theirs is an "infinite country" with unlimited wealth. They extract as much as they can and destroy as they please, showing no concern for what they are leaving behind for their children and grandchildren. Their almost total destruction of the forest that once covered the country's Atlantic seaboard is only one example. It is almost as though they do not view themselves as permanent residents. As the twentieth century draws to a close, the consequences of these attitudes are becoming all too apparent.

One of the first Brazilians to sound an ecological warning that reached a mass audience was Ignácio de Loyola Brandão. His successful 1982 novel *Não Verás País Nenhum* (translated into English under the title *And Still the Earth*) conjures up a nightmarish vision of a São Paulo to come: parched, haze shrouded, stifling, overcrowded, garbage strewn, crime ridden, and segregated by social class.

As Loyola later revealed in a videotaped lecture, the inspiration for the book came from an incident in his neighborhood involving the mysterious, sudden death of a beautiful tree. After conducting an investigation, authorities discovered that one of the neighbors had poisoned it. When asked why she had done it, the woman explained that the tree's yellow flowers fell on and stained the sidewalk in front of her home. This utter lack of consciousness about the natural environment got Loyola started on a futuristic novel that, as he pointed out in an 1986 interview, "is no longer futuristic."

*        *        *

The São Paulo of the 1990s has yet to attain the degree of unlivability Loyola's book portrays, but the city gives every indication of edging in that direction. With seventeen million inhabitants in its metropolitan area and a population of more than twenty-one million projected for the year 2000, Brazil's mightiest city shows the effects of a long period of uncontrolled, explosive growth that presently strains municipal services to the breaking point, poses serious health hazards, and adversely affects the quality of life for all of the city's residents.

On first seeing São Paulo, one is immediately struck by its overwhelming size. At certain locations one can make a 360 degree scan and see imposing clusters of high-rises extending to the horizon in every direction. At most hours of the day and evening the elevated highways that crisscross the city groan under eight lanes of solid traffic either hurtling at high speeds or impatiently lurching forward in fits and starts.

What makes São Paulo even more bewildering to the visitor is the absence of any touristic landmark to lend the city a picture-postcard identity. One finds no Empire State Building, Eiffel Tower, or Sugar Loaf Mountain. In a sense, there is no "there" there. Instead this city of more than five hundred square miles is one vast beehive, a center of serious enterprise, the capital of an enormously productive state fond of describing itself as the locomotive that pulls the rest of the country.

Founded as a Jesuit missionary outpost in 1554, the town of São Paulo emerged as an economic power at the dawn of the twentieth century because the soil and climate of the surrounding area proved particularly favorable to the cultivation of coffee trees. Between 1906 and 1910 Brazil's production of coffee reached 78 percent of the world's total. The boom attracted to São Paulo a flood of settlers from abroad. Between 1890 and 1920, an influx of foreigners into the state, and their subsequent migration to the city, tripled the state's population and increased the city's by nearly tenfold.

Some of the wealth generated by the coffee boom was invested in the creation of small enterprises in and around São Paulo during the period between 1870 and 1920. The city had always been receptive to progressive ideas and exuded a dynamism, as well as a strong independent streak, that could be traced back to the heyday of the *bandeirantes*. Its location was particularly favorable to industrial development. A network of railways and roads linked it to the port of Santos, to the interior of the state, and to Rio de Janeiro to the north. Raw materials were easily accessible, and the increase in the region's population generated an internal market for new products. By 1920 the industrial output of the city of São Paulo had surpassed that of Rio.

In the wake of the Great Depression the city experienced its second major industrial growth spurt. The dictatorial regime of President Getúlio Vargas sought to make Brazil more self-sufficient and less dependent on imported goods by prioritizing industrialization. São Paulo, with its abundant supply of skilled and semiskilled labor, took advantage of the added energy made available by the construction of several new hydroelectric facilities on its outskirts. By 1940 factories in the metropolitan area were churning out 43 percent of Brazil's entire industrial production.

The next burst of industrial expansion came with the presidency of Juscelino Kubitschek. Metropolitan São Paulo played a leading role. In 1957 Volkswagen founded Brazil's first automobile assembly plant in the town of São Bernardo do Campo, thirteen miles from São Paulo. Before long, the "ABC" suburbs (Santo André, São Bernardo do Campo, and São Caetano do Sul) could boast of harboring Latin America's largest automotive industry.

The heady years of the Brazilian "miracle" marked yet another stage in the explosive burgeoning of São Paulo. Success bred success, as the area attracted foreign investment that facilitated the construction of new industrial plants. São Paulo by now was the fastest growing city in the world. It had become the most powerful commercial and financial center in the Western Hemisphere, outside of the United States.

The city and its environs, along with the manufacturing enterprises that gave the region its economic muscle, expanded in a very Brazilian way: with great optimism, exuberance, and spontaneity. There was no serious long-range planning to take into account the environmental impact of the region's growth. The hardworking *paulistas* were so bent on charging ahead into the future that they failed to pause and consider what kind of future they were bringing upon themselves.

In the 1960s it was already becoming evident that the city was suffering from both air and water pollution. The two major rivers of the region had become sewage canals, and industrial chimneys were emitting dark smoke that at times made breathing difficult and reduced visibility. But most people accepted these circumstances as a price of progress.

By the 1970s, however, the quality of Greater São Paulo's atmosphere had worsened to a point where public anxiety began to displace acquiescence. A 1973 government report found that the air in the "ABC" suburbs, where some 750,000 people lived, contained so much sulfur dioxide that it was "'unbreathable." Moreover, since this huge industrial park was located south and east of São Paulo, the prevailing winds often pushed its pollutants in the direction of the capital (providing yet another example of the bitter fruits of unplanned growth).

Smog generated by tens of thousands of factories in and around the city, more than a million motor vehicles, three garbage incinerators, and a thermoelectric plant was especially troublesome during the winter months, when temperature inversions trapped foul air over the city. Within the city, air pollution affected the breathing of all citizens, rich and poor alike, but people living in substandard housing, and especially children, suffered from higher rates of respiratory illnesses.

In 1973 a well-known artist generated widespread publicity when he appeared in public with an oxygen mask strapped to his face. Two years later, a Gallup poll indicated that 82 percent of the people of Greater São Paulo considered the air pollution "very serious."

Moreover, the flood of migrants into São Paulo and its suburbs increased the dumping of nontreated sewage into nearby rivers and streams, which were already contaminated by industrial waste from factories. Scientists suspected that this added pollution, in turn, was contributing to the high rate of infant mortality in the slum areas of the city and its environs.

As São Paulo grew, the quality of life in the megalopolis kept deteriorating. The amount of open, green space (public parks, plazas, and so on) per inhabitant dropped to less than one third of the amount generally recommended for urban areas. This deficiency helped produce the "heat-island" effect, a phenomenon that causes sharp increases in temperature—as much as ten degrees Celsius—in isolated areas of the city. The heat from these "islands" can cause severe discomfort and even intestinal diseases; it can also generate sudden, heavy rains that produce flooding.

The pollution problems afflicting São Paulo were but one part of a larger situation that forced Brazil's military regime to back away from the development-at-any-cost rhetoric it had used at the 1972 United Nations conference in Stockholm. Mainly addressing the need to rationalize the exploitation of the country's natural resources, the federal government created an environmental-protection agency within the Ministry of the Interior. This was another example of the *para inglês ver* syndrome, because the agency was woefully underfunded and had limited authority.

State governments were still elected by popular vote during this period, and although the military placed limits on the democratic process, voters could still make their concerns felt on a number of issues. As public apprehension about pollution mounted, São Paulo politicians found it prudent to address the issue, and as a result, on the state level a number of environmental-protection initiatives were launched.

In 1973 the state took its first important step by creating the Company of Technology for Basic Sanitation and Water Pollution Control (or CETESB, to use its Portuguese acronym). Attached to the Secretariat of Public Works, CETESB was a corporate entity operating as both a regulator and a consultant to industry.* CETESB was granted legal authority to establish sanitation standards for the public water supply and to set emissions standards governing air pollution. It also monitored polluting activities and granted licenses for enterprises that might cause environmental damage.

CETESB found it easier to require new industries to install emissions controls than to force existing plants to take pollution-abatement measures. The costs of abatement were often substantial, and businessmen were hesitant to incur them without

---

* The latter role is troublesome, since an enterprise's compliance with advice from CETESB makes it difficult for the agency to take subsequent regulatory action against that "client."

public subsidies. Using its authority to levy fines and penalties, CETESB concentrated on lowering industrial emissions of particulates and sulfur dioxide, which came from a relatively small percentage of the area's factories, and achieved some degree of success.

However, the number of motor vehicles in Greater São Paulo has passed the four million mark, and they now cause some 90 percent of the city's air pollution. Cars, trucks, and buses dump five thousand tons of carbon monoxide into the atmosphere each day, and breathing in São Paulo remains less than salubrious. Regulation of auto emissions is considered a matter for the federal government, and the cost of cutting down emission rates in both new and old vehicles would be substantial.

CETESB is also struggling with the problem of water pollution. The need to construct new sewage-treatment facilities has reached a critical stage, and it remains to be seen whether the state of São Paulo can find the financial resources necessary for funding these projects. Meanwhile, the internal migration to the periphery of the capital continues, and the new arrivals build more privies and dig more wells. Disease-laden waste from the privies can seep into underground streams and from there into the wells. As one scientist has noted, "there is a sanitation bomb around São Paulo, waiting to detonate."

If there is one dramatic success story to which CETESB can point, it is the recovery of Cubatão. While some environmental-protection officials have suggested privately that the original uproar over the "Valley of Death" might have been somewhat exaggerated, it is beyond cavil that Cubatão had become both a national and an international symbol of ecological devastation. This awareness created a political climate that enabled CETESB to mount an aggressive program designed to place limitations on the amount of pollutants emanating from the city's industrial plants.

Between 1983 and 1990 CETESB identified 230 sources of pollution and brought 206 of them under control. These measures sharply reduced the levels of air and water pollution. Over this period industry spent $450 million on pollution abatement, and the government levied $2.5 million in fines against recalcitrant polluters.

The air in downtown Cubatão is now better than that in some parts of São Paulo. Fish have returned to the region's streams. The foul odors that used to permeate the city on a daily basis are now a problem about every four months. Vila Parisi is but a memory, having been torn down to make room for a truck terminal. In 1989 helicopters sprayed two tons of "seed bombs" (gelatine balls containing seeds of twenty-five plant species) on the nearby slopes in an effort to regenerate vegetation.

"Cubatão is not a paradise by any means," a CETESB engineer remarked in 1992. "We are not euphoric. There are still many problems here." The toxic diseases brought on by past exposures to the pollution in Cubatão continue to afflict many among the city's residents. On the other hand, as the engineer pointed out in the same interview, the city has an unusually high proportion of track-and-field athletes who do well in state competitions—a remarkable tribute to the adaptability and toughness of the human species.*

Although elements of Brazilianness bear some responsibility for the violence wreaked on the environment in parts of Brazil, the burgeoning of a grassroots environmental movement stirs hope that public concern will nudge indifference aside, and that the wanton destruction of the country's natural endowments will soon cease. Citizens are becoming increasingly aware of the high costs of ecological degradation, having learned from the media about the effects of pollution on both urban and rural life, disasters like Cubatão, and the international controversy over Brazil's exploitation of the Amazon basin (a subject explored in detail in Chapter Twelve). Attitudes toward the environment are definitely in transition—further evidence of the evolving essence of national character.

The roots of the environmental movement go back to 1958 and the creation of the Brazilian Foundation for the Conservation of Nature. This was a private group, composed of agronomists, botanists, and ecologists who were concerned that the developmental-

---

* In the 1985 Rio de Janeiro marathon, one of the finishers wore a Cubatão T-shirt. This had to be either sardonic social commentary or a remarkable physiological feat.

ist policies the government was pushing would cause serious damage to the natural environment. It operated in a discreet, genteel way to educate Brazilians about the need for conservation, and to persuade public officials to pay some heed to the preservation of Brazil's forests, rivers, and animal life. As the historical record demonstrates, the foundation was a voice crying in the wilderness.

The first aggressively activist environmental organization came into being in 1971 in Rio Grande do Sul. A prime mover of the Gaucho Association for the Protection of the Natural Environment (AGAPAN) was José Lutzenberger, an indefatigable, freewheeling, somewhat eccentric scientist who once worked for the pesticide industry but left because he felt he was prostituting himself.

As Brazil made the transition to democracy in the early 1980s, more environmental groups came into being. Fábio Feldman, the founder of the Union of Defenders of the Land (OIKOS), became the first politician to be elected to the Congress by campaigning on environmental issues. With his influence a "green" political party came into being. Conservationists began to make use of an unusual feature of Brazilian law, the *ação popular,* or "popular action," which enables citizens to bring suits against government agencies or officials for failing to protect the public patrimony.

The new Constitution of 1988 contained an article that began by assuring every citizen the right to an "ecologically balanced environment," and charged the government with preserving the environment for future generations. The article went on to impose a number of specific duties on the executive branch. Of course, these are aspirations rather than enforceable obligations, but their very presence in the nation's Magna Carta has to be considered a major triumph for the environmental movement.

The notoriety Cubatão generated in the early 1980s both internally and abroad helped create public awareness of environmental issues within Brazil, but an even more heightened degree of consciousness came into being as a result of an assault on nature that dwarfed what was happening in the Valley of Death. Brazilian efforts to exploit the vast resources of the Amazon basin involved some of the aspects of the national character that contributed to environmental devastation generally, but it also dramatized the clash between the country's immediate (and enormous) economic needs and the less tangible but equally urgent necessity to preserve one of the earth's unique ecosystems. The story of the rain forests is a complex one, shedding light on courage, foolishness, persistence, violence, suffering, and greed—the story of a dream threatening to become a nightmare—and it requires a detailed look.

# Chapter 12

# The Amazon Basin

## A Case Study of Violence

*T*he view from above is one of pillars of grey smoke converging into dark, orange-fringed clouds that hover ominously over the green canopy, rendering cities and settlements invisible, and even causing air traffic to seek alternate routes. At ground level hellish flames hold majestic tree trunks in a serpentine embrace and lick their way up toward the topmost branches to spurt skyward and glow like the fire on a candle wick.

The purposeful torching of vast stretches of the tropical forest in the Amazon basin during the 1970s and 1980s was the most visible aspect of extensive ecological violence perpetrated there, and but just one episode in a larger, more general pattern of regional violence that included the extermination of Indians and bloody conflicts over landownership.

At first little heed was paid to the fires, because there seemed to be an inexhaustible expanse of forest for Brazilians to burn. The Amazon Basin comprises the north of Brazil, as defined by the Brazilian Institute of Geography and Statistics, and embraces seven states and an area of over 1.3 million square miles, or 42 percent of the entire country.*

Yet by the end of the 1970s, deforestation was provoking intense concern in some quarters. Photographs from satellites circling the earth produced solid evidence of what had previously been a

---

* Amazônia, another official designation used for administrative purposes, includes this region as well as large, densely forested segments of the states of Mato Grosso and Maranhão.

matter of speculation: as much as one tenth of the Brazilian Amazon forest had already been razed. The soil beneath the dense tree cover was turning out to be infertile and highly vulnerable to erosion. There were those who grimly predicted that if the wholesale destruction were allowed to continue unchecked, an area two thirds that of the continental United States would one day become an immense wasteland—perhaps not the Brazilian Sahara that the most pessimistic commentators were projecting, but at the very least a wilderness of scrub.

Such a cataclysmic change could have mind-boggling implications. The Amazon basin contains anywhere from one to fifteen million (or more) species of animal and plant life, according to recent estimates. Within this astonishingly diverse ecosystem may be undiscovered pharmaceutical and genetic treasures of incalculable value (perhaps cures for AIDS and cancer, as some have suggested). Moreover, the burning of the forest was discharging large quantities of carbon dioxide into the atmosphere, thereby contributing to what some scientists had identified as a trend toward global warming (the greenhouse effect) that might one day lead to the melting of the polar ice caps and the consequent flooding of coastal regions everywhere.

In the 1980s the rate of deforestation kept increasing, especially in western Amazônia. Although there were disagreements about the size of the fires and exactly how much of the rain forest had been destroyed (statistics relating to the Amazon are notoriously inexact), the situation clearly was out of hand. Environmentalists both abroad and inside Brazil, where the movement was still suffering from birth pangs, protested energetically but with little effect.

In 1988 two events combined to focus increased worldwide attention on Amazônia. The press coverage of the fires ravaging Yellowstone Park during a particularly dry summer in the United States increased public awareness of the global-warming phenomenon. Later that year Chico Mendes, the internationally known leader of Brazilian rubber tappers who were trying to save the rain forest, was shot down in cold blood by assassins in Xapuri, in the state of Acre on the western edge of Amazônia. The murder provoked universal outrage from human-rights advocates and from groups and individuals opposed to the senseless destruction of the biological wonderland in northern Brazil.

The destruction of the Amazon basin is much more than a threat to animal and plant life, as the death of Chico Mendes suggested. The survival of Brazil's remaining tribal Indians, as well as the intrepid forest people who live by collecting latex and other products from jungle trees, is at stake. Also hanging in the balance is the fate of the hundreds of thousands of poor Brazilians lured into Amazônia by promises of land and work that could never be fulfilled. Yet at the same time Brazil, with its heavy foreign debt, pressing economic and social needs, and dreams of grandeur, can hardly be expected to turn its back on the untapped wealth and hydroelectric potential of the region.

Certain aspects of Brazilianness have contributed to the staggering ecological and social problems of Amazônia. These traits include a penchant for grandiose projects, shortsightedness, reliance on good intentions even though they might fly in the face of logic and experience, an extractive mentality (part of the country's heritage as a Portuguese colony), a lack of respect for nature, and a propensity for violence.

Ever since the first adventurers made their way inland on the Amazon River and its tributaries in search of South America's legendary city of gold (or "El Dorado"), the notion that Amazônia was a potential source of hidden wealth, in one form or another, has never left the Brazilian imagination. But the impenetrability of the rain forest, the rigors of the tropical climate, and the ever-present risk of injury or death from disease, insects, snakes, carnivores, and hostile Indian tribes made exploration and settlement of what many called the "Green Hell" exceedingly difficult. The rubber boom at the turn of the nineteenth century brought a brief period of giddy growth to Manaus, Belém, and other towns along the Amazon, but when Brazil's rubber monopoly ended, Amazônia once again became a backwater, cut off by the vast distances and geographical barriers that separated it from the rest of the country.

In 1950 the population of Amazônia had not yet reached two million. The number of tribal Indians was steadily diminishing, although the sexual unions of Indians and settlers from other parts of the country made the native Brazilian presence felt throughout the region. One subgroup to which Indian blood made an important contribution was the rubber tappers, or *seringueiros,* the descendants of northeasterners who came to the jungles during the rubber boom, as well as more recent migrants who answered the call for "rubber soldiers" to help the Allied war effort in World War II, when the Japanese cut off the supply of rubber from Malaya.

Exploited mercilessly by their bosses during the boom years, the *seringueiros* remained in the tropical forest after the rubber market collapsed. Many took Indian women as wives or companions. They survived by working on their own, clearing away small plots for farming, extracting latex from wild rubber trees, and harvesting nuts from jungle trees and plants. It is ironic that the *seringueiros* were slaughtering Indians during the height of the rubber boom (an episode that is described in Chapter Three), and afterward they were embracing the ways of the remaining tribe members and learning how to live in harmony with the rain forest.

The *seringueiros* developed a hybrid culture of their own, neither northeastern nor Indian but with traces of both. Despite the extreme isolation in which they lived, they retained contact with the rest of Brazil by listening to the radio, their only link to the larger society to which they knew they belonged. Although they could neither read nor write and had no access to health care, they managed to lead simple, reasonably decent, reasonably happy lives, at least in comparison with their compatriots who faced grinding poverty in the coastal cities or rural areas of the Northeast and south.

During the presidency of Juscelino Kubitschek, life began to change in Amazônia. In conjunction with the building of a new capital in the interior, the federal government set out to construct a highway that would link Brasília to Belém, on the mouth of the Amazon River. This was a critical first step in the integration of Amazônia with the rest of the country. The road would open the way for the colonization of the southeastern sector of the Amazon basin and mark the first step in a process of destructive exploitation.*

---

* Perhaps the forces of nature knew what was coming and resented it. Just before the final segment of the highway was completed, as the engineer in charge of the project napped in a hammock, a strong wind caused a nearby tree to topple on him, and he was killed.

The fear that if they did not populate Amazônia they would lose it was a key concern motivating the Brazilians' push northward. The military governments of the 1960s and 1970s took the view that considerations of national security required the settlement of land adjacent to Brazil's northern and northwestern borders, to create a buffer against the infiltration of subversive elements based in other South American countries. (They had in mind, among other things, Che Guevara's ill-fated frolic in Bolivia.)

There was another, more subtle apprehension lurking in Brazilian minds—the notion that foreigners had designs on the natural resources to be found in Amazônia. The prime suspect was Uncle Sam. A long-standing, if seldom openly expressed apprehension was that the United States was going to send African Americans to live in the region, as a prelude to annexation. When the Hudson Institute, an American think tank, proposed the construction of a gigantic dam that would flood much of Amazônia, in order to create a huge source of hydroelectric power as well as to facilitate ship traffic in the region, Brazilians saw this as part of the "grand design."

By quickly dismissing these concerns as paranoia, we ignore the nationalism and national pride that animated them, and the deeply rooted conviction of Brazilians that if their nation was to achieve its rightful destiny, Brazil itself would have to exploit the natural resources of the Amazon basin. Moreover, it was highly predictable that when foreigners decried the destruction of the rain forest, nationalistic Brazilians would view the protest as part of a conspiracy to keep them from developing, and that they would denounce it as unacceptable intervention in their domestic affairs.

The program of road building between Brasília and Belém continued after the military seized power in 1964. An even more ambitious scheme sought to connect Northeast Brazil with the western Amazon basin, and work began on the trans-Amazon highway, which would one day provide an overland route between Recife and the Peruvian border.

At the same time the regime launched a program of incentives designed to attract capital to the north. Companies could invest in Amazonian enterprises the funds they would otherwise have had to pay as taxes to the federal government. There was no requirement that the new businesses be labor intensive. Corporations from the south of Brazil as well as multinationals purchased huge tracts of land in the north for the purpose of setting up cattle ranches that would have been unprofitable but for the subsidies that the military government was offering.

Plans for the construction of the trans-Amazon highway drew major inspiration from the serious drought ravaging the Northeast in 1970 and causing backlanders to migrate to coastal cities that were already seriously overcrowded and hard-pressed to provide rudimentary public services. The hope was that the new highway system would relieve this social pressure by encouraging migration to Amazônia. Prior colonization schemes had been unsuccessful because the government had failed to provide migrants with the kind of education and technical support (such as credit that would enable them to purchase farm implements and seeds) they needed to thrive (or at least survive) in a new environment. But experience had taught the authorities nothing, so with typical Brazilian optimism and reliance on improvisation, the regime set out to fulfill the slogan "Land without people for people without land."

Although Amazônia might have been a "land without people," it was surely not a land without landowners. Not only were big corporations snatching up huge patches of virgin forest, but speculators were also busy along the new roads. Chronic inflation and the absence of a capital-gains tax in Brazil make land speculation an attractive pursuit for the rich and the powerful, and they were quick to take advantage of the opening up of Amazônia. Often relying on fraudulent land titles, and selling the same property to two or more purchasers, they traded briskly or held land in the expectation that it would appreciate in value. Neither the federal nor the state governments had the administrative or law-enforcement resources (or the will) to put an end to these fraudulent practices.

The result was that when migrants began to arrive and looked for plots to farm—the dream of every landless peasant—they often discovered to their dismay that they were settling on property claimed by someone with a valid or apparently valid legal title to the premises. This chaos inevitably led to conflicts, often culminating in the loss of life.

The social and economic structure of rural Brazil has reflected a concentration of landownership, wealth, and power in the hands of an elite that could always count on the civil authorities to protect their interests. Attempts to change this status quo have traditionally provoked violent responses. A 1988 study by Amnesty International found that more than a thousand peasants had been slain since 1980, generally over land disputes, and that "[r]eports of violence and killings in the context of land tenure . . . have increased in the last five years, particularly in the eastern Amazon and northeastern Brazil."

In remote areas landowners would employ gunmen to threaten, expel, or kill settlers and organizers of rural workers. They could count on the support of all the available local authorities, including the police. The torturing of settlers was not uncommon. Efforts to investigate charges of wrongdoing often foundered because of dilatory tactics or outright obstruction on the part of government officials. The Amnesty International report uncovered only two instances of hired killers being convicted and sentenced, and no instances of an individual accused of committing a murder being brought to justice.

Occasionally colonists or workers would fight back, and an owner or "hit man" would lose his life.* The atmosphere resembled the American Wild West. Many squatters opted to move and search for new land or to go to work for some powerful landowner, often under conditions of debt peonage that could scarcely be distinguished from slavery.

During the military regime the only effective support for landless peasants in Amazônia came from the Catholic Church. Priests and bishops spoke out for social justice and helped settlers organize to defend their rights. For their efforts they occasionally became the targets of violence, and some paid with their lives. When extreme leftists launched a guerrilla-warfare campaign in the early 1970s in the southeastern corner of the Amazon basin—a pitiful effort involving some seventy participants with no chance of success—the military seized on this as a pretext for clamping down heavily on any manifestations of unrest in the region.

---

* In 1976 a cattle rancher and his two sons, United States citizens who had settled in Amazônia, were shot down by peasants in a dispute over land.

The human violence erupting from struggles over land matched the violence the invaders of Amazônia were perpetrating on the environment. There may be a psychological factor that helps explain this behavior. Because the unknown dangers of the tropical rain forests terrified the early settlers, their descendants may be playing out these fears by destroying as much of the forest as they can.

The establishment of new cattle ranches in the region required extensive deforestation, which was accomplished by the use of fire and bulldozers. As highways began to penetrate the tropical forests, squatters cleared the adjacent properties and often pushed deep into the surrounding areas. Eventually, along some stretches of roadway, there were no trees to be seen.

The trans-Amazon highway cost nearly a billion dollars, increasing the national debt and enriching contractors. But it has never achieved the goals intended by the federal government of providing a link between eastern and western Amazônia (one writer has called it the "highway to nowhere") and populating the vastness of the central Amazon basin. The jungle and its adverse weather patterns make the road difficult to traverse. Most of the resettlement projects collapsed because the government failed to furnish settlers with the technical assistance necessary for them to survive in a hostile environment.

In addition to attempting to promote a greater human presence in Amazônia, the regime also sought to exploit the natural resources of the region. One of the more highly publicized initiatives was the concession granted to the reclusive American billionaire Daniel Ludwig in 1967. For $3 million he purchased a tract of jungle of more than five thousand square miles (larger than the area of Austria) on the Jari River, a tributary of the Amazon. His original plan was to harvest lumber, to be derived from groves of fast-growing trees transplanted from Asia. He floated two sections of a wood-pulp plant from Japan, where it had been built, across the Indian and Atlantic Oceans on thirty-ton barges. The gigantic operation eventually employed over seven thousand workers. The enterprise extended to the production of rice and kaolin, a valuable clay discovered by chance on the property, and the raising of the world's largest herd of water buffalo.

The Jari enterprise foundered, as did a smaller scale project undertaken by Henry Ford four decades earlier. The automobile magnate had attempted to create rubber plantations in the Amazon jungle but had failed because of plant diseases that spread among closely planted groves of trees (wild rubber trees are scattered and hence are less susceptible to contagion). So, too, Ludwig's trees and their replacements failed to survive in the thin Amazonian soil, and high costs made growing rice uneconomical.

Moreover, during the transition to civilian rule in the late 1970s and early 1980s, the deeply rooted Brazilian paranoia about foreign occupation of Amazônia fed on the excessive secrecy that shrouded the Ludwig operation. There were unfounded rumors that workers were being held as slaves, and that the Jari complex was in reality a U.S. military base. The resulting atmosphere of distrust, combined with the snarl of red tape to which the government subjected Ludwig's enterprise, raised frustration levels far beyond toleration. Having earned nothing on what amounted to a $1 billion investment, Ludwig surrendered and in 1982 sold out to a Brazilian consortium at a substantial loss.

The fate of the Jari project demonstrated the awesome power of the Amazon jungle, bureaucracy, and paranoia when they joined forces to bring the world's richest man to his knees. But a second "pharaonic" enterprise, set in motion as Ludwig was liquidating his Jari holding, proved that Brazilians on their own were capable of undertaking the taming of Amazônia and taking full advantage of its untold wealth. Carajás, the shorthand expression for a mining operation in the southeastern Amazon basin, promises to yield enormous profits from the export of iron ore, gold, manganese, nickel, copper, and bauxite. But the mining operation has also dramatically illustrated the enormity of the environmental damage that can be inflicted by the flamboyant projects Brazilians delight in launching.

In 1967 a young Brazilian geologist working for a Brazilian subsidiary of the U.S. Steel Corporation was copiloting a company helicopter that set down by chance on a bare hilltop in the Serra dos Carajás, remote highlands situated in the jungles south and east of Belém. He was astonished to discover he was perched on a bed of solid iron ore. It turned out to be the world's largest concentration of high-grade iron ore, estimated to contain eighteen billion tons of 66 percent pure iron compound. Indeed, the entire region, covering an area larger than the state of California, was found to be a vast treasure trove of minerals.

Because of the magnitude of the capital investment that would be required to exploit what came to be known as "Grand Carajás," the Brazilians had to move with caution. At first U.S. Steel entered into a joint venture with the Vale do Rio Doce Company (or CVRD), a state-owned mining company. In 1977 the Brazilians dissolved the relationship and bought out the Americans. By 1980 they had drawn up their own plans for the development of Grand Carajás, and the project was typically monumental.

Pressure to pay off their foreign debt, which was approaching $80 billion, and to underwrite oil imports motivated Brazilians to undertake the Grand Carajás program, which they hoped would greatly increase export earnings. In addition, the project was meant to stimulate new industry and agricultural production as well as create new jobs in the region, all of which they hoped would begin to alleviate the nation's internal social and economic problems.

The centerpiece of Carajás was an ambitious operation at the site of the 1967 discovery, where the CVRD dug an open-pit mine and installed ore-processing facilities. The government constructed a 550-mile railway line linking the mine with docks just south of São Luis, the capital of the state of Maranhão, where an ore-loading terminal and other deepwater port facilities were built. In Tucuruí on the Tocantins River 150 miles from Carajás, an enormous hydroelectric dam and power plant were built to send electricity to the mine and other industrial enterprises to be located in the vicinity. A number of other dams were planned. They would supply energy to various other mining and industrial projects, including a chain of pig-iron smelters to be set up along the railroad line. Finally, the project called for the encouragement in the immediate area of farming, cattle-raising, and forestry enterprises that would provide food and other products for domestic consumption as well as work and land for settlers.

The Grand Carajás program required a massive commitment of capital. Indeed, one observer has called it "the world's most expensive mining-based project." More than half the $3.5 billion spent by the CVRD between 1985 and 1987 came from Japan, Western Europe, and the World Bank. Foreign financing of the project evoked the usual outcry from Brazilian nationalists quick to denounce the "surrender" of Amazônia to multinational corporations.

Less vocal but equally urgent protests originated from ecologists who were alarmed at the damage that aspects of the program could potentially inflict on the environment. They expressed particular anxiety about the projected pig-iron smelters. Subsequent events have validated many of their concerns.

The Carajás iron mine itself, under the ownership of the CVRD, has in fact been a model operation from the ecological perspective. Sensitive to criticisms from abroad about the despoliation of Amazônia, the state company spent $54 million on studying and implementing environmental conservation plans between 1981 and 1985. The settlement of the area around the mine has been well organized and orderly, and damage has been confined to the unavoidable effects of a large-scale mining operation.

But planners apparently assumed that the other components of the Grand Carajás project did not need the type of controls that were being enforced at the mine. They undoubtedly hoped that the massive development they were triggering would not do more harm than good, exhibiting the typically Brazilian attitude that if one hopes with sufficient fervor, things will turn out well. Reality, however, often finds a way of obtruding on the best of intentions.

The pig-iron smelters furnish a perfect example. Tax incentives were devised to encourage the location of smelters in the region, and licenses were granted to twenty-two of them. The only way they would be able to compete on the world market was by using cheap, readily available fuel—charcoal obtained from wood. The hope was that the new enterprises would at some point obtain half their fuel needs from eucalyptus plantations they would create or from trees cultivated through sustainable forest management practices.

But there was no way to force these methods on the smelter owners, who would naturally opt to maximize their short-term profits. As some critics had predicted, the first two pig-iron operations to come on-line cut down trees with abandon, triggering extensive deforestation, because this was the cheapest way to fuel their smelters, especially after the world price of pig iron fell. What began to happen along the Carajás–São Luis railway was an exact repeat of what had previously occurred in Minas Gerais; there pig-iron production had destroyed almost two thirds of the forests in the state.

The method the smelters used to obtain cheap fuel for their furnaces appeared to violate the terms of a World Bank loan granted to the CVRD for its Carajás project, which stipulated the observation of measures to protect the environment. But CVRD officials took the position that the loan clause applied only to property actually owned by the CVRD and not to the virgin forests that were being destroyed to provide charcoal for the smelters. By washing its hands of responsibility for the deforestation, the CVRD was not only ignoring the plain language of the clause, which clearly applied to more than company land; it was also hiding behind the cynical indifference and indolent fatalism that an authoritarian social tradition had imposed on Brazilian culture.

Central to the grand design of industrializing the eastern Amazon basin was the construction of a series of hydroelectric installations that would provide cheap sources of energy for new factories to be located in the region. The Tucuruí dam on the Tocantins River would be the first of these projects, the world's fourth largest hydroelectric complex and the largest ever built in a tropical forest. The first stage of the installation cost in the vicinity of $5 billion and provided thirty-nine hundred megawatts of electricity. When completed, it would generate eight thousand megawatts.

While the dam was under construction, film director John Boorman used the site as a setting for his film *The Emerald Forest*, because he wanted to capture visual images of the devastation modern society was visiting on the Amazon basin. According to critics, much worse was yet to come.

The Tucuruí project called for the flooding of nearly a thousand square miles of virgin woodlands. A contract for the removal of commercially valuable trees from this area was given to a company with no experience in clearing trees. The company, whose main business up to this point had been the management of a military pension fund, succeeded in going bankrupt, after receiving large sums of money from the government and recovering very little wood.

At the same time another scandal brewed as a result of allegations that harmful herbicides were being used by work crews clearing strips of jungle for the installation of power lines in the vicinity of Tucuruí. Press reports claimed that the deaths of forty settlers were associated with these chemicals, but the manufacturer (Dow Chemical) denied any connection between the chemicals and the fatalities.

Attorneys filed suits to enjoin the flooding that was scheduled to begin on October 1, 1984. The president of Electronorte, the state utility running the dam, first hid from process servers and then ordered that the flood gates be opened on September 6. Although he was subsequently fired by the Minister of Energy and Mines, the president of the utility succeeded in making it impossible for the courts to delay the project.

Treetops rise eerily from the placid waters of the lake at Tucuruí, a tacit testament to the novel form of deforestation employed there as well as to the loss of millions of dollars' worth of wood because of incompetence and corruption. Some scientists have predicted that the decomposition of trees and of secondary growth will not only turn the lake into a dead body of water but will also corrode and render useless the turbines of the hydroelectric plant within a relatively short period of time.

Even with its shortcomings, the Tucuruí project is a roaring success when compared to the dam and hydroelectric plant at Balbina, on a tributary of the Amazon ninety miles north of Manaus. Conceived under the military regime and inaugurated in 1989 despite the warnings of ecologists and others, Balbina demonstrates the validity of a conclusion drawn from bitter experience by Paulo Nogueira Neto, once the head of Brazil's federal environmental protection agency, to the effect that ill-advised "pharaonic" undertakings must be stopped in the planning stage. "Once work begins, there is not much we can do."

What made the Balbina project highly questionable was that the flatness of the region necessitated that a great deal of water be amassed in order to run the generators. The Balbina dam has flooded nine hundred square miles of jungle, yet it provides only one fifteenth the amount of electricity created at Tucuruí, at a cost of $750 million. The Balbina dam and plant have displaced tribal Indians and badly damaged the ecosystem of the region. Its reputation as a major ecological disaster even convinced President José Sarney to absent himself from its inauguration ceremonies.

If hydroelectric projects have brought high technology to Amazônia, the search for gold has lured northward hundreds of thousands of ordinary people, most of them poor northeasterners. They have been using brute force and willpower in efforts to wrest the precious metal from the jungle by hand or with relatively simple implements. Just as modern applied science has taken its toll on the region, so too has the unbridled foraging of the *garimpeiros,* or "gold prospectors." At the same time, their blood, sweat, and grit has made Brazil the world's fifth largest producer of gold.

Although *garimpeiros* had long been scouring the length and breadth of Amazônia, one dramatic find riveted the world's attention during the 1980s. In January of 1980 a storm felled a tree on the Serra Pelada (or Bald Mountain), near the Carajás complex. Among its roots were found several large gold nuggets. This is a generally accepted version of the beginning of an extraordinary find that eventually yielded forty-two tons of gold by 1987. The discovery also produced a matchless spectacle that at its zenith involved perhaps as many as eighty thousand *garimpeiros,* aptly nicknamed "ants," playing in what could have been a silent-movie extravaganza worthy of Cecil B. De Mille.

Reporter Norman Gall has termed it "a scene that calls to mind Dante's *Inferno.*" In the words of Brian Kelly and Mark London, in their book *Amazon,* "It was as if Hieronymus Bosch's chaotic, multidimensional painting of the 'Garden of Earthly Delights' had been brought to life." (They also dub it "an amphitheater for Gullivers but populated by perpetually moving Lilliputians.") To journalist Marlise Simons it was "a staggering scene, seeming to belong in a time in which slaves built monumental works for pharoahs and kings." The *garimpeiros* themselves referred to the mine as "Babylon."

What was once a mountain soon became a gaping six-hundred-foot crater, perhaps the largest hole ever dug by human hands alone, as countless individual prospectors working tiny plots excavated uneven shafts straight down into the earth. An army of mud-caked "ants" carried sacks of dirt and rock from each claim up wooden ladders leaning precariously against the shelved walls of the mine. They brought their sacks to the owners, who sifted the contents for gold. The "ants" earned a daily wage, or were paid by the bag, or received a share of the find from their employers.

It was a perilous occupation. Ladders slipped, mud slid, and violence could erupt at any moment over claim jumping, as well as more mundane matters such as conflicts over women. Within months things grew so chaotic at the mine site that the government, fearing that the *garimpeiros* might smuggle gold out of Serra Pelada, had a pretext to intervene. Agents of the Bank of Brazil arrived and paid Brazilian currency for gold extracted from the mine. (The price was set at slightly above the world dollar price for gold.)

Moreover, the whole operation was placed under the control of the National Intelligence Service, which seems an odd choice until one recalls that the agency had been active in the counterinsurgency campaign against leftist guerrillas in the region during the 1970s, and that several veterans of the campaign were available for the new assignment.

One of them, Major Sebastião Rodrigues Moura, took charge of the site and quickly imposed order. Known to the *garimpeiros* as Major Curió (Major Black Bird, a nickname supposedly derived from his way of making his prisoners sing like birds), he ruled with an iron hand, banning firearms, liquor, and women from Serra Pelada, settling disputes, limiting claims to about a thousand owners, and taking steps to prevent the mine laborers from being exploited. The *garimpeiros,* fearing that the government might take over the mine at any moment and expel them, looked on the charismatic major as a hero and protector.

In his honor they gave the name Curionópolis to the settlement they built for themselves just outside Serra Pelada. "A horrible place, a ghost-town-to-be," was the way a gold-mining expert described the settlement in 1986, "full of whorehouses, where the miners catch diseases, and pharmacies, where they buy what they hope will cure them." Loud, garish, and beset by constant violence (bodies would turn up on its dusty streets every morning), Curio-nópolis at its peak was home to some sixty thousand residents.

In 1982 Major Curió ran for the Chamber of Deputies, at the behest of President João Figueiredo, who recognized the value of the major's popularity and recruited him into the government's political party. The *garimpeiros* voted him into office, and he left for Brasília, where he soon found himself at odds with the president. He did not run for re-election in 1986, nor did he return to Serra Pelada.

Meanwhile, things were deteriorating at the mine. Most of the gold that could be extracted by hand had already been removed. Moreover, the primitive methods used by the *garimpeiros* made the site vulnerable to flooding and cave-ins, so working in the pit was becoming increasingly dangerous. Operations had to be suspended on several occasions, and in 1987 the mine was closed for repairs for almost a year. The *garimpeiros* desperately sought government help to restore the mine to a workable state, and they clashed frequently with the authorities.

In December 1987 a contingent from Serra Pelada seized the railroad bridge over the Tocantins River in the municipality of Marabá. The governor of the state sent military police to reopen the bridge. In carrying out their mission the authorities may have killed as many as ten protesters. (As of June 1988, according to an Amnesty International report, about fifty of the demonstrators still remained unaccounted for, and the state government was dragging its feet instead of responding to demands that the matter be fully investigated.) The crackdown on the protesters at the Tocantins River broke the back of the miners' political movement.

Some miners made fortunes from Serra Pelada, but the great majority of the tens of thousands who toiled in "Babylon" left as impoverished as they had been when they arrived. According to Alain Lestra, a French geologist living in Belém and serving as a consultant to gold-mining enterprises, people who came to the Amazon from the Northeast in search of gold tended to be from the lower class and had the unfortunate compulsion to spend heavily on drink and women whenever they made a find. "They had to show others that they had money, and would squander everything in one day. The *garimpeiro* who transcended this could become rich."

The ecological damage from the Serra Pelada strike did not spread beyond the mountain itself and the surrounding areas where the *garimpeiros* lived. But the swarms of prospectors searching for gold in the streams and riverbeds throughout the Amazon basin may have inflicted enormous long-term harm by using large amounts of mercury to separate gold from fluvial sediments and then dumping the mix into waterways. The highly toxic metal, for a time freely available in stores selling supplies for dentists, has turned up in fish, which are an essential part of the diet of the people of Amazônia. Goldminers and others who live in mining areas have already been treated for mercury poisoning, and many cases may go unrecognized because the symptoms are easily confused with those of malaria.

Between 1979 and 1987, it is estimated that three hundred tons of mercury contaminated the Madeira River along a two-hundred-mile stretch in Rondônia where some twenty-five thousand *garimpeiros* labored. Moreover, as many as three thousand tons may have been thrown into the Amazon since the 1950s. This is about three times the amount of the toxic substance that was discarded into Minamata Bay on the southern coast of Japan. Thus in the long run the equivalent to the Japanese disaster may occur not in Cubatão, but rather in Amazônia.

The struggle to exploit the natural resources of the Amazon basin had a certain logic to it, in terms of Brazil's aspirations for long-term development. But efforts to populate the "Green Hell" never made much sense. This was especially true with respect to the massive effort to attract substantial numbers of settlers to southwestern Amazônia. The enterprise was marked by greed, stupidity, and shortsightedness, as well as a dollop of romanticism, as dramatized by the final scene in the film *Bye, Bye, Brazil,* when the hero, having failed to find his fortune in eastern Amazônia, sets off on a new odyssey with the cry "Rondônia!"

Rondônia first caught the public eye in the period between 1872 and 1912, when it was still an outlying territory of the empire (and then the republic). Waterfalls and rapids along the Marmoré and Madeira Rivers, which flow into the Amazon, made it impossible to ship rubber from northwestern Brazil and neighboring Bolivia to the Atlantic Ocean. One solution was to build a railroad line that would skirt the unnavigable portions of these waterways, from the town of Guajará-Mirim on the Bolivian border to Porto Velho, a riverbank settlement that would eventually become the capital of the territory (now the state) of Rondônia.

Jungle diseases, hostile Indians, and the maddeningly difficult terrain defeated the efforts of an American contractor and his British subcontractor to build the railroad line during the last decades of the nineteenth century. In 1907, to fulfill their part of a treaty that permitted them to annex the territory of Acre from Bolivia, the Brazilians engaged another American contractor to build the Madeira–Marmoré railroad. He managed to complete the project by 1912. The railroad line stretched for 220 miles, cost over $30 million, and over the years claimed the lives of thousands of workers.

Known variously as the "Devil's Railway," the "Railroad to Nowhere," and the "Mad Maria" (the latter serving as the title of Márcio Souza's riveting fictional account of the undertaking), the railroad line opened just as the rubber boom collapsed. It became a sort of phantom railroad, operating sporadically until 1972, when the government finally shut it down. Today tourists can ride wagons drawn by a wood-burning steam locomotive from the railroad museum in Porto Velho along a five-mile section of track to the nearby town of Santo Antônio. This train ride is all that remains of one of Brazil's earliest "pharaonic" enterprises.

When the rubber boom came to an end, the territory of Rondônia became once again a forgotten corner of Brazil's vast frontier. Its northern section, covered by dense rain forest, had access to rivers that provided a link with Manaus and Belém, but the trip to these far-off places took weeks to complete. Southern Rondônia had some fertile soil that might potentially be converted into farmland, but it was totally isolated from the rest of the country.

In 1970 Rondônia had a population of only 116,620. But it would soon become a magnet for increasingly large numbers of settlers. Although the government's highway construction and colonization programs focused on eastern Amazônia, the same pressures that forced migrants up the Belém-Brasília highway and along newly opened portions of the trans-Amazon highway encouraged the development of Rondônia. BR-364, a dirt road linking Cuiabá, the capital of Mato Grosso, with Porto Velho had been completed in the mid-1960s. It was impassable during the rainy season, but nonetheless it provided a route for the dispossessed rural workers of southern Brazil who had been forced to migrate when the large agricultural enterprises that employed them switched to soybean production, which is capital-intensive.

By 1975 Rondônia's population had grown by 250 percent. But the colonization of the territory foundered against the same obstacles that hindered the settlement of eastern Amazônia—violent land conflicts between squatters and those claiming legal ownership, and the failure of the government to provide funds for necessary technical assistance.

By decade's end, a concatenation of factors converted the flow of migrants into a flood. Conditions in rural Brazil, especially in the south, were growing even worse, and landless peasants saw in southwestern Amazônia their last best hope to acquire a piece of farmland of their own. Governors and mayors in southern Brazil saw a chance to export their social problems by encouraging emigration northward. Ambitious politicians in Rondônia saw a chance to increase their territory's population and thereby win statehood, which would give them greater access to federal funds. Highway construction firms and bus companies saw chances to make big money. And the military regime saw yet another chance to stabilize the country by colonizing Brazil's frontier.

What emerged was a new development plan called "Polonoroeste" (the Northwest Pole), the cornerstone of which was the paving of BR-364. With the help of loans from abroad, the road was modernized and access to Rondônia became possible throughout the year. What followed, in the words of journalist Tyler Bridges, was "perhaps the greatest land rush since the settling of the American West."

Every month thousands of migrants were arriving, not only from the south but also from eastern Amazônia. Over a six-month period in 1981, 37,000 residents of the state of Pará, in eastern Amazônia, made the 1,200-mile trek westward to Rondônia in search of land. It was the equivalent of a trip from Spain to central Poland. Local officials were confidently predicting that Rondônia's population would reach 1.6 million by the year 2000.

The World Bank and other international financial institutions that helped underwrite Polonoroeste included in their loans certain stipulations for safeguarding the natural environment as well as the Indians whose lands abutted BR-364. The Brazilians solemnly promised to observe these conditions, and the banks solemnly accepted the assurances they were given.

Yet it is difficult to believe that either side was serious about protecting the tropical forest and its human inhabitants. The international banks had money they needed to lend but no institutional mechanisms that could accurately assess compliance with environmental stipulations. On the basis of Brazil's past performance in matters involving both Indians and the ecology of Amazônia, the bankers should not have placed much stock in the promises of the Brazilian government.

Moreover, Brazilians were unlikely to treat loan conditions with any more seriousness than they observed in respect to their own laws that provided for the protection of the rain forest and the Indians. They viewed formal legal restrictions as either goals to which they aspired, but only in the abstract, or inconveniences that could easily be surmounted by the rich and powerful. In any contest between Brazil's long-standing national policy for the development of Amazônia and measures stipulated to assure the survival of trees and Indians, it should have been obvious which would prevail.

BR-364, once paved, became a "highway to the promised land" for Brazil's poor. In 1986 the number of migrants pouring annually into Rondônia, which was now a full-fledged state (the first ever to be named after a person, Cândido Rondon), reached 165,899. By 1988 the state's population exceeded one million.

There was little that either the federal or the state government could have done to avoid environmental damage. Burning was the most efficient way to clear away tropical forest, and the government would not have been able to increase the scope of its law-enforcement activities enough to stop the fires. Even the best of intentions went astray. The national land-reform program, designed to facilitate the distribution of property not being put to productive use, encouraged landowners of forested tracts to burn them and convert them into cattle pasture, so as to avoid expropriation.

Moreover it was impossible to stop the incursions of settlers onto Indian land, especially when new roads skirted or crossed territory that the government had supposedly set aside for native Brazilians. The Indians occasionally resisted, killing colonists and destroying their homes, but it was a futile effort, since modern technology and sheer numbers favored the intruders.

The mass migration to Rondônia may have eased social pressures elsewhere in Brazil, but those problems didn't disappear; they were only transplanted into a particularly inhospitable setting. The governor of Rondônia, in a memorable speech captured in Adrian Cowell's powerful documentary film *Decade of Destruction*, had issued an invitation for "Brazilians from all over Brazil" to "bring your dreams, hopes and illusions," and he had declared that his state "offers work, solidarity, and respect." Those who took him at his word found a different reality.

The region's new rural workers had no special farming skills and had to confront a tropical environment totally foreign to them. The federal land-reform agency, following a policy that amounted to a cruel joke, settled them on infertile land where they could not possibly make a go of it. The settlers burned down trees and planted annual crops, such as beans, manioc, and rice. But once the protective cover of the forest had been removed, the relentless rays of the equatorial sun converted the thin soil into clay, which was not hospitable to plant growth. Settlers' efforts yielded returns so paltry that within two or three years many had to abandon their farms. They would seek land elsewhere and repeat the cycle of burning and sowing, with the same results, or hire out as workers or sharecroppers on someone else's farmland—thus returning to the social status they had fled northward to escape—or seek work in Porto Velho or one of the other burgeoning cities of the region.

All the while the settlers endured the hardships of tropical illnesses such as malaria, which ravaged the new farming colonies.* The absence of health care and other basic services that the gov-

---

* According to one study, many settlers actually believed that something in the air or the water caused malaria, an indication of the backwardness of most of the migrants.

ernment had promised but failed to provide made life on Brazil's new frontier a grim struggle for survival. Yet most of the newcomers insisted that they would not return to where they came from—a bleak indicator of conditions elsewhere in the country.

The settlement of Rondônia was a massive experiment in social Darwinism. Those few who possessed intelligence and technical skills as well as grit had some hope of success. Perennial crops such as cacao and coffee could be cultivated profitably and did not require deforestation, although before they could harvest these crops farmers had to wait several years after planting.

The promises that lured settlers into Rondônia have proved hollow. Only about 9 percent of the state has turned out to be capable of supporting agricultural production, and as a result people have been abandoning their farmland. As a government official told a *New York Times* reporter in a 1991 interview: "In 1980, Rondônia was 70 percent rural. Today, it is 60 percent urban." Brush is now reclaiming land that had once been cleared.

The explosive growth of Rondônia and the senseless destruction of its tropical forests became emblematic of the folly of much of the traditional Brazilian thinking on how to develop the Amazon basin, and environmentalists overseas began to denounce what was happening there and level harsh criticism at the World Bank for its complicity. But it was not until the tragedy of Rondônia threatened to repeat itself in the adjacent state of Acre that meaningful pressure was brought to bear against the Brazilian government and the international lending institutions.

During the boom years, Acre was a rich source of natural rubber. Then nominally a part of Bolivia, the region faced constant pressure from Brazilians determined to extend their country's frontiers and exploit the tropical forests of this remote corner of the Amazon basin. In 1903 a treaty between Brazil and Bolivia gave Brazil the territory of Acre, which in a short time became a state; in return Bolivia was granted access to the Madeira River and thence to the Atlantic Ocean.

What distinguished Acre from neighboring Rondônia was the presence of large numbers of *seringueiros*, who had remained there after the rubber boom came to an end. They made a modest living off the tropical forest, which they exploited without destroying. But they could not insulate themselves against the same forces that were laying waste to large portions of Rondônia.

Powerful landowners cast covetous eyes on the forests of Acre and saw opportunities for cattle ranching. And population pressures in Rondônia inevitably would send migrants into the relatively empty lands of Acre. When plans were announced to pave BR-364 from Porto Velho to Rio Branco, the capital of Acre, and advertisements hailing Acre as the "filet mignon of Amazônia" began to appear in magazines, the handwriting was on the wall. Yet fate intervened and brought the attention of the entire world to this remote edge of the Amazon basin.

On December 22, 1988, a forty-four-year-old Acre rubber tapper named Francisco Alves Mendes de Almeida fell victim to a cold-blooded ambush at the back door of his modest home in the small town of Xapuri. In one sense, there was nothing remarkable about the assassination of Chico Mendes, the name by which the Acrean *seringueiro* was known. Beginning in 1964, conflicts over land and labor disputes in Amazônia and throughout rural Brazil had resulted in an estimated sixteen hundred killings.

But this case turned out to be different. Chico Mendes was no ordinary tapper. A man of uncommon intelligence and charisma, he had risen from the ranks to become not only a leader of Acre's *seringueiros*, but also an effective advocate abroad for his people's interests.

There is a good deal of drama in the life story of Chico Mendes. His grandfather, a northeasterner, migrated to Acre and became a freelance tapper, roaming the tropical forest, draining latex from wild rubber trees, and joining the descendants of other northeasterners who had been lured to the region during the rubber boom, ruthlessly exploited, and then left to their own devices when Brazil's rubber monopoly ended.

Chico mastered the ways of the tropical forest at an early age, and then he learned to read and write from a mysterious stranger, who was in fact a footloose fugitive who had participated in the Communist uprising in Brazil in the mid-1930s.* The political edu-

---

* This could have been an instance of life imitating art, since Jorge Amado's 1940 novel *Os Subterrâneos da Liberdade* depicted the adventures of a Communist agent who went into the jungle to radicalize exploited peasants.

cation his tutor gave him shaped his early participation in collective efforts by the *seringueiros* to better their lives.

When landowners began to convert tropical forest groves into pasture for raising cattle, Chico played a key role in devising a strategy by which the rubber tappers could engage in nonviolent resistance. Realizing that his people needed broader bases of support in their struggles, he became an early supporter of the Workers' party in Acre. But politics in Acre, as is true in most rural areas of Brazil, was controlled by wealthy landowners who could purchase votes, and a humble rubber tapper had little hope of gaining a following.

Then Chico and Brazil's nascent environmental movement discovered each other. Chico quickly recognized the tactical advantage of raising the banner of ecology as a means of defending the way of life of tropical-forest dwellers. The environmentalists, stung in the past by charges that they were elitists who cared only about flora and fauna, realized the value of incorporating into their struggle real-life working people who lived off the tropical forest. For them Chico and the *seringueiros* were a godsend.

Before long Chico was traveling to the United States to lobby Senators and officials of the World Bank. His was a fresh face, and the message he brought was simple and straightforward. Not only would the unbridled exploitation of Acre destroy vegetation and animal life; it would also have a devastating impact on human beings who had learned to live in harmony with nature.

Filmmaker Adrian Cowell was the first outsider to stumble on the gentle, moonfaced Chico. The footage Cowell compiled while following the exploits of the Acrean rubber tappers provides a vivid portrait of the man and his movement. It contains glimpses of Chico trekking through the tropical forest; Chico campaigning (unsuccessfully) for state deputy, as little boys try to sell him the votes of their families; Chico discussing tactics with fellow tappers; Chico playing with his children (one of whom was named Sandino, after the Nicaraguan hero); Chico meeting with World Bank officials; and finally, Chico being buried during a heavy rain.

The uproar over Chico's assassination forced the government to undertake an investigation that eventually resulted in the filing of charges against a local landowner, Darly Alves da Silva, and his son Darci. The son was indicted for carrying out the foul deed, the father for having instigated and planned it.

The trial attracted international attention. Darly turned out to be a larger-than-life character with an insatiable sexual appetite and a past tainted by suspicions of involvement in various prior killings both in Acre and elsewhere. Two years after the murder of Chico Mendes, both father and son were found guilty by a jury and received prison sentences.

Many both inside and outside Brazil rejoiced at the convictions. The shield of impunity, at least in this one instance, had been breached, and justice had been done. But celebration was premature. First an appellate court in Acre set aside the jury verdict against Darly on the ground that the evidence convicting him was insufficient. He remained in jail, however, awaiting trial for a murder charge that had been brought against him in the southern state of Paraná. But on February 15, 1993, both Darly and Darci escaped through a hole they had made by sawing through the bars of their cell window, and they disappeared, probably into nearby Bolivia.

It was difficult to believe that this could have happened without the connivance of local authorities. The prison, as subsequent investigations revealed, was woefully lacking in security measures, and the convicted killers had received all kinds of special privileges, ranging from the use of a color television and a freezer to overnight visits from women.

The flight of Darly and Darci was but one of several blows to the memory of Chico Mendes. In the aftermath of his death, an unseemly spat broke out among his surviving relatives, friends, and associates over the sale of motion picture rights to his life story. And two months after the conviction of his killers, hired assassins shot down the leader of a rural union in a town in the south of the state of Pará in Amazônia.

The full range and depth of the social and environmental problems plaguing Amazônia have lent themselves to pessimistic forecasts for the future. Yet the vastness of the region has made it difficult to get an accurate fix on the true dimensions of these problems. The true extent of deforestation is but one example. Original forecasts based on 1978 satellite images calculated that an average of fifteen thousand square miles of rain forest were being lost each year. A recent study has found that the average is more like fifty-eight hundred square miles.

The exaggeration occasionally employed by advocates hoping to dramatize the plight of the rain forest and its inhabitants, and thereby bring pressure to bear on the Brazilian government and international institutions, serves only to provide ammunition to those who do not accept the proposition that the resources of the Amazon basin should be rationally exploited. Examples of overstatement include predictions that the artificial lake at Tucuruí would not support life because the decomposition of the trees submerged there is using up the available oxygen. In fact, fish are now thriving in the dammed waters of the Tocantins River. Moreover, lumber that was said to have been lost forever as a result of the flooding is being successfully recovered by an entrepreneur who has mastered the art of underwater logging.

In the wake of the Chico Mendes murder and the international outcry over the destruction of the Amazon rain forest, President José Sarney raised the well-worn banner of nationalism to decry foreign intervention in Brazil's domestic affairs and to hint that beneath the criticism being leveled against Brazil's environmental policies lurked a hidden agenda: the desire of wealthy nations to exploit Amazônia for their own benefit. But he also launched the "Our Nature" program, designed to slow down deforestation and control (but not ban) the use of mercury by goldminers.

The March 1990 inauguration of Fernando Collor de Mello as president brought about an apparent shift in official attitudes toward conservation. Evidencing a new sensitivity to criticism from abroad (and evidently with an eye on the U.N. Earth Summit to be held in Rio in 1992), Collor surprised everyone by naming José Lutzenberger as his Secretary of the Environment.* The enforcement of laws regulating deforestation and the decision to dynamite airstrips used by goldminers who were encroaching on Indian tribal preserves were other indications that Collor took the environment issue seriously.

---

* The idiosyncratic Lutzenberger turned out to be a loose cannon, blessed with neither tact nor administrative skills; he was later dismissed.

Yet at the same time, as a reminder of the strength of opponents of conservationism, the voters of Amazonas in late 1990 chose as their governor Gilberto Mestrinho, whose campaign rhetoric included promises to give every peasant a chain saw and to legalize the hunting of endangered species. His mastery of the sound bite was evident in aphorisms such as "Ten million people can't be condemned to die of hunger so the animals and trees can grow," and "The environmentalists want to keep the Amazon like a circus, with us as the monkeys." He also stressed a point that struck a chord with his compatriots: atmospheric pollutants from automobiles in the "First World" (and especially the United States) far exceeded those discharged by fires in Amazônia.

The rate of deforestation decreased noticeably during the Collor presidency. Stricter law enforcement, the discontinuation of government subsidies for cattle ranching in Amazônia, heavier than usual rains, and the economic recession all contributed to the turnaround.

This improvement in turn took much of the heat off the Brazilian government, which had been apprehensive about the possibility of a public-relations disaster at the 1992 Earth Summit in Rio. The event proved to be a success, from the Brazilian point of view. When thirty thousand delegates from all over the world were gathered in Rio de Janeiro, the government opened a lovely new highway that sped visitors from the airport to the conference centers, ordered the street kids and the homeless off the streets, occupied strategic neighborhoods with troops and tanks, and otherwise cleaned up the city. It was a classic example of *para inglês ver.*

Of much more import is the extent to which the *para inglês ver* syndrome applies more generally to Brazilian efforts to rationalize the exploitation of the Amazon basin. A decision to send the army into parts of northern Amazônia to facilitate oil exploration in the region may encourage further road construction, with results that are all too predictable. There has always been a gap between rhetoric and reality in Brazil, and lofty pronouncements about conservation and "sustainable development" do not necessarily reflect what is actually happening on the front lines.

Events unfolding elsewhere in Brazil will also affect the future of Amazônia. If the economic recovery of late 1994 leads to an end to the recession and an increase in industrial growth in the South, the creation of new jobs will stem migration northward. If the administration of President Fernando Henrique Cardoso adopts a strong, sensible policy toward the Amazon basin and does not abandon stewardship of the region to those who would extract from the rain forest as much profit as possible as quickly as possible, there is hope that Amazônia can be preserved as an invaluable natural resource for both Brazil and the rest of the planet.

*Part Four*

# Spiritual Brazil

# Chapter 13

# Roman Catholicism

$\mathcal{T}$he Roman Catholic hierarchy got off to an inauspicious start in Brazil. The first bishop assigned to the colony, Dom Pero Fernandes Sardinha, got tangled up in a bitter controversy with the govenor-general, which was sparked by the bishop's outspoken disapproval of the sinful life-style of the governor-general's son. In 1556 the King of Portugal persuaded the bishop to return to Europe in order to allow tempers to cool. The vessel carrying Dom Pero went down off the coast of northeastern Brazil. The bishop managed to make his way to shore, where he was seized and eaten by Indians.

During the five centuries it has been a part of Brazil, the Catholic Church has traveled great distances both literally and figuratively. The institution has produced not only the ill-starred Dom Pero but also the bishop who was kidnapped, tortured, and sprayed with red paint by right-wing paramilitary vigilantes in Nova Iguaçu in 1976; not only the priests who accompanied the first Portuguese expeditions in order to spread the "One True Faith" throughout the New World, but also the Brazilian theologians who have contributed heavily to the shaping, popularizing, and concretizing of what has come to be known as liberation theology; not only the curates who faithfully served the interests of rural landowners during the colonial era but also the priests and nuns now exercising a "preferential option for the poor" by working in Brazil's urban slums and rural settlements.

Today, like many other components of Brazilian society, the Church is in crisis, facing challenges from within and from without. Progressive bishops are under pressure from their conservative colleagues (and the Vatican) to return the "Bark of Peter" to its traditional soul-saving course, while evangelical Protestant denominations continue to gain converts from Catholic ranks.

The history of the Catholic Church in Brazil is more than the trajectory of an institution. It also reflects the unique religiosity of the Brazilian people, and the interaction of this element of Brazilianness with Roman Catholicism. The mysticism brought to Brazil by Portuguese settlers took on a life of its own, especially as it shaped religious beliefs in the backlands of the Northeast. Strong traces of this unsophisticated spirituality survive to the present day and complicate the ongoing struggles within the Catholic community.

The Catholic Church in colonial Brazil differed markedly from the branches of Catholicism in Hispanic America. The Portuguese enjoyed a special status in the eyes of the Holy See because they defeated the Moors in North Africa and the Iberian peninsula on a number of occasions. When the Portuguese committed themselves to spreading the faith as they explored Africa and Asia and established commercial footholds wherever they went, they reinforced the prestige they already enjoyed in Rome. Indeed, there were those who believed that the destiny of the Lusitanians was to enable the Catholic Church to offset losses inflicted by the Protestant Reformation. When the Holy See encouraged Spain and Portugal to sign the Treaty of Tordesillas and divide the globe between them, the granting of the land mass of Brazil to the Portuguese seemed a fitting reward for their faithful service.

As a further reward, Rome granted to the Portuguese Crown broad authority over the Church in Brazil. The king could name bishops and other members of the high clergy, administer the financial affairs of the Church, distribute all benefices, approve ecclesiastical documents, control the influx of priests into the colony, and even settle appeals on decisions rendered by ecclesiastical courts. What resulted was a de facto merger between Church and State, a condition that made it difficult for the Church in Brazil to develop a separate identity of its own.

This did not prevent the Church in Brazil from assuming certain characteristics that reflected its Portuguese roots as well as the new environment. The malleability and tolerance that were peculiarly Lusitanian and produced a soft Catholicism contrasted sharply with the quasi-fanaticism of the Spaniards that gave a hard edge to the Catholicism implanted by the Spaniards elsewhere in Latin America. The isolation imposed by the vast size of Brazil, the temptations of the flesh intensified by the tropical setting, and the fact that raising a family was the only way a local priest could provide for his own care in sickness and old age combined to turn a number of local clerics from their obligation of chastity, and it was common for them to keep concubines and father illegitimate offspring.

Since colonial Brazil was primarily a rural society, the focal point of religious life for most settlers was the plantation rather than the parish. This was another point of difference with Spanish America, which could boast of a number of important towns with large Catholic churches. On the great sugar estates of the Northeast, the priest became the patriarch's adjunct (indeed, he was occasionally the patriarch's son). He was paid by the landowner, celebrated mass in the chapel customarily located near the "big house," and otherwise ministered to the spiritual needs of the owner's family and slaves.

If there was one group that had a broader vision of the role Catholicism should play in the New World, it was the Jesuits, whom the Pope charged with spreading Catholicism in Brazil. When the first governor-general of the colony arrived in Salvador in 1549, six black-robed members of the Society of Jesus accompanied him. Over the next half-century, 122 more would follow. Although other religious communities, such as the Franciscan and the Carmelite orders, sent missionaries to Brazil, it was the Jesuits who made the most significant impact. With remarkable energy and zeal, they undertook to instill religious values in the colonists and European civilization in the colony by setting up and maintaining the colony's educational system.

The Jesuits also sought to carry out the Pope's mandate to convert the Indians to Roman Catholicism. As has been described in Chapter Three, they built villages where they gathered natives and taught them religion as well as agricultural methods and various arts and crafts. In so doing, the Jesuits were pursuing long-term designs that looked to the future of Brazil. Their approach differed drastically from the extractive mind-set of most of the colonists, so it was inevitable that the members of the Society of Jesus would come into conflict with the landowners who wanted to enslave the Indians and put them to work on plantations. The Jesuits resisted, but in the end, as depicted vividly in the film *The Mission,* their theocratic outposts succumbed to armed attacks by the settlers.

Although the Jesuits and other members of the clergy opposed the enslavement of the Indians, they generally accepted the African slave trade and the establishment of involuntary servitude on a massive scale in Brazil. Perhaps it was because slavery had been a fact of life in Portugal and the missionaries brought their acceptance of it with them to the New World. They baptized manacled Africans arriving in the colony, and in some instances missionaries even procured slaves for their own use. Although there were priests who later spoke out forcefully against the "excesses" of slavery, the attitude of the Church remained pragmatic, in thrall to the economic necessities of the ruling class in Brazil.

Catholicism's relationship to the Crown in colonial Brazil enabled it to serve as both a formalizing and a unifying element in the society that was evolving, yet this role benefited the temporal authorities much more than it did the Church. In rural areas parish priests took their place alongside the landowners and local government officials and were accorded a certain degree of respect, but they exercised little real influence, except with the wives, daughters, and spinsters who attended church regularly. The men in the community were married in the church but were otherwise disposed to ignore Catholic rituals and look on the priestly presence with benign toleration.

Catholicism in Portugal's prize colony tended to be nearly a continent wide and an inch deep. As Thomas C. Bruneau points out in his monograph *The Church in Brazil,* "the king was Catholic, therefore, so were all his subjects. With adherence to the religion guaranteed, not to say imposed, there was no need for the faithful to develop a personal sense of commitment or belief." This meant that the institutional Church became especially vulnerable to shifts in the political wind, and that religious conviction became similarly susceptible to the tug of unorthodoxy.

Thus when the Jesuits were expelled from Brazil in 1759, the colony lost its most dedicated and independent-minded curates, the

Jesuit seminaries, and the educational institutions that they had administered. Later, under the empire, the government suppressed all religious orders, and the number of priests and nuns in Brazil dwindled. Young men entering religious life were not well prepared. They often attached themselves to a local pastor, picked up a smattering of Latin, and were thereafter ordained.

Pedro II, a lukewarm Catholic at best, assumed that the powers the Portuguese Crown had traditionally exercised over the Brazilian Church were his to exercise as well, and Rome acquiesced. He deplored the state of moral decay into which the Brazilian clergy had plunged, so he sent candidates for the priesthood to study in Europe. At the same time, he kept his distance from the Vatican. When Rome proposed to install a cardinal in Brazil, which would have been a first for Latin America, the emperor declined the offer.

Dom Pedro's decision to permit aspiring priests to be trained in Europe improved the intellectual and moral qualities of the clergy in Brazil, but it also had an unintended effect. The new clerics became inculcated with the notion that national churches should submit to the authority of the papacy, a doctrine that the Holy See was actively promoting at the time.

The disagreement over papal authority produced a serious Church-State conflict in Brazil when the Vatican condemned Masonry in 1864. The anticlericalism of these secret societies in Europe had not infected the Brazilian lodges, and hence Dom Pedro saw no reason to permit a papal encyclical critical of Freemasonry to be published in Brazil. But several bishops who subscribed to the principle of papal supremacy defied the emperor's wishes and took disciplinary action against Catholic organizations accepting Masons as members. Dom Pedro bridled at this challenge to his authority, and in 1874 two bishops ended up in prison as a result of the dispute.

These tensions ultimately led to the separation of Church and State in Brazil. When a republican form of government replaced the monarchy, a new Constitution promulgated in 1891 abolished the special status enjoyed by Roman Catholicism. Freedom of religion was guaranteed, only civil marriages could receive legal recognition, and religious education was barred from the public schools. The Church was left to fend for itself, a turn of events that proved to be a blessing in disguise.

The formal, superficial Catholicism prevalent in Brazil during the colonial period not only prevented the Church from developing apart from the State, and thereby from attaining a degree of institutional strength that would enable it to resist the dictates of the temporal rulers of the country; but the weakness of the Church also created a favorable climate for the spread of a variety of unconventional religious beliefs and practices on or beyond the fringes of the "One True Faith." This was especially true as settlers pushed into the vast interior of the colony.

The isolated backlands of the Northeast, for example, produced a unique brand of religiosity that combined superstition, mysticism, and elements of Portuguese, Indian, and African folk culture. Given that life in the hostile environment of the *sertão* was a constant struggle, it is not difficult to understand how aberrant forms of Catholicism could flourish.

What emerged was a mixture of very traditional, primitive Lusitanian Catholicism that had gone to seed and elements of both Indian and African spiritual beliefs. The shortage of priests in Brazil meant that for many of the backlanders, contact with the institutional Church was an annual or semiannual event. Moreover, those clerics who did occasionally minister to the spiritual needs of the *sertanejos* often attributed the harshness of life in the backlands, and especially the periodic droughts, to God's wrath, deeming it punishment for the sins of mankind. This, in turn, generated beliefs that not only prayer but also a variety of unorthodox religious practices would ameliorate life's tribulations. Of the latter, one of the most common was the *promessa,* or "promise" to perform some sacrificial act, like carrying a large wooden cross for many miles, in return for the fulfillment of a supplicant's petition.*

The appearances of individuals thought to possess saintly properties were not uncommon in the *sertão.* At times these holy men

---

* This custom was the theme of the gripping film *O Pagador de Promessas* (the title in English was *The Given Word*), which won a prize at the 1962 Cannes Film Festival.

or women did nothing more than care for churches, shrines, and cemeteries that had fallen into a state of disrepair. At other times, they caused major disruptions.

Wild-eyed prophets, often bearded and wrapped in tattered robes, periodically played on the frustrations and superstitions of backlanders, and plunged them into various forms of fanaticism. Deeply rooted elements of popular culture, such as the messianic movement that held that the lost Portuguese monarch, Sebastian, would one day return and reward those who believed in him, provided the catalyst for some of these outbursts.

For example, in 1836, a psychotic prophet gathered together a group of followers who erected a pair of pillars in a remote part of the interior of the state of Pernambuco. From the top of one of the pillars he led religious services and preached that King Sebastian would return to reward those who believed in him, but only if the foot of one of the columns were washed in blood. For three days the faithful indulged in a sacrificial orgy, during which mothers threw their offspring from the adjacent column, and, as the frenzy spread, adults jumped or were pushed. In the end thirty children, twelve men, eleven women, and fourteen dogs lost their lives.

The most famous of the religion-related disturbances in the Northeast had nothing to do with Sebastianism. The movement led by Antônio Conselheiro did not await the return of a missing Portuguese king, but instead called on the faithful to reject all worldly goods and purify themselves in preparation for the second coming of Christ.

Antônio Vicente Mendes Maciel was a small businessman from the interior of the state of Bahia. His mother died when he was six, and his childhood was an unhappy one, owing to his father's heavy drinking. Antônio attended both primary and secondary school and helped out in his father's store. His father had a poor head for business and sank heavily into debt. When his father died, Antônio inherited the debts. In an attempt to shake off the financial burden thrust on him, Antônio did some tutoring as well as odd jobs. Having married his fifteen-year-old cousin and siring two children, he now had a family to support.

In 1860 his young wife ran off with a soldier. As Robert E. Levine points out in his excellent study *Vale of Tears*, "The backland code of honor gave him little choice in this unhappy situation: he could either avenge himself by killing his wife and her lover, or he could do nothing and suffer endless humiliation. In the end, flight proved a third option."

Maciel spent fifteen years wandering through the backlands, and eventually became a penitent. He prayed and fasted and inflicted all kinds of physical hardship on himself. Soon he acquired a reputation as a holy man, and people began to follow him. He and his growing entourage repaired chapels and burial grounds, and during the drought of 1877 they built wells and water tanks. Because he preached sermons and dispensed advice for those who sought it, he earned a new name, Antônio Conselheiro (Antônio the Counselor).

The traditional explanation for the activities of Antônio Conselheiro rests on the contention that he was a psychopath. Euclides da Cunha, in his classic *Rebellion in the Backlands*, embraces this interpretation and stresses the Counselor's "mental aberrations," "absurd conceptions," and "mad ravings." This conclusion rests on dubious scientific evidence—a study of the size of the Counselor's brain, which was taken to the medical school in Salvador after he was killed and decapitated during the final battle at Canudos. (The head disappeared after a fire in 1904.)

More recently, intellectuals on the Left have sought to rehabilitate Antônio Conselheiro by portraying him as a proto-Marxist revolutionary leader of the region's dispossessed. But this characterization overlooks the fact that he never attacked the inequitable concentration of landownership in the Northeast, and that capitalism and private property existed in Canudos, the town his followers occupied and fortified.

Antônio Conselheiro was in fact a devout (if excessive) Catholic in the tradition of *beatos* (pious men) who roamed the interior of the Northeast. He helped parish priests and attained the status of a "counselor," which meant, among other things, that he could conduct public prayer on his own, without specific clerical authorization. The advice he gave was not inconsistent with Catholic doctrine.

What pushed him and his followers into rebellion was his refusal to accept the separation of Church and State decreed by the new Brazilian republic. This stance put him in conflict not only with local authorities but also with the Church itself, which was willing to adapt to the new political climate and instructed the faithful to respect the new national government. In addition, landowners who were losing workers to Antônio Conselheiro's movement feared the economic consequences of a serious reduction in the region's labor force, and they demanded that the federal authorities take military action against Canudos. The result was the bloodly anni-hilation of the settlement in 1897.

The disturbances caused by Antônio Conselheiro and his motley band of disciples were not the only manifestations of religious ex-tremism in the Northeast at the end of the nineteenth century. North of Canudos, in a fertile valley located in the midst of arid backlands where the states of Ceará, Paraíba, and Pernambuco con-verge, a tiny priest named Cícero Romão Batista was developing a mystique that would attract a devoted following and also translate into political power. His influence is still evident today.

The institutional Church, in the process of becoming "Roman-ized" and seeking to assert centralized authority over its far-flung flock, looked with disapproval on the activities of Father Cícero and took direct action against him. That their official sanctions failed demonstrates once again the vitality of grassroots religious move-ments that were emerging from the unique spirituality of the Bra-zilian people.

Father Cícero studied for the priesthood at the diocesan semi-nary in Fortaleza, the capital of Ceará, and took the sacrament of holy orders in 1870. He planned to teach at the seminary, but in 1872, during a visit to the hamlet of Joaseiro (today called Juazeiro do Norte) he had a dream in which Christ ordered him to minister to the impoverished peasants of the region. Resolving to obey, the little curate became the town's parish priest, and in the ensuing years he earned a reputation as a hardworking, selfless person, who lived with the poverty endemic to the area.

One of the religious activities he initiated was the assembling of a group of pious women for instruction and devotion. Some of them came to live in the modest house he shared with his mother and sisters. It was one of these *beatas*, a twenty-eight-year-old laundress, who would play a key role in the events that propelled Father Cícero into regional prominence. On March 1, 1889, while she was taking communion from him at the chapel in Joaseiro, the white host she had received into her mouth became stained with blood, a phenomenon that repeated itself over the next two months. Not only Father Cícero but also other priests from nearby cities and towns proclaimed imaginatively that what was appearing on the communion wafers in the laundress's mouth was in fact the blood of Christ.

The miracle at Joaseiro fired the imagination of the people of the Northeast. Poor people from all over the region began to make pilgrimages to the hamlet. Prominent citizens from neighboring municipalities declared their belief in the miracle. (The economic stimulation occasioned by the pilgrimages may have influenced their professions of faith.) Believers began to venerate unconsumed communion wafers and pieces of cloth bearing visible stains of what was alleged to be the blood of Christ. At the center of it all was Father Cícero, whose reputation for holiness lent credibility to the claim that supernatural events were occurring.

The bishop of Fortaleza, firmly convinced of the need for ecclesiastical discipline, was greatly displeased that Father Cícero and the other priests who had legitimated the miracle had not gone through the proper channels within the Church to verify such phenomena, and he took steps to curb what he saw as an affront to his authority. In his view the implications of the supposed miracle violated Catholic doctrine. In 1894 he suspended Father Cícero from exercising many of his priestly functions.

The diminutive priest followed Church procedures in efforts to clear himself, to the point of traveling to Rome in 1898. The Sacred Congregation of the Holy Office did not absolve him, but neither was he forced to make any formal recantations, as his bishop had demanded, nor was he ordered to leave Joaseiro. He also had a brief audience with Pope Leo XIII. When he returned home, his followers had not lost any of their enthusiasm. Indeed, the fact that he had been to Rome and had met the pope raised their estimation of him. They continued to regard him as a saint and venerated him as such.

By now the faithful believed that Joaseiro was the "New Jerusalem," a holy place chosen to be the location for the second coming of Jesus Christ. Even though Father Cícero remained under ecclesiastical sanctions that limited the religious functions he could exercise, multitudes emerging from the backlands of the Northeast streamed into the town he had made famous, in the hope that through his intercession they would find some relief from the harshness of a drought or from the many social injustices routinely visited on the region's have-nots.

In the second decade of the new century, the growth of Joaseiro helped elevate it to the status of a municipality, and Father Cícero soon found himself abandoning the strict neutrality he had carefully followed in political matters. Although his primary concern remained focused on his ongoing struggle with the hierarchy over the suspension of some of his priestly duties, he became the first mayor of Joaseiro in 1911 and, shortly thereafter, third vice president of Ceará.

At the time the state was in political turmoil, so when government forces attacked Joaseiro in 1913 under the pretext of rooting out bandits who had taken refuge there, Father Cícero urged his followers to defend the New Jerusalem. Convinced that their spiritual leader would afford them divine protection in battle, a motley assortment of defenders turned back the aggressors and then, shifting from resistance to a revolutionary mode, they marched to Fortaleza and overthrew the state government.

Father Cícero was now the most powerful figure in the state, if not the region, and his new status made him a force to be reckoned with on the national scene as well. Though politically naive, he relied heavily on a close adviser, whom some accused of manipulating him. Moreover, during the 1920s he became, in the words of his biographer Ralph della Cava, the " 'labor czar' of the entire Northeast," as he mobilized manpower for public-works projects and cotton harvests and encouraged workers to work hard, say their prayers, and respect authority.

By this time he was an old man, and his advanced age took its toll on him. During the last decade of his life he lived in virtual isolation, still hoping to obtain full reconciliation with his Church, and still venerated by his followers and by pilgrims from all over the Northeast. He died in 1934 at the age of ninety.

Joaseiro remains to the present day the destination of miracle seekers and pious folk who believe that Father Cícero will one day

return to earth. A fifty-two-foot, five-hundred-ton statue of him—
one of the tallest monuments in Brazil—stands as a testament to
the permanence of his appeal to the have-nots of the Northeast.

A diminutive Italian Capuchin missionary, Friar Damião, is
widely believed to be a reincarnation of Father Cícero. He, too, has
been subject to disciplinary action by the Church, but these efforts
have not in the least diminished the reverence paid him by backlanders. During the 1989 presidential campaign, Fernando Collor
made several highly publicized visits to Friar Damião, just as politicians from Ceará had routinely made calls on Father Cícero. How
many votes Collor received as a result of his invocation of the
memory of the miracle worker from Joaseiro cannot be determined, but the young candidate from Alagoas did very well in the
interior of the Northeast.

The religiosity of the Brazilian people has inspired a number
of devotions that have challenged the Church. The Church's response to one of them, the widespread veneration of the image of
the Virgin Mary in Aparecida, demonstrates its success in adapting
and channeling the intense religiosity of the Brazilian people, while
at the same time strengthening and imposing unity and discipline
on an institution that had been severely weakened by a long history of subservience to the State.

In 1717 three fishermen retrieved the two broken parts of a
black terra-cotta statue of the Virgin Mary from the waters of the
Paraíba River in the northern part of the state of São Paulo. Immediately thereafter, they began to catch so many fish that they
had to stop or risk sinking their boat. One of the fishermen kept
the image in a sanctuary in his home, and people from the neighborhood began to pray before it. Over the years, miracles were attributed to the statue, and eventually an increasing number of
people began to make pilgrimages to Aparecida, the name given to
the place where the figure had been placed on display in a modest
chapel.

It was Dom Pedro I who promised to make Our Lady of Aparecida the patron saint of Brazil. The tremendous popularity of the
image, aided by the location of the chapel midway between the
population centers of São Paulo and Rio de Janiero, no doubt
helped to persuade the Catholic hierarchy to look with favor on

the veneration it inspired. In 1929 the Brazilian Church petitioned the Vatican to have Our Lady of Aparecida declared the "Principal Patron Saint of Brazil before God." Pope Pius XI granted the request, and the black Virgin of Aparecida became for the nation of Brazil what Our Lady of Fátima was to Portugal, and Our Lady of Lourdes was to France.

Today pilgrims continue to flock to Aparecida. Many of them come to fulfill promises they have made to the Virgin in return for some spiritual or temporal benefit. For those unable to make the trip, the statue of the Blessed Virgin is occasionally transported to and exhibited in other parts of the country.*

Unlike the cult of Father Cícero, which had (and continues to have) a life of its own, devotion to Our Lady of Aparecida has been under firm ecclesiastical control ever since the process of "Romanization" began to gather momentum in the late nineteenth century. After the separation of Church and State in 1891, the Church hierarchy accepted its new status but at the same time sought to insert Catholic symbols into the national fabric. Our Lady of Aparecida was one way to achieve this end.†

A continuing shortage of priests often made it difficult for the Church to deal with widespread popular beliefs and practices rooted in superstition and ignorance. For that reason, the hierarchy put greater emphasis on reviving and deepening the faith of middle-class Brazilians. Priests and nuns streaming into Brazil from the Old World spread a contemporary European brand of Catholicism. They also established secondary schools, mostly for the middle class, and prepared the way for a better educated laity. At the same time, Church officials went about establishing a relationship with the state that enabled them to influence Brazilian society on matters they felt were of vital concern.

---

* In 1987 Church dignitaries brought the image of Our Lady of Fátima from Portugal for exhibition in about forty Brazilian cities, and during the visit had it pay what might be deemed a "courtesy call" on the statue in the shrine at Aparecida.

† The erection of the huge statue of Christ on the Corcovado Mountain in Rio de Janeiro in 1922 was another, as the Redeemer with his outstretched arms became one of the city's symbols.

Thus, beginning in the 1920s and continuing for three decades, the Church promoted a more muscular Catholicism to counter the secularist tendencies that had been gaining a strong foothold in the country. With this renewed faith, the Church succeeded in influencing the principal institutions of Brazilian society. Catholic intellectuals rose to prominence, while lay Catholic organizations mobilized the middle class, students, women, and workers and affirmed within the social fabric the presence of the Church and its teachings. The hierarchy, moreover, was able to maintain a firm control over the lay groups.

The newly activated Catholic laity permitted the Church to pursue political goals. As Scott Mainwaring has pointed out in his excellent study *The Catholic Church and Politics in Brazil, 1916-1985,* "The Church wanted the state to reinstitute informally the favored relationship that disestablishment had legally ended. The state, realizing it had much to gain through an alliance with the Church, grasped the opportunity to trade some privileges for religious sanction."

In the political arena, the Church looked out for matters it considered to be within its sphere of interest, such as issues affecting education and the family. Although an encyclical issued by Pope Leo XIII in 1891 called for a more equitable relationship between labor and capital and inspired a new social consciousness within the Church, the hierarchy remained fundamentally conservative. In response to the revolutionary currents emanating from the Russian Revolution, the Church declared that Communism was intrinsically evil. In Brazil this led the Church to cultivate close ties to the anticommunist and antiliberal regime of Getúlio Vargas, and to turn a blind eye to Vargas's human-rights abuses. The Church's political strategy bore fruit in the new Constitution of 1934, which provided for state subsidies to the Church and to Catholic schools, and for a prohibition of divorce.

With the fall of the Vargas dictatorship and the reinstitution of democratic rule after World War II, Catholicism in Brazil faced new challenges. Its long-standing resistance to secularism ran counter to the pressures for modernization and development sweeping the country. With the Communist party's rise to political prominence the Church realized it would pay a big price if it kept ignoring the just demands of workers and peasants. But the broadening of the democratic process in Brazil made it somewhat awkward for an authoritarian, hierarchical institution to exert political influence.

The Church responded in a number of ways. Institutionally, it established the Conferência Nacional dos Bispos do Brasil (CNBB) (or the National Conference of Brazilian Bishops), which became a forum for the hierarchy to discuss both ecclesiastical and non-ecclesiastical issues and a vehicle for the Church to take positions on such matters. The Church became increasingly concerned with the lack of social justice in Brazil. The CNBB spoke out in favor of land reform, and Church-sponsored social programs began to address the temporal problems of slumdwellers.

The late 1950s and early 1960s saw the emergence of an embryonic, heterogeneous movement known as the Catholic Left. It was composed mainly of Catholic students and intellectuals who pushed Catholic social doctrine in new directions and advocated radical changes within Brazilian society. They worked at the grassroots level, especially among young people in universities, factories, urban slums, and the countryside. They organized workers and peasants and set up literacy programs for the poor.

These lay Catholic activists either embraced Marxism or found much in it that was congenial to their analysis of the structural inequities they saw around them. Conflicts arose between the Catholic Left and the Church hierarchy, which disassociated itself from the new breed of Catholic radicals and in some instances disowned them.

The turbulence that destabilized the Goulart administration in the early 1960s and the apparent political influence the Communist party and other elements of the extreme Left had managed to gain among a number of Brazilians created deep apprehension within the Church, which remained a conservative force despite the activities of a number of its clerics and lay people who were working on behalf of Brazil's have-nots. Right-wing Catholics, supported by several bishops, formed a group called "Tradition, Family, and Property," which organized demonstrations against the government. Shortly after the military overthrew Goulart in 1964, the CNBB released a statement cautiously praising the armed forces for preventing "the implementation of a Bolshevik regime in our country."

In the early months of the military regime, the army and the police moved quickly, ruthlessly, and efficiently to annihilate the various youth components of the Catholic Left. This brought only indirect murmurs of protest from the Church hierarchy. But as the authoritarian rule became increasingly repressive in the late 1960s, the Church gradually tempered its support for the government and began to denounce the human-rights abuses that were becoming prevalent. The enlightened spirit of the Second Vatican Council, which began a process of renewal within Roman Catholicism, contributed to the shift of the Church in Brazil. In addition, as the dictatorship stifled all outlets for political dissent, the Church found itself to be the only institutional voice that could speak out effectively on behalf of individual rights in Brazil.

Prominent among the Church officials taking action on behalf of human rights were two prelates who did not hesitate to put themselves at personal risk to do what they believed was right. Dom Hélder Pessoa Câmara and Dom Paulo Evaristo Arns may have come from opposite ends of Brazil and from dissimilar backgrounds, and they may have had entirely different personalities, but the archbishop of Olinda and Recife and the cardinal of São Paulo shared a basic commitment to a distinctly Christian vision of social and economic justice.

Hélder Câmara was born in 1909 in the state of Ceará, which meant that he grew up during the heyday of Father Cícero. Indeed, while studying for the priesthood in Fortaleza, he had the opportunity to meet the legendary cleric, who made a vivid impression on the young seminarian. Five years after his ordination in 1931, Father Hélder was transferred to Rio de Janeiro, where he quickly ascended the hierarchical ladder, from priest to monsignor to auxiliary bishop to auxiliary archbishop.

He was charismatic, articulate, and dramatic. Scholar Ralph della Cava once noted that he "hardly has to lift an eyebrow to draw a sigh from the crowd." Although he stood no taller than most altar boys, his size, like Father Cícero's, worked to his advantage. He became tremendously popular not only because of his personal magnetism but also because of the social projects he organized for Rio's poor, and he gained great respect as a result of his contribution to the founding of the CNBB.*

The political odyssey of Hélder Câmara began on the far Right during the 1930s, when he flirted with Integralism, the Brazilian version of fascism. During the Rio phase of his career, Dom Hélder's social consciousness surfaced, and he involved himself in efforts to better the lives of the *favelados*. However, his efforts focused on the symptoms rather than the causes of poverty. Although he was called the "Bishop of Development" and the "Bishop of the Poor," Dom Hélder remained committed to a basically conservative outlook. For a while he was close to Carlos Lacerda, the mercurial right-wing editor, and during the 1960 presidential campaign, Dom Hélder published a letter declaring that Catholics could not in conscience vote for one of the candidates because of that candidate's permissive stands on divorce and Communism.

It was not until after Dom Hélder's appointment as archbishop of Recife, which coincided with the military coup of 1964, that the little priest's concern for the poor turned to outspoken criticism of what he saw as economic, social, and political injustice not only in the Northeast but in the whole of Brazilian society as well.

He organized the bishops of the region and persuaded them to issue statements and reports condemning the exploitation of peasants and rural workers, and the inequitable distribution of land in the Northeast. He made no secret of his own preference for democratic socialism, and for dialogue with Marxists. He also denounced torture and other forms of repression the military regime was using against those it suspected of subversion, whether they opposed the government or worked at the grass roots in an effort to improve the lot of the impoverished.

Dom Hélder's outspokenness at a time when Brazil's men in uniform had silenced political dissent made him a target, and over the years there were a number of attempts to intimidate him. He

---

* The Holy See approved the founding of the CNBB because of Dom Hélder's success in selling the idea to an official in the Vatican Secretariat of State, Giovanni Battista Montini. The latter remained Dom Hélder's friend, and later, upon assuming the throne of Peter as Pope Paul VI, became his most powerful protector.

received telephone threats, and armed men in passing cars sprayed archdiocesan buildings with bullets. In 1969 unknown assailants brutally murdered a young priest who worked with Dom Hélder.

David Nasser, a renowned "attack-dog" journalist, wrote of the archbishop, "He has . . . dressed the Rabbi of Galilee in the tunic of Mao, putting on him the ideological beard of Fidel." Sociologist Gilberto Freyre, an enthusiastic supporter of the military regime and an abashed apologist for its excesses, engaged in a scurrilous, nonstop campaign to discredit Dom Hélder, and he even managed to accuse the archbishop of being a "Brazilian Dr. Goebbels" and a "Brazilian Kerensky" in the same newspaper article.

Dom Hélder seemed to thrive on adversity. In his sixties, he retained an air of impishness and projected the charm of a precocious child, qualities that made him a poor target for those who sought to villify him. He moved out of the Archbishop's Palace and into a sparsely furnished room at the rear of a church in a residential neighborhood not far from downtown Recife, where assassins might easily have reached him.

Yet he survived, in part because he had become famous outside Brazil and had remained close to Pope Paul VI. Moreover, inflicting physical harm on an archibishop would surely have had untold negative consequences for the military rulers of the country. So instead they turned him into a nonperson. The censored press stopped writing about him or even mentioning his name. Many people in the south of Brazil thought he had died.

Friendly critics of Dom Hélder maintained that he was more "show" than "go," an intellectual butterfly who fluttered from one idea to another and looked good in the process but lacked the patience to organize for the long haul. There is perhaps some truth in this, but the fact remains that he did follow up on an idea that he had embraced while he was an auxiliary bishop in Rio—the encouraging of a greater degree of lay involvement in Church matters—an idea that foreshadowed and facilitated the subsequent spread of the Ecclesiastical Base Communities.

Dom Hélder was but the most visible of a growing number of bishops, priests, and nuns who were not only advocating social and economic justice, but also putting their lives on the line to achieve it during the 1960s and 1970s. For example, the Bishop of Nova Iguaçu, Dom Adriano Hipólito, was smeared with red paint and beaten by unknown kidnappers because of his protests against human-rights abuses in the Baixada Fluminense outside Rio de Janeiro. When the regime's policy of developing Amazônia resulted in a growing number of violent conflicts over landownership in the region, the Church came out squarely on the side of the peasants. The police and private gunmen hired by the landowners threatened and occasionally tortured religious workers. The government expelled foreign priests considered to be "agitators."

What was emerging as a full-scale Church-State conflict provoked the hierarchy to close ranks. Even right-wing prelates joined in denunciations of the government repression. The CNBB, which had been taken over by conservatives in 1964, remained mute, but regional subdivisions of the conference spoke out boldly in defense of the poor. When the CNBB came under the control of progressive bishops in 1968, it too began to raise its voice against the repressive and regressive policies of the military regime.

Yet it was not until Dom Paulo Evaristo Arns took over the archdiocese of São Paulo in 1970 that the Church gained its most influential and substantive spokesman for its opposition to the excesses of the dictatorship. He was as self-effacing as Dom Hélder was flashy. But because Pope Paul VI put him in charge of the world's largest Catholic diocese and then made him a cardinal in 1973, he found himself inexorably drawn into a fight that was not of his making but from which he did not shrink.

Paulo Arns was born in 1922, the fourth of thirteen children, in a modest German colony where most of the population was bilingual. He was descended from German immigrants who had settled three generations ago in the southern state of Santa Catarina. He entered a Franciscan seminary and was ordained a priest shortly after the end of World War II. His order sent him to France, where he studied at the Sorbonne, and upon his return to Brazil he spent some thirteen years teaching in high schools in the state of São Paulo and at the Franciscan seminary in Petrópolis, near Rio de Janeiro. His next post took him to the city of São Paulo, where he became an auxiliary bishop, and four years later he succeeded the conservative Dom Agnelo Rossi at the head of the archdiocese.

Up to this point Dom Paulo had not been involved in any activities that would suggest that he held radical ideas about the Church or its role in society. He had shown himself to be cautious, relatively moderate, and traditional, and like most of his colleagues he had supported the 1964 military coup. But his outlook would soon change.

It was exposure to the tragedy of Brazil's "disappeareds" that changed Dom Paulo. The families and friends of the victims of the military regime kept coming to him for help, and he could not refuse them. His efforts to obtain information brought him into direct contact with prisoners who had been tortured. He set up the Archdiocesan Peace and Justice Commission to deal with the hundreds of requests he was receiving. He also made certain that Pope Paul VI became aware of what was happening, and the pontiff himself spoke out against human-rights abuses in Brazil.

Dom Paulo's crowning achievement, in his crusade against torture, was the 1985 publication of *Brasil: Nunca Mais (Brazil: Never Again*, published in English as *Torture in Brazil)*, an analysis of military court proceedings that documented in horrific detail the work of the repressive apparatus of the regime. The book was the product of an extraordinary five-year project undertaken in secret by the cardinal and a group of trusted associates. It sought to place in the historical record a dark corner of the recent past, and to convince Brazilians of the need to abolish the official use of torture.

The physical abuse inflicted on prisoners was not the only injustice that concerned Dom Paulo during this period. He was astute enough to perceive what the "Brazilian miracle" was doing to the workers of São Paulo and its environs, and to the masses of poor people everywhere, and he felt the need to address these problems from a structural rather than a palliative approach. Thus, he permitted archdiocesan churches to serve as assembly halls for workers at a time when the regime sought to keep a tight lid on all forms of self-expression by labor, and he supported impoverished squatters who invaded unused land—a phenomenon that was occurring with growing frequency on the periphery of São Paulo.

Even more significant were his steadfast support of a grassroots movement that encouraged lay Catholics to organize themselves into so-called Ecclesiastical Base Communities (or CEBs, the Portuguese acronym), and his espousal of liberation theology, a new way of relating Catholicism to the earthly concerns of the poor.

The CEBs brought small groups of lay people together, originally to hold Sunday religious services in localities only occasionally visited by a priest. Many of the CEBs encouraged participants to discuss the Bible and its relevance to their everyday lives. The CEBs became instruments for greater lay participation in Church activities and parish governance, as well as launching pads for poor people becoming involved in collective efforts to improve living conditions in local communities. The CEB movement originated in Brazil and then spread to the rest of Latin America.

Liberation theology posited that Christ became flesh not just to point the way to eternal salvation but also to free mankind from hunger, misery, ignorance, and oppression. This branch of theology sought to deduce a liberating message from the Christian tradition, and to link faith with practice by recognizing the political essence of faith.

There was a symbiotic relationship between the CEBs and the new theological movement, with the CEBs inspiring the theology as well as serving as the operational base for carrying out liberation theology. Both challenged the ecclesiastical status quo and aroused the opposition of some traditionalists within the Church: the CEBs because they fostered a spirit of self-awareness that made it difficult for the hierarchy to control them, and liberation theology because it used Marxist analysis to look at social and economic problems.

The CEBs were in part a response to the continuing shortage of priests in rural areas, in part an effort to offset gains being made by evangelical Protestant sects, and in part a reflection of Catholic anxiety over the threat of Communist penetration of the Brazilian countryside, especially in the immediate aftermath of the Cuban Revolution. Yet at the same time the CEBs were authentic expressions of grassroots Catholicism.

What would later be called CEBs began to appear in 1963 in remote parts of Brazil. They were organized by priests, nuns, or lay pastoral workers who had secured the approval of the local bishop and were operating under his aegis. The usual practice was for pastoral agents to visit the CEBs on a regular, periodic basis. The degree of autonomy enjoyed by the communities depended on the outlook of the bishops: conservative prelates tended to keep the CEBs on a short leash; whereas progressives permitted them to function freely on their own. The progressives outnumbered the conservatives in the vast countryside of Brazil.

It was not until 1965 that the CNBB took note of the existence of the Ecclesiastical Base Communities, and three years later the Latin American Bishops Conference at Medellín, Colombia, deemed the CEBs one of the most promising new developments to emerge from the Church in Latin America.

In their formative years, the Brazilian Ecclesiastical Base Communities came to serve as vehicles for consciousness-raising among the poor, as participants began to realize the nexus between their lowly status in society and their passivity. They understood that they had been conditioned to view themselves as objects to which things happened, rather than as human beings who could make things happen and thereby effect their own destiny.*

Thus it should come as no surprise that many of the CEBs soon turned from purely religious activity to spirited involvement in the larger communities around them. This increased activity occurred at a time when the military regime was stifling most forms of dissent. The Ecclesiastical Base Communities, because of their Church "cover," were able to survive relatively intact even when the authorities looked askance at what they were doing. By the early 1970s CEBs were sprouting in many of Brazil's urban slums.

Eventually, as the dictatorship committed itself to a gradual return to democratic, civilian rule and began to ease up on many of the restrictions it had placed on civil rights and civil liberties, the CEBs provided a great deal of the leadership as well as the rank and file for new political groups that were forming. The Ecclesiastical Base Communities themselves often became involved in politics,

---

* In this regard, they borrowed from the literacy method developed by Paulo Freire, a lay Catholic northeasterner who devised a system of motivating illiterates to learn to read and write by making them see the connection between their ignorance and the living conditions to which society had condemned them.

to the extent that they discussed issues and mobilized members to support candidates.

Many of the priests and nuns working with the Ecclesiastical Base Communities had no problem with the direction the CEBs were taking. They were experiencing firsthand the harsh realities of life among Brazil's have-nots, and were radicalized by it. They also communicated these realities to their bishops, who in turn supported what they were doing. Indeed, one of the staunchest supporters of the CEB movement was Cardinal Arns, and CEBs flourished in the slums on the periphery of São Paulo.

This Church involvement in political activities had implications that went unnoticed at the time. It was one thing to denounce human-rights abuses and the heavy hand of military dictatorship (even though it put a serious strain on Church relations with the regime and compromised the Church's ability to resist becoming involved in legislative measures of interest to it, such as the legalization of divorce). But to make the leap into advocacy of radical social and economic change meant fashioning alternatives to the status quo. And later, when full political rights were revived in Brazil, it meant risking the possibility that candidates supported by the Church would win elections and have to produce positive results.

The politicization of some of the CEBs became a cause for concern among some conservative members of the Church hierarchy. Yet it was a natural outgrowth of the process of consciousness-raising that was going on within the movement. It was also a natural consequence of the new theology that was both taking sustenance from and nourishing the Ecclesiastical Base Communities.

What came to be known as liberation theology evolved from the liberalizing currents emanating from the 1962-65 Vatican Council, which stressed the social mission of the Church and advocated a greater role for the laity, and from the 1968 Latin American Bishops Conference in Medellín, Colombia, during which the hierarchy came out firmly on the side of social and economic justice and structural change that would improve the lot of the region's have-nots. At that conference in Medellín the Latin American Church committed itself to a "preferential option for the poor," and liberation theology received an indispensable boost.

Although its origins predated the 1968 conference, the new theology gained legitimacy when the Latin bishops requested that Catholics involve themselves in the struggle to transform the earthly society in which they lived. This directive raised the question of how Church officials and the laity could relate Catholic teaching to Latin American reality, and some of the region's theologians warmed to the task. Contributors to the evolution of liberation theology came from all over Latin America, but it was in Brazil, where the Ecclesiastical Base Communities were rapidly multiplying, that this innovative way of thinking about and reformulating the Christian message made the greatest impact.

The leading Brazilian contributor to the movement was Friar Leonardo Boff, a bearded, charismatic Franciscan who taught at the seminary in Petrópolis. Boff was a protégé of Cardinal Arns, who had taught him at the seminary and arranged for him to be sent to Munich for doctoral studies. Later, when the Vatican took measures to silence the friar, the cardinal would become his principal protector.

Liberation theology as espoused by Friar Leonardo adapted the religious message of Catholicism to the realities of social and economic injustice that were oppressing Brazil's have-nots and condemning them to a lifetime of suffering. The goal of liberation theology was to enable the oppressed to free themselves by using faith as an instrument for transforming the very structure of society. The new theological movement was explicitly critical of capitalism, which was seen as enabling one social class to exploit another, and was explicitly sympathetic to socialism. It used Marxist analysis and accepted the notion of class struggle, yet it rejected Marxist materialism, along with the totalitarian tendencies of Leninism and Stalinism.

At the same time, liberation theology embraced the idea of a more democratic, less centralized "People's Church," as it came to be called, with an increased role for the laity. On this point it both drew inspiration from and gave an intellectual framework to Brazil's Ecclesiastical Base Communities.

Boff believed that "faith is not only 'also' political, but [is] *above all else* political." Thus it was natural for those who accepted his teachings to involve themselves in political struggles against oppression. Because of the widespread study of liberation theology in Brazil's seminaries, an increasing number of priests began to play active roles, at the grassroots level, in the process of redemocratization the country was experiencing in the late 1970s and early 1980s.

Conservative elements within the Brazilian Church found this trend toward political involvement alarming. Led by the authoritarian Cardinal of Rio de Janeiro, Dom Eugênio Sales, they criticized what they saw as the left-wing politics of many of Brazil's bishops, priests, nuns, and pastoral workers, and they communicated their concerns to like-minded officials within the Vatican. Because of the Brazilian distaste for confrontation and controversy, bishops on both sides of the issue maintained a spirit of collegiality within the CNBB and in public utterances, but they could not hide the gravity of the disagreements among them.

The winds of ecclesiastical change loosed by the Second Vatican Council had by this time begun to provoke the beginnings of a backlash, first in Europe and then in the New World. Traditionalists gained control of the Latin American Bishops Conference and attempted to shape the outcome of a meeting of the region's bishops, who were scheduled to convene in Puebla, Mexico, in January of 1979 and continue the work begun in Medellín. They argued that the proper business of the Church was not politics, but rather saving souls, and that the leftward drift of many clergy and laypeople in Latin America seriously threatened institutional unity.

Shortly before the meeting in Puebla was scheduled to open, the newly elected Pope John Paul I suddenly died, and a Polish cardinal was chosen to succeed him. Although neither John Paul I nor his predecessor, Paul VI, had planned to attend the conference, John Paul II opted to cross the Atlantic and open the proceedings.

The Puebla conference ended in a stalemate, since the pope made statements that both sides could claim as supporting their positions. The conservatives failed in their effort to shape the final document issued by the bishops, because Brazilian prelates and theologians played a critical role in persuading the assembly to hold fast to the Church's "preferential option for the poor." The traditionalists, however, kept control of the bishops conference.

John Paul II turned out to be hostile to key elements of liberation theology. Having experienced the fruits of Marxism firsthand in his native Poland, he was decidedly unsympathetic to any suggestion that the Church view the world through a Marxist lens. Although he often displayed great compassion for the wretched of the earth and voiced harsh criticisms of exploitative capitalism, the pontiff made it abundantly clear that he did not want the Church to become involved in political activity, which at this time meant left-wing politics.

Thus in the mid-1980s, on his 17,500-mile, thirteen-city tour of Brazil, the abject poverty he witnessed firsthand visibly moved him, and he spoke out firmly in favor of the "preferential option for the poor," the right of workers to a decent wage, the right of peasants to have access to land, and the right of Indians to survive. But at the same time he cautioned Catholic activists against class violence and the use of Marxist, rather than Christian concepts.

While the progressive and conservative wings of the Brazilian Church argued over the meaning of the pope's words, both sides seemed to overlook an important aspect of the papal visit. The large crowds attracted by John Paul II did not really pay much heed to the substance of what he was saying. It was his image, and the magic surrounding it, that brought them beyond the brink of euphoria. The outpouring of emotion he inspired—some Brazilians even began to refer to him as "our king"—was reminiscent of that evoked by Antônio Conselheiro and Father Cícero.

In the years following the visit, the Vatican left no doubt about the pope's position on the controversy dividing the Brazilian Church. A series of measures launched by the Holy See set the progressives back on their heels and severely challenged the concept of the People's Church.

The most highly publicized of these initiatives were disciplinary actions taken against Friar Leonardo Boff. In 1984 the Vatican's Congregation for the Doctrine of the Faith decided to interrogate Boff and summoned him to Rome. The immediate provocation was his publication of a book questioning the hierarchical structure of the Church, but it was widely recognized that liberation theology itself was on trial. Despite the presence of Dom Paulo and one of his fellow Brazilian cardinals at Boff's side, the Vatican eventually imposed a harsh penalty on the theologian. He was forbidden to write, teach, or speak in public for an indefinite period of time, a ban that lasted for about eleven months. In the years that followed, Boff had to endure other restrictions on his work.

On another level, the Vatican did its best to undercut the progressive wing of the Brazilian Church by nominating conservatives to positions in the hierarchy. The most dramatic of these appointments came in 1985, when Dom Hélder Câmara reached the age of retirement, and Dom José Cardoso Sobrinho was named to replace him at the head of the Archdiocese of Olinda and Recife. A northeasterner by birth, Dom José was a member of the Carmelite order and had spent twenty-six years in Rome, where he taught canon law. As archbishop, he went about dismantling many of the lay organizations Dom Hélder had created. He also closed down two seminaries where liberation theology was an important part of the curriculum, and he ordered the priests of the archdiocese to stay out of politics. In 1988 the pope installed conservative cardinals in Salvador and Brasília.

What to do about Dom Paulo Arns remained a problem for the Vatican. His relationship with John Paul II was correct but tepid. (On the wall of the cardinal's receiving room in São Paulo hangs an enlarged photograph of Dom Paulo and the pope embracing, a distant expression on their faces.) The bureaucrats in Rome came up with an imaginative ploy. In 1988 the Vatican decreed the division of Dom Paulo's archdiocese. With the creation of four new dioceses, covering many of the impoverished regions of Greater São Paulo, the archdiocese that had once contained 14.5 million faithful (it had been the largest diocese in the world), was reduced to 7 million.

The Vatican's efforts to bring to heel the People's Church in Brazil forced progressive Catholics to consider the option of breaking off on their own. However, there was never any serious talk of schism. If, as liberation theology taught, there was no difference between faith and politics, leaving the institutional Church might decimate the political influence of the progressives. The powerful hold Catholic symbols exercised over the hearts and minds of the Brazilian people led the progressives to remain with the Church and continue the fight for control over those symbols. As Friar Boff put it when he submitted to the first of the restrictions placed on him by the Vatican, "I prefer to walk with the Church rather than walk alone with my theology."

Yet within the institutional Church progressives faced much more than a simple power struggle with conservatives, both lay and religious, who clung to a pre-1960 European style of Catholicism. They also had to contend with at least two other types of Catholicism in Brazil: the old-fashioned "popular" Catholicism, the roots of which trace back to the colonial era, and a Catholicism containing strong elements drawn from Afro-Brazilian religions (a matter to be explored in Chapter Fourteen). Each of the four strands of Catholicism had its own saints, its own theology, and its own ecclesiology. It was not uncommon for all forms to coexist within individual parishes, a legacy of the tradition of accommodation the Portuguese brought to Brazil.

Folk Catholicism and what might be termed Afro-Catholicism were deeply ingrained in the consciousness of lower-class Brazilians and resonated with their unique sense of religiosity. Both strands of Catholicism tended to reinforce passivity and hinder the development of political awareness. For example, the practice of the *promessa* signified acceptance of one's dependence on supernatural forces for relief from earthly travails. In an effort to modify this mind-set, some priests abolished religious processions and other traditional devotions in their parishes, but they often encountered resistance when they did this.

At the same time, liberation theology offered little to replace some of the customary practices of which it disapproved. Nancy Scheper-Hughes points out in *Death Without Weeping,* her excellent study of infant mortality and its consequences in Northeast Brazil, that disciples of the liberation theologians discouraged the religious ceremonies that traditionally followed the passing of babies and that reinforced the notion that infant death was a blessing. These representatives of the Church told mothers that God wanted their babies to live, but they did not offer the women any concrete way to limit the number of children their husbands, companions, or lovers forced them to conceive. Since progressive priests and nuns continued to accept Catholic teaching about female sexuality and reproduction, they left poor women in what Scheper-Hughes calls a state of "moral and theological confusion."

On the purely political front, liberation theology advocates were so hostile to capitalism and so enamored of socialism that they turned a blind eye to the human-rights violations that routinely occurred in Communist countries. Left-wing Catholics from Brazil were unswerving in their continued support for Cuba. Indeed, in late 1988 Cardinal Arns sent a laudatory letter to Fidel Castro in celebration of the thirtieth anniversary of the Cuban Revolution. The Cuban Communist party newspaper published it, and Dom Paulo came under criticism not only from Brazilians but also from two Cuban bishops. Even more controversial were Friar Boff's ingenuous declarations, on his return from a visit to the Soviet Union in 1987, that socialist countries were "highly ethical and physically as well as morally clean," and that he had not noticed any restrictions on freedom of expression during his trip to the USSR.

The electoral defeat of the Sandinista regime in Nicaragua and the fall of Communism in the Soviet Union and Eastern Europe must certainly have shaken the liberation theologians. Catholic progressives had become identified with the left-wing Workers' party (PT) since its inception, and the PT platform was uncompromisingly socialist. With the apparent collapse of socialism as a viable mode of government outside Brazil and the defeat of the PT candidate in the 1989 presidential elections, the religious as well as the secular Left had to confront the necessity of rethinking their principles and priorities.

Finally, the rapid growth of Pentecostalism and other forms of evangelical Protestantism among the Brazilian lower classes over the past decade (to be discussed in Chapter Fifteen) is posing a direct challenge to the hegemony the Catholic Church has always enjoyed in Brazil. Some critics have pointed the finger of blame at liberation theology and argued that the Brazilian masses prefer that their religion be spiritually rather than politically centered. Once again, the Catholic progressives in Brazil have been put on the defensive.

Although the 1992 meeting of the Latin American Bishops Conference in Santo Domingo, the capital of the Dominican Republic, did not produce a disavowal of liberation theology, as many of its advocates had feared, doubt continues to cloud the question of what degree of freedom the Brazilian Church will be granted for continuing to exercise its "preferential option for the poor." The appointment of conservative prelates is bound to take a toll in the near future. In 1990, for the first time in a number of years, the theme of the annual meeting of the CNBB was religious rather than political. In its 1994 Fraternity Campaign, the CNBB proclaimed its unswerving opposition to the use of artificial contraceptives—an inevitably fatal proscription in a country with a rampant AIDS epidemic.*

Given Brazil's social problems, it seems most unlikely that the bishops will turn back the clock. Yet the shift in the balance of power toward the conservatives within the hierarchy will force some progressive members of the Church to seriously rethink the role the Church should play in ministering to Brazil's have-nots.

Meanwhile, in mid-1992 a weary Leonardo Boff announced that he was leaving both his order and the priesthood. Having been subjected to discipline by the Vatican five times since being summoned to Rome in 1984, he stated that he would remain a theologian and would resume the name Genésio Darcy, which he had abandoned when he first entered a Franciscan monastery.

---

* Even the otherwise progressive Cardinal Arns adhered to this traditional Catholic position. Moreover, his sister was appointed to a key post in the Ministry of Health, the division in charge of family planning, where she was expected to put into practice the Jurassic teachings of the Church on birth control.

# Chapter 14

# The *Orixás*

$\mathcal{T}$echnically, it was not her first appearance on television. Cacilda de Assis had once taken part in a musical program on a Rio de Janeiro channel. But on this occasion, an August evening in 1971, as the forty-eight-year-old faith healer stepped before the camera, she was not quite herself. Wrapped in a black and red cape bearing the design of a lyre, a cane at her side, a cigar dangling from her lips, a bottle of *cachaça* (Brazilian rum) within reach, she was but a corporeal form through which an *exu* (pronounced ei-*shu'*) called "Seu Sete da Lira" reached out to the mass audience.

Most Brazilians know what *exus* are. A heritage of the nation's African descendants, the original Exu was a divinity who served as a guardian of temples, homes, and individuals, as well as an intermediary between the other *orixás*, or "deities," and mankind. Cunning, vain, and virile, he represented energy or life force. As Afro-Brazilian religious beliefs evolved over the centuries, Exu assumed multiple forms and came to embody mischievousness, trickery, and evil, which brought his persona close to that of the Devil of the Christian tradition.

Seu Sete da Lira undoubtedly had a good deal of mischief in him this particular night, when he took possession of Cacilda de Assis as she appeared on popular, back-to-back, live programs in front of a large studio audience and an untold number of viewers. The body of the forty-eight-year-old woman began to shake, as Seu Sete made her strut about the stage. The host of the TV program began to cry like a baby. A collective hysteria gripped the specta-

351

tors gathered in the studio of TV Tupi in Urca (once the site of a casino where Carmen Miranda performed) and spread to homes throughout the city. Soon hundreds of delirious, shouting people had gathered outside the studio and were besieging the auditorium, while a delighted Seu Sete da Lira sang Carnival songs.

These scenes might have leapt off the pages of a Jorge Amado novel, but they actually happened and had real-life consequences. Two viewers engaged in a violent argument over whether Seu Sete was male or female, and one ended up killing the other. Another viewer shot himself in the head with a pistol. Catholic officials protested that allowing Seu Sete to appear on television threatened the psychological well-being of the public and damaged Brazil's reputation abroad. Two state deputies who belonged to an Afro-Brazilian religion criticized the Church's criticism of Seu Sete. The military regime responded by taking steps to tighten its censorship of TV.

African religions have left a deep and permanent mark on Brazil's culture and consciousness. References to the *orixás* abound in literature, art, film, music, and the *telenovela*. Floats in carnival processions in Rio de Janeiro and other cities routinely include allusions to cult beliefs and practices. In her study of judicial records of the government repression of Afro-Brazilian religions during the 1930s, anthropologist Yvonne Maggie found that the judges were very familiar with the terminology associated with the cults, because they never had to ask what the words meant when they were used during legal proceedings.

Religious beliefs originating in Africa have penetrated every corner of Brazilian society. They have even attracted the descendants of non-Portuguese immigrants. In the deep south, some cults primarily draw members of German or Italian ancestry. In São Paulo there are cult groups composed almost exclusively of Brazilians of Japanese descent. Afro-Brazilian religions have even spread to Uruguay and Argentina.*

---

* Indeed, José López Rega, the notorious "warlock" who was the power behind the government of Argentine President Isabel Perón in the mid-1970s, participated actively in one of the Afro-Brazilian sects.

People from all social classes belong to Afro-Brazilian cults. Businessmen follow cult rituals before making important deals. The poor find comfort and hope in places of cult worship. Engineers, lawyers, and other professionals often take part in cult ceremonies. Many government officials are quite candid about their ties to cults. Politicians in search of votes regularly court cult leaders. Celebrities such as Jorge Amado and singer Caetano Veloso are devoted cult members.

Every New Year's Eve millions dressed in white stream to the beaches of Copacabana and elsewhere along Brazil's long coast to leave offerings for Iemanjá, the goddess of the sea. In 1986 when the ninety-two-year-old Mãe (Mother) Menininha died in Salvador, two cabinet ministers, the state governor, and the mayor appeared at the wake to pay their respects to Afro-Brazil's most famous and revered high priestess.

Shops catering to worshipers are ubiquitous. In a book about the cults, Fran O'Gorman describes an informal survey she took in Rio de Janeiro: "Walking from Copacabana to Botafogo I once started counting the stores that sell Afro-Brazilian religious articles. I ended up with an average of one store per block." The signs of Afro-Brazilian worship are also ubiquitous. Offerings of food, drink, cigars, and makeup are left at crossroads, often in such profusion as to create trash-removal problems for city authorities. Oblational candles cast flickering shadows against certain walls, curbstones, and tree trunks.

In a country where 90 percent of the people list themselves as Roman Catholic, as many as one in three may participate actively at one time or another in some form of Afro-Brazilian worship. It is perhaps safe to say that all but a small percentage of Brazilians have at least a tolerant attitude toward the cults. Indeed, recent attacks by fundamentalist Protestants on cult members in Rio de Janeiro seem profoundly un-Brazilian.

The dynamic process by which African religious traditions have taken root and prospered in Brazil is a remarkable if exceedingly complex story. The *orixás* have survived the cultural genocide implicit in slavery as well as official campaigns to suppress them. They have found a congenial environment amidst the peculiar religiosity of the Roman Catholicism brought to the New World by the Portuguese and amidst the animist beliefs of the Brazilian Indians. The *orixás* are central figures in *candomblé,* the cult that has remained closest to its African origins, in *umbanda,* wherein the deities blend with elements of primitive Catholicism and French spiritism to form what some call the first uniquely Brazilian religion, and in a bewildering welter of variations.

Indeed, the African deities contribute heavily to, and in turn draw heavily on, an essential element of Brazilianness, a proclivity toward magic and mysticism. This trait has nourished such diverse contemporary unorthodoxies as the postmodernist cult of Santo Daime, whose members drink a trance- (and vomit-) inducing substance derived from a jungle plant (the properties of which were first discovered by Indians), and the colorfully costumed spiritualist sect that seeks cosmic energy in the Vale do Amanhecer (Dawn Valley) just outside the city of Brasília.

The Africa from which Brazil's slaves were uprooted was far from uniform in its levels of social, economic, and political development from tribe to tribe and from region to region; likewise religious beliefs and practices varied. The three main civilizations to which the slaves belonged were the Sudanese, whose territory extended from the southern part of the Sahara down the west coast of Africa (with concentrations in what is now Liberia, Nigeria, Dahomey, and the Gold Coast); the Bantu, which permeated the southern and south-central regions (mainly what is now Angola, Mozambique, and Zaire); and the Islamic, which had spread from the Niger Valley.

The Sudanese group, within which the Yorubans, the Dahomans, and the Fanti-Ashantis exercised predominant influence, practiced various forms of polytheistic religions in which the *orixás* assumed critical roles. Some of these divinities had been in life remarkable individuals—kings, warriors, wizards—and like all humankind they possessed certain powers, virtues, and foibles. When their first worshipers endowed them with supernatural powers, the deities assumed the capability to relieve mankind's feelings of panic and despondency.

These gods and goddesses inspired awe, reverence, confidence, affection, and fear. Their mysterious forces could work on nature to cure infertility, improve harvests, defeat the enemy, and solve baffling crises. The deities were summoned when the irrational, the unbearable, or the unknown seemed to call for celestial intervention, and also when the cycles of life demanded it. The priests and their followers would pray, dance, and perform all the required rituals, and the ceremony would culminate with a chosen medium entering into a mystic trance. In this way a god would answer the worshipers' calls and possess one of the faithful as a way of addressing the congregation. The *orixá* would comfort the faithful, give advice, and predict what the future held in store.

The Bantu, a peaceful people, worshiped their ancestors and nature spirits. Their beliefs and rituals were closely bound to their immediate surroundings. Thus geographic dislocation severely weakened the foundations on which their religion rested.

The African Moslems were animists who had converted to Islam without completely abandoning their prior beliefs. They adhered strictly to the precepts of Islam—including circumcision, fasting, abstinence from alcoholic beverages, and the reading of the Koran—but they also used amulets and talismans possessing magical properties.

The blacks brought to Brazil came from each of these civilizations, because the slave merchants first raided coastal tribes and later ventured into the heart of the continent in search of their human quarry. Both on the slave ships and after their arrival in the New World, Africans were thrown together indiscriminately, a practice that generated friction, rivalries, and even bloody conflicts. Indeed, it is a wonder that the various religious groups did not self-destruct in the process.

What happened instead was that the peculiar features of slavery in Brazil facilitated not only the survival but also the evolution of African religious beliefs. The process has been remarkably dynamic. For the past four hundred years the African religions interacted with the Roman Catholicism of the Portuguese and the animist beliefs of the native Indians. They eventually assumed different forms in different regions of Brazil, and they have become a rich mosaic of ritual and creed. Although the Yoruban cult originating with slaves from the Sudan may have left the deepest mark on Afro-Brazilian religion, the influences of other sects from other regions, except for that of Islam, have remained vigorous.

One of the factors that helped African religions to survive was the sheer magnitude of the institution of slavery in Brazil. On the large sugar plantations of Northeast Brazil, Africans were so numerous that they could regroup, select their own "kings," fight or befriend slaves from other regions of Africa, and practice their own cults. The white masters were generally indifferent to anything other than the way their field slaves worked and reproduced themselves. Their attitudes toward the Africans ranged from racist condescension to thinly disguised fear, the latter a consequence of the numerical advantage the slaves had over the white population and the awe in which the Portuguese held the "black magic" associated with the slave quarters.

The slave owners actually encouraged certain African religious celebrations because they believed that their slaves worked better when they were permitted to play their drums and amuse themselves in their own peculiar ways. In addition, the slaves' dances appeared to provoke sexual arousal, which in turn would lead to the procreation of new generations of slaves.

The slave trade, for as long as it continued, also served to help perpetuate African cultural traditions. The traders often unwittingly included in their shipments of new slaves African priests and nobles whose presence in Brazil rejuvenated the religious and political hierarchies of the groups of slaves struggling to keep their identities alive in hostile, alien surroundings.

Plantation life revolved around the owner's family, which lived in virtual sequestration in the mansion or "big house," as it was called. The social structure was firmly and unabashedly patriarchal. The master exercised total control over every member of the household, as well as over the slaves and other laborers who worked in his fields.

The spiritual glue holding this vast conglomerate together was the Catholic religion. Every big house had its own chapel, and many had their own resident chaplains. The slaves, who were forced to undergo the Roman Catholic rite of baptism both when they were loaded into vessels in African ports and again on their disembarkation in Brazil, were never really instructed in the particulars of the faith. They were required to participate in Catholic rituals, although they remained outside the walls of the chapel and merely watched. For them the magic of the white man's god had to be much more powerful than theirs, because the whites were absolute rulers in Brazil. Therefore, the slaves prayed to the god of the whites for deliverance, and they did so using their African ways and languages.

In the process the slaves juxtaposed Catholic and African religious symbols and adapted both religions to their own necessities. On African altars, likenesses of the *orixás* disappeared behind the statues of the Catholic saints. Divinities, saints, and guardian angels could be worshiped together because they had certain similarities. Africans could easily adopt patron saints and accept the notion of a guardian angel who looked over them, because they related to their *orixás* in much the same way that Portuguese Catholics related to their favorite saints and guardian angels—in a personal, heavily superstitious way.

There were parallels in the ways that Catholic saints acted as mediators between humans and God Almighty and the ways in which the *orixás* acted as the links between men and Olorum, the highest divinity in the African pantheon. There were also specific correspondences (some rather tenuous, others more obvious) between the functions or characteristics of certain saints and those of some of the *orixás*. For example, Ogum, the god of iron and war, could easily be identified with St. George. Iemanjá, the goddess of the sea and of fertility, was associated with the Virgin Mary. This process of syncretization turned out to be exceedingly complex because of the decentralized evolution of Afro-Brazilian religions. Thus, various cults matched different saints with different *orixás*.

Syncretization worked both ways. The Africans tinted Portuguese Catholicism black, just as whites incorporated African religious elements into their own religious beliefs and practices. The slaves copied from Portuguese Catholicism the tradition of petitioning the saints for favors in exchange for promises, but they attributed fulfillment of their appeals to the supernatural powers exercised by their own *orixás*. The colonists, meanwhile, absorbed some of the African traditions they learned from their storytelling nannies, and they often used magic potions or charms obtained from a local sorcerer.

Because masters had little interest in saving the souls of their slaves and there were not enough Catholic priests in the colony to enforce religious orthodoxy, the Africans remained free to view Catholic teaching through the lens of their own customary beliefs.

The syncretization of African religion and Roman Catholicism was not the only spiritual merger taking place in Brazil. Those blacks who ended up in the backlands of Northeast Brazil and in the Amazon region (mostly Bantus) encountered rituals practiced by people of mixed Portuguese and Indian blood *(caboclos)*. The latter had combined elements of Catholicism with traditional Indian beliefs. The cults that evolved from that mix tended to be messianic and permeated with the resentment the oppressed felt toward their oppressors. They used an initiation rite similar to baptism, carried crosses, and staged processions, but they also included Indian elements such as the practice of polygamy, the performing of songs and dances, the smoking of tobacco and the ingestion of sacred herbs, animist beliefs, mystic trances, and the consumption of a mind-altering drink.

The blacks who came into contact with these cults soon added their own ingredients to the religious observances. They brought with them their own spirits, who tended to be more playful than the proud, wild spirits of the Indians, a knowledge of narcotics (the Africans brought marijuana to Brazil), and the gift of divination.

In urban areas several factors enhanced the survival of Afro-Brazilian cults. Free blacks were able to live together in communities and combine their resources to help purchase freedom for their enslaved brothers and sisters. As the number of ex-slaves grew, it became easier for African religious beliefs to permeate the new enclaves.

Some free blacks saw in the religion of the whites a road to success in the mixed-race society that was developing in the cities. The Catholic Church welcomed them, but it imposed a type of de facto segregation on its flock. Special brotherhoods were created for blacks and mulattoes. They had their own chapels and their own rites, and they provided separate burial services for members.

By sponsoring these brotherhoods, the Catholic Church inadvertently nourished the continued growth of Afro-Brazilian religion. Blacks were permitted to speak their ancestral languages, dance, play their own music, and worship dark Virgins and saints. The same people who attended brotherhood meetings by day participated in cult rituals late at night.

The cults deriving from each of the three major African civilizations represented among Brazil's black population had to overcome serious obstacles in the New World. The sophisticated polytheism of the Sudanese was based on lineage. Each believer had a private *orixá*, who was passed down through his or her father. In the sexual anarchy of the slave quarters, where women might have several partners in a single night, it was often difficult for mothers to know whose child she had borne. If the father was unknown, the child's *orixá* could not be identified. Therefore, other ways had to be devised for determining which individuals belonged to which divinities. In time it was decided that each person had one major and several minor *orixás*. The head of a cult was believed to possess the power to detect the particular *orixás* who protected a believer.

In Africa each major *orixá* had exclusive priests and exclusive temples. In Brazil this proved impossible because of the lack of resources. Hence a single temple had to do the tasks of many temples and provide the means for worshiping many *orixás*.

Moreover, a process of weeding out *orixás* had to take place. In Africa certain divinities protected crops. In Brazil there was no reason to pray to them, since abundant harvests enriched only the white masters. A shift in emphasis was inevitable, and greater attention was paid to *orixás* who might safeguard the faithful from the horrors of slavery.

The Bantus had problems transplanting their traditional cult of the dead. The breakup of family groups and the dispersal of family members to far-flung parts of the huge colony made it difficult to maintain a style of worship intimately associated with domestic life and the family. Some Bantus opted to believe that after death souls returned to their old "nation," where they either were reincarnated as free human beings or became divine ancestors—a conviction that encouraged suicide.

The animism and ancestor worship of the Bantus did not transfer well to a foreign environment (except in the Northeast and north, where the Bantus found kindred souls among the *caboclos*).

But their sensual dances did find a prominent place in the Afro-Brazilian culture.

The Islam some slaves brought with them from Africa eventually disappeared leaving nary a trace. Proud and puritanical, Brazil's black Moslem slaves resisted the encroachments of Christianity, remained apart from their African brothers and sisters, and refused even to proselytize them. They steadfastly resisted slavery, and many were either slaughtered or deported to Africa after an unsuccessful revolt in 1813.

Over time a variety of Afro-Brazilian religions gradually and ultimately took shape. In Bahia, where slaves of Sudanese origin predominated, blacks practiced what came to be known as *candomblé*. A version of *candomblé* that rooted itself in Recife was called *xangô*. Cults that emerged from a marriage of African religions with *caboclo* religions were given names such as *candomblés do caboclo*. *Macumba*, which combined *candomblé* with elements of black magic and Indian animism, became popular in Rio de Janeiro.

This is but a rough and highly oversimplified sketch of a number of religious developments the complexity of which has absorbed scores of anthropologists and scholars from other disciplines for nearly a century. It would take several volumes to describe and analyze all of them in depth. Two, however, merit a closer look: *candomblé*, the popular Afro-Brazilian religion that has remained close to its African origins; and *umbanda*, a more recent phenomenon that qualifies as the most Brazilian of the cults.

Kept alive in the collective hearts and minds of peoples unwilling to abandon their cultural heritage and values, what came to be known as *candomblé* survived and adapted despite having been torn from its life-giving sources, having to exist in a social environment that forced it into clandestinity, and having to compete with other creeds.

A critical stage in its development was the founding of the first known place of formal *candomblé* worship in downtown Salvador in 1830. The location was a small house behind the Church of the Barroquinha. Members of a black brotherhood associated with the church administered the cult. It operated in daylight as well as at night, followed a calendar of specific ceremonies, worshiped in accordance with a prescribed liturgy, and was controlled by a defined hierarchy.

The abolition of slavery in 1888 stimulated the proliferation of overt *candomblé* temples. They became centers of solidarity for blacks struggling to overcome social and economic barriers and the sense of atomization they felt as they had to make their way in society at large. Freedom meant losing the structured life slaves were used to, as well as the slave master who served as a father figure. *Candomblé* provided a refuge, a source of mutual assistance, and a substitute protector, in the form of the cult leader.

Over the years *candomblé* has continued to serve as a vital support in the lives of black Brazilians, even as increasing numbers of nonblacks have joined *terreiros* (*candomblé* temples). Indeed, the sight of middle- and upper-class whites prostrating themselves before a black cult leader has served to enhance the self-image of Afro-Brazilians.

Although *terreiros* may be found in the crowded residential districts of Salvador and other cities (the cult has spread to both the north and south of Brazil), some of the older temple complexes closely replicate African villages in form as well as in spirit, and for this reason they tend to be situated in wooded areas on the outskirts of town. The design is simple and functional: a large main hall where the principal ceremonies take place; lodgings for the high priest or priestess and others who live on the premises; various shrines dedicated to the *orixás* (a small house with a padlocked red door belongs to Exu; the house of Oxum, the queen of rivers, must be near a fountain, if possible). The shrines of Iemanjá and Oxalá, two of the most important of the *orixás*, by tradition are installed in the main building.

The initial phase of most ceremonies requires the actual sacrifice of animals (principally goats, chickens, and pigeons), a ritual to which, for obvious reasons, only initiates are admitted. Both the blood and some of the cooked meat of the victims are offered to the *orixás*. The rest of the meat is consumed in a communal meal. The beating of drums then heralds the beginning of the main service, at which visitors are welcome.

The congregation gathers on benches around an open area. On one side are the drummers and a throne for the high priest or priestess, called the *pai* or *mãe do santo* (father or mother of the saint). There are special chairs for the *ogãs*, special friends and protectors of the *candomblé* (often prestigious whites, whose presence in ceremonies dates back to the period when *candomblé* was persecuted by the authorities and needed protection). Against one wall is an altar with likenesses of Catholic saints.

The opening ritual involves placating (and getting rid of) the troublesome Exu. A glass of water and an offering of food placed in the center of the floor accomplishes this end. Then the initiates, known as *filhos* or *filhas do santo* (sons or daughters of the saint), enter in procession and perform certain prescribed rituals, which include dancing and chanting in Yoruban or a related African tongue. They dress in costumes (some evoking the colonial period) whose colors and accessories match the divinity to whom the *filha* or *filho* is dedicated.

The focal event is the appearance of *orixás* who take possession of participants. At the essence of *candomblé* is the very personal relationship between the initiate and his or her *orixá*. During ceremonies, the *orixás* will "mount" various *filhos* or *filhas do santo*, who thereupon become the *orixá*'s "horse" and enter into a trance. These are dramatic episodes. The person possessed will shake convulsively, scream, gyrate wildly about the room, and flop to the floor like a rag doll. The voice and movements of the medium will become those of the *orixá*. The subsequent departure of the divinity also follows certain ritualized steps.

The trance, according to some observers, has always provided a way for worshipers to resolve the tensions besetting the slave, and later the free Afro-Brazilian. It permits believers to identify with their gods and thereby shed, at least for the moment, the sense of inferiority imposed by slavery and racism. The trance also represents an affirmation of faith in the power of the *orixás*, and in ancient traditions passed down from generation to generation.

For whites *candomblé* creates a similar sense of relief from tension, a welcome state not only for those struggling with poverty but also for middle-class Brazilians beset by financial difficulties and other strains of urban life. In addition, the absence of notions of sin and guilt within the Afro-Brazilian religious context has appealed to many. An affinity for the supernatural has such deep roots in Brazilianness that Brazilians have been able to easily reconcile the contradiction between rationality and spiritism. Jorge Amado, for example, had no problem belonging to both the Communist party and a *candomblé* temple. (He ultimately left the party.)

To become a *filho* or *filha do santo* and to qualify to receive an *orixá* takes months of training. Aspirants must live at the *terreiro* for a fixed period of time and learn the various chants, dances, myths, and taboos. This religious training will prepare them to behave in accordance with the personality of the *orixás* who will one day take possession of them. They must also find some way, either on their own or with the help of friends, neighbors, or ad hoc "godparents," to defray the cost of the prescribed costumes and animals to be sacrificed during their final initiation rites.

The *filhos* or *filhas do santo* occupy the bottom rungs of a complex hierarchy. The high priest or priestess of each *terreiro* is the *pai* or *mãe do santo*, who serves as a kind of ambassador to the land of the *orixás* and a keeper of ancient secrets. The *pais* or *mães do santo* exercise total control over their domains. The faithful consult them about everything. The high priests foresee the future and dispense all kinds of advice. Officials in charge of particular ceremonies occupy intermediate positions within the *terreiro*.

The early efforts of the Catholic Church to encourage those elements of Afro-Brazilian religion conceivably consistent with Catholic doctrine and to purge the irreconcilable elements were not particularly successful. Over the course of time *candomblé* has taken advantage of Catholicism more than Catholicism has used *candomblé*. Members of the cult are encouraged to belong to the Church. Indeed, Mãe Menininha insisted throughout her lifetime that she was a Catholic in good standing.

One of *candomblé*'s major feast days brings a huge multitude every January to the front of the Church of Nosso Senhor do Bonfim (Our Lord of the Good End) in Salvador. A group of white-clad *filhas do santo* perform a ritualized washing of the steps, in homage to Oxalá, the *orixá* identified with the Lord of the Good End.* Periodically Catholic Church officials have announced that they would no longer tolerate what they viewed as a sacrilegious

---

* There is a vivid description of the event in Jorge Amado's recent novel, *O Sumiço da Santa* (published in English under the title *The War of the Saints*).

use of Church property. Each time they have found it prudent to back off from their threats.

Cut off from their source, the African religions transplanted in Brazil evolved quite differently from those that remained on the other side of the Atlantic. They incorporated elements of Catholicism and Indian animism, yet at the same time they maintained traditions deeply imbedded in the collective memory of Brazilians of African descent. According to Pierre Verger, a white-haired Frenchman who has lived for three decades in a humble neighborhood of Salvador and has closely followed Afro-Brazilian religion, the rituals are better kept in Brazil than in Africa. Indeed, he insists that "Brazil is now the Mecca."

Yet there are signs of a movement to re-Africanize the Brazilian cults. Travel between Brazil and Africa is on the increase, and individual Brazilians are making the trip and bringing back with them a wide range of religious articles. Moreover, some of the *terreiros* have become wealthy because they have acquired a middle-class congregation willing and able to pay for certain religious (and magical) rituals, so *pais* and *mães do santo* have been able to afford to cross the Atlantic. In addition, there is a burgeoning interest in learning contemporary African languages. (The Yoruban used in *candomblé* rituals has become archaic, like the English spoken in certain remote parts of Appalachia.)

The most significant aspect of the re-Africanization trend is the movement to extirpate from *candomblé* all traces of Catholicism. But the decentralization long characteristic of *candomblé*, whereby the head of each *terreiro* has wide discretion in all matters except for hierarchical structure, ritual, and language, provides a buffer against these efforts, which would change the very essence of the religion by eliminating its Brazilian elements.

*Umbanda*, in contrast, glories in its Brazilianness. This twentieth-century sect was born in Brazil and incorporates quintessentially Brazilian myths and symbols. Yet it also draws sufficiently on the country's African religious traditions to qualify as an Afro-Brazilian religion.

*Umbanda* has traveled a tortuous path. Its immediate roots date back to the 1850s, when a Frenchman who claimed to have been possessed by a Druid spirit adopted the name Alain Kardec and wrote a number of books that launched a new spiritist cult. Kardecism was the highly rationalized belief in the existence of incorporeal beings in interplanetary space, and in the possibility of communicating with them. Because of its emphasis on Christian virtues such as charity and universal brotherhood, followers were required to engage in philanthropic enterprises. The cult also imposed strict moral standards on believers. The gospel according to Kardec attracted intellectuals inclined toward parapsychology as well as individuals eager to make contact with departed relatives.

Kardecism found fertile ground in Brazil, where it gained numerous converts during the late nineteenth and early twentieth centuries. Kardecists kept their distance from the Afro-Brazilian religions, which they considered a "low" form of spiritism. The white middle-class Brazilians who joined the cult, however, gave it a new wrinkle. They shifted its focus to curing, so that spirits were summoned to alleviate members' physical as well as spiritual ills.

In the 1920s novel offshoots of Kardecism came into being in Rio de Janeiro, Niterói, and São Paulo. Scholars dispute which of these cities may rightfully claim credit for having been the birthplace of what amounted to a new cult, but this seems of little real import. What matters is that Kardecist mediums began to claim that they were summoning different kinds of spirits representing deeply rooted elements of Brazilian culture. From this trend emerged *umbanda,* an intriguing projection of both Brazilianness and the nationalism that was gripping the country in the 1930s.

Although *umbanda* disavowed any link to the Afro-Brazilian religious tradition, in fact it was greatly influenced by *macumba,* the variant of *candomblé* that had achieved considerable popularity in Rio de Janeiro. *Macumba* emerged among the increasing concentration of blacks in and around Brazil's capital. It was less faithful to its African roots and more susceptible to syncretization with folk Catholicism, Indian animism, and even Kardecism itself. The spirits of long-dead Africans and Indians as well as *orixás* made appearances in *macumba* ceremonies.

*Umbanda* applied the rationality of Kardecism to elements of *macumba.* The animal sacrifices and wildly ecstatic trances of

*macumba* were eliminated. The *orixás* were recognized and venerated, most spectacularly in the December 31 rituals honoring Iemanjá. But African gods did not put in appearances at cult sessions.
Instead mythical figures from Brazilian culture occupied *umbanda*'s
pantheon.

The most important of these came by way of *macumba*. These
mythical figures are known generically as *caboclos* (in this context,
the word means "Indians") and *pretos velhos* (old blacks). Within
each category may be found a number of individual spirits, each
with a particular name and history.

*Caboclos* represent both a romanticized notion of nature and the
myth of the Brazilian Indian as a noble savage. The *caboclo* is proud
and hyperactive, always on his feet, always puffing on a cigar. He
likes to shout and beat his chest and gesture as though he is shooting an arrow. In the words of *umbanda* scholar Patrícia Birman, he
is a "veritable lord of the jungle." Often he wears a headdress that
has nothing to do with Brazilian Indians, but instead comes right
out of Hollywood westerns—a curious contemporary spin on syncretization. The *caboclo*'s name will generally relate to the place
from which he comes, or his tribe.

The *preto velho* depicts another Brazilian stereotype. He smokes
a pipe, walks slowly with a cane, often wears a straw hat, and
speaks bad Portuguese. Bent with age, he is a fatherly or grandfa-
therly figure, kind, humble, generous, and submissive. He represents the ex-slave who loyally ministered to his master and his
master's family in the big house. There are female versions, too,
embodying black women who became surrogate mothers, aunts,
or grandmothers for the whites they served.

If the *preto velho* embodies notions of home, civilization, and
the "good Negro," on the reverse side of the coin one finds perhaps the most intriguing of the *umbanda* spirits, the *exu*. In the African religious tradition, Exu was an *orixá* representing life force.
*Candomblé* turned him into a trickster who sows disorder, more
demigod than divinity. *Umbanda* viewed Exu in the Christian context, and he became a type, rather than an individual deity, identified with the Devil or the fallen angel. His image became
unabashedly Mephistophelean, complete with black cloak, horns,
turned-up moustache, and satanic grin.

As *umbanda* spread to the lower classes, the *exu* figure underwent yet another reinterpretation, and it came to represent the quintessentially Brazilian antihero called the *malandro*. This figure originated in the slum-covered hills of Rio de Janeiro. A hustler who invents his own rules, the *malandro* often dresses in a white suit with a striped shirt and spats or white shoes. He is ambiguous, in the sense that he operates on society's margin, somewhere between living by his wits and outright criminality.

Some of the *exus* in *umbanda* cults frequented by the poor appear as *malandros*. They wear the typical *malandro* garb and help people escape from difficult situations. They will listen to all kinds of appeals (even requests to have negative things happen to the petitioner's enemies). From time to time, efforts have been made to rid *umbanda* of the *exu-malandro* character, but without avail. As Liana Trindade, a scholar who has written on the subject, has observed, "People say: 'How can I throw him out? He's a part of me.'" The popularity of Seu Sete da Lira attests to the staying power of the *exus*.

Not wanting to neglect the distaff side of society's fringe, *umbanda* features a female *exu*, called the *pomba gira*. She represents sensuality and rebelliousness and takes the form of another familiar figure from Brazilian culture— the prostitute. The *pomba gira* wears red and black. In some of her incarnations she likes to make obscene gestures and use dirty words. But there is also a *pomba gira* called Maria Padilha, a seventeenth-century Spanish courtesan of noble birth. People ask the female *exus* for advice relating to love.

*Umbanda* has continued to demonstrate its flexibility by incorporating other spirits drawn from folklore. One can find gypsies, sailors, cattle-drivers from the south, and backlanders from the Northeast in some of the lower-class cult centers. There seems to be room for everyone.

Each temple has a high priest or priestess (also known as the *pai* or *mãe do santo*) who exercises the same kind of absolute authority as the counterpart figure in *candomblé* does. However, it is easier to attain this leadership status in *umbanda* than in *candomblé*, where it usually takes about seven years. As Lisias Nogueiro Negrão, another student of the cults, has observed, regarding *umbanda*, "When people believe in you, you become a *pai do santo*."

*Umbanda* sects also have their equivalent of the *filho* and *filha do santo*. They dress normally in white costumes with turbans and beaded necklaces, and they serve as mediums, along with the *pai* or *mãe do santo*, receiving the various spirits that possess them during ceremonies.

*Umbanda* temples are known as *centros espíritas* (spirit centers) or *tendas* (tents) as well as *terreiros*. The interior layout of the main hall is longitudinal, more like a Catholic church than a place of *candomblé* worship. At one end is a main altar, decorated by statues, paintings, flowers, palm leaves, candles, and other religious objects. In front of the altar is a space where the ceremonies are conducted. A barrier separates the ceremonial space from the rows of benches for spectators, who are often segregated by sex.

The rituals of *umbanda* vary depending on the tendency of the particular branch of the cult. They may be closer to what is practiced in Kardecism, or to *macumba*, or somewhere between the two. The services open with rites designed to protect the temple from evil. The burning of aromatic herbs purifies the premises. The *pai* or *mãe do santo* may pray or preach. The mediums sing songs to the spirits associated with the group. If the temple is located in a highly populated area, the beating of drums may be forbidden, and the rhythm may have to be kept by the clapping of hands.

The main part of each session unfolds when the various spirits descend. The *pai* or *mãe do santo* is the first to be possessed, and the other mediums then receive their "saints." The possession of the medium is not nearly so dramatic in *umbanda* as in *candomblé* ceremonies. The worshiper in a trance will do some spinning and adopt the characteristics of the "saint." Thus, when a *caboclo* is received, the medium (whether male or female) will generally light up a cigar.*

At this point, members of the congregation go forward and consult with one of the mediums. They generally seek very practical advice about problems relating to work, marriage, health, or any other type of personal matter. The spirit will suggest offerings to be made and courses of action. The responses are down-to-earth

---

* Seventy percent of Brazil's internal market for domestically produced cigars goes to *umbanda* centers.

rather than moralistic. Some spirit centers will charge nonmembers for consultations.

Although the *umbanda* sects insisted that they were a national rather than an Afro-Brazilian religion, they suffered persecution during the 1930s when the government decided to repress manifestations of black culture. The sects survived, and when the situation eased, they sought a rapprochement with the authorities. Since cult leaders were perceived as controlling the votes of their followers, politicians began to woo them once democracy was restored in 1946.

After the 1964 military coup, when the Catholic Church became the main source of opposition to the military dictatorship, *umbanda's* brand of nationalism, and Brazilianness, found favor with those in power. Some *pais do santo* received decorations from the regime. State governments included *umbanda* feast days on their calendars and invited *umbanda* representatives to official functions. Suddenly the cult had gained legitimacy.

Although *umbanda* believers have traditionally defined themselves as Roman Catholic, they now have a growing tendency to see their sect as a bona fide religion in its own right, on a par with the other established creeds in Brazil. One manifestation of this trend is the performance of marriage ceremonies in *umbanda* temples, a relatively recent occurrence.

Afro-Brazilian religions share as common traits diversity, decentralization, and a lack of clearly defined dogma. In these respects *umbanda* is no different from the rest. There may be as many as ten *umbanda* federations in the state of Rio de Janeiro alone, and not all of the estimated forty thousand spirit centers in the state belong to a federation.

This diversification has facilitated the emergence of phenomena such as Cacilda de Assis, who in her heydey operated an enormous "Spiritist Tent" in the Fluminense Lowlands, where tens of thousands of believers would gather to welcome Seu Sete, as he entered Cacilda and sang popular songs, sprinkled *cachaça* on the faithful, and cured the sick and the disabled.* How much money

---

* Even Assis Chateaubriand, after suffering a severe stroke, visited Cacilda's tent and had Seu Sete blow cigar smoke on him, in an effort to achieve a cure.

Cacilda herself made from all this is uncertain, but weekend sessions generated a tremendous demand for food and drink, which were sold on the premises, and someone had the savvy to produce *cachaça* and glasses bearing the mark of Seu Sete. The *umbanda* establishment eventually frowned on Cacilda, and Seu Sete eventually lost his appeal, but the extent to which official disapproval contributed to his decline is uncertain.

The dividing line between *candomblé* and *umbanda* can be difficult to draw. As Patrícia Birman noted in a 1992 interview: "I have been to rituals I would have sworn were *candomblé,* and the people there said it was *umbanda.*" Obviously there appears to be a certain amount of leeway for improvisation at the intersection of the two cults.

Yet at the same time the two sects seem to be on the verge of heading in opposite directions. *Candomblé* is evidencing a trend toward returning to its African origins and removing all traces of Roman Catholicism and Indian animism. *Umbanda* continues to display remarkable flexibility and pragmatism in its ability to incorporate the concerns and aspirations of Brazilians. In so doing, it has become a projection of Brazil's urban society.

Beginning in the postwar era, *umbanda* made substantial gains at the expense of *candomblé.* But with the emergence of black consciousness in the late 1970s, the tide shifted in favor of *candomblé,* and a number of *pais* and *mães do santo* from spiritist centers switched to *candomblé* and took their flocks with them.

More recently a new dynamic is underway, as *candomblé* and *umbanda* worshipers from the lower classes have been abandoning their Afro-Brazilian faith to join Christian evangelical churches. Alma Guillermoprieto, in a perceptive *New Yorker* piece, has pointed out that the appeal of Afro-Brazilian religion has been "to imagine an alternative reality better than the present dreary one," but that "to a large extent the evangelical sects' genius is to have helped their followers *change* reality." How this has come to pass merits a closer look.

# Chapter 15

# Evangelicals
# on the Move

*T*he gates to Maracanã opened at 5 A.M., and in a matter of hours nearly 160,000 people had filled both the ground-level seats and the upper-deck benches, as well as the sunken standing-room area surrounding the grassy surface where Brazil's elite soccer players normally cavort.

On one side of the playing field a precariously anchored cross towered over a stage that covered nearly a hundred square yards. A sixty-thousand-watt sound system amplified religious hymns, some of which borrowed melodies from popular favorites such as "Bridge Over Troubled Waters." The multitude, which had come on foot and by public transportation from Rio de Janeiro's poorer neighborhoods, and on chartered buses from other regions of the country, sang with unabashed enthusiasm. Many were in wheelchairs or on crutches or displayed other physical infirmities.

They belonged to the Universal Church of the Kingdom of God, and had assembled to hear their soi-disant bishop, Edir Macedo, who mounted the platform shortly after ten A.M. to proclaim the living Christ and to ask those of his flock beset by health problems to stand up and place their hands on the afflicted parts of their bodies.

"In the name of the Lord," he intoned, "let the evil forces that possess a husband, a wife, or a child, that bring AIDS or cancer, let them leave now." The spectators began to chant "Out! Out!" and soon people on all sides were emitting loud cries, or convulsing, or fainting.

As a follow-up, the bishop called on persons with eyeglasses to pass them up to the stage, and scores of believers immediately complied. Macedo and several of his assistants arranged them in a pile. "God will make you see," the bishop declared, whereupon he joined his aides in stomping on the glasses and reducing them to fragments.

In the final portion of the service, neatly dressed church workers passed among the multitude with sacks that soon bulged with cash contributions, as Bishop Macedo instructed his flock, "The more you give, the more you'll receive."

The Universal Church of the Kingdom of God is but one of a number of Pentecostal sects that are in the forefront in the vertiginous growth of evangelical Protestantism in Brazil, a development that threatens to rob the country of its status as the largest Roman Catholic nation in the world, and to bring about dramatic, far-reaching changes in the texture of Brazilian society.

A confidential study undertaken by Brazil's Roman Catholic bishops and sent to the Vatican on the eve of Pope John Paul II's 1991 trip to Brazil estimated that the Brazilian Catholic Church was losing six hundred thousand members a year to Protestant denominations and other religious groups, and that the number of Brazilian Catholics who actually practiced their faith did not match the number of practicing Protestants.

Moreover, it is evident that the most rapidly expanding Protestant congregations are those of the "new Pentecostals," who not only claim direct inspiration from the Holy Spirit and speak in tongues but also perform cures and exorcisms and preach here-and-now self-improvement through individual initiative. These fundamentalist sects operate independently of one another. The larger churches make extensive use of radio and television. The smaller ones operate out of renovated storefronts in slum neighborhoods. They all stress personal responsibility and sacrifice, qualities that mesh nicely with notions of free enterprise and decentralized authority. Hence, it is not surprising that these churches tend to support a conservative political agenda.

In addition, the new Pentecostals are specifically targeting the Afro-Brazilian cults, whose *orixás* are considered rivals of the Holy Spirit. The Pentecostals have not only aggressively (and successfully) attracted converts from the ranks of the cults; they have even, upon occasion, launched physical attacks on cult members.

The followers of Bishop Macedo and the numerous other Pentecostal pastors are a distinctly new breed of Brazilian Protestant, a far cry from the non-Catholics who began to settle in Brazil during the nineteenth century.

In point of fact, the first Protestants to attempt to gain a foothold in Brazil were the Huguenots who took part in the unsuccessful 1555 French invasion of Rio de Janeiro. Neither they nor the Dutch Protestants who occupied Northeast Brazil in the seventeenth century made any lasting mark on the religious landscape of the country.

It was not until German immigrants began to arrive in the early nineteenth century that Protestantism gained a permanent foothold in Brazil. But as they arrived in greater numbers, the German settlers made no attempts to attract converts, choosing to keep their Lutheran faith to themselves.

A Scotsman named Robert Kakkey is credited with launching the first Protestant missionary effort in Brazil. In 1855 he and his wife founded a Congregational church in Rio de Janeiro. Presbyterian missionaries from the United States arrived in 1859. In addition to proselytizing, they founded private educational institutions, such as the American School (now Mackenzie University) in São Paulo. American Methodists, Baptists, and Episcopalians also opened churches and sought Brazilian converts.

These historical or classical Protestants from the United States came to Brazil with social and political ideas that were quite different from those of the people they hoped to attract. Their goal was not only to implant new religious beliefs in Brazil, but also to introduce a new culture. They brought with them American patterns of behavior and reproduced, both physically and institutionally, the American churches they had left behind them. In their view, Brazilian music, dancing, and feast-day celebrations such as Carnival were sinful.

When Brazilians adopted one of the new Protestant religions, they rejected much of their native culture. They became more rational and less spontaneous and emotional. As David Martin points out in his book *Tongues of Fire*, Brazil's early Protestants were "a peculiar people marked by their dislike of alcohol, promiscuity, and dancing, and by their attachment to work and social mobility." They even dressed differently, by wearing ties. Curiously, the word used to designate them was not "Protestants," but rather *"crentes,"* or "believers."

The Protestant churches enjoyed modest success in attracting converts from the Brazilian middle class. The only denomination to make any headway within the lower classes was the Baptist, perhaps because of the drama and emotion associated with baptism by immersion.

The *crentes* might have remained an insignificant minority within a predominantly Roman Catholic country had it not been for the arrival of a new type of Protestant in the second decade of the twentieth century. The first Pentecostals to found churches in Brazil came from the United States and belonged to a unique, charismatic religious movement that had recently broken away from historic Protestantism. The faith they brought with them resonated in Brazil, especially among the poor.

Pentecostalism called on its believers to seek a religious experience that matched the appearance of the Holy Ghost before the apostles of Christ. This "baptism with the Holy Spirit" brought with it the ability to speak in tongues, as well as to cure the sick and make prophesies. Pentecostalism taught a literal interpretation of the Bible, and it urged on its followers a strict moral code. Services were highly emotional and spontaneous, in stark contrast to the formalized worship to be found in classical Protestant churches.

One of the key features of Pentecostalism was its emphasis on autonomy and individualism. For Pentecostals, bureaucracy and hierarchy were anathema. They never united into a single church but instead remained a heterogeneous lot, although several large denominations did eventually emerge within the movement.

The first Brazilian Pentecostals materialized in the state of São Paulo in 1910 and in Belém in 1911. The latter belonged to a sect called the Assembly of God; whereas the former named themselves the Christian Congregation of Brazil. For several decades these sects remained very much on the fringes of the religious scene, as they disdained not only Roman Catholicism but also the established

Protestant denominations, which, in turn, looked with scorn on their fundamentalist rivals.

It was not until the 1950s and 1960s that Pentecostalism began to enjoy rapid growth, a phenomenon that has continued to the present day. What sparked their success in gaining converts was Brazil's industrial revolution, which increased the size of the working class and fostered a sense of alienation and bewilderment among the urban poor. In search of community and certainty, many of them turned to Pentecostalism.

An important factor in the upsurge of popularity of this fundamentalist religion was that the Pentecostals did not openly seek to transplant a new culture to Brazil, as the mainstream Protestants had done. Indeed, their freewheeling style of worship was well suited to the Brazilian temperament. Believers could sing, shout, and applaud in an improvised fashion and bring Brazilian musical instruments into their churches. Moreover, Pentecostalism addressed the day-to-day concerns of its members. It taught that miracles can happen at any moment and can transform people's lives. In 1930 one in ten Protestants belonged to a Pentecostal sect. By 1964 that proportion had grown to seven out of eight (if one discounts the German-Brazilian Lutherans).

The most aggressive of the first wave of Pentecostals belonged to the Assembly of God. From their humble beginnings in northern Brazil they eventually spread to every state and territory in the union; they were especially effective at gaining converts in rural areas. In 1930 this denomination accounted for 31 percent of all Pentecostals in Brazil; by 1970 its presence had increased to 53 percent.

Over time, as the Assembly of God has matured, it has grown more institutionalized than most other Brazilian Pentecostal denominations. The assembly established a seminary, a national headquarters, and a publishing house. These institutions, in turn, have provided a solid base and a continuity that have made the denomination an important social force.

With the appearance of the new Pentecostals, however, the Assembly of God found itself relegated to the category of historical Pentecostalism. In recent decades a more autonomous, unruly style of Pentecostalism has burst on the scene and shaken up the religious establishments of Brazil.

These new Pentecostals brought with them old-style Pentecostalism and a willingness to use the modern mass media to promote it. In addition, they engaged in assertive fund-raising among their flocks, and some churches have amassed substantial fortunes. They categorically rejected any form of ecumenicalism and were openly hostile to Roman Catholicism, the Afro-Brazilian religions, and the traditional Protestant churches, although they have formed political alliances with non-Pentecostal evangelicals (Protestants who believe the Bible should be read literally).

A survey conducted several years ago by the Institute for the Study of Religion in Rio de Janeiro gives a strong sense of the growth of the evangelical movement. It found that over a specified period of time in Greater Rio, an area with a population of ten million, a new evangelical church opened its doors about once a day. Nine out of ten new churches belonged to a Pentecostal denomination. Over the same time span and within the same geographical limits, 214 new spiritist centers and one new Catholic parish were inaugurated. The study calculated that about 20 percent of the residents of the heavily populated Fluminense Lowlands are Protestant.

As might be expected, Brazilians dismayed by this trend (including members of the Roman Catholic hierarchy) have blamed it on nefarious foreign influences, or more specifically, the Central Intelligence Agency, working on its own and with the help of American missionaries and multinational corporations. This theory posits that the CIA saw fundamentalist Protestants first as a bulwark against the spread of Communism in Brazil, and then as an antidote to liberation theology, which the agency viewed as a threat to American economic hegemony in Brazil.

The conviction that Brazilians on their own could not possibly produce the vast amount of growth in the Pentecostal churches without outside help provides yet another example of the Brazilian inferiority complex. This view not only lacks factual support; it also conveniently sidesteps the possibility that a connection might exist between the rise of Pentecostalism and popular dissatisfaction with liberation theology and its emphasis on community (and political) action. Moreover, this view also betrays a fundamental misperception of the social forces that are propelling Pentecostalism and evangelical Protestantism in Brazil.

Some observers make the argument that liberation theology has drained much of the emotional content from Roman Catholicism. According to them, the lower classes in Brazil have always responded to the spiritual, mystical, at times magical elements of Catholicism, but when these elements are deemphasized, the poor seek them elsewhere.*

Moreover, the poor have run out of patience when it comes to waiting for social and political change to have an impact on their lives. Although through the mechanism of the Ecclesiastical Base Communities, liberation theology advocates the need for community action to achieve social and political change, the Pentecostals offer personal salvation through personal transformation. Individual metamorphosis is within the control of the individual, and it is more likely to produce tangible, positive results.

Fundamentalist Protestantism has obviously connected in a very basic way with Brazil's have-nots, and has been much more successful in doing so than progressive Catholicism. As a Brazilian minister noted in a *New York Times* interview, "The irony is that the Catholics opted for the poor, and the poor opted for the Evangelicals."

The responsibility liberation theology may bear for the spread of the Pentecostal movement in Brazil is a highly debatable point. Defenders of progressive Roman Catholicism contend that the Pentecostals are for the most part converting people who are Catholic in name only, and that the Church would be suffering even greater defections were it not for the renewal associated with liberation theology and the Ecclesiastical Base Communities.

Whatever the contribution of liberation theology, it is clear beyond cavil that the economic situation in the country in the 1980s and early 1990s has played a major role in expanding the ranks of the Pentecostals. The crisis has caused a recession with devastating

---

* As a counterresponse, the Catholic Church has begun to develop its own charismatic movement.

consequences for millions of Brazilians. Daily life for them has become a constant struggle for survival. In addition, the peasants and rural workers who have migrated to city slums find themselves adrift in a strange at times hostile environment. The new Pentecostals have responded to the slumdwellers' needs by providing them with a community to which they can belong, and a conviction that they can improve their lot in life.

Three pillars form the basis for the new Pentecostalism. The first is a view of illness as a manifestation of the Devil's presence. The historical Pentecostals did not make cures a central element of their religious practice but instead relegated them to a peripheral status. The new Pentecostal pastors stress therapy through the exorcism of Satan. In a country where health care for the poor is woefully inadequate, where the hardships of daily life produce not only disease and injury but also a multitude of neuroses, and where society in general disregards the suffering of the have-nots, it is not difficult to understand the appeal of a religion that speaks of healing. It is also conceivable that the emotional experience provided by the new Pentecostalism may have an ameliorating effect on people suffering from psychosomatic ailments, which are not uncommon among the lower and lower middle classes.

Closely related to the stress on healing is the use of exorcism to drive out the diabolic forces that corrupt an individual's character and behavior. Urban life uproots traditional values, and this upheaval, in turn, can foster a deep sense of insecurity. The culture of poverty in city slums destroys family relationships and turns young men toward lives of crime and young women toward the abyss of prostitution. The new Pentecostalism sees this set of circumstances as the work of Satan and offers exorcism as a remedy.

Finally, the new Pentecostals preach the virtues of self-improvement, individual initiative, and hard work. Believers are urged to seek better jobs. Making money, they are told, is an indication of God's blessing. Support networks within the churches relay information about employment openings. Moreover, Pentecostals' reputation as honest, diligent workers has led employers to give Pentecostals preference when they are hiring or making promotion decisions. Since the churches require their members to abstain from alcoholic beverages and leisure activities such as dancing, many Pentecostals have begun to accumulate savings.

The attitude of the new Pentecostals toward money has generated charges of abuses within the movement. Critics claim that Pentecostal pastors play on the misery and gullibility of lower-class Brazilians to persuade them to part with cash they can ill afford to do without. The total autonomy that characterizes Pentecostal denominations does create opportunities for charismatic entrepreneurs to become pastors and use their churches to raise funds of which no account is kept. Moreover, the financial muscle developed by highly successful new Pentecostals, such as Bishop Edir Macedo and his Universal Church of the Kingdom of God, has raised concerns about where all this money is being spent.

Edir Macedo is undoubtedly the most prosperous of the new Pentecostals. He was born in 1945 in Rio das Flores, a small town in the state of Rio de Janeiro near the Minas Gerais border. His father had migrated from the Northeast and was a merchant of modest means. The family moved several times before settling down in São Cristóvão, a neighborhood in the north zone of the city of Rio de Janeiro.

By his own account, Macedo took courses at a university but never obtained a degree. He claims to have worked at the State Secretariat of Finances for sixteen years. (Press reports aver that his job was selling tickets for the state lottery.) Macedo's ambition, however, ran to higher levels, and he soon discovered he had a religious calling.

A Roman Catholic by birth, Macedo had dabbled in *umbanda* before becoming a pastor in one of Brazil's numerous Pentecostal sects. How much actual preparation he underwent before assuming this position is unknown, but it was probably minimal, since the new Pentecostals generally did not require seminary training for their ministers-to-be. In 1977 he struck out on his own and founded the Universal Church of the Kingdom of God, which held its first services in a rented house that had once served as a funeral parlor.

Over the next decade and a half, Edir Macedo established himself as Brazil's most successful religious entrepreneur. Perhaps his greatest triumph occurred in October 1991, when he attracted four hundred thousand to simultaneous prayer meetings in Rio de Janeiro, São Paulo, and Salvador on the same day that Pope John Paul II was drawing only a hundred thousand to a mass in Brasília. While reliable statistics are nonexistent, it is estimated that the Universal Church has between five hundred thousand and two million members frequenting some 850 houses of worship in Brazil. Moreover, Macedo claims to have affiliated churches in Argentina, Uruguay, Portugal, Spain, and the United States. As befitting his newly attained status, he has declared himself a bishop, much to the consternation of not only the Roman Catholic Church but also the Protestant churches.

The charismatic preaching style of Edir Macedo has had much to do with the rapid expansion of the Universal Church. Whether appearing before tens of thousands in soccer stadiums, or reaching untold millions through radio broadcasts and telecasts, Bishop Macedo has won over a large and loyal following with his promises to heal the physically and spiritually afflicted by freeing them from the grip of Satan. At the same time, he has convinced his flock that miracles depend on faith, and that the size of one's financial contribution to the church is a dependable measure of the strength of one's faith. The fact that the Universal Church does not require that its members give up smoking, drinking, and dancing differentiates this denomination from other Pentecostal churches and makes it even more attractive to many Brazilians.

Bishop Macedo created a highly successful spiritual enterprise, and he also put together a business empire that includes a publishing house, a company that builds churches, and a chain of radio stations. But it was not until he purchased Brazil's fifth-largest television network for $45 million in 1989 that public criticism of him reached a crescendo.

Brazilian journalists swarmed over Macedo and his Universal Church. The press investigated the sale of the network and uncovered a number of alleged irregularities. Macedo, who personally controls all the funds of the Universal Church, was also accused of tax evasion, illegally sending money abroad (he owns property just outside New York City, where he established a residence in 1986), and, more mundanely, breaking the law by promising cures in return for cash contributions.

The charges against Bishop Macedo will undoubtedly strike some American observers as drab, especially when placed alongside the colorful scandals involving the "TV evangelists" in the United States. Macedo's followers claim that their leader is being unjustly persecuted by people who disapprove of the growth in membership enjoyed by the flagship church of the new Pentecostalism. There may be elements of truth in this suspicion. The bishop may also be paying a price for the open, aggressive hostility the Universal Church has demonstrated toward the Afro-Brazilian religions, and for the right-wing politics that he and his flock, as well as other new Pentecostals and evangelical Protestants, have embraced.

The relationship between Brazilian Pentecostalism and Afro-Brazilian religious beliefs is closer than one would imagine. Both share the same concept of the supernatural, except that for the Afro-Brazilians the *orixás* are deities, but for the Pentacostals they are Satanic spirits. The Pentecostals preach that the Holy Spirit is stronger than the *orixás,* and they advocate the use of exorcism for freeing believers in *candomblé* or *umbanda* from the spiritual entities that possess them. Thus the rites performed by Pentecostal pastors more often than not specifically target the Afro-Brazilian *orixás.*

Some Pentecostals, including members of Bishop Macedo's Universal Church, have not been satisfied with the high number of conversions they have achieved among members of Afro-Brazilian religions. Responding to the violent rhetoric of their pastors, they have launched physical attacks on both *terreiros* and people they suspect of frequenting them. Devotees of *umbanda* dress in white for their ceremonies, and Pentecostals have occasionally assaulted white-clad individuals (who at times have been *umbandistas* and at other times health-care workers). These outbreaks of violence constitute dramatic departures from the Brazilian tradition of religious tolerance and, in the eyes of many, put Pentecostals in a negative light.

The ultraconservative politics of the Pentecostals and other evangelical Protestants has been more open and more aggressive in recent years. However, it is worth noting that not all politically active Pentecostals have located themselves on the conservative side of the spectrum. In the late 1950s and early 1960s, many of the rural workers who joined peasant leagues in the Northeast belonged to the Assembly of God. And Benedita da Silva, one of the rising stars of the left-wing Workers' party and a successful candidate for the Senate from the state of Rio de Janeiro in 1994, is an active member of a Pentecostal church.

But over the past decade, it has been the right-wing Pentecostals and evangelicals who have thrust themselves into political prominence. Although they have not launched any religiously oriented party to serve as a specific vehicle for their agenda, they have elected a number of federal and state deputies. The Congress that served during the late 1980s included thirty-four evangelical deputies, of whom eighteen were Pentecostals. They formed a block that helped keep an amendment legalizing abortion out of the Constitution; they also acted in concert to promote other conservative causes.

Bishop Macedo was only one of a large number of leading Pentecostals and evangelicals who endorsed Fernando Collor for the presidency in 1989 and claim credit for providing him with more than ten million votes. While this may be an exaggeration, most of Brazil's political parties now pay close attention to the Protestant vote.

The rapid growth of Pentecostalism and evangelical Protestantism may eventually impose significant changes on Brazilian culture. The traditional Protestants originally tried to influence Brazilian culture but failed, because they did not connect with the local ethos. The new fundamentalists have adapted themselves to certain elements of Brazilianness, and use these links to attract converts. But at the same time they induce their membership to undergo behavioral changes, such as abstention from dancing and drinking and dedication to the work ethic and the accumulation of wealth.

Some see these changes in behavior as essential preconditions to the modernization of Brazil. Thus an article in *Forbes* magazine concludes that "the growth of Protestantism in Brazil and throughout Latin America offers solid clues to the future—a capitalist, bourgeois future, not a Marxist or traditional future."

Yet this future will depend on the sort of economic development that will reach Brazil's poor, who fill the ranks of the new Pentecostals, and will transform them into members of the middle class. Such a change will require more than faith healing and exorcism.

## Part Five

# In Search of What Makes Brazilians Brazilian

# Chapter 16

# Soccer Madness

*O*n July 16, 1950, as the world's largest stadium embraced the largest crowd ever to witness a soccer game, a palpable sense of unease blanketed the more than two hundred thousand Brazilians who thought they had gathered to celebrate the consecration of their national team as the best on the planet. A mere tie would enable the host squad to drink champagne from the coveted World Cup, since this was the final contest in a round-robin championship series and Brazil had entered with a slight lead in the standings. But when the Uruguayans knotted the score at 1–1 early in the second half, the anxiety emanating from the huge throng began to weigh heavily on the Brazilian players, and the team's overconfidence quickly gave way to hesitation and excessive caution.

Then, with eleven minutes remaining in regulation time, there came a moment that remains emblazoned in the collective consciousness of a nation otherwise noted for its lack of historical memory. Alcides Ghiggia, a slender Uruguayan winger nicknamed Perrito (Puppy), worked a perfect give-and-go pass with a teammate and darted past his defender, Bigode. Deep on the right side, he pushed the ball into the penalty area. Juvenal, another Brazilian defender, retreated in a desperate but tardy effort to mark his opponent but left a Uruguayan attacker free in front of the net. The Brazilian goalkeeper, Barbosa, anticipated a centering pass, but Ghiggia opted to shoot from a very difficult angle, and he put the ball past the goalie on the short side and into the twine.

When the English referee blew his whistle to end the game, the assembled multitude as well as a radio audience composed of the rest of the country wept tears of blood. In the words of a local reporter, the Brazilian team left the field "like sleepwalkers." Dazed spectators exited in slow motion, "a battalion of living dead," as one author described them. It was a catastrophe the extent of which is difficult for outsiders to grasp. A number of Brazilians reportedly took their own lives. Many could never again bring themselves to set foot in Maracanã stadium.

Athletes expecting enshrinement in the national pantheon found themselves plunging into a lifelong nightmare. The secret police summoned Barbosa to headquarters to ask him whether he was a Communist. Bigode had been voted the most popular player in Rio, but after the game the company sponsoring the poll refused to pay him the prize money that was due him. Juvenal could not bring himself to set foot outside his home for weeks. The team's top goal scorer suffered a temporary loss of memory.

More than four decades after their bitter loss, the players still talk about it, point fingers of blame at one another and their coach, and provide grist for books and newspaper articles. Barbosa continues to claim that Ghiggia meant to pass the ball, but somehow the misdirected spheroid found its way into the goal. His assertion is an understandable yet vain attempt to erase the indelible stain of the phrase "Barbosa's chicken" ("chicken" being Brazilian soccer slang for an easy shot that somehow eludes the goalkeeper), which will follow him to the grave.

On that fateful afternoon, Brazil took second place in the World Cup competition, a result that would have produced some degree of satisfaction in most other countries. But Brazilians felt only frustration, betrayal, anguish, and despair. For them soccer was not just a game; it was the embodiment of their Brazilianness, a sport they had elevated to an art form, and a game they had taken to new heights. All they lacked was the stamp of official recognition a World Cup championship would bring. Their loss was all the more painful because it occurred at home where they were heavily favored, at a time when the traditional European soccer powers had still not fully recovered from the effects of World War II, and in a showdown match against a team from a tiny neighboring country.

This tragic loss also brought to the surface not only the self-doubt Brazilians have always harbored, but also the racism that lurked beneath their inferiority complex. Both Barbosa and Bigode, the principal scapegoats, were dark-skinned, and many Brazilians were willing to believe that their country would never win the World Cup with a racially mixed team.

The soccer madness that has never relaxed its hold on Brazil began at the turn of the century, caused the entire nation to plunge into depression in 1950, later lifted it to peaks of euphoria between 1958 and 1970, contributed to the malaise caused by the political, social, and economic difficulties afflicting the country in the 1980s, and in 1994 gave Brazil's collective self-esteem a badly needed boost.

The oft-used expression "Soccer Country" defines Brazil as accurately as the descriptive "Carnival Country." Indeed, the game has managed to captivate Brazilians in every corner of the land, from Amazônia to the deep south, with an equal measure of devotion; in fact, it has sustained a degree of popularity that even Carnival has never been able to match. The sport has played a major role in unifying both nation and community. Everyone follows the national team and takes great pride in its successes. Newcomers, whether from abroad or from another part of the country, are able to integrate themselves into the social life of a city or town by becoming fans of a local team or by participating in the game themselves.

Sailors from Great Britain, where the game of soccer originated, were the first to play soccer on Brazilian soil, but it was a teenager named Charles Miller who receives credit for introducing the sport to Brazilians. In 1894 this native-born son of British parents brought back with him from a trip to England two soccer balls and a rule book. He had played soccer during his trip abroad, and upon returning helped organize several teams in São Paulo.

At first soccer players were mostly British employees of British-owned firms. Then Mackenzie University organized a squad composed primarily of Brazilians, the first such soccer club. Enthusiasm for the game spread among young Brazilians from the upper class, many of whom had been exposed to soccer during visits to Europe, and they began to organize teams of their own. The formation of a league in São Paulo inspired sportsmen in Rio de Janeiro to follow suit.

Many of the early soccer teams in São Paulo and Rio were sponsored by societies that catered to the wealthy, and games were played on fields provided by exclusive clubs. This atmosphere made it respectable as well as fashionable for young women of good breeding to don their Parisian finery and attend matches.

In the second decade of the twentieth century, soccer received a further boost with the influx of European immigrants who began to form teams of their own. Many of the employers for whom the newcomers worked encouraged them to play the game, since it diverted them from involvement in trade-union militancy, which was beginning to disrupt labor relations in Brazil.

At the same time, the sport was spreading rapidly throughout the country. Leagues in Pernambuco, Bahia, Minas Gerais, Paraná, and Rio Grande do Sul were established, and soccer clubs were organized even in faraway Amazônia.

For a long time soccer in Brazil remained very British. Beginning with the name of the game, "football" (later evolving into the Portuguese word "futebol"), the terminology generally used was English. Players who committed fouls that injured an opponent customarily apologized by saying, "I'm sorry." Teams exchanged the "Hip, hip, hooray" salute after a match.

Lower-class Brazilians soon developed their own fascination with soccer. For the poor it was an ideal sport, requiring only a ball and some empty space. They would stand on walls surrounding playing areas or on the fringes of unfenced fields to watch games in progress. Before long they too were practicing the sport. However, with very few exceptions, nonwhites found themselves excluded from high-level competition. Those who were permitted to play were either fair-skinned or used rice powder to lighten their complexions.

The color line was not really breached until 1923, when Vasco da Gama, a club founded by Portuguese immigrants, fielded a squad composed primarily of black and mulatto workers, and the team won the Rio championship. Initially there was much resistance to integration on the soccer fields, but by the 1930s it receded.

By this time the face of soccer in Brazil had changed dramatically. It was no longer a pastime for aristocrats. The elegant young ladies who once graced the sidelines withdrew to more genteel surroundings. Ordinary people took the game to their hearts and shaped it accordingly.

Soccer swept Brazil in large part because there was no other sport to compete with it. In the United States, baseball was already the national pastime, so immigrants and their children found it prudent to embrace the sport as a means of asserting their Americanness. Brazil, on the other hand, had lacked a sport to call its own. Soccer filled that void. Indeed, it became as much a monoculture as the production of sugar or coffee.

These explanations alone, of course, do not adequately explain why soccer ignited the passions of Brazilians throughout the country. The game proved ideally suited to the Brazilian temperament and became a consummate mechanism for both individual and collective self-expression. It seemed as though soccer had been invented just for Brazilians. They adopted it as their own, identified with it, and went about transforming it.

What Brazilians imprinted on the game was their strong reliance on individuality and improvisation, a faith in magic (exemplified by the conviction that in the relationship between the human body and the soccer ball, anything was possible), the slyness of Pedro Malasartes (a legendary folk hero who survived by outwitting his social superiors), and, above all, the sense of overwhelming joy shared by players and spectators alike.

Betty Milan has aptly described the improvisational style of Brazilian soccer as deriving from the Brazilian way of overcoming poverty. "The Brazilian player invents in every possible way, for . . . he has been schooled in invention. If we have no money, then we'll make a tambourine out of an old tin can. We haven't got a hat for a fancy dress? An old cheese box will serve the purpose."

Soccer seemed to merge sport and samba. During games fans often beat drums from start to finish, and in so doing they reinforced the rhythms of the players, who converted dribbling into a form of dance. Their moves always exuded spontaneity, one of the characteristics of the samba.

Anthropologist Roberto da Matta and others have advanced another explanation for soccer's popularity. They regard the existence of fixed, universally respected rules as the key to the sport's hold over the Brazilian masses. In a society where laws that inconvenience the rich and powerful are either ignored or easily changed, soccer stands apart as an enterprise governed by norms with which everyone is familiar, and which guarantee that talent, rather than money or personal ties, will prevail. The sport thus demonstrates to the common people of Brazil that the social justice they do not see in their everyday lives is possible, and their love for the game represents their embrace of that possibility.

Sociologist Gilberto Freyre hit upon yet another aspect of soccer's appeal to Brazilians when he observed, in the course of a television documentary, that when ordinary people took soccer away from the elite and adopted it as their national pastime, "[i]t ceased to be a sport for Apollos, and became a sport of the Dionysia." Indeed, over the years soccer became "carnivalized."

Thus crowds attending major matches are not mere onlookers; they are participants in an ecstatic rite that begins when the teams take the field. Waving banners, setting off firecrackers, tossing talcum powder, and chanting cheers, the fans enter into a symbiotic relationship with the players, who feed off the energy that comes from the stands. The mass frenzy reaches the point of orgasm with the scoring of a goal.

It was only natural that Brazilian soccer, with its emphasis on individual genius, should develop idols. One of the earliest was Arthur Friedenreich, who could trace his green eyes and steely determination to a father of German descent, and his dark skin and irreverence to a mulatto mother. The first nonwhite to gain recognition as a topflight player in Brazil, the "Tiger" scored 1,329 goals during his career—a record not even Pelé would match.

Another hero was Leônidas da Silva, the legendary "Black Diamond," who has been credited with inventing the "bicycle kick" (an acrobatic maneuver he performed by doing a half somersault backward and at the same time kicking the ball in the direction opposite to that which he had been facing). He was the top goal scorer in the 1938 World Cup tournament in France.

The chance to play in international soccer matches permitted Brazilians to test their skills against the rest of the world. A necessary prerequisite was the organization of a national body that would supervise the scheduling of these contests and the formation of national teams. In 1914 the Brazilian Sports Federation came into being, and soon a Brazilian squad was competing sporadically against other South American teams. But Brazilian soccer was not up to the level of play in Argentina and Uruguay, where the sport had been introduced several decades before its arrival in Brazil and had been immediately taken up by working-class youths.

Brazil did not send a soccer team to participate in the 1924 Olympic Games in Paris, nor in the 1928 Amsterdam Games. Teams from Uruguay won gold medals in soccer at both events, and in so doing astonished the Europeans with their style of play—fast and tricky.

It was during this period that soccer became a professional sport in a number of European countries. This meant that many of the world's best players would be ineligible to compete in the Olympic Games. As a consequence, FIFA (the International Federation of Football Associations), an organization founded in 1904 to encourage and standardize international soccer competition, decided to sponsor a new tournament, called the World Cup, that would be open to professionals. As a result of their Olympic triumphs, the Uruguayans were selected by FIFA in 1930 to host the first of what would become a quadrennial event. They agreed and proceeded to win the Cup.

For the first several tournaments, participation was by invitation rather than through qualification in preliminary matches. FIFA asked Brazil to play in the 1930 World Cup. In 1934 and 1938 Brazil also took part in the event, to replace other South American countries that were not able to send teams to Italy and France, where the matches were held.

By this time soccer in Brazil had also become professionalized. There had been some opposition to the change, but when Argentine play-for-pay teams began to lure away Brazilians in the early 1930s, Brazil had no option but to permit the teams in its various leagues to compensate their players.

The Brazilian national teams showed great progress and promise during their performances in the three World Cup tournaments in the 1930s. Their lack of experience and organization cost them dearly, and they were ousted in the first round in Uruguay (although a 4–0 victory over Bolivia served notice to the world that the Brazilians could score goals). In 1934 the team did not survive a single-elimination preliminary round, but in 1938 it at last came into its own. Leônidas put on a spectacular offensive show, and Brazil made it to the semifinals, where the team self-destructed and lost, 2–0, to the eventual World Cup winner, Italy.

By now Brazilians were convinced that they were the best in the world at soccer, but because of World War II they had to wait twelve years for another chance to prove it. When FIFA decided to resume the competition in 1950, it accepted Brazil's offer to host the event, and a nation of soccer-crazed fans reached new peaks of frenzy.

To provide an appropriate backdrop for the games, the Brazilians embarked on a prototypically "pharaonic" project, the construction of a stadium the likes of which had never been seen anywhere on earth. On the site of a racetrack not far from Rio de Janeiro's downtown, work began in 1948 on what would become soccer's most grandiose temple, its most splendid cathedral, its most magnificent theater.

Nearly two years and five hundred thousand sacks of cement later, Brazilians could look with pride on what came to be known as Maracanã stadium, an area capable of seating 178,000, and of crowding (cheek by jowl) 42,000 standees in a sunken area surrounding the playing field. A moat ten feet wide and ten feet deep separates the field from the fans and makes it impossible for them to reach the players and the officials, who enter through tunnels. Maracanã represented Brazilian architecture at its most imaginative. It was a facility expressly designed for the future (although locating it in a densely populated area that provided no separate space for parking has turned out in the long run to be a serious shortcoming).

Because of its size, Maracanã does not offer the average spectator a close-up view of the action on the field. But the arena does serve as a perfect setting for soccer madness. Brazilians go to matches not just to watch but to participate, and the antics of the crowds are often as diverting as the plays on the field. Maracanã merely increased the scale of the spectacle.

Brazilians rejoiced in the construction of Maracanã because they believed that it would be on its grass that their beloved allstars would win their first World Cup. Few doubted this. After all, the home advantage had been decisive in two of the first three World Cup tournaments. Germany, Hungary, and Argentina, perennial favorites to win the Cup, were not sending squads to Brazil, and the Italian team had been decimated by the loss of ten players in a 1948 airplane crash. The bottom line was that the Brazilians would field a team with talent far superior to that of the competition.

In its first appearance in the stadium, the Brazilian team trounced Mexico 4–0 to open Cup play, and the home team went on to compile a near perfect record (blemished only by a tie with Switzerland) in the preliminaries. Brazil, Sweden, Spain, and Uruguay qualified for the championship series, which would be round-robin rather than single-elimination. (Constant modification of its format has been a feature of the World Cup.) The Brazilians overwhelmed the Swedes, 7–1, and the Spaniards, 6–1. The latter contest was one big party, as a throng of two hundred thousand waved handkerchiefs, released yellow and blue balloons, and sang "Touradas de Madrid" ("Bullfights in Madrid"), a popular Brazilian song that seemed appropriate for the occasion.

Now only Uruguay remained. The Uruguayans had struggled to beat Sweden and had tied their game with Spain. Hence, a draw would give Brazil the coveted Cup. At this point the optimism of the locals was out of control. An unwise decision was made to move the team's training camp closer to Maracanã. In the several days before the final game, publicity-seeking politicians (1950 was an election year), endorsement-seeking merchants, and well-wishers in general were so relentless in imposing themselves on the team that the players had no respite from their attentions. The press assured readers that Brazil would not only win but would run up a lopsided score.

On that fateful, memorable afternoon the unreserved sections of the stadium were packed solid by noontime. When the Brazilians took the field, pandemonium erupted. The mayor of Rio, in a pregame speech, hailed the team as "world champions."

The Uruguayans had nothing to lose. Before the match their captain led them in a ceremonial mass urination on a stack of copies of a Rio newspaper heralding Brazil's impending triumph. He then led them to the most stunning upset in World Cup history.

One interpretation of Brazil's loss likens it to a Greek trag-edy—a classic case of punishment visited by the gods on a people whose fatal flaw was hubris. But perhaps immaturity is a more suit-able explanation. The Brazilians were behaving like adolescents, flaunting an overconfidence that gave them a sense of invincibil-ity. This overestimation of their skills put too much pressure on the players, who turned out to be human after all. So the Brazilian people would have to wait a while, until the lessons of 1950 had been fully absorbed, and until a new crop of superheroes arrived on the scene.

Among the millions who sat by their radios and wept on that Sunday afternoon in 1950 was a skinny little nine-year-old black boy in the city of Bauru in the interior of the state of São Paulo. His given name was Edson Arantes do Nascimento, but his friends called him Pelé, the meaning and origin of which remain unknown even to the present day. His father played soccer professionally but never made it to the top leagues. Pelé would more than make up for this by becoming the greatest soccer star the planet has ever seen.

Pelé was shining shoes at the age of seven and had only four years of formal education. But his uncommon skill with a soccer ball brought him to the attention of talent hunters, and he soon left home to play for the Santos team, in the port of the same name not far from the city of São Paulo. Although it was expected that he would remain for a while with the Santos youth squad, within a short time he found himself promoted to the main team, which competed with the major clubs from São Paulo. On September 7, 1956, the five foot eight, 130-pound, fifteen-year-old phenomenon scored his first goal in an official game against topflight competi-tion.

The youthful Pelé converted a strong Santos team into what one author has called "an astonishing goalscoring machine." His offensive abilities were prodigious. He had it all: speed, mobility, a sense of oneness with the ball, uncanny vision, a fearsome shot off either foot, and, the crowning touch, an audacious, instinctive cre-ativity. On July 7, 1957, Pelé made his debut on the national team in Maracanã. Entering a South American championship game against Argentina in the second half, he scored Brazil's only goal in a 2–1 loss. A year later, despite his tender years, he was called to join the squad that would travel to Sweden for the World Cup tournament.

Brazil had still not recovered from its calamitous 1950 defeat at the hands of the Uruguayans. In 1954, under a new system of regional qualifying matches, Brazil beat Chile and Paraguay to earn a chance to compete for the Cup in Switzerland. But in a bloody, brawl-marred quarterfinal match against a Hungarian team that had not lost in four years, the Brazilians bowed out, 4–2.

But in 1958 things were different. The team benefited from better organization and coaching. The new crop of stars was truly exceptional, clearly the best group that the Brazilians had ever assembled. There were no weaknesses at any position. The attacking front line displayed awesome talent. The squad that would travel to Sweden for the 1958 World Cup featured not only Pelé, but Mané Garrincha, a twenty-four-year-old mulatto forward who brought to the game an exuberant artistry that endeared him to spectators on both sides of the Atlantic.

Garrincha did not look much like a soccer player. But his hunched body and crooked legs, the results of malnutrition, enabled him to perform "now-you-see-it-now-you-don't" feats of legerdemain once he gained control of the ball. When he embarked on one of his patented dribbling sorties, he would more often than not leave in his wake a trail of frustrated defenders.

Garrincha came from Pau Grande, thirty-one miles from Rio at the foot of the steep climb to Petrópolis. The descendants of slaves seeking work at a nearby textile factory were the first settlers of Pau Grande, and to this day it remains an impoverished backwater. Garrincha was born Manoel dos Santos, but as a boy he received the nickname Garrincha, after a small bird indigenous to the region. The additional sobriquet Mané would come later.

As a teenager, Garrincha liked to drink, chase girls, and play soccer, pursuits at which he excelled. Because of his threadbare clothes and unathletic physique, he had difficulty obtaining a tryout with the professional teams of Rio. One coach, upon seeing his twisted legs, remarked "They're bringing everyone here now— even cripples." But Garrincha eventually secured a chance to show off his talents to the officials and fans of one of the elite Rio teams.

He played in a preliminary game for the junior team of Botafogo and scored three goals. It was a quick trip from there to full-fledged stardom, and in 1958 he earned a berth on the national squad that would play in Sweden.

Brazil entered the World Cup tournament with a reputation for choking in critical games. In an attempt to turn this around, the coach installed a new formation better suited to the freewheeling talents of his players. He also followed the advice of the team psychologist (one of the additions to the Brazilian contingent), whose tests told him that Pelé was too immature and Garrincha too undisciplined to be effective in World Cup play. (Some say that the two players were also too dark, since Brazilian officials seemed to want to field as white a team as possible.) The two sat on the bench as Brazil beat Austria and tied England in its first two matches.

The next game, against a strong squad from the Soviet Union, would decide who got a berth in the quarterfinals. On the night before, some of the players urged the coach to turn loose Pelé and Garrincha, and he gave in to their entreaties.

From the opening whistle Garrincha drove the Soviets to distraction with his dribbling. Pelé, though nervous at first, flashed the brilliance that suggested of his capacity to transcend mere stardom. Although neither player scored, they were instrumental in Brazil's 2–0 triumph.

Victories over Wales, France, and host team, Sweden, brought the Cup to Brazil at long last. Pelé, Garrincha, and the rest of the team put on a display of crowd-pleasing soccer that left spectators breathless. The Brazilian style of play had clearly established itself as transcendent. Moreover, several ghosts had finally been put to rest. The Brazilians had demonstrated that they could win when the chips were down, and that they could do so with a racially mixed team. All Brazil exploded in celebration.

In 1962 Brazil captured its second World Cup championship in Chile. Most of those who had played on the Brazilian squad in Sweden returned. The extent of the Brazilian players' talent became obvious when Pelé suffered a serious groin pull in the second game and was lost to the team for the rest of the tournament, yet the irrepressible Garrincha and his teammates did not miss a beat.

A third championship would have allowed Brazil to retire the Cup permanently, but the 1966 event in England turned out badly for them. This time the squad as a whole was less talented. Moreover, World Cup officials had apparently decided that European teams would have a better chance against Brazil and the other South American teams if the referees allowed a more "manly" (that is, rough) brand of play. Against Bulgaria, Pelé was fouled incessantly, and in a subsequent game a defender on the team from Portugal finally put him out of action with a brutal, blatant foul. An angry Pelé swore he would never play in World Cup competition again. Brazil did not survive the first round.

By 1970 Pelé had changed his mind, and the regenerative faculty of Brazilian soccer had given the national team another crop of gifted athletes to compete for the Cup, this time in Mexico. Though perhaps not quite at the overall level of the 1958 squad (the goalkeeper, for example, was a bit unsteady), the team featured a mature Pelé at his prime and other splendid offensive players whose talents more than compensated for defensive lapses. Jairzinho, for example, scored a spectacular goal off a pass from Pelé to beat England 1–0 in a critical first-round match. In the semifinals, the Brazilians downed Uruguay, 3–1, and satisfied themselves with a large measure of revenge for 1950. Then, with an impressive 4–1 victory over Italy in the championship match, Brazil became the first country ever to capture three world titles.

In the course of two decades Brazilian soccer had gone from pit to pinnacle. This trajectory mirrored certain trends in Brazilian society as a whole during this same period. Indeed, there was a complex interrelationship between the course of the national soccer team and larger events that were transforming the country. This was especially true in 1950, 1958, and 1970.

Midcentury found Brazil still searching for an identity, still uncertain of its destiny, still seeking to realize its aspirations. The nation's self-image continued to reflect serious reservations about its racially mixed heritage and doubts about whether an underdeveloped tropical nation could ever compete successfully with the countries of Europe and North America, countries where Brazilians felt they were regarded as "savages." What happened on the grass at Maracanã in 1950 intensified their worst fears.

By 1958 Brazilians had reason to believe that they were at last on the verge of finding themselves. The Kubitschek era had begun, and the country at last was moving forward toward a realization of its potential. The victory in Sweden was a tremendous confidence booster. Moreover, winning had not required slavish imitation of foreign models. The Brazilians could win in their own way, and the rest of the world admired not only their triumph but also the Brazilianness they stamped on it.

In the late 1960s the military regime in Brazil decreed a new economic policy designed to encourage rapid growth, and the "Brazilian miracle" dawned. In order to divert the millions of Brazilians left out of the "miracle" and to defuse any discontent they might harbor, the government took full advantage of the opiate qualities of soccer.

Thus, for the first time teams from all over the country (not just the powerhouses of Rio and São Paulo) were permitted to compete in a tournament for the national championship. As an important component of the regime's ambitious program of "pharaonic" public works, a number of large stadiums mushroomed in population centers throughout the country. A national lottery based on results of major soccer games was instituted. The TV networks improved their technical capacity to transmit games involving the national team from anywhere in the world.

Clearly, as far as the military was concerned, as an instrument for promoting national integration, soccer was on a par with building highways to the Amazon, and its promotion even became a matter of national security. To the surprise of no one, Brazil's rulers gave top priority to the winning of World Cups, and they spared no expense in the effort.

General Emílio Médici, who took over as president in 1969, was a passionate devotee of the game, and his public-relations people made the most of the leader's love for the game. Indeed, most of the popularity he achieved during his presidency came from his image as Brazil's number one soccer fan. He boldly predicted that Brazil would bring home the Cup from Mexico in 1970, and he even tried to influence the selection of the squad. Moreover, many suspect that the president engineered the ouster of the team's coach (who had once belonged to the Communist party and had ties to opposition politicians) five days before its departure for the tournament in order to monopolize the political dividends he would reap from a Brazilian victory.

When Brazil won its third championship, Médici seemed to assume personal credit for it. He flew the team directly to Brasília, where he presented cash bonuses to the players and posed with them for photographers. The government organized a reception in Rio, where a carnival-like celebration reached such a pitch of uncontrolled frenzy that forty-four people lost their lives.

The success of the Brazilian style of play delighted soccer connoisseurs. One analyst described it as "soccer with a smile, fluid, entertaining, immensely skilled and acrobatic." The Europeans traditionally relied on technical factors such as hard-nosed tackling (as practiced by the English), brute strength and physical conditioning (German characteristics), tactical discipline (a Soviet specialty), and cautious defensive play (the contribution of the Italians). All this added up to dull soccer when compared to the way the Brazilians performed.

After the 1970 victory the glory soon faded. The pressures of international competition grew more intense, yet at the same time the Brazilian people came to expect nothing less than championships. Other countries improved their level of play. The Europeans further refined their defensive tactics and physical approach to the game. It became increasingly evident that although Brazilian soccer entertained spectators, it no longer guaranteed favorable numbers on the scoreboard.

Indeed, the very Brazilianness at the heart and soul of Brazilian soccer now seemed to be a drawback. Improvisation, creativity, and slyness might once have bewildered opponents, but the element of surprise had worn off, and the lack of discipline inherent in the Brazilian approach to the game made adjustments to opposing counter-tactics difficult.

Moreover, Brazilian soccer put great reliance on individual effort, which meant that success in international competition depended on the genius of superstars. Brazilians cherished the conviction that because they were inherently superior at the game, there was no need for them to train, and that their genes could consistently produce soccer prodigies who would maintain Brazil's position at the top of the soccer world. This was yet another version of the extractive mentality that has long plagued the country. This mindset led the Brazilians to believe that they could dispense with thoughtful preparation and hard work, because all that was required was the harvesting of a crop of plentiful talent that grew naturally in the country's soccer-rich environment.

The government did everything it could to field a squad that would win again in 1974, and it spent an estimated $6 million in preparations for the event, which was to be hosted by the West Germans. But the military advisers with no special soccer expertise who received appointments to Brazil's burgeoning soccer bureaucracy interfered clumsily with the management of the team. Moreover, Pelé and a number of other stars from the 1970 squad decided not to play, and their replacements were less talented. The Brazilians had to struggle to reach the semifinals, where an excellent Dutch team trounced them.

At this point Brazilian soccer found itself at a crossroads. One option was to maintain the status quo and hold fast to the notion that the country would continue to produce uncommonly talented players who could win World Cups if they were allowed free rein on the field. The other choice was to "Europeanize."

In the wake of the 1974 defeat, the military men who controlled the Brazilian soccer program chose the second option, deciding to mimic the transatlantic strategies of defensive play and teamwork. An army officer who specialized in physical education became the coach of the national team and tried to convert his players into Europeans by exalting tactics and physical conditioning over raw talent. At the 1978 World Cup in Argentina, the Brazilians were neither themselves nor a passable imitation of European players. Although they did not lose a game, they nonetheless suffered the sting of elimination in the second round.

This disappointing outcome settled nothing about the direction Brazilian soccer should take. A debate continued to rage, with some urging a return to the freewheeling days, and others insisting that Brazil had to adapt its game to the European style. Yet at the same time it was obvious that certain aspects of the European style, such as long passes and constant running, were ill-suited to a tropical climate.

Those in the status quo camp could point to the difficulty some Brazilians with rare natural talent had when forced to play within a structured system. They argued that an overly disciplined approach to soccer could kill off the type of idiosyncratic genius that had been the foundation of Brazil's extraordinary successes in international competition.

On the other hand, those who endorsed the Europeanization of Brazilian soccer could point to the national team's failures in 1982 and 1986, when aggregations of extremely talented Brazilian players delighted World Cup spectators with their dazzling performances, only to suffer heartbreaking defeats in critical matches against European opponents.

It was not until 1994 that a Brazilian national team successfully melded the soccer styles of both Brazil and Europe. The squad that won the World Cup in Pasadena, California, featured a skilled, disciplined, well-conceived defense playing behind a pair of uncommonly gifted goal scorers. Although the championship team displayed less flair than prior Brazilian teams (much to the dismay of critics back home), it proved that greatness was still within Brazil's grasp.

The plight of Brazilians in international play between 1974 and 1994 mirrored the deterioration of the game within Brazil. This latter aspect of the "soccer crisis," in turn, reflected trends and developments within Brazilian society at large during this same period of time.

The game suffered from the economic problems that beset the country after the collapse of the "miracle." The overcrowding of cities by migrants from the countryside drove up property values and caused the utilization of empty spaces that had previously served as soccer fields. Urban children thus had fewer opportunities to play the game. Depressed wages made it difficult for fans to afford tickets to matches, and attendance slipped, imposing financial hardships on the various local teams.

European soccer clubs found it easy to purchase Brazilian players from their cash-starved teams. The players preferred to go abroad, where they could earn more. Before long, a number of Brazilian *craques* (crack, or star, players) were performing in Europe. In 1991 there were thirteen of them in the top Italian league alone. Their departures lowered the quality of the professional game in Brazil. It became difficult to put together a cohesive national squad every four years, since those invited to participate had a limited time to practice as a team.

For those Brazilians not playing overseas, the quadrennial World Cup became a showcase for them to market their individual talents and secure lucrative contracts with European teams. So the players did not have the kind of team spirit needed to bring the championship back to Brazil. The Brazilian public became resentful of what it perceived as the mercenary motives of its quondam heroes. In 1990, after an indifferent performance by the team in the World Cup tournament in Italy, disenchanted fans met returning players at the airport in Rio and pelted them with coins.

The structure of organized soccer in Brazil has also contributed to the slump the game has experienced. Although soccer has long been a professional sport, the people who run it are amateurs in the worst sense of the term and have coped clumsily with changing conditions in the country.

Unlike North American pro teams, many of which are the private property (and often playthings) of millionaires or the subsidiaries of corporate conglomerates, soccer teams in Brazil have always remained under the sponsorship and control of nonprofit clubs that serve a particular local community. These entities make available to members a wide range of social and recreational activities.

This organizational structure dates back to the turn of the century, when clubs catering to the upper classes or organized by immigrants to serve their leisure-time needs put together soccer squads composed of their own members. The subsequent professionalization of the sport did not change its club-based structure. The clubs simply went out and hired players, who became employees. In time the clubs not only stocked Brazil's topflight soccer leagues but also created teams for younger players in various age groups as a means of discovering and developing new talent.

Clubs are organized in democratic fashion, so that members in good standing elect the directors and officers. The administrators serve two-year terms and manage social and recreational activities as well as the soccer team. They are not professionals and hence receive no direct payment for their efforts.

Many directors are self-made men devoted to their clubs and prone to acting emotionally rather than rationally. As one Rio soccer expert put it, "they do in the clubs all kinds of stupid things they would never think of doing in their businesses." Since their terms in office are limited, they have been known to make shortsighted decisions, such as taking out heavy loans to sign a star player, that in the long run have devastating financial consequences.

Service as an officer or director may have its rewards. A position in the leadership of a major urban club can function as a springboard for entering politics, or it can facilitate the cultivation of important business contacts. Directors and officers also gain a substantial amount of community prestige, which helps explain why bankers of Rio's illegal lottery have become involved with the administration of certain clubs.

The financial straits into which Brazilian soccer has fallen have, of course, had a negative impact on the players. Like the rest of the country's workers, they have been hit hard by the economic downturn and have been powerless to do anything about it. Exploitation has always defined the relationship between employers and employees in Brazil, and the boys and men who play professional soccer are no exception.

The physical demands on them are brutal, to say the least. The schedule may cover as many as forty-nine weeks of the year. Occasionally, the elite teams play exhibition games in other parts of the country or abroad in the middle of state or national competitions, and keeping to that kind of schedule requires exhausting travel. In addition, playing in tropical heat can subject players to the sort of wear and tear that can shorten careers.

The majority of Brazil's professional soccer players receive meager wages. Their contracts tie them to a team for long periods of time, and they are usually at the mercy of their employers during salary negotiations. They have no agents and no unions to represent their interests.

Until recently, professional soccer has been in large part the sphere of boys from impoverished backgrounds, who look on it as a vehicle for social advancement. Dreaming of fame and fortune, they devote their early years to the game, and more often than not acquire very little formal education along the way. This pattern has produced the stereotype of the ignorant soccer player, best illustrated by the anecdote about the member of the national team who, while participating in the 1966 World Cup in Munich, refused to buy a Telefunken radio because it "spoke only German." Ill-prepared for life after soccer, many of these men eventually slide back into the poverty from which they thought they had escaped.

There is some evidence that this pattern is beginning to change. A 1991 survey of soccer teams in the state of São Paulo found that players were predominantly white, middle class, and reasonably well educated. One fourth had attended university classes. More than 50 percent identified as the main factor motivating them to become professional athletes the pleasure they derived from playing the game.

The Brazil of the 1990s differs significantly from the nation that produced World Cup champions in 1958, 1962, and 1970. Soccer has found itself competing with other sports, such as basketball and volleyball, with the latter gaining a tremendous boost when the men's team won an Olympic gold medal in 1992. Images of the youthful, yuppie-ish president Collor practicing karate and wind surfing set a tone that was difficult to ignore.

Attendance at soccer matches has suffered because of an increase in the savage behavior of fans and the security problems confronting spectators who leave large urban stadiums like Maracanã in Rio. The toll of such violence has not yet reached the level of casualties experienced at soccer stadiums elsewhere in the world, but it should come as no surprise that the violence afflicting Brazilian society at large has spread to soccer stadiums.

Despite its problems, soccer continues to reign supreme as the country's most popular sport. Brazil has more stadiums (five) with a capacity in excess of one hundred thousand than any other country. The terminology of the game remains embedded in everyday conversation. The favorite fantasy of boys and grown men alike is to imagine themselves playing on the grass at Maracanã in front of a huge crowd. That Brazil is the only country in the world to have participated in every single World Cup tournament since the Cup's inception and that it is the first country to win the Cup four times remain matters of enormous national pride.

Moreover, soccer has produced Brazil's only enduring, undisputed national hero, the peerless Pelé, as well as perhaps a more beloved idol, Garrincha, both of whom have bestirred the hearts and minds of their compatriots in ways that illuminate key aspects of Brazilianness.

While he played soccer both for Santos and for the national squad, Pelé enjoyed the veneration of his fellow Brazilians for the contributions he made to three World Cup triumphs and for the consistent brilliance he displayed while reigning for two decades as the sport's undisputed king. Garrincha, likewise admired for his performances in international competition, endeared himself to Brazilian fans with his unique style of play, earning from them the epithet *alegria do povo* (joy of the common people).

The successes Pelé achieved promoting soccer in the United States, where he played several years for the New York Cosmos, and in business ventures before as well as after his retirement from the game, have actually tended to diminish his stature in certain quarters of Brazil. Garrincha, who made a tragic mess of his post-soccer life and eventually drank himself to a premature death, has become an even greater folk hero than he was during his playing career.

Although both men's lives followed "poor-boys-make-good" trajectories, Pelé rose far above his background. He went about educating himself and took full social and financial advantage of the fame and fortune that came his way. Garrincha never tried to become anything other than what he was: an uncomplicated, ingenuous Brazilian from the bottom of the societal pyramid.

One important key to understanding how they differed lies in the way they approached the game of soccer. Pelé manifested Brazilian qualities such as inventiveness and spontaneity, but he melded them into an offensive style of play that reached a level of classic perfection recognized by soccer aficionados throughout the world. Garrincha, on the other hand, was pure *malandro* on as well as off the soccer field, and therein lay the secret of the adoration he attracted from his fellow Brazilians.

The *malandro* is a heroic figure with roots in Brazilian folklore. Struggling to escape the poverty into which he was born, the *malandro* lives by his wits, converting his weaknesses into strengths and standing reality on its head, to the utter consternation of his betters. He refuses to accept the injustice inherent in a society without social mobility, and in doing something to rectify the situation, he acts on behalf of all the have-nots. He is not a criminal, but he lives on the thin line between legality and illegality. Neither conventions nor laws hold him back because of his expertise in bending them or finding ways around them. He is an individualist and a survivor, yet there is an unmistakable joie de vivre about him.

Although *malandragem* (the art of being a malandro) had always been a characteristic of Brazilian soccer, Garrincha brought it to a new level (and a level that it has never again attained). He turned his deformed legs, a physical defect, into formidable weapons. His skill at dribbling a soccer ball left opponents lunging at thin air or sprawling on the turf. He cared not a whit who they were, referring to all of them as "João" (John), and his fans often roared with laughter at his tricky moves. Indeed, at times he seemed to convert the grass of the soccer field into the sawdust of the circus ring. The childishness he often projected was merely one of his *malandro* guises.

Pelé, meanwhile, accomplished the signal feat of becoming the first Afro-Brazilian to earn recognition as a truly national hero. To a much greater extent than Garrincha, he drew fans across social lines because of the prodigiousness of his goal scoring and the acclaim he won in every corner of the globe.* All Brazilians identified with him.

In 1960 the Brazilian Congress enacted a law declaring him a "national treasure" and forbidding Santos from selling his contract to a foreign team. There was a subtle irony here. The adulation Pelé received was often cited as evidence that there was no racial prejudice in Brazil, yet the government was willing to impose a sort of slavery on him by limiting his right to work where he pleased.

---

* Nigeria and Biafra once declared a twenty-four-hour cease-fire in the war between them in order to permit Pelé to play in an exhibition match.

After his retirement, the restriction no longer applied, and the lure of a multimillion-dollar contract brought the superstar to New York, where he performed for three years with the Cosmos of the North American Soccer League and undertook to do public-relations work for Warner Communications, the owner of the team, and for other American companies. It was at this point that some of his compatriots, especially intellectuals of the Left, began to criticize him for being a "mercenary." They apparently would have preferred that he refrain from displaying entrepreneurial initiative.

Pelé himself made matters worse by issuing statements that could be construed as supportive of the military regime, and by not only ignoring, but also denying, the existence of racial prejudice in Brazil. He also did not conceal his enjoyment of the good life, and after divorcing his wife of twelve years, he often appeared in the company of young, beautiful women.

A multimillionaire as a result of his continuing association with Warner, as well as product promotions, movie roles, and real-estate investments, Pelé remains an international celebrity of the first magnitude. In 1994, a World Cup year, his endorsements and other business deals may have topped basketball legend Michael Jordan's off-court income of $30 million. A nonsmoker and nondrinker, Pelé looks as fit as he was during his playing days.

Whereas Pelé prospered after he hung up his cleats for good, Garrincha could not adjust to the loss of his soccer skills. Botafogo, the team to which he was under contract, exploited him as much as it could, forcing him to play on an injured knee rather than allowing him to undergo treatment that would have kept him out of the lineup for a while (and would have reduced the club's gate receipts, since he was their principal attraction). The knee injury, along with his inability to give up drinking and carousing, reduced him to a shadow of his former self. After Botafogo finally released him, he bounced from team to team, in Brazil and abroad, before finally retiring in 1973, at the age of forty.

Garrincha's personal life was grist for the tabloids. At nineteen he married a local girl, who bore him nine daughters. In the early 1960s he abandoned her for Elza Soares, a popular singer who introduced him to the nightlife of Rio. Elza stood by him support-

ively during all the hard years, even after his drunk driving caused
an auto accident that claimed the life of her mother, but in 1977,
after he gave her a severe beating during one of his bouts with the
bottle, she finally left him. After being hospitalized repeatedly for
his alcoholism, he eventually succumbed to the effects of the disease in 1983.

The soccer stadium in Brasília, as well as the field where
Botafogo plays, bears the name of Mané Garrincha. Brazilians continue to cherish his memory for a number of reasons, several of
which are contradictory. A key figure on two of the World Cup
championship teams, he raised the Brazilian style of soccer to new
heights and at the same time entertained spectators with his happy-
go-lucky brilliance. A consummate *malandro*, he was admired as
such, yet in the end he did not triumph over adversity in the tradition of the mythical hustler.

The story of Garrincha is one of triumph and tragedy. For Brazilians to celebrate their hero's success is only natural, a matter of
national (or class) pride; for them to be moved by the sad turn his
life took reflects the intense sentimentality that is an integral part
of their Brazilianness.

The idolization of Pelé derives from his contributions to Brazil's World Cup triumphs and from his worldwide deification as the
King of Soccer. Recognition abroad is a highly prized commodity
in an underdeveloped country like Brazil, even though Brazilians
at times have a tendency to depreciate compatriots who have prospered in foreign lands (as occurred in the case of Carmen Miranda).

The tendency of some intellectuals to glorify Garrincha, and at
the same time to snub Pelé, points to a rejection of material success and a celebration of the virtues of being poor and uneducated.
Yet this proclivity also risks fortifying the sense of inferiority, and
of defeat, that Brazilian society has traditionally drummed into its
have-nots.

Brazilian intellectuals have not always discounted Pelé. Once
upon a time, a group of them accompanied Jean-Paul Sartre on a
lecture tour to Araraquara, in the interior of the state of São Paulo.
They surrounded him as he made his way on foot to the place
where he was scheduled to speak. Suddenly and unexpectedly, in
the opposite direction came Pelé, encircled by a group of children,

on his way to the soccer stadium, where Santos was scheduled to play a local team. The two groups converged on a street corner. When they separated, all the intellectuals were following Pelé and the children, and Sartre was walking alone, until his erstwhile companions remembered what they were doing in Araraquara and dashed back to the Frenchman. To this day many residents refer to the spot as the "Pelé-Sartre Corner."

# Chapter 17

# The Lesser Gods

## *Brazil's Heroes*

*A*s the stories of Pelé and Garrincha demonstrate, the idols a nation worships as its "lesser gods" embody the common dreams, aspirations, and values of an entire population or broad segments of it. But the venerated ones are neither supernatural beings nor humans who have achieved sainthood by serving as intermediaries of divine forces; rather they are flesh-and-blood creatures whose earthly feats have earned more than mere admiration. The conferral of hero or idol status signifies that the recipient has come to symbolize something people want and need to say about themselves.

Some have questioned whether Brazil has any genuine national heroes, apart from Pelé.* Throughout its history there have been no military commanders who led their compatriots to truly epic victories over foreign foes on the field of battle,† nor have there been towering political figures who guided the country through difficult times and into a brighter tomorrow.‡ Moreover, most Brazilians lack historical memory, which means that they

---

* Ayrton Senna, a race-car driver who won three Formula 1 championships, might have approached Pelé's level as a national hero had it not been for his untimely death in a 1994 crash.

† Indeed, Brazil's most notable victories over foreign rivals occurred in the diplomatic arena, the handiwork of José Maria da Silva Paranhos Júnior, the Baron of Rio-Branco, who used quiet, effective negotiation to gain favorable settlements in many of Brazil's outstanding border disputes with neighboring countries at the end of the nineteenth century. Many Brazilians would rank him as a national hero.

‡ Some Brazilians might place the controversial Getúlio Vargas in this category.

don't profit from remembering heroic figures from the past such as Tiradentes, who led an early uprising against Portuguese rule, and Maria Quitéria, an extraordinary woman who fought bravely and well in the war for independence.*

This does not mean, however, that heroes or idols are in short supply in Brazil. Since Brazilian society is fragmented along lines of class, race, sex, region, religion, education, and profession, there are many who are heroes to some but not all sectors of the social mosaic. Zumbi, the rebel slave, for example, is idolized by many Afro-Brazilians. Padre Cícero remains a hero to many poor northeasterners. Oswaldo Cruz, the physician responsible for eradicating yellow fever from Rio de Janeiro at the turn of the century, deserves the admiration he receives from public-health professionals. Heitor Villa-Lobos thrilled classical-music lovers when he gained worldwide recognition as a composer who wove Brazilian musical themes into his works. More recently, Herbert de Souza, a hemophiliac sociologist infected with the AIDS virus as a result of a blood transfusion, has won the undying adulation of public-spirited Brazilians for his inspirational leadership of a national campaign against hunger. Even though these figures may appeal to citizens in only one or several of the subgroups that make up Brazilian society, they share some common characteristics that shed light on the concept of Brazilianness.

It would, of course, be impossible to discuss more than a handful of them. The following selection represents a limited cross section designed to illustrate who gains admission to Brazil's gallery of lesser gods, and what this process tells us about the country's national character. Those discussed include

- aviation pioneer Alberto Santos-Dumont;

- Vinicius de Moraes, diplomat, poet, performer, and Bohemian par excellence—an intellectual who turned to popular music

---

* Maria Quitéria, a young woman who grew up in the interior of Bahia, where she learned to hunt with firearms, disguised herself as a man and joined the new army Dom Pedro I was raising to expel the Portuguese. Assigned to the infantry, she assaulted enemy trenches, took prisoners, and later organized a battalion of women soldiers, whom she led in battle. A street in Rio de Janeiro's Ipanema neighborhood bears her name.

and became famous, in spite of himself, among young people not only in Brazil but throughout Latin America;

- Luiz Carlos Prestes, a quasi-mythical figure who held the unique distinction of being esteemed, albeit begrudgingly, by the military and worshiped by the political Left;

- Maria da Graça Meneghel, better known as Xuxa, a creation of television and the idol of Brazilian children; and

- Ivo Pitanguy, the plastic surgeon whose sure-handed efforts to keep patients looking young and beautiful has made him an icon among well-off Brazilians.

In the resort town of Petrópolis where the Brazilian royal family once repaired to avoid the tropical diseases that ravaged Rio de Janeiro during the summer, a peculiar structure resembling an oversized birdhouse in the style of a Swiss chalet perches unobtrusively on the side of a hill. The steps from the street are so narrow that a visitor must turn sideways to climb them. The tiny abode, painted white with green trim and topped by a rust red roof, houses curiosities such as a dining table twice the height of standard furniture, with chairs to match, and what a placard celebrates as the first hot-and-cold-water shower in Brazil, a contraption dating back to 1918.

There is a strong scent of eccentricity in every corner of what has come to be known as the "Enchanted House." And rightly so, for the house was designed and inhabited by one of Brazil's most original and lovable eccentrics, Alberto Santos-Dumont.

In his native land he is hailed as the "Father of Brazilian Aviation." The French, among whom he lived for many years, bestowed on him the affectionate nickname Petit Santos (Little Santos). Márcio Souza called him *o brasileiro voador* (the flying Brazilian) and used the phrase as the title of his fictionalized biography of the fearless birdman whose derring-do was the talk of Paris during the belle époque.

Santos-Dumont is an unusual denizen of the Brazilian pantheon of national heroes because he performed his epic feats abroad. Yet the accomplishments of this fascinating aviation pioneer were so extraordinary and his style so Brazilian that his fellow citizens took, and continue to take, great pride in him.

Alberto Santos-Dumont, the last of eight children, was born in 1873 in the sugar-growing region of southern Minas Gerais, near what is now the main highway between Rio de Janeiro and Belo Horizonte. His father acquired a coffee plantation in the state of São Paulo in 1879. Using modern technology to increase its production, he soon became a wealthy man.

The young Alberto was a wiry wisp of a lad with dark hair and eyes and large ears. The machinery he encountered on the farm intrigued him, and he set about learning how everything worked. Shy and full of dreams, he immersed himself in the novels of Jules Verne and fantasized about air travel.

In 1891 a fall from a horse left Alberto's father partially paralyzed. He took Alberto with him on a trip to Lisbon and Paris, where he consulted with specialists about his condition. The boy fell under the spell of the City of Lights.

Realizing that he did not have long to live, Alberto's father decided to let his youngest son go his own way, so he allowed Alberto to return to Paris to continue his education. "We'll see whether you'll make a man of yourself," he wrote in a letter to the nineteen-year-old boy, whom he advised to study physics and chemistry. "Don't forget," he wrote, "that the future of the world lies in mechanics." Alberto followed his father's counsel. On his own in Paris, he took private classes in the applied sciences and also attended lectures at the University of Bristol in England.

The turn of the century was an exciting time for anyone interested in technology, which was bursting beyond its frontiers, and the young Brazilian became fascinated with the infant science of ballooning. Making use of the financial resources his father had put at his disposal, Alberto set up a workshop on the outskirts of Paris and turned his attention with remarkable single-mindedness to lighter-than-air flight.

Within a short time Santos-Dumont was a leading figure within a small group of intrepid adventurers who designed and produced their own spherical balloons and flew them with the aid of air currents. After becoming an accomplished free-flyer, Alberto designed and constructed a cylindrical airship powered by an engine mounted in a basket suspended from an elongated balloon. It was the first in a series of dirigibles he would fly.

When the Aéro Club of France offered a prize for the first person who could pilot a dirigible along a prescribed route around the Eiffel Tower in thirty minutes, Santos-Dumont rose to the challenge. He made several attempts, one of which almost ended in tragedy when his airship crashed onto the roof of the Trocadero Hotel and he had to be rescued by firemen. But on September 19, 1901, he successfully completed the course and became the toast of Paris.

Santos-Dumont's popularity derived from not only what he did but also how he did it. The Brazilian had a way about him that captivated Parisians. A shade under five feet in height and weighing less than 110 pounds, he was a curious amalgam of cockiness and reticence, courage and primness. He was also somewhat of a man-about-town, dining regularly at Maxim's, the famous restaurant.

Then there was the matter of his appearance. To offset his lack of size, he wore elevated heels, striped suits, a high starched collar, a red scarf, and a broad-brimmed Panama hat. He became the delight of the French press, which publicized his adventures in words and photographs, a novelty at the time. He also became the favorite subject of one of his friends, the caricaturist Georges Goursat. Before long, people began to imitate his style of dress.

He bought a house on the Champs Élysées, not far from the Arch of Triumph, and set up in the dining room a table and chair that hung by wires from the high ceiling, six feet from the floor. Mounting the chair with the use of stilts, he would sway back and forth as he ate his meals, in order to acclimate himself to dining in a balloon.

Always impeccably dressed, he would electrify Parisians by engaging in unannounced descents from the sky. He would even steer his airship along the streets of the city. Once he tied up at his apartment building, went inside for a cup of coffee, and then resumed his flight. On another occasion he landed in front of a café on the Avenue du Bois de Boulogne and sauntered in for an aperitif. He took the young son of a United States diplomat with him on one ascent, and on another he let a dazzlingly attractive Cuban woman solo in one of his dirigibles (both firsts). He was totally unflappable, even during the mishaps that inevitably occurred.

One explanation for Santos-Dumont's eccentric behavior, which has been put forward by one of his biographers (Henrique Lins de Barros), was that he wanted to be accepted by the French aristocracy. He disdained the pursuit of profit, considered a bourgeois notion, and looked on what he was doing as a gentleman's pastime. Thus, when he won a contest for being the first person to fly a dirigible around the Eiffel Tower, he gave away the prize money. He would not patent any of his numerous inventions, and he allowed them to enter the public domain, for anyone to copy and use freely.

Although he would have preferred to continue experimenting with dirigibles, a growing worldwide interest in the possibilities of flight in heavier-than-air machines soon captured his attention. Reports that the Wright Brothers had flown an airplane in 1903 in the United States were greeted with skepticism in Europe, and the Aéro Club of France offered a prize for the first aviator to make a flight of 650 feet. The diminutive Brazilian decided to enter the competition.

By late 1906 he was ready to give it a try. He constructed an odd-shaped biplane that resembled a series of box kites, with a horizontal stabilizer in front, rather than in the back as a tail. He called his invention the *14 Bis* (an accurate translation into English would be the *14 a*, since it was a variation on his fourteenth airship). On November 12, before an enthusiastic crowd on a field in the outskirts of Paris, after several inconclusive attempts, he and the *14 Bis* managed to traverse more than the required distance at an altitude that exceeded twenty feet.

The publicity generated by Santos-Dumont's feat gave a tremendous boost to the work of others. He was prominent among the handful of individuals who made Europe air-conscious during this period. Moreover, his total openness contributed to the rapid progress in aviation that was to follow, since anyone was free to copy and improve upon what he had done.

Petit Santos clung stubbornly to his belief that aviation should be an avocation for the rich, and he shuddered at the thought that airplanes might be mass-produced in factories. He built a new craft, which he christened the *Demoiselle,* or *Dragonfly,* an elegant little monoplane that his British biographer, Peter Wykeham, described as "beautifully made and finished, . . . the last and perhaps the most satisfying realisation of his genius." Santos-Dumont once landed it on the lawn of the château of a French count, who invited him in for tea—an exploit that gave him the distinction of making the first social call in an airplane. The *Demoiselle* was soon copied by others.

In November of 1909 Santos-Dumont made his last flight. Several months later, the news broke that he had suffered what was described as a nervous breakdown. Wykeham hypothesizes that French doctors had in fact discovered that the aviator had multiple sclerosis, and he preferred to keep his condition a secret.

With the passing of the belle époque and the coming of World War I, Santos-Dumont's world came to a sudden end. Although in 1913 the French Aéro Club built a monument in St. Cloud, just outside Paris, to commemorate his 1901 dirigible trip around the Eiffel Tower and the flight of the *14 Bis* in 1906, he was increasingly marginalized. When he amused himself with a telescope in a seaside town he was visiting in 1914 and the overzealous police chief arrested him on suspicion of being a German spy, he decided to leave the country, despite the prompt apologies of the French government. He then returned to Brazil.

By this time Santos-Dumont was beginning to show signs of premature aging, the effects of multiple sclerosis. The use of airplanes during the war profoundly depressed him, and he sought refuge in the little house he built for himself in Petrópolis. As soon as hostilities in Europe ended, he sailed back to the continent for medical treatment. He could not seem to adjust to the changed times.

On another return to Brazil in December 1928, his compatriots planned a gala reception as his steamship entered Guanabara Bay. A seaplane, named the *Santos-Dumont* and carrying a number of notable Brazilian scientists, was to take off, fly over the vessel, and drop a packet containing a message of homage to "the great Brazilian who by achieving the conquest of air honored the country's name abroad." As the plane glided toward the ship, a wingtip caught a wave and the plane crashed. There were no survivors.

By now a very sick man, Santos-Dumont bounced back and forth between Brazil and European sanitariums. In 1930 the French government awarded him its coveted Legion of Honor decoration. In late 1931, as the depression he suffered him grew worse, he went home to Brazil for the last time.

The 1930 revolution that had brought Getúlio Vargas to power provoked an armed revolt in São Paulo in 1932, and the regime used aerial bombardments to suppress it. Santos-Dumont, who had gone to live at the seashore resort of Guarujá not far from São Paulo, could watch military planes from his hotel room as they deployed to attack a rebel fortress near the coast. When his nephew, who was caring for him, went off to buy some cigarettes and left Santos-Dumont alone for a few minutes, the old man headed straight for the bathroom and hanged himself. Santos-Dumont today lies at rest beneath a statue of Icarus (a copy of the St. Cloud monument) in the São João Batista Cemetery in Rio de Janeiro.

Alberto Santos-Dumont exemplifies the mix of sweetness and greatness that marks the most seductive aspect of Brazilianness. Because of the recognition he achieved abroad for Brazil, his fellow citizens idolized him (although some grumbled at his refusal to make flights in his native land). The town where he was born and the downtown airport in Rio de Janeiro bear his name, and the Brazilian air force has made him their hero (despite his well-known opposition to military aviation).

He was the only early flier who had significant successes in both lighter-than-air and heavier-than-air flight. He may have been the first to build a hangar for dirigibles. He made the first flight in a powered aircraft in public before an official commission. His dirigibles and his *Demoiselle* were clear contributions to the state of the art in aviation development. And when he told a friend, Louis Cartier, that he could not manipulate the controls of his airships and at the same time consult his pocket timepiece, the two of them came up with the design for the first wristwatch for men.

But this is just part of the story. Santos-Dumont was truly unique: a complex, dapper daredevil; a comet who blazed briefly but brightly; both a shaper of his era and a mirror for his contemporaries; a legend in his own time; and ultimately a tortured soul to whom fate dealt a cruel hand.

The star-crossed quality of his life (perhaps a fate that leads Brazilians to see him as flawed, and therefore to doubt his greatness, and by extension, their own) seems to have remained with him after death. A major international film project to be based on Márcio Souza's O *Brasileiro Voador* and likely to secure for Santos-Dumont the recognition that he richly deserves has been shelved indefinitely because of a lack of financing.

In the winter of 1962, several blocks from one of Rio's better beaches, at an intersection throbbing with vehicular and pedestrian traffic, two men sat drinking beer in the Veloso Bar and studied the forms of human life that swirled by them. It was an almost daily ritual, one of the more popular pastimes of *cariocas* who inhabit the south zone of the "Wonderful City."

The high point of their routine occurred when a stunning, green-eyed fifteen-year-old made her way past them on the street, or entered the bar to buy cigarettes for her mother. These regular appearances at first rendered them speechless and later inspired a running dialogue about her abundant charms. She was, in the words of one of them, "a golden girl, part flower, part siren, full of light and grace."

Eventually they decided to write a song about her. The younger of the pair, a painfully shy pianist named Antônio Carlos Jobim, composed the music. His companion, a ruddy-faced poet and diplomat named Vinicius de Moraes, wrote the lyrics. The piece, which they called "A Garota de Ipanema" ("The Girl from Ipanema"), became not just a hit but a classic, not just in Brazil but everywhere.

Both Marcos Vinicius Cruz de Mello Moraes and Antônio Carlos Jobim qualify as authentic Brazilian heroes. The choice to focus on Vinicius in no way signifies a lack of appreciation of the musical genius known to his friends simply as Tom; it merely reflects a preference for the powerful element of Brazilianness that shaped and colored the unique career of Vinicius. As the American writer Waldo Frank once pointed out succinctly, "There is in him so much of Brazil."

He exuded many of the idiosyncracies of his native land. He was captivating, easygoing, sensual, musical, and totally anarchic.

Within him one could detect strong traces of Macunaíma, the roguish, prototypically Brazilian hero immortalized in Mário de Andrade's classic novel of the same name.

"Life is a big rat trap," he used to say, "and you have to eat the cheese." Vinicius himself never hesitated to pounce on the cheese, and he never let the trap bother him.

He was born in 1913 in the pleasant neighborhood of Gávea, a stone's throw from Rio de Janeiro's botanical gardens. His family was comfortably upper middle class, with blood lines that were mainly Portuguese, though he could identify ancestors who were German, Italian, Hungarian, and Argentine.

The young Vinicius grew up in a home environment that placed value on the intellect and an appreciation of the arts. His father had no real profession and pursued various moneymaking schemes that came to naught, when he was not writing poetry or strumming the guitar. Following in his father's footsteps, Vinicius penned his first verses at the age of eight.

He found music particularly appealing. Vinicius sang in the choir of the Jesuit high school he attended in Botafogo and taught himself to play the guitar by ear, so that he could perform in a musical trio at parties. At fifteen he composed his first song lyrics.

After three years at the university, where he obtained a law degree without sacrificing his consuming interests in literature, philosophy, dance, music, cinema, and the pursuit of women, he published his first book of verse, which won critical acclaim. Two years later a second collection of poems won him a prize. He began to live the life of an intellectual, which did not prevent him from taking a job as the film censor for the Federal Ministry of Education. (He never censored a single film.) In 1938 Vinicius's poetry won him a fellowship at Oxford.

When he left his native land, Vinicius was a dashing, romantic figure. His past followed him to England, and in 1939 he interrupted his studies to wed a beautiful, strong-willed young woman he had met just prior to his departure from Brazil. Beatriz Azevedo de Mello (nicknamed Tati) came from an old São Paulo family that was displeased by her decision to link her destiny with that of a poet. She defied them, married Vinicius by proxy in Rio, sold some of her jewelry, and set out across the Atlantic.

The outbreak of hostilities on the Continent forced Vinicius and Tati to return home later that same year. Soon he was scrambling to support her and the two children she bore him, the profession of poet being not even minimally remunerative. Journalism provided him with his only steady income. He took a position as literary-supplement editor and film critic for a Rio daily.

The film critic position enabled him to promote his somewhat eccentric ideas about cinema and fight a rearguard action against talking pictures, which he despised. He was such a purist in this regard that he even deplored the practice of piano accompaniment with silent films.

Being the head of a family did not check the Bohemian tendencies that he had indulged during his bachelor days, and he resumed active participation in the intellectual and artistic life of Rio de Janeiro. When Orson Welles arrived in early 1942 to shoot a documentary film about Brazil, Vinicius the film buff was irresistibly drawn to the "boy genius" who had stunned the cinema world with *Citizen Kane*. Unchecked by Vinicius, who became his friend and companion, Welles quickly gave himself over to the carnal delights of the city.

Another American visitor in 1942 brought out the serious side of Vinicius and helped transform him politically. Up to that time he had manifested decidedly profascist sympathies. But this alignment changed when Waldo Frank, a well-known novelist and critic with an interest in Latin America, came to Brazil as part of a continental speaking and writing tour intended to promote support for the Allies and the ideals for which they were fighting. Vinicius served as his companion and secretary during an excursion Frank made to Amazônia, the Northeast, and the heart of the state of Mato Grosso in central Brazil.

Today most Brazilians from the south know relatively little about the rest of their country; *a fortiori*, in the 1940s, when travel was extremely difficult, this ignorance was much more pervasive. For Vinicius, the consummate *carioca*, the trip revealed a Brazil he had scarcely imagined existed. It put him in touch with the most backward and poverty-stricken areas of the country and radicalized him. At one point he even contemplated signing up with the Communist party, but its leader, Luiz Carlos Prestes, advised him not to join, since he could be more useful to the party from the outside.

By 1943 family responsibilities weighed so heavily on Vinicius that he joined Brazil's foreign service. For several years his new profession did not noticeably interfere with his lifestyle in Rio. In 1946 he was offered posts in Moscow or southern California. Hedonism triumphed over ideology, and Vinicius chose the assignment in the Brazilian consulate in Los Angeles, a post that would enable him to sample Dionysian living on a major-league scale.

Motion pictures were still the preeminent form of popular entertainment in the United States, and the studio system still had firm control of Hollywood. The film industry was booming in the immediate postwar period, and Vinicius had a front-row seat.

He studied moviemaking with Orson Welles. Carmen Miranda was a big star, and she and Vinicius (as well as Tati) became close friends. He met (and fell under the spell of) the young Ava Gardner and hobnobbed with other celebrities. He also wrote about cinema and jazz for Brazilian newspapers. Like all of his assignments throughout his long diplomatic career, the job of vice-consul seemed to occupy only a small portion of his time and attention.

He returned to Brazil in 1950. Shortly afterward, his marriage came apart. At this time that his Bohemian tendencies were gaining irresistible momentum. He moved in with another woman, the first of eight successors to Tati.* He began to gain weight. Because the foreign service poorly compensated its officials serving within the country, he returned to the field of journalism and began writing film criticism as well as an advice-to-the-lovelorn column, under a pseudonym, for a Rio daily.

It was during the fifties that Vinicius took the step that was to earn him fame and fortune: he devoted serious attention to the writing of popular songs. He did not, however, completely abandon his intellectual bent. Indeed, his major opus of the decade was

---

* When he broke up with a companion, he would take with him only a toothbrush. "This is the fifth Encyclopedia Britannica I've bought," he once told his daughter Susana as he established yet another new household.

a musical play written in verse and based on the Greek myth of Orpheus and Eurydice. Perhaps inspired by the success of the American musical play *Cabin in the Sky*, it retold the ancient fable as a tragedy befalling blacks in a Rio *favela* during Carnival. To provide the music, Vinicius engaged a young and vastly talented composer who would become his partner for a number of years— Antônio Carlos (Tom) Jobim. It was an association that would leave an indelible mark on Brazilian music.

Some of his literary friends looked with disapproval on Vinicius's incursion into the "pop" field. They insisted that what he was doing was inconsistent with the career of a serious poet. Vinicius reacted in a way that became a trademark: he made it clear that he could not care less what others thought of him, and that he would march to his own drummer.

The beat would evolve toward the end of the decade, as Vinicius joined the small nucleus of creative young Brazilians who followed the lead of a quirky musical genius named João Gilberto and gave the world a synthesis of samba and cool jazz known as bossa nova. This new musical form was a classic example of Brazilian anthropophagy. Gilberto began with the Afro-Brazilian beat of the samba, as refined by his fellow Bahian Dorival Caymmi, who superimposed on it rhythms produced by the fishermen and street vendors of the city of Salvador. Along with this style he digested American jazz, and what emerged was something fresh, beguiling, and distinctively Brazilian.

Up to that point popular music in Brazil had been under the controlling influence of instinctive musicians from the lower classes. Now people with university degrees began to bring sophistication to the pop music scene. Bossa nova reflected a different esthetic, rooted not in the *favelas* but in the comfortable apartments of the South Zone of Rio.

The new beat became a worldwide craze in large measure owing to the popularity of the motion picture adaptation of Vinicius's play *Orfeu da Conceição*. The French producers of the film, entitled *Orfeu Negro (Black Orpheus)*, decided not to use the songs performed in the stage version; instead they asked Vinicius and Tom Jobim (along with Luiz Bonfá) to compose new musical numbers. These songs were driven by the bossa nova beat that was catching fire in

Rio and São Paulo. Moviegoers everywhere found them irresistible.*

Vinicius was on a creative roll in the early 1960s. His songs were being performed by some of Brazil's best singers. He was working in collaboration with some of Brazil's best composers: besides Tom Jobim, among others there were Pixinguinha, a legendary figure in Brazilian popular music, and Ary Barroso, another idol best known for his classic song "Aquarela do Brasil" ("Brazil").

In 1962 Vinicius took another quantitative leap and began to perform in person before nightclub audiences. The fact that he was an active-duty official of the foreign service gave him a certain cachet and even more popular appeal. Throughout the many years he appeared on stages in Brazil and abroad, he sang and played his guitar with some notably talented partners.

In making the transition from serious poet to pop artist, Vinicius influenced a generation of university-educated musicians who saw that music designed for mass audiences could incorporate a considerable degree of sophistication. Caetano Veloso and Chico Buarque were in the forefront of the new movement.

Meanwhile, Vinicius became an avatar of the mood of liberation that reached Brazil in the 1960s. Letting his hair grow long, he preached (and practiced) sexual freedom. During his performances onstage, he drank heavily and openly from a bottle of Scotch. His political views remained progressive, so he was what might be termed a "left-wing hedonist." During the military dictatorship he did and said whatever he pleased, confident that his international fame would protect him. Finally, in 1969, he was expelled from the foreign service. On that occasion the president of Brazil, General Artur Costa e Silva, is said to have remarked, "Let that bum go to work."

Like Garrincha and Santos-Dumont, Vinicius did not worry about material things. He was completely carefree and insisted on doing things his own way (which meant in whatever way his mood

---

* Ironically, Vinicius hated the film. According to his daughter Susana, he stormed out of the premier at the Laranjeiras presidential palace in Rio in the middle of the screening, went home, and got roaringly drunk. He thought the movie presented a fake version of both Brazil and his play.

at the moment dictated), no matter what his friends advised him, to the point of that he sold for practically nothing the rights to his intellectual labors.*

In 1980, at the age of sixty-six, Vinicius died of natural causes in his bathtub, where he customarily drank whiskey, did his writing, and received visitors. He left behind a legacy of creative work that lives on, and an approach to life so direct and uncompromising, so charming and at the same time so exasperating that it is impossible to imagine him as anything other than Brazilian.

If Vinicius de Moraes was quintessentially Brazilian, Luiz Carlos Prestes embodied traits that were in certain respects antithetical to Brazilianness. Cerebral, organized, uncompromising, unemotional, impersonal, and puritanical, on paper he appears to be an implausible prospect for inclusion in the nation's gallery of immortals. Yet he achieved heroic status as the symbol of hope for Brazil's have-nots—an exalted position he maintained for six decades.

Contradictions among his devotees abounded, not the least of which was that the Brazilian nationalists who deified him saw no problem with his long years of loyal service to the Soviet Union. The Brazilian military, anticommunist to the core, could never completely cure itself of admiration for him. The Brazilian Communist party, which ostensibly placed principle above the "cult of personality," accepted the fact that without Prestes's popularity it would have limited appeal, and the party played a critical role in making a mythical figure out of him. And when Prestes died in 1990, no less a pillar of the establishment than Roberto Marinho wrote an editorial calling him a "brave revolutionary leader," and had these words read to the nation on the Globo network's evening news.

The man who one day would be known as the "Cavalier of Hope" was born in 1898 in Porto Alegre, the capital of Rio Grande do Sul, into a middle-class family of modest means. His father, an army officer, was transferred to Rio de Janeiro and brought his fam-

---

* His chaotic distribution of the rights to the songs in *Black Orpheus* has blocked a contemporary production of a musical play based on the film.

ily there with him. Several years later he died from illness, a tragedy that qualified his only son for admission to a military preparatory school. The boy was an excellent student and easily gained acceptance into the Military Academy in Rio de Janeiro.

Short and slender, Luiz Carlos did not have the physique of a soldier, but he was extremely bright and serious, and his willingness to help classmates with their studies made him popular with them. He graduated at the top of his class in 1920 and then received a commission in the army engineers. Two years later, having been assigned to a railroad-construction battalion, he became involved for the first time in a plot against the government.

Although the armed forces had been instrumental in the overthrow of the monarchy in 1889, after the first turbulent years of the Old Republic they had generally maintained a hands-off policy toward the civilian government that ruled Brazil.* But now discontent with the way government officials were treating the armed forces began to intensify. In addition, younger officers imbued with the positivist vision of progress and a sense of their own responsibility for the fate of the nation displayed impatience with what they saw as the corruption and incompetence of politicians and bureaucrats. The public came to know them as the *tenentes* (lieutenants).

In 1922 the *tenentes* sparked an easily suppressed rebellion in Rio de Janeiro. Lieutenant Luiz Carlos Prestes participated in the planning, but when the moment of truth arrived, an attack of typhoid fever kept him from the actual insurgency. As a result, his superiors never identified him as one of the conspirators. In 1924 he received an assignment with a railroad battalion in the interior of his home state, Rio Grande do Sul. He was at this post when a *tenente* rebellion broke out in São Paulo.

This time the insurgents had more success and managed to hold São Paulo for about three weeks. Meanwhile, revolts erupted in other parts of the country. Prestes, now a captain, led a column of troops northward, to the interior of the state of São Paulo, where

---

* One exception was a curious uprising in 1904, when cadets from the academy joined civilians in a revolt against a law making smallpox vaccinations compulsory. It was a vivid example of the influence wielded by the French positivist Auguste Comte, who vigorously opposed the newly developed smallpox vaccine.

they linked up with rebel forces that had been driven from the capital. At this point the revolutionaries numbered about fifteen hundred. Captain Prestes took command, and his troops set out on a march into both history and mythology—the two-and-a-half-year, fifteen-thousand-mile, thirteen-state odyssey of what would soon become known as the Prestes Column.

It was an incredible journey by any standard. The Column crisscrossed much of the vast interior of the country, from the edge of the Pantanal swamp in Mato Grosso to the tablelands of Goiás, into the bowels of the Northeast, across the Chapada Diamantina (Diamond Plateau) of central Bahia, and finally to the border of Bolivia. And it was the wiry, diminutive Captain Prestes, now sporting a bushy black beard, who held things together with the force of his personality, his intelligence, and his capacity to inspire fierce loyalty from the officers and men in his charge.

Prestes's goal was to inspire others to rise up against the government. But there were very few along the way who were sufficiently moved by the Column's exploits to follow suit. Moreover, when his troops reached the Northeast, the mass of impoverished backlanders who should have in theory flocked to his side generally kept their distance. They were not at all ready for revolutionary change, being easily persuaded by the local landowners to regard the rebels as their enemies. The fact that members of the Column occasionally treated them with cruelty fueled their hostility. Many of the outlaws in the region enlisted in the effort to repel the invaders, and there were occasional bloody clashes.

The Prestes Column eventually had to withdraw from the Northeast because of the armed resistance of the backlanders. Prestes's forces returned through Goiás and Mato Grosso and traversed the marshlands of the Pantanal. On February 26, 1927, the main body of men, now numbering 620, crossed into Bolivia and laid down their arms. About a month later, the remnants of the rebel force, 66 men, crossed into Paraguay.

Throughout its "long march," the goals of the Column remained vague. Prestes and his fellow *tenentes* issued various proclamations calling for honest elections, social legislation, and an end to corruption in government, excessive taxes, and political persecution, but this was hardly a coherent blueprint for renovation, and it is not surprising that the *tenentes* failed to attract broad segments of the population to their cause. But they did succeed in electrifying the nation, once word of their courage and dedication spread. As Neill Macauley, author of an excellent book on Prestes's "long march" put it, "In 1927 Brazil wanted heroes and not a revolution."

Once the revolt had ended, the press glorified the Prestes Column and it leader. Reporters for Assis Chateaubriand's newspaper, *O Jornal*, interviewed Prestes in Bolivia. Their stories helped feed a public demand for news about him. A leftist newspaper called him the "Cavalier of Hope," and the epithet stuck.

The *tenentes* became a strong political force in Brazil. Popular dissatisfaction with the government was cresting, and those seeking to force a change in direction found it expedient to court the survivors of the "long march." Of course, the big prize would be Prestes, and it was the Brazilian Communist party that took the most decisive and immediate steps to recruit him. A Communist leader traveled to Bolivia and brought Prestes books by Marx, Engels, and Lenin. In them the captain found a theoretical framework that was in accord with his revolutionary impulses, and he continued to study these revolutionary theorists after he moved on to Buenos Aires. Meanwhile, the Communist press in Brazil glorified him, to the point of commemorating his birthday each year.

The *tenentes* who had marched with Prestes returned to Brazil, and many of them joined the movement that eventually produced the revolution of 1930. Prestes remained aloof. In the end he proclaimed his opposition to the 1930 coup and formally applied for membership in the Communist party.

In 1931 Prestes, his mother, and his siblings went to Moscow. The Cavalier of Hope worked as an engineer there for several years, and while there he also rubbed elbows with revolutionaries from the four corners of the planet. He became a member of the executive committee of the Comintern (the international organization of Communist parties under Soviet control), and thereby joined with such luminaries as Mao Zedong, Italy's Palmiro Togliatti, and Spain's Dolores ("La Pasionaria") Ibarruri.

During his sojourn, leaders of the Brazilian Communist party sent to Moscow reports that were increasingly optimistic about the possibilities of armed revolution in Brazil. Soviet officials accepted their assessment at face value. This was a period during which the Comintern was debating the wisdom of adopting a policy of forming "popular fronts" with noncommunists who opposed the growth of fascism. The Comintern decided to encourage popular fronts in some Latin American countries, such as Chile, but to go ahead with armed revolution in Brazil. Luiz Carlos Prestes was ordered to return to his native land and take charge of efforts designed to pave the way for a "dictatorship of the proletariat."

The Soviets assigned an experienced agent to accompany Prestes. She was a German Jewess by birth, young, attractive, a committed Communist, fluent in four languages (but not Portuguese), an excellent shot, a pilot, and a parachutist. Her name was Olga Benario. She and Prestes were to travel as a married couple, even though she was already married to a Soviet official. On the ocean voyage from Brest to New York, the two fell in love; later they began to live together in an actual conjugal relationship. Prestes was thirty-seven. According to Olga's biographer, Fernando Morais, this was his first sexual experience with a woman.

Brazil's 1935 "revolution," which recently-released documents from Communist archives reveal was planned, financed, and directed from Moscow, turned out to be a colossal blunder. Loyalist troops easily crushed Communist-directed military revolts in Natal and Recife. Undaunted, Prestes ordered an uprising in Rio; it suffered the same fate. The fact that the rebels killed several army officers in the process of the uprising would have long-term implications, as it provided the basis for an implacable hatred of Communism within Brazil's armed forces.

Unlike those who planned the coup, the regime had excellent intelligence. Government security forces knew in advance virtually every move the rebels intended to make. When order was restored, Vargas unleashed a wave of repression. The Cavalier of Hope escaped detection for a while, but in the end the police tracked him down and surrounded the house in Rio where he and Olga were hiding. On March 5, 1936, both were arrested. At the time Olga was pregnant.

When the two were separated at police headquarters, it was the last time they saw each other. The Vargas regime deported Olga to Germany, where she delivered her child. She was eventually taken to a concentration camp and perished in a Nazi gas chamber in 1942.

Prestes was condemned to forty-seven years' imprisonment. The international Communist movement agitated ceaselessly for his release, and Jorge Amado wrote an adoring biography of him.* But it was not until World War II was drawing to a close in Europe that Vargas released Prestes from prison.

Broad segments of the population now regarded Prestes as a hero. They remembered the exploits of the Prestes Column, sympathized with him over the tragic death of Olga, and identified him with the wartime bravery of the Soviet people, on whose side Brazil had fought. Moreover, the Communists' intransigent opposition to the Vargas dictatorship had won the admiration of many of Brazil's intellectuals and students, and Prestes still embodied his party.

It came as a shock to many when the Cavalier of Hope spoke out in support of Getúlio while the rest of the opposition mobilized to force the leader's resignation. The Communists felt they were better off with Vargas remaining in power and committing himself to free elections than they would be under the rule of the military, which remained firmly anticommunist and would exert significant influence on any successor regime. Prestes even appeared on the same platform with the man who had delivered Olga over to the Nazis.† For the sentimental, personalizing Brazilians, this was a breathtaking display of discipline and commitment to a political cause, and they have never ceased to marvel at it.

---

* In 1979, with the reissuance of the biography, Amado stated in a new preface, "I feel proud to be the author of this book." Besides glorifying Prestes, it contained the following description of the USSR: ". . . friend, fatherland of the workers of the world, fatherland of science, of art, of culture, of beauty and of liberty. Fatherland of human justice."

Elected federal deputy on the Communist ticket in 1945, Amado broke with the party in the wake of Nikita Khrushchev's revelations about the horrors of Stalinism. After that Amado's novels became much less political, and he soon gained recognition as Brazil's most beloved and famous writer.

† Prestes had earlier appeared on a balcony of the American Embassy with U.S. Ambassador Adolf Berle in a tribute to Franklin D. Roosevelt, who had recently died.

Prestes and the Communists could not stop the military ouster of Vargas, but in the general elections on December 2, 1945, they were permitted to participate, and they succeeded as never before (and never since) in attracting voters. Their presidential candidate garnered 10 percent of the total, and Luiz Carlos Prestes won not only a seat in the Senate, but also (because of a peculiarity in Brazilian election law) seats in the Chamber of Deputies from four different states.

The onset of the cold war doomed Communist participation in Brazil's democratic process. The party was declared illegal, and its elected representatives were expelled from office. A major pretext was Prestes's statement that the Communists would oppose Brazilian participation in a hypothetical war between the United States and the USSR. The Cavalier of Hope went underground in 1948 and lived clandestinely in Brazil for ten years.

The government of Juscelino Kubitschek eased the restrictions on the Communist party, and Prestes resurfaced. In the 1960s he openly supported João Goulart and became a bête noire for Goulart's political opponents, who charged that the president's administration was being infiltrated by Communists. As they had done in 1935, Prestes and his party miscalculated their ability to influence events. When the military overthrew Goulart in 1964, the Communists once again paid dearly for their optimism.

Prestes escaped capture. Despite the fact that his name topped the first list of persons the dictatorship deprived of their rights as citizens, the armed forces did not make his arrest a priority. He repaired to São Paulo, where he lived clandestinely for seven years. Since neither he nor the Communist party supported armed insurrection at this time, the security forces left them alone and pursued those who were organizing urban and rural guerrilla warfare in Brazil (a strategy Prestes firmly opposed).

In 1971, when the military tightened its grip, Prestes once again slipped out of Brazil and made his way to Moscow. By this time he had a new wife, with whom he would eventually produce eight children, and he took his family with him. He returned to Brazil when the regime declared a general amnesty in 1979.

For five decades Luiz Carlos Prestes had faithfully followed the Communist party line, as dictated from Moscow. He was a devoted

Stalinist under Stalin, adjusted to the anti-Stalinism of Nikita Khrushchev, and supported the Soviet repression of uprisings in Hungary and Czechoslovakia. By the 1980s he had become an anachronism. Shortly after his arrival in Brazil he lost his position as secretary-general of the Brazilian Communist party, which he had held since the 1930s, and in 1984 he was expelled from the party.

In the last years of his life he criticized his former comrades but never spoke ill of the Soviet Union or the international Communist movement. He continued to make known his views on Brazilian politics, but his influence was minimal. Because he was by this time virtually penniless, architect Oscar Niemeyer, a longtime party member, provided him with financial support. Prestes died of a heart attack on March 7, 1990.

Although the Brazilian Communist party and its sympathizers, as well as the Soviet Union itself, labored diligently to expand and preserve the legendary aura of Luiz Carlos Prestes, it would be a mistake to regard his renown as an artificial construct. His courage, endurance, and persistence during the "long march" were qualities that understandably earned for him the undying admiration of his compatriots. The army, sorely in need of heroic figures, could not help but respect his remarkable feat. Civilians yearning for someone to lead the country out of the doldrums into which it had sunk during the 1920s were quick to accept him as the Cavalier of Hope.

Yet for nearly six decades Prestes dedicated his life unquestioningly to a totalitarian ideology that had little relevance to Brazil, Brazilians, and Brazilianness, and that ultimately collapsed of rot in its country of origin. Moreover, he committed serious strategic and tactical errors during his long tenure at the helm of the Brazilian Communist party.

In many ways Prestes embodied the opposite of Brazilianness, yet many Brazilians elevated him to the status of a lesser god. This might reflect a tendency to undervalue their own national character and to admire traits found in other peoples. The prestige Prestes enjoyed abroad—and his lionization by the international Communist movement—no doubt greatly impressed many of his compatriots. That there were no limits to his willingness to suffer for his principles, that he was perpetually becoming involved in lost causes, and that he suffered a horrible personal tragedy with the loss of Olga—all these details appealed to Brazilian sentimentality.

A proposed memorial to Prestes has set off a controversy among not only his political friends and enemies but also among his children. Projected to cost about $300,000, designed by Oscar Niemeyer, and planned for Rio's Barra de Tijuca (a chic neighborhood far removed from any working-class district), it has a ground plan that faintly resembles a hammer and sickle.*

That Luiz Carlos Prestes and Xuxa, the TV star worshiped by millions of Brazilian children, would have anything in common might seem far-fetched, but both share not only a birthplace in Rio Grande do Sul but also fathers who as career army officers brought their families to Rio de Janeiro as a result of military assignments. At that point the similarities come to an abrupt halt.

Maria da Graça Meneghel, known professionally as Xuxa (pronounced *Shoo*-shah), is a megacelebrity in the eyes of the preteen set, not only in Brazil but throughout Latin America. In addition to starring on her own morning TV program five times a week, the tall, pigtailed blonde is a mini-industry, churning out records, making films, doing live shows, and licensing her name for use on dolls, stuffed animals, games, articles of clothing, yogurt, cosmetics, and posters. What makes her success remarkable is that the spell she casts over Brazil's children has an unmistakably erotic tinge to it.

The *Xou de Xuxa (Xuxa Show)* is a chaotic blend of songs, dances, games, cartoons, and general frenzy, presided over by a young hostess who connects with her live audience, and the millions watching her all over Brazil, by behaving as a child and exuding a carefree innocence that almost, but not quite, camouflages the sexiness that once made her a successful model and the starlet in a soft-porn

---

* Niemeyer likes *épater la bourgeoisie* (to shock the middle class), as the French would say. The design of his Memorial to Juscelino Kubitschek in Brasília also conjures up a suggestion of the Communist symbol. Moreover, according to some Brazilians, the arch the architect conceived for the Apotheosis Plaza at the end of the Sambadrome in Rio, where the annual Carnival parade ends, recalls the shape of a woman's buttocks.

film. Clad in boots, hot pants that flatter her shapely rump, and a jacket often sequined and shortened to reveal her midriff, she prances and wiggles, shouts with glee, and bestows generous kisses that leave the mark of her bright-red lipstick on the *baixinhos,* or "shorties," as she calls the youngsters who crowd the stage behind her, fill the auditorium in front of her, and gaze lovingly at her image on the TV screen.

Little girls imitate her way of dressing; little boys send her adoring fan mail; fathers watch her whenever they can; and critics fulminate that she is prematurely stimulating the sexual drives of Brazilian children. One unflattering commentary in the *Jornal do Brasil* compared Xuxa and her fans with Snow White and the latter's seven "shorties"; both women, according to the authors, project a "masturbatory, infantilized fantasy."*

The story of Xuxa began in 1963 in the little town of Santa Rosa. Her mother, who liked to give her children unusual names, had been planning to christen her next child Ivanhoé Jandrei, if a boy, or Morgana Saionara, if a girl, but because the birth was a difficult one, she chose a more traditional, religious appellation, Maria da Graça (Mary Full of Grace). Maria's two older brothers bestowed upon their new sister the nickname Xuxa, and it stuck.

It was after the close-knit family's move to Rio de Janeiro that its youngest member grew into a stunning teenager. Her flaxen hair and blue-green eyes, the legacy of German and Polish ancestors, caused heads to turn, and one day a man began to follow her. Terrified, Xuxa hurried home. The doorbell rang. It was her pursuer, a photographer from *Manchete* magazine. The rest, as they say, is history.

In 1979, at the age of sixteen, Xuxa launched a modeling career that would put her face on the covers of fifty-nine magazines two years later. She also posed in the nude, a common practice in the profession. Her fresh-faced looks and innocence intensified the sexuality she projected. Her looks proved irresistible to Pelé when the two appeared together on a magazine cover, and soon the mists

---

* Xuxa has been the target of much overheated, convoluted criticism, mostly from intellectuals who blame her for such misdeeds as reinforcing racism, sexism, and mindless consumerism in Brazil.

of romance enveloped the former "King of Soccer" and the future "Queen of the Shorties."

In 1982 Xuxa made her motion picture debut in *Amor Estranho Amor* (Love Strange Love), in which she played a young prostitute whom a prepubescent boy secretly observes nude and making love to a customer. Several years later Xuxa was presented with another opportunity to perform before prepubescents when the young Manchete TV network, whose owner also published magazines that often featured Xuxa, decided to make her the hostess of a children's program.

At first she was awkward, uncomfortable, and even rude to the children, but Manchete stuck with her and she soon developed an unusual rapport with her young viewers. Instead of talking down to them, as many performers on Brazilian children's TV shows did, Xuxa managed to become one of them. She learned to enter their world, connect with their interests, and speak their language.

The rise in her ratings did not go unnoticed, and soon the powerful Globo network hired her away from their upstart competitor. Roberto Marinho's communications empire gave her much greater national exposure, and children from the four corners of Brazil soon developed a ravenous craving for the indefatigable Xuxa and her trademark mantra, *"Beijinho, beijinho"* ("Kissie, kissie"). Her program played five mornings a week for more than four hours.

Astute business advice from her manager, Marlene Mattos, enabled Xuxa to keep control of her persona and her career. Anyone using her name without her permission could expect a lawsuit. Marlene created Xuxa Promotions, Inc., and several other companies to handle Xuxa's various spin-off enterprises, and later set up Xuxa's own charitable foundation. Xuxa's records sold in the millions, and permission to use her name on a product or service guaranteed booming sales.

At a time when the motion picture industry in Brazil had all but disappeared because the federal government had stopped subsidizing it, Xuxa made movies that attracted the "shorties" in droves and turned profits. The films were generally simple-minded fare, but one of them had some subtle cinematic touches betraying the hand of its director, Tizuka Yamasaki.

Xuxa soon became a multinational enterprise. She began to make television shows and recordings in Spanish and to target youth audiences in the rest of Latin America. The Spanish-language programs attracted a vast new audience and even penetrated the market in the United States. In 1991 she placed thirty-seventh on *Forbes* magazine's list of show business' top earners, just behind Sylvester Stallone, Arsenio Hall, and author Tom Clancy, and just ahead of Mel Gibson and Matt Groening (creator of *The Simpsons*). Two years later, she had vaulted to twenty-eighth place, leaving in her wake such luminaries as Harrison Ford, Clint Eastwood, and Andrew Lloyd Webber. In 1992 *People* magazine listed her among the world's fifty most beautiful people.

Throughout her meteoric rise, Xuxa remained a simple, rather lonely soul, eschewing cigarettes and alcoholic beverages, and always wearing her heart on her sleeve. Her relationship with Pelé came to an end, and she then took up for a while with auto racer Ayrton Senna. She lived in a Rio mansion with only her fifteen dogs for steady company.

This phase of her life ended abruptly in August of 1991, when Rio's ubiquitous violence touched her directly. Only thirty yards from a studio where she was in the process of taping her TV show, two men parked an automobile stocked with weapons and tear-gas bombs. Police discovered them, and in an exchange of gunfire, one of the suspected kidnappers was killed and the other critically wounded. A distraught Xuxa immediately abandoned Brazil for Buenos Aires. She returned regularly to record her program but established her residence in the Argentine capital.

Hoping to hit the jackpot in the land of Uncle Sam, Xuxa launched a syndicated television program for children in the United States in 1993. But her failure to master English created an awkwardness that reduced the show's appeal to young people, and since the puritanical predisposition of North American society forced her to turn off much of her sex appeal, she was unable to capitalize on what helped make her a megastar in Brazil.

The sensual vibrations Xuxa projects and their impact on Brazilian children are part and parcel of Brazilian sexuality, which has somehow managed to reconcile the carefree attitude inherent in the popular saying "There is no sin south of the equator" with a repressive, patriarchal social structure that exalts both virility and virginity. The manifestations of eroticism emerging from such sources as the mass displays of flesh to be seen during Carnival, the popularity of a bathing suit known as the *fio dental*, or "dental floss" (an indication of how much female flesh it covers), television commercials for undergarments, and the Xuxa Show reflect a peculiarly Brazilian attitude toward sex that is much less permissive than it appears.

One possible explanation for this contradiction posits that Brazilians are exibitionists about sex and sexuality. A European-born resident of Rio de Janeiro described how a delegation of her neighbors came to her to ask that her seven-year-old daughter stop going around naked to the waist. The woman added, "But if she put a flower on her ear and danced, everyone would watch and be delighted." Thus the costumes and cavortings of both Xuxa and her youthful imitators may amount to the sort of exhibitionism that one sees on beaches throughout the year and on streets during Carnival, and this exhibitionism may be acceptable because it serves as a means of escaping from pressures imposed by traditional values.

Xuxa herself has shrugged off complaints. At one point she poked fun at her critics by creating the character of a sex-education teacher on her program. But she dropped the bit when she undertook an explanation of how babies came out of their mother's body, and a little boy asked her how they got in. On another occasion, when queried by a reporter about the sexiness of the youngsters appearing on her show, she replied, "If they're sensual, it's because they were born that way." An American who lived for several years in Rio disputes that notion and attributes to the influence of the Xuxa Show the behavior of her three-year-old daughter, who once sidled up to a mirror in a department store, tucked up her shorts, and asked, "Mommy, do you think I've got a pretty *bumbum* [Brazilian slang for "buttocks"]?"

The city of Niterói faces Rio de Janeiro across the waters of Guanabara Bay, a distant backdrop that gives the impression of being an afterthought in the overall design of things. On December 17, 1961, it provided the setting for one of those mass disasters that occur in

Brazil from time to time, when a circus tent caught fire during a performance and collapsed on 2,500 trapped spectators, most of them children. A surgeon from a Rio hospital rushed to the scene by boat and helped treat the hundreds of burn victims. He worked day and night without rest, doing what he could to save lives (323 were lost), and then later to repair horribly disfiguring injuries.

In his autobiography, Ivo Pitanguy describes this experience as altering the course of his destiny. He was already a plastic surgeon at the time, but he claimed that working with the survivors of the circus fire brought home to him that physical appearance could be as important as life itself, an insight that dawned on him when some of his patients expressed a wish to die when they saw how deformed they had become. He concluded that cosmetic surgery was as important as reconstructive surgery, rather than a poor relation meriting the neglect and even disdain of his professon.

The Niterói calamity and the sudden conversion it supposedly triggered furnish drama befitting the curriculum vitae of a man *Time* magazine once described as "theatrically handsome," a personality who has fused professional skill and panache to create an aura that has placed him close to Pelé at the top of any list of Brazilian celebrities—indeed, a quasi-divine dispenser of beauty and youthful looks.* Yet if the story of Pitanguy's reaction to the circus fire is true, it contains a certain irony, since it means that the suffering of badly scarred slum children served as the catalyst for his rise to worldwide fame as a "cutaneous cutter" to the international jet set.

Harold Robbins has mentioned Ivo Pitanguy in one of his novels. The *New York Times* has made him the subject of an extended profile (entitled "Dr. Vanity"). An American cable network featured him in a TV documentary, "The Man with the Golden Touch." Jimmy Carter stayed with him on the island Pitanguy owns off the coast of Angra dos Reis when the U.S. President visited Brazil. Sev-

---

* Since Dr. Pitanguy was already an established plastic surgeon at the time, his flare for the dramatic may have caused a bit of exaggeration here. One cannot be too critical of Pitanguy's poetic license, however; his autobiography and his 425-page treatise on plastic surgery gained for him election to the Brazilian Academy of Letters.

eral Brazilian *telenovelas* have featured characters loosely based on
him. A Rio samba school has used his image to adorn one of its
enormous floats in the annual Carnival parade. Vinicius de Moraes
once coined the verb *"pitanguizar"* (to change face). In one of its
advertisements American Express has run a photo of him holding
a mirror to his face as he sits by the sea and gazes intently at the
statue of an ancient goddess.

Ivo Pitanguy is a hero to those who have benefited from his
prodigious skills with the scalpel. This group includes patients bearing natural or inflicted disfigurements that keep them from functioning in society, as well as people fortunate enough to be able to
afford elective treatment designed to improve their appearance or
postpone the aging process. Yet he is much more than a successful
plastic surgeon. By virtue of the force of his personality and the
life he has chosen to lead apart from the practice of surgery, he
has become a symbol of Rio de Janeiro's upper class, despite the
fact that he was not born into it and in many ways is atypical of
*carioca* high society.

Rio de Janeiro has become a mecca for cosmetic surgery. A recent newspaper account estimates that about two thousand aesthetic operations a month are performed there, at an annual cost
of $120 million. (Indeed, the city has more plastic surgeons than
public-health physicians.) Women of means regularly resort to cosmetic surgery, and even middle-class women eager to imitate their
social superiors often use their savings to seek help from one of
the many practitioners who perform face-lifts, tummy tucks, and
other surgical alterations of body parts.

In part this demand for plastic surgery reflects the influence of
the city's beaches, where life is a perennial beauty contest and increasingly skimpy beachwear leaves nothing to the imagination.
The Brazilian concept of beauty grants elevated status to small
breasts and well-shaped buttocks, features that can be obtained, or
at least approximated, by artificial means. Moreover, the exulta-
tion of youthfulness, a legacy of the tropics and long an element
of Brazilianness, provides yet another incentive for resorting to cosmetic surgery.

There is a suggestion here of a certain shallowness, which Warren Hoge underscored in his aforementioned *New York Times* pro-

file of Pitanguy, when he wrote: "Looks count for almost everything in Rio society because very little else is in contention. . . . One can spend long sunny days on the beaches and at the clubs where the rich idle and never see anyone reading."

Thus it is hardly surprising that Rio has produced the world's foremost plastic surgeon. Yet the Professor, as Pitanguy prefers to be called, is not a *carioca* by birth, but rather a *mineiro* (from the state of Minas Gerais), and far from being an empty bathing suit—if that is a proper symbol for Rio's leisure class—he is a complex, driven, highly talented individual who has labored long and hard both to earn his status and to shape his image as one of Brazil's lesser gods.

Just as fun-loving *cariocas* are a product of their lush environment, *mineiros* bear the imprint of the mountains that fill their home state and isolate its communities. *Mineiros* tend to be cautious, steady, distrustful, and averse to emotional extremes. They also shun extravagance, a trait that has earned for them the reputation of being tight-fisted, or *"pão duro"* (an expression referring to people who keep bread until it hardens). Minas Gerais has generated an intense religiosity and is perhaps more Catholic than any other state in the country. It produced Brazil's first serious independence movement and the first military uprising against the government of João Goulart. Minas Gerais has given Brazil Pelé, Juscelino Kubitschek, Tiradentes, singer Milton Nascimento, novelist João Guimarães Rosa,* and sculptor Aleijadinho.

As Ivo Pitanguy once put it, the rough terrain of his home state has forced its inhabitants to realize that "behind each mountain is still another mountain." This insight motivates *mineiros* to think ahead carefully, to be modest about their accomplishments, and to go forward relentlessly toward bigger and better things rather than to be content with the horizon before them—all of which are qualities that the Professor has demonstrated.

---

* One of Brazil's greatest writers, João Guimarães Rosa was a country doctor turned diplomat who captured the language, rhythm, color, and magic of the *mineiro* interior in his masterpiece *Grande Sertão: Veredas* (translated into English as *The Devil to Pay in the Backlands*).

Belo Horizonte, the capital of the state, was his birthplace in 1926, but he was brought up in Diamantina, 180 miles to the north, in the diamond-mining region. His father was a general surgeon, his mother a devotee of literature and art. A very competitive boy (perhaps owing to his lack of height), he excelled at swimming and tennis. Although he fainted the first time he watched his father perform surgery, he resolved to attend medical school, and he gained early entry by lying about his age.

Compulsory military service interrupted his studies and took him to Rio de Janeiro, and like many other *mineiros,* he felt a strong attraction to the "River of January." He eventually completed his medical studies there, doing his internship in an emergency room. Two years of study abroad at the Bethesda Hospital in Cincinnati brought him into contact with Dr. John Longacre, a reconstructive surgeon who taught him that plastic surgery can serve important humanitarian and aesthetic functions, and that the notion that people should accept whatever deformities nature or trauma has inflicted on them is anachronistic. After a brief interlude in Rio, Pitanguy set off for France and England, where he studied plastic surgery with pioneering practitioners in the new field. He was now ready to return to Brazil and set up his own school.

In 1953 he began performing plastic surgery at the Santa Casa de Misericórdia Hospital and assembling a team to work with him. Eight years later he experienced the Niterói circus fire, and shortly thereafter he inaugurated a twenty-three-room private clinic in the neighborhood of Botafogo, where he began to assemble and train a team of specialists, and to perform cosmetic surgery on patients eager to improve their appearance, and willing to pay handsomely for what would become known as the Pitanguy touch. Soon his name would become a household word not only in Rio but throughout the world.

Although Pitanguy maintains absolute silence about the identity of his patients, enough of them have talked about their visits to his clinic (and the press has dug up enough names) that it is possible to get a sense of the type of clientele he has attracted. Anita Ekberg, Zsa Zsa Gabor, Gina Lollobrigida, the former empress of Iran, ballerina Natalia Makarova, actress-politician Melina Mercouri, the Duchess of Windsor, Ultra Violet, and Viva are among those on the list. After suffering serious accidents, actress Marisa Berensen and race-car driver Niki Lauda went to Pitanguy for reconstructive surgery.* He speaks six languages fluently, which enables him to communicate with many of his foreign patients in their native tongue.

The artist in Pitanguy comes to the fore in his approach to cosmetic surgery. He insists that there is beauty inside everyone, and that a little help from his scalpel will make it visible. On the other hand, he also realizes that unlike the painter or the sculptor, he must work within certain physical limitations the Creator has imposed on individual men and women.

Pitanguy's broad face, bushy eyebrows, and big brown eyes appear often on the society pages of Rio's newspapers, and the gossip columnists chronicle his comings and goings assiduously. He participates so actively in the city's social whirl that people often identify him with the leisure-class patients to whom he frequently ministers. Indeed, the Carnival float bearing his likeness had a caption reading "Champagne, Caviar and Pitanguy."

However, Pitanguy's frenetic lifestyle and the breadth of his interests set him apart from most of Rio's elite. He is a patron of the arts, an avid skier, a voracious reader, a pilot, the holder of a black belt in karate, and a conservationist. He has converted his private island into a nature preserve where he has gathered various species of birds and animals. In addition, unlike many members of Brazil's leisure class, Pitanguy has a social conscience, and it motivates him to spend one day a week operating free of charge at a public hospital.

Ivo Pitanguy's entry into the galaxy of Brazil's lesser gods suggests how international fame can excite the esteem of Brazilians of every social class. Moreover, the man and his environment are a perfect fit, since it is difficult to imagine him performing plastic surgery procedures, cavorting, and starring in any other venue except Rio de Janeiro.

---

* In the TV documentary about Pitanguy, a grateful Lauda comments: "He did more than I asked him to do."

# Chapter 18

# The *Telenovela*
## *A National Obsession*

*F*rom June 24, 1985, until February 21, 1986, the whole of Brazil was held in thrall by the tale of a small town that had become rich and famous because of the reputation of a local martyr but stood to lose everything when the supposedly dead saint returned home to reveal himself as alive and altogether unsaintly. Weekdays and Saturdays just before 8:30 P.M., restaurants, bars, theaters, and cinemas emptied. Telephone lines fell silent, and Brazilians from Belém to Porto Alegre sat transfixed in front of their television sets, as the continuing saga of *Roque Santeiro (Roque the Saint-Maker)* unfolded.

The setting for the Globo network's hit *telenovela* was a small town called Asa Branca somewhere in the hinterlands of Brazil. The story line went like this: Seventeen years have passed since a young man who made a humble living carving images of saints lost his life while defending the town against bandits. The killers threw the body of Roque Santeiro into a river, and it was never recovered. Then a sick girl claimed that she saw him rise from the waters and that the apparition miraculously cured her. The common folk began to venerate the dead man as a saint, and Asa Branca, like some giant magnet, began to draw pilgrims from all over the country. But the sudden, mysterious reappearance of Roque threatened to undermine the foundation on which the town's prosperity rested.

Among the nearly forty characters were Asa Branca's ruthless political boss, a wealthy landowner who has been pretending that his mistress married Roque Santeiro just before his death, in order to profit from her status as a town celebrity; Roque's real sweetheart, who has remained faithful to him; the owner of a factory that produces medallions with Roque's likeness on them; the weak-kneed mayor of Asa Branca and his domineering wife; an old priest who defends traditional Catholicism and a young priest committed to the cause of social justice; the owner of the town bordello; and members of a television crew in town to make a film about Roque.

The remarkable success of *Roque Santeiro*, which earned audience ratings that from time to time reached 100 percent, stemmed from, first of all, the superb quality of its script, direction, and cast. Its author was Alfredo Dias Gomes, one of Brazil's most talented dramatists. Some of the country's best actors and actresses lent lustre to the *telenovela*'s colorful characters.

In addition *Roque Santeiro* appeared at a pivotal moment in the life of the country. Brazil was in the process of emerging from two decades of authoritarian rule and was struggling to find itself. The *telenovela*, with its biting satire of small-town corruption and hypocrisy, gentle spoof on Brazilian mysticism, and deft incorporation of topical concerns, struck viewers as holding a mirror to Brazilian society. Even the ending, which permitted the villain to depart unrepentant and unpunished, seemed typically Brazilian. As a bellhop in a Salvador hotel observed, "We see ourselves and our reality in it."

Finally, there was the element of curiosity. The Globo network had actually begun filming episodes of *Roque Santeiro* in 1975, but the military regime's censors would not permit the series to be televised because they considered it an "offense to public morality and a threat to national security." As the regime eased restrictions on what Brazilians could watch on television, viewers clearly relished a taste of previously forbidden fruit.

The *Roque Santeiro* phenomenon brought renewed attention to an art form that had attained the level of a national institution. Some observers hailed the *telenovela* as the consummate articulation of popular culture in Brazil; others complained that the *telenovela* was in fact destroying the ways in which Brazil's common people expressed themselves artistically, and that it was implanting hollow values throughout the country.

Both sides of the debate shared the assumption that *telenovelas* were having a significant impact on Brazilian society from top to bottom. There was also general agreement that these television programs were affecting the way the rest of the world looked at Brazil, because the Globo network was aggressively exporting its distinctive *telenovelas* to 128 countries.

An understanding of Brazilian *telenovelas* (or *novelas*, to use the shortened expression) must begin with the recognition that it would be misleading to call them soap operas, a term that conveys a particular meaning to North Americans. The *novelas* have a beginning, a linear plot, and an ending, as opposed to American "soaps," which are virtually interminable. *Telenovelas* reach television screens six nights a week over an eight-month (or longer) span during prime time, whereas in the United States soap operas are televised either every weekday afternoon or once a week during prime time. *Novelas* may be romantic, tragic, or comic (and occasionally all three). They may deal with contemporary or historical themes. Or their plots may derive from classics of Brazilian literature, such as the novels of Machado de Assis or Jorge Amado. And they have had a cultural impact, both nationally and internationally, far beyond anything the U.S. soaps have been able to effect.

In Brazil, where fact operates on several discrete levels, the *telenovela* often merges with or supersedes reality. For example, when the death throes of President-elect Tancredo Neves paralyzed the entire country in 1985, there were those who were convinced that the dramatic events filling television screens were part of a *telenovela*. As Alex Shoumatoff points out in his absorbing book *The World Is Burning*, when rubber tapper Chico Mendes was assassinated, there were those who thought that the killer might be the same person who had murdered a leading character on a popular *novela* that was being broadcast at the time.

But perhaps the most astonishing blending of life and the art of the *novela* occurred on December 28, 1992, when police discovered the body of Daniela Perez, punctured eighteen times with a pair of scissors, on a road above the Rio neighborhood of Barra de Tijuca. The twenty-two-year-old actress had been appearing in *De Corpo e Alma (With Body and Soul)*, a very popular *novela* written by her mother. Indeed, several hours before she was murdered, she had filmed a scene in which her character had angrily broken up with her boyfriend, a jealous, violent, and possessive punk rocker. When the actor who played the boyfriend and his nineteen-year-old pregnant wife were arrested for the crime, the country obsessed on the incident. Even the announced resignation of President Collor the day after the murder seemed to fade into irrelevance.*

*Telenovelas* serve a validating function. The late Cláudio Abramo, a distinguished São Paulo journalist, claimed in a 1987 interview that "many people here realized there was torture [during the military regime] only after they heard about it on *Roda de Fogo* [a *novela*]." The popularity of *Pantanal*, a Manchete network *telenovela* about the struggle to protect the ecology of the great Pantanal marshlands of central Brazil, did more to raise public awareness about conservation than all prior agitation on the part of the country's environmentalists.

The addictive appeal of the *telenovelas* has become a kind of glue that binds together the disparate elements of Brazilian society. Residents of shacks in frontier towns in Amazônia and high-rise apartments in São Paulo, wealthy matrons and humble maids, children and their grandparents, attorneys and janitors (and even many intellectuals who insist that they despise television) all share a common fascination with the characters and the plot convolutions of hit *novelas*. One French writer has dubbed this phenomenon "a strange and fleeting televisual democracy."

Being very communicative individuals who love to chat with neighbors and friends at home, through open windows, on the street, in the beauty parlor, or at the beach, Brazilians everywhere have made the characters of the *telenovelas* a major source of their daily gossip. Moreover, as talented television director Guel Arraes once noted wryly, "*Telenovelas* are the great aspirin of Brazil." People have become so dependent on them that they feel deprived and

---

* The actor, who in real life had reportedly worked as a male prostitute in Belo Horizonte and an exotic dancer in a Rio drag show, confessed to the murder and then accused his wife. The press speculated first that there was a romantic involvement between the actor and his victim, and then that the killing was part of a satanic rite. The victim's character was written out of *De Corpo e Alma* by having her accept a job offer to work on a Caribbean island.

upset, and complain vehemently whenever one of the *telenovelas* does not live up to the standards they have come to expect.

The *novelas* have also become an integral part of the national culture, for better or for worse. The most successful of them convey the aspirations and concerns of large segments of the population. Critics who complain that *novelas* manufacture the aspirations and concerns of the viewing public with some hidden agenda in mind are overestimating the manipulative powers of the medium. *Roque Santeiro* was clearly a reflection of what was in many people's minds at the time, as was *Vale Tudo (Anything Goes)*, a subsequent Globo series that matched *Roque's* ratings by capturing the mood of cynicism that was gripping the country at the time.

It is, of course, true that *novelas* promote consumerism in numerous ways, from the luxurious Rio and São Paulo lifestyles they often depict to the not very subliminal product advertising that is woven ceaselessly and shamelessly into their plot lines. They have also affected the way people throughout Brazil talk and dress, and have influenced tastes in popular music by their insinuating use of theme songs.

But the link between the *telenovela* and its audience is perhaps better described as interactive, since the impact of the *novela* on viewers is matched by the impact of viewers on the *novela*. The networks use polling and specially organized discussion groups to determine how viewers are reacting to a program in progress. Depending on the viewer response, there may be script alterations, and the roles of characters may be expanded or contracted depending on their popularity.

A more serious charge is that the *telenovela* is destroying the ways Brazil's lower classes express themselves. Brazilian popular culture has been amazingly rich, especially in rural areas, where traditions rooted in the country's Portuguese, African, and Indian past have survived intact or have blended to produce new forms. As television has spread to the far corners of the land, viewing is consuming leisure time that used to be spent on these cultural pursuits. As a result, there has been a marked decline in creative activities such as the production of *cordel* literature, the narrative folk poetry that is composed by literate or semiliterate poets mainly from the Northeast, printed in cheap booklets, and sold in market-places, bus and railroad stations, and public plazas.

Of course, it would be unfair to place all the blame for this decline on the *telenovela*. The inexorable process of modernization and the population shift from countryside to city probably bear a much greater responsibility. Indeed, if the *telenovela* did not exist, there would be other new forms of distraction that would have a similar impact.

Like most elements of popular culture, the *telenovela* is the result of a process of evolution. Its roots date back to the feuilleton, or serialized novel, which was highly popular in nineteenth-century France. Technical advances in printing and increases in levels of literacy, especially within the middle class, contributed to the success of these tales of romance and adventure, which appeared in newspapers and pamphlets. The feuilleton also crossed the Atlantic and found an avid readership in Brazil and other parts of Latin America. Most of the Brazilian versions were translations from the French.

The advent of radio in the United States produced an unrelated yet parallel phenomenon, when the need to attract daytime audiences composed mainly of housewives triggered the development of what came to be known as the soap opera, pioneered by corporations seeking to market, by the most cost-effective means possible, detergents and similar household products. The soap opera differed from the feuilleton in that it continued indefinitely and did not tell one principal story.

The same companies that were instrumental in inventing the soap opera in the United States transplanted this type of radio programming to Latin America. The most fertile new market turned out to be in Cuba, because its proximity to the United States made the island nation highly vulnerable to North American influence, and because Cuba was the Latin American country with the largest number of radio sets. What was called a *radionovela* went out over the Cuban airwaves for the first time in 1935 and captivated large numbers of listeners. The *radionovela* blended the structure of the soap opera with the tradition of the feuilleton, which had a long history in Cuba. The Cubans soon became so skilled at pro-

ducing *radionovelas* that they began to export them to the rest of
Latin America.

The genre, however, went through a process of adaptation in
Latin hands. Elements of the feuilleton found their way into the
*radionovelas,* the plots of which tended to be much more romantic
and melodramatic than the U.S. soap operas. Before long the emergence of a "Latin formula" could be detected. The American companies that sponsored the programs throughout the region
maintained control over them but realized that they were dealing
with a distinctive audience, so they allowed their soaps to be Lati-
nized.

In Brazil the first *radionovela* arrived in São Paulo in 1941. It
was an Argentine production, sponsored by Colgate-Palmolive.
That same year a Rio station aired the translation of a Cuban *radio-*
*novela.* Soon these programs were staples of Brazilian broadcasting.

When television began to replace radio as the preeminent instrument of mass communication, logic dictated that the *radionovela*
would assume a visual form. The same corporate advertisers that
underwrote radio soaps in Latin America pushed ahead with the
development of the *telenovela.* It was a relatively cheap type of programming, since the same set and cast could be used repeatedly
over an extended period of time. It would fill the same daytime
hours as the *radionovelas,* and with luck it would attract and hold
the same kind of audience. Cuba became the center of *telenovela*
production for all of Latin America, as this type of programming
became as popular as the *radionovela.* Argentina and Mexico were
vigorous competitors and picked up the slack when the revolution
of 1960 disrupted the filming of *novelas* in Cuba.

In 1951 a São Paulo television station brought a *telenovela* to
Brazilian viewers for the first time. It may not have been love at
first sight, but at this point in time there were very few television
sets in use, and television was, in the words of one writer, "an elec-
tronic toy for Brazilian elites." However, over the next twelve years
São Paulo channels televised an average of about fourteen *novelas*
annually. Most were either purchased from Argentina or Mexico
and dubbed into Portuguese, or produced locally from Argentine
or Mexican scripts.

These programs generally aired only twice a week, and each chapter lasted about twenty minutes. The made-in-Brazil *novelas* were telecast live and were low budget, so there were all kinds of imperfections. The actors often came from radio, so they were much better at conveying emotion verbally than with the physicality that a visual medium demanded.

In July 1963 Brazilian viewers in Rio and São Paulo were for the first time treated to a *novela* televised on a daily basis. *2-5499 Ocupado (Line 2-5499 Is Busy)* told the story of a man who fell in love with a prison telephone operator, without ever seeing her face or knowing she was a convict. It was a case of history repeating itself: as with the first *radionovela* to be broadcast in Brazil, this groundbreaking *telenovela* was of Argentine origin and was sponsored by Colgate-Palmolive.

The shift to a daily format reflected a hope of replicating the success enjoyed by daily *telenovelas* in Argentina. It was also a way of catering to a mass audience, because the number of TV sets in use in Brazil had passed the one million mark. Shortly afterward, Brazilian producers decided to lengthen *telenovelas* from four to six weeks to eight to ten months, a change the marketing implications of which pleased Colgate-Palmolive and other foreign companies selling soap and dental products in Brazil. Also each episode was expanded, eventually stabilizing at about fifty minutes.

It did not take long for these changes to pay handsome dividends. In 1964 TV Tupi of São Paulo, part of the Chateaubriand chain, scored a smash hit with the melodramatic *O Direito de Nascer (The Right to Be Born)*, originally a Cuban *radionovela* and first broadcast in Brazil back in the 1950s. It depicted the travails of a bastard son who is rejected and threatened by his moralistic grandfather. He is rescued by the family maid, who takes him to another town and raises him. Finally he gains ultimate vindication when, after becoming a physician, he saves the life of his grandfather.

Although set in agrarian, preindustrial Cuba, *Direito* struck a chord with Brazilian viewers. Some named their sons after the leading man. The use of toilets fell off dramatically while the show was on the air. When the *novela* came to an end, rallies filled indoor stadiums in Rio and São Paulo. Succumbing to mass hysteria, the crowds wept and chanted the names of the *novela*'s characters.

With the popularity of the *novela* now demonstrated beyond cavil, the genre underwent a crucial process of adaptation with the televising of *Beto Rockfeller*, a TV Tupi production that is generally credited with being the first significantly Brazilianized *telenovela*. Running from November 1968 to November 1969, it featured a typical Brazilian rogue (a São Paulo shoe salesman passing himself off as a millionaire), used Brazilian colloquialisms, and brought to life the contemporary urban scene in Brazil. In place of the heavy melodrama of the standard Latin American *novela*, it substituted wit and satire. Instead of starring a brave, romantic, idealized hero, it offered as its title character a deceitful social climber. And it was the first *telenovela* to use musical themes for each of its main characters.

*Beto Rockfeller* had its flaws. The *novela* ran for too long, characters occasionally disappeared from the plot because the actors who played them went on holiday, and the writing was uneven. Yet it offered an unmistakable glimpse into the future of the Brazilian *telenovela*.

TV Tupi was unable to replicate its hit. At this point the Chateaubriand empire was in an advancing state of creative as well as financial disarray, which produced increasingly frequent flashes of incompetence. The TV Tupi people proved incapable of identifying and reproducing the elements that had endeared *Beto Rockfeller* to Brazilian TV viewers.

It was a competitor network that fully understood the lessons of TV Tupi's hit and how to take full advantage of them. The rise of Roberto Marinho's Rede Globo has been described in some detail in Chapter Six. The economic strength and technical know-how of the new chain of TV stations enabled the network to nudge aside the foreign advertisers that had been exercising substantial control over the production of *telenovelas* and other aspects of TV programming in Brazil.

In pursuit of as large and wide an audience as possible, the Globo people did their homework. They knew that they had to draw on themes and develop approaches with which a Brazilian mass audience could identify. The serialized novel was an obvious type of programming that could serve Globo's purposes, and *Beto Rockfeller* had demonstrated what type of *novela* could dominate the ratings.

By not stinting on expenses, the Globo network was able to hire the best directors, writers, and actors and to construct a state-of-the-art facility in the Jardim Botánico neighborhood of Rio de Janeiro. The emphasis at Rede Globo was on quality and professionalism, and the other networks found themselves unable even to approximate the standards being set by Globo.

In the 1970s *telenovelas* produced by Globo totally swept the field. Although the other networks attempted to compete, they were unable to keep pace. TV Tupi screened *The Return of Beto Rockfeller* and a remake of *O Direito de Nascer*, but neither created much excitement among viewers. The financial woes of the Chateaubriand chain grew steadily worse.* In 1980 the Tupi network finally collapsed.

The Globo *telenovelas* of the 1970s were remarkable for the level of excellence they achieved and maintained, while at the same time appealing to a mass audience. In targeting the masses producers had to give critical heed to the fact that most of their viewers were illiterate and unsophisticated.

As one writer of *novelas* elaborated, "The artistic roots of us Brazilians don't come from the Greek theater, they come from the circus. We are a people of the Third World, a poor and ignorant people. I want to talk to my people in language they understand." Thus neither humor nor imagery could be overly subtle. Moreover, human passions had to be magnified, often to the verge of paroxysm, usually with the generous use of close-up shots.

In spite of these prescriptions the *telenovelas* were sufficiently well crafted to appeal to an educated audience. The photography was excellent, the acting sure-handed, and the storytelling techniques effective. Of course, not every *novela* succeeded, but the

---

* According to one anecdote, a TV Tupi director had a salary of $5,000 a month but was never paid. At the end of the year, he was informed that he was to receive a $2,000 raise. He politely refused, pointing out that he had steeled himself not to receive $5,000, but he didn't think he could bear not to receive $7,000.

quality of Globo's output during the 1970s was extraordinarily good.

The Globo *novelas* were also exceptional for their variety. Works of Brazilian literature made their way to television screens in the form of *novelas*, the most notable being the superproduction of Jorge Amado's classic novel *Gabriela, Cravo e Canela (Gabriela, Clove and Cinnamon)*, to commemorate the network's tenth anniversary in 1975. Some *novelas* re-created segments of Brazil's past. One of the more successful was *Escrava Isaura (The Slave-Girl Isaura)*, an adaptation of a historical novel written in 1875 and relating the story of the passion of a coffee-plantation owner for one of his slaves, the child of a white father and a mulatto mother.

Although Globo carried on the process of Brazilianizing the *telenovela*, its authors did not hesitate to borrow ideas from abroad. Thus Janete Clair, the wife of Dias Gomes and a highly successful writer, used a version of the central theme of Theodore Dreiser's *An American Tragedy* (and the film *A Place in the Sun*) in her hit *Selva de Pedra (Stone Jungle)*, the first Globo *novela* to achieve a one-night audience rating of 100 percent. Dias Gomes incorporated the "magical realism" of Gabriel García Márquez into one of his hits, *Saramandaia*, which spun a tale of bizarre happenings in a small town in the interior of Brazil. Parts of the ending of *Roque Santeiro* came straight out of the film *Casablanca*.

The distinctive Brazilianness of Globo's *telenovelas*, far from hindering their exportation, seemed to make these programs more appealing to foreign viewers, especially elsewhere in the Third World. The first of its *novelas* to be sold abroad was *O Bem-Amado (The Well-Loved Man)*, which also happened to be the first of its *novelas* to be filmed in color. But it was not until four years later, in 1980, that the company began to export its *novelas* aggressively, and the results surprised even Globo's own executives.

The high quality of Globo's *novelas* and the universality of their themes obviously had much to do with their success abroad, but there were other important contributing factors. Tropical sensuality, exotic locales, and multiracial casts proved appealing not only to Latin Americans and Europeans, but also to Africans and Asians. In Managua, Nicaragua, at the height of the civil war, a power shortage combined with the excessive demand for power created by a Brazilian *telenovela* that was mesmerizing the city every night forced the Sandinista regime to cut the flow of electricity into many neighborhoods. In Luanda, the capital of Angola, a huge market on the outskirts of town bears the name Roque Santeiro. *The Slave-Girl Isaura* was a smash hit in places like Cuba, Mozambique, Nigeria, Algeria, Morocco, and the People's Republic of China.*

The *telenovela* has become the major source of worldwide impressions of Brazil everywhere but in the United States, where the viewing public's strong distaste for dubbed programs has been cited as the reason for Globo's failure to penetrate the lucrative American mass market. Indeed, the only *novela*-related export from Brazil to find success in the land of Uncle Sam has been Sônia Braga.

*Newsweek* once called her the "queen of Brazil's TV soap operas." This designation smacks of journalistic hyperbole; Regina Duarte, who starred in *Roque Santeiro* and numerous other hit *novelas*, has a much better claim to the title. Nonetheless, the sultry Sônia did make her initial mark on Brazilian television screens. Her debut was in 1970 as a minor character in *Irmaõs Coragem (The Coragem Brothers)*, the Globo network's first megahit *novela*. After several other small parts, she secured the title role in *Gabriela*, after the producers had conducted a highly publicized search that shamelessly mimicked David O. Selznick's campaign to find an actress to play Scarlett O'Hara in *Gone With the Wind*.

With traces of Brazil's three major racial groups in her blood and on her countenance, Sônia Braga was perfect for the part of Gabriela, the sensual child-woman from the backlands who becomes the servant of a Lebanese-Brazilian bar owner, beds and weds him, and then finds herself suffocated by his insistence on a conventional married life. The *novela* brilliantly reproduced the languid ambience of Ilhéus, a town in the cacao-growing region of Bahia, and a society dominated by powerful "colonels."

---

* Lucélia Santos, the young actress who played the title role, was dumbfounded by the enthusiastic reception she received from mobs of Chinese on a visit to Beijing. According to some estimates, as many as five hundred million viewers around the world have seen *Isaura*.

The leisurely pace of the *telenovela* format proved far more congenial to Jorge Amado's masterpiece than the condensation perpetrated by MGM in its subsequent movie version, which starred Sônia Braga and a miscast Marcello Mastroianni. But the American studio had secured worldwide rights from Amado just after the initial publication of the book in 1958 and gave Globo permission to telecast its *novela* only in Brazil. Therefore the network was unable to distribute its production outside the country.

This arrangement did not prevent Sônia from exporting herself. Having become a big star in Brazil as a result of *Gabriela,* she gained international fame from her stellar performance in *Dancin' Days,* a widely marketed *novela* about a woman who serves an eleven-year prison term and then returns home in search of reconciliation with her daughter and reintegration into society. In addition, she was brilliant in the erotically charged title role of *Dona Flor e Seus Dois Maridos (Dona Flor and Her Two Husbands),* a Brazilian film adaptation of another of Jorge Amado's novels.

*Dona Flor* found a North American audience, and Sônia became the first (and thus far only) graduate of the Brazilian *telenovela* to make a career in Hollywood. Yet the fact of the matter is that despite the hype that greeted her arrival in the United States, where she has been hailed as a "sex goddess" and the "thrill from Brazil," she has not yet been given roles worthy of her talent*, and she has thus far failed to recapture the heights she reached in the television version of *Gabriela.*

The Globo network continued to prosper during the 1980s, despite its inability to follow in Sônia Braga's footsteps and claim a U.S. audience. The success it enjoyed inevitably bred renewed competition, and in 1982 Rede Manchete (the Manchete network) came into being. The offspring of a magazine-publishing chain, the new kid on the block made the bold decision to challenge its powerful competitor at its strongest game, the production of *telenovelas.*

Manchete did well with its maiden voyage into the field, a two-month miniseries entitled *Marchesa dos Santos (The Marquise dos San-*

---

* A recent example of how her talents have been wasted is the minor, virtually nonspeaking role she played in *The Burning Season,* the Home Box Office made-for-television movie about rubber-tapper Chico Mendes.

*tos).* Based on the steamy extramarital affair of the Emperor Pedro I with Domitila de Castro Canto e Mello, the program won critical acclaim and a respectable audience. More important for Manchete, it also made a superstar of Maitê Proença.

If Sônia Braga embodies the cliché of the dark-skinned Brazilian woman radiating raw eroticism, Maitê Proença provides a more contemporary, less exotic look. Projecting a classic beauty that turns male knees to putty, she is also an intelligent, plucky woman who has managed to survive the trauma she endured as a teenager, when her father, a law professor and public prosecutor, stabbed her mother to death with a knife during an argument about the mother's infidelity. (He was later acquitted on the ground that he had killed in "defense of his honor.")

Though she had previously graced Globo *novelas,* it was her performance as the Marquise dos Santos that propelled her to stardom and induced Manchete to gamble on producing a costly major project that would serve as a vehicle for her talents. Wisely waiting until *Roque Santeiro* had ended, the new network then launched *Dona Beija (Lady Beija),* a historical *telenovela* based on the life of a nineteenth-century courtesan from the diamond-mining region of Minas Gerais.

Maitê brought *Dona Beija* to life with a gritty, memorable performance. Moreover, Manchete capitalized on her physical charms by using, in the credits after each chapter, spectacular shots of her bathing in the buff beneath a waterfall. This was the first time that nudity had been used in a *novela,* and it obviously contributed to the popularity of the program.

*Dona Beija* established Manchete as a creditable competitor to Globo in the *telenovela* field. Globo still scored much higher in the ratings and still had at its disposal resources that were far superior to those of Manchete, but *novela* enthusiasts (that is, most Brazilians) now had options.

Indeed, television viewers seemed to have an insatiable appetite for *novelas.* Globo responded by regularly screening three of them per night. This schedule has required an output that compares favorably with that of Hollywood studios during the 1930s.

The filming of a *telenovela* occupies the cast and crew five days a week, from 10:00 A.M. to 6:00 P.M., and occasionally evenings. It takes five days of work to complete six 50-minute chapters. Given Globo's high standards, this would be the equivalent of churning out six episodes of *Melrose Place* every week.

Interior scenes are taped at the large Globo studio in Jardim Botánico. Exteriors are shot wherever necessary. For *novelas* like *Roque Santeiro*, elaborate outdoor sets are constructed at sites not far from the city of Rio de Janeiro. Because it is often necessary to work at Jardim Botánico and on location simultaneously, most *telenovelas* have two directors.

The writing of a *novela* is an exhausting chore. Until relatively recently, with the adoption of the practice of assigning assistants to authors, a single person was responsible for the script of an entire *novela*. The customary practice is to complete twenty or thirty chapters before the actual filming begins. Thereafter, the writer must produce a chapter (or about twenty-six pages) a day, and six chapters a week.

"I lose from 15 to 20 pounds when I'm writing a *novela*," disclosed Mário Prata in a 1989 interview in which he emphasized the "physical wear and tear" of the job. A versatile author of short stories, plays, and movie scripts as well as *telenovelas*, Prata described how he jots down ideas on napkins in restaurants. "You are the owner of forty persons [the *novela's* characters]," he pointed out, "and you have to think of them 24 hours a day for eight months."

Since it programs three *novelas* every night in prime time beginning at about 6:00 P.M., Globo must keep nine writers on the payroll simultaneously. Three work on the current *novelas*, three work on the next ones, and three rest. There are only about fifteen active *telenovela* authors in Brazil. As one observer put it in jest, "If you kidnapped all of them, you could bring the entire country to a standstill."

One of the fascinating aspects of the Brazilian *telenovela* is that it does not have a rigid or immutable story line. The author begins by coming up with the rough idea of a plot, a cast of characters, and the conflicts among them. But in the course of writing and filming the actual *novela*, two sets of circumstances may dictate changes: real-life exigencies and audience reaction.

"It's impossible to predict what's going to happen in the actual lives of all the people involved in the making of a *telenovela*," explained Sílvio de Abreu, a highly successful author specializing in humorous *novelas*. "Over an eight-month period some die, some go crazy, some separate from their husbands or wives, some become dissatisfied with what they're doing, some become too famous for what they're doing." The author may find himself caught between the fantasy of his project and the realities that may interfere with its realization. Abreu provided two examples.

"I had written one hundred chapters of *Guerra dos Sexos (War of the Sexes)* when suddenly I got a call from Paulo Autran, my 70-year-old male lead and one of the most beloved personalities in Brazil. He told me he was in the hospital, about to have serious surgery. There I was, with the biggest hit of the year, about to lose my principal actor. I had a responsibility to the 50 million viewers who were watching the program and to the rest of the cast, and I had only half a day to figure out how to deal with the situation.

"Everything turned out well because I was able to create an explanation for his absence and work it into the plot. The public followed closely both Autran's actual recovery and the unfolding of the *novela*, to find out whether and how he would return. It was a wonderful mixture of fantasy and reality."

A second instance occurred in a *novela* that featured an actress who was much older than the other members of the cast. "She began to feel depressed being around all these young people, and she had anxiety attacks. The only solution was to permit her to go off and have plastic surgery. So I dropped her out of the story. Later, when she had recuperated from her operation, I had her return, looking more or less like the character she had been playing, but younger. This created a mood of suspense that greatly helped the *novela*, as viewers wondered whether it was the original actress or a double."

Another kind of unexpected news that drives authors to distraction is a last-minute order from the network to extend the length of a *telenovela* in progress. Often this happens because of a delay in preparations for the next *novela* that was scheduled for the same time slot. It occasionally results from a desire to cash in on the success of an ongoing *novela*, as was the case when Manchete told the author of *Dona Beija* he had to add twenty more chapters.

He received this news *after* the taping of the episode in which he had killed off one of the major characters (Beija's true love).

Both Globo and Manchete keep their fingers on the pulse of their audiences by constantly polling housewives. This device is especially useful when a *novela* is not connecting with its audience. Reactions of viewers may force the cutting back, or even the elimination, of a character or the augmentation of a role that has caught the fancy of the public.

The author himself gets constant feedback, since he hears people talking about his *novela* in elevators, on the street, and in restaurants. He also enters into a symbiotic relationship with some of his characters, who take on a life of their own and begin to "dictate" to the author.

"It's amazing," was the way Mário Prata decribed it. "At a certain point in time, after you see episodes that have been shot, a character begins to dominate and becomes stronger than you. He grows on you and does things you never imagined he would do. Every *telenovela* has two or three characters who engage in this remarkable dance with the author."

The strain on the author of an ongoing *novela* is at least equal to that to which the actors submit themselves. Each chapter contains about 40 scenes, which means that some 240 scenes are televised each week. The principal characters appear in about 200 of these scenes, and thus the number of lines they must commit to memory on a weekly basis is staggering. Unlike moviemaking, which permits careful preparation for each shot, the production of a *telenovela* must move along at a brisk pace. The demands of the schedule make the actors virtual prisoners in a hectic process often bordering on madness and lasting for months on end.

While Globo enjoyed its total dominance of the *telenovela* market, the network could dictate terms of employment and salary levels. During the military dictatorship, which clamped down heavily on the legitimate theater, the steady work provided by the network's *novelas* became extremely attractive to the best and the brightest in Brazil's entertainment industry, and they were willing to accept whatever Globo offered. This meant a straight salary, with no overtime pay and no residuals for repeated screenings or foreign sales.

With the rise of Manchete and the pioneering work of Maitê Proença, who became the first star to move back and forth between the networks, a bit more leverage has been created for actors, directors, and writers. Yet they continue to be unorganized, lack representation by agents, and are generally at the mercy of the networks, which continue to exercise control reminiscent of that wielded by Hollywood studios in the 1930s.

Globo and its competitors have a considerable stake in maintaining the status quo because of the enormous profitability of the *telenovelas*. A recent study has estimated that the average cost of a *novela* ranges from $1 million to $2.5 million, which would put the cost per chapter at about $10,000. In 1988, according to the same study, Globo was charging $19,800 per thirty seconds of air time for commercials during the *novelas* it aired at 8:30 P.M.

Moreover, Globo has raised to a fine (and lucrative) art a device the Brazilians call, borrowing an English term, *merchandising*, which refers to advertisements inserted into the body of a *telenovela*. When a character drives up in a new automobile, opens a refrigerator door, sips a soft drink, or thumbs through the pages of a book on the coffee table, Globo is making money for promoting the sale of a product. Even the T-shirts worn by younger cast members may serve as commercial billboards.

The price for each plug exceeds by 20 to 30 percent the cost of a one-minute commercial during the same program. The rate also varies depending on whether one of the actors actually uses the product, or whether the product appears only in the background. There may be as many as 130 plugs woven into a *novela* over the course of the months it is on the air. Globo has a special subsidiary that lines up contracts for *merchandising* before the airing of a series. Income from this type of product placement may cover as much as 30 percent of the cost of the program.

The imagination devoted to *merchandising* has produced remarkable results such as an ad campaign for women's panties that became a part of *Roque Santeiro*. A billboard promoting the panties appeared in the main square of Asa Branca. The town drunk became convinced that the young panty-clad woman pictured on the billboard was shaking her hips at him. He even scaled the structure to find out whether the billboard was using "one of those Japanese computers." Later the respectable ladies of Asa Branca grew outraged at the billboard and organized a protest to have it removed. These clever snippets caused the sales of the featured panties to hit new highs.

Another income-generating facet of the *telenovela* derives from the promotion of its sound track. Each *novela* has a musical score that may or may not be original, and many of the sound tracks feature songs performed by well-known artists. Globo has a subsidiary that markets long-playing records, cassettes, and compact discs derived from *novelas'* sound tracks, an operation that has proved to be highly profitable. The exposure given to musical numbers over the course of a popular *telenovela* seems to guarantee their popularity. Indeed, the same phenomenon obtains when a *novela* features the work of classical composers such as Chopin.

Given the profitability of *telenovelas*, it was inevitable that Globo would face intensified competition. Manchete, having tasted success with *Dona Beija*, spent an estimated $7 million on an ambitious series called *Kananga do Japão*. Spanning the years between the 1929 stock-market crash and the bombing of Pearl Harbor (the latter coinciding with Ary Barroso's composition of the immortal song "Aquarela do Brasil," or "Brazil," as it is called in English), the series took its name from its setting, a fictitious Rio nightclub (which was named after a trendy perfume). It incorporated historical events and actual persons, such as Carmen Miranda and Luiz Carlos Prestes, and improved Manchete's position in the ratings.

It was not, however, until the production of *Pantanal* that Manchete gave Globo cause for real concern. Filmed in the breathtaking setting of Brazil's south-central swampland, *Pantanal* regaled viewers with a natural beauty that many of them did not realize existed within their country's borders. It also made ecology fashionable and popularized country music from the interior. Following a trail blazed by *Dona Beija*, it offered renewed proof of the selling power of sex.

*Pantanal* starred the beautiful young actress Cristina Oliveira in the role of a sensual, rifle-toting backwoods woman. Her naked dips in alligator-infested rivers had a hypnotic effect on viewers. The *novela* also featured love scenes that were more erotic than any previously seen on television. The program stirred up a real-life debate reminiscent of the controversy over the near naked panty-clad woman on the billboard in Asa Branca.

Near nudity and steamy romance had long been components of Brazilian *telenovelas*, and they also made the programs marketable abroad. (Indeed, even commercials on Brazilian television occasionally displayed performers in advanced stages of undress.) The images projected on television were merely reflecting the carefree sexuality that permeates Brazilian society, at least on a surface level and in urban environments. But there had always been limits set on what could be aired.

Until the adoption of the new Constitution in 1988, the federal government had the legal authority to censor television programs. During the dictatorship, the regime exercised constant prior restraint over what the networks televised. The Sarney administration sharply curtailed this practice, although occasionally problems arose. For example, in *Mandala*, a 1987 Globo *novela* based loosely on Sophocles' *Oedipus Rex*, the federal censors permitted only an innocent kiss and prohibited an act of intercourse between Édipo and his mother Jocasta.* Incest, even though unwitting, was declared unsuitable for family viewing during prime time.

But in the wake of *Pantanal* and under a new Constitution that contained vague, aspirational, and by itself unenforceable language about the content of television programs, Brazilian television networks seemed to be adopting an "anything goes" philosophy in the interest of winning the battle for ratings. Globo, plainly shaken by Manchete's success with *Pantanal*, responded with doses of nudity and eroticism in its own *novelas*. General programming on all the networks contained increased levels of violence. A survey reported by the magazine *Veja* in July 1990 found that in the course of a single week Brazilian television recorded 1,145 scenes of partial or total nudity, 188 references to homosexuality, 23 incidents of torture, and 1,940 gunshots.

---

* The use of the original Greek names in a *novela* set in contemporary Brazil was perfectly normal, since Brazilians customarily use all manner of imagination, literary or otherwise, in naming their children.

While debate raged about whether the government should institute a ratings system with teeth, and whether the television industry should impose voluntary restraints on itself, the SBT network of Sílvio Santos, which had not been a serious player in the *telenovela* arena, scored a surprise coup in 1991 with an imported Mexican *novela*. Although badly dubbed from the Spanish and rudimentary in style, the program scored ratings that cut deeply into Globo's supposedly untouchable national newscast, which had customarily dominated the 8:00 P.M. time slot.

*Telenovela* imports, however, had a limited appeal to Brazilian audiences. Moreover, the high costs involved in producing first-rate *novelas* were a factor in the subsequent decline of the Manchete network, which became mired in serious financial difficulties.* Thus Globo soon reclaimed its undisputed supremacy in the field.

Nevertheless, it had by now become apparent that Globo network was losing its edge. The production of its *novelas* had become increasingly bureaucratized, which hindered the launching of innovative ideas. (For example, Globo turned down a chance to produce *Pantanal* because of what were perceived as the risks of shooting on location.) The network's repeated use of well-worn plot lines and characters in the *novelas* ran the risk of boring audiences.

Moreover, Globo had failed to invest any of its substantial earnings in the development of new writers. There was no way, other than by actually doing it, for aspirants to learn the craft. Given the high costs of production, it was safer to rely on experienced writers. But by doing so, the network neglected to provide for an infusion of fresh talent. As Mário Prata put it, "What young person is ever going to sit down and write a 180-chapter *telenovela* just for practice?"

---

* Manchete's demise resulted from bad management. Its principal owner acquired the network as a result of contacts with the military regime. He was unable to build on the successes of shows like *Dona Beija* and *Pantanal*, discovered and then lost Xuxa to Globo, and was reported to have engaged in dubious financial maneuvers in his efforts to keep afloat and then sell Manchete.

Even if the "golden age" of the Globo *telenovela* has passed (and it is by no means clear that this has happened), the success the *novelas* have enjoyed both at home and abroad should encourage Brazilians to have a positive regard for their creative abilities. The heights to which Globo has taken this form of popular art by blending talent, creativity, and administrative skill demonstrates that Brazilians, in spite of their self-doubt, can plan, organize, and execute projects well without losing their Brazilianness in the process.

If the *telenovela* proves that people from the business and entertainment communities have this capability, another uniquely Brazilian institution—the Rio Carnival—indicates that *favela*-dwellers, when given the opportunity, are able to do likewise.

# Chapter 19

# In the Land of Carnival

*O*n the surface it is a spectacle that beggars the imagination, a feast for the eyes and ears, a plunge into the realm of ecstasy for participants and onlookers alike. This unique blend of music, dance, and pageantry proudly (and without apologies to the Ringling Brothers and Barnum & Bailey Circus) lays claim to being the "Greatest Show on Earth," and as such Carnival takes its place as one more jewel in Brazil's crown of superlatives. Indeed, the festival and Brazil are so closely intertwined that Brazil has been referred to as "Carnival Country" (a phrase used by Jorge Amado for the title of his first novel).

The parade is the ne plus ultra event of the orgiastic, end-of-summer, pre-Lenten, nonstop festivities that suffuse Rio de Janeiro with an irresistible delirium and have become multitextured metaphors for many aspects of Brazilianness.

The annual procession unfolds within the narrow confines of a facility designed by Oscar Niemeyer and inaugurated in 1984. Brazil's premier architect converted a mile-long stretch of paved roadway next to a nondescript brewery in downtown Rio into a corridor capable of channeling the energies of a flood tide of marchers numbering in the thousands. Criticized by some for its ultra-sterility, what has come to be known as the Sambadrome explodes into life during Carnival week, when it welcomes an enthusiastic audience of ninety thousand who occupy steeply banked concrete bleachers, luxury boxes, and ground-level seating, and some fifty thousand marchers representing neighborhood associations called samba schools. The parade route ends in an open area aptly named the Plaza of the Apotheosis, with a huge arch, also designed by Niemeyer, spanning the far end of the area.*

To accommodate the number of schools constituting what is now called the *grupo especial* (special group), the parade unfolds on two consecutive nights. The first marchers enter the Sambadrome before the sun sets; the last do not cross the finish line until well into the next morning. The heat may be stifling and torrential rains may drench participants and spectators to the bone, yet the show has always gone on, even during the darkest years of World War II and the uncertain days just before the 1964 military coup.

The foreign tourists who flock to the Sambadrome in ever-increasing numbers delight in the audiovisual aspects of the parade. The gut-pounding beat of drums accompanies relentless waves of humans awash in dazzling color who swirl and bob in synchronized movement. Many of the costumes are astonishing, many of the floats breathtaking. And then there is the surfeit of bare flesh, glistening with sweat and the generous application of glitter—gorgeous young men cavorting in the skimpiest of raiments, gorgeous young women exposing their breasts.

Virtually every Brazilian in the crowd is familiar with each school's theme song because it has been available on tapes and records for several months and is repeated over and over again during that school's performance. Many in the audience add their voices to those of the marchers. The samba beat of the percussionists makes the earth reverberate, and soon most of the spectators are on their feet, arms swaying, hips twirling, in communion with the procession passing before them.

For Brazilians the parade has layers of meaning. Indeed, and incredible as it may seem, there is much more to this sumptuous spectacle than what meets the eye. It has provoked all manner of passionate debate. The scores given to the presentation of each samba school by an official jury mean for the winners a year of

---

*Some *cariocas* say that the design of the arch represents the *bumbum da mulata*, or "mulatto woman's buttocks," a national obsession.

special glory (including lucrative engagements for some members of the school); while the losers are relegated to the "minor league" and do not get to participate in the next year's parade of the *grupo especial*. Naturally there are always sharp disagreements about the judging.

Arguments often touch on subjects beyond the competitive aspect of the show. Attempts to censor nudity and supposedly sacrilegious floats have produced spirited polemics. Moreover, there has most recently been a great deal of discussion of the fundamental issue of whether the parade has been transformed from an authentic vehicle of self-expression by Rio's poor (and mostly black) neighborhoods to a highly commercialized enterprise aimed primarily at foreign tourists and unduly influenced by the underworld characters who bankroll many of the samba schools.

Brazilians may also take note of the elements of drama often involved in the staging of each group's procession. A Brazilian professor who has worked to produce samba-school presentations puts it this way: "There are all kinds of things that can go wrong in the staging area. A float might collapse, people might not show up or might show up drunk, the leaders might get into arguments with one another. Nothing happens exactly the way you expect. The tension is tremendous."

During the march itself crises may occur that may become apparent to those who know where to look for them. For example, a costumed starlet perched high above a float may suddenly become faint and appear to be about to fall, and there may be no way to reach her except with the use of cranes on trucks stationed in the Plaza of the Apotheosis.

The themes elaborated by the floats and costumes interpret and reinterpret the nation's past, culture, mood, and sense of identity, often in a very critical way. (Recent topics have included the abolition of slavery, the exploitation of Amazônia, and the evils of consumerism.) Each samba school has a tradition and a complex personality of its own that attracts the partisan support of spectators as well as television viewers. Celebrities from the sports, arts, and entertainment worlds appear as "stars" on the floats or mingle with rank-and-file marchers.

The parade brings to a fitting end the annual Carnival of Rio de Janeiro, which in the eyes of many is one of the defining elements of Brazil. The festival opens on the Friday before Ash Wednesday, when "King Momo" (for many years a jolly, obese young man nicknamed Bola) is proclaimed temporary mayor, in a ceremony in which he orders all his subjects to enjoy themselves to the fullest. Thereafter, for five nights and four days, a marathon of merrymaking convulses the city, as delirious celebrants shed all their inhibitions (along with most of their outer garments) and respond to the ubiquitous, nonstop pulsing of drums conveying the infectious beat of the samba.

Anthropologist Richard G. Parker has defined the ethic of the Brazilian Carnival as "the conviction that in spite of all the evidence to the contrary, there still exists a time and place where complete freedom is possible." As the tropical summer draws to a close, society suspends its rules, hierarchies reverse themselves, and the struggles of daily life give way to the uninhibited pursuit of fun and pleasure.

In the "anything goes" atmosphere of Carnival, neighborhood groups called *blocos* adopt imaginative or outrageous names: for instance, *Simpatia é Quase Amor*, or "Sympathy Is Almost Love," an Ipanema *bloco*; and *Sovaco de Cristo*, or "Christ's Armpit," the designation adopted by people who live beneath the outstretched arms of the statue of the Redeemer atop Corcovado Mountain. In costumes or *bloco* T-shirts, they take to the streets and cause monumental traffic jams, which the authorities as well as the trapped motorists tolerate with surprising equanimity in the spirit of the season.

Exhibitionism, a natural outgrowth of the *cariocas'* fixation on physical appearance, bubbles irrepressibly to the surface, most noticeably at gala balls in social clubs and nightspots, where the city's "beautiful people" mix with local as well as international celebrities and display their bodies with or without the help of dazzling costumes.

At all levels of society cross-dressing has long been a popular practice during Carnival. Heterosexual men do not hesitate to parade about in feminine attire that has in many instances been made for them by their wives. Even young boys customarily disguise themselves as girls. For avowed transvestites, Carnival is a time when society permits them to have free rein, and they cavort about with wild and often hilarious abandon, blocking or directing the flow of vehicles on the main arteries of Copacabana and Ipanema.

Hugh Gibson, in his 1937 book *Rio*, notes that although many writers have sought to capture the Carnival of Rio de Janeiro, the event eludes description. "The strange thing is that none of [them] seem to realize that Carnival is not nearly so much what they saw as what they felt; a feeling which enables two million people to be turned loose in the streets for four days and nights with little or no restraint."

The masked faces of Carnival revelers in a sense represent the real countenance of Brazil. Indeed, to make use of an insight offered by the Argentine writer Luisa Valenzuela, in a certain sense Brazilians go about in costumes during the rest of the year and regard what they wear during Carnival as indicative of their real selves.

To be a genuine Brazilian, it is said, one must be able to succumb willingly and wholeheartedly to the enchantment, the delirium, and the splendor of what has become a national allegory. Although this claim is perhaps an exaggeration, the inversion of reality that defines the event—whereby males dress as females, virtuous women as prostitutes, good Christians as devils, the living as the dead, the old as the young, and the poor as nobility from Brazil's past—matches the surreal quality that lies near the essence of all things Brazilian. People from every walk of life transform themselves into whatever they want to be. The Brazilian mania for spontaneity and disorder, sparkle and noise, and pleasure and pathos assumes its ultimate expression.

Yet the Rio Carnival has its critics: those who say that it has deteriorated from a genuine manifestation of popular culture to a media extravaganza concocted by professionals, exploited by publicity seekers, totally commercialized, and increasingly staged for the entertainment of foreign tourists. The samba schools, they aver, are no longer associations serving the needs and aspirations of the slum (and predominantly black) neighborhoods from which they sprang, but rather unwieldy conglomerations struggling to meet the pressures of putting together an elaborate spectacle that calls for expenditures far beyond their means. Thus it has become fashionable in some quarters to belittle the Rio event and point to the street celebrations in Salvador and Olinda in the Northeast as much closer to the true tradition of Carnival.

The exact origins of Carnival are unknown. Some point to the prehistoric practice of painting the body and wearing masks and feathers during rites intended to exorcise demons. Others trace it back to Egyptian, Greek, and Roman festivals during which pleasure-seeking celebrants behaved in a crazed manner and set out to disrupt the established order. Momus, the name given to today's "King of Carnival," was the god of mockery in ancient Greek mythology.

Despite its pagan roots, Carnival eventually gained acceptance, with some modification, in the Roman Catholic world of the Middle Ages, where it became a pre-Lenten occasion to feast and bid goodbye to the indulgence of the flesh before the season of fasting and penance began. Singing, dancing, and the wearing of disguises enlivened the festivities. Masked balls gained great popularity in Italy and France, especially among the upper classes and intellectuals, who brought to the celebration displays of wealth and refined taste. But by the end of the nineteenth century, Carnival had became virtually extinct in Europe.

In the New World, however, Carnival flourished. Its evolution in Brazil reflected the peculiar nature of the festival brought across the Atlantic by Portuguese colonists. The pre-Lenten affair in Lisbon had a distinctively unruly character. The Carnival, or *entrudo*, as it was called, was dirty, boisterous, and at times involved criminal activities. People fought on the street with eggs and eggshells filled with flour, gypsum, and even mud. From windows pranksters emptied bags of sand on top of onlookers and hurled rolls, cakes, and oranges filled with water and perfume. For the rich and powerful, it was merely another excuse to eat well and indulge other appetites.

It was this vulgar and violent *entrudo* that the Portuguese transplanted to their New World colony. In the street battles that raged in Rio de Janeiro, the weapons of choice were the *limões-de-cheiro*, or wax balls filled with water or urine, and large bottles from which revelers squirted red or black ink on passers-by. Gentler pranks involved people pouring talcum powder or whitewash from the balconies of their town houses. When the royal court relocated to Rio de Janeiro in the first decade of the nineteenth century, the festivities were so disorderly and in such bad taste that foreign visitors to Brazil assumed that the observances had indigenous rather than Portuguese origins.

From time to time, the authorities attempted to suppress Carnival, but without success. Indeed, King João's son, who later became Pedro I, and the latter's bookish son, Pedro II, enjoyed the *entrudo* enormously and immersed themselves in the spirit of the occasion by soaking other members of the royal family with water and perfume.

Throughout the years the gadgets used to inflict Carnival mischief became increasingly sophisticated. Wax *limões-de-cheiro* gave way to balls made of rubber, celluloid, and then plastic. In 1892 the French invented the *serpentina*, a coil of thin paper that would unwind as a streamer, and the Brazilians immediately put them to use during Carnival. At about the same time they also adopted paper confetti, a Spanish fabrication. Watches and guns that could project water made their appearances at the beginning of the twentieth century. Perfume squirters in all sizes came from France. What made them particularly popular was the fact that their contents might include ether, which produced the same intoxicating effect as *cachaça*, the national drink the government banned during Carnival.

In imitation of the extravaganzas that had become exceedingly fashionable in Europe, an Italian resident of Rio organized the first masked ball in 1840. The affair, staged at the Hotel de Itália, became an annual Carnival event and was so successful that theaters began to sponsor their own Carnival galas. By the end of the century the balls were competing with one another to produce the best decorations, orchestras, and special guests. The hosts also used gimmicks; for instance, one highly popular 1879 masked ball was staged at a roller rink, with participants dancing on skates. There were scandals, such as that of the 1890 ball where the French cancan was first performed in Brazil. Initially polkas were played at the galas, but later other musical numbers were included—waltzes, tangos, cakewalks, and even Charlestons.

Most of the ideas for costumes at the Carnival balls originated in France. The most popular disguises assumed by ladies were Gypsies, Orientals, Indians, and Moors; while men dressed as Satan, Dominoes, royalty, hustlers, smugglers, and clowns. Boys donned jockey outfits.

The institution of the Carnival ball continued to evolve in the modern era. Galas proliferated in 1932, when the government sanctioned the celebration of Carnival. Their venues spread from hotels and theaters to social clubs and nightclubs, and they were traditionally scheduled during the five nights before Ash Wednesday. Today the Carnival balls draw abundant media coverage. Glossy magazines devote page after page to photos of the famous faces, scantily clad bodies, and extravagant costumes on display at affairs such as the "Sugar Loaf Ball" on Urca Hill and the "Champagne Ball" at the Scala nightclub.

The Carnival ball provides yet another example of how Brazilians from the upper, middle, and intellectual classes aped European fashions. As an institution it coexisted with the *entrudo* as a means of celebrating the arrival of Lent. At the same time other traditions with a more distinctively Brazilian flavor began to evolve.

In 1855 a Rio newspaper announced that the members of a new aristocratic organization that had recently been created planned to parade in costume along the streets on the Sunday of Carnival week. The emperor and his daughters were among those in attendance when the eighty members of the group staged what was the first Carnival parade in the history of Brazil. A martial band of "Cossacks from the Ukraine" opened the march. They were followed by lavish floats bearing such notables as "Don Quixote" and "King Ferdinand the Catholic," along with Chinese mandarins, assorted dancers, and other figures. A group of mounted horsemen brought up the rear.

The enthusiastic applause of the spectators at the march was evidence that a trend had been set. Similar groups, which came to be known as *grandes sociedades* (great societies), began to be formed from the ranks of students, intellectuals, journalists, high government functionaries, and others who could afford the expense of membership. Before long the Carnival parade of the *grandes sociedades* became an institution. The presentations began to reflect

the political views of the group members. During the imperial period, some societies advocated the adoption of a democratic form
of government. Many urged the abolition of slavery. One way of
communicating this message was to buy certificates of freedom for
a group of slaves and then let them ride on one of the allegorical
floats.

The *grandes sociedades* swiftly grew very competitive, often trying to outdo one another in sophistication and learning. They
fought their battles through the newspapers, and the weapon of
choice was poetry. This spirit of contentiousness occasionally
turned inward, producing squabbles that caused members to leave
and form their own new societies (a tendency that would later be
repeated at the samba schools).

Elegance and sophistication bordering on preciosity graced virtually everything connected with the *grandes sociedades*. Yet the care
with which the presentations were staged did not prevent complaints from both elements of the public and the police when the
allegorical floats carried women in stages of undress that offended
contemporary sensibilities.

In addition to the balls and the parades of the *grandes sociedades*,
Rio's elite had another outlet for celebrating Carnival. The *corso*,
which originated in 1907, was a procession of open motor vehicles
carrying gaily costumed *cariocas* who tossed confetti, *serpentinas*,
perfume, and bons mots at onlookers as they passed along some of
Rio's broad avenues. The *corso* enjoyed a high degree of popularity,
until the proliferation of automobiles and resulting traffic conges-
tion brought an end to the practice in the 1930s.

The parades of the *grandes sociedades* and the *corsos* served as
occasions when people from the wealthy and intellectual classes
performed for the amusement of spectators of humbler origins.
Eventually the roles of performer and onlooker would be reversed.
For in the late nineteenth century, other groups began to march
during Carnival week, and one day they would replace the *sociedades* and the *corsos* as the principal attractions of Carnival.

The first organized effort on the part of Afro-Brazilians to participate in Carnival appears to have occurred in 1885, when a group
of blacks of Congolese origin took to the streets to criticize Brazil's
imperial regime. Disguising themselves as figures such as old men,

devils, clowns, kings, queens, and the dead, they carried their banners through Rio's downtown at Carnival time to give vent to the frustrations of the common people. A *mestre*, or "master," blowing a whistle acted as leader; percussionists supplied the rhythm; the "old men" performed certain steps; and the clowns sang a refrain. Called *cordões*, these groups multiplied in succeeding years. They came to represent sharp satire cloaked in anonymity.

Another distinct type of Carnival group was the *rancho*. Some say that blacks from the Sudan created the first *ranchos*. They began as rather closed societies that maintained totemic traditions in their names and colors, and evolved into associations drawing members from the working and lower-middle classes. More refined than the *cordões*, the *ranchos* permitted women to participate, and they accompanied their presentations with string instruments, clarinets, and flutes as well as drums. Instead of one *mestre*, the *ranchos* had three: one for the orchestra, one for the chorus, and the *mestre de sala*, who was in charge of choreography. The themes they adopted were generally mythological (involving gods of the forest, satyrs, nymphs, and goddesses), and the music they played was original.

The most modest of the Carnival groups were the *blocos* (also known as *blocos de sujos*, or "blocks of dirty ones"), formed by friends living on the same blocks in lower-class neighborhoods. In 1889 the police for the first time authorized the participation of some twenty *blocos* in the festivities. These groups improvised everything, from their costumes to their parade steps. Their spirited and boisterous behavior, which more than occasionally led to street fights, kept alive the tradition of the *entrudo*. The newspapers sponsored contests to crown the yearly champion of the *blocos*, as well as of the *cordões* and *ranchos*.

Out of these various strands emerged the organizations that today dominate the Carnival scene. The exact origins of what came to be known as "samba schools" remain shrouded in doubt. Several claim the distinction of being the first. Police repression of the *blocos* and the "respectable" *cariocas'* disdain for the samba music that had evolved on the *morros* (hills) in and around Rio inspired the formation of new associations rooted in lower-class communities, modeled after the *ranchos* but incorporating the spirit (and some of the personnel) of the *blocos*. These new groups were called samba schools.

Some say that inspiration for the name came from the presence of a nearby teacher-training school. Others insist that the founders of the schools saw their institutions as vehicles for teaching and passing from generation to generation the forms of music and dance indigenous to Rio's poor (predominantly black and mulatto) neighborhoods. Moreover, referring to the new organizations as schools would lend them prestige.

The samba schools succeeded in transforming the pre-Lenten festivities in Rio de Janeiro. They made samba the music of Carnival, used mass culture as a vehicle for protest for both the lower and middle classes, served as showcases of "racial democracy" in Brazil, and eventually became an indispensable source of revenue for the city.

During the 1920s the samba schools came down from the *morros* to the Praça Onze (Eleventh of July Plaza), located less than a mile from Rio's downtown, on the Sunday and Tuesday of Carnival week. Female members dressed like Bahian women, with long, wide skirts, turbans, necklaces, and bracelets; the men generally preferred either striped, pajamalike outfits or the shirts and hats worn by the city's *malandros,* or hustlers. Crowds gathered to watch them dance and sing sambas that dealt with contemporary national or local themes.

At a time when modern technology, in the forms of the radio set, the phonograph, and phonograph record, was rescuing the samba from disrepute and was converting it into a national craze, the regime of President Getúlio Vargas decided to promote the samba schools from their position on the fringes of Carnival and to make them bona fide participants in the annual affair—a measure consistent with the myth of racial democracy that the government was promoting. In 1932 the first official samba-school competition was one of the events of the Carnival celebration. This was the beginning of a tradition that continues to the present day.

The price the schools paid for recognition was the necessity of submitting to government control and the condition of dependency that went with it. The authorities set the criteria for judging the annual contest and placed limitations on the themes that costumes, songs, and floats could convey. One of the early regulations limited presentations to events or personalities drawn from Brazilian history. In 1939 a school that had selected "Snow White and the Seven Dwarfs" for its theme suffered the indignity of disqualification.

The community organizers and samba composers who held positions of leadership within the schools prized acceptance and recognition by society above the creative independence they had enjoyed during the 1920s. Therefore they did not resist the imposition of ground rules that put restraints on articulations of discontent they might otherwise have incorporated into their Carnival presentations.

In the six decades between the first official authorization of the samba-school parade and the present day, the route along which the schools march has undergone several changes that have taken the procession from the Praça Onze to Rio Branco Avenue in the heart of the downtown district, then to the broad Avenida Getúlio Vargas nearby, and finally to Niemeyer's colossal Sambadrome. Each new site permitted a larger number of spectators than before to witness the event.

Throughout the years the Rio Carnival has gained an ever-increasing measure of worldwide renown. The film *Black Orpheus* might have done more than anything else to bring the event to the attention of people everywhere and to assure its immortality. In his film French director Marcel Camus demonstrates with powerful sensitivity how the illusion of Carnival takes over the lives of samba-school members. Although the score by Luiz Bonfá and Tom Jobim uses more bossa nova than samba, the lyrics that poet Vinicius de Moraes wrote for one of the songs captures the essence of Carnival in a way that has never been matched. "Sadness has no end," the song proclaims, "but happiness does."

The actual scenes of the Carnival parade in *Black Orpheus* have mesmerized moviegoers for years. Other films, such as the James Bond epic *Moonraker,* and books such as like Gregory McDonald's *Carioca Fletch,* have used the parade as an exotic backdrop for plots that have little to do with Brazil, and this publicizing of the event has contributed to the building up of Carnival as an international tourist attraction. But *Black Orpheus* makes viewers yearn not only to attend the festivities themselves but also to understand more about the context that the movie vividly portrays.

Participants in the Carnival parade must follow a stylized format that at the same time leaves room for enormous creativity. Each school selects an *enredo*, or "plot," for its annual march. The compulsory components of the group's presentation permit the *enredo* to unfold.

Thus the school's marchers must include a *comissão de frente* (front commission), or welcoming committee, which leads the procession and introduces the school's *enredo*;* a dance master (male) and a flag bearer (female) who perform an exquisite pas de deux, the latter carrying the colors of the school and spinning about with such remarkable grace and economy of motion that her feet seem never to touch the pavement; the *bateria*, or percussion section, providing the samba beat to which the school marches; the allegoric floats, decorated to illustrate the *enredo* and carrying the school's *destaques*, or dazzlingly costumed "stars"; and the *alas*, or "wings," discrete groups of dancers, each with its own outfits and colors. The *alas* must include *baianas*, a group of older women dressed in versions of the traditional hoopskirts worn by black women in the city of Salvador. The *baianas* dance in a whirling motion that produces one of the most spectacular visual effects of the parade. All marchers sing their school's theme song, the *samba enredo*, which conveys the story they have come to tell.

Samba schools have customarily served as strong community organizations that absorb the energies of their members throughout the entire year. Shortly after one Carnival, preparation for the next one begins. The *enredo* is developed, composers compete fiercely to have their song selected as the annual *samba enredo*, costumes are sewn, and floats are constructed. Beginning in November, weekly meetings bring participants together to rehearse the

---

*Once the *comissão de frente* was customarily composed of the school's elders, dressed in black tie and tails. Today the costumes of the lead marchers may be more elaborate and imaginative. In 1989 one of the schools had twelve pregnant women dressed in white in its front row. In 1993 a *comissão de frente* featured a group of tall black men in shorts and imported sneakers, their heads shaved, basketballs in hand, representing the U.S. Olympic "Dream Team."

music and dances they will present in their march. The need to scrimp on meager salaries in order to pay for their costumes does not dampen in the least the enthusiasm of the *favela*-dwellers for whom appearing in Carnival is an all-consuming pursuit.

Over the years the samba schools and their performances have undergone a dramatic transition. In the 1960s an increasing number of people from Rio's upper and middle classes "discovered" the schools, whose rehearsal halls they began to frequent and in whose *alas* they began to enlist. As a result, the samba schools underwent a degree of bleaching, although they remain predominantly black.

In addition, there was a change in the process by which the schools put together their shows. Traditionally this had been the province of people from the neighborhoods that produced the schools. But by the 1960s the march of the samba schools was turning into a complex tableau emphasizing the visual and requiring the help of outside professionals. Indeed, a school's presentation became increasingly dependent on the genius and leadership of one person, the *carnavalesco,* or "Carnival master," who coordinates the efforts of costume designers, artisans, composers, and performers. These directors have become the luminaries of the Rio Carnival, and for a number of years the brightest and most controversial star in the galaxy was a short, round-faced, curley-haired, self-educated, wildly imaginative virtuoso whom everyone calls Joãozinho Trinta (a name that translates into English as Johnny Thirty).

Born in 1933 in São Luis, the capital of the northern state of Maranhão, João Clemente Jorge Trinta lost his father at the age of two and grew up in very modest circumstances. As a teenager he migrated to Rio de Janeiro, and in 1956 he joined the corps de ballet of the Municipal Theater, where he performed on the same boards with Dame Margot Fontaine and Alicia Alonso. His first love was spectacle, and he learned as much as he could about the staging of ballets and operas from set designers, wardrobe people, and other specialists at the Municipal Theater. The transition from the legitimate stage to the Carnival parade route was a natural and inevitable step for him.

"Carnival spectaculars are the Brazilian equivalent of opera," he has explained. "The *samba enredo* is the libretto, the *bateria* the orchestra, the *sambistas* [samba dancers] the ballet corps, the *destaques* the prima donnas, and the allegoric floats the sets."

Serving as *carnavalesco* first for Salgueiro, one of the well-established Rio samba schools, and then for Beija-Flor, a newer school from Nilópolis in the impoverished Baixada Fluminese, Joãozinho compiled an enviable winning record in the Carnival competitions of the 1970s and 1980s. From his first *enredo* with Salgueiro—portraying the conquest of Maranhão by the French, as seen through the eyes of the eight-year-old French King Louis XIII—his sumptuous presentations went far beyond anything that had previously been attempted in the parade. He did not shrink from daring themes, such as the supposed presence of the ancient Phoenicians on the Amazon River (and their transport of precious gems back to the court of King Solomon), and developed them with costumes and stately floats that raised lavishness to new levels. He has been innovative on many fronts. Indeed, the first woman to bare her breasts during the parade, and the first male nude, marched with Beija-Flor.

Critics accused Joãozinho of deforming the true spirit and tradition of the Carnival parade. They claimed, among other things, that he was ignoring the wretchedness of everyday life in Brazil and was imposing unwarranted financial burdens on the poor people who made up the bulk of the membership of the samba schools.

Joãozinho's response was characteristically vigorous. "If I made an *enredo* out of poverty," he said in a 1987 interview, "no one would march. These people are poor all year long. Why would they want to parade as wretches?" The classic, oft-quoted rejoinder he aimed at his detractors was "The poor like luxuriousness. It is the intellectuals who like misery."

Yet Joãozinho could not resist fashioning another, quite different reply to his critics. In 1989, staging one of the most astonishing and revolutionary pageants in the history of Carnival, he concocted an *enredo* whose title translates as "Rats and Vultures—Let Go of My *Fantasia*" (a play on a word that in Portuguese means both "Carnival costume" and "fantasy"). It succeeded brilliantly in converting *lixo* (garbage) into *luxo* (luxuriousness). The *comissão de frente* and one of the *alas* (wings) dressed as beggars in tattered, multicolored rags. Another of the *alas* represented a group of lunatics and performed as though they were straight out of the theater of the absurd. Dancers disguised as prostitutes and young street thieves cavorted wildly. There was a float piled high with surrealistic "garbage" and labeled Beggars' Banquet. The directors of Beija-Flor, including Joãozinho himself, paraded as uniformed garbage collectors. It was a stunningly original tribute by the poor to the poor, the likes of which had never been seen on the streets of Rio. The panel of jurors found it excessively avant-garde and awarded Beija-Flor only second place, but many impartial observers disagreed.

Staging elaborate presentations in the Carnival parade did not, of course, originate with Joãozinho Trinta. He merely turned out to be consistently better at pulling it off than any other *carnavalesco*. Moreover, Beija-Flor's former guiding light has insisted that the costumes and floats his school uses look much more expensive than they actually are. "We are very creative in the use of cheap materials, yet we have gotten the reputation of being extravagant."

Criticisms of Joãozinho have related to matters beyond his alleged extravagance. Purists have faulted him for deviating from hallowed traditions that date back to the very first parades of the samba schools. They have argued that by orienting his presentations to please foreign tourists and by imposing his own peculiar views and tastes, he has lost contact with the real meaning of the Carnival parade, which has always been a form of self-expression for Rio's slum communities.

There is another way to view the negative reactions Joãozinho has stirred. He was an outsider from the north, rather than a product of Rio's Carnival culture. He was a poor boy who made good on his own rather than a Rio intellectual. In addition, his Beija-Flor samba school was located in Nilópolis, an impoverished suburb populated by migrant northeasterners who are not part of the local Carnival tradition.

Joãozinho insists that Beija-Flor brings tremendous benefits to the community. "Nilópolis is a poor suburb, but we are showing people what they can accomplish on their own, with the right kind of leadership. Young people work with our carpenters, sculptors, and seamstresses, and learn trades. Our school has created a day-care center for 300 children. From October to March, members of the school perform three nights a week in Rio for tourists. We have traveled and paraded in Paris, Nice, Morocco, Jordan, and Zaire.

"Some say that Carnival is an opiate, a way of deceiving the poor; but it's exactly the opposite: a way to open people's eyes and show them that life has other qualities, other emotions, other possibilities."*

A number of forces have shaped the current figuration of the Rio Carnival. The completion of the Sambadrome in 1984 increased the scale of things and reinforced an already existing trend toward more and more elaborate costumes and allegoric floats. With the economic decline of Rio de Janeiro, tourism became its most important "industry," making inevitable the transformation of Carnival into a major attraction for foreign visitors (which in turn necessitated a large-scale facility to accommodate spectators).

Moreover, the tremendous power of the mass media in Brazil has influenced the Carnival parade, which has become a major television event. The television cameras have tended to focus on the participating celebrities (and on displays of nudity, before they were banned from prime time) rather than on the traditional and collective aspects of each school's presentation. The networks have also insisted on a degree of scheduling control over the parade, so that they can maximize their exposure to the nationwide viewing audience.

The samba schools have felt the effects of these changes. The expenses of staging a Carnival march have skyrocketed far beyond the financial capacities of the lower-class neighborhoods that continue to serve as the hearts and souls of the schools. The government, though maintaining control over Carnival, contributes but a modest percentage of what the parade costs each school. Therefore, the schools have had to search for other sources of income. Rehearsals for the parade have become weekly fund-raising events, through the charging of admissions fees and the sale of refresh-

---

*Joãozinho lost his position with Beija-Flor, reportedly over the scandal that accompanied his path-breaking use of a fully nude male *destaque*. In 1994 he staged the performance of the Viradouro samba school.

ments and souvenirs—practices that have drawn the diluting presence of tourists and people from Rio's middle class. Indeed, because of the dire financial straits in which many of the schools have found themselves, anyone with the proper connections has been able to buy his or her way into participating in the march down the Marquês de Sapucaí Avenue.

This has made the schools vulnerable to the importunings of "civic-minded" *bicheiros*. The *jogo do bicho*, or "animal game," is so intimate a part of the fabric of Brazilian culture that its link to other staples of Brazilianness, such as Carnival, should not be surprising. It was logical that the *bicheiros*, in search of respectability and goodwill in the communities that patronize their business, would become backers of many of the samba schools.

The first of the *bicheiros* to identify with a school was an Afro-Brazilian named Natalino José de Oliveira. Beginning in the 1950s until his death in 1975, this charismatic "sugar daddy" not only channeled some of his earnings from the *jogo do bicho* into neighborhood social projects; he also became the patron of the local samba school, Portela. This earned for him the sobriquet Natal da Portela and an aura of legend that continues to the present day. The school paid tribute to him in its 1987 Carnival presentation, and a motion picture released two years later presented a glorified version of his life.

A number of other *bicheiros* have followed in his footsteps. They have arranged to have themselves named presidents or honorary presidents of samba schools, upon which they have then bestowed substantial sums of money. They have also combined forces to form the Independent League of Samba Schools, an entity that has successfully pressured the government of the city of Rio de Janeiro for a larger share of the tourist and television revenues generated by Carnival.

Those who decry the current state of the parade of the samba schools seem to forget that this hallowed institution has been in a constant state of evolution since its birth. In a sense, the "crisis" of today results from the success of the samba schools in producing a sight-and-sound extravaganza that has deeply touched and excited Brazilians and people from all over the globe. The universal appeal of the parade has taken it far beyond the precincts of folklore, and turning the clock back to a more innocent, less complicated era hardly seems feasible.

Nor is it at all clear that most of the poor people who annually electrify the Sambadrome would want to deprive themselves of the experience. A United States consular official who paraded with one of the schools for several years described it in terms that Americans might understand: "There are 90,000 spectators cheering you on, millions are watching on TV, and you are just ordinary folks. It's like playing in the Superbowl, or the World Series, all compressed into an hour and a half."

Heated debate over the Carnival parade erupted after the 1991 event, when Mocidade Independente spent nearly $800,000 on its winning presentation; Mangueira, a popular school that had refused to take money from any *bicheiro*, did so badly that it nearly lost the right to march with the *grupo especial*. At the same time, the *bicheiros* threatened to withdraw their schools from the official parade and stage their own Carnival show, an act of defiance that for better or for worse would completely privatize the parade.

The samba schools' subservience to the *bicheiros* has been an unavoidable sequel to their submission to control by the government, and this symbiotic relationship mirrors the dependency of other enterprises on privileges and subsidies provided by the state. Unfortunately, the *bicheiros*, as well as government officials, have their own agendas, which probably do not feature the promotion of the self-expression of the lower classes that has traditionally been the defining element of the samba-school performances.

It would indeed be tragic if the Carnival parade became totally commercialized. Several years ago entrepreneurs were concocting a scheme for constructing luxury hotels along Rio's southwest beaches, far from the center of town, where a new "sambadrome" would be installed and weekly samba-school marches would be staged for the benefit of tourists. Although this scenario remains on the drawing boards, a version of it comes to life in *O Samba dos Vagalumes (The Samba of the Fireflies)*, a novel by Rodolfo Motta Rezende, whose imagination conjures up a nightmarish, nonstop parade in the existing Sambadrome, attracting hordes of enthusiastic foreign visitors, some of whom watch from their windows in a new hotel overlooking the Marquês de Sapucaí Avenue.

Although truly unique in its impact on the emotions of spectators and participants alike, the Rio de Janeiro Carnival parade is perhaps most remarkable for the evidence it offers, year after year, that lower-class Brazilians are adept at conceiving, organizing, and successfully executing a highly artistic pageant that compares favorably with entertainment offered anywhere in the world. The samba schools have somehow managed to overcome the various crises associated with the event and the staggering difficulties in staging it.

The parade is a legitimate source of national pride, and it should be taken to heart by all those who would doubt the capabilities of Brazil's common folk. At least in expressing their Brazilianness year after year in the defining event of the Rio Carnival, they demonstrate to anyone with eyes to see and ears to hear their ability to plan, work together, and produce. The challenge facing the country is to harness this dedication, diligence, imagination, and enthusiasm and apply them to other areas of endeavor, in ways that will do the most good for the ordinary people of Brazil.

# Chapter 20

# Whither Brazil?

*I* know . . . that I am Brazilian and not North American because I like to eat *feijoada* and not hamburger; . . . because
I speak Portuguese and not English; because when I hear
popular music, I know immediately how to tell a *frevo* from a
samba; because football for me is a game played with the feet
and not the hands; . . . because I know that at Carnival I bring
into the light my social and sexual fantasies; because I know
that there never exists a "no" in the face of formal barriers,
and that there is no such barrier that does not admit of a *jeitinho* through the mechanism of personal relationships or
friendship; because I believe in Catholic saints and also African *orixás;* because I know that destiny exists and yet I still
have faith in study, education, and the future of Brazil; because I am loyal to my friends and cannot deny anything to
my family; because, finally, I know that I have personal relationships that will not let me walk alone in this world, as happens to my American friends, who always see themselves and
exist as individuals.

**Roberto da Matta,** *O que faz o Brasil, Brasil?*

The uniqueness that makes Brazilians Brazilian has left its mark
on the political, economic, and social development of the country.
Spontaneity, improvisation, youthful immaturity, tropical languor,
individualism, the patriarchal mind-set, the authoritarian tradition

and its corollary of impunity for the rich and powerful, and the various legacies of slavery are among the aspects of Brazilianness that have contributed in some way to the evolution of Brazil as a society and a nation. Thus national character must bear some responsibility for the chronic crisis of the past decade and a half. By the same token, this unique set of traits will surely help shape, for better and for worse, the Brazil of the twenty-first century.

An understanding of Brazilianness, however, does not assure one of success in predicting the direction Brazil will take as the third millennium approaches. It is obvious that external economic and political considerations, such as the easy availability of loans from foreign banks and the sudden increase in the price of imported petroleum in the 1970s, have seriously affected events in Brazil,* and factors such as the collapse of international Communism and future shifts in the balance of economic power among the European Economic Community, Japan, and the United States will certainly affect Brazil in important ways.

Moreover, national character is not static, but rather dynamic. Just as the Britishness of the epoch of Robin Hood and his merry men eventually became the Britishness of Victorian England, which was quite different from the Britishness of the age of Margaret Thatcher, so the contours of Brazilianness may evolve as the country continues its painful passage past adolescence. Changes in how Brazilians think and behave will complicate even further the task of attempting to answer the question Whither Brazil?

Brazil has experienced a cycle of ups and downs since the end of World War II. The disarray of the 1980s and early 1990s may represent a dip that is extended yet temporary—a period of adjustment constituting a transitory phase in the process of national maturation. Increased foreign investments in Brazil in the latter months of 1993, booming exports during that same period, and the

---

*Economic determinists place total responsibility for Brazil's crisis on external factors, and especially the dependent relationship imposed on Brazil by the United States. Assigning some blame to national character signifies a rejection of this view but should not be taken as an embrace of the opposite extreme. Obviously outside pressures have also played an important role in influencing the course of events in Brazil.

government's success in halting inflation in 1994 are indications that Brazil is regaining its balance and is about to move forward again toward the realization of its destiny.

Those who remain realistically optimistic about Brazil's future no longer entertain grandiose visions that Brazil is a superpower in the making, or that a "Brazilian century" is about to dawn. Instead, invoking a new mood of cautious enthusiasm, they point to positive signs, such as the development of effective government and relative prosperity in some of the country's less populous states and municipalities. On the top of everyone's list is Curitiba, which in recent years has become known variously as Brazil's "livable," "ecological," and "model" city.

The national as well as international attention generated by Curitiba during the past decade contrasts sharply with the unobtrusiveness the city had previously worn for centuries almost as a badge of honor. Originally founded as a mining camp on the banks of the Atuba River some three hundred years ago, the settlement languished when gold turned out to be present in only sparse amounts. Remaining modest in both size and bent, the town nestled peacefully on a broad plateau about three thousand feet above sea level, cut off from the nearby Atlantic coast by a ridge of mountains, at a comfortable distance from the bloody frontier wars and civil strife that beset Rio Grande do Sul, and far removed from the main currents of Brazilian history and culture. Originally part of the captaincy of São Paulo, the region surrounding the town became the separate province of Paraná in 1853, and Curitiba was named its capital.

Paraná was fortunate in that slave labor was not introduced there on a large scale, and thus it escaped some of the pernicious effects of involuntary servitude seen in much of the rest of Brazil. By the time its agricultural potential began to be fully appreciated, which did not occur until the nineteenth century, abolition had become inevitable. The farming operations that began in Paraná for the most part did not utilize slave labor. Instead, a steady influx of German, Italian, and Polish immigrants (along with lesser numbers of Japanese, who came later) founded small- and medium-sized farms and worked the land themselves. The system of large, individual landholding prevalent elsewhere in the country was not widely established in Paraná, a factor that was altogether to the state's advantage.

Curitiba itself attracted German colonists and soon took on the look of a small German city. A subsequent influx of settlers from Poland did not alter its reserved, cautious, provincial air. In 1940 the population of the municipality had barely reached a hundred thousand. Yet the city was already earning a reputation as a salubrious place to live. Statistics for 1941 revealed that it had the lowest infant mortality rate of any of Brazil's state capitals.

In the early 1960s conservative Curitiba escaped the turbulence that roiled within other large metropolitan areas. The city's tranquility was due in part to the dominance of the centrist Christian Democratic party, which advocated a progressive conservatism modeled after European Christian Democracy, and supported the 1964 military coup.

At the beginning of the 1970s, the city was still not much more than the administrative capital of an agricultural state, and it was growing at a slower pace than other large Brazilian urban centers. But that would soon change. The mechanization of agriculture in Paraná forced a number of workers off the land and led to the absorption of small- and medium-sized farms by large enterprises. Some of those who had been displaced found reasons to go north to Rondônia; others migrated to the city and state of São Paulo. A goodly number made their way to Curitiba.

What set Curitiba apart from other Brazilian municipalities confronted by the challenge of the influx of migrants from the countryside was that a team of technocrats who had been thinking about how the city should grow drew up a plan for the future. The Institute for Research and Urban Planning of Curitiba had been set up in 1965 to advise both the city and the state governments. In 1971 its president, a round-faced architect named Jaime Lerner, was designated mayor of Curitiba, and he set out to put into action a strategy the institute had developed.

In the course of three terms as the city's chief executive (he was appointed twice and elected once), the energetic Lerner transformed Curitiba into a showcase. Among his accomplishments are an excellent system of bus transportation that has made Curitibans less dependent on private automobiles and has facilitated decentralized urban growth; taking resolute measures to reduce the level of atmospheric air pollution and increase the amount of green space in the city; the encouragement of waste recycling by imaginative methods such as providing food to the poor if they would collect and deliver trash; and the development of a safe, clean, pleasant downtown. During the same period, Lerner even found time to co-author some song lyrics with Vinicius de Moraes.

Today the population of Curitiba has reached 1.6 million. The municipality has a large middle class, and the contrast between haves and have-nots is not nearly so striking as in other Brazilian cities. The *favelas* that have cropped up on the periphery seem much less wretched than the urban slums of São Paulo and Rio de Janeiro. The quality of life is reasonably decent, and one senses an attitude of civic pride among *curitibanos* of every class, even though some outsiders may find the city provincial and dull.

Lerner, on his part, has become a widely respected figure, and he is unabashedly upbeat about the future of the country. "Curitiba proves that Brazil is possible," he said in a 1992 interview. The secret, in his view, is to work to improve the quality of urban life by taking creative low-cost initiatives at the local level.* "Curitiba is different because the city made itself different. You have to believe you can do it." In 1994 he was elected governor of Paraná.

But whether the Curitiba model can be replicated elsewhere is open to question. Despite the fact that companies often test-market new products there, in many ways Curitiba is atypical of the rest of Brazil. *Curitibanos* tend to be more docile, more orderly, and less aggressive than their compatriots further north. The cold climate of Paraná has tended to discourage migration from the tropical regions of the country. As is true of southern Brazil generally, the population of Curitiba is "whiter" than the rest of the country, even in the *favelas*.

The city has remained conservative (it went heavily for Collor in 1989) and relatively immune to the sort of demagoguery that often permeates Brazilian politics. Since the 1940s careful planning

---

*One example is the conversion of buses no longer fit for transport use into classrooms where people from poor neighborhoods can take, free of charge, courses in subjects such as typing, hairdressing, carpentry, and knitting.

rather than improvisation has been the modus operandi. The manufacturing enterprises that have been attracted to the area in the last decade have developed in an orderly fashion, mostly within the confines of an industrial park on the city's outskirts.

What perhaps redounds most to Curitiba's advantage is that it has never allowed itself to be overwhelmed by the extensive, oppressive poverty that renders it difficult for a city to know where to begin looking for more than faintly palliative solutions. Because the region has been able to avoid a flood of immigration and to plan for the influx that did occur (and because it "exported" some of its potential social problems to Rondônia in the 1970s), Curitiba has managed to cope well with the challenges it faced during the 1980s and 1990s. Yet by being rational and farsighted rather than emotive and spontaneous, *curitibanos* seem rather less Brazilian than Brazilians elsewhere.

Other small and mid-sized municipalities have been able to create for their residents a quality of life superior to that found in Brazil's mega-metropolises. They have accomplished this by planning for growth and by permitting citizens to take control of their own lives and establish for themselves the elements of a livable urban environment. A good illustration of a municipality that has used this strategy is Uberlândia, a prosperous city of over 500,000 inhabitants in the *"Mineiro* Triangle" of western Minas Gerais, where forward-looking administrators have consulted with Jaime Lerner and borrowed from the Curitiba model to prepare for an expected population increase. Maringá, a municipality of 240,000 in the state of Paraná to the northwest of Curitiba, exemplifies reliance on grassroots initiatives to provide decent housing and child care for every citizen.

This trend toward self-sufficiency reflects an important shift in Brazilian attitudes toward the role of the federal government. Originating in the absolute authority vested in the Portuguese Crown, the notion of government as a highly centralized administration with tight control over the disbursement of revenues and broad authority to regulate private activity fostered a relationship of dependency between citizens and the state. Today people at the local level, and especially in the cities and towns, are becoming convinced that they can do a better job of dealing with local problems by mobilizing their own resources and developing their own ideas. Corruption, incompetence, and bureaucratic inertia in Brasília have disenchanted many Brazilians, to the degree that they realize it is fruitless to expect the federal government to improve their daily lives to any meaningful degree.

The upbeat news from Curitiba and other cities has been matched in recent years by success stories generated by several state governments, which have demonstrated what honest and intelligent administration can accomplish. The most remarkable record of progress comes from Ceará, once the bailiwick of Father Cícero and, as recently as the mid-1980s, the preserve of powerful "colonels" who placed the state government at the service of their private interests. But in 1986 a split within the elite permitted a young businessman named Tasso Jereissati to win the governorship, and he managed to convert the impoverished northeastern state into a model for the rest of the country.

Tasso eliminated the traditional system of patronage, reduced the number of government jobs, and insisted that state employees work for their salaries. He adopted an austerity program, reformed the system of tax collection, and was soon able to devote increased revenues to infrastructure investment, which in turn attracted new industries to the state. His governorship was so popular that he was able to secure the election of a young protégé, Ciro Gomes, as his successor, and Ceará has enjoyed a period of administrative continuity unusual for Brazil.

As the national economic growth rate stalled at 0 in 1992, Ceará's exceeded 3 percent. The state's sandy beaches and year-long sunny weather were attracting tens of thousands of visitors from Europe, Argentina, and southern Brazil, who supported a thriving tourism industry, which in turn has stimulated the construction of new hotels. Meanwhile, public opinion polls showed Ciro was the most highly regarded of Brazil's governors.

The Jereissati-Gomes administrations have not ignored social needs, which are considerable in a state that is still one of the nation's poorest. One of their most interesting initiatives is an imaginative, effective, low-cost program, hailed as "an example to the world" by UNICEF, which trains local people to visit remote villages in the interior and supply rudimentary health services; this medical care has succeeded in reducing the rate of infant mortality.

Both Tasso and Ciro relinquished control of a number of services previously supplied by the state and gave municipalities authority to address matters that can be dealt with more efficiently at the local level. Yet at the same time they demonstrated that a lean, serious-minded government can accomplish wonders, in the Brazilian context, if it sets priorities and then works hard to realize them.

The trend toward decentralization in Brazil is yielding positive results, but it can have a dark side as well. Some municipalities, adopting a "dog-in-the-manger" attitude, are resisting the influx of migrants from other parts of the country. For example, Canoas, a city not far from Porto Alegre in Rio Grande do Sul, has been physically barring or expelling migrants in an effort to protect its per capita income of $7,200.

This phenomenon is related to the mood of separatism that has been rekindled recently in southern Brazil. There have always been southerners urging the secession of the states of Paraná, Santa Catarina, and Rio Grande do Sul, which would then join together to create an independent, agriculture-based republic. During the early 1990s, this kind of talk intensified, to the degree of attracting national concern, but a breakup of Brazil is hardly likely to happen because of the opposition it would incite in the rest of the country (and especially from the military, who have never backed away from their self-appointed role as guardians of the nation).

A more likely separatist scenario is the evolution of a system of de facto social and economic segregation within a unitary Brazil. Indeed, there are signs that this has already begun to happen. The notion of reshaping Brazilian society to exclude the increasingly unmanageable poor is already being played out in the proliferation of residential communities and apartment complexes walled off from the misery around them, where affluent city dwellers can live in safety and comfort.

This trend toward what amounts to a new form of apartheid is evident in the growth of Barra de Tijuca (or Barra, as it is com-

monly called), a community of high-rises and luxury homes situated along a glistening Atlantic beach on the far edge of the
municipality of Rio de Janeiro. Well-to-do *cariocas* fed up with the
violence and grime of the older sections of Rio have been moving
beyond the Hill of the Two Brothers at the end of Leblon, and beyond São Conrado, the fashionable neighborhood on the ocean-
front at the foot of the Rocinha *favela,* and are in the process of
creating what some have called a *"Carioca* California."

The rapid growth of Barra makes it possible to fantasize a future in which it becomes an independent city and takes over as
the center of commerce and tourism for the area; while the center
of Rio, along with the nearby middle-class neighborhoods in both
the south and north zones, disintegrates into an extensive ruin, reclaimed in whole or in part by tropical vegetation, abandoned by
all but the very poor, and perhaps converted into a museum maintained by funding from UNESCO (United Nations Educational, Scientific, and Cultural Organization).

Yet at the same time what has actually been happening in Barra
is a reminder that the planned growth pioneered by Curitiba and
undertaken elsewhere has not totally replaced the haphazardness
and spontaneity at or near the heart of Brazilianness. The expansion of the *"Carioca* California" has not been orderly and well
thought out in advance, but rather chaotic, careless, and ecologically indifferent—so myopic that in the long run there are real dangers lurking in this idyllic environment.

Moreover, *favela*-dwellers have followed the upper and upper-
middle class to Barra, and slums are mushrooming in the flatlands
behind the high-rise apartments along the shore. People who purchased expensive houses and lots in Barra and adjoining neighborhoods now find themselves besieged by *favelados* who are invading
their properties or adjacent lots and constructing shanties. Thus, as
the magazine *Veja* has noted, it is conceivable that the *"Carioca* California" may be forced to coexist with a *"megafavelópolis"* housing
two hundred thousand and stretching from Leblon to Rocinha to
Barra.

Were the socioeconomic separatism of Brazil to occur, it would
ultimately require authoritarian government and the unyielding
application of brute force to keep the majoritarian have-nots away

from the minoritarian haves and maintain the existing distribution of wealth and power. Only the military could accomplish this, most probably by the deployment of force in urban centers. The army not only would have to provide security for the upper and middle classes (as occurred in Rio de Janeiro during the U.N. Earth Summit in 1992); it would also be forced to send troops into slum areas in order to disarm the organized gangs that use them as safe havens, an assignment that the federal government finally forced on the military in late 1994. But long-term occupation of the cities is hardly a proper role for the nation's armed forces.

A coup such as occurred in 1964 is conceivable, especially as years pass and memories of the failures of dictatorial rule fade. But the institution that presided over the massive enrichment of Brazil's haves can hardly be relied on to solve a crisis for which it bears heavy responsibility.

Of the two competing paradigms for twenty-first-century Brazil— the model of planned growth and local autonomy on the one hand, and separate societies for rich and poor on the other—it seems clear that the latter can never succeed; whereas the former offers a future worthy of Brazil.

By erecting physical and legal barriers that would consign the have-nots to permanent status as outsiders, Brazil would be embracing what South Africa has dismantled. Instead of building a nation in which citizens could participate on an equal basis, the country would be institutionalizing a permanent state of social and economic injustice. Brazilianness, to which Brazilians from all sectors of society have made important contributions, would be torn asunder, and Brazil would become an international pariah.

On the other hand, the ideal of planned growth and local autonomy could mean the dispersion of the country's populace away from coastal urban areas and into the vast interior of the country, fulfilling a dream long entertained by Brazilians. It would enable the nation to develop its vast human resources and exploit to the maximum its productive potential.

Of course, this grand strategy will succeed only if the exodus from overpopulated cities is gradual and evenly distributed, and the new population centers prepare themselves in advance for steady growth. It also requires a continuation of the current trend of giving local governments the resources and autonomy that will enable them to develop and prosper on their own.

The dilemma facing policymakers is easy to state: a market-oriented laissez-faire approach relying on private initiative to unleash the productive forces of the country will exacerbate even more an already unacceptable gap between rich and poor and will demand even more suffering from those at the base of the societal pyramid, in exchange for the speculative hope that at some future time prosperity will filter down to the less fortunate; a socially oriented economic policy designed to meet the minimum needs of Brazilians below the poverty level and redistribute existing wealth risks stifling the productive forces of the country and impeding the growth that is essential to economic recovery.

To find a way out of this predicament will not be an easy task. Indeed, Brazil's record under the linked criteria of growth plus equitable wealth distribution has been remarkably unbalanced up to now. As the Mexican political scientist Jorge G. Castañeda points out in his thoughtful study *Utopia Unarmed: The Latin American Left After the Cold War,* "Brazil . . . has perhaps combined growth and *inequity* in greater doses than any other Latin American nation over the past forty years." The fact that no other Latins have managed to solve this problem merely underscores the historic opportunity facing Brazil, which has always aspired to greatness and now has a chance to redefine it.

Thus Brazil's desperate need is to develop a strategy that will bring about growth *plus* economic and social justice. If the country's vocation, in the words of Roberto Mangabeira Unger, is to synthesize sweetness and greatness, Brazilians can make no greater contribution to humanity than to demonstrate that it is possible to expand production and at the same time close the tremendous gap between rich and poor. To do so, they will have to abandon their fondness for foreign models and chart their own course, in a way that capitalizes on particular Brazilian strengths (such as the existence of a strong manufacturing base and the potential to expand the domestic market for consumer goods).

Perhaps Brazilians will have to resort to their penchant for metaphoric cannibalism, which has heretofore operated mainly in the cultural realm, enabling them to chew, swallow, and digest borrowings from abroad, and convert them into something uniquely their own. In recent years Brazilians seem to be losing their anthropophagic touch.* The time may be ripe to revive it and apply it to the socioeconomic sphere.

Change will require a certain degree of self-confidence that must replace the self-doubt long lurking within the soul of Brazilianness. The evolving dynamics of national character place this achievement within the realm of possibility. There are already signs that Brazilians are changing. The impeachment proceedings against President Fernando Collor, and the criminal conviction of the owners of the tour boat that capsized in Guanabara Bay, causing the deaths of fifty-five persons, signal an erosion of the cloak of impunity that had previously sheltered the powerful and the wealthy; such justice would have been unthinkable in the past. Indeed, Brazilians are now for the first time going to jail for tax evasion.

Moreover, the proliferation of grassroots groups advocating the interests of the poor, as well as nongovernmental organizations promoting environmental protection, the well-being of women and children, and other causes suggests a trend toward greater citizen participation in civic life and a sense of societal responsibility that represent a healthy divergence from the traditional attitudes of passivity and individualism.

The Brazil of the past captured the fancy of outsiders because it connected with a widely shared dream that there could exist somewhere on this planet a place of beauty, sensuality, magic, racial harmony, playfulness, and innocence. The Brazil of present no longer nourishes these illusions, as the realities long lurking behind the beguiling aspects of Brazilianness have become impossible to ignore or downplay.

---

*For example, they have been importing foreign music, such as reggae and rap, intact, rather than Brazilianizing it.

Yet there is reason to hope for and believe in the birth of a new dream, grounded in the Brazil that is and imagining a Brazil that could be, building on the irrepressible vitality of its people, accepting the magnitude and gravity of the problems that need to be solved, and moving ahead with a renewed sense of self-confidence and optimism into the twenty-first century.

# Selected Bibliography

## Introduction

### Books, Parts of Books, and Pamphlets

Barbosa, L. *O Jeitinho Brasileiro: A Arte de Ser Mais Igual Que os Outros*. Rio de Janeiro: Editora Campus, 1992.

Bishop, E. *Brazil*. New York: Time, Inc., 1962.

Brasília. Departamento de Turismo. *Brasília Mística: Roteiro Místico-Religioso*. Undated.

Buarque de Hollanda, S. *Raizes do Brasil*. Rio de Janeiro: José Olympio, 1984.

Burns, E. *A History of Brazil*. 3d ed. New York: Columbia University Press, 1993.

Cooper, C. *The Brazilians and Their Country*. New York: Frederick A. Stokes, 1917.

Diégues, M. *O Brasil e os Brasileiros*. São Paulo: Livraria Martins, 1964.

Harding, J. *I Like Brazil: A Close-up of a Good Neighbor*. Indianapolis: Bobbs-Merrill, 1941.

Jaguaribe, H., et al. *Brasil, 2.000: Para um Novo Pacto Social*. Rio de Janeiro: Editora Paz e Terra, 1986.

———. *Brasil: Reforma ou Caos*. Rio de Janeiro: Editora Paz e Terra, 1989.

Kellemen, P. *Brasil para Principiantes*. Rio de Janeiro: Civilização Brasileira, 1963.

Leite, D. *O Carácter Nacional Brasileiro*. São Paulo: Livraria Pioneira Editora, 1983.

da Matta, R. *O Que Faz o Brasil, Brasil?* Rio de Janeiro: Rocco, 1986.

Porto, M. *Os Brasileiros: Uma Tragi-Comédia*. São Paulo: Massao Ohno, 1984.

Rodrigues, J. *The Brazilians: Their Character and Aspirations*. Translated by R. Dimmick. Austin: University of Texas Press, 1967.

Sabino, F. *Zélia, Uma Paixão*. Rio de Janeiro: Editora Record, 1991.

Zweig, S. *Brazil: Land of the Future*. Translated by A. St. James. New York: Viking, 1941.

### Periodicals

"O azarão da segunda divisão." *Veja*, June 30, 1993, 82.

Bernard, A. "Exile's Return." *New York Review of Books*, January 13, 1994, 15.

"Brazil" (Survey). *The Economist*, April 25, 1987.

"Brazil" (Survey). *The Economist*, December 7, 1991.

"Brazil" (Survey). *South*, July 1988, 49.

Brooke, J. "Looting Brazil." *New York Times Magazine*, November 8, 1992, 31.

Cesar, A. "O voto em plena guerra." *Veja*, September 21, 1994, 56.

Corrêa, M. "O Brasil se expande." *Veja*, September 7, 1994, 70.

Friedman, M. "Economic Miracles." *Newsweek*, January 21, 1974, 80.

Guillermoprieto, A. "Obsessed in Rio." *The New Yorker*, August 16, 1993, 44.

Long, W. "Brazilians: A Laid-Back Breed Apart." *Los Angeles Times*, October 14, 1988, part 1, p. 1.

López Torregrosa, L. "*Escândalo* in Brazil." *Vanity Fair*, February 1993, 132.

Macrae, N. "Oh, Brazil" (Survey). *The Economist*, August 4, 1979.

Margolis, M. "Reinventing Brazil." *World Monitor,* November 1989, 31.

"A multiplicação das desigualdades." *Jornal do Brasil,* December 20, 1992, 17–21.

Rosenn, K. "Brazil's New Constitution: An Exercise in Transient Constitutionalism for a Transitional Society." *American Journal of Comparative Law* 38 (1990): 773.

———. "Brazil's Legal Culture: The Jeito Revisited." *Florida International Law Journal* 1 (1984): 1.

Schwartz, L. "Elizabeth Bishop and Brazil." *The New Yorker,* September 30, 1991, 85.

Seabra, C. "O profeta do futebol." *O Globo,* July 11, 1993, 54.

Simon, W. "Social Theory and Political Practice: Unger's Brazilian Journalism." *Northwestern University Law Review* 81 (1987): 832.

Vesilind, P. "Brazil: Moment of Promise and Pain." *National Geographic,* March 1987, 348.

White, P. "Giant Brazil." *National Geographic,* September 1962, 299.

# Chapter 1

### Books, Parts of Books, and Pamphlets

de Barros, T. *História de Portugal.* Porto: Editora Educação Nacional, undated.

Bethell, L., ed. *Brazil: Empire and Republic, 1822–1930.* Cambridge, England: Cambridge University Press, 1989.

Boxer, C. *The Golden Age of Brazil, 1695–1750: Growing Pains of a Colonial Society.* Berkeley: University of California Press, 1962.

Burns, E. *A History of Brazil.* 3d ed. New York: Columbia University Press, 1993.

Cooper, C. *The Brazilians and Their Country.* New York: Frederick A. Stokes, 1917.

Correa de Costa, S. *Every Inch a King: A Biography of Dom Pedro I, First Emperor of Brazil.* Translated by S. Putnam. New York: Macmillan, 1950.

Freyre, G. *New World in the Tropics: The Culture of Modern Brazil.* New York: Vintage, 1963.

———. *The Masters and the Slaves: A Study in the Development of Brazilian Civilization.* Translated by S. Putnam. New York: Alfred A. Knopf, 1964.

Gil-Montero, M. *Brazilian Bombshell: The Biography of Carmen Miranda.* New York: Donald I. Fine, 1989.

Harding, B. *Amazon Throne: The Story of the Braganzas of Brazil.* Indianapolis: Bobbs-Merrill, 1941.

Hayes, R. "The Formation of the Brazilian Army and the Military Class Mystique, 1500–1889." In *Perspectives on Armed Politics in Brazil,* edited by H. Keith and R. Hayes. Tempe: Center for Latin American Studies, Arizona State University, 1976.

Jaguaribe, H. *Economic and Political Development: A Theoretical Approach and a Brazilian Case Study.* Translated by S. Macedo. Cambridge, Mass.: Harvard University Press, 1968.

Livermore, H. *A New History of Portugal.* 2d ed. London: Cambridge University Press, 1976.

Livermore, H., ed. *Portugal and Brazil: An Introduction.* London: Oxford University Press, 1953.

Moog, V. *Bandeirantes and Pioneers.* Translated by L. Barrett. New York: George Braziller, 1964.

Poppino, R. *Brazil: The Land and People.* 2d ed. New York: Oxford University Press, 1973.

Prado, C., Jr. *The Colonial Background of Modern Brazil.* Translated by S. Macedo. Berkeley: University of California Press, 1967.

Rippy, J. *Latin America: A Modern History.* Ann Arbor: University of Michigan Press, 1968.

*U.S. Army Area Handbook for Brazil.* Department of the Army, July 1964.

Williams, M. *Dom Pedro the Magnanimous, Second Emperor of Brazil.* New York: Octagon Books, 1978.

# Chapter 2

## Books, Parts of Books, and Pamphlets

Andrews, G. *Blacks and Whites in São Paulo, Brazil, 1888–1988.* Madison: University of Wisconsin Press, 1991.

Bastide, R. *Les Religions Africaines au Brésil.* Paris: Presses Universitaires de France, 1960.

Comissão dos Religiosos, Seminaristas e Padres Negros do Estado do Rio de Janeiro. *Ouvi o Clamor deste Povo . . . Negro!* Petrópolis: Editora Vozes, 1987.

Conferência Nacional dos Bispos do Brasil. *Ouvi o Clamor deste Povo: Texto-Base.* Brasília: Editora Gráfica, 1988.

Costa, H. *Fala, Crioulo.* Rio de Janeiro: Editora Record, 1982.

Degler, C. *Neither Black nor White: Slavery and Race Relations in Brazil and the United States.* New York: Macmillan, 1971.

Dos Passos, J. *Brazil on the Move.* Garden City, N.Y.: Doubleday & Co., 1963.

Fernandes, F. *The Negro in Brazilian Society.* Translated by J. Skiles, A. Brunel, and A. Rothwell. New York: Atheneum, 1971.

Fontaine, P.-M., ed. *Race, Class and Power in Brazil.* Los Angeles: Center for Afro-American Studies, University of California, 1985.

Frank, W. *South American Journey.* New York: Duell, Sloan and Pierce, 1943.

Freyre, G. *New World in the Tropics: The Culture of Modern Brazil.* New York: Vintage Books, 1963.

———. *The Masters and the Slaves: A Study in the Development of Brazilian Civilization.* Translated by S. Putnam. New York: Alfred A. Knopf, 1964.

Hasenbalg, C. *Discriminação e Desigualdades Raciais no Brasil.* Translated by P. Burglin. Rio de Janeiro: Edições Graal, 1979.

Hasenbalg, C., and N. Silva. *Estrutura Social, Mobilidade e Raça.* Rio de Janeiro: Vértice & IUPERJ, 1988.

IBASE. *Negros no Brasil: Dados da Realidade.* Petrópolis: Editora Vozes, 1989.

do Nascimento, A. *O Genocídio do Negro Brasileiro: Processo de um Racismo Mascarado.* Rio de Janeiro: Editora Paz e Terra, 1978.

———. *O Negro Revoltado.* Rio de Janeiro: Editora Nova Fronteira, 1982.

———. *Brazil: Mixture or Massacre?* Translated by E. Nascimento. Dover, Mass.: The Majority Press, 1989.

Ortiz, R. *Cultura Brasileira e Identidade Nacional*. São Paulo: Editora Brasiliense, 1986.

Ramos, A. *The Negro in Brazil*. Translated by R. Pattee. Philadelphia: Porcupine Press, 1980.

Russell-Wood, A. *The Black Man in Slavery and Freedom in Colonial Brazil*. New York: St. Martin's Press, 1982.

dos Santos, J. *Zumbi*. São Paulo: Editora Moderna, 1987.

Skidmore, T. *Black into White: Race and Nationality in Brazilian Thought*. New York: Oxford University Press, 1974.

Valente, A. *Ser Negro No Brasil Hoje*. São Paulo: Editora Moderna, 1988.

**Periodicals**

Brooke, J. "In Nigeria, Touches of Brazilian Style." *New York Times*, March 26, 1987, C12.

————. "If It's 'Black Brazil,' Why Is the Elite So White?" *New York Times*, September 24, 1991, A4.

————. "Black Woman in Race to Be Mayor of Rio." *New York Times*, November 4, 1992, 3.

Cavalcanti, P. "Tráfico de escravos foi cartel dos corruptos." *O Estado de São Paulo*, March 31, 1991, 20.

"Centenário de um mau século." *Veja*, May 11, 1988, 20.

"A Cinderela negra." *Veja*, July 7, 1993.

Corrêa, M. "Candidata em pele de eleitor." *Veja*, October 14, 1992, 60.

Degler, C. "The Negro in America—Where Myrdal Went Wrong." *New York Times Magazine*, December 7, 1969, 64.

Gaspari, E. "As vozes da África." *Veja*, September 25, 1991, 124.

Kalili, N., and O. de Mattos. "Existe preconceito de côr no Brasil." *Realidade*, October 1967, 36.

Long, W. "Brazil: No Equality for Blacks Yet." *Los Angeles Times*, April 9, 1988, part 1, p. 1.

"Negros no governo." *Veja*, December 5, 1990, 40.

Podesta, D. "Black Slums Belie Brazil's Self-Image: Equality Is the Law, Inequality the Fact." *Washington Post*, August 17, 1993, A9.

Subervi-Vélez, F., and O. Oliveira. "Blacks (and Other Ethnics) in Brazilian Television Commercials: An Exploratory Inquiry." *Los Ensayistas*, nos. 28–29 (1990): 129.

Thompson, E. "Does Amalgamation Work in Brazil?" *Ebony*, July 1965, 27; August 1965, 33.

# Chapter 3

**Books, Parts of Books, and Pamphlets**

Bodard, L. *Green Hell: Massacre of the Brazilian Indians*. Translated by J. Monaghan. New York: Outerbridge & Dienstfrey, 1971.

Burns, E. *Nationalism in Brazil: A Historical Survey*. New York: Frederick A. Praeger, 1968.

————. *A History of Brazil*. 3d ed. New York: Columbia University Press, 1993.

Collier, R. *The River That God Forgot: The Amazon Rubber Boom.* New York: E. P. Dutton, 1968.

Davis, S. *Victims of the Miracle: Development and the Indians of Brazil.* Cambridge, England: Cambridge University Press, 1977.

Freyre, G. *The Masters and the Slaves: A Study in the Development of Brazilian Civilization.* Translated by S. Putnam. New York: Alfred A. Knopf, 1964.

"Genocídio sem trégua." *Retrato do Brasil: Da Monarquia ao Estado Militar.* Vol. 1. São Paulo: Editora Política, 1984, 145.

Hemming, D. *Red Gold: The Conquest of the Brazilian Indians, 1500–1760.* Cambridge, Mass.: Harvard University Press, 1978.

———. *Amazon Frontier: The Defeat of the Brazilian Indians.* Cambridge, Mass.: Harvard University Press, 1988.

Kelsey, V. *Seven Keys to Brazil.* New York: Funk & Wagnalls, 1941.

Lévi-Strauss, C. *Tristes Tropiques.* Translated by J. and D. Weightman. New York: Washington Square Press, 1973.

### Periodicals

Barros, A. "O país se assenta." *Veja,* September 7, 1994, 78.

Gorney, C. "Tribes in the Amazon Reel under Impact of Development." *Washington Post,* December 19, 1981, A23.

———. "Brazilian Practices Dying Art of Making Contact with Indians." *Washington Post,* December 20, 1981, A23.

"O índio brasileiro numa aula de sertão." *Jornal do Brasil,* March 13, 1973, Caderno B, p. 1.

Lewis, N. "Brazil's Dead Indians: The Killing of an Unwanted Race." *Atlas,* January 1970, 22.

"Os marajás da madeira." *Veja,* June 17, 1992, 83.

"The Savage Can Also Be Ignoble." *The Economist,* June 12, 1993, 54.

Simons, M. "The Amazon's Savvy Indians." *New York Times Magazine,* February 26, 1989, 36.

Villas Bôas, C. and O. "A tragédia dos índios." *Jornal do Brasil,* May 7, 1989, Caderno B, p. 6.

———. "A cultura dos índios." *Jornal do Brasil,* May 14, 1989, Caderno B, p. 6.

## Chapter 4
### ON JAPANESE IMMIGRANTS

### Books, Parts of Books, and Pamphlets

Kumasaka, Y., and H. Saito. "Kachigumi: Uma delusão coletiva entre os japoneses e seus descendentes no Brasil." In *Assimilação e Integração dos Japoneses no Brasil,* edited by H. Saito and T. Maeyama. Petrópolis: Editora Vozes, 1973.

### Periodicals

"Amargo regresso." *Veja,* November 10, 1993, 71.

Brooke, J. "A Rising Sun Beckons, to Highly Paid Drudgery." *New York Times,* February 23, 1990, A4.

Corrêa, M. "O Brasil se expande." *Veja,* September 7, 1994, 70.

Diuguid, L. "Japanese in Brazil Prosper, Draw Nations Together." *Washington Post,* September 23, 1971, F1.

Gaillard, P. "L'irresistible ascension de la communauté japonaise." *Autrement,* no. 44 (November 1982): 176.

Maeyama, T. "Ethnicity, Secret Societies, and Associations: The Japanese in Brazil." *Comparative Studies in Society and History* 21 (October 1979): 589.

Martins, M. "Tomie Ohtake: The Essence of Simplicity." *Américas,* January/February 1994, 46.

Nader, R. "Brazil Taps Farm Potential as Japanese Pioneer." *Christian Science Monitor,* November 29, 1963.

"Nisei sofre preconceito no Japão e em São Paulo." *Jornal do Brasil,* October 12, 1986, 31.

"Reino do sol nascente." *Veja,* July 12, 1989, 74.

Saito, M. "Mergulho na ilusão." *Veja,* June 12, 1991, 34.

Simons, M. "Japanese Gone Brazilian: Unhurried Workaholics." *New York Times,* May 8, 1988, 14.

## ON ITALIAN IMMIGRANTS

**Books, Parts of Books, and Pamphlets**

Cenni, F. *Italianos no Brasil.* São Paulo: Editora Universidade de São Paulo, 1975.

Gattai, Z. *Anarquistas, Graças a Deus.* Rio de Janeiro: Editora Record, 1985.

Leão, J., and R. Kent. *Portinari: His Life and Art.* Chicago: University of Chicago Press, 1940.

**Periodicals**

Callado, A. "Portinari." *Ícaro,* no. 12, 1985, 9.

Hoge, W. "Brazil Gathers Archive on Its Painter, Portinari." *New York Times,* May 10, 1983, 11.

## ON GERMAN IMMIGRANTS

**Books, Parts of Books, and Pamphlets**

Luebke, F. *Germans in Brazil: A Comparative History of Cultural Conflict During World War I.* Baton Rouge: Louisiana State University Press, 1987.

Oberacker, C., Jr. *A Contribuição Teuta á Formação da Nação Brasileira.* 2 vols. Rio de Janeiro: Presença, 1985.

Pinsdorf, M. *German-Speaking Entrepreneurs: Builders of Business in Brazil.* New York: Peter Lang, 1990.

## ON OTHER IMMIGRANTS

**Books, Parts of Books, and Pamphlets**

Harter, E. *The Lost Colony of the Confederacy.* Jackson: University Press of Mississippi, 1985.

Piñon, N. *The Republic of Dreams.* Translated by H. Lane. New York: Alfred A. Knopf, 1989.

**Periodicals**

Page, J. "Brazil's Foremost Book Keeper." *Américas* 44, no. 6, 1992, 40.

Ross, M., and F. Kerner. "Stars and Bars Along the Amazon." *The Reporter,* September 18, 1958, 34.

# Chapter 5

## Books, Parts of Books, and Pamphlets

Aquino, C., ed. *História Empresarial Vivida: Depoimentos de Empresários Brasileiros Bem Sucedidos.* 2 vols. São Paulo: Gazeta Mercantil, 1986.

Burns, E. *Nationalism in Brazil: A Historical Survey.* New York: Frederick A. Praeger, 1968.

———. *A History of Brazil.* 3d ed. New York: Columbia University Press, 1993.

Conniff, M., and F. McCann, eds. *Modern Brazil: Elites and Masses in Historical Perspective.* Lincoln: University of Nebraska Press, 1991.

Dean, W. *The Industrialization of São Paulo, 1880–1945.* Austin: University of Texas Press, 1969.

"Emírio e as seis irmãs." *Retrato do Brasil: Da Monarquia ao Estado Militar.* Vol. 1. São Paulo: Editora Política, 1984, 83.

Freyre, G. "The Patriarchal Basis of Brazilian Society." In *Politics of Change in Latin America,* edited by J. Maier and R. Weatherhead. New York: Frederick A. Praeger, 1964.

Jaguaribe, H. *Economic and Political Development: A Theoretical Approach and a Brazilian Case Study.* Cambridge, Mass.: Harvard University Press, 1968.

Johnson, J. *The Military and Society in Latin America.* Stanford, Calif.: Stanford University Press, 1964.

Levi, D. *The Prados of São Paulo, Brazil: An Elite Family and Social Change, 1840–1930.* Athens: University of Georgia Press, 1987.

Morse, R. *From Community to Metropolis: A Biography of São Paulo, Brazil.* New York: Octagon Books, 1974.

Payne, L. *Brazilian Industrialists and Democratic Change.* Baltimore: Johns Hopkins University Press, 1994.

Prado, C., Jr. *The Colonial Background of Modern Brazil.* Translated by S. Macedo. Berkeley: University of California Press, 1967.

de Scantimburgo, J. *José Emírio de Moraes: O Homem—A Obra.* São Paulo: Companhia Editora Nacional, 1975.

Schneider, R. *Politics within the States: Elite Bureaucrats and Industrial Policy in Authoritarian Brazil.* Pittsburgh: University of Pittsburgh Press, 1991.

Simmons, C. "Military Leaders in National Politics, 1853–1889." In *Perspectives on Armed Politics in Brazil,* edited by H. Keith and R. Hayes. Tempe: Center for Latin American Studies, Arizona State University, 1976.

Skidmore, T. *The Politics of Military Rule in Brazil, 1964–85.* New York: Oxford University Press, 1988.

Sodré, N. *História Militar do Brasil.* Rio de Janeiro: Civilização Brasileira, 1965.

Vilaça, M., and R. de Albuquerque. *Coronel, Coroneis.* Rio de Janeiro: Tempo Brasileiro, 1965.

Wythe, G. *Industry in Latin America.* 2d ed. New York: Greenwood Press, 1969.

## Periodicals

Barham, J. "The Man Who Built Brazil." *Fortune,* October 12, 1987, 185.

———. "A Slow Handover by Brazil's Entrepreneurs: Management Succession." *Financial Times,* June 27, 1988, 14.

Cavalcanti, P. "Tráfico de escravos foi cartel dos corruptos." *O Estado de São Paulo,* March 31, 1991, 20.

"Damas em crise." *Veja*, May 12, 1993, 76.

Gall, N. "Brazil at the Brink." *Forbes*, February 4, 1980, 67.

Hoge, W. "Brazilian Go-Getter Sets Sight on the Presidency." *New York Times*, September 13, 1982, A2.

Kandell, J. "The Bonus Babies of Brazil." *New York Times*, July 11, 1976, F3.

Simonetti, E. "O império loteado." *Veja*, December 16, 1992, 90.

"Variações em torno de uma foto de família." *Veja*, July 29, 1992, 82.

## Chapter 6

### Books, Parts of Books, and Pamphlets

Barata, M. *Presença de Assis Chateaubriand na Vida Brasileira*. São Paulo: Livraria Martins, 1971.

Calmon, J. *O Livro Negro da Invasão Branca*. Rio de Janeiro: Edições O Cruzeiro, 1966.

Clark, W., with G. Priolli. *O Campeão de Audiência: Uma Autobiografia*. São Paulo: Editora Best Seller, 1991.

Dos Passos, J. *Brazil on the Move*. Garden City, N.Y.: Doubleday & Co., 1963.

Dulles, J. *Carlos Lacerda, Brazilian Crusader*. Vol. 1, *The Years 1914–1960*. Austin: University of Texas Press, 1991.

Gauld, C. *The Last Titan: Percival Farquhar, American Entrepreneur in Latin America*. Stanford, Calif.: Institute of Hispanic Studies and Luso-Brazilian Studies, Stanford University, 1964.

Herz, D. *A História Secreta da Rede Globo*. Porto Alegre: Tchê!, 1987.

Levine, R. *Vale of Tears: Revisiting the Canudos Massacre in Northeastern Brazil, 1893–97*. Berkeley: University of California Press, 1992.

Mattos, S. *The Impact of the 1964 Revolution on Brazilian Television*. San Antonio, Tex.: V. Klingensmith Independent Publisher, 1982.

Mello e Souza, C. *15 Anos de História*. Rio de Janeiro: Rede Globo, 1984.

Melo, J. *As Telenovelas da Globo: Produção e Exportação*. São Paulo: Summus Editorial, 1988.

Morais, F. *Chatô: O Rei do Brasil*. São Paulo: Companhia das Letras, 1994.

Pompeu, S. "Uma instituição nacional." *Retrato do Brasil: Da Monarquia ao Estado Militar*. Vol. 2. São Paulo: Editora Política, 1984, 397.

Simões, I., A. da Costa, and M. Kehl. *Um País no Ar: História da TV Brasileira em Três Canais*. São Paulo: Editora Brasiliense, 1986.

Skidmore, T. *Politics in Brazil, 1930–1964*. New York: Oxford University Press, 1967.

———. *The Politics of Military Rule in Brazil, 1964–85*. New York: Oxford University Press, 1988.

Sodré, N. *História da Imprensa no Brasil*. Rio de Janeiro: Civilização Brasileira, 1966.

Straubhaar, J. "Mass Communication and the Elites." In *Modern Brazil: Elites and Masses in Historical Perspective*, edited by M. Conniff and F. McCann. Lincoln: University of Nebraska Press, 1991.

### Periodicals

Blum, E. "Brazil's Yankee Network." *The Nation*, May 29, 1967, 678.

Couri, N. "No ar, o herdeiro do mundo da Globo." *Playboy*, October 31, 1986, 67.

"O engenheiro quer demolir a Globo." *Imprensa*, July 1989, 24.

"O fazedor de reis." *IstoÉ*, December 12, 1984, 18.

Hinchberger, B. "Brazil's Media Monopoly." *Multinational Monitor*, January/February 1991, 37.

Long, W. "Brazil's Globo: Tuning in to TV's Influence." *Los Angeles Times*, December 26, 1987, part 5, p. 1.

Preston, J. "Brazil's Power of the Press." *Washington Post*, December 9, 1992, C1.

Riding, A. "On TV, Brazil Is Getting a Clearer Picture of Itself." *New York Times*, December 13, 1984, A2.

————. "One Man's Political Views Color Brazil's TV Eye." *New York Times*, January 12, 1987, A4.

"Romance electrizante." *Veja*, June 21, 1989.

Tartaglia, C. "O império Roberto Marinho." *Pasquim*, March 10–16, 1983, 14.

Themer, M. "Um assunto de jornal." *Realidade*, August 1967, 152.

"The World According to Globo." *The Economist*, July 4, 1987.

**Dissertations, Reports, and Working Papers**

Straubhaar, J. The Transformation of Cultural Dependence: The Decline of American Influence on the Brazilian Television Industry. Ph.D. diss., Fletcher School of Law and Diplomacy, 1981.

# Chapter 7

**Books, Parts of Books, and Pamphlets**

Americas Watch. *Forced Labor in Brazil*. December 30, 1990.

de Castro, J. *Documentário do Nordeste*. São Paulo: Editora Brasiliense, 1959.

CPT, CEPAC, IBASE. *O Genocídio do Nordeste, 1979–1983*. São Paulo: Editora Hucitec, undated.

Craveiro, P. *Prefácio da Cidade: Crônicas do Recife*. Prefeitura do Recife: Departamento de Documentação e Cultura, 1961.

Freyre, G. *Guia Práctico, Histórico e Sentimental da Cidade do Recife*. Rio de Janeiro: José Olympio, 1968.

IBASE. *Nordeste: Seca, Fome, Miséria*. Rio de Janeiro: IBASE, April 17, 1984.

O'Gorman, F., ed. *Hillside Woman*. Rio de Janeiro: Francisco Alves, 1985.

Page, J. *The Revolution That Never Was: Northeast Brazil, 1955–1964*. New York: Grossman, 1972.

Ramos, G. *Barren Lives*. Translated by R. Dimmick. Austin: University of Texas Press, 1965.

Scheper-Hughes, N. *Death Without Weeping: The Violence of Everyday Life in Brazil*. Berkeley: University of California Press, 1992.

Smith, T. *Brazil: People and Institutions*. Baton Rouge: Louisiana State University Press, 1946.

Suassuna, A. *Auto da Compadecida*. Rio de Janeiro: Editora Agir, 1986.

Zaluar, A. *A Máquina e a Revolta: As Organizações Populares e o Significado da Pobreza*. São Paulo: Editora Brasiliense, 1985.

**Periodicals**

"A derrota do atraso." *Veja*, June 13, 1990.

"Desespero no sertao." *Veja*, March 24, 1993.

McDowell, E. "Famine in the Backlands." *The Atlantic*, March 1984, 22.

Page, J. "Brazil's 'Shadow City' Seems Worse Off Than 20 Years Ago." *Christian Science Monitor,* October 10, 1984, 16.

Scheper-Hughes, N. "Death Without Weeping." *Natural History,* October 1989, 8.

**Dissertations, Reports, and Working Papers**

Sanders, T. "Northeastern Brazilian Environmental Refugees: Part I: Why They Leave." *American Universities Field Staff Reports, Latin America,* no. 20, 1990–91.

# Chapter 8

**Books, Parts of Books, and Pamphlets**

Alexander, R. *Communism in Latin America.* New Brunswick, N.J.: Rutgers University Press, 1957.

———. *Labor Relations in Argentina, Brazil, and Chile.* New York: McGraw-Hill, 1962.

Amado, J. *Os Subterrâneos da Liberdade.* Rio de Janeiro: Editora Record, 1987.

Betto, F. *Lula: Biografia Política de um Operário.* São Paulo: Editora Clube do Livro, 1989.

Dantas, A., Jr., ed. *Lula Sem Censura.* Petrópolis: Editora Vozes, 1982.

Dulles, J. *Carlos Lacerda, Brazilian Crusader.* Vol. 1, *The Years 1914–1960.* Austin: University of Texas Press, 1991.

Guattari, F. *Lula: Entrevista.* São Paulo: Editora Brasiliense, 1982.

Hahner, J. *Poverty and Politics: The Urban Poor in Brazil, 1870–1920.* Albuquerque: University of New Mexico Press, 1986.

Hall, M., and M. Garcia. "Urban Labor." In *Modern Brazil: Elites and Masses in Historical Perspective,* edited by M. Conniff and F. McCann. Lincoln: University of Nebraska Press, 1989.

Hewlett, S. *The Cruel Dilemmas of Development: Twentieth-Century Brazil.* New York: Basic Books, 1980.

Keck, M. *The Workers' Party and Democratization in Brazil.* New Haven, Conn.: Yale University Press, 1992.

Sader, E., and K. Silverstein. *Without Fear of Being Happy: Lula, the Workers Party and Brazil.* London: Verso, 1991.

Skidmore, T. *The Politics of Military Rule in Brazil, 1964–85.* New York: Oxford University Press, 1988.

**Periodicals**

Carvalho, L. "Lula tem 17 irmãos dispostos a percorrer todo o país." *Jornal do Brasil,* May 21, 1989, 5.

Kandell, J. "Brazil's Economic 'Miracle' Appears of Little Benefit to Workers." *New York Times,* January 25, 1976, 3.

Lanzetta, L. "Manifesto socialisto de Lula será lançado em Agosto." *Jornal do Brasil,* July 21, 1991, 5.

"O PT sobe a rampa." *Veja,* February 17, 1993, 22.

"Sem pedir licença." *Veja,* June 21, 1989, 34.

**Dissertations, Reports, and Working Papers**

Keck, M. From Movement to Politics: The Formation of the Workers' Party in Brazil. Ph.D. thesis, Columbia University, 1986. Ann Arbor: University Microfilms International.

# Chapter 9

**Books, Parts of Books, and Pamphlets**

Alves, M. *Torturas e Torturados*. Rio de Janeiro: Idade Nova, 1966.

Amado, J. *Seara Vermelha*. Rio de Janeiro: Editora Record, 1987.

Americas Watch. *Prison Conditions* in Brazil. April 1989.

———. *Rural Violence in Brazil*. February 1991.

———. *Criminal Injustice: Violence Against Women in Brazil*. October 1991.

Amnesty International. *Brazil*. June 1990.

Archdiocese of São Paulo. *Torture in Brazil*. Translated by J. Wright. New York: Vintage Books, 1986.

"Assassinos de aluguel." *Retrato do Brasil: Da Monarquia ao Estado Militar*. Vol 1. São Paulo: Editora Política, 1984, 258.

Barros, S. *Messianismo e Violência de Massa no Brasil*. Rio de Janeiro: Civilização Brasileira, 1986.

Bicudo, H. *Do Esquadrão da Morte aos Justiceiros*. São Paulo: Edições Paulinas, 1988.

Buarque de Hollanda, S. *Raizes do Brasil*. Rio de Janeiro: José Olympio, 1984.

Burns, E. *A History of Brazil*. 3d ed. New York: Columbia University Press, 1993.

Camus, A. *American Journals*. Translated by H. Levick. New York: Paragon House, 1987.

Carvalho, M. *Sangue da Terra: A Luta Armada no Campo*. São Paulo: Editora Brasil Debates, 1980.

da Cunha, E. *Rebellion in the Backlands*. Translated by S. Putnam. Chicago: University of Chicago Press, 1957.

Keith, H. "The Nonviolent Tradition in Brazilian History: A Myth in Need of Explosion?" In *Conflict and Continuity in Brazilian Society*, edited by H. Keith and S. Edwards. Columbia: University of South Carolina Press, 1969.

Kidder, D., and J. Fletcher. *Brazil and the Brazilians*. Philadelphia: Childs and Peterson, 1857.

Leite, D. *O Carácter Nacional Brasileiro*. São Paulo: Livraria Pioneira Editora, 1983.

Levine, R. *Vale of Tears: Revisiting the Canudos Massacre in Northeastern Brazil, 1893–97*. Berkeley: University of California Press, 1992.

Love, J. *Rio Grande do Sul and Brazilian Regionalism, 1882–1930*. Stanford, Calif.: Stanford University Press, 1971.

Pires, C. *A Violência no Brasil*. São Paulo: Editora Moderna, 1985.

Reverbel, C. *Maragatos e Pica-Paus: Guerra Civil e Degola no Rio Grande*. Porto Alegre: L & PM Editores, 1985.

Scheper-Hughes, N. *Death Without Weeping: The Violence of Everyday Life in Brazil*. Berkeley: University of California Press, 1992.

Skidmore, T. *The Politics of Military Rule in Brazil, 1964–85*. New York: Oxford University Press, 1988.

Vellinho, M. *Brazil South: Its Conquest and Settlement*. Translated by L. and M. Barrett. New York: Alfred A. Knopf, 1968.

Ventura, Z. *Cidade Partida*. São Paulo: Companhia das Letras, 1994.

Veríssimo, É. *Time and the Wind.* Translated by L. Barrett. New York: Macmillan Co., 1951.

Zweig, S. *Brazil: Land of the Future.* Translated by A. St. James. New York: Viking, 1941.

**Periodicals**

"Ataque ao defensor." *Veja,* March 23, 1994, 26.

"Batalha no campo." *Veja,* March 22, 1989.

Blount, J. "Gunmen Slay Children Asleep on Streets of Rio." *Washington Post,* July 24, 1993, A1.

Brooke, J. "Brazil Tries to Curb Crimes Against Women." *New York Times,* November 17, 1981.

———. "Machismo on Trial." *Washington Post,* December 6, 1981, L1.

———. "Kidnappings Unnerve Rio's Business Leaders." *New York Times,* June 25, 1990, A9.

———. " 'Honor' Killing of Wives Is Outlawed in Brazil." *New York Times,* March 29, 1991.

Bussab, J. "Assassinos matam com oito tiros a Nenê da Brasilândia." *Folha da Tarde,* March 3, 1989.

"As caras do Brasil." *Veja,* March 31, 1993, 76.

César, A. "Sindicato de ladrões." *Veja,* September 1, 1993, 50.

Cohen, R. "Brazilian Youths Get Macho Thrills Riding Atop Trains." *Wall Street Journal,* November 1, 1988, 1.

"O dia da sorte." *Veja,* April 13, 1994, 20.

"Enfim, na cadeia." *Veja,* May 19, 1993, 34.

Epstein, J. "Documents Link Brazilian Lottery to Drug Ring." *Dallas Morning News,* April 17, 1994, 18A.

Hoge, W. "Brazilian Police Routinely Torturing Criminal Suspects to Extract Confessions and Few Citizens Object." *New York Times,* October 5, 1979, A10.

———. "Machismo 'Absolved' in Notorious Brazilian Trial." *New York Times,* October 28, 1979.

———. "Brazil's Crime Rate Produces Lynchings." *New York Times,* December 2, 1979, 11.

———. "Death Squad Is Spreading Terror in Rio Shantytowns." *New York Times,* March 15, 1980, A3.

"Os homens de bem." *Veja,* April 3, 1991.

"Inocência da contravenção esconde o rastro do crime." *Jornal do Brasil,* November 2, 1986, p. 34, col. 1.

"A juíza deu o troco." *Veja,* May 26, 1993, 32.

Kamm, T. "Next He Will Leap Some Tall Buildings in a Single Bound." *Wall Street Journal,* May 3, 1990, A1.

Long, W. "Squads of Death Stalk Brazil Slums: Police Implicated." *Los Angeles Times,* April 18, 1988, p. 1, col. 1.

———. " 'Animal Lottery': A 'Mafia' Thrives on Brazil Game." *Los Angeles Times,* July 12, 1988, p. 1, col. 1.

Lourenço, L. " 'Surfistas' ainda correm perigo nos trens." *O Globo,* March 15, 1992, 23.

"Marajás do xadrez." *Veja,* January 12, 1994, 24.

Margolis, M. "Rio Drug Lords Reign with Fear and Favor." *Washington Post,* May 13, 1988, A15.

————. "Last Samba for Brazil's Powerful Lottery Lords?" *Los Angeles Times,* May 25, 1993, 5.

McDowell, E. "The Murderous Policemen of Brazil." *Wall Street Journal,* November 1, 1974.

Moreira, D. "Atenção, bolinhas rolando." *O Globo,* September 7, 1986, p. 30, col. 1.

Moreira, M. "Troca de chefes leva os traficantes á guerra." *Jornal do Brasil,* June 27, 1993, 33.

"A morte no fogo." *Veja,* February 6, 1991, 77.

"Na lista de Castor." *Veja,* April 6, 1994, 34.

"No Rio o pó cala os governantes." *Veja,* June 1, 1988.

Novitski, J. "10 Petty Criminals Killed in São Paulo by a 'Death Squad.' " *New York Times,* July 21, 1970, p. 1, col. 3.

Orsini, E. "As confissões da eterna missa." *Jornal do Brasil,* June 13, 1993, B4.

Pedrosa, F. "Os 80 anos da morte de Euclides da Cunha." *Jornal do Brasil,* August 15, 1989, 6.

"O perigo mora ao lado." *Veja,* April 12, 1989, 66.

Perin, O. "Homicídios no Brasil crescem." *Jornal do Brasil,* November 19, 1986, 14.

Pimenta, A. "O pau-de-arara na praça." *Veja,* September 1, 1993, 111.

Renato, C. " 'Comando' se transforma numa máfia." *O Globo,* February 24, 1991, 26.

Riding, A. "Brazilians Turn to Lynchings to Fight Soaring Crime Rate." *New York Times,* April 15, 1984, 1.

"O Rio de cara com o medo." *Veja,* December 16, 1992, 20.

Robinson, E. "Rio's Carnival of Carnage." *Washington Post,* October 27, 1991, F1.

Rocha, J. "Lottery Bribes Scandal Snares Rio's Elite." *The Guardian,* April 9, 1994, 16.

Sampaio, F. "Quadrilhas espalham pânico entre caminhoneiros." *O Globo,* October 12, 1988, 24.

"A terceira geração." *Veja,* November 12, 1986, 48.

"Tráfico é o crime mais rentável hoje." *O Globo,* September 8, 1991, 2.

Valério, M. "Quadrilhas assaltam 'muambeiros.' " *Jornal do Brasil,* October 27, 1991, 8.

"Viola calibre 38." *Veja,* November 10, 1993, 32.

Weschler, L. "A Miracle, A Universe." *The New Yorker,* May 25, 1987, 69; June 1, 1987, 72.

# Chapter 10

## Books, Parts of Books, and Pamphlets

Alves, M. *São Paulo: Sementes de Democracia.* São Paulo: Companhia Editora Nacional, 1985, ch. 8.

Amado, J. *Capitães da Areia.* Rio de Janeiro: Editora Record, 1987.

Bierrenbach, M., E. Sader, and C. Figueiredo. *Fogo no Pavilhão: Uma Proposta de Liberdade para o Menor.* São Paulo: Editora Brasiliense, 1987.

Conferência Nacional dos Bispos do Brasil, Campanha da Fraternidade. *Quem Acolhe o Menor, a Mim Acolhe: Texto Base.* Brasília: Editora Gráfica, 1987.

Dimenstein, G. *A Guerra dos Meninos: Assassinatos dos Menores no Brasil.* São Paulo: Editora Brasiliense, 1990.

———. *Meninas da Noite: A Prostituição de Meninas-Escravas no Brasil.* São Paulo: Editora Ática, 1992.

Drexel, J., and L. Iannone. *Criança e Miséria: Vida ou Morte?* São Paulo: Editora Moderna, 1989.

Iannone, L. *Eu Gosto Tanto de Você . . .* São Paulo: Editora Moderna, 1988.

Luppi, C. *Agora e na Hora de Nossa Morte: O Massacre do Menor no Brasil.* São Paulo: Editora Brasil Debates, 1982.

Movimento Nacional de Meninos e Meninas da Rua et al. *Vidas em Risco: Assassinatos de Crianças e Adolescentes no Brasil.* Rio de Janeiro, 1992.

"Nossos Pixotes." *Retrato do Brasil: Da Monarquia ao Estado Militar.* Vol. 2. São Paulo: Editora Política, 1984, 301.

*A Situação da Infância Brasileira* (Pamphlet). *Retrato do Brasil: Da Monarquia ao Estado Militar.* Vol. 3. São Paulo: Editora Política, 1985.

### Periodicals

Arruda, R. "Praça da Sé vive guerrilha de meninos." *O Estado de São Paulo,* August 18, 1991, 22.

Dourado, A. "A voz e a vez das meninas." *Jornal do Comércio* (Recife), June 19, 1989, 14.

Eleutério, R. "Droga, a mortal companheira do menor da rua." *O Globo,* June 28, 1987, 15.

França, M. "O descaso cobra seu preço." *Visão,* March 4, 1992, 34.

Helena, L., and C. Renato. "Crianças de 10 a 15 anos se vendem na noite do Rio." *O Globo,* August 18, 1991, 16.

Hoge, W. " 'For Every One We Reach There Are 1,000 We Don't Touch.' " *New York Times,* September 11, 1983, 8E.

"Infância maltrapilha." *Veja,* September 16, 1992, 78.

Nunes, T. "Vida cruel mata cedo as meninas da rua da capital pernambucana." *Jornal do Brasil,* August 26, 1988, 12.

Pereira, R. "Em busca da infância perdida." *Veja,* March 16, 1994, 66.

Prado, G. "A pousada das esquecidas." *Diário de Pernambuco,* May 21, 1989, A26.

Riding, A. "Brazil's Time Bomb: Poor Children by the Millions." *New York Times,* October 23, 1985, A2.

———. "Brazil's Street Children: New Attempt at Rescue." *New York Times,* May 11, 1987, A6.

Vanvolsem, W. "Jungle Sex Teenagers Join Gold Rush." *Daily Telegraph,* September 2, 1990, 16.

"A vida e a morte das crianças nas ruas do Brasil." *Veja,* May 29, 1991, 34.

# Chapter 11

**Books, Parts of Books, and Pamphlets**

"As duas caras do milagre." *Retrato do Brasil: Da Monarquia ao Estado Militar.* Vol. 1. São Paulo: Editora Política, 1984, 136.

Branco, S. *O Fenómeno Cubatão.* São Paulo: CETESB, 1984.

Brandão, I. *And Still the Earth.* Translated by E. Watson. New York: Avon Books, 1985.

Bryce, J. *South America: Observations and Impressions.* Detroit: Macmillan, 1912.

Dean, W. *The Industrialization of São Paulo, 1880–1945.* Austin: University of Texas Press, 1969.

Gattai, Z. *Anarquistas, Graças a Deus.* Rio de Janeiro: Editora Record, 1985.

Morse, R. *From Community to Metropolis: A Biography of São Paulo, Brazil.* New York: Octagon Books, 1974.

Prefeitura Municipal de Cubatão. *O Município de Cubatão e a Poluição do Ar na Baixada Santista.* 1970.

**Periodicals**

Acevedo, C. "Esta cidade não parou para pensar." *Realidade,* June 1967, 81.

"All Things Come to Towns That Wait." *The Economist,* September 3, 1988, 46.

Bridges, T. "Brazilian City Battles Pollution." *Christian Science Monitor,* May 23, 1988, 9.

Chang, L. "The New Emerald Hunters: Brazilian Environmental Jurisprudence, 1988–1989." *Georgetown International Environmental Law Review* 3 (1990): 395.

Duarte, S. "Guanabara: a lenta morte de uma baía." *O Globo,* December 6, 1987, 38.

Findley, R. "Pollution Control in Brazil." *Ecology Law Quarterly* 15, no. 1 (1988): 1.

Hoge, W. "New Menace in Brazil's 'Valley of Death' Strikes at Unborn." *New York Times,* September 23, 1980, A2.

Howe, M. "São Paulo Is Setting a Growth Record, and Its Problems Keep Pace." *New York Times,* February 4, 1973, 10.

————. "São Paulo Caught Between Pollution and Progress." *New York Times,* June 16, 1975, 8.

Joyce, C. "The Price of Progress." *New Scientist,* July 25, 1985, 46.

Macklin, D. "Rebirth in Death Valley." *South,* March 1989, 86.

Margolis, M. "Perils of Developing Too Fast: Brazil's Case Study of Pollution." *Christian Science Monitor,* March 18, 1983, 18.

Novitski, J. "Brazil Shunning Pollution Curbs." *New York Times,* February 13, 1972, 11.

Robinson, E. "São Paulo, Brazil's Economic Engine, Overheats." *Washington Post,* June 26, 1989, A1.

Schuster, L. "Industrialization of Brazilian Village Brings Jobs at Cost of Heavy Pollution and Even Death." *Wall Street Journal,* April 15, 1985, 32.

Simons, M. "The Bay's a Thing of Beauty; Pity It's a Cesspool." *New York Times,* September 16, 1987, A4.

"Verde profissional." *Veja,* March 29, 1989.

Worcman, N. "Brazil's Thriving Environmental Movement." *Technology Review,* October 1990, 42.

**Dissertations, Reports, and Working Papers**

Estado do São Paulo. *Relatório Final, Comissão Especial de Inquérito para Apurar Possíveis Irregularidades no Município de Cubatão e Dar Solução aos Problemas da Poluição Ambiental. Diário Oficial do Estado.* Sec. I, São Paulo, 91 (096), May 23, 1981, 78.

World Bank Staff. "Pollution Control in São Paulo, Brazil: Costs, Benefits and Effects on Industrial Location." Working Paper No. 501, November 1981.

# Chapter 12

**Books, Parts of Books, and Pamphlets**

Amado, J. *Os Subterrâneos da Liberdade.* Rio de Janeiro: Editora Record, 1987.

Branford, S., and O. Glock. *The Last Frontier: Fighting Over Land in the Amazon.* London: Zed Books Ltd., 1985.

Kelly, B., and M. London. *Amazon.* New York: Holt, Rinehart & Winston, 1983.

Pinto, L. *Jari: Todo a Verdade Sobre o Projecto de Ludwig.* São Paulo: Editora Marco Zero, 1986.

Revkin, A. *The Burning Season: The Murder of Chico Mendes and the Fight for the Amazon Rain Forest.* Boston: Houghton Mifflin Co., 1990.

Shoumatoff, A. *The World Is Burning.* Boston: Little, Brown and Co., 1990.

Stone, R. *Dreams of Amazonia.* New York: Viking, 1985.

**Periodicals**

Adam, J. "Plundering the Amazon for Power." *Washington Post,* November 27, 1988, D3.

"Agressão mineral." *Veja,* December 9, 1987, 105.

"Amazônia, 1984" (Symposium). *Ciência Hoje,* January/February 1984.

Bennett, P. "Destroying the Amazon, Part II: Industry and Peril in Brazil." *Boston Globe,* December 19, 1988.

"Billionaire Ludwig's Brazilian Gamble." *Newsweek,* September 10, 1979, 76.

Brasiliense, R. "Serra Pelada faz 10 anos e ouro é cada vez mais raro." *Jornal do Brasil,* January 14, 1990, 9.

Bridges, T. "The Rain Forest's Road to Ruin?" *Washington Post,* July 24, 1988, H2.

Brooke, J. "Billionaire's Dream Founders in Amazon Jungle." *Washington Post,* May 31, 1981, A1.

————. "In an Amazon Lake, Underwater Logging Blooms." *New York Times,* August 14, 1990, A4.

————. "Ecologists' Foe to Become Amazon Governor." *New York Times,* October 21, 1990, 19.

————. "Amazon Advocate's Unsettling Vision." *New York Times,* April 30, 1991, C4.

————. "Plan to Develop Amazon a Failure." *New York Times,* August 25, 1991, 9.

————. "Brazilian Sequel: A Jailbreak, a Bitter Widow." *New York Times,* February 17, 1993, A5.

"O cerco do verde." *Veja,* February 1, 1989, 24.

"Ciranda da impunidade." *Veja,* February 24, 1993.

Diuguid, L. "An Amazon Frontier." *Washington Post,* January 9, 1972, C2.

"Empires of the Chainsaws." *The Economist,* August 10, 1991, 36.

"Esta estrada é uma rua." *Realidade,* December 1970, 75.

"Extinção no ato." *Veja,* March 25, 1992, 22.

Gailliard, P. "Ludwig, éclipse d'un pharaon." *Autrement,* no. 44 (November 1982): 184.

Gall, N. "The Last Gold Rush." *Harpers,* December 1984, 59.

Goodsell, J. "Amazônia: Problems and Promise." *Christian Science Monitor,* January 3, 1968, 9; January 9, 1968, 9; January 17, 1968, 11; January 24, 1968, 9; January 31, 1968, 9; February 7, 1968, 11; February 14, 1968, 11; February 20, 1968, 11.

Gorney, C. "The Last Frontier: Venturing into the Amazon." *Washington Post,* December 13, 1981, A1; December 14, 1981, A1; December 15, 1981, A1; December 16, 1981, A1; December 17, 1981, A1; December 18, 1981, A26; December 19, 1981, A23.

Hertsgaard, M. "Meanwhile, People Die." *The Independent* (Sunday Review Section), July 5, 1992, 12.

Hummerstone, R. "Cutting a Road Through Brazil's 'Green Hell.' " *New York Times Magazine,* March 5, 1972, 14.

Kamm, T. "Rain Forest Advocates Have Local Foe." *Wall Street Journal,* September 9, 1991, A8.

Kepp, M. "Mercury Slowly Poisons Amazon." *Times of the Americas,* October 16, 1991, 2.

Lamb, C. "Brazil Builds Boom Towns on Fallen Forests." *Financial Times,* August 17, 1990, 5.

"Mar de peixes." *Veja,* December 3, 1986, 106.

Margolis, M. "Amazon Ablaze." *World Monitor,* February 1989, 20.

Martins, E. "Serra Pelada: Onde a luxúria é o ouro." *Jornal do Brasil,* July 1, 1984, 22.

Maxwell, K. "The Tragedy of the Amazon." *New York Review of Books,* March 7, 1991, 24.

———. "The Mystery of Chico Mendes." *New York Review of Books,* March 28, 1991, 39.

McDowell, E. "By Train to the Middle of the Amazon Jungle." *New York Times* (Travel Section), November 26, 1989, 20.

Novitski, J. "Brazil Is Challenging a Last Frontier." *New York Times,* July 7, 1970, 1.

"Orgia amazônica." *IstoÉ,* July 15, 1987.

"Playing with Fires." *Time,* September 18, 1989, 76.

Pompeu, K. "Balbina: O choque do futuro." *Manchete,* May 20, 1989.

"As promessas do oeste." *Veja,* January 6, 1982, 52.

Riding, A. "Brazil Is Studying Use of Herbicides." *New York Times,* February 24, 1984, A5.

Rohter, L. "Amazon Basin's Forest Going Up in Smoke," *Washington Post,* January 5, 1979, A14.

Sanches, V. "Resistir até a última grama de ouro." *Afinal,* June 2, 1986, 4.

Shaw, A. "CVRD's Carajas Project." *Mining Magazine,* August 1990, 90.

Shoumatoff, A. "A Threatened World." *Washington Post,* May 1, 1977, C1.

Silverstein, K. "The Murders Go on in Amazonia." *The Nation,* April 1, 1991, 410.

Simons, M. "An Epic Struggle for Gold." *New York Times Magazine,* June 7, 1987, 34.

———. "Brazil, Smarting from the Outcry over the Amazon, Charges Foreign Plot." *New York Times,* March 23, 1989, A14.

"A sombra de Xapuri." *IstoÉ,* February 13, 1991.

Stevens, W. "Scientists Confront Renewed Backlash on Global Warming." *New York Times,* September 14, 1993, C1.

Werner, L. "The Mad Mary—All Aboard to Nowhere." *Américas* 42, no. 4, 1990, 6.

**Dissertations, Reports, and Working Papers**

Gall, N. "Letter from Rondônia." *American Universities Field Staff Reports,* nos. 9–13, 1978.

**Film**

Cowell, A. *A Decade of Destruction* (documentary film).

# Chapter 13

**Books, Parts of Books, and Pamphlets**

Alves, M. *O Cristo do Povo.* Rio de Janeiro: Editora Sabiá, 1978.

Archdiocese of São Paulo. *Torture in Brazil.* Translated by J. Wright. New York: Vintage Books, 1986.

de Azevedo, T. *A Religião Civil Brasileira: Um Instrumento Político.* Petrópolis: Editora Vozes, 1981.

Berryman, P. *Liberation Theology.* New York: Pantheon, 1987.

Boff, L. and C. *Liberation Theology: From Confrontation to Dialogue.* Translated by R. Barr. San Francisco: Harper & Row, 1986.

———. *Introducing Liberation Theology.* Translated by P. Burns. Maryknoll, N.Y.: Orbis Books, 1989.

de Broucker, J. *Dom Hélder Camara: The Violence of a Peacemaker.* Translated by H. Briffault. Maryknoll, N.Y.: Orbis Books, 1970.

Bruneau, T. *The Church in Brazil: The Politics of Religion.* Austin: University of Texas Press, 1982.

della Cava, R. *Miracle at Joaseiro.* New York: Columbia University Press, 1970.

Claudino, A. *O Monstro Sagrado e o Amarelinho Comunisto: Gilberto Freyre, Dom Hélder e a Revolução de 64.* Recife: Editora Opção, 1985.

da Cunha, E. *Rebellion in the Backlands.* Translated by S. Putnam. Chicago: University of Chicago Press, 1957.

Filgueiras, O. "Crenças da miséria." *Retrato do Brasil: Da Monarquia ao Estado Militar.* Vol. 1. São Paulo: Editora Política, 1984, 101.

Guimarães, A. *Comunidades de Base no Brasil: Uma Nova Maneira de Ser em Igreja.* Petrópolis: Editora Vozes, 1978.

Lernoux, P. *Cry of the People: United States Involvement in the Rise of Fascism, Torture, and Murder and the Persecution of the Church in Latin America.* Garden City, N.Y.: Doubleday & Co., 1980.

———. *People of God: The Struggle for World Catholicism.* New York: Viking, 1989.

Levine, R. *Vale of Tears: Revisiting the Canudos Massacre in Northeastern Brazil, 1893–97.* Berkeley: University of California Press, 1992.

Mainwaring, S. *The Catholic Church and Politics in Brazil, 1916–1985.* Stanford, Calif.: Stanford University Press, 1986.

———. "Grass-Roots Catholic Groups and Politics in Brazil." In *The Progressive Church in Latin America,* edited by S. Mainwaring and A. Wildes. Notre Dame, Ind.: University of Notre Dame Press, 1989.

O'Gorman, F. *Base Communities in Brazil: Dynamics of a Journey.* Rio de Janeiro: Francisco Alves, 1983.

Santayana, M. *No Meio do Povo: Perfil Biográfico de Dom Paulo Evaristo Arns.* São Paulo: Editora Salesiana Dom Bosco, 1983.

de Souza, L. *Classes Populares e a Igreja nos Caminhos da História.* Petrópolis: Editora Vozes, 1982.

Valente, W. *Misticismo e Região: Aspectos do Sebastianismo Nordestino.* Recife: Instituto Joaquim Nabuco de Pesquisas Sociais, 1963.

**Periodicals**

Bruneau, T. "The Church Moves Left." *Commonweal,* February 2, 1968, 535.

"Camisinha é pecado." *Veja,* February 23, 1994, 73.

"A fé retomada." *Veja,* May 9, 1990.

Jabusch, W. "Brazilian Tapestry." *The Tablet,* October 17, 1992, 1293.

Kramer, J. "Letter from the Elysian Fields." *The New Yorker,* March 2, 1987, 40.

"Look Over Your Shoulder." *The Tablet,* October 26, 1991, 1306.

Pope, C. "Human Rights and the Catholic Church in Brazil, 1970–1983: The Pontifical Justice and Peace Commission of the São Paulo Archdiocese." *Journal of Church and State* 27 (August 1985): 429.

Ribeiro, H. "A força da igreja." *Realidade,* December 1970, 30.

Weschler, L. "A Miracle, A Universe." *The New Yorker,* May 25, 1987, 69; June 1, 1987, 72.

# Chapter 14

**Books, Parts of Books, and Pamphlets**

Bastide, R. *Les Religions Africaines au Brésil.* Paris: Presses Universitaires de France, 1960.

Bastos, A. *Os Cultos Mágico-Religiosos no Brasil.* São Paulo: Editora Hucitec, 1979.

Birman, P. *O que é Umbanda.* São Paulo: Editora Brasiliense, 1985.

Camargo, C. *Kardecismo e Umbanda: Uma Interpretação Sociológica.* São Paulo: Livraria Pioneira Editora, 1961.

Carneiro, E. *Candomblés da Bahia.* Rio de Janeiro: Civilização Brasileira, 1978.

Conconi, M. *Umbanda: Uma Religião Brasileira.* São Paulo: Faculdade de Filosofia, Letras e Ciências Humanas, Universidade de São Paulo, 1987.

Ortiz, R. *A Morte Branca do Feticeiro Negro: Umbanda, Integração de uma Religião numa Sociedade de Classes.* Petrópolis: Editora Vozes, 1978.

Sangirardi, Jr., *Deuses da África e do Brasil: Candomblé e Umbanda.* Rio de Janeiro: Civilização Brasileira, 1988.

Trindade, L. *Exu: Simbolo e Função.* São Paulo: Faculdade de Filosofia, Letras e Ciências Humanas, Universidade de São Paulo, 1985.

Velho, Y. *Guerra de Orixá: Um Estudo de Ritual e Conflito.* Rio de Janeiro: Jorge Zahar Editores, 1977.

**Periodicals**

Goshko, J. "Africa's Ancient Gods Live on in Brazil." *Washington Post*, July 10, 1966, E5.

Guillermoprieto, A. "Letter from Rio." *The New Yorker*, December 2, 1991, 116.

Hoge, W. "Macumba: Brazil's Pervasive Cults." *New York Times Magazine*, August 21, 1983, 30.

Long, W. "Brazil's Umbanda Religion Finds Strength in Its Credo of Flexibility." *Los Angeles Times*, November 26, 1988, 2–6.

Maggie, Y. "O medo do feitiço: Verdades e mentiras sobre a repressão das religiões mediúnicas." *Religião e Sociedade*, March 1986.

Page, J. "In Search of Afro-Brazil." *The Reporter*, November 4, 1965, 44.

Riding, A. "Rio Journal: As '88 Dawns, Brazil is Spellbound." *New York Times*, January 1, 1988, 1–4.

Simons, M. "Brazilians High and Low Mourn a Cult Priestess." *New York Times*, October 13, 1986.

**Dissertations, Reports, and Working Papers**

Maggie, Y. O Medo do Feitiço: Relações entre Mágia e Poder no Brasil. Doctoral diss., Departamento de Antropologia, Museu Nacional, Universidade Federal do Rio de Janeiro, 1988.

# Chapter 15

**Books, Parts of Books, and Pamphlets**

Landim, L., ed. *Sinais dos Tempos: Diversidade Religiosa no Brasil*. Rio de Janeiro: Instituto de Estudos da Religião, 1990.

Martin, D. *Tongues of Fire: The Explosion of Protestantism in Latin America*. Oxford: Basil Blackwell Ltd., 1990.

Mendonça, A. "Um panorama do protestantismo brasileiro actual." In *Sinais dos Tempos: Tradiçoes Religiosas no Brasil*, edited by L. Landim. Rio de Janeiro: Instituto de Estudos da Religião, 1989.

**Periodicals**

Azevedo, E. "Fé explosiva." *Veja*, December 16, 1992, 82.

Brooke, J. "Pragmatic Protestants Win Catholic Converts in Brazil." *New York Times*, July 4, 1993, p. 1, col. 1.

"A fé multiplicada." *Veja*, July 19, 1989, 54.

"A fé que move multidões avança no país." *Veja*, May 16, 1990, 46.

"A força dos crentes." *O Estado de São Paulo*, May 17, 1992, 3; May 24, 1992, 3.

Freitas, M. "Fisco pode pegar bispo." *Jornal do Brasil*, June 23, 1991, 1, 14.

Marcom, J. "The Fire down South." *Forbes*, October 15, 1990, 56.

Marqueiro, P. " 'Sexta-feira da cura' mata um no Maracanã." *O Globo*, April 14, 1990.

"The Pastor Is Faster." *The Economist*, April 17, 1993, 42.

Prado, A., and N. Letaif. "O céu na terra." *IstoÉ/Senhor*, June 2, 1990.

Riding, A. "In Brazil, Evangelicals Are on Rise." *New York Times*, October 15, 1987, 16.

———. "A Spirited 'Holy War' in an Easygoing Land." *New York Times*, December 31, 1988, p. 4, col. 4.

## Chapter 16

### Books, Parts of Books, and Pamphlets

Henshaw, R. *The Encyclopedia of World Soccer.* Washington: New Republic Books, 1979.

Hollander, Z., ed. *The American Encyclopedia of Soccer.* New York: Everest House Publishers, 1989.

Lever, J. *A Loucura do Futebol.* Translated by A. Lemos. Rio de Janeiro: Editora Record, undated.

da Matta, R. *Carnavais, Malandros e Heróis: Para uma Sociologia do Dilema Brasileiro.* Rio de Janeiro: Jorge Zahar Editores, 1978.

da Matta, R., et al. *Universo do Futebol.* Rio de Janeiro: Edições Pinakotheke, 1982.

Milan, B. *Brasil, O País da Bola.* São Paulo: Biblioteca Eucatex de Cultura Brasileira, 1989.

Pelé, with R. Fish. *My Life and the Beautiful Game: Autobiography of Pelé.* New York: Doubleday, 1977.

Perdigão, P. *Anatomia de uma Derrota.* Porto Alegre: L & PM Editores, 1986.

Zanini, T. *Mané Garrincha.* São Paulo: Editora Brasiliense, 1984.

### Periodicals

Alcântara, E. "A sombra das chuteiras milionárias." *Veja,* December 22, 1993, 86.

Araujo, R. "Força estranha." *Ciência Hoje,* July/August 1982, 32.

Areas, J. "O dia em que o Uruguai roubou a festa." *O Globo,* July 16, 1989, 54.

"Atleta de meio século." *Veja,* October 31, 1990, 80.

Carelli, W. "O ex-país do futebol." *Folha de São Paulo,* July 9, 1989, 22.

Duarte, T. "Pesquisa mostra face elitista do futebol." *O Estado de São Paulo,* August 18, 1991, 37.

Frias Filho, O. "Saudosismo revela herança de subdesenvolvimento." *Folha de São Paulo,* July 16, 1989, D3.

Keerdoja, E. "Pelé: There Is Life After Soccer." *Newsweek,* June 11, 1979, 19.

Laurence, M. "1990: Uma grande indústria chamada Pelé." *Realidade,* January 1971, 16.

Martins, P. "Os 'abnegados,' que tiram a fortuna da cartola." *O Globo,* October 12, 1986, 52.

Moraes Neto, G. "Retrato falado de uma dor brasileira." *Jornal do Brasil,* July 14, 1991, 36.

Motta, A. "Derrota de 50 é só história para jogadores." *Jornal do Brasil,* July 16, 1989, 44.

"Soccer Great Keeps Busy with Big Deals." *USA Today,* May 3, 1994, 1C.

## Chapter 17

### Periodicals

"Cara a cara com o Brasil." *Veja,* December 29, 1993, 66.

Kamm, T. "Year-Round Santa Strikes Blow Against Poverty in Brazil." *Wall Street Journal,* February 22, 1994, A14.

## ALBERTO SANTOS-DUMONT

### Books, Parts of Books, and Pamphlets

de Barros, H. *Alberto Santos-Dumont*. Rio de Janeiro: Editora Index, 1986.

da Costa, F. *Alberto Santos-Dumont: The Father of Aviation*. Centro de Relações Públicas da Aeronáutica, undated.

Senna, O. *Alberto Santos-Dumont*. São Paulo: Editora Brasiliense, 1984.

Souza, M. *O Brasileiro Voador*. Rio de Janeiro: Editora Marco Zero, 1986.

Wykeham, P. *Santos-Dumont: A Study in Obsession*. London: Putnam, 1962.

### Periodicals

Davison, P. "A Daring Old Man and His Flying Machine." *The Independent* (Foreign News), April 11, 1993, 15.

## VINICIUS DE MORAES

### Books, Parts of Books, and Pamphlets

Cabral, S. *Tom Jobim*. Rio de Janeiro: Companhia Brasileira de Projectos e Obras, 1987.

Carneiro, G. *Vinicius de Moraes*. São Paulo: Editora Brasiliense, 1984.

Castello, J. *O Poeta da Paixão: Uma Biografia*. São Paulo: Companhia das Letras, 1994.

Castro, R. *Chega de Saudade: A História e as Histórias da Bossa Nova*. São Paulo: Companhia das Letras, 1990.

de Moraes, V. *Poesia Completa e Prosa*. Rio de Janeiro: Editora Nova Aguilar, 1980.

### Periodicals

"A herança do poeta." *Veja*, May 29, 1991, 78.

Mayrink, G. "Coração fingidor." *Veja*, March 2, 1994, 92.

de Souza, T. "Music, the Pulse of a People: Brazilian Music." *UNESCO Courier*, December 1986, 29.

## LUIZ CARLOS PRESTES

### Books, Parts of Books, and Pamphlets

Alexander, R. *Communism in Latin America*. New Brunswick, N.J.: Rutgers University Press, 1957.

Amado, J. *O Cavaleiro da Esperança*. Rio de Janeiro: Editora Record, 1987.

Burns, E. *A History of Brazil*. 3d ed. New York: Columbia University Press, 1993.

Cavalcanti, P. *Nos Tempos de Prestes: Memórias Políticas*. Vol. 3. Recife: Editora Guararapes, 1982.

Custódio, P. *Luis Carlos Prestes*. Porto Alegre: Tchê!, 1985.

Dulles, J. *Anarchists and Communists in Brazil, 1900–1935*. Austin: University of Texas Press, 1973.

———. *Brazilian Communism, 1935–1945*. Austin: University of Texas Press, 1983.

Macauley, N. *The Prestes Column: Revolution in Brazil*. New York: New Viewpoints, 1974.

Morais, F. *Olga*. São Paulo: Editora Alfa-Omega, 1987.

Sodré, N. *A Coluna Prestes*. Rio de Janeiro: Civilização Brasileira, 1980.

### Periodicals

"Fim da longa marcha." *Veja*, March 14, 1990, 90.

"Luis Carlos Prestes: Brazil's Lenin and 'Knight of Hope.' " *Los Angeles Times*, March 11, 1990, A40.

"Obituary of Luiz Carlos Prestes." *Daily Telegraph*, March 8, 1990, 23.

Riding, A. "Brazil's Red Knight of Hope: Unhorsed But Undaunted." *New York Times*, April 4, 1984, p. A2, col. 3.

#### MARIA DA GRAÇA MENEGHEL—"XUXA"

### Books, Parts of Books, and Pamphlets

Cardozo, I. *Retratos: Entrevistas de Playboy*. Porto Alegre: L & PM Editores, 1984.

Parker, R. *Bodies, Pleasures and Passions: Sexual Culture in Contemporary Brazil*. Boston: Beacon Press, 1991.

Simpson, A. *Xuxa: The Mega-Marketing of Gender, Race, and Modernity*. Philadelphia: Temple University Press, 1993.

### Periodicals

Andrade, P. "A multinacional rainha dos 'bajitos.' " *O Globo*, September 8, 1991, 1.

Batista, T. "Xuxa." *Gente*, June 15, 1981.

Braga, T. "Apresentadora é alvo de ataques na TV americana." *Jornal do Brasil*, January 11, 1992.

Dapieve, A. "Midas aos 23 anos." *Jornal do Brasil*, November 1, 1986.

Duncan, A. "Meet Brazil's Queen of Kid TV." *Christian Science Monitor*, January 22, 1991, 14.

Durst, R. " 'Lua de Cristal': Caça-níquel de baixinhos." *Jornal do Brasil*, June 26, 1990, B4.

Guatimosim, P. "Xuxa é hoje marca de sucesso internacional." *Jornal do Brasil* (Negócios e Finanças), March 24, 1991, 6.

"A loirinha chegou lá." *Veja*, September 25, 1991, 102.

Motta, A. "O país perdeu a graça." *IstoÉ/Senhor*, September 25, 1992, 22.

Newcomb, P., and L. Gubernick. "The Top 40." *Forbes*, September 27, 1993, 97.

Preston, J. "Brazil's Tot-to-Teen Idol." *Washington Post*, December 2, 1991, B1.

Ribeiro, B. "Só falta 'Beijinho, Beijinho' na vida de Xuxa." *Playboy*, August 1987, 69.

Sodré, M., and F. Doria. "Xuxa de neve e os seus baixinhos." *Jornal do Brasil*, January 1, 1989; reprinted in M. Sodré, *O Brasil Simulado e o Real: Ensaio Sobre o Quotidiano Nacional*. Rio de Janeiro: Editora Rio Fundo, 1991.

#### IVO PITANGUY

### Books, Parts of Books, and Pamphlets

Cardozo, I. *Retratos: Entrevistas de Playboy*. Porto Alegre: L & PM Editores, 1984.

Pitanguy, I. *Les chemins de la beauté: Un maître de la chirurgie plastique témoigne*. Paris: Éditions J.-C. Lattès, 1983.

### Periodicals

Carmo, M. "Bisturi popular." *Veja*, February 20, 1991, 14.

Cony, C. "O fantástico Dr. Pitanguy." *Manchete*, August 2, 1975.

Dunningham, A. "Brasileiras gastam US$ 1 bilhão por ano para manter a beleza em dia." *O Globo,* August 9, 1992, 44.

Gandra, J., and R. Goulart. "Ele agora quer ser imortal." *Exame Vip,* July 25, 1990.

Gil-Montero, M. "Ivo Pitanguy: Master of Artful Surgery." *Américas* 43, no. 2, 1991, 24.

Hoge, W. "Doctor Vanity: The Jet Set's Man in Rio." *New York Times Magazine,* June 8, 1980, 44.

Knox, P. "Plastic Surgeon Improves Nature." *Toronto Globe and Mail,* June 26, 1989.

"As mãos da beleza." *IstoÉ,* May 2, 1984, 36.

# Chapter 18

## Books, Parts of Books, and Pamphlets

Campedelli, S. *A Telenovela.* São Paulo: Editora Ática, 1985.

Fernandes, I. *Memória da Telenovela Brasileira.* São Paulo: Editora Brasiliense, 1987.

Leal, O. *A Leitura Social da Novela das Oito.* Petrópolis: Editora Vozes, 1986.

Melo, J. *As Telenovelas da Globo: Produção e Exportação.* São Paulo: Summus Editorial, 1988.

Ortiz, R., S. Borelli, and J. Ramos. *Telenovela: História e Produção.* São Paulo: Editora Brasiliense, 1988.

## Periodicals

Cesar, A. "O motor da destruição." *Veja,* May 26, 1993, 98.

Curran, M. "Brazil's *Literatura de Cordel:* Its Distribution and Adaptation to the Brazilian Mass Market." *Studies in Latin American Popular Culture* 1 (1982): 164.

Diehl, J. "Brazilian TV Challenges U.S. Hold on Soap Operas." *Washington Post,* May 3, 1984, A31.

"Entrevista com Lima Duarte." *Playboy* (Brazil), June 1989, 35.

Guillermoprieto, A. "Obsessed in Rio." *The New Yorker,* August 16, 1993, 44.

Margolis, M. "Once Censored Soap Opera Carves Niche in Everyday Brazilian Life." *Christian Science Monitor,* December 9, 1985, 25.

Michaels, J. "In-Script TV Ads Get Brazilian Boost." *Advertising Age,* January 27, 1986, 58.

Nash, N. "A Slaying Stuns Brazil: It's Right Out of the Soaps." *New York Times,* January 1, 1993, A4.

"Pacto rompido." *Veja,* September 1, 1993.

Riding, A. "Brazilian Soap Operas Appeal to Global Tastes." *New York Times,* October 20, 1985, H25.

———. "On Brazilian TV, the Subtle Sell Pays Off Big, Too." *New York Times,* June 3, 1988, D15.

"Sexo, socos e babás." *Veja,* July 4, 1990, 50.

Silva, B. "A novela brasileira ganha as telas do mundo." *O Globo,* June 6, 1985, part 2, p. 1.

Straubhaar, J. "The Development of the Telenovela as the Pre-Eminent Form of Popular Culture in Brazil." *Studies in Latin American Popular Culture* 1 (1982): 138.

"Tiroteio no video." *Veja,* May 9, 1990.

Valladão, A. "La fabuleuse alchimie du feuilleton télévisé." *Autrement*, no. 44 (November 1982): 192.

# Chapter 19

## Books, Parts of Books, and Pamphlets

Amado, J. *País do Carnaval*. Rio de Janeiro: Editora Record, 1987.

Azedo, M. "Superescolas S/A." *Retrato do Brasil: Da Monarquia ao Estado Militar.* Vol. 1. São Paulo: Editora Política, 1984, 66.

Botting, D. *Rio de Janeiro*. Amsterdam: Time-Life Books, 1977, ch. 6.

Cabral, S. *As Escolas de Samba*. Rio de Janeiro: Editora Fontana, 1974.

Costa, H. *Salgueiro: Academia de Samba*. Rio de Janeiro: Editora Record, 1984.

Guillermoprieto, A. *Samba*. New York: Alfred A. Knopf, 1990.

Kritch, J. *Why Is This Country Dancing? A One-Man Samba to the Beat of Brazil*. New York: Simon & Schuster, 1993.

da Matta, R. *Carnavais, Malandros e Heróis: Para uma Sociologia do Dilema Brasileiro*. Rio de Janeiro: Zahar Editores, 1978.

McDonald, G. *Carioca Fletch*. New York: Warner Books, 1984.

Moraes, E. *História do Carnaval Carioca*. Rio de Janeiro: Editora Record, 1987.

Moura, R. *Carnaval: Da Redentora a Praça do Apocalipse*. Rio de Janeiro: Jorge Zahar Editor, 1986.

Parker, R. *Bodies, Pleasures and Passions: Sexual Culture in Contemporary Brazil*. Boston: Beacon Press, 1991.

Rezende, R. *O Samba dos Vagalumes*. Rio de Janeiro: José Olympio, 1990.

## Periodicals

Costa, H. "The History of the Brazilian Carnival." *Ícaro*, no. 19, 1986, 22.

Maranhão, A. "Bicheiros dominam Carnaval do Rio." *O Estado de São Paulo*, February 17, 1991, 22.

Marques, F. "Cabeças cortadas na avenida." *Veja*, February 13, 1991.

Miller, M. "Carnival in Rio." *Holiday*, February 1965, 40.

"Samba Cia. Ltda." *IstoÉ/Senhor*, February 13, 1991, 30.

Smith, G. "The Colors of Carnival." *Américas*, November/December 1986, 21.

Valenzuela, L. "The Samba, Feathers, Glitter, and Sweat." *Vanity Fair*, February 1986, 50.

## Dissertations, Reports, and Working Papers

Raphael, A. Samba and Social Control: Popular Culture and Racial Democracy in Rio de Janeiro. Ph.D. thesis, Columbia University, 1981. Ann Arbor: University Microfilms International.

# Chapter 20

## Books, Parts of Books, and Pamphlets

Castañeda, J. *Utopia Unarmed: The Latin American Left After the Cold War*. New York: Alfred A. Knopf, 1993.

Smith, T. *Brazil: People and Institutions*. Baton Rouge: Louisiana State University Press, 1946.

## Periodicals

Araripe, S., and S. Maços. "Barra vive uma nova febre de construções." *Jornal do Brasil*, June 27, 1993, 28.

Barros, A. "Cidades proibidas." *Veja*, March 3, 1993, 44.

Blount, J. "In Brazil's Ceará State, a Reversal of Fortune." *Christian Science Monitor*, March 18, 1993, 8.

"Brazil" (Survey). *The Economist*, December 7, 1991.

Brooke, J. "The Secret of a Livable City? It's Simplicity Itself." *New York Times*, May 28, 1992, A4.

———. "White Flight in Brazil? Secessionist Caldron Boils." *New York Times*, May 12, 1993, A4.

———. "Brazilian State Leads Way in Saving Children." *New York Times*, May 14, 1993, A1.

———. "Mighty Brazil Rides a Free-Market Wave." *New York Times*, October 31, 1993, F5.

———. "Bouquets for a State as Brazil's Dust Bowl Flowers." *New York Times*, April 15, 1994, A4.

"Cidade-modelo do Brasil faz 300 anos amanhã." *O Estado de São Paulo*, March 28, 1993, Cidade, p. 1.

Corrêa, M. "As boas idéias estão nas prefeituras." *Veja*, September 30, 1992, 71.

Ferraz, S. "Lá no morro o estopim está aceso." *Veja*, April 20, 1994, 38.

Gomes, L. "O agito cearense." *Veja*, December 1, 1993.

Gomes, L., and M. Silva. "A capital de uma país viável." *Veja*, March 31, 1993, 68.

Hoge, W. "For Brazilians, Curitiba Serves as a Model City." *New York Times*, March 8, 1981, 5.

"Home Remedies Are Best." *The Economist*, April 17, 1993, 45.

Kamm, T. "Urban Problems Yield to Innovative Spirit of a City in Brazil." *Wall Street Journal*, January 10, 1992, A1.

Lara, M. "Uberlândia não quer crescer para manter padrão de vida." *Jornal do Brasil*, August 4, 1991, 18.

Marqueiro, P. "Barra: um bairro com vocação para cidade." *O Globo*, July 28, 1991, 18.

"A metrópole cobaia." *Veja*, May 15, 1991, 64.

Pedreira, M., and C. Goodstein. "Blueprint for an Eco-Safe City." *Américas* 44, no. 4, 1992, 6.

Pinheiro, F. "A Califórnia carioca." *Veja*, June 12, 1991, 58.

"No reino da utopia." *Veja*, June 29, 1988, 76.

"Nos braços do povo." *Veja*, July 12, 1989, 42.

Riding, A. "Political Maverick Tilts at the Lords of Patronage." *New York Times*, May 4, 1988, A4.

Spíndola, R. "Ceará reduz em 32% taxa de mortalidade infantil." *O Estado de São Paulo*, June 30, 1991, 30.

# Index